CLARENCE BYRD

Clarence Byrd Inc.

IDA CHEN

Clarence Byrd Inc.

With contributions by
GARY DONELL

Byrd & Chen's
Canadian
Tax
Principles

2018–2019 EDITION

Volume II

Pearson

Pearson Canada Inc., 26 Prince Andrew Place, North York, Ontario M3C 2H4.

978-0-13-526020-3

1   19

PREFACE

Complete Preface In Volume I

The complete preface to this three volume set of **Byrd & Chen's Canadian Tax Principles** can be found in Volume I.

Online Student Supplements

MyLab Accounting

MyLab Accounting for *Canadian Tax Principles* contains a great deal of additional material that will provide significant assistance to users of this text. Instructions on how to access MyLab can be found on the access card provided with this package. The URL for MyLab is:

www.pearsoncanada.ca/byrdchen/ctp2019

The various items that are included on MyLab can be described as follows:

- Corrections to the textbook and Study Guide. Please check periodically to help avoid frustration.
- Pearson eText of the complete set - 2 Volumes plus Study Guide
- Self Study Problems (The solutions are in the print and online Study Guide)
- Supplementary Self Study Problems and Solutions
- Access to CPA Canada's Federal Income Tax Collection (FITAC)
- Access to Intuit Canada's ProFile tax return preparation software
- Practice Examinations and Solutions
- Power Point Presentations
- Glossary Flashcards
- 2018 tax rates, credits and common CCA Classes (PDF file)
- Tax Returns for examples and Self Study tax return problems

2018 Rates, Credits And Other Data

> For your convenience, this information, as well as the Chapter 5
> Appendix of common CCA rates, is available **online** as a .PDF file.

Information Applicable To Individuals

Federal Tax Rates For Individuals

Taxable Income In Excess Of	Federal Tax	Marginal Rate On Excess
$ -0-	$ -0-	15.0%
46,605	6,991	20.5%
93,208	16,544	26.0%
144,489	29,877	29.0%
205,842	47,670	33.0%

Federal Tax Credits For Individuals - Personal Credits (ITA 118)

Reference

118(1)(a) **Married Persons** 15% of $11,809 ($1,771).

118(1)(a) **Spousal** 15% of $11,809 ($1,771), less 15% of the spouse's Net Income For Tax Purposes. Base amount increased by $2,182 (to $13,991) if the spouse is mentally or physically infirm. Not available when the spouse's income is more than $11,809 (or $13,991).

118(1)(b) **Eligible Dependant** 15% of $11,809 ($1,771), less 15% of the eligible dependant's Net Income For Tax Purposes. Base amount increased by $2,182 (to $13,991) if the eligible dependant is mentally or physically infirm. Not available when the eligible dependant's income is more than $11,809 (or $13,991).

118(1)(b.1) **Canada Caregiver For Child Under 18** 15% of $2,182 ($327).

118(1)(c) **Single Persons** 15% of $11,809 ($1,771).

118(1)(d) **Canada Caregiver** 15% of $6,986 ($1,048), reduced by 15% of the dependant's income in excess of $16,405.

118(1)(e) **Canada Caregiver - Additional Amount** If either the income adjusted infirm spousal credit base or the income adjusted infirm eligible dependant credit base is less than the spouse or eligible dependant's income adjusted credit base ($6,986 - less the spouse or dependant's income in excess of $16,405), an additional Canada caregiver credit is available based on 15% of the deficiency.

118(2) **Age** 15% of $7,333 ($1,100). The base for this credit is reduced by the lesser of $7,333 and 15% of the individual's net income in excess of $36,976. Not available when income is more than $85,863. If the individual cannot use this credit, it can be transferred to a spouse or common-law partner.

118(3) **Pension** 15% of up to $2,000 of eligible pension income for a maximum credit of $300 [(15%)($2,000)]. If the individual cannot use this credit, it can be transferred to a spouse or common-law partner.

118(10) **Canada Employment Credit** 15% of up to $1,195. This produces a maximum credit of $179.

Other Common Federal Personal Credits (Various ITA)

118.01   **Adoption Expenses Credit** 15% of eligible expenses (reduced by any reimbursements) up to a maximum of $15,905 per adoption. This results in a maximum credit of $2,386.

118.02   **Public Transit Passes Credit** Repealed for 2018 and subsequent years.

118.031   **Children's Arts Credit**   Repealed for 2017 and subsequent years.

118.041   **Home Accessibility Credit**   15% of lesser of $10,000 and the amount of qualifying expenditures for the year.

118.05   **First Time Home Buyer's Credit** 15% of $5,000 ($750) of the cost of an eligible home.

118.06   **Volunteer Firefighters Credit** 15% of $3,000 ($450) for qualifying volunteers.

118.07   **Volunteer Search And Rescue Workers Credit** 15% of $3,000 ($450) for qualifying volunteers.

118.1   **Charitable Donations - Regular** The general limit on amounts for this credit is 75% of Net Income. There is an addition to this general limit equal to 25% of any taxable capital gains and 25% of any recapture of CCA resulting from a gift of capital property. In addition, the income inclusion on capital gains arising from a gift of some publicly traded shares is reduced from one-half to nil. For individuals, the credit is equal to:

$$[(15\%)(A)] + [(33\%)(B)] + [(29\%)(C)]$$ where:

A = The first $200 of eligible gifts.
B = The lesser of:
  • Total gifts, less $200; and
  • Taxable Income, less $205,842.
C = The excess, if any, by which the individual's total gifts exceed the sum of $200 plus the amount determined in B.

118.1(3.1)   **Charitable Donations - First-Time Donor's Super Credit** Not available after 2017.

118.2   **Medical Expenses** The medical expense tax credit is determined by the following formula:

$$[15\%] [(B - C) + D]$$, where:

B   is the total of an individual's medical expenses for himself, his spouse or common-law partner, and any of his children who have not reached 18 years of age at the end of the year.
C   is the lesser of 3% of the individual's Net Income For Tax Purposes and $2,302 (2018 figure).
D   is the total of all amounts each of which is, in respect of a dependant of the individual (other than a child of the individual who has not attained the age of 18 years before the end of the taxation year), an amount determined by the formula:

$$E - F$$, where:

E   is the total of the dependant's medical expenses
F   is the lesser of 3% of the dependant's Net Income For Tax Purposes and $2,302 (2018 figure).

118.3   **Disability - All Ages** 15% of $8,235 ($1,235). If not used by the disabled individual, it can be transferred to a person claiming that individual as a dependant.

118.3 **Disability Supplement - Under 18 And Qualifies For The Disability Tax Credit** 15% of $4,804 ($721), reduced by the total of amounts paid for attendant care or supervision in excess of $2,814 that are deducted as child care costs, deducted as a disability support amount, or claimed as a medical expense in calculating the medical expense tax credit.

Education Related Credits

118.5 • **Tuition Fees Which Includes Examination And Ancillary Fees**
  • 15% of qualifying tuition fees
  • 15% of examination fees for both post-secondary examinations and examinations required in a professional program
  • 15% of ancillary fees that are imposed by a post-secondary educational institution on all of their full or part-time students. Up to $250 in such ancillary fees can be claimed even if not required of all students.

118.6(2) • **Education** Repealed for 2017 and subsequent years.

118.6(2.1) • **Textbook** Repealed for 2017 and subsequent years.

118.62 • **Interest On Student Loans**
  15% of interest paid on qualifying student loans.

118.9 • **Transfer Of Tuition Credit**
  If the individual cannot use the credit, is not claimed as a dependant by his spouse, and does not transfer the unused credit to a spouse or common-law partner, then a parent or grandparent of the individual can claim up to $750 [(15%)($5,000)] of any unused tuition credit. The amount that can be transferred is reduced by the amount of the credit claimed by the student for the year.

118.7 **Employment Insurance** 15% of amounts paid by employees up to the maximum Employment Insurance premium of $858 (1.66% of $51,700). This produces a maximum tax credit of $129 [(15%)($858)].

118.7 **Canada Pension Plan** 15% of amounts paid by employees up to the maximum Canada Pension Plan contribution of $2,594 [4.95% of ($55,900 less $3,500)]. This produces a maximum tax credit of $389 [(15%)($2,594)]. For self-employed individuals, the payment is $5,188 ($2,594 times 2).

122.51 **Refundable Medical Expense Supplement** The individual claiming this amount must be over 17 and have earned income of at least $3,566. The amount is equal to the lesser of $1,222 and 25/15 of the medical expense tax credit. The refundable amount is then reduced by 5% of family Net Income in excess of $27,044. Not available when family income is more than $51,484.

122.8 **Refundable Child Fitness Credit** Repealed for 2017 and subsequent years.

122.9 **Refundable Teacher And Early Childhood Educator School Supply Tax Credit** A maximum of 15% of up to $1,000 ($150) of eligible expenditures that are made by eligible educators.

127(3) **Political Donations** Three-quarters of the first $400, one-half of the next $350, one-third of the next $525, to a maximum credit of $650 on donations of $1,275.

127.4 **Labour Sponsored Venture Capital Corporations (LSVCC) Credit** The federal credit is equal to 15 percent of acquisitions of provincially registered LSVCCs.

ITA 82 and **Dividend Tax Credit**
ITA 121

- **Eligible Dividends** These dividends are grossed up by 38%. The federal dividend tax credit is equal to 6/11 of the gross up. The credit can also be calculated as 15.02% of the grossed up dividends, or 20.7272% of the actual dividends received.

- **Non-Eligible Dividends** These dividends are grossed up by 16%. The federal dividend tax credit is equal to 8/11 of the gross up. The credit can also be calculated as 10.0313% of the grossed up dividends, or 11.6363% of the actual dividends received.

Other Data For Individuals

ITA 82 **Dividend Gross Up**

Eligible Dividends For these dividends, the gross up is 38% of dividends received.

Non-Eligible Dividends For these dividends, the gross up is 16% of dividends received.

Chapter 4 **OAS Clawback Limits** The tax (clawback) on Old Age Security (OAS) benefits is based on the lesser of 100% of OAS benefits received, and 15% of the amount by which "threshold income" (Net Income For Tax Purposes, calculated without the OAS clawback) exceeds $75,910.

Chapter 4 **EI Clawback Limits** The tax (clawback) on Employment Insurance (EI) benefits under the *Employment Insurance Act* is based on the lesser of 30% of the EI benefits received, and 30% of the amount by which "threshold income" exceeds $64,625 (1.25 times the maximum insurable earnings of $51,700). For this purpose, "threshold income" is Net Income For Tax Purposes, calculated without the OAS or EI clawbacks.

Chapter 9 **Child Care Expenses** The least of three amounts:

1. The amount actually paid for child care services. If the child is at a camp or boarding school, this amount is limited to a weekly amount $275 (any age if eligible for disability tax credit), $200 (under 7 year of age), or $125 (age 7 through 16 or over 16 with a mental or physical impairment).

2. The sum of the **Annual Child Care Expense Amounts** for the taxpayer's eligible children. The per child amounts are $11,000 (any age if eligible for disability tax credit), $8,000 (under 7 year of age), or $5,000 (age 7 through 16 or over 16 with a mental or physical impairment).

3. 2/3 of the taxpayer's **Earned Income** (for child care expenses purposes).

Chapter 10 **RRSP Deduction Room** For 2018, the addition to RRSP deduction room is equal to:

- the lesser of $26,230 and 18% of 2017 Earned Income,
- reduced by the 2017 Pension Adjustment and any 2018 Past Service Pension Adjustment,
- and increased by any 2018 Pension Adjustment Reversal.

Chapter 11 **Lifetime Capital Gains Deduction** For 2018, the deduction limit for dispositions of shares of qualified small business corporations is $848,252. There is an additional amount for farm or fishing properties of $151,748, providing a total of $1,000,000 for such properties.

Provincial Tax Rates And Provincial Credits For Individuals Provincial taxes are based on Taxable Income, with most provinces adopting multiple rates. The number of brackets range from three to five. Provincial tax credits are generally based on the minimum provincial rate applied to a credit base that is similar to that used for federal credits. In addition to regular rates, two provinces use surtaxes.

Information Applicable To Individuals And Corporations

ITR 4301   **Prescribed Rate**   The following figures show the base rate that would be used in calculations such as imputed interest on loans. It also shows the rates applicable on amounts owing to and from the CRA.   For recent quarters, the interest rates were as follows:

Year	Quarter	Base Rate	Owing From*	Owing To
2016	All	1%	3%	5%
2017	All	1%	3%	5%
2018	**I**	**1%**	**3%**	**5%**
2018	**II**	**2%**	**4%**	**6%**

*The rate on refunds to corporations is limited to the base rate, without the additional 2%.

Automobile Deduction Limits

- CCA is limited to the first $30,000 of the automobiles cost, plus applicable GST/HST/PST (not including amounts that will be refunded through input tax credits).
- Interest on financing of automobiles is limited to $10 per day.
- Deductible leasing costs are limited to $800 per month (other constraints apply).
- Operating Cost Benefit = $0.26 per kilometre.
- Deductible Rates = $0.55 for first 5,000 kilometres, $0.49 for additional kilometres.

CCA Rates   See Appendix to Chapter 5.

Quick Method Rates (GST Only)

	Percentage On GST Included Sales	
	First $30,000	On Excess
Retailers And Wholesalers	0.8%	1.8%
Service Providers And Manufacturers	2.6%	3.6%

Note   Different rates apply in the provinces that have adopted an HST system.

Information Applicable To Corporations

Federal Corporate Tax Rates   are as follows (federal tax abatement removed):

General Business (Before General Rate Reduction)	28%
General Business (After General Rate Reduction Of 13%)	15%
Income Eligible For M&P Deduction	15%
Income Eligible For Small Business Deduction	10%
Part IV Refundable Tax	38-1/3%
Part I Refundable Tax On Investment Income Of CCPC (ART)	10-2/3%

Reference
125(1)   **Small Business Deduction**   is equal to 18% of the least of:

A.   Net Canadian active business income.

B.   Taxable Income, less:

    1.   100/28 times the ITA 126(1) credit for taxes paid on foreign non-business income, calculated without consideration of the additional refundable tax under ITA 123.3 or the general rate reduction under ITA 123.4; and

    2.   4 times the ITA 126(2) credit for taxes paid on foreign business income, calculated without consideration of the general rate reduction under ITA 123.4.

C.   The annual business limit of $500,000, less any portion allocated to associated corporations, less the reduction for large corporations.

125.1   **Manufacturing And Processing Deduction** is equal to 13% of the lesser of:

     A.   Manufacturing and processing profits, less amounts eligible for the small business deduction; and

     B.   Taxable Income, less the sum of:

         1.   the amount eligible for the small business deduction;
         2.   4 times the foreign tax credit for business income calculated without consideration of the ITA 123.4 general rate reduction; and
         3.   "aggregate investment income" (of CCPCs) as defined in ITA 129(4).

123.4(2)   **General Rate Reduction** is equal to 13% of Full Rate Taxable Income. This is Taxable Income, reduced by; income eligible for the small business deduction, income eligible for the M&P deduction and the corporation's "aggregate investment income" for the year.

126(1)   **Foreign Tax Credits For Corporations** The Foreign Non-Business Income Tax Credit is the lesser of:

     •   The tax paid to the foreign government (for corporations, there is no 15% limit on the foreign non-business taxes paid); and

     •   An amount determined by the following formula:

$$\left[\frac{\text{Foreign Non} - \text{Business Income}}{\text{Adjusted Division B Income}}\right][\text{Tax Otherwise Payable}]$$

126(2)   The Foreign Business Income Tax Credit is equal to the least of:

     •   The tax paid to the foreign government;

     •   An amount determined by the following formula:

$$\left[\frac{\text{Foreign Business Income}}{\text{Adjusted Division B Income}}\right][\text{Tax Otherwise Payable}]; \quad \text{and}$$

     •   Tax Otherwise Payable for the year, less any foreign tax credit taken on non-business income under ITA 126(1).

129(4)   **Aggregate Investment Income** is the sum of:

     •   net taxable capital gains for the year, reduced by any net capital loss carry overs deducted during the year; and

     •   income from property including interest, rents, and royalties, but excluding dividends that are deductible in computing Taxable Income. Since foreign dividends are generally not deductible, they would be included in aggregate investment income.

123.3   **Additional Refundable Tax On Investment Income (ART)** is equal to 10-2/3% of the lesser of:

     •   the corporation's "aggregate investment income" for the year [as defined in ITA 129(4)]; and

     •   the amount, if any, by which the corporation's Taxable Income for the year exceeds the amount that is eligible for the small business deduction.

186(1)   **Part IV Tax** is assessed at a rate of 38-1/3% of portfolio dividends, plus dividends received from a connected company that gave rise to a dividend refund for the connected company as a result of the payment.

129(3)(a)   **Refundable Portion Of Part I Tax Payable** is defined as the least of three items:

1. the amount determined by the formula

$$A - B, \text{ where}$$

A   is 30-2/3% of the corporation's aggregate investment income for the year, and

B   is the amount, if any, by which the foreign non-business income tax credit exceeds 8% of its foreign investment income for the year.

2. 30-2/3% of the amount, if any, by which the corporation's taxable income for the year exceeds the total of:

- the amount eligible for the small business deduction;
- $100 \div 38\text{-}2/3$ of the tax credit for foreign non-business income; and
- 4 times the tax credit for foreign business income.

3. the corporation's tax for the year payable under Part I.

129(3)   **Refundable Dividend Tax On Hand (RDTOH)** is defined as follows:

- The corporation's RDTOH at the end of the preceding year; less
- The corporation's dividend refund for its preceding taxation year; plus
- The Refundable Portion Of Part I tax for the year; plus
- The total of the taxes under Part IV for the year.

89(1)   **General Rate Income Pool**   A CCPC's General Rate Income Pool (GRIP) is defined as follows:

- The GRIP balance at the end of the preceding year; plus
- 72% of the CCPC's Taxable Income after it has been reduced by amounts eligible for the small business deduction and aggregate investment income; plus
- 100% of eligible dividends received during the year; plus
- adjustments related to amalgamations and wind-ups; less
- eligible dividends paid during the preceding year.

Tax Related Web Sites

GOVERNMENT

Canada Revenue Agency   www.cra.gc.ca

Department of Finance Canada   www.fin.gc.ca

CPA FIRMS

BDO   www.bdo.ca/en-ca/services/tax/domestic-tax-services/overview/

Deloitte.   www2.deloitte.com/ca/en/pages/tax/topics/tax.html

Ernst & Young   www.ey.com/CA/en/Services/Tax

KPMG   www.kpmg.com/ca/en/services/tax

PricewaterhouseCoopers   www.pwc.com/ca/en/tax/publications.jhtml

OTHER

CPA Canada   www.CPAcanada.ca

Canadian Tax Foundation   www.ctf.ca

ProFile Tax Suite   www.intuit.ca/professional-tax-software/index.jsp

CONTENTS

The textbook is published in two Volumes:	Volume I = Chapters 1 to 10 Volume II = Chapters 11 to 21

Chapter	VOLUME I
1	Introduction To Federal Taxation In Canada
2	Procedures and Administration
3	Income Or Loss From An Office Or Employment
4	Taxable Income and Tax Payable For Individuals
5	Capital Cost Allowance
6	Income Or Loss From A Business
7	Income From Property
8	Capital Gains And Capital Losses
9	Other Income, Other Deductions And Other Issues
10	Retirement Savings And Other Special Income Arrangements

Chapter	VOLUME II
11	Taxable Income and Tax Payable For Individuals Revisited
12	Taxable Income and Tax Payable For Corporations
13	Taxation of Corporate Investment Income
14	Other Issues In Corporate Taxation
15	Corporate Taxation and Management Decisions
16	Rollovers Under Section 85
17	Other Rollovers and Sale Of An Incorporated Business
18	Partnerships
19	Trusts And Estate Planning
20	International Issues In Taxation
21	GST/HST
Glossary	Located at the back of the print and online Study Guide.

Detailed contents of Volume II, Chapters 11 to 21 follows.

CHAPTER 11
Taxable Income And Tax Payable For Individuals Revisited

Introduction 511

Taxable Income Overview 512

Lump-Sum Payments 512

Treatment Of Losses 513
   Carry Over Provisions 513
   Personal Use Property Losses 516
   Listed Personal Property Losses 516
   Non-Capital Losses 517
   Net Capital Losses 518
   Net Capital Losses At Death 520
   Allowable Business Investment Losses . . . 521
   Farm Losses 523

Lifetime Capital Gains Deduction 524
   Current And Future Limits 524
   Qualified Property 524
   Determining The Deductible Amount . . . 525
   Comprehensive Example 528

Ordering Of Deductions And Losses 530
   Ordering In Computing Net Income . . . 530
   Ordering In Computing Taxable Income . . 530

Tax Payable Overview 532

Tax On Split Income (TOSI) 533
   What Is Split Income? 535
   Applicability Of The TOSI 535
   Calculation Of The Tax 537

Tax Credits Revisited 539
   Transfer Of Dividends To A Spouse . . . 539
   Charitable Donations Credit Revisited . . . 540
   Foreign Tax Credits Revisited 545

Alternative Minimum Tax 547
   Minimum Tax Calculation 547
   Tax Credits For AMT 549

Key Terms Used In This Chapter 550

References 551

Appendix - Returns For Deceased Taxpayers 551
   Special Rules At Death 551

Problems For Self Study (Online) 557

Assignment Problems 557

CHAPTER 12
Taxable Income And Tax Payable For Corporations

Note On Current Developments 583

Computation Of Net Income 585

Computation Of Taxable Income 586
   Deductions Available To Corporations . . . 586
   Dividends From Other Corporations 587
   Non-Capital Loss Carry Over - Corporations . 590
   Ordering Of Taxable Income Deductions . . 593

Geographical Allocation Of Income 593

Federal Tax Payable 595
   Basic Rate 595
   Federal Tax Abatement 595
   General Rate Reduction 595

Provincial Tax Payable 596
   General Rate 596
   Manufacturing And Processing Rate 596
   Small Business Rate 596
   Investment Income Rates 597

Small Business Deduction 598
   Canadian Controlled Private Corporation . . 599
   Active Business Income 599
   Annual Business Limit 601
   Allocation Among Associated Companies . . 601
   Elimination For Large CCPCs 604
   Personal Services And
    Professional Corporations 606

**Manufacturing And Processing
Profits Deduction** 608
   Calculating The Deduction 608
   Eligibility 610

General Rate Reduction - ITA 123.4(2) . . . 611
   Full Rate Taxable Income 611
   Application To Companies Other Than CCPCs 611
   Application To CCPCs 612

Foreign Tax Credits For Corporations 613

Key Terms Used In This Chapter 616

References 616

Problems For Self Study (Online) 617

Assignment Problems 617

CHAPTER 13
Taxation Of Corporate Investment Income

Note On Current Developments 625

Integration 625
    The Basic Concept 625
    Dividend Gross Up And Tax Credit Procedures 626
    Integration And Business Income 627

Refundable Taxes On Investment Income . 630
    Meaning Of Aggregate Investment Income . . 630
    Basic Concepts 631

Refundable Part I Tax - Investment Income. 633
    Additional Refundable Tax
      On Investment Income (ART) 633
    Problem One: Excessive Tax Rates - Flow
      Through Of A CCPC's Investment Income. . 634
    Solution To Problem One:
      Refundable Portion Of Part I Tax 636

Refundable Part IV Tax - Dividends 639
    Problem Two: Use Of Multi-Level Affiliations
      To Defer Taxes On Investment Income . . . 639
    Solution To Problem Two:
      Refundable Part IV Tax 640
    Part IV Tax On Portfolio Dividends Received . 641
    Dividends From A Connected Corporation . . 642
    Dividends Paid Out Of Mixed Income
      Of A Connected Corporation 644
    Other Part IV Tax Considerations 645

Refundable Dividend Tax On Hand 645
    RDTOH - General Definition 646
    Refundable Portion Of Part I Tax Payable . . 646
    The Dividend Refund 648
    Example Of RDTOH Calculations 649

**Working Through Large Corporate
Tax Problems** 652

Designation Of Eligible Dividends 652
    CCPCs And Their GRIP 654
    Non-CCPCs And Their LRIP 655
    Part III.1 Tax On Excessive Designations . . 656

Key Terms Used In This Chapter 658

References 658

Problems For Self Study (Online) 659

Assignment Problems 659

CHAPTER 14
Other Issues In Corporate Taxation

Introduction 671

Acquisition Of Control Rules 671
    Economic Background. 671
    Acquisition Of Control Legislation 672
    Deemed Year End 672
    Restrictions On Use Of Charitable Donations . 673
    Restrictions On The Use Of Losses 673
    Unrecognized Losses At Deemed Year End. . 674
    Deemed Disposition Election 675

Associated Companies. 677
    Definitions 678
    Examples - Associated Corporation Rules . . 679

Investment Tax Credits 682
    Procedures 682
    Eligible Expenditures 683
    Rates 683
    Refundable Investment Tax Credits. 684
    Carry Overs Of Investment Tax Credits . . . 685
    Effect Of Acquisition Of
      Control On Investment Tax Credits 685

Tax Basis Shareholders' Equity 686
    Shareholders' Equity Under GAAP 686
    Paid Up Capital (Tax Basis Contributed Capital) 686
    Tax Basis Retained Earnings. 687
    Capital Dividend Account (CDA). 688

Distributions Of Corporate Surplus 690
    Regular Cash Dividends 690
    Stock Dividends 691
    Dividends In Kind 692
    Capital Dividends 693
    Deemed Dividends - Increase In PUC. . . . 693
    Deemed Dividends - Winding-Up 695
    Deemed Dividends On Redemption,
      Acquisition, Or Cancellation Of Shares . . . 697
    Deemed Dividends - Liquidating 698

Key Terms Used In This Chapter 699

References 700

Problems For Self Study (Online) 701

Assignment Problems 701

Tax Software Assignment Problem 711

CHAPTER 15

Corporate Taxation And Management Decisions

The Decision To Incorporate **715**
Basic Tax Considerations. 715
Other Advantages And Disadvantages. . . . 716

Tax Reduction And Deferral **717**
Basic Example 718
Public Corporation 720
CCPC - Active Business Income 721
CCPC - Investment Income Other
Than Dividends. 724
CCPC - Dividend Income 725
Conclusions On Tax Reductions And Deferrals 726

Provincial Taxes And Integration **729**
Tax Deferral 729
Tax Reduction 730
Examples - Effects Of Provincial
Rates On Integration 731
Summary: Tax Deferral And Tax Reduction . 734

Tax Free Dividends **734**
Tax Rates On Dividends 734
Use Of Tax Credits 735
Tax Free Amounts For 2018 736

Income Splitting **737**
Basic Concept 737

Shareholder Benefits Including Loans. . . . **737**
The Owner-Manager Environment 737
Shareholder Benefits Other Than Loans . . . 738
Shareholder Loans 738

Management Compensation **741**
General Principles 741
Salary Vs. Dividends 742

Salary Vs. Dividends For
The Owner - Manager. **742**
The Basic Trade-Off 742
Other Considerations 743

Key Terms Used In This Chapter **753**

References **753**

Problems For Self Study (Online) **754**

Assignment Problems **754**

CHAPTER 16

Rollovers Under Section 85

Rollovers Under Section 85 . . . . **761**

General Rules For The Transfer **762**
Transferor And Transferee 762
Eligible Property 762
Consideration To Transferor 763
Making The Election 763
Establishing The Transfer Price 763

Transfer Prices - Detailed Rules. **765**
Rules Applicable To All Assets. 765
Accounts Receivable 766
Inventories, Non-Depreciable Capital Property 767
Disallowed Capital Losses 768
Depreciable Property 770
Disallowed Terminal Losses 772
Summary Of Transfer Price Rules 772

Allocation Of The Elected Value. **773**
Consideration Received By The Transferor . . 773
Assets Acquired By The Corporation 774

Paid Up Capital (PUC) Of Shares Issued . . **776**
Paid Up Capital Reduction 776
More Than One Class Of Shares 777

Comprehensive Example
Section 85 Rollovers. **779**

Gift To Related Party - Section 85 . . . . . . **782**
General Rules 782
Example 782

Excess Consideration - Section 85. . . . . . **784**

Dividend Stripping — ITA 84.1 . . . . **786**
Applicability Of ITA 84.1. 787
Dividend Stripping Example 787

Capital Gains Stripping — ITA 55(2) **790**
Application Of ITA 55(2). 791
Capital Gains Stripping - Examples 793

Key Terms Used In This Chapter **795**

References **795**

Problems For Self Study (Online) **796**

Assignment Problems **796**

CHAPTER 17
Other Rollovers And Sale Of An Incorporated Business

Introduction 807

Share For Share Exchanges - ITA 85.1 807
  General Rules 807
  Conditions For The Application Of ITA 85.1 . 808
  Example 808

Exchange Of Shares In A Reorganization - ITA 86 810
  Conditions For The Reorganization 811
  Procedures 812
  Example Using ITA 86(1) In An Estate Freeze . 813
  Gift To Related Person - ITA 86(2) 816
  Using ITA 86(1) - Tax Planning Considerations 819

Amalgamations - ITA 87 819
  Position Of The Amalgamated Company . . 820
  Position Of The Shareholders 821
  Vertical Amalgamations 822
  Asset Bump-Ups 822
  Non-Tax Considerations 822
  Amalgamations - Tax Planning Considerations 822

Winding-Up Of A 90% Owned Subsidiary . 823
  Acquisition Of Assets 824
  Disposition Of Shares 827
  Tax Planning Considerations Amalgamation Vs. Winding-Up 827

Winding-Up Of A Canadian Corporation . . 829

Convertible Properties 832

Sale Of An Incorporated Business 833
  Alternatives 833
  Restrictive Covenants (a.k.a. Non-Competition Agreements) . . . 833
  Sale Of Individual Assets 834
  Sale Of Assets As A Going Concern 835
  Sale Of Shares 836
  Evaluation Of Alternatives 837
  Example 839

Key Terms Used In This Chapter 841

References 842

Problems For Self Study (Online) 843

Assignment Problems 843

CHAPTER 18
Partnerships

Introduction 853
  Taxable Entities In Canada 853
  Chapter Coverage 854

Partnerships Defined 854
  The Importance Of Defining A Partnership . . 854
  Basic Partnership Elements 855
  Types Of Partnerships 855

Co-Ownership, Joint Ventures, And Syndicates 857
  Co-Ownership 857
  Joint Ventures 857
  Syndicates 858

Partnership Income, Losses, And Tax Credits 858
  Applicable Concepts 859
  Calculating The Amounts To Be Allocated . . 861
  Methods Of Allocation 866

The Partnership Interest 867
  The Concept 867
  Acquiring A Partnership Interest 867
  Adjusted Cost Base Of Partnership Interest . . 869
  Disposition Of A Partnership Interest 872

Limited Partnerships And Limited Partners . 873
  Definitions 873
  At-Risk Rules 874

Transfer Of Property To And From A Partnership 876
  Definition Of Canadian Partnership . . . 876
  Transfers With No Rollover Provision . . . 876
  Common Partnership Rollovers 877

Specified Investment Flow Through Partnerships 881

Key Terms Used In This Chapter 881

References 882

Problems For Self Study (Online) 883

Assignment Problems 883

CHAPTER 19
Trusts And Estate Planning

Introduction **892**

Basic Concepts. **893**
What Is A Trust? 893
Establishing A Trust 895
Returns And Payments - Trusts 896
Non-Tax Reasons For Using Trusts 896

Classification Of Trusts **896**
Personal Trusts 897
Testamentary Trusts Vs. Inter Vivos Trusts . . 897

Taxation Of Trusts. **900**
The Basic Taxation Model 900
Rollovers To A Trust And Beneficiaries . . . 901

Net Income For Tax Purposes Of A Trust . . **905**
Preferred Beneficiary Election 905
Amounts Deemed Not Paid 906
Amounts Retained For A Beneficiary . . . 906

Taxable Income Of A Trust **907**

Income Allocations To Beneficiaries . . . **907**
General Rules 907
Discretionary Vs. Non-Discretionary . . . 908
Flow Through Provisions 908
Principal Residence Exemption 910

Tax Payable Of Personal Trusts **910**
Calculation Of Basic Amount 910
Other Tax Payable Considerations 911

Income Attribution - Trusts **912**

Purchase Or Sale Of An Interest In A Trust . **914**
Income Interest 914
Capital Interest 914

Tax Planning. **915**
Qualifying Spousal Trusts 917
Alter Ego Trusts 917
Joint Spousal Trusts 918

Estate Planning. **918**

Estate Freeze. **920**

Key Terms Used In This Chapter **923**

References **924**

Problems For Self Study (Online) **925**

Assignment Problems **925**

CHAPTER 20
International Issues In Taxation

Introduction **933**
Subjects Covered. 933
The Role of International Tax Treaties. . . . 934

Part I Tax On Non-Residents **934**
Carrying on Business in Canada 935
Canadian Source Employment Income . . . 937
Dispositions of Taxable Canadian Property. . 938

Part XIII Tax On Non-Residents **940**
Interest Payments 941
Dividend Payments. 942
Royalty Payments 942
Rental Income. 942
Pension Payments And Other
Retirement Related Benefits 944
Shareholder Loans To Non-Residents . . . 945

Immigration And Emigration **946**
Entering Canada - Immigration 946
Departures From Canada - Emigration . . . 946
Unwinding A Deemed Disposition 949
Short-Term Residents 949

**Foreign Source Income
Of Canadian Residents** **950**
Foreign Investment Reporting Requirements . 951
Foreign Source Employment Income 952
Foreign Source Business Income
(Unincorporated Sources) 953
Foreign Source Interest Income 954
Foreign Source Capital Gains 954
Foreign Source Dividend Income - Problems . 955
Foreign Source Dividends
Received By Individuals. 956
Foreign Dividends Received
From Non-Affiliated Corporations 957
Dividends Received
From Non-Controlled Foreign Affiliates. . . 957
Dividends Received From
Controlled Foreign Affiliates 961
Foreign Accrual Property Income (FAPI) . . . 962

Key Terms Used In This Chapter **964**

References **965**

Problems For Self Study (Online) **966**

Assignment Problems **966**

CHAPTER 21
GST/HST

Introduction 975

Transaction Tax Concepts 977
Example 978
Single Stage Transaction Taxes
Retail Sales Tax 978
Multi-Stage Transaction Taxes
Turnover Tax 978
Value Added Tax (VAT) 979

Liability For GST/HST 981
Basic Charging Provision 981
The Concept Of Supply 981

Supply Categories 982
Taxable Supplies 982
Exempt Supplies 983

Applying the GST/HST Rate 984
Place Of Supply 984
Applying The Rate 985

Collection And Remittance Of GST/HST . . 985

Registration 986
Meaning Of Person For GST/HST 986
Who Must Register 986
Exemption For Small Suppliers 987

Input Tax Credits 989
Vendors Of Fully Taxable
And Zero-Rated Supplies 989
Vendors Of Exempt Supplies 991
Accounting vs. Income Tax vs. GST/HST . . . 991
Examples 992

Relief For Small Businesses 995
Quick Method Of Accounting 995
Small Suppliers Exemption 998
Streamlined Input Tax Credit Method 998

GST/HST Procedures And Administration . . 999
GST/HST Returns And Payments 999
Associated Persons 1001
Refunds And Rebates 1001
Books And Records 1001
Appeals 1002
General Anti-Avoidance Rule 1002

Employee And Partner GST/HST Rebate . . 1003
Calculating The GST/HST Rebate Amount . 1003
Example 1003

Residential Property And
New Housing Rebate 1004
General Rules For Residential Property . . . 1004
New Housing Rebate 1005

Sale Of A Business 1005
Sale Of Assets 1005
Sale Of Shares 1006
Other Situations 1006

Specific Applications 1007

Partnerships And GST/HST 1008

Trusts And GST/HST 1009

Key Terms Used In This Chapter 1010

Problems For Self Study (Online) 1011

Assignment Problems 1011

Study Guide

Your two volume textbook is accompanied by a separate Study Guide that is available in print and online.

The chapters of this Study Guide correspond to the chapters of *Byrd & Chen's Canadian Tax Principles*.

Each of these Study Guide chapters contains the following:

- Detailed guidance on how to work through the text and problems in the chapter.
- Detailed solutions to the Exercises and Self Study Problems in the textbook for the chapter.
- A list of learning objectives for the material in the chapter.

In addition, the Study Guide contains:

- Two sample personal tax returns and two Self Study Tax Software Problems in Chapters 4 and 11.
- A sample corporate tax return in Chapter 13.
- An extensive Glossary.

CHAPTER 11

Taxable Income And Tax Payable For Individuals Revisited

Introduction

The Problem

11-1. The subjects of Taxable Income for individuals and Tax Payable for individuals were introduced in Chapter 4. This earlier Chapter provided a general overview of how we arrive at the Taxable Income figure and, in addition, covered in detail the majority of credits that can be applied in the determination of Tax Payable. We chose to cover this material in Chapter 4 in order to enhance your understanding of some of the material dealing with specific types of income in Chapters 5 through 9.

11-2. The problem with this early coverage of these subjects is that there are some concepts and procedures involved in determining Taxable Income and Tax Payable for individuals that cannot be explained without some understanding of the additional components of Net Income For Tax Purposes that are covered in subsequent chapters.

11-3. For example, it is not possible to meaningfully discuss the deduction of loss carry overs in calculating Taxable Income without knowledge of the difference between capital and non-capital losses, a subject that is not covered until Chapter 8. A similar problem arises in dealing with the transfer of dividend tax credits to a spouse. This idea is not comprehensible to an individual who does not have an understanding of the dividend gross up and tax credit procedures which are not introduced until Chapter 7.

Our Solution

11-4. Our solution to this problem is this second chapter on Taxable Income and Tax Payable for individuals. At this point, we have provided comprehensive coverage of all of the components of Net Income For Tax Purposes. Chapter 3, dealt with employment income, Chapters 5 and 6 dealt with CCA and business income, Chapter 7 provided coverage of property income, and Chapter 8 dealt with taxable capital gains and allowable capital losses. This coverage of income components concluded with Chapter 9's coverage of miscellaneous sources of, and deductions from, Net Income For Tax Purposes.

11-5. With this background, we can now finish our coverage of Taxable Income and Tax Payable for individuals. With respect to Taxable Income, we will provide complete coverage of both loss carry overs and the lifetime capital gains deduction. We will also be able to deal with the additional credits required in the determination of Tax Payable, as well as the procedures associated with the determination of alternative minimum tax.

Taxable Income Overview

11-6.   As was discussed in Chapter 4, Taxable Income is calculated by deducting certain specified items from Net Income For Tax Purposes. These deductions, which are found in Division C of the *Income Tax Act*, are as follows:

ITA 110(1)(d), (d.01), and (d.1) - Employee Stock Options   Our basic coverage of stock options and stock option deductions was included in Chapter 3. Adding to this coverage in this Chapter 11, we deal with some special rules that are associated with gifts of shares that have been acquired through the exercise of stock options.

ITA 110(1)(f) - Deductions For Payments   This deduction is designed to ensure that certain amounts are not subject to tax. Included here are such amounts as social assistance received, workers' compensation received (covered in Chapter 4), and amounts exempted from Canadian tax by tax treaty (covered in Chapter 20). Also included here are deductions for employment income received from certain prescribed international organizations and employment income earned by a member of the Canadian forces serving in certain prescribed missions.

ITA 110.2 - Lump-Sum Payments   This Section provides a deduction for certain lump-sum payments (e.g., an amount received as a court-ordered termination benefit and included in employment income). It provides the basis for taxing this amount as though it was received over several periods (a.k.a. income averaging). Limited coverage of this provision can be found in the next section of this Chapter.

ITA 110.6 - Lifetime Capital Gains Deduction   The provisions related to this deduction are very complex and require a fairly complete understanding of capital gains. As a consequence, it was not covered in Chapter 4 and will be given coverage in this Chapter.

ITA 110.7 - Residing In Prescribed Zone (Northern Residents Deductions)   These deductions, which are limited to individuals living in prescribed regions of northern Canada, were covered in Chapter 4.

ITA 111 - Losses Deductible   This is a group of deductions that is available for carrying over various types of losses from preceding or subsequent taxation years. The application of these provisions can be complex and requires a fairly complete understanding of business income, property income, and capital gains. As a consequence, this group of deductions was not covered in Chapter 4 and will be covered in detail in this Chapter.

11-7.   The material in this Chapter will complete our coverage of Taxable Income for individuals. Of the Taxable Income deductions available to individuals, only amounts exempted by treaty under ITA 110(1)(f) and loss carry overs under ITA 111 are available to corporations. There are, however, additional deductions available to corporate taxpayers for charitable contributions and dividends received from other taxable Canadian corporations. These additional deductions are covered in Chapter 12.

Lump-Sum Payments

The Problem

11-8.   Individuals sometimes receive lump-sum payments that relate to services provided in one or more previous years. An example of this would be an employment termination payment that included amounts that related to service provided in previous years.

lump sum payments , tax relief for

11-9.   There is an advantage in such situations in that there has been some deferral of the tax on these amounts. However, because of the presence of progressive rates in the Canadian tax system, the tax liability on such lump-sum payments may be higher than would have been the case had the payments been received and taxed over multiple years. This would be a particularly severe problem in situations where a very large taxable amount is involved. Because of this problem, there is <u>tax relief available for certain lump-sum payments</u>.

Qualifying Amounts

11-10.   The relief can be applied to payments that are referred to as "qualifying amounts". These are given a technical definition in ITA 110.2(1). In the Explanatory Notes that accompany the legislation, the following more general description is found:

> A **qualifying amount** is the principal portion (e.g. not including interest) of certain amounts included in income. Those amounts are: spousal or child support amounts, superannuation or pension benefits otherwise payable on a periodic basis, employment insurance benefits and benefits paid under wage loss replacement plans. Also included is the income received from an office or employment (or because of a termination of an office or employment) under the terms of a court order or judgment, an arbitration award or in settlement of a lawsuit.

Relief Mechanism

11-11.   ITA 110.2(2) provides a deduction for the "specified portion" of a "qualifying amount" that was received by an individual during a particular taxation year. The "specified portion" is the fraction of the qualifying amount that relates to an "eligible taxation year". An "eligible taxation year" is any prior year after 1977 in which the individual was a resident of Canada throughout the year and during which the individual did not become bankrupt. No deduction is available if the qualifying amount is less than $3,000. In somewhat simplified terms, this means that an individual can remove the types of payments described as qualifying amounts from the current year's income, to the extent that they relate to prior years.

11-12.   ITA 120.31 describes an alternative tax that will be payable on the amounts that are deducted under ITA 110.2(2). This tax is the total of the additional taxes that would have been triggered for each relevant preceding year, if the portion of the qualifying amount that relates to that preceding year was added to the individual's Taxable Income for that year. In addition to the tax for those years, a notional amount of interest is added to reflect the fact that the tax was not paid in the relevant years. This interest is accrued from May 1 of the year following the relevant preceding year, through the end of the year prior to the receipt of the lump-sum payment.

tax the person would have paid if lump sum had been included

interest added to account for time value of money

11-13.   The goal of these procedures is to <u>spread the lump-sum payment over earlier years, thereby eliminating the influence of progressive rates on the total tax bill</u>. For example, if a 2018 court settlement reflected a wage adjustment for the years 2013 through 2017, the recipient would pay the amount of taxes that would have been due if he had received the amounts in those earlier years, reduced by the amount of taxes that were paid on these amounts in 2018. In many cases this will provide significant tax relief. However, there may be some situations in which, because of differing marginal tax rates in the years under consideration, using this approach could result in higher taxes because of the addition of the notional amount of interest. In such cases, the taxpayer would not make the deduction under ITA 110.2(2).

can sometimes mean that the individual pays more tax if marginal tax rates in preceding years are higher

Treatment Of Losses

Carry Over Provisions

General Rules

11-14.   In earlier Chapters there have been references to a taxpayer's ability to carry back or carry forward losses. Before covering the carry over rules related to specific types of losses, we will consider the general procedures associated with these carry overs.

11-15.   If a taxpayer experiences a loss in the current year with respect to a particular type of income, it must be used, to the extent possible, to offset other types of income in the current year. The taxpayer does not have any real discretion in this matter. If he is in a position to apply a loss to other types of income that are available in the loss year and he chooses not to do so, the loss cannot be carried over to either earlier or later years.

11-16.   However, there are situations in which one or more losses cannot be used during the current year. There are two basic reasons why this may be the case:

- The taxpayer may not have sufficient other sources of income to absorb the loss (e.g., a business loss that is greater than all other current sources of income).

- The taxpayer may not have sufficient income of the right type to absorb the loss (e.g., an allowable capital loss that is greater than current taxable capital gains).

11-17.   If either of these situations arises in the current year, the taxpayer can either carry the loss back to apply against Taxable Income in previous years or, alternatively, carry the loss forward to apply against Taxable Income in future years. Unlike the situation with current year losses, provided that the use is within the specified carry back and carry forward periods, the decision as to when a loss carry over should be used is at the discretion of the taxpayer.

Carry Backs

11-18.   With one exception, all types of current year losses can be applied against income in the three preceding taxation years. The one exception is limited partnership losses which cannot be carried back (see Chapter 18). When the loss is applied, the carry back will result in a refund of some or all of the taxes that were paid in the carry back year.

11-19.   Note that, with several types of losses, the carry back amount can only be applied against income of the same type. More specifically:

- Net capital losses can only be applied against net taxable capital gains realized in the carry back year.

- Net listed personal property losses (see Chapter 8) can only be applied against listed personal property gains realized in the carry back year.

- Restricted farm losses (see Chapter 6) can only be applied against farm income realized in the carry back year.

Carry Forwards

11-20.   In general, because of the certainty of a refund, taxpayers will want to carry losses back if there is sufficient income of the appropriate type in any of the three preceding years. While variations in applicable tax rates for the relevant years might generate a situation where a taxpayer might wish to risk carrying an amount forward on the possibility that it would eliminate income that is being taxed at a higher rate in the carry forward period, this is unlikely to be a common choice.

11-21.   Any amount of current year loss that is not carried back will become a loss carry forward. Unlike the situation with carry backs, there is some variation in the carry forward period for different types of losses. The current rules are as follows:

Non-Capital Losses And Farm Losses For non-capital and farm losses, the carry forward period is 20 years. Non-capital and regular farm losses can be applied against any type of income in the carry forward year. If the farm loss is restricted, it can only be applied against farm income in the carry forward year.

Net Capital Losses Net capital losses can be carried forward indefinitely, limited only by the life of the taxpayer. However, they can only be applied against taxable capital gains that arise in the carry forward year. As will be discussed later in this Chapter, there is an exception for deceased taxpayers who can generally deduct any unused net capital losses against any type of income in the year immediately preceding death and in the year of death. Note that, as this term is used in the *Income*

Tax Act, net capital loss refers to the excess of the allowable (one-half) portion of capital losses, over the taxable (one-half) portion of capital gains.

7 years **Net Listed Personal Property Losses**   Listed personal property losses can be carried forward for 7 years. As noted previously, they can only be deducted against net listed personal property gains that arise in the carry forward year.

Segregation By Type

11-22.   We have noted that, with both loss carry backs and loss carry forwards, some types of losses can only be applied against income of the same type. Because of this requirement, loss carry forward balances must be segregated by type. More specifically, the separate balances that must be tracked are:

- Non-Capital Losses [employment losses, business losses, property losses, and business investment losses (defined in Paragraph 11-55)]
- Net Capital Losses
- Regular Farm Losses   *3 difference?*
- Restricted Farm Losses

Applying The Deduction

11-23.   With the exception of listed personal property losses (see coverage beginning in Paragraph 11-31), loss carry overs are deducted from Net Income For Tax Purposes in the determination of Taxable Income. *loss carry overs deducted from NIFTP*

11-24.   In the case of a carry back, there is a reduction of both Taxable Income and Tax Payable in the carry back year. Provided the taxes for that year have been paid, the result will be a refund. As you would expect, the refund will be based on the tax rates applicable to the carry back year.

11-25.   With respect to carry forwards, they serve to reduce Taxable Income and Tax Payable in the carry forward year. As was the case with carry backs, the loss carry forward benefit will accrue at the tax rates applicable to the carry forward year.

Loss Carry Overs And Tax Credits

11-26.   You will recall from Chapter 4 that most of the credits against Tax Payable that are available to individuals are not refundable. Further, most of them cannot be carried over to be used in subsequent taxation years. This means that, in the absence of sufficient Tax Payable to absorb these credits, they will be permanently lost.

11-27.   These facts relate to loss carry overs in that, given that many tax credits have no value in the absence of a Tax Payable amount, it is generally not advisable to use loss carry overs to reduce Taxable Income to nil in the carry over year.

> **EXAMPLE** In 2017, Jan Teason had employment income of $25,000 and a net rental loss of $55,000. She had no reported income in the three preceding years. In 2018, she has no employment income and net rental income of $25,000. Ms. Teason's only tax credit is the basic personal credit of $1,771 [(15%)($11,809)].

> **ANALYSIS** In 2017, Ms. Teason had Net Income For Tax Purposes of nil and, at the end of the year, non-capital loss carry forward of $30,000. Note that she did not have the option of reducing the amount of the 2017 rental loss in order to use her personal tax credit.

> If she wished to do so, Ms. Teason could reduce her 2018 Taxable Income to nil by applying $25,000 of the 2017 non-capital loss carry forward. However, if she limits her carry forward deduction to $13,191 ($25,000 - $11,809), her Taxable Income will be reduced to $11,809. The tax on this would be $1,771 [(15%)($11,809)], an amount that would be eliminated by her basic personal credit. This approach leaves an unused carry forward balance of $16,809 ($30,000 - $13,191).

11-28.   What this example illustrates is that, in practical situations, loss carry overs should not be used to reduce Taxable Income to nil. In the real world, tax preparation software should automatically limit loss carry overs to prevent this from happening. However, trying to build this consideration into the examples and problems included in this text can have the effect of significantly complicating material that is already very difficult to understand. As a result, in some problems we ask that you ignore this issue.

11-29.   While this approach is not consistent with real world tax planning considerations, we feel that it can be justified in terms of aiding your understanding of this difficult material on loss carry overs.

Personal Use Property Losses

11-30.   You will recall that personal use property is defined as "property owned by the taxpayer that is used primarily for the personal use or enjoyment of the taxpayer, or for the personal use or enjoyment of one or more individuals related to the taxpayer". As covered in Chapter 8, taxable capital gains on personal use property, determined on the assumption that both the proceeds of disposition and the adjusted cost base are at least $1,000, are included in the calculation of Net Income For Tax Purposes. However, unless the personal use property qualifies as "listed personal property" as described in the following material, losses on personal use property are never deductible.

Listed Personal Property Losses
General Rules

11-31.   Listed personal property is a designation that has been given to 5 specific categories of personal use property. As listed in ITA 54, these categories are:

- a print, etching, drawing, painting, sculpture, or other similar work of art;
- jewelry;
- a rare folio, rare manuscript, or rare book;
- a stamp; or
- a coin.

11-32.   As was the case with personal use property, taxable capital gains on listed personal property are included in Net Income For Tax Purposes, and are also calculated on the assumption that both the proceeds of disposition and the adjusted cost base are at least $1,000 (as noted in Chapter 8, this rule may not be applicable when a charitable donation is involved).

11-33.   The difference with these categories of personal use property is that allowable capital losses on listed personal property can be deducted. However, they can only be deducted against taxable capital gains on listed personal property. They cannot be used to reduce taxes on any other type of income, including taxable capital gains on property that is not listed personal property.

Carry Over Provisions

11-34.   If a loss on listed personal property cannot be used in the current year, it can be carried back three years or forward for seven years. In the carry over year, the loss can only be used to the extent that there are gains on listed personal property in that year.

11-35.   Unlike other loss carry overs, listed personal property losses are not deducted from Net Income For Tax Purposes in the calculation of Taxable Income. Under ITA 41(2), the net gain on listed personal property is defined as the gains for the current year, reduced by the carry over amounts from the seven preceding years, or the three subsequent years. If this amount is positive, it is added in the calculation of Net Income For Tax Purposes under ITA 3(b). While the process is somewhat different, the final result is the same reduction in Taxable Income that would result from the carry over of some other type of loss.

Exercise Eleven - 1

Subject: Listed Personal Property Losses

During 2017, Mr. Ronald Smothers was unemployed and had no income of any kind. In order to survive, he sold a painting on December 1, 2017 for $89,000. This painting had been left to Mr. Smothers by his mother and, at the time of her death, it had a fair market value of $100,000. During 2018, Mr. Smothers finds a job and has employment income of $62,000. In addition, during June he sells a second painting for $5,000. He had purchased this painting several years ago for $1,000. Determine Mr. Smothers' minimum Net Income For Tax Purposes and Taxable Income for 2018. Indicate the amount and type of any losses available for carry forward at the end of the year. Assume the December 1, 2017 sale had been of publicly traded shares instead of a painting. How would this change your solution?

SOLUTION available in print and online Study Guide.

Non-Capital Losses
General Rules
11-36.   In terms of a simple dictionary meaning, the term non-capital would mean any loss other than a loss on the disposition of a capital asset. In fact, in many situations, this non-technical approach would provide the correct result. However, ITA 111(8) contains a very technical definition that must be used in more complex situations in order to ensure that we arrive at the appropriate answer. In simplified form, this definition is as follows:

ITA 111(8) The non-capital loss of a taxpayer for a taxation year means the amount determined by the formula:

$$A - D, \text{ where}$$

A   is the amount determined by the formula:

$$E - F, \text{ where}$$

E   is the total of all amounts each of which is the taxpayer's loss for the year from an office, employment, business or property (including farm losses), the taxpayer's allowable business investment loss for the year, and net capital loss carry overs deducted in the calculation of Taxable Income for the year (this net capital loss amount cannot exceed the taxable capital gains for the year).

F   is the amount of income determined under ITA 3(c). [Sum of ITA 3(a) non-capital positive sources and ITA 3(b) net taxable capital gains, less Division B, Subdivision e deductions.]

D   is the taxpayer's farm loss for the year (amount included in E).

11-37.   Note that this definition excludes both current year capital losses and farm losses. These two types of losses are subject to different rules and, as a consequence, their balances must be tracked separately. The inclusion of net capital losses in this definition will be explained in our later discussion of net capital losses.

11-38.   As can be seen in the definition, non-capital losses can result from the calculation of income from employment, income from a business, or income from property. However, given the limited number of deductions from employment income, it is very unlikely that an individual will experience an employment loss. Normally, non-capital losses would result from the operation of a business or the ownership of property. For example, a non-capital loss on a rental property could occur when expenses associated with the property exceed the rental revenues.

Exercise Eleven - 2

Subject: Non-Capital Losses

During 2018, Janice McMann has net employment income of $35,000, as well as a taxable capital gain of $13,000. In addition, she has a business loss of $58,000 and a farm loss of $2,200. Determine her 2018 non-capital loss.

SOLUTION available in print and online Study Guide.

Carry Over Provisions

11-39.   Non-capital losses are defined in ITA 111(8) in such a fashion that a carry over is only available after the current year's income is reduced to nil. Stated alternatively, a carry over is only possible after all current year losses, other than current year capital losses, have been deducted. If losses remain and are available for carry over, they can be applied, at the taxpayer's discretion, to any of the eligible carry over years. However, ITA 111(3) indicates that a non-capital loss carry over for a particular year cannot be used until the available non-capital loss carry overs from all preceding years have been exhausted.

11-40.   As we have noted, such losses may be carried back three years and applied against any type of income in those years. If there is not sufficient income in those years to absorb the full amount of these non-capital losses, any remaining balance can be carried forward for a period of 20 years. Whether the amounts are carried back or forward, they will be deducted under ITA 111(1)(a) in the computation of Taxable Income.

Net Capital Losses

General Rules

11-41.   The term "net capital loss" is defined in ITA 111(8) as the excess of allowable capital losses over taxable capital gains for the current taxation year. Note carefully that, as the term is used in the *Act*, "net capital loss" refers to the deductible portion of capital losses, not to the 100 percent amounts. When these annual amounts are carried forward, the resulting balance is normally referred to as the "net capital loss balance".

Carry Over Provisions

11-42.   While a net capital loss for the current year cannot be deducted in the calculation of the current year's Net Income For Tax Purposes, this amount is available for carry over to other years. Such losses may be carried back three years and forward to any subsequent year.

11-43.   When they are carried forward or back, they will be deducted under ITA 111(1)(b) in the calculation of Taxable Income. However, ITA 111(1.1) restricts the deduction of such carry over amounts to the amount included in Net Income For Tax Purposes under ITA 3(b) (net taxable capital gains). Expressed in less technical terms, you can only deduct a net capital loss carry over to the extent that you have net taxable capital gains in the carry over year.

11-44.   You will recall from Chapter 8 that the inclusion rate for capital gains has varied over the years. Further, the relevant legislation is such that, when net capital losses are carried over they must be deducted at the rate that is applicable to the carry over year. However, the inclusion rate for capital gains has been one-half since 2000. Given this, our only coverage of situations involving different inclusion rates for capital gains will be in our discussion of net capital losses that are present when a taxpayer dies.

Conversion Of A Net Capital Loss Carry Over
To A Non-Capital Loss Carry Over

11-45.   A problem can arise when a taxpayer has a net capital loss carry over, taxable capital gains in the current year, and a current year business or property loss that is large enough to reduce his Net Income For Tax Purposes to nil. As a net capital loss carry over can only be deducted to the extent of current year net taxable capital gains, the taxpayer usually prefers to use such carry overs whenever current year taxable capital gains are available. A simple example will illustrate this problem.

EXAMPLE For 2018, Mr. Waring has property income of $25,000, taxable capital gains of $45,000 [(1/2)($90,000)], and a business loss of $150,000. He also has a net capital loss carry forward from 2017 of $60,000 [(1/2)($120,000)]. He does not antic-ipate having any further taxable capital gains in the foreseeable future.

11-46. The usual ITA 3 calculation of Net Income For Tax Purposes would be as follows:

ITA 3(a) Non-Capital Positive Sources	$ 25,000
ITA 3(b) Net Taxable Capital Gains	45,000
ITA 3(c) Sum Of ITA 3(a) And 3(b)	$ 70,000
ITA 3(d) Business Loss	(150,000)
Net Income For Tax Purposes	Nil

11-47. The business loss reduced Net Income For Tax Purposes to nil and this is a problem for Mr. Waring in that he does not anticipate having further taxable capital gains in the near future. Given this, it would appear that he has lost the ability to use this year's net taxable capital gains to absorb the 2017 net capital loss carry forward.

11-48. Fortunately, this is not the case. You will recall that, in the definition of non-capital loss in Paragraph 11-36, the taxpayer can add to the E component of the definition, any net capital loss carry overs deducted in the current year. This means that, if we assume that Mr. Waring chooses to deduct the maximum amount of his net capital loss carry forward in 2018, the non-capital loss carry over for 2018 would be as follows:

Business Loss For Year	$150,000
Net Capital Loss Carry Forward Deducted (Limited To Taxable Capital Gains)	45,000
Total For Amount E	$195,000
Amount F = Income Under ITA 3(c) ($25,000 + $45,000)	(70,000)
Non-Capital Loss Available For Carry Over	$125,000

11-49. There are two points that should be made with respect to this analysis:

• The amount of the net capital loss carry forward deducted is limited to the $45,000 in net taxable capital gains that were realized during the year. As a result, he has utilized $45,000 of the $60,000 net capital loss carry forward from 2017.

• The deduction of the net capital loss carry over is discretionary. That is, the taxpayer can deduct any amount between $1 and the maximum value of $45,000. In the solution presented, he has deducted the maximum amount, which results in a non-capital loss carry over of $125,000 and leaves a net capital loss carry forward of $15,000 ($60,000 - $45,000). An alternative would have been to deduct none of the net capital loss carry forward, leaving a net capital loss carry forward of $60,000. Under this scenario, the non-capital loss for the year would be calculated as follows:

Business Loss For Year (Amount E)	$150,000
Amount F = Income Under ITA 3(c) ($25,000 + $45,000)	(70,000)
Non-Capital Loss Available For Carry Over	$ 80,000

As this calculation illustrates, the combined non-capital and net capital loss total will be the same in these situations, without regard to what amount of the net capital loss is used. If $45,000 of the net capital loss is used, the total loss remaining is $140,000 ($15,000 + $125,000). If none is used, the total is still $140,000 ($60,000 + $80,000). In simple economic terms, this procedure allows the taxpayer to convert a net capital loss balance with restricted deductibility, into a non-capital loss balance that can be deducted against any type of income.

Exercise Eleven - 3

Subject: Net Capital Loss Carry Overs

During 2017, Ms. Laura Macky had an allowable capital loss of $15,000. Prior to 2018, she had no taxable capital gains and, as a consequence, she has not been able to deduct this loss. In 2018, her income consists of a taxable capital gain of $40,000 [(1/2)($80,000)] and a net rental loss of $30,000. She does not anticipate any future capital gains. Determine Ms. Macky's minimum 2018 Net Income For Tax Purposes and minimum 2018 Taxable Income, as well as the amount and type of any losses available for carry over at the end of the year. Ignore the effects of her tax credits.

SOLUTION available in print and online Study Guide.

Net Capital Losses At Death

11-50.   One of the difficulties with net capital loss carry overs is that they can normally only be deducted against taxable capital gains. As there is no time limit on the carry forward of such undeducted losses, an individual can die with a substantial balance of these amounts on hand. Capital losses may also arise in the year of death, either through a disposition prior to death or through a deemed disposition at death.

11-51.   ITA 111(2) contains a special provision with respect to both net capital losses from years prior to death and to allowable capital losses arising in the year of death. Essentially, this provision allows these accumulated losses to be applied against any type of income in the year of death, or the immediately preceding year.

11-52.   An example will illustrate these provisions:

EXAMPLE   Ms. Vincent dies in December, 2018. She has a net capital loss carry forward of $25,300 [(1/2)($50,600)]. Her final return has a Net Income For Tax Purposes of $40,000 which includes a taxable capital gain of $4,500 [(1/2)($9,000)]. The only tax credit on her final return is her basic personal tax credit.

ANALYSIS   If Ms. Vincent was alive, her 2018 taxable capital gain would limit the use of her net capital loss carry forward in 2018. This limitation does not apply in the year of death. To maximize tax savings, her final return should have a Taxable Income of 11,809, the 2018 basic personal amount (see Paragraph 11-27). This means that $28,191 ($40,000 - $11,809) of the net capital loss carry forward should be deducted. This can be applied against any type of income in 2018. The $11,809 can be carried back to 2017 in an amended return and applied against any type of income.

11-53.   Capital losses realized by the estate on dispositions of an individual's property in the first taxation year after his death can be carried back and applied against any type of income in the final return of the deceased. Note, however, that these losses cannot be carried back to the tax return for the year preceding death.

11-54.   The inclusion rate has been at one-half since 2000. As a result, calculations where an inclusion rate that is not one-half is relevant are increasingly rare. However, we would note the following points:

- If there are taxable capital gains in the year of death, the net capital loss must first be applied at the inclusion rate for the current year to the extent of those gains. If a net capital loss balance remains, ITA 111(2) allows it to be applied against other types of income, using the inclusion rate that prevailed in the year in which the net capital loss was realized.

- The ability to use this provision is reduced by the previous deduction of amounts under the lifetime capital gains provision (see discussion later in this Chapter). This reduction reflects the actual amount of the lifetime capital gains deduction made, without regard to the capital gains inclusion rate that was applicable at the time.

- Unlike the usual procedure with capital loss carry overs, this carry over deduction is applied at the capital gain/loss inclusion rate that prevailed in the year in which the capital loss was realized.

Exercise Eleven - 4

Subject: Net Capital Losses At Death

Mr. Derek Barnes dies during 2018. He has a net capital loss carry forward of $20,000 [(1/2)($40,000)] at the time of his death. His final return has a Net Income For Tax Purposes of $23,800 which includes a taxable capital gain of $9,200 [(1/2)($18,400)]. The only tax credit on his final return is his basic personal tax credit. Describe the optimal tax treatment of Derek's net capital loss carry forward.

SOLUTION available in print and online Study Guide.

Allowable Business Investment Losses

Defined

11-55. A Business Investment Loss (BIL), as defined in ITA 39(1)(c), is a special type of capital loss resulting from the disposition of shares or debt of a "small business corporation". In addition to losses on arm's length sales, business investment losses can be incurred when there is a deemed disposition for nil proceeds. This could occur for shares of a small business corporation due to bankruptcy or insolvency, or if the debt is considered uncollectible.

11-56. A small business corporation is defined in ITA 248(1) as a Canadian controlled private corporation (CCPC) of which "all or substantially all", of the fair market value of its assets are used in an active business carried on "primarily" in Canada. In tax work, the term "substantially all" generally means 90 percent or more, while "primarily" is generally interpreted to mean more than 50 percent.

11-57. In making this determination, shares or debt of a connected small business corporation would count towards the required 90 percent. A corporation is connected if the potential small business corporation either controls it, or owns more than 10 percent of its voting shares and shares that represent more than 10 percent of the fair market value of all of the corporation's outstanding shares. As you would expect, an Allowable Business Investment Loss (ABIL) is the deductible one-half of a BIL.

Special Treatment

11-58. In general, allowable capital losses can only be deducted against taxable capital gains. However, ABILs are given special treatment in that the taxpayer is permitted to deduct these amounts from any source of income.

> **EXAMPLE** An individual with net employment income of $50,000 has an ABIL of $10,500 [(1/2)($21,000)].

> **ANALYSIS** This individual would be able to deduct the $10,500 ABIL against the employment income, resulting in a Net Income For Tax Purposes of $39,500. If this had been an ordinary allowable capital loss, the taxpayer's Net Income For Tax Purposes would be $50,000 and the unapplied allowable capital loss would become a net capital loss for the year which would be available for carry over to other years.

11-59. If there is sufficient income, the ABIL must be deducted in the year in which it is realized. However, if other sources of income are not sufficient for deducting all or part of an ABIL under ITA 3(d) in the current year, it becomes a part of the non-capital loss carry over balance. This permits this special type of allowable capital loss to be deducted against any type of income when they are carried back or carried forward.

11-60.   If the ABIL has not been applied during the 10 years subsequent to its occurrence, it reverts to its original status as an allowable capital loss and becomes a component of the net capital loss carry forward balance. While this restricts the types of income that the loss can be applied against, it gives the loss an unlimited carry forward period.

Effect Of The ITA 110.6 Lifetime Capital Gains Deduction

11-61.   As we shall see in our discussion of the ITA 110.6 lifetime capital gains deduction, beginning in Paragraph 11-68, the realization of a Business Investment Loss reduces the taxpayer's ability to take advantage of this deduction. Of note here, however, is the fact that under ITA 39(9), Business Investment Losses are disallowed by the use of the ITA 110.6 lifetime capital gains deduction. What this means is, to the extent that the individual has made a deduction under ITA 110.6, an equivalent portion of the Business Investment Loss will be disallowed (i.e., converted to an ordinary capital loss).

> **EXAMPLE**   Mr. Mercer had a taxable capital gain in 2011 of $8,000 [(1/2)($16,000)] and deducted this amount under the provisions of the ITA 110.6 lifetime capital gains deduction. In July, 2018, he has a $60,000 loss on the sale of shares of a small business corporation. Mr. Mercer has no capital gains or losses in any other year.
>
> **ANALYSIS**   If Mr. Mercer had made no use of ITA 110.6, he would have an allowable business investment loss of $30,000 [(1/2)($60,000)] in 2018. However, since he has made a deduction under ITA 110.6, the business investment loss would be reduced as follows:
>
> | | |
> |---|---:|
> | Actual Loss On Disposition | $60,000 |
> | Disallowed By Lifetime Capital Gains Deduction Use | (16,000) |
> | Business Investment Loss | $44,000 |
> | Inclusion Rate | 1/2 |
> | Allowable Business Investment Loss (ABIL) | $22,000 |

11-62.   As we have noted, the disallowed $16,000 does not disappear. It becomes an ordinary capital loss, subject to the usual restriction that it can only be deducted against capital gains. The remaining $22,000 ABIL can be deducted in 2018 against any source of income. If it is not deducted in that year or carried back, it becomes part of the non-capital loss carry forward for 10 (not 20) years. If it is still not used after 10 years, in year 11, it becomes part of the net capital loss carry forward.

Exercise Eleven - 5

Subject: Business Investment Losses

During 2017, Mr. Lawrence Latvik used his lifetime capital gains deduction to eliminate a taxable capital gain of $13,000 [(1/2)($26,000)]. During 2018, he has capital gains on publicly traded securities of $18,000, and a loss of $50,000 on the disposition of shares of a small business corporation. His employment income for 2018 is over $200,000. Determine the amount of the Allowable Business Investment Loss that can be deducted in 2018, as well as the amount and type of any losses available for carry over at the end of the year.

SOLUTION available in print and online Study Guide.

We suggest you work Self Study Problem Eleven-1 at this point.

Farm Losses

Regular Farm Losses

11-63.   For full time farmers, farm losses are not restricted. They are treated in the same manner as non-capital losses in that they can be carried back 3 years and forward for 20 years. Unlike restricted farm losses (see the following Paragraph), when they are deducted on a carry over basis, regular farm losses can be applied against any type of income.

Restricted Farm Losses

11-64.   As noted in Chapter 6, if a farm operation does not have a reasonable expectation of profit (the so-called hobby farm), none of the losses associated with the operation will be deductible. However, even if there is a reasonable expectation of profit, farm losses may be restricted. More specifically, under ITA 31, farm losses are restricted if:

> ... a farmer's chief source of income for a taxation year is neither farming nor a combination of farming and some other source of income that **is a subordinate source of income** for the taxpayer ...

11-65.   In effect, if farming is only a secondary source of income, farm losses will be restricted, even if the farming operation has a reasonable expectation of a profit. The restriction limits losses that can be deducted against other sources of income to the first $2,500 of such losses, plus one-half of the next $30,000, for a maximum deduction of $17,500 [$2,500 + (1/2) ($32,500 maximum - $2,500)] on farm losses of $32,500 or greater. Any amount of the farm loss that is not deductible in the current year is commonly referred to as a "restricted farm loss".

11-66.   Restricted farm losses can be carried over to other years. Such losses can be carried back 3 years and forward for a maximum of 20 years. In carry over periods, restricted farm losses can only be deducted to the extent that income from farming has been included in Net Income For Tax Purposes. For example, if a restricted farm loss carry forward of $15,000 was available at the beginning of 2018 and 2018 farming income totaled $12,000, only $12,000 of the carry forward could be deducted in calculating 2018 Taxable Income. The remaining $3,000 of the restricted loss could not be deducted, even if the taxpayer had large amounts of other types of income available.

11-67.   If land used in a farming business is disposed of before the taxpayer has an opportunity to fully utilize restricted farm losses carried forward, a part of the undeducted losses can be used to increase the adjusted cost base of the property. This would have the effect of reducing any capital gains arising on the disposition of the property. This treatment is only possible to the extent that the loss was created by property taxes or interest payments on the farm property.

Exercise Eleven - 6

Subject: Farm Losses

Ms. Elena Bodkin has a full time appointment as a professor at a Canadian university. As she has considerable free time, she is developing an organic vegetable farm. In 2017, the first year of operation, she had a loss of $36,000 and deducted the maximum allowable amount. In 2018, in addition to her employment income of $85,000, her farming operation showed a profit of $3,500. Determine Ms. Bodkin's minimum 2018 Net Income For Tax Purposes and Taxable Income, as well as the amount and type of any losses available for carry forward at the end of the year.

SOLUTION available in print and online Study Guide.

We suggest you work Self Study Problem Eleven-2 at this point.

Lifetime Capital Gains Deduction

Background

The Original Legislation

11-68.   The lifetime capital gains legislation was first introduced in 1985 and, in its original form, it allowed every individual resident in Canada to enjoy up to $100,000 in tax free capital gains during the course of their lifetime. This privilege was available without regard to the type of property on which the gain accrued. A resident Canadian could acquire a major tax benefit through the process of owning and disposing of a Florida condominium. This original legislation was modified in 1988, providing an enhanced $500,000 deduction for shares in qualified small business corporations and for qualified farm properties.

Limiting Its Scope

11-69.   Without reviewing the long history of this legislation, changes to the original legislation have limited the use of this valuable deduction to dispositions involving qualified farm properties, qualified fishing properties, and shares of qualified small business corporations. These changes left in place a number of issues related to determining the adjusted cost base of assets that had previously qualified for the deduction. However, at this time, these issues are no longer of sufficient importance to warrant coverage in a general text such as this.

Current And Future Limits

11-70.   As of 2018, the deduction limit for dispositions of shares of qualified small business corporations is $848,252. This is an indexed figure that was established at $800,000 in 2014 and is indexed each year for inflation. The available deduction for qualified farm property and qualified fishing property was increased to $1,000,000 for dispositions after April 20, 2015. The $1,000,000 limit will remain unchanged until the indexed limit for qualified small business shares exceeds $1,000,000. At that time the same indexed figure will apply to all types of qualified property. For 2018, the extra amount for farm or fishing properties is $151,748 ($1,000,000 - $848,252).

11-71.   You should note that the limits are cumulative for all three types of qualified property. That is, you do not get $848,252 for qualified small business shares and an additional $1,000,000 for qualified farm and fishing property. Given that we have two different limits, there is a problem in applying a cumulative limit. The solution is that gains on all three types of qualified property are accumulated until they reach the indexed figure ($848,252 for 2018). To go beyond this to the $1,000,000 limit, only gains on dispositions of farm or fishing property are eligible, even if gains on these types of property are included in the first $848,252.

> **EXAMPLE**   In 2017, Mary Geary has a $500,000 gain on a qualified farm property and a $300,000 gain on shares of a qualified small business corporation. In October, 2018, Mary has a $75,000 gain on a qualified farm property and a $100,000 gain on shares of a qualified small business corporation.

> **ANALYSIS**   In 2017, both gains, a total of $800,000, would qualify for the lifetime capital gains deduction. In 2018, only $48,252 of the gain on the qualified small business shares could be eliminated through the use of the lifetime capital gains deduction. The remaining $51,748 ($100,000 - $48,252) would not be eligible as it exceeds the indexed limit for qualified small business shares. However, the $75,000 gain on the qualified farm property could be eliminated with the lifetime capital gains deduction, bringing the total claimed to $923,252 ($800,000 + $48,252 + $75,000).

Qualified Property

Types Of Property

11-72.   The ITA 110.6 lifetime capital gains deduction is available on a disposition of shares of a qualified small business corporation, and interests in qualified farm and fishing properties. As it is the most common application of this provision, we will focus our attention on shares of qualified small business corporations. With respect to the other two types of qualified property, they can be generally described as follows:

> **Qualified Farm or Fishing Property** Qualified farm property and qualified fishing property are defined in ITA 110.6(1). They include real property and eligible capital property used in Canada for farming or fishing by a taxpayer, the taxpayer's spouse, or their children. The definition also includes a share of a family farm or fishing corporation and an interest in a family farm or fishing partnership. To qualify, during the 24 months preceding the disposition, the property must not be owned by anyone other than the selling taxpayer, his spouse or common-law partner, his children or his parents.

Small Business Corporations

11-73.   As noted in our discussion of Business Investment Losses in Paragraph 11-55, ITA 248(1) defines a small business corporation as a Canadian controlled private corporation (CCPC) of which all, or substantially all (90 percent or more), of the fair market value of its assets are used in an active business carried on primarily (more than 50 percent) in Canada. In order to be a qualified small business corporation for the purposes of the lifetime capital gains deduction, the corporation is only required to satisfy this definition of a small business corporation at the point in time at which the shares are sold.

11-74.   In many cases this is not a difficult criterion to satisfy. If, at a particular point in time, less than 90 percent of the fair market value of the corporation's assets are involved in producing active business income, it is often a simple matter to sell some of the non-qualifying assets and distribute the proceeds to the shareholders. This process, commonly referred to as "the purification of a small business corporation", can normally be carried out in a short period of time, thereby satisfying the small business corporation criteria prior to the disposition of the shares.

Qualified Small Business Corporations

11-75.   Not all small business corporations are qualified small business corporations. To achieve this stature, ITA 110.6(1) requires that two other conditions be met. In somewhat simplified terms, they are:

- the shares must not be owned by anyone other than the taxpayer or a related person for at least 24 months preceding the disposition; and
- throughout this 24 month period, more than 50 percent of the fair market value of the corporation's assets must be used in an active business carried on primarily in Canada.

11-76.   There are additional rules that are applicable when intercorporate investments are involved in the preceding determinations. More specifically, additional requirements apply when the condition that 50 percent of the assets must be used in active business for a 24 month period can only be met by adding in the shares of another small business corporation. These special rules go beyond the scope of this text and, as a result, will not be covered here.

11-77.   As compared to meeting the small business corporation criteria, a failure to meet these additional qualifying criteria is more difficult to correct. As they involve measurements made over a period of time, a failure to satisfy them can only be corrected by the passage of time.

Determining The Deductible Amount
General Rules

11-78.   The determination of the amount of the lifetime capital gains deduction that can be deducted in a year involves calculations that can be complex. In general terms, the available deduction is the least of the following three items:

- Capital Gains Deduction Available
- Annual Gains Limit
- Cumulative Gains Limit

11-79.   These items will be explained in detail in the following material.

Capital Gains Deduction Available

11-80.   The "capital gains deduction available" is the lifetime maximum for the capital gains deduction, less any amounts that have been used up in preceding years. As discussed and illustrated with an example in Paragraph 11-71, there are two limits:

- For shares of qualified small business corporations, the limit for 2018 is $424,126 [(1/2)($848,252)].

- For qualified farm and fishing properties the limit is $500,000 [(1/2)($1,000,000)] for dispositions after April 20, 2015.

11-81.   A problem can arise in determining the amounts used up in years prior to 2000. Clearly, it would not be appropriate to subtract a $12,000 deduction made in 1990 which represented the taxable three-quarters of a $16,000 capital gain, from the 2018 limit of $424,126, which is based on one-half of the limit. However, as noted in Paragraph 11-44, the inclusion rate has been at one-half since 2000. Given this, we will not complicate our lifetime capital gains deduction calculations with this issue as it is now much less common.

Annual Gains Limit

11-82.   The annual gains limit is defined in ITA 110.6(1) as follows:

Annual Gains Limit of an individual for a taxation year means the amount determined by the formula

$$A - B, \text{ where}$$

A is equal to the lesser of:

- net taxable capital gains for the current year on all capital asset dispositions [ITA 3(b)]; and
- net taxable capital gains for the current year on dispositions of qualified farm property, qualified fishing property, and qualified small business corporation shares.

B is equal to the total of:

- The amount, if any, by which net capital loss carry overs deducted for the year under ITA 111(1)(b), exceeds the excess of net taxable capital gains for the year [ITA 3(b)] over the amount determined in Part A of this formula; and
- Allowable Business Investment Losses realized during the current year.

11-83.   The annual gains limit formula is made complex by the possibility of having a capital gain on an asset that is not eligible for the deduction in the same year that there is a capital gain on a qualified property. In a year in which there is a capital gain on a qualified property and no other capital gains, the formula can be stated more simply as follows:

Annual Gains Limit is equal to the taxable capital gains on qualified property, less:

- Allowable capital losses realized.
- Net capital loss carry overs deducted.
- Allowable Business Investment Losses realized.

11-84.   We will make use of this abbreviated formula when the only capital gains during the year are those on qualified property.

11-85.   Additional points here are as follows:

- With respect to the Allowable Business Investment Losses realized, the full amount is subtracted in the preceding formula, without regard to whether they have been deducted in the calculation of Net Income For Tax Purposes. Also keep in mind that the amount of Allowable Business Investment Losses realized is based only on those amounts that have not been disallowed by the previous use of the lifetime capital gains deduction.

• As a further point here, the deduction of net capital loss carry forwards is discretionary. This means that, in cases where there is the possibility of using either the lifetime capital gains deduction or a net capital loss carry forward, the individual must choose between the two alternatives. This is inherent in the annual gains limit formula which, in most situations, will reduce the limit on a dollar for dollar basis for net capital loss carry overs deducted.

While this choice between the two alternatives may have no influence on the current year's Taxable Income, we would suggest a preference for making maximum use of the lifetime capital gains deduction. There is no time limit on using the net capital loss carry forward and, more importantly, it can be used when any type of taxable capital gain is realized. In contrast, the lifetime capital gains deduction can only be used for particular types of capital gains.

Exercise Eleven - 7

Subject: Annual Gains Limit

On January 1, 2018, your client, Miss Jana Slovena, has a net capital loss carry forward from 2016 of $45,000. During 2018, Miss Slovena has the following:

• taxable capital gains on sales of real estate in the amount of $114,000
• allowable capital losses of $82,000
• a taxable capital gain of $42,000 on sales of shares in a qualified small business corporation
• an Allowable Business Investment Loss of $3,000 on sales of shares of a small business corporation that does not qualify for the lifetime capital gains deduction

As she does not expect to have additional capital gains in the near future, Miss Slovena has asked you to deduct the full $45,000 of the 2016 net capital loss during 2018. Determine her annual gains limit for 2018 using this approach. What advice would you give Ms. Slovena regarding her net capital loss?

SOLUTION available in print and online Study Guide.

Cumulative Net Investment Loss (CNIL)

11-86. Many individuals who have high income, invest in products that are, in general, referred to as tax shelters. Such products include limited partnerships, certain types of investments in resource properties and, in some situations, real estate. These investments, while producing positive overall results for investors, also generate significant tax savings. Hence, the name tax shelter. The government concluded that it was inequitable for individuals to simultaneously deduct such investment losses while sheltering capital gains through the use of the lifetime capital gains deduction. As a result, the legislation restricts the use of the lifetime capital gains deduction by an individual's Cumulative Net Investment Losses (CNIL).

11-87. CNIL is defined as the amount by which the aggregate of investment expenses for the current year and prior years ending after 1987, exceeds the aggregate of investment income for that period. That is, the CNIL consists of post-1987 investment expenses minus investment income. You should note that, in this context, both investment income and investment expense are defined in the *Income Tax Act*. As a consequence, they have a meaning that can be different from the meaning associated with the everyday use of these terms.

11-88.   As will be explained in the following material, individuals who have a CNIL will have their ability to use the lifetime capital gains deduction reduced. As a result, if qualified capital gains are anticipated, it is advantageous to minimize any CNIL. Some examples of ways in which the impact of the CNIL can be reduced are as follows:

- Realizing capital gains on qualified assets early, if Cumulative Net Investment Losses are anticipated in future years.

- Delaying the disposition of qualified assets with accrued capital gains until the CNIL has been eliminated or reduced as much as possible.

- For owner/managers, having their corporation pay dividends or interest on shareholder loan accounts, rather than salaries, to increase investment income.

Cumulative Gains Limit

11-89.   In somewhat simplified form, the cumulative gains limit can be defined as follows:

The sum of all annual gains limits for the current and previous years, unadjusted for changes in the capital gains inclusion rate. This total is reduced by:

- The sum of all amounts deducted under the lifetime capital gains deduction provision in computing the individual's taxable incomes for preceding taxation years (unadjusted for changes in the capital gains inclusion rate); and

- the individual's CNIL at the end of the year.

11-90.   In the absence of a CNIL balance, this formula would simply be the sum of all annual gains limits, reduced by all of the lifetime capital gains deductions made in previous years. As individuals will normally deduct the full amount of their annual gains limit, this balance will usually be equal to the annual gains limit for the current year. This result can be altered by an individual's failure to deduct the full amount of the annual gains limit in some previous year, either as a tax planning choice or as the result of a CNIL balance.

11-91.   The following is a simple example of cumulative gains limit calculations.

EXAMPLE   In 2018, Ms. Nolan has $5,600 of deductible interest on loans for investment purposes and $2,600 of net rental income. She has had no investment income or investment expenses in years prior to 2018, so her Cumulative Net Investment Loss (CNIL) is $3,000 ($5,600 - $2,600). During August, 2018, she has a $60,000 taxable capital gain on the sale of shares in a qualified small corporation. Ms. Nolan has no other capital gains or losses in 2018.

ANALYSIS   As she has made no previous use of her lifetime capital gains deduction, her unused lifetime limit for qualified small business shares is $424,126. While her annual gains limit would be $60,000, the amount of the taxable capital gain, her ability to use the lifetime capital gains deduction would be reduced by her CNIL as her cumulative gains limit is only $57,000 ($60,000 - $3,000).

Comprehensive Example

11-92.   The example that follows illustrates the basic rules involved in the application of the lifetime capital gains deduction.

EXAMPLE   Dwight Treadway's 2018 Net Income For Tax Purposes is as follows:

Employment Income	$ 60,000
Taxable Capital Gain On The Sale Of	
Shares In A Qualified Small Business Corporation	200,000
Net Income For Tax Purposes	$260,000

In 2012, Mr. Treadway realized a $20,000 taxable capital gain [(1/2)($40,000)] from the sale of shares in a qualified small business corporation and used his lifetime capital gains deduction to claim a deduction for this amount. In 2011, Mr. Treadway realized an allowable capital loss of $9,000 [(1/2)($18,000)]. He was not able to use the loss in that year, or any other year, and he intends to deduct it as a net capital loss carry forward in 2018. Other than the 2012 taxable capital gain of $20,000 and the 2011 allowable capital loss of $9,000, Mr. Treadway had no capital gains, capital losses, loss carry overs, or Business Investment Losses from 2011 through 2018. He has no CNIL balance in 2018.

ANALYSIS For 2018, the maximum deduction under ITA 110.6 would be the least of the following amounts:

- **Capital Gains Deduction Available = $404,126** ($424,126 - $20,000).

- **Annual Gains Limit = $191,000** As Mr. Treadway has had no capital gains on non-qualified property in 2018, we can use the simplified version of this calculation. (See Paragraph 11-83.) This would result in an annual gains limit of $191,000, the $200,000 taxable capital gain for the year, less the 2011 net capital loss carry forward of $9,000 deducted under ITA 111(1)(b).

- **Cumulative Gains Limit = $191,000** As the annual gains limit for 2012 would be equal to the $20,000 taxable capital gain on qualifying property, the sum of the annual gains limits would be $211,000 ($20,000 + $191,000). Subtracting from this the $20,000 lifetime capital gains deduction for 2012 leaves the cumulative gains limit of $191,000.

11-93. Given these calculations, the maximum deduction for 2018 would be $191,000, the amount of both the annual gains limit and the cumulative gains limit. The full $200,000 gain on the shares could have been deducted if Mr. Treadway had not chosen to deduct the net capital loss carry forward. The deduction of this amount reduced both the annual gains limit and the cumulative gains limit by $9,000. It would be advisable for Mr. Treadway not to deduct any of the net capital loss carry forward. If he did this, his annual gains limit would increase to $200,000. Although he would have used $9,000 more of his lifetime capital gains deduction, his tax liability for 2018 would not change and he would still have a net capital loss carry forward of $9,000 that could be applied against any type of capital gain for an unlimited period of time.

Exercise Eleven - 8

Subject: Lifetime Capital Gains Deduction (ITA 110.6 Deduction)

Mr. Edwin Loussier had a 2011 taxable capital gain on shares of a qualified small business corporation of $5,000 [(1/2)($10,000)] and a 2013 taxable capital gain on shares of a qualified small business corporation of $13,000 [(1/2)($26,000)]. He used his ITA 110.6 lifetime capital gains deduction to eliminate both of these gains. He has no other capital gains, capital losses, or Business Investment Losses in the period 2011 through 2016. In December, 2017, he has a $63,000 capital loss which, because he has no capital gains in that year, he cannot deduct. In 2018, he has a $510,000 capital gain on the sale of shares of a qualified small business corporation. In addition, he deducts the $63,000 capital loss from 2017. Mr. Loussier does not have a CNIL balance. Determine Mr. Loussier's maximum lifetime capital gains deduction for 2018. Provide all of the calculations required to determine the maximum ITA 110.6 deduction.

SOLUTION available in print and online Study Guide.

We suggest you work Self Study Problem Eleven-3 at this point.

Ordering Of Deductions And Losses

Significance Of Ordering

11-94.   If an individual has sufficient income to absorb all of the losses and deductions that are available in the calculation of Taxable Income, the question of ordering is not important. The real significance of provisions covering the ordering of losses and other deductions is in the determination of the amounts and types of items that can be carried over to previous or subsequent years.

11-95.   For example, assume that a taxpayer has taxable capital gains of $25,000, a business loss of $25,000, and allowable capital losses of $25,000. No matter how these items are ordered, the Net Income For Tax Purposes will be nil. However, it does make a difference whether the loss carry over is for the business loss, or for the net capital losses. A net capital loss carry forward can only be deducted to the extent of taxable capital gains in the carry forward period. On the other hand, the non-capital losses can only be used for a limited period of time (20 years) while, by contrast, the net capital losses can be carried forward indefinitely. Note, however, with a time limit of 20 years, having a limited carry forward period of this length is not likely to be a significant factor in most situations.

Ordering In Computing Net Income For Tax Purposes

11-96.   The basic rules for the computation of Net Income For Tax Purposes under Division B are found in ITA 3. In computing Net Income For Tax Purposes, ITA 3 indicates that we begin by adding together positive amounts of income from non-capital sources, plus net taxable capital gains. Net taxable capital gains are defined as the amount, if any, by which the current year's taxable capital gains exceed the current year's allowable capital losses. This, in effect, requires that capital losses, to the extent there are capital gains during the year, be deducted prior to the deduction of any other type of loss.

11-97.   The various deductions available under Subdivision e (RRSP deductions, spousal support paid, child care costs, moving expenses, etc.) are subtracted from this total. If a positive balance remains, the final step in computing Net Income For Tax Purposes is to subtract any employment, business, or property losses, as well as Allowable Business Investment Losses. If this process does not seem familiar to you, you might want to review the material on ITA 3 that is contained in Chapter 1.

Ordering In Computing Taxable Income

11-98.   The ordering rules in ITA 3 are applicable to all taxpayers - individuals, corporation and trusts. Further, they are not discretionary. Items that occur during a given taxation year, must be added or deducted in that year. In contrast, the ordering rule in ITA 111.1 only applies to individuals. Under this rule, the order in which Division C items must be deducted is as follows:

- Various deductions provided by ITA 110 (e.g., stock options)
- Retroactive lump-sum payments under ITA 110.2
- Loss carry overs under ITA 111 (non-capital, net capital and farm)
- Lifetime capital gains deduction under ITA 110.6
- Northern residents deductions under ITA 110.7

11-99.   Within ITA 111 (loss carry overs), available amounts can be deducted in any order the taxpayer wishes. The only constraint is the ITA 111(3)(b) requirement that, within a particular type of loss (e.g., non-capital losses), the oldest losses have to be deducted first.

11-100.   When several different types of loss carry overs are available, decisions in this area can be difficult. On the one hand, certain types of carry overs have a limited period of availability (i.e., non-capital losses and farm losses can be carried forward for 20 years). In contrast, net capital losses have no time limit, but can only be deducted to the extent of taxable capital gains that have been realized in the year. Restricted farm loss carry overs and carry overs of losses on listed personal property have more onerous limitations. These losses are restricted with respect to both time and type of income (e.g., restricted farm loss carry forwards are available for 20 years and can only be deducted to the extent of farm income earned in the year).

11-101. Decisions in this area will involve a careful weighing of which type of loss carry over is most likely to have continued usefulness in future years. For example, if a non-capital loss carry forward is 19 years old and the business is expecting no Taxable Income in the following year, then use of this carry forward would appear to be a prudent course of action. An additional constraint is that the deduction of loss carry overs should leave sufficient Taxable Income that Tax Payable does not become less than the amount of available tax credits. As discussed in Paragraph 11-26 through 11-29, tax credits that are not used during the current taxation year are, in general, permanently lost.

Example

11-102. The following is an example of the ordering rules used in computing Taxable Income for individuals:

EXAMPLE At the beginning of 2018, Miss Farnum had the following loss carry forwards available:

Non-Capital Losses	$40,000
Net Capital Losses [(1/2)($20,000)]	10,000
Restricted Farm Losses	5,000

For 2018, she can claim only the basic personal amount of $11,809. Also during 2018, she has no available subdivision e deductions. For this year, she had the following income amounts as calculated under Division B rules:

Employment Income	$15,000
Property Income (Interest)	4,000
Farm Income	2,000
Income From Sole Proprietorship	15,000
Capital Gains	12,000

ANALYSIS Miss Farnum's 2018 Net Income For Tax Purposes and Taxable Income would be calculated as follows:

Income Under ITA 3(a):		
Employment Income	$15,000	
Property Income	4,000	
Farming Income	2,000	
Business Income (Proprietorship)	15,000	$36,000
Income Under ITA 3(b):		
Taxable Capital Gains [(1/2)($12,000)]		6,000
Net Income For Tax Purposes		**$42,000**
Restricted Farm Loss Carry Forward (Limited to farming income)		(2,000)
Net Capital Loss Carry Forward (Limited to taxable capital gains)		(6,000)
Subtotal		$34,000
Non-Capital Loss Carry Forward ($34,000 - $11,809)		(22,191)
Taxable Income = Basic Personal Amount		**$11,809**

Loss Carry Forwards

• Restricted farm loss carry forward ($5,000 - $2,000)	$ 3,000
• Net capital loss carry forward ($10,000 - $6,000)	4,000
• Non-capital loss carry forward ($40,000 - $22,191)	17,809

11-103.   Note that, in this example, the amount of net capital and restricted farm losses deducted was limited by the amount of the taxable capital gains and farm income. The non-capital loss deducted was limited to the amount that would reduce her Taxable Income to her basic personal amount of $11,809. Since her Tax Payable will be nil at this point, there is no reason to deduct any further amount of the non-capital loss available.

Exercise Eleven - 9

Subject: Ordering Of Losses

At the beginning of 2018, Alan Barter had the following loss carry forwards available:

Restricted Farm Losses	$ 8,000
Non-Capital Losses	36,000
Net Capital Losses [(1/2)($40,000)]	20,000

During 2018, he had the following amounts of income:

Taxable Capital Gains	$ 9,000
Business Income	12,000
Employment Income	56,000
Farm Income	3,500

Determine Alan's Net Income For Tax Purposes, as well as his minimum Taxable Income for 2018. Indicate the amount and type of any losses available for carry forward at the end of the year.

SOLUTION available in print and online Study Guide.

Tax Payable Overview

General

11-104.   Chapter 4 provided detailed coverage of the application of federal tax rates to Taxable Income in order to provide an initial figure for an individual's Tax Payable. In addition, coverage of most of the tax credits available to individuals was provided. The coverage of tax credits was extended in Chapter 7 with coverage of the dividend tax credit, as well as the credit for taxes withheld on foreign source income.

11-105.   None of this material will be repeated in this Chapter. However, as many of the Self Study and Assignment Problems that accompany this Chapter are comprehensive in nature and will require you to apply tax calculations and credits, you might wish to review the material in Chapters 4 and 7 before working the problems in this Chapter.

11-106.   As was the case with the material on Taxable Income, there are issues involved with the determination of Tax Payable for individuals that could not be dealt with in Chapter 4 because of the need to understand income concepts not presented until subsequent chapters. As a result, additional coverage of Tax Payable is included in this Chapter. Specifically, the following concepts and procedures are discussed in this material:

Tax On Split Income (TOSI)   This is a special tax, assessed at the maximum federal rate of 33 percent on certain types of income received from a related source. It was originally designed to limit income splitting to minor children. However, as of 2018 it has been extended to cover related adults.

Transfer Of Dividends To A Spouse Or Common-Law Partner   The calculations related to this tax credit require an understanding of the dividend gross up and tax credit procedures which were not introduced until Chapter 7.

Charitable Donations   The basic calculation of this tax credit was presented in Chapter 4. However, it was not possible to deal with gifts of capital property until the material in Chapters 5 through 8 on business income, property income and capital gains had been covered.

Foreign Tax Credits   These credits were introduced in Chapter 7. However, the full determination of the eligible amounts requires the additional material on Taxable Income that is included in this Chapter.

11-107.   Now that we have covered the material in Chapters 5 to 10, we are in a position to complete our coverage of the determination of Tax Payable for individuals.

Basic Federal Tax Payable

11-108.   Basic federal Tax Payable is a figure from which some, but not all tax credits have been deducted. At one time, this was an important figure in that it was the base that the provinces and territories used in calculating their respective provincial Tax Payable. Since the provinces now base provincial taxes on Taxable Income, the basic federal tax figure is no longer of general importance.

11-109.   This concept does have some limited use in specialized situations and, because of this, you will see references to this figure in the T1 tax return. The most important of these is that it is used to calculate the additional federal Tax Payable that must be paid by individuals who are deemed Canadian residents but do not reside in a province (e.g., members of the Canadian Armed Forces stationed outside of Canada). However, other than indicating that this concept exists, we will give basic federal Tax Payable no further consideration.

Tax On Split Income (TOSI)

Background
The Problem
11-110.   As discussed in Chapter 1, income splitting is one of the most powerful weapons in tax planner's arsenal. For example, if an Ontario taxpayer with over $300,000 of Net Income For Tax Purposes receives $30,000 of 2018 additional income in the form of eligible dividends, the combined federal/provincial tax on these dividends would be $11,802 [($30,000)(39.34%)]. Alternatively, if this taxpayer can find a way to channel this income to a related individual with no other source of income, this individual would receive the dividends tax free (see discussion of tax free dividends in Chapter 15), resulting in a 2018 savings of $11,802. Further, a similar savings can occur year-after-year, provided the high income taxpayer can find a way to regularly re-allocate the $30,000 of eligible dividends

11-111.   Given the attractiveness of income splitting, it is not surprising that taxpayers have created many different and sometimes complex arrangements to implement the required transfers of income.

11-112.   In situations where the government believes the use of income splitting is appropriate, tax legislation provides for some use of this technique. Examples of this would be spousal RRSPs and pension income splitting. However, the government is not prepared to allow unlimited use of this technique and various anti-avoidance provisions have been put into place over the years (e.g., the income attribution rules).

1999 - Introduction Of The Tax On Split Income (Kiddie Tax)
11-113.   The 1999 federal budget introduced the Tax On Split Income (TOSI, hereafter). As introduced at that time, it only applied to what the legislation referred to as Specified Individuals. Specified Individuals were originally defined as:

- children who were under the age of 18 at the end of the taxation year;
- were residents of Canada throughout the year; and
- had a parent who was a resident of Canada sometime during the year.

11-114.   This new tax, quickly dubbed by tax professionals as the "kiddie tax", was assessed at the maximum federal rate (29 percent at that time, 33 percent, currently). This rate was applied to all Split Income, beginning with the first dollar received. In addition, only limited tax credits were available against the resulting tax payable.

11-115.   In the 1999 legislation, the concept of Split Income included:

- Dividends from private companies received directly or indirectly through a trust or partnership.
- Shareholder benefits or loans received from a private corporation.
- In some circumstances, income from a partnership or trust if the income is derived from the provision of property or services to a business.

11-116.   It is important to note that the new legislation on Split Income does not alter the application of this concept to individuals under the age of 18. Also important is the fact that none of the exceptions to Split Income treatment are available to this group. If the recipient of such income meets the definition of a Specified Individual, is under 18, and the income falls into the categories described in the preceding paragraph, 100 percent of it will be taxed at the maximum federal tax rate.

11-117.   These changes served to significantly curtail the use of income splitting with minor children. With Split Income amounts being taxed at the maximum federal rate, there was no longer any monetary incentive to allocate these types of income to a minor child with little or no other income.

Consultation On Changes

11-118.   Even after the 1999 introduction of the Kiddie Tax, the government believed that private companies were being used in tax planning procedures that were offensive. Reflecting this view, the 2017 Federal Budget announced that a study was underway to develop legislation that would place additional constraints on the use of private companies in tax planning. This study was released in July, 2017 and included draft legislation dealing with income sprinkling by private companies, as well as issues related to the accumulation of passive investments by private companies.

11-119.   Many of the provisions in this first draft were subject to heavy and, in some cases, well deserved criticism. As planned, the government set out a 90 day period for receiving submissions from critics. After extensive consultation with users and careful consideration of the views heard, the government released revised legislation in December, 2017. The provisions related to income splitting came into effect for 2018. Other provisions related to the accumulation of passive investments by private companies will become effective for 2019. As we have noted, coverage of the latter provisions is deferred until the next edition of this text.

2018 - Expansion Of The TOSI

11-120.   The new legislation expanded the applicability of the TOSI in two important ways:

Types Of Income   The original TOSI legislation generally limited its coverage to private company dividends, shareholder benefits, and some types of partnership and trust income. Under the new legislation, its coverage has been expanded to include interest received on debt issued by a private corporation, as well as capital gains.

Specified Individuals   The definition of a Specified Individual has been expanded to include all residents of Canada, in addition to those under 18 who have a parent who is a resident of Canada.

11-121.   These new provisions, commonly referred to as "income sprinkling" legislation, came into effect January 1, 2018. These provisions are presented largely as amendments to the original provisions that were found in ITA 120.4 of the *Income Tax Act*. This revised section is both lengthy and complex. In addition, some of the provisions are sufficiently subjective that there is likely to be many disputes with respect to their implementation.

11-122.   Complete coverage of these provisions could occupy an entire Chapter in this text, a result that would not be appropriate in a general text such as this. Our coverage will be limited to fairly basic situations and will not deal with the many complications that are found in the complete legislative provisions. While this will provide both students and professionals with a basic understanding of these provisions, this presentation will not provide a satisfactory reference for individuals dealing with complex, real-world cases.

What Is Split Income?
Terminology
11-123.   The TOSI may be applicable when a Specified Individual (previously defined) receives certain types of income. In the case of individuals over 17, it must be received from a related business. In general, a business is related when a person related to a Specified Individual is connected to the business. This latter individual is referred to as a Source Individual. This connection occurs when the Source Individual:

- carries on the business as a proprietorship; or
- is actively engaged in a private corporation in which he owns shares.

11-124.   Where the business is a partnership, the Source Individual must have a direct or indirect interest in the partnership and be actively engaged in its business. If the business is carried on by a corporation, the business will be a related business if the Source Individual owns shares that represent 10 percent or more of the fair market value of all of the corporation's issued shares. As was the case with the definition of a Specified Individual, the definition of Source Individual requires the individual to be a Canadian resident.

11-125.   Consider the following simple example:

EXAMPLE   John Russo owns 100 percent of the voting shares of JR Inc., a Canadian private company. He is actively engaged in the business. He has issued a class of non-voting shares to his 25 year old son, Jerry. Jerry has never been active in his father's business. During 2018, these shares pay dividends of $20,000.

11-126.   This is a classic example of the type of situation that the TOSI was designed to prevent. Using the terminology of the legislation, John would be referred to as a Source Individual and Jerry would be referred to as a Specified Individual. While there are complications, these terms refer to individuals who are residents of Canada.

11-127.   The dividends received by Jerry would clearly be Split Income and subject to the TOSI. They are received from a corporation controlled by a Source Individual that is related to Jerry, the Specified Individual. While we have not discussed any of the exceptions to the definition of Split Income, none of them would be applicable in this situation.

11-128.   As an additional point here, only amounts that are subject to the TOSI are considered to be Split Income. If, because of one of the exceptions which we will be discussing shortly, the TOSI is not applicable to a particular income stream, the amounts will not be considered Split Income.

Types Of Income
11-129.   While the original TOSI largely applied to dividends, the current version generally covers dividends, interest and capital gains. It does not, however, cover employment income or compound income resulting from the investment of Split Income amounts.

11-130.   The TOSI is also applicable to indirect receipts of income. For example, if a private corporation pays dividends to a family trust and that trust distributes the income to minor children, the TOSI would apply to the income distributed.

Applicability Of The TOSI
Default Application
11-131.   If a taxpayer has received amounts that are potentially subject to the TOSI, the default position is that 100 percent of these amounts will be subject to federal tax at the

current maximum rate of 33 percent. Further, credits against the resulting Tax Payable will be limited to dividend tax credits and foreign tax credits to the extent that they relate to the amounts subject to the TOSI.

11-132.   Fortunately, a fairly large number of potential Split Income amounts can be excluded from the definition. These amounts will not be considered Split Income and, as a consequence, will not be subject to the TOSI.

Excluded Amounts

11-133.   There are a number of exceptions to the general rules that allow amounts that might be considered Split Income to be excluded from the default treatment. Understanding these exceptions is further complicated by the fact that several of them have exceptions to their basic rules.

11-134.   Further complicating the situation is the fact that whether an exception applies is dependent on the age of the Specified Individual. We have already noted that none of these exceptions apply to the under 18 age group. With respect to other age groups, some exceptions only apply to those 25 years of age or older, some apply to those between 18 and 24 years of age, and one is applicable only when the Specified Individual's spouse or common-law partner is aged 65 or older.

11-135.   The major exceptions, presented in a somewhat simplified manner, can be described as follows:

EXCLUDED BUSINESS (Taxpayers Age 18 And Over)   Amounts received from an Excluded Business are not considered to be Split Income and are not subject to the TOSI. An Excluded Business is one in which the taxpayer is actively engaged on a regular, continuous and substantial basis. This active engagement must be in the current taxation year or in at least 5 prior taxation years. Note, however, the years do not have to be current or consecutive. That is, any 5 years of active engagement will satisfy this condition.

To simplify the application of this rule, the CRA guidance on TOSI has provided what is referred to as a "bright line" test. This test requires that the taxpayer work in the business an average of at least 20 hours per week during the time the business is in operation. Note that, if the business is seasonal (e.g., a landscaping business), the 20 hours per week requirement is only required for the portion of the year during which the business operates.

The CRA materials also note that a failure to meet this bright line test does not necessarily prevent the taxpayer from using the Excluded Business exception. Whether or not an individual is actively engaged will depend on the facts and circumstances in individual cases.

EXCLUDED SHARES (Taxpayers Age 25 And Over)   Amounts received from Excluded Shares are not considered to be Split Income and are not subject to the TOSI. For shares to be classified as Excluded Shares, the taxpayer must be aged 25 or older and must own, in terms of both fair market value and voting rights, at least 10 percent of the outstanding shares of the corporation. In addition, the corporation must meet the following conditions:

- It must not be a professional corporation. ITA 248(1) defines a professional corporation as a corporation that carries on the professional practice of an accountant, dentist, lawyer, medical doctor, veterinarian, or chiropractor. Corporations carrying on the practice of other professionals, for example architects, do not fall within this definition.
- Less than 90 percent of its income in the previous year is from the provision of services.
- Less than 10 percent of its income in the previous year was from a related business.

REASONABLENESS TEST (Taxpayers Age 25 And Over)   For taxpayers age 25 or older, Split Income amounts that represent a Reasonable Return for contributions made to the business are not subject to the TOSI. The measurement of a Reasonable Return requires consideration of labour contributions, capital contributions, as well as the assumption of business risk.

REASONABLENESS TEST (Taxpayers Age 18 To 24)   For individuals between the age of 18 and 24, the reasonableness test is more restrictive. It does not take into consideration either active engagement in the business or business related risk assumed. It is based solely on capital contributions to the business.

For these individuals, this exclusion from Split Income requires that the return be limited to either a "safe harbour" capital return or a "reasonable return" on "arm's length" capital.

The safe harbour capital return would be based on the highest prescribed rate for any quarter in the year. Note that it is the basic prescribed rate and does not include the extra amounts that are applicable for amounts owing to the CRA or amounts owing by the CRA to the taxpayer.

The alternative reasonable return is limited to investment capital acquired from an arm's length source. That is, the reasonable return does not apply to capital that the Specified Individual has acquired from a related business, or a loan or a transfer from a related person.

SPOUSE IS 65 OR OLDER   For a number of years, legislation has allowed spouses and common-law partners to split pension income (see coverage in Chapter 9). An additional exception has been added to the TOSI legislation to allow a similar result for amounts that might be considered Split Income.

Specifically, Split Income does not include income received by a spouse of any age, if that income would not have been Split Income if it had been received by their spouse who is 65 years of age or older.

PROPERTY ACQUIRED THROUGH MARRIAGE BREAKDOWN   Split Income does not include amounts that a Specified Individual receives from a property that is acquired as a result of a marriage breakdown agreement. This only applies to property received under a written agreement. Further, it does not apply to property that the Specified Individual owned prior to the marriage breakdown.

CAPITAL GAINS ON QUALIFIED PROPERTY   Split Income does not include capital gains on qualified property that is eligible for the lifetime capital gains deduction. This is true, even if the lifetime capital gains deduction is not claimed.

11-136.   These are the more important of the amounts that are excluded from the Split Income classification. As indicated, this is a somewhat simplified presentation of these exceptions. In addition, you should be aware that there are other exceptions which we have not covered.

Calculation Of The Tax
The Tax Credit Problem
11-137.   When a Specified Individual has received Split Income, their Tax Payable is made up of two components. The first component is based on a calculation that, under ITA 20(1)(ww), removes the Specified Individual's Split Income from the total. This can create a problem in determining tax credits that are income tested.

     EXAMPLE   Josh Browning has taxable income of $250,000, while his spouse Maria has Taxable Income of $15,000, all of which is Split Income. When the deduction is made under ITA 20(1)(ww), the remaining balance of Maria's Income will be nil.

ANALYSIS The problem with this result is that if the nil amount was used for calculating income tested tax credits, the subtraction of the Split Income would result in the creation of a spousal tax credit for Josh of 1,771 [(15%)($11,809 - nil)]. In contrast, if there had been no Split Income subtraction, Maria's income would exceed the 2018 base for the spousal tax credit of $11,809, resulting in no spousal tax credit for Josh.

The government did not believe that this was an appropriate result and added ITA 118(4)(a.2). This provision indicates that for purposes of determining personal tax credits, the Net Income figure that would be used would be before the ITA 20(1)(ww) deduction. This means that Josh's spousal tax credit would be nil ($11,809 - $15,000).

Two Components

11-138.   With the ITA 20(1)(ww) subtraction, the taxpayer's income is made up of two components:

Split Income Component   This component will be subject to a federal flat rate of 33 percent. The only credits against the resulting Tax Payable will be dividend tax credits and/or foreign tax credits that relate to the amounts included in Split Income.

Regular Income Component   This component will be subject to the regular graduated rates and will be eligible, subject to the ITA 118(4)(a.2) provision, for the usual tax credits.

11-139.   A simple example will serve to illustrate these calculations.

EXAMPLE   Helen, who is 25 years old, receives non-eligible dividends of $20,000 from a private company controlled by her father. In addition, she has interest income of $5,500 from a savings account funded by an inheritance. Her only tax credits are the basic personal credit and the dividend tax credit. She is not eligible for any exclusion from the application of the TOSI.

ANALYSIS   The initial calculation involves determining the tax on total income, reduced by amounts that fall within the definition of Split Income (the non-eligible dividends). All of the usual tax credits can be claimed in this calculation.

Taxable Non-Eligible Dividends [(116%)($20,000)]	$23,200
Interest Income	5,500
Deduction For Split Income - Non-Eligible Dividends	(23,200)
Net Income For Tax Purposes = Taxable Income	$ 5,500
Tax Rate	15%
Tax Payable Before Credits	$ 825
Basic Personal Credit [(15%)($11,809)]	(1,771)
Federal Tax Payable On Regular Income	Nil

The TOSI Payable would be calculated as follows:

Split Income - Taxable Non-Eligible Dividends	$23,200
Tax Rate	33%
Tax Payable Before Dividend Tax Credit	$ 7,656
Dividend Tax Credit [(8/11)(16%)($20,000)]	(2,327)
TOSI Payable	$ 5,329

With the regular component being nil, the total Tax Payable will be $5,329, the amount based on the Split Income sources.

11-140.   In some circumstances, Source Individuals may be liable for payment of the TOSI if the Specified Individual fails to make the required payment.

Evaluation

11-141.   Both the original Kiddie Tax legislation, as well as the expansion of the TOSI coverage to adult taxpayers, were met with howls of protest from many in the tax community. In our view, these changes represented appropriate modifications. The type of income splitting that is being attacked in these provisions is, in general, only available to higher income Canadians. It would be difficult to describe our tax system as fair if such arrangements were allowed to continue.

Exercise Eleven - 10

Subject: Tax On Split Income

During 2018, Norton James, who is 16 years old, receives non-eligible dividends of $15,000 from a private corporation controlled by his mother. He also has income of $13,200 from contracts to create computer games. As he has used the income that he has earned from these contracts in previous years to invest in the stock market, he has eligible dividends from publicly traded companies of $8,600. Assume his only tax credits are his basic personal credit and dividend tax credits on the shares that he owns. Determine Norton's federal Tax Payable for 2018.

SOLUTION available in print and online Study Guide.

We suggest you work Self Study Problem Eleven-4 at this point.

Tax Credits Revisited

Transfer Of Dividends To A Spouse Or Common-Law Partner

11-142   There may be situations in which a taxpayer's spousal credit has been reduced or eliminated by dividends received by that spouse. The ITA 82(3) election permits a transfer of all of the dividends from the spouse or common-law partner's income to that of the taxpayer, if it creates or increases the spousal credit. Consider the following example:

EXAMPLE   Mrs. Barba's total income consisted of $12,000 in eligible dividends received from taxable Canadian corporations. Mrs. Barba's basic personal tax credit, along with part of the dividend tax credit, eliminate all taxation on the grossed up amount of $16,560 [(138%)($12,000)]. However, because she has this income receipt, Mr. Barba is not able to claim a spousal tax credit.

ANALYSIS   In this situation, the transfer of dividends under ITA 82(3) would eliminate all of Mrs. Barba's income, and Mr. Barba would be able to claim the full spousal credit of $1,771. Mr. Barba would then be taxed on the $16,560 of grossed up dividends. He would, however, be eligible for the dividend tax credit associated with these dividends. Whether this is a good alternative or not depends on Mr. Barba's marginal tax rate, as can be seen in the following calculations:

Mr. Barba's Tax Bracket	15%	33%
Increase In Taxable Income	$16,560	$16,560
Tax On $16,560	$ 2,484	$ 5,465
Increase In Spousal Credit	(1,771)	(1,771)
Dividend Tax Credit [(6/11)(38%)($12,000)]	(2,487)	(2,487)
Increase (Decrease) In Tax Payable	($ 1,774)	$ 1,207

As can be seen in the table, if Mr. Barba is in the 15 percent tax bracket, his federal tax would be decreased by $1,774. Alternatively, if he is in the 33 percent bracket, the transfer would not be desirable as his federal tax would be increased by $1,207.

Exercise Eleven - 11

Subject: Transfer Of Dividends To A Spouse

Mr. Albert Ho is 38 years old and has over $250,000 in 2018 Taxable Income. His wife's only 2018 source of income is $8,500 in eligible dividends received from taxable Canadian corporations. In terms of federal Tax Payable, would Mr. Ho benefit from the use of the ITA 82(3) election to include the eligible dividends received by his spouse in his Net Income For Tax Purposes? Justify your conclusion.

SOLUTION available in print and online Study Guide.

We suggest you work Self Study Problems Eleven-5 and 6 at this point.

Charitable Donations Credit Revisited

Introduction

11-143. A basic treatment of this credit was provided in Chapter 4. In that Chapter, we noted that, for individuals, the first $200 of donations was eligible for a tax credit of 15 percent. The rate applicable to additional amounts was either 29 percent or 33 percent depending on the Taxable Income of the donor. In general, the base for calculating this credit was limited to 75 percent of the taxpayer's Net Income For Tax Purposes.

11-144. In Chapter 4, we dealt only with simple situations involving gifts of cash. Coverage of more complex issues involving gifts of various types of capital property was deferred and is included in this Chapter 11.

11-145. As many of you are aware, in recent years, a number of gift giving programs have been developed that appear to provide the taxpayer with benefits that exceed his cost and, in some cases, the value of the gift to the recipient charity.

11-146. A classic example of this was the so-called art flips. Such arrangements might involve a taxpayer buying a large block of paintings directly from the inventories of the artist. The cost of the block was essentially a wholesale value and was significantly lower than the sum of the retail prices of the individual paintings. The paintings would then be appraised on the basis of individual retail values, followed by a gift of the art works to a registered charity. The taxpayer would then claim a tax credit based on the significantly higher appraised value, often resulting in a tax credit that was worth more than the original cost of the paintings.

11-147. Because of problems such as this, ITA 248(30) through ITA 248(41) were added to the *Income Tax Act*. These subsections are intended to curtail the ability of taxpayers to use schemes which abuse the intent of the basic charitable donations legislation.

Donations Classified

11-148. ITA 118.1 defines four types of charitable donations:

1. **Total Charitable Gifts** is defined to include all eligible amounts donated by an individual to a registered charity, a registered Canadian amateur athletic association, a Canadian municipality, the United Nations or an agency thereof, a university outside of Canada which normally enrolls Canadian students, and a charitable organization outside of Canada to which Her Majesty in right of Canada has made a gift in the year or in the immediately preceding year.

2. **Total Crown Gifts** is defined as the aggregate of eligible amounts donated to Her Majesty in right of Canada or a province.

3. **Total Cultural Gifts** is defined as the aggregate of all eligible gifts of objects that the Canadian Cultural Property Export Review Board has determined meet the criteria of the *Cultural Property And Import Act*.

4. **Total Ecological Gifts** is defined as all eligible gifts of land certified by the Minister of the Environment to be ecologically sensitive land, the conservation and protection of which is important to the preservation of Canada's environmental heritage. The beneficiary of the gift can be any level of government. The beneficiary can also be a registered charity, provided its primary purpose is the conservation and protection of Canada's environmental heritage.

11-149.   In addition to the items specified in the *Act*, under the U.S./Canada tax treaty, Canadians can claim gifts to any qualifying U.S. charity in amounts up to 75 percent of their net U.S. income (75 percent of their net world income if the Canadian resident lives near the U.S. border and commutes to a U.S. place of business or employment).

Eligible Amounts

11-150.   In the preceding material on the classification of donations, each of the definitions contains the term "eligible amounts". The term is defined as follows:

> **ITA 248(31)** The eligible amount of a gift or monetary contribution is the amount by which the fair market value of the property that is the subject of the gift or monetary contribution exceeds the amount of the advantage, if any, in respect of the gift or monetary contribution.

11-151.   ITA 248(32) defines "advantage" very broadly to include a benefit to the taxpayer that is in any way related to the gift, including benefits that are contingent on future events.

> **EXAMPLE** As an example of an advantage, consider a gift of real property with a fair market value of $300,000. If the charity receiving the gift were to assume a $100,000 mortgage on the property, this would be considered an advantage. The resulting eligible amount of the donation is $200,000 ($300,000 - $100,000).

11-152.   In addition to this eligibility requirement, ITA 248(30) includes the concept of "intention to give". The basic idea here is that, if the advantage to the taxpayer resulting from making the gift exceeds 80 percent of the value of the gift, the gift will be disallowed unless the taxpayer can convince the Minister that the transfer was made with a real intention to make a gift.

Deemed Fair Market Value

11-153.   In order to eliminate arrangements such as the art flip that was described in Paragraph 11-146, ITA 248(35) introduces the concept of "deemed fair market value". This Subsection indicates that, if a taxpayer acquires a property less than three years prior to its donation as a gift or, if a taxpayer acquires a property less than 10 years before the gift is made and it is reasonable to conclude that the taxpayer acquired the property with an intent to make a gift, the value of the gift will be based on the lesser of the cost to the taxpayer and the actual fair market value at the time of the gift. There is an exception to this rule for gifts made as a consequence of a taxpayer's death.

Gifts Of Capital Property - Transfer At Elected Value

11-154.   When an individual makes a charitable, Crown, or ecological (but not cultural) gift of capital property, an election is available under ITA 118.1(6). On such properties, there will usually be a difference between the tax cost of the property (i.e., adjusted cost base for non-depreciable properties or UCC for depreciable properties) and its fair market value. If the fair market value is the higher value, the taxpayer can elect to transfer the property at any value between the tax cost of the property and its fair market value. There are special rules applicable to gifts of publicly traded securities and ecologically sensitive land that will be covered in Paragraph 11-161.

11-155.   With respect to non-depreciable assets, if the fair market value of the donated asset exceeds the adjusted cost base of the asset, it is advisable to elect the fair market value. Any amount of elected value in excess of $200 will be eligible for a tax credit at either 29 percent or 33 percent. In contrast, only one-half of any capital gain that results from the disposition will be taxed.

EXAMPLE Mr. Vignesh Menan has a piece of land with an adjusted cost base of $100,000 and a fair market value of $150,000. During 2018, he intends to gift this land to a registered Canadian charity and would like to know whether he should elect to make the donation at $100,000 or alternatively, at $150,000. Before consideration of any income resulting from making the gift, Mr. Menan has Taxable Income of more than $400,000. Given this, any amount of donations in excess of $200 will receive a credit based on the maximum tax rate of 33 percent.

ANALYSIS The tax consequences of the two alternatives are as follows:

Elected Value	$100,000	$150,000
Tax Credit [(15%)($200) + (33%)($99,800)]	$ 32,964	
Tax Credit [(15%)($200) + (33%)($149,800)]		$ 49,464
Tax On Gain	N/A	
Tax On Gain [(1/2)($150,000 - $100,000)(33%)]		(8,250)
Credit Net Of Tax	$ 32,964	$ 41,214

11-156.   It should be noted that ITA 118.1(6) places a floor on this election. The elected value cannot be below the amount of any advantage received by the taxpayer as a consequence of the gift.

EXAMPLE - Extended Mr. Vignesh Menan has a piece of land with an adjusted cost base of $100,000 and a fair market value of $150,000. In return for making this gift, he receives a cash payment from the registered charity of $110,000.

ANALYSIS Mr. Menan cannot elect a value below $110,000. Assuming he elects to transfer the asset at the maximum value of $150,000, the eligible amount of his gift will be $40,000 ($150,000 - $110,000).

11-157.   The situation is not so clear when depreciable assets are involved. This results from the fact that an election at fair market value may create fully taxable recapture. The taxes on such recapture may be a bit more than the credit generated by the donation as the credit on the first $200 is at 15 percent.

Gifts Of Capital Property - Income Limits
11-158.   In most cases, an individual's eligible donations are restricted to 75 percent of Net Income For Tax Purposes for the year (see Chapter 4). A potential problem with electing a value that creates income is that making a gift and electing to use the fair market value may result in income that cannot be eliminated with the related tax credit. In other words, making a gift could result in the payment of taxes. To avoid this problem, two other components are added to the Net Income base for charitable donations, resulting in a total base equal to:

- 75 percent of Net Income For Tax Purposes for the year; plus
- 25 percent of any taxable capital gain resulting from a gift; plus
- 25 percent of any recaptured CCA resulting from a gift.

11-159.   An example will illustrate the importance of these additions to the overall limit:

EXAMPLE In July, 2018, Jonas Anderson gifts a customized bus that was used in his proprietorship to a registered Canadian charity. The bus has a fair market value of $130,000, a capital cost of $100,000, and a UCC of $65,000. He elects to make the gift at the fair market value of $130,000. He has no other source of income, other than amounts arising as a result of the gift.

ANALYSIS The election to make the gift at the fair market value of $130,000 will result in a total increase in Net Income For Tax Purposes of $50,000. This is comprised of a taxable capital gain of $15,000 [(1/2)($130,000 - $100,000)] and recaptured CCA of $35,000 ($100,000 - $65,000).

As Mr. Anderson has no other source of income, his basic limit for charitable dona-tions would be $37,500 [(75%)($50,000)]. If his limit was $37,500, he would be faced with paying tax on $12,500 ($50,000 - $37,500) less his personal tax credits, as a result of his generosity in making the gift. However, with the additions to the limit, his charitable donations credit base limit is as follows:

75 Percent Of Net Income For Tax Purposes [(75%)($50,000)]	$37,500
25 Percent Of Taxable Capital Gain [(25%)($15,000)]	3,750
25 Percent Of Recaptured CCA [(25%)($35,000)]	8,750
Total Limit (Equals Income From Donation)	$50,000

11-160.   As you can see, the additions to the limit serve the purpose of creating a base for charitable donations that includes 100 percent of any income resulting from gifts of capital property. Note, however, Mr. Anderson will not want to use the full $50,000 in 2018. As amounts over $200 will generate a credit at a rate of 29 percent (the 33 percent rate is not rele-vant as Mr. Anderson's Taxable Income is well below the $205,842 threshold for that rate) and all of Mr. Anderson's income will be taxed at a lower rate, use of the full $50,000 would produce a credit that is larger than his Tax Payable. In addition, he will want to make use of any non-refundable tax credits that are available for 2018. The following Exercise illustrates the determination of the amount of an available tax credit that should be taken in order to reduce Tax Payable to nil.

Exercise Eleven - 12

Subject: Donation Of Depreciable Property

Ms. Sally Felder donates some food preparation equipment to the local food bank, a registered Canadian charity. The assets have a fair market value of $85,000, a capital cost of $62,000, and a UCC of $28,000. She elects to make the donation at the fair market value of $85,000. She has no other source of income during the year and her only tax credit other than the charitable donations tax credit is her basic personal credit of $1,771. Determine her maximum charitable donations tax credit for 2018. In addition, determine the amount of the donation she should claim in 2018 in order to reduce her federal Tax Payable to nil. Calculate any carry forward of unused amounts that will be available in future years.

SOLUTION available in print and online Study Guide.

Gifts Of Publicly Traded Securities And Ecologically Sensitive Land
11-161.   Gifts of publicly traded securities and ecologically sensitive land benefit from special rules that make gifting these assets particularly attractive. While a donor can receive a donations tax credit based on the full fair market value of such assets, ITA 38(a.1) deems the capital gain on gifts of publicly traded securities to be zero. Using the same approach, ITA 38(a.2) deems the capital gain on gifts of ecologically sensitive land to be zero.

Gifts Of Publicly Traded Securities Acquired Through Stock Options
11-162.   Without special rules, there is a potential problem for donations of publicly traded shares purchased through stock options. You will recall from Chapter 3 that, in the case of these shares, any accrued gain that is present at the time the options are exercised is treated as an employment income inclusion. In order to give such gains effective capital gains treat-ment, a deduction of one-half is provided in the determination of Taxable Income.

EXAMPLE Roberto Cerutti is provided with options to buy 1,000 of his employer's shares at an option price of $20 per share, the fair market value of the shares at the time the options are granted. Roberto exercises these options when the shares are trading at $32 per share. He gifts the shares immediately to a registered charity.

ANALYSIS Roberto will have an increase in Taxable Income calculated as follows:

Employment Income [(1,000)($32 - $20)]	$12,000
Deduction Under ITA 110(1)(d) [(1/2)($12,000)]	(6,000)
Increase In Taxable Income	$ 6,000

11-163. As this increase in Taxable Income is not a capital gain, it will not be deemed to be zero by ITA 38(a.1). In the absence of a further special provision, this $6,000 would be subject to tax. Fortunately, ITA 110(1)(d.01) contains a provision which acts to eliminate this tax. This paragraph provides an additional deduction equal to one-half of the Employment Income inclusion. Using this additional provision, the results would be as follows:

Employment Income [(1,000)($32 - $20)]	$12,000
Deduction Under ITA 110(1)(d) [(1/2)($12,000)]	(6,000)
Deduction Under ITA 110(1)(d.01) [(1/2)($12,000)]	(6,000)
Increase In Taxable Income	Nil

Exercise Eleven - 13

Subject: Donation Of Listed Shares

Mr. Saheed Radeem has employment income of $90,000. He owns shares that are listed on the Toronto Stock Exchange. These shares have a fair market value of $110,000 and an adjusted cost base of $30,000. During 2018, these shares are given to a registered Canadian charity. He has no deductions in the calculation of Taxable Income (i.e., his Taxable Income is equal to his Net Income For Tax Purposes). His tax credits, other than the charitable donations credit, total $4,000. Determine Mr. Radeem's maximum charitable donations tax credit for 2018 and the amount of the donation he should claim in 2018 in order to reduce his federal Tax Payable to nil. Calculate any carry forward of unused amounts that will be available in future years.

SOLUTION available in print and online Study Guide.

Canadian Cultural Property

11-164. We have noted that, when an individual makes a charitable, Crown or ecological gift of capital property, they can elect to have the proceeds of disposition be any value between the tax cost of the property and the fair market value. In the case of cultural gifts of capital property, ITA 118.1(10.1) deems the proceeds of disposition to be the fair market value of the property in all cases. Note, however, that this same Subsection indicates that the value established by the Canadian Cultural Property Export Review Board or the Minister of the Environment is deemed to be the fair market value of the donated asset.

11-165. This fair market value rule must be considered in conjunction with the fact that a provision in ITA 39(1)(a)(i.1) indicates that, with respect to gifts of Canadian cultural property, the difference between the fair market value and the adjusted cost base of the asset does not fall within the meaning of capital gain. As a consequence, any gain on a gift of Canadian cultural property is not subject to tax. Losses, however, would be treated as normal capital losses. Given this, it is not unreasonable to require that the proceeds of disposition on cultural gifts of capital property be equal to the fair market value of the property.

Limits On Amount Claimed And Carry Forward Provisions

11-166. As noted in Chapter 4, it is the policy of the government to limit charitable donations that are eligible for the tax credit to a portion of a taxpayer's Net Income For Tax Purposes. Note that, while corporations deduct their donations as opposed to receiving a credit against Tax Payable, the limits on the amount of eligible donations are the same for corporations as they are for individuals.

11-167.   The limit on eligible amounts of charitable gifts is 75 percent of Net Income For Tax Purposes, but there are exceptions to this general limit. For individuals, this limit is increased to 100 percent of Net Income For Tax Purposes in the year of death and the preceding year. In those situations where a gift of capital property resulted in a capital gain and/or recaptured CCA, the overall limit is increased by 25 percent of the taxable capital gain and 25 percent of any recaptured CCA resulting from such a gift. There is no income limit on the amount of Crown gifts, cultural gifts, or ecological gifts. Credits can be claimed for these gifts up to their full eligible amounts.

11-168.   The *Income Tax Act* does not require that charitable donations be claimed in the year that they are made. Unused charitable donations can be carried forward and claimed in the subsequent 5 year period (10 years for ecological gifts). In the carry forward period, the same income based limits will apply in determining eligible amounts.

Foreign Tax Credits Revisited
Rules For Corporations
11-169.   Corporations are allowed to use foreign non-business income and foreign business income tax paid as a basis for a credit against Canadian Tax Payable. The rules for corporations are somewhat different from those for individuals and, in addition, require an understanding of some concepts that have not been introduced at this stage in the material. As a result, the foreign tax credit rules applicable to corporations are discussed in Chapter 12.

Foreign Non-Business (Property) Income Tax Credit For Individuals
11-170.   ITA 126(1) provides for a tax credit in situations where a Canadian resident has paid foreign taxes on non-business income. We introduced coverage of foreign tax credits in Chapter 7, but could not fully discuss the calculations as we had not yet covered loss carry overs and the lifetime capital gains deduction.

11-171.   As was noted in Chapter 7, the full amount of foreign non-business income earned, including amounts withheld for taxes in the foreign jurisdiction, must be added to the taxpayer's Net Income For Tax Purposes. This 100 percent amount is then subject to Canadian taxes, with the amount withheld in the foreign jurisdiction being allowed as a credit against Canadian Tax Payable. The objective of this procedure is to tax non-business income earned in a foreign jurisdiction at the same overall rate as would apply to non-business income earned in Canada.

11-172.   There are a number of complications with this procedure. The first of these is that, for individuals, amounts withheld that exceed 15 percent of the total foreign non-business income must be deducted under ITA 20(11). If, for example, an individual earned $1,000 in a jurisdiction that withheld $200, $150 of this amount would serve as a credit against Tax Payable, with the remaining $50 being deducted under ITA 20(11).

11-173.   A further problem is that the federal government wants to ensure that taxpayers do not receive a credit that is greater than the Canadian taxes that would have been paid on the foreign non-business income. This is accomplished by limiting the foreign non-business tax credit to the lesser of the amount withheld, and the amount determined by multiplying the ratio of foreign non-business income to total income by Canadian Tax Payable. This approach is reflected in the following formula:

The **Foreign Non-Business Income Tax Credit** is the lesser of:

- The tax paid to the foreign government. For individuals, this is limited to 15 percent of foreign non-business income, and

- An amount determined by the following formula:

$$\left[\frac{\text{Foreign Non} - \text{Business Income}}{\text{Adjusted Division B Income}}\right][\text{Tax Otherwise Payable}]$$

11-174.   The "Adjusted Division B Income" in this formula is defined as follows:

Division B Income (i.e., Net Income For Tax Purposes), less:
- net capital loss carry overs deducted under ITA 111(1)(b);
- any lifetime capital gains deduction taken;
- any amounts deductible for stock options under ITA 110(1)(d) and (d.1); and
- any amounts deductible under ITA 110(1)(f) for workers' compensation, social assistance or exempt foreign income.

11-175.   "Tax Otherwise Payable" in this calculation consists of:

Part I Tax Payable before the deduction of:
- dividend tax credits;
- employment outside of Canada tax credits;
- political contributions tax credits;
- investment tax credits; and
- labour sponsored funds tax credits.

11-176.   You should note that the preceding definition of Adjusted Division B Income is unique to the calculation of foreign tax credits. It starts with Net Income For Tax Purposes (Division B Income), and proceeds to deduct some, but not all, of an individual's available Division C deductions. The most important omission is the fact that non-capital losses are not deducted. As a result, "Adjusted Division B Income" is a figure that is neither Net Income For Tax Purposes nor Taxable Income.

11-177.   The preceding rules would have to be applied on a country by country basis if non-business income was received from more than one foreign source. If the amount of foreign non-business taxes withheld exceeds the amount determined by the formula, there is no carry over of the unused amount as a tax credit. However, ITA 20(12) allows a taxpayer to deduct such amounts in the determination of Net Income For Tax Purposes.

Foreign Business Income Tax Credit For Individuals

11-178.   If a Canadian resident has income from an unincorporated business in a foreign country, ITA 126(2) provides for a credit for foreign taxes paid that is similar to that for non-business income. As is the case with foreign non-business income tax credits, individuals must include 100 percent of the foreign business income in their Net Income For Tax Purposes, with foreign taxes withheld being allowed as a credit against Tax Payable.

11-179.   While the amount of the credit that can be used does not have the 15 percent limit that is applicable to foreign non-business income tax credits, it is limited by a formula that is similar to the formula applicable to the foreign non-business income tax credit. One of the main differences between these two formulas is that, with respect to the foreign business income tax credit, there is an additional limit based on the tax otherwise payable for the year, reduced by any foreign non-business income tax credit deducted. The calculation of the foreign business income tax credit is as follows:

The **Foreign Business Income Tax Credit** is the least of:

- The tax paid to the foreign government (no 15 percent limit).

- An amount determined by the following formula:

$$\left[\frac{\text{Foreign Business Income}}{\text{Adjusted Division B Income}}\right][\text{Tax Otherwise Payable}]$$

- Tax Otherwise Payable for the year, less any foreign tax credit taken on non-business income under ITA 126(1).

11-180.   A further important difference between the two foreign tax credits is that, when foreign business income taxes paid exceed the amount that can be used as a credit during the current year, there is a three year carry back and ten year carry forward available. That is, if a taxpayer does not have sufficient Tax Payable to use all of the foreign business income tax credit during the current year, the excess can be claimed against Tax Payable in any of the 3 preceding years, or in any of the 10 subsequent years. Note, however, that it can only be used in those years within the constraints provided by the formula in Paragraph 11-179.

Exercise Eleven - 14

Subject: Foreign Tax Credits

During 2018, Sarah Cheung has net rental income of $44,000, net taxable capital gains of $2,500 and foreign non-business income of $3,500. The foreign jurisdiction withheld 11 percent of this amount, resulting in a net receipt of $3,115. In calculating Taxable Income, she deducts a $4,000 non-capital loss carry forward and a $2,500 net capital loss carry forward. Her only tax credits are the basic personal credit and the credit for foreign tax paid. Calculate her federal Tax Payable for 2018. Include a detailed calculation of her foreign non-business income tax credit. Ignore the fact that Sarah could deduct any excess of the withholding amount ($385) over the actual credit in the determination of Net Income For Tax Purposes.

SOLUTION available in print and online Study Guide.

Alternative Minimum Tax

General Concept

11-181.   There is a strong public feeling that allowing wealthy individuals with high levels of income to pay little or no tax is not an equitable situation. While such cases usually involve no more than taking full advantage of the various provisions in the *Act* that allow individuals to reduce their Tax Payable, the government felt that it was necessary to have legislation in place to deal with this public relations problem. As a result, an alternative minimum tax (AMT) was introduced.

11-182.   This tax is directed at individuals who take advantage of tax shelters and other "tax preference" items. The basic idea is that individuals who have certain types of income, deductions, or credits, must calculate an adjusted taxable income by adding back all of the "tax preferences" that have been used in the calculation of regular taxable income. As will be discussed in Chapter 19, for income tax purposes, trusts are considered to be individuals. Given this, with a few exceptions, trusts are subject to the AMT.

11-183.   After deducting a basic $40,000 exemption, a flat rate of 15 percent is applied to the remaining net adjusted taxable income. The resulting Tax Payable is reduced by some, but not all, of the individual's regular tax credits to arrive at a minimum tax. The taxpayer must pay the greater of the regular Tax Payable and the minimum tax. Again, as will be discussed in Chapter 19, the $40,000 exemption is not available to trusts in calculating their minimum tax. The one exception to this is a testamentary trust that has been designated as a graduated rate estate.

Minimum Tax Calculation
Definition
11-184.   The minimum tax is specified in ITA 127.51 as follows:

An individual's minimum amount for a taxation year is the amount determined by the formula

$$A (B - C) - D, \text{ where}$$

A is the appropriate percentage for the year (15 percent for 2018);
B is his adjusted taxable income for the year determined under section 127.52;
C is his basic exemption for the year (currently $40,000); and
D is his basic minimum tax credit for the year determined under section 127.531.

Adjusted Taxable Income

11-185.   The calculation of adjusted taxable income that is described in ITA 127.52 is illustrated in a somewhat more comprehensible fashion in Form T691. The basic idea behind this adjusted taxable income is to put back into regular taxable income those items that are felt to be "tax preferences". Examples of such preference items would be losses on tax shelters and the non-taxable portion of capital gains.

11-186.   The calculation of adjusted taxable income described in ITA 127.52 is as follows:

Regular Taxable Income

Plus Additions:
* 30 percent of the excess of capital gains over capital losses (see Paragraph 11-187).
* 3/5 of the employee stock option deductions under ITA 110(1)(d) and (d.1).
* Amounts of CCA on Certified Canadian Films.
* The excess of CCA and interest charges claimed on rental and leasing property, over the net income or loss reported for such property.
* Amounts deducted for Canadian Exploration Expense (CEE), Canadian Development Expense (CDE), or depletion, net of certain resource related income.
* Losses deducted by limited partners, and members of a partnership who have been specified members at all times since becoming partners, in respect of their partnership interests, net of certain gains allocated from the same partnership.
* Deductions related to investments identified or required to be identified under the tax shelter identification rules.

Less Deductions:
* The gross up of Canadian dividends.
* 60 percent of ABILs deducted (see Paragraph 11-188).
* 60 percent of net capital loss carry overs deducted.

Equals: Adjusted Taxable Income For Minimum Tax Purposes

11-187.   Rather than require that all of the non-taxable component of capital gains be added back, which could result in an excessive number of taxpayers being exposed to alternative minimum tax, only 30 percent of the total capital gain is added in the Adjusted Taxable Income calculation. This brings the total inclusion of the excess of capital gains over capital losses to 80 percent (50 percent is already included in regular income, plus the additional 30 percent).

11-188.   The government also decided that this 80 percent treatment was appropriate for ABILs. The Adjusted Taxable Income calculation requires an additional deduction of 60 percent of any ABILs deducted in the year. Since 60 percent of an ABIL is equal to 30 percent of the total Business Investment Loss and 50 percent is already deducted from regular income, this effectively provides for a total deduction equal to 80 percent of the Business Investment Loss.

Tax Payable Before Credits

11-189.   A basic exemption of $40,000 is subtracted from the adjusted taxable income figure. As noted, this $40,000 exemption is not available to trusts, other than those testamentary trusts that have been designated as graduated rate estates.

11-190.   After subtraction of the basic exemption, a flat rate is applied to the resulting balance. This rate is referred to in the ITA 127.51 formula as the "appropriate percentage". Appropriate percentage is defined in ITA 248 as the lowest percentage applicable in calculating federal Tax Payable. Since 2007, this rate has been 15 percent. The resulting figure could be described as the alternative minimum tax before the deduction of tax credits.

Tax Credits For AMT

11-191. ITA 127.531 specifies the tax credits, as calculated for the determination of regular Tax Payable, which can be applied against the alternative minimum tax. The credits specified are as follows:

- Personal credits under ITA 118(1)
- Age credit under ITA 118(2), but not the transfer from a spouse
- Canada employment credit under ITA 118(10)
- Adoption expenses credit under ITA 118.01
- Home accessibility credit under ITA 118.041
- First time home buyer's credit under ITA 118.05
- Volunteer firefighters credit under ITA 118.06
- Volunteer search and rescue workers credit under ITA 118.07
- Charitable donations credit under ITA 118.1
- Medical expense credit under ITA 118.2
- Disability credit under ITA 118.3, but not the transfer from a spouse or other dependant
- Tuition credit under ITA 118.5, but not the transfer from a spouse or other dependant
- Interest on student loans credit under 118.62
- CPP and EI credits under ITA 118.7

11-192. The deduction of these credits will produce the alternative minimum tax payable. If this amount exceeds the regular taxes that are payable on the regular taxable income, the amount of alternative tax must be paid.

AMT Carry Forward - ITA 120.2

11-193. There will be individuals who become subject to this alternative minimum tax in only some taxation years. The most common example of this situation is the realization of a large capital gain that can be eliminated by the use of the lifetime capital gains deduction.

11-194. To provide for this, an excess of alternative minimum tax over regular Tax Payable can be carried forward for up to 7 years to be applied against any future excess of regular Tax Payable over the alternative minimum tax.

Exercise Eleven - 15

Subject: Alternative Minimum Tax

Mr. Norton Blouson has Taxable Income for 2018 of $85,000. This includes taxable capital gains of $22,500 and taxable eligible dividends of $27,600 [(138%)($20,000)]. In addition, he received a $50,000 retiring allowance that was contributed to his RRSP. The full contribution was deductible. His only tax credits are the basic personal credit and the dividend tax credit. Determine whether Mr. Blouson would have a liability for alternative minimum tax and, if so, the total amount of such tax.

SOLUTION available in print and online Study Guide.

Sample Comprehensive Personal Tax Return

11-195. In the separate paper Study Guide, there is a comprehensive example containing a completed personal tax return, as well as a Tax Software Self Study Problem, included in the material for Chapter 11. The sample return illustrates tax savings possible through pension income splitting.

We suggest you work Self Study Problems Eleven-7 through Eleven-11.

Additional Supplementary Self Study Problems Are Available Online.

Key Terms Used In This Chapter

11-196.   The following is a list of the key terms used in this Chapter. These terms, and their meanings, are compiled in the Glossary located at the back of the Study Guide.

Active Business
Active Business Income
Adjusted Taxable Income
Allowable Business Investment Loss
Alternative Minimum Tax (AMT)
Annual Gains Limit
Business Investment Loss
Carry Over
Charitable Donations Tax Credit
Charitable Gifts
Crown Gifts
Cultural Gifts
Cumulative Gains Limit
Cumulative Net Investment Loss
Ecological Gifts
Excluded Business
Excluded Shares
Farm Property
Fishing Property
Foreign Taxes Paid Credit
Lifetime Capital Gains Deduction
Listed Personal Property

Loss Carry Back
Loss Carry Forward
Lump-Sum Payments
Net Capital Loss
Net Income For Tax Purposes
Non-Capital Loss
Ordering Rule
Personal Use Property
Purification Of A
   Small Business Corporation
Professional Corporation
Qualified Farm Property
Qualified Fishing Property
Qualified Small Business Corporation
Restricted Farm Loss
Small Business Corporation
Source Individual
Specified Individual
Split Income
Stock Option
Taxable Income
TOSI

References

11-197. For more detailed study of the material in this Chapter, we would refer you to the following:

ITA 82(3)	Dividends Received By Spouse Or Common-Law Partner
ITA 110	Deductions Permitted
ITA 110.6	Lifetime Capital Gains Deduction
ITA 111	Losses Deductible
ITA 111.1	Order Of Applying Provisions
ITA 118.1	Charitable Gifts
ITA 120.2	Minimum Tax Carry Over
ITA 127.5-.55	Obligation To Pay Minimum Tax
IC 75-23	Tuition Fees And Charitable Donations Paid To Privately Supported Secular and Religious Schools
S5-F2-C1	Foreign Tax Credit
S7-F1-C1	Split-receipting and Deemed Fair Market Value
IT-113R4	Benefits To Employees — Stock Options
IT-226R	Gift To A Charity Of A Residual Interest In Real Property Or An Equitable Interest In A Trust
IT-232R3	Losses - Their Deductibility In The Loss Years Or In Other Years
IT-244R3	Gifts By Individuals Of Life Insurance Policies As Charitable Donations
IT-288R2	Gifts Of Capital Properties To A Charity And Others
IT-295R4	Taxable Dividends Received After 1987 By A Spouse
IT-322R	Farm Losses
IT-523	Order Of Provisions Applicable In Computing An Individual's Taxable Income And Tax Payable

Appendix - Returns For Deceased Taxpayers

Special Rules At Death

Coverage In Text

11A-1. Filing requirements on the death of an individual can be very complicated and complex, especially if the individual left a significant amount of various types of assets. There are a number of special rules that are applicable when an individual dies. Some of these are covered in various chapters in the text. The following is a short summary of the special rules covered in the text, as well as where more information related to the rules can be found in the text. This Appendix also covers the special filing requirements and elective returns for deceased taxpayers. Note that death benefits are income of the recipient and have no effect on the final return of the deceased. Death benefits are covered in Chapter 9.

Charitable Donations - Special Rules At Death

11A-2. Charitable donations made in the year of death, or through bequests in the will and carried out by the executors of the will, can be claimed for tax credit purposes subject to a limit of 100 percent of Net Income, as opposed to the normal limit of 75 percent. Any charitable donations that are not claimed in the final return can be carried back to the immediately preceding year, subject to the 100 percent of Net Income limit.

Medical Expenses - Special Rules At Death

11A-3. Medical expenses paid can normally be claimed for any 12 month period ending in the year to the extent they exceed a threshold amount (see Chapter 4). In the year of death, the time period is extended to the 24 month period prior to death.

Deemed Disposition Of Capital Property At Death

11A-4.   The deceased taxpayer is deemed to have disposed of capital property at fair market value immediately before his death. When the capital cost of a depreciable property for the deceased taxpayer exceeds its fair market value, the beneficiary is required to retain the original capital cost, with the difference being treated as deemed CCA.

11A-5.   An exception to the general rules is available where the transfer is to a spouse, a common-law partner, or a testamentary spousal or common-law partner trust. This is a rollover provision that allows the transfer of non-depreciable property at its adjusted cost base and depreciable property at its UCC. There are other tax free transfers involving specific types of farm and fishing assets. Deemed dispositions at death are covered in Chapter 9.

Deferred Income Plans At Death

11A-6.   In many cases, a deceased individual will have a Tax Free Savings Account (TFSA), a Registered Retirement Savings Plan (RRSP) or a Registered Retirement Income Fund (RRIF) at the time of death. There are a number of special rules associated with this situation and these are covered in Chapter 9 (TFSA) and Chapter 10 (RRSP and RRIF).

Capital Losses - Special Rules At Death

11A-7.   There are special rules that apply to both net capital losses from years prior to death and to allowable capital losses arising in the year of death. These accumulated losses can be applied against any type of income in the year of death, or the immediately preceding year. Any capital gains deductions claimed to the date of death reduce the net capital losses that can be claimed on an unrestricted basis. The treatment of capital losses at death is covered in this Chapter 11.

Representation

11A-8.   The deceased do not, of course, file tax returns. However, a considerable amount of filing and other tax work may need to be done by the legal representative of the deceased. This legal representative may be an executor. This is an individual or institution appointed in the will to act as the legal representative of the deceased in handling his estate.

11A-9.   In the absence of a will, or in situations where an executor is not appointed in the will, a court will generally appoint an administrator as the legal representative of the deceased. This administrator will normally be the spouse or next of kin of the deceased.

11A-10.   The basic tax related responsibilities of the legal representative of an estate are as follows:

- filing all necessary tax returns;
- paying all taxes owing;
- obtaining a clearance certificate from the CRA for all tax years, before property under his control is distributed to the beneficiaries (a failure to do this can result in a personal liability for taxes owing); and
- advising beneficiaries of the amounts of income from the estate that will be taxable in their hands.

11A-11.   In order to deal with the CRA in these matters, the legal representative will have to provide a copy of the deceased person's death certificate, as well as a copy of the will or other document identifying him as the legal representative of the deceased. Without this documentation, the CRA will not provide any of the deceased person's income tax information.

Procedures For Specific Returns

Ordinary Return(s)

11A-12.   As noted previously, the legal representative of the deceased is responsible for filing a return for the year of death (a.k.a., final return) and, if required, a return for the previous year. This return would contain the usual sources of income, including employment income, business income, property income, and net taxable capital gains. With respect to employment income, it would include salary or wages from the end of the last pay period to the date of death.

EXAMPLE A taxpayer dies on June 4. His last pay period is from May 16 through May 31, with the amount being payable on June 7.

ANALYSIS The accrual for the period from June 1, the first day after the end of his last pay period, through the June 4 date of his death, must be included in his ordinary return for the year of death. With respect to the amount that is accrued but unpaid at his death, this can either be included in the taxpayer's ordinary return or, alternatively, in a separate "rights or things" return.

Rights Or Things Return

11A-13.   Rights or things are defined as unpaid amounts that would have been included in the deceased's income when they were realized or disposed of, had the taxpayer not died. Included would be:

- unpaid salaries, commissions, and vacation pay for pay periods which ended before the date of death (e.g., the salary for the period May 16 through May 31 in the example in Paragraph 11A-12)
- uncashed matured bond coupons, provided they were not required to be included in a previous year's income
- harvested farm crops and livestock on hand
- inventory and accounts receivable of taxpayers using the cash method
- declared, but unpaid dividends

11A-14.   While some of these amounts could be included in the ordinary return of the taxpayer, it is generally advisable, provided the amounts are material, to file this separate return as it permits a doubling up of certain tax credits and, in many cases, will result in additional amounts being taxed at the lowest federal rate.

11A-15.   Interest accrued at the time of death is somewhat problematical. If, at the time of his death, a taxpayer owns a term deposit or similar investment that pays interest on a periodic basis, ITA 70(1)(a) requires that interest accrued to the date of death be included in the taxpayer's ordinary return of income. This would be the case even if the taxpayer ordinarily used the cash basis of interest recognition. Under ITA 70(2), any accrued interest that is required to be included in the final ordinary return cannot be included in the rights or things return.

11A-16.   In contrast, if the debt instrument does not pay periodic interest, the accrued interest can be treated as a right or thing. As examples of this, IT-210R2, "Income Of Deceased Persons - Periodic Payments", Paragraph 2 refers to a matured treasury bill that has not been realized and to matured, but uncashed bond coupons as follows:

> If a deceased taxpayer owned a term deposit or other similar investment on which interest was payable periodically, interest accrued from the last date on which interest was payable up to the date of death would be included in income for the year of death under paragraph 70(1)(a). However, if the taxpayer also had on hand a matured investment (such as a matured Treasury Bill or uncashed matured bond interest coupons) at the date of death, any interest that was owing to the deceased taxpayer on the matured investment immediately before the date of death would be considered a right or thing for the purposes of subsection 70(2) to the extent the amount was not included or required to be included in the deceased's income for the year or a preceding year.

> For information about the tax treatment of "rights or things," refer to IT-212R3, Income of Deceased Persons — Rights or Things.

11A-17.   As a final point, note that rights or things can be transferred to a beneficiary, provided this is done within the time limit for filing a separate rights or things return. If this election is made, the amounts will be included in the beneficiary's income when they are realized, and should not be included in either the ordinary, or the rights or things return of the deceased.

Other Elective Returns

11A-18.   There are other elective returns that will be given limited attention in the following material.

Filing Requirements

Prior Year Returns

11A-19.   If an individual dies between October of the prior year and the normal due date for the prior year's return (April 30 of the current year or, if the individual or his spouse or common-law partner had business income, June 15 of the current year), it is likely that he will not have filed the return for the prior year. In this situation, the due date for the prior year's return is the later of six months after the date of death and the normal filing date.   For example, if a taxpayer whose normal due date is April 30, died on December 12, 2018, his representative would have until June 12, 2019 to file his 2018 tax return. Alternatively, if his normal due date was June 15, his representatives would have until June 15, 2019 to file his return

11A-20.   Under ITA 111(2), a deceased taxpayer is allowed to deduct unused capital losses against any source of income in the year of death and the immediately preceding year. However, any capital gains deductions claimed to the date of death reduce the net capital losses that can be claimed on an unrestricted basis. Charitable donations can also be carried back to the preceding year if not needed on the final return. If either item is applied to the preceding year, the prior year's return must be amended if it has been filed.

Multiple Returns

11A-21.   Filing the appropriate tax returns in the most advantageous manner for a deceased taxpayer can be complicated as there are a number of exceptions to the normal rules. In addition, there are special rules for final returns.

11A-22.   In fact, in some situations, more than one return will be filed on behalf of a deceased individual. Some of these are required by the ordinary provisions of the *Income Tax Act*. Other can be filed on the basis of an election and may or may not be filed in particular cases. The potential returns and their deadlines can be described as follows:

- **Ordinary Return - Year Of Death**   The ordinary return for the year of death, also referred to as the final or terminal return, will be due on April 30 or June 15 of the subsequent year. However, if the death occurs between November 1 and December 31 of the current year, the deceased taxpayer's representative has until the later of the normal filing date and six months after the date of death to file the current year's return. For example, if a taxpayer died on December 1, 2018 and his normal filing date was April 30, 2019, his representative would have until June 1, 2019 to file his 2018 tax return. Alternatively, if his return contained business income, his normal filing date of June 15, 2019 would be applicable.

- **Elective Return - Rights Or Things**   Under ITA 70(2), this special return is due the later of one year from the date of death or 90 days after the mailing date of the notice of assessment of the final return. (See Paragraph 11A-13, which explains rights or things.)

- **Elective Return - Non-Calendar Fiscal Year End**   If the deceased had business income from a partnership or proprietorship with a non-calendar taxation year, the taxpayer's death may or may not create a year end for the business. Usually, this will not be the case. However, if the taxpayer's death does create a deemed year end for the business, and that year end occurs after the end of the fiscal period of the business, ITA 150(4) provides for an elective return to include the income of the business for the period between the deemed year end and the end of the calendar year. This avoids having two years of business income accruing in a single taxation year.

For example, if Mr. Samuel Rosen had a proprietorship with a June 30 year end and he died on November 23, 2018, his representative could file a separate return for the period July 1 through November 23, 2018. This would allow the representative to limit the business income in his final return to the 12 month period ending June 30, 2018. The filing deadline for this return is the same as the one applicable to the final return.

- **Elective Return - Testamentary Trust Beneficiary** Under ITA 104(23)(d), if the deceased is an income beneficiary of a testamentary trust that has a non-calendar taxation year, the representative may elect to file a separate return for the period between the end of the trust's fiscal year and the date of the taxpayer's death. The filing deadline is the same as the one applicable to the final return.

11A-23. There are two basic reasons for filing as many tax returns as possible. The first relates to the fact that the income tax rates are progressive and income starts at nil in each return. This means that the first $46,605 (for 2018) in each return has the advantage of being taxed at the lowest federal rate of 15 percent. If multiple returns are not filed, there may be amounts taxed at rates higher than 15 percent that would have been taxed at the lower rate if multiple returns had been filed.

11A-24. The second advantage of filing multiple returns is that some personal tax credits can be deducted in each return. As will be discussed in the following material, this could save the deceased taxpayer's estate several thousand dollars for each tax return filed.

Use Of Deductions And Credits
Multiple Usage
11A-25. The full amount of applicable personal credits is claimed, regardless of when the individual died in the year. As previously noted, one of the major advantages of being able to file multiple returns is that some personal tax credits can be used in all of the returns filed. It appears that the rationale for claiming certain tax credits on multiple returns is to recognize the fact that the income reported on the different returns could have been included in a later year's tax return if the deceased had lived. In that later year, personal tax credits would have been available to reduce Tax Payable.

11A-26. The CRA's Guide, "Preparing Returns For Deceased Persons" (T4011) provides a great deal of information relevant to the returns of deceased taxpayers. In the Guide, it notes that there are three groups of amounts that can be claimed on optional returns. More specifically, the following non-refundable credits can be claimed in the final return and in each optional return filed:

- basic personal credit
- age credit
- spousal credit (including infirm amount if applicable)
- credit for an eligible dependant (including infirm amount if applicable)
- Canada caregiver for a child under 18 credit
- Canada caregiver credit

11A-27. The combined value of these federal tax credits, if applicable, can represent a significant tax savings if multiple tax returns can be filed. There are similar credits available in the various provinces. Achieving these savings is, of course, conditional on each of the individual returns having sufficient Tax Payable to make use of the credits.

Elective Usage
11A-28. Other non-refundable credits can be split between, or deducted in full, in any of the returns filed. However, the total claimed cannot exceed the amount that would be included in the ordinary return for the year of death. These credits include the following:

- adoption expenses
- disability amount for the deceased person

- disability amount for a dependant other than a spouse
- tuition amount for the deceased person
- tuition amount transferred from a child
- interest paid on certain student loans
- charitable donations, including amounts gifted in the will (limited to 100 percent of Net Income)
- first time home buyer's amount
- medical expenses (note that the total expenses must be reduced by the lesser of $2,302 (2018 figure) and 3 percent of the total Net Income reported on all returns)

Usage With Related Income

11A-29.   With respect to the following deductions and non-refundable credits, they can only be claimed in the return in which the related income is reported:

- Canada or Quebec Pension Plan contributions credit
- Employment Insurance premiums credit
- Canada Employment credit
- pension income credit
- dividend tax credits
- stock option deduction
- social benefits repayment (clawback)

Usage With Ordinary Return

11A-30.   Deductions and credits that cannot be claimed on elective returns are claimed on the final return. The following deductions and non-refundable credits are listed in the CRA Guide as amounts that cannot be claimed on an optional return, but that can be claimed in the deceased's ordinary final return (it is not a complete list):

- Registered Pension Plan deduction
- Registered Retirement Savings Plan deduction
- annual union or professional dues
- amounts transferred from a spouse or common-law partner
- child care expenses
- carrying charges and interest expenses
- disability supports deduction
- allowable business investment losses
- moving expenses
- support payments made
- losses from other years
- lifetime capital gains deduction
- northern residents deduction
- exploration and development expenses

Payment Of Taxes

11A-31.   Regardless of the extension of filing dates for the final and elective returns, the tax owing is normally due on April 30 of the year following the year of death.   We would also remind you that the due date for payment of taxes is unchanged by the deferral of the normal filing date to June 15 for taxpayers with business income.

11A-32.   However, if death occurs between November 1 of the prior year and April 30 of the current year, the due date for the payment of taxes is six months after the date of death.

11A-33.   With respect to income from the value of rights or things and from deemed disposi-tions of capital property at death, the legal representative for the deceased individual can elect to defer the payment of taxes. Under ITA 159(5), payment can be made in ten equal annual instalments, with the first payment due on the regular payment due date of the final return. Security acceptable to the Minister must be furnished to guarantee payment of the deferred taxes. Interest will be charged on amounts outstanding and, as is the usual case, such interest is not deductible.

Sample Tax Return And Tax Software SS Problem

The Chapter 11 Sample Tax Return and the Tax Software Self Study Problem for Chapter 11 can be found in the print and online Study Guide.

Problems For Self Study (Online)

To provide practice in problem solving, there are Self Study and Supplementary Self Study problems available on MyLab Accounting.

Within the text we have provided an indication of when it would be appropriate to work each Self Study problem. The detailed solutions for Self Study problems can be found in the print and online Study Guide.

We provide the Supplementary Self Study problems for those who would like additional practice in problem solving. The detailed solutions for the Supplementary Self Study problems are available online, not in the Study Guide.

The .PDF file "Self Study Problems for Volume 2" on MyLab contains the following for Chapter 11:

- 11 Self Study problems,
- 6 Supplementary Self Study problems, and
- detailed solutions for the Supplementary Self Study problems.

Assignment Problems

(The solutions for these problems are only available in
the solutions manual that has been provided to your instructor.)

Assignment Problem Eleven - 1
(Loss Carry Overs - Individual)
Martin Dornet opens a new retail business operation on January 1, 2015. Relevant information for 2015 and the subsequent three taxation years follows.

Year Ending December 31, 2015

During this first year of operations, Martin's net business income is $32,600. In addition to his new retail business, he begins a farming operation which loses $14,200 during its first year of operation. He has always been an active investor in the stock market and, during 2015, he has the following results:

Eligible Dividends	$3,050
Taxable Capital Gains	1,150
Allowable Capital Losses	6,860

Year Ending December 31, 2016

The 2016 operations of his retail business result in a net business loss of $23,700. His farming operation produces a net income of $3,600. His investment results for 2016 are as follows:

Eligible Dividends	$3,850
Taxable Capital Gains	3,470

Year Ending December 31, 2017

His retail operation produces net business income of $53,200 for 2017. The farming operation is also profitable, producing a net income of $5,480. His 2017 investment results are as follows:

Eligible Dividends	$4,860
Taxable Capital Gains	3,870

Year Ending December 31, 2018

For 2018, his retail business experiences a net business loss of $32,670. In addition, he has a net farm loss of $2,460. Investment results are as follows:

Eligible Dividends	$ 7,920
Taxable Capital Gains	23,360
Allowable Capital Losses	24,940

Because his farming activities are secondary to his business activities, his losses are restricted.

In each of the four years 2015 through 2018, Martin needs $23,618 in Taxable Income to absorb his personal tax credits.

When he has a choice, Martin would prefer to deduct maximum net capital loss carry overs. He will also carry back any current losses to the earliest possible year.

Prior to 2015, because of significant health issues, Martin had no amounts of Tax Payable. This means that it would not be useful to carry back any type of loss to years prior to 2015.

Required: Calculate Martin's minimum Net Income For Tax Purposes and Taxable Income for each of the four years. Indicate the amended figures for any years to which losses are carried back. Also indicate the amount and types of loss carry overs that would be available at the end of each year.

Assignment Problem Eleven - 2

(Allowable Business Investment Losses)

In 2015, after several years of working part time at McDonald's, Lucinda McIvor was fortunate enough to win a lottery prize of more than $1,000,000. She quickly blew through over $100,000 of this on recreational drugs, alcohol, and luxury travel. However, in early 2016 after an overdose that very nearly ended her life, Lucinda checked herself into rehab and emerged from treatment a changed woman.

She embarked on a program of actively investing in rental properties, and in the shares and debt of small private companies. Her investment income during the three years 2016 through 2018 were as follows:

2016   During this year she realized a large capital gain on the sale of shares in a wildly successful, qualified small business corporation. She used $156,000 of her lifetime capital gains deduction to reduce her 2016 Taxable Income to be equal to her basic personal amount leaving her with a nil Tax Payable.

2017   During this year she had the following amounts of income:

Taxable Capital Gains	$ 17,300
Net Rental Income	91,450
Interest Income	38,275
Total	$147,025

2018   Income amounts during this year were as follows:

Taxable Capital Gains	$ 18,620
Net Rental Income	86,300
Interest Income	27,438
Total	$132,358

During 2018, Recovery Inc., a small business corporation to which she had extended a loan of

$675,000, went into bankruptcy. Lucinda has been advised that it is extremely unlikely that she will recover any of this amount. Given this, Lucinda is writing off the entire balance.

The only tax credit available to Lucinda in 2017 or 2018 is the basic personal credit (basic personal amount of $11,635 in 2017 and $11,809 in 2018). For several years prior to 2016, Lucinda's Tax Payable was eliminated by various credits. She did not have any loss carry forwards from years prior to 2018.

Required: Determine Lucinda's optimum Taxable Income for the years ending December 31, 2017 and December 31, 2018. In your solution, consider the effect of the basic personal credit. Indicate any loss carry over that is present at the end of either year, and the rules applicable to claiming the loss carry over.

Assignment Problem Eleven - 3
(ABILs and Lifetime Capital Gains Deduction)
The following information is for Dirk Flack for the year ending December 31, 2018:

- Dirk had net rental income of $187,000.
- Dirk sold shares of Stix Inc., a qualified small business corporation, for $360,000. The adjusted cost base of these shares was $57,000. Selling costs were $2,000.
- Dirk sold shares of Sugrass Inc., a small business corporation that did not qualify for the lifetime capital gains deduction. The shares had cost $295,000. The net proceeds of disposition were $71,000.
- At the end of 2018, Dirk had a Cumulative Net Investment Loss of $3,600.
- On January 1, 2018, Dirk had a net capital loss carry forward of $6,400 [(1/2)($12,800)].

Dirk has used the ITA 110.6 lifetime capital gains deduction to eliminate a 2013 capital gain of $78,500, as well as a 2015 capital gain of $39,000. Dirk has not deducted any other amounts under ITA 110.6 in the years prior to 2018.

Required: Calculate Dirk's minimum Net Income For Tax Purposes and Taxable Income for 2018. Provide all of the calculations required to determine the maximum ITA 110.6 deduction assuming:

A. Dirk would prefer to make the maximum deduction of his net capital loss carry forward, prior to making any use of the lifetime capital gains deduction.

B. Dirk would prefer to make the maximum use of the lifetime capital gains deduction.

Assignment Problem Eleven - 4
(Tax On Split Income)
In the following five cases, one or more taxpayers receive dividends from a private company. For each taxpayer, determine whether the dividends received will be classified as Split Income. Explain your conclusion.

CASE 1   Sam and Sandra are both 23 years old and have been married for five years. They each own 50 percent of the shares of Mobus, a corporation that is actively involved mobile applications. The shares were acquired, in return for a nominal investment, when the corporation was formed. All of the shares have the same fair market value and the same voting rights.

Sam works full time for another corporation, while Sandra has a part time job in health care. They both spend time managing and operating Mobus. Neither Sam or Sandra work more than 20 hours per week in the business. However, the nature of the corporation's business is such that additional employees are not required.

During 2018, because one of its applications has been very successful, Mobus is able to pay dividends of $200,000, with Sam and Sandra each receiving $100,000.

CASE 2 GoGreen is a Canadian private corporation that runs a seasonal landscaping business. The business operates from May 1 through September 30. Ninety percent of the shares are owned by John Go, with his twin children, Max and Mary Go, owning the remaining 10 percent (5 percent each).

The twins are 22 years old and attending university in another city during the period from mid-September until the end of April. During the period May through mid-September, they work full time with their father in operating the GoGreen business.

During 2018, each twin receives $10,000 in dividends from GoGreen.

CASE 3 Edward and Elsie Cole were married in 2005. Elsie has been the family's primary bread winner, a role she satisfied by operating Cole Industries, a Canadian private company involved in an active business. Elsie was the sole shareholder of this company and worked full time in its operations. In late 2017, citing irreconcilable differences, the couple was divorced.

As part of the settlement agreement, Elsie was required to have Cole Industries issue a second class of shares to Edward. During 2018, as required by the divorce decree, these shares pay dividends to Edward in the amount of $50,000.

CASE 4 Larry and Louise Martin own respectively 95 percent and 5 percent of the shares of Musken Enterprises, a Canadian private company. Larry is 66 years old and Louise is 59 years old. They have been married for over 20 years.

From 2005, when Musken started operations, until 2017, Larry worked full time in the business. In 2017, Larry retired and turned the operation of the business over to a salaried manager. Louise has never been involved in the business.

During 2018, Musken pays dividends of $190,000 to Larry and $10,000 to Louise.

CASE 5 Donald Rump owned all of the shares of Dontar during the period 2010 through 2017. Dontar is a private Canadian company involved in an active business in manufacturing. Donald has worked full time in the business since its inception in 2010.

After graduating from high school at 18 years of age, Donald's son David worked full time in the business during the years 2015 through 2017. However, in January, 2018, he enrolled in a full time university program and no longer spends any time working in the business. He is 22 years old at the end of 2018.

In late 2017, in order to assist David with the cost of attending university, Donald issues a second class of shares to his son. David uses his savings to acquire the shares. These new shares have a fair market value equal to 20 percent of the total value of all outstanding shares, pay dividends at an annual rate of 5 percent and are non-voting. Assume that the basic prescribed rate is 2 percent throughout 2018.

During 2018, Dontar pays $105,000 in dividends to Donald and $6,000 in dividends to David.

Assignment Problem Eleven - 5
(Comprehensive Tax Credits With Dividend Transfer)

Despite being 75 years old, Mr. Igor Resso has retained a full time position with a Canadian university. His salary for 2018 is $95,000. While the university continues to deduct maximum EI contributions ($858 for 2018), he is collecting CPP payments of $9,500 per year and no longer makes contributions to the plan. Because of the continuing high level of his income, he has never applied for or received Old Age Security (OAS) benefits.

When Mr. Resso turned 69, he could no longer make contributions to the university's pension plan and had to begin receiving pension payments from the plan. For 2018, these payments totaled $31,000. In addition to his other sources of income Mr. Resso was required to withdraw $18,000 from his RRIF in 2018.

In 2017, while visiting family in Russia, Mr. Resso met Ivana and they were married later in that year. Unfortunately, as the result of a stroke suffered during their whirlwind honeymoon in 2017, Ivana was disabled to such a degree that she qualified for the disability tax credit after she moved to Canada.

In the 2016 divorce from her Russian husband, Ivana received a substantial settlement. After her marriage, she invested much of it in blue chip Canadian public companies. During 2018, she receives eligible dividends from Canadian companies in the amount $14,000. While Ivana is 68 years old, she does not meet the residency requirements for receiving Old Age Security (OAS payments).

Beyond personal credits and employment related credits, the only other 2018 credit available to the couple is based on qualifying medical expenses of $16,000.

Assume that Mr. and Mrs. Resso do not elect to use the pension income splitting provisions.

Required:

A. Calculate Mr. and Mrs. Resso's 2018 minimum federal Tax Payable and any social benefits repayment assuming that no transfer of dividends is made under ITA 82(3).

B. Determine whether a transfer of dividends under ITA 82(3) would be permitted.

C. Calculate Mr. and Mrs. Resso's 2018 minimum federal Tax Payable and any social benefits repayment assuming that all of Mrs. Resso's dividends are transferred to Mr. Resso under ITA 82(3). Comment on whether the dividend transfer should be done.

Assignment Problem Eleven - 6
(Alternative Minimum Tax)

The two cases which follow are designed to illustrate the basic features of the alternative minimum tax procedures. In both cases, you are given information about an individual taxpayer's income and deductions for the 2018 taxation year. The two cases are independent of each other.

Case One   Marita Ulman provides the following estimates of her various types of income and deductions for the year ending December 31, 2018:

Net Employment Income	$ 32,000
Net Taxable Capital Gains	206,000
Lifetime Capital Gains Deduction Claimed	206,000

Case Two   Fiona Acevedo provides the following estimates of her various types of income and deductions for the year ending December 31, 2018:

Net Employment Income	$149,000
Taxable Capital Gains	12,000
Eligible Dividends Received	41,000
Net Rental Loss (Note)	17,000
Stock Option Deduction [(1/2)($63,000)]	31,500
RRSP Deduction (Due To A Good Night At The Casino)	32,000

Note   The net rental loss consisted of gross rental income of $18,000, interest paid of $15,000 and other rental expenses of $20,000. No CCA was taken on the property.

In both Cases, assume the only tax credits available are the basic personal tax credit and the dividend tax credit related to any dividends received.

Required: For both Cases, determine whether there is a liability for alternative minimum tax and, if so, the total amount of such tax. In addition, calculate any related carry forwards available.

Assignment Problem Eleven - 7
(Death Of A Taxpayer)
Family Information

On July 7, 2018, Mrs. Rachelle Flax was killed in an automobile accident. At the time of her death, Rachelle was 47 years old. She is survived by her 44 year old husband, Martin Flax and her 24 year old daughter, Roxanne Flax.

Martin has spent most of his adult life volunteering for worthy causes. During 2018, he has employment income of $2,100 that was paid to him for services performed for Rachelle's unincorporated business prior to her death, as well as $1,700 in interest income. This interest was earned on a guaranteed investment certificate that had been given to him by Rachelle several years ago.

Roxanne is a very successful home decorator and is not a dependant of Rachelle.

Business Income

For several years, Rachelle has been the proprietor of a dog boutique and restaurant. The business had a December 31 fiscal year end. Until the date of her death, the proprietorship had net business income for tax purposes of $69,400. At the time of her death, the fair market value of the business assets was $5,900 greater than their UCC. None of the individual assets had fair market values that exceeded their capital cost.

As noted, prior to her death, the business had paid her husband, Martin a total of $2,100. This was for serving as bartender in the restaurant for discerning dogs. As Martin did not feel capable of carrying on the business on his own, he immediately sold the assets for their fair market value to a regular customer.

Rental Property

Rachelle had owned a residential rental property for 5 years prior to her death. In 2018, prior to her death, the property had rents of $46,300 and expenses other than CCA of $31,400. The property had been purchased for $312,000, of which $210,000 was allocated to the building and $102,000 to the land. An appraisal indicated that, at the time of her death, the total value of the property was $355,000, which was allocated $243,000 to the building and $112,000 to the land. At January 1, 2018, the building had a UCC of $174,795.

Rachelle's will leaves this property to her daughter, Roxanne.

Investments And Other Assets

Information related to the other assets that Rachelle owned at the time of her death is as follows:

Art Collection   Rachelle had collected Inuit art for a number of years. Her collection had an adjusted cost base of $23,400. At the time of her death, the fair market value of the collection was $57,000. The collection was left to her daughter who immediately sold the collection for its fair market value of $57,000.

Jewelry   Over the years, Rachelle had spent $32,000 on various pieces of jewelry. At the time of her death, their fair market value was only $8,300. The collection was left to her daughter who immediately sold them for their fair market value of $8,300.

Shares In RAF Ltd.   RAF Ltd. is a Canadian public company. The common shares were purchased for $12,400 and, prior to her death, paid Rachelle eligible dividends of $860. At the time of her death, their fair market value was $28,600. Her will leaves these shares to the Humane Society. The Humane Society issues a charitable donation receipt for $28,600 on receiving the shares.

Shares In Flax Fittings Inc.   This is a company that was started by Rachelle's father with an investment of $20,000. He left all of the shares to Rachelle in his will. At that time, their fair market value was $72,000. Prior to her death, the shares paid Rachelle non-eligible dividends of $6,200. At the time of her death, their fair market value was

$104,000. The shares are not eligible for the lifetime capital gains deduction. Her will leaves these shares to Martin.

RRSP   At the time of her death, Rachelle had an RRSP with a total fair market value of $1,123,000. Martin is named as beneficiary of the RRSP.

Family Residence   The family home is in Rachelle's name only. It had been purchased at a cost of $382,600. At the time of her death, the appraised value of the property was $507,000. This property is left to Martin.

Other Information

At the time of her death, Rachelle had a net capital loss carry forward of $89,400 and a listed personal property loss carry forward (100 percent) of $5,400. Rachelle has never claimed the lifetime capital gains deduction.

Due to her business income, Rachelle will pay the maximum CPP contributions for a self employed proprietor.

The terms of Rachelle's will requires the executor of her estate to elect out of the ITA 70(6) spousal rollover in the case of all properties bequeathed to Martin.

Required: Calculate Rachelle's minimum Net Income For Tax Purposes for the 2018 taxation year, her minimum Taxable income for that year, and her 2018 federal Tax Payable.

Assignment Problem Eleven - 8
(Comprehensive Tax Payable With Donations)
Family Information

Lyla and Clark Beaston are both 45 years of age. They have been happily married for 23 years. When they first met, they found that they both shared a strong dislike for dogs, cats and small children. Given this, they have no children and have never had a pet.

Both of them are lawyers and have had very successful careers in a variety of jobs. At this point, their net worth is over $5 million. Lyla is currently employed by a large public company. While Clark has been an employee in the past, he currently spends his time managing the family's investments. For a variety of reasons, all of these investments are solely owned by Clark.

While both Lyla and Clark enjoy generally good health, Clark has significant back problems related to a childhood accident. As these have worsened in recent years, in 2018, he decides to go to a clinic in the U.S. for surgery. The total cost of this surgery is US$52,000. At the time of this surgery, the exchange rate was US$1.00 = C$1.35, providing a translated value of $70,200. The travel costs associated with this surgery were US$8,000, resulting in a translated value of $10,800. Clark's Canadian doctor has provided a letter indicating that a similar surgery would have required a wait time of at least two years in Canada.

The couple have qualifying medical expenses in Canada consisting of prescriptions and regular dental work of $4,800.

Because they attribute much of their success to the excellent education they received at the University of Toronto, they make a 2018 donation of $175,000 to this institution when Clark receives a large and unexpected inheritance. As a result of this donation, they do not make their annual donation to the Canadian Cancer Society, or any other donations during the year.

Lyla's Employment information

Lyla's gross salary for 2018 is $270,000. Her employer withholds the maximum 2018 contributions to Employment Insurance ($858) and the Canada Pension Plan ($2,594). She does all of her work in her employer's office and is not required to travel. Given this, she has no deductible travel or other employment related expenses.

Her employer sponsors a defined benefit pension plan. Her contribution, which is withheld from her salary payments, is $12,450. Her employer makes a matching contribution.

Assignment Problems

Her employer provides a group disability plan for its employees. The 2018 premium on this plan is $2,500, one-half of which is paid by Lyla through withholdings. Her employer also provides for a generous medical insurance plan that covers 100 percent of any prescription costs and dental fees paid in Canada by employees for themselves or their families.

Clark's Investment Results

During 2018, the results for the investments that Clark manages are as follows:

Interest	$ 28,600
Eligible Dividends From Canadian Public Companies	136,000
Net Taxable Capital Gains	77,000

In order to increase his investment holdings, Clark assumed a mortgage on the family residence. This residence had been purchased for cash and, at the time the mortgage was arranged, there was no debt on the property. The proceeds of the mortgage were immediately invested in shares of Canadian public companies. Interest on the mortgage for 2018 was $12,000.

Required:

A. Determine the combined federal Tax Payable for Lyla and Clark, assuming that Lyla claims all of the medical expenses and all of the charitable donations.

B. Determine the combined federal Tax Payable for Lyla and Clark, assuming that Clark claims all of the medical expenses and all of the charitable donations.

C. Determine whether there is an allocation of medical expenses and charitable donations that would produce a lower combined federal Tax Payable than either the Part A results or the Part B results. Show your calculations.

Assignment Problem Eleven - 9
(Comprehensive Personal Tax Payable)

On January 10, 2018, Ms. Arlene Arsenault formally separated from her husband and retained custody of her 15 year old son, Jerry. Jerry has no income during 2018. Ms. Arsenault is also responsible for her 20 year old daughter, Janine, who has a severe and prolonged disability (a medical doctor has certified her disability on Form T2201). Janine has 2018 income of $6,000, resulting from income on investments that were left to her by her grandmother.

In order to get a fresh start in life, Ms. Arsenault found a new job. She resigned from her position in Ottawa and moved to a similar position in Toronto. The move took place on October 31, 2018. She has asked for your assistance in preparing an estimate of her 2018 personal tax liability and, in order to assist you with your calculations, she has prepared the following list of transactions that occurred during 2018:

1. Her gross salary from her Ottawa employer, a large public company, for the first 10 months of the year was $82,000. Her employer withheld from this amount CPP contributions of $2,594, EI premiums of $858, and RPP contributions of $2,500. The employer also contributed $2,500 to the company's RPP on her behalf.

    Before leaving her Ottawa employer, she exercised stock options to acquire 2,000 of the company's shares at a price of $15 per share. The options were issued in 2016, when the market price of the shares was $12 per share. On August 12, 2018, the day that she exercised the options, the shares were trading at $20 per share. Ms. Arsenault sells the shares as soon as she acquires them. Brokerage fees totalled $350 on the sale.

2. During November and December, her gross wages with her Toronto employer amounted to $13,000. Her new employer withheld CPP contributions of $500, EI premiums of $390, and $650 in RPP contributions. Her Toronto employer also contributed $650 to the company's money purchase RPP on her behalf.

Ms. Arsenault found a new home in Toronto during her September house hunting trip there. The legal arrangements for the house purchase were finalized on October 10. In Ottawa, she and her husband had lived for 10 years in a home that they rented. Her agreement with her new employer requires that they pay her moving costs. In order to simplify the record keeping, the employer paid her an allowance of $7,500 and did not require a detailed accounting of expenses. Her actual expenses were as follows:

Moving company charges	$3,800
Airfare for September Toronto trip to acquire new home	350
Meals and lodging on September Toronto trip	275
Gas for October 31 move to Toronto	65
Lodging in Ottawa on October 30	110
Meals on October 30 and October 31 While Moving	250
Charges for cancellation of lease on Ottawa home	935
Legal and other fees on acquisition of Toronto home	1,500
Total	$7,285

Ms. Arsenault did not use the simplified method of calculating vehicle expenses and moving costs.

3. In 2015, Ms. Arsenault's mother died, leaving her 5,000 shares of Lintz Industries, a private company. These shares had cost her mother $50,000, and had a fair market value at the time of her death of $95,000. Ms. Arsenault received non-eligible dividends of $7,500 on these shares in May and, in December, she sells the shares for $105,000. Selling costs were $850.

4. Ms. Arsenault made $1,500 in donations to a registered Canadian charity and $900 in contributions to the Libcon Rebloc Party, a registered federal political party.

5. Ms. Arsenault incurred the following child care costs:

Payments To Individuals For Jerry And Janine	$7,160
Fees For Jerry To Attend Camp (4 Weeks At $200 Per Week)	800
Food And Clothing For The Children	6,400
Total	$14,360

6. Ms. Arsenault paid the following medical expenses:

For Herself	$ 9,700
Jerry	900
Janine	7,250
Total	$17,850

7. In previous years, Ms. Arsenault's husband took care of her financial affairs. She has no understanding of either RPPs or RRSPs, but will make the maximum deductible RRSP contribution for 2018 as soon as you have calculated it. Her RRSP Deduction Limit Statement from the CRA states that her 2017 Earned Income was $81,100 and that, at the end of 2017, she had no Unused RRSP Deduction Room. Her 2017 T4 from her employer indicates a Pension Adjustment of $4,500. There are no undeducted contributions in her RRSP.

8. During the year, Ms. Arsenault paid legal fees of $2,500 in connection with her separation agreement. This settlement requires her husband to make a lump sum payment of $25,000 on March 1, 2018, as well as child support payments of $4,000 at the end of each month beginning on January 31, 2018. All required payments were received for the year.

9. In addition to her employment income, Ms. Arsenault operates an unincorporated mail order business with a December 31 year end. Her net business income for 2018 totaled $22,500. Included in this amount is a deduction of $950 for interest that she paid on a

demand loan taken out to finance inventory purchases. During the year ending December 31, 2018, Ms. Arsenault withdraws $27,000 from the bank account maintained by the business.

10. Ms. Arsenault's father owns and operates a very successful CCPC. In 2017, he gave Arlene a block of non-voting shares in his company. During 2018, these shares paid non-eligible dividends to Arlene in the amount of $10,000. Arlene has never been involved in this company's activities.

Required:

A. Determine Ms. Arsenault's minimum Net Income For Tax Purposes and her minimum Taxable Income for 2018. Ignore any HST considerations. In the Net Income For Tax Purposes calculation, provide separate disclosure of:

  - Net Employment Income,
  - Net Business And Property Income,
  - Net Taxable Capital Gains,
  - Other Sources Of Income, And
  - Other Deductions From Income.

B. Based on your answer to Part A, calculate Ms. Arsenault's minimum federal Tax Payable and any other amounts owing to (refundable from) the CRA for 2018. Ignore any income tax withholdings that her employers would have made.

Assignment Problem Eleven - 10
(Personal Tax Payable, TFSA and RRSP)

Mr. Wilson Kim is married and has a 19 year old son. Mr. Kim's wife had 2018 Net Income For Tax Purposes of $3,400.

The son lives at home and, during the summer of 2018, he earned employment income of $3,300. At the end of the summer, he began full time studies at a university. His tuition fees, which totaled $6,500 for 2018, were paid for by his father. The son's only other source of income was $2,200 of eligible dividends on a $40,000 portfolio of public company shares that were given to him by his father on his 16th birthday. The son has agreed to transfer any unused tuition credit to Mr. Kim.

Mr. Kim has asked you to assist him in preparing his 2018 tax return. To this end, he provides you with the following list of receipts and disbursements for the 2018 taxation year:

Receipts

Director's Fees	$ 1,372
Royalties On Patent Purchased In 2010	29,400
TFSA Withdrawal In January	10,000
Bond Interest	960

Disbursements

Spousal RRSP Contribution In July	$ 4,200
TFSA Contribution In December (Less Than Contribution Limit)	4,000
Rent Paid To Employer For Living Accommodation	18,000
Financial Support Of His Father*	17,100

*You ascertain that his father is physically infirm, is wholly dependent on Mr. Kim for support, had income of $4,200 during the year, and lives in Arizona for health reasons.

Mr. Kim is employed by a large publicly traded corporation. His basic salary for 2018 is $71,500. Other information related to his employment is as follows:

- As part of his compensation package, his employer provides living accommodations that have a fair market value of $2,500 per month.

- Mr. Kim is provided with a performance award of $3,600 in recognition of his outstanding performance.

- His employer sponsors a defined contribution RPP. For 2018, Mr. Kim and his employer each contributed $3,100 to this plan. These contributions are the same as those made in 2017.

- His employer withheld the maximum for CPP contributions and EI premiums for 2018.

- On September 1, 2018, Mr. Kim's employer granted him an option to purchase 500 of its shares at a price of $5 per share. The market price of the shares at that time was $4 per share. On December 1, 2018, the market price of the shares had increased to $9 per share. On that date, Mr. Kim exercises his option and purchases the 500 shares. He is still holding the shares on December 31, 2018.

- His employer provides him with a vehicle to use in his employment duties. The vehicle cost $41,000 in 2017. In the company's tax records it has a January 1, 2018 UCC of $25,500. The Company pays all of the operating costs which totaled $12,300 for 2018. Mr. Kim drives the vehicle 42,000 kilometers during 2018, of which 38,000 related to his employer's business. The car was available to Mr. Kim throughout 2018.

Mr. Kim provides you with the following information on his dispositions of property during the year:

	Proceeds	Cost
Diamond Necklace	$1,100	$ 750
Oil Painting	3,800	5,100
Graphic Novel Collection	800	2,500
Assault Rifle Collection	8,000	6,200

Assume Mr. Kim's 2017 Earned Income for RRSP purposes was equal to his 2018 Earned Income. At January 1, 2018, Mr. Kim had no unused deduction room and no undeducted contributions in his RRSP account.

Required: For Parts A to F, compute the required amounts for Mr. Kim for 2018. Show all calculations, including all those necessary to determine the maximum RRSP deduction for the year.

- A. Net employment income.
- B. Income from property.
- C. Net taxable capital gains.
- D. Net Income For Tax Purposes.
- E. Taxable Income.
- F. Federal Tax Payable.
- G. Indicate any available carry over amounts for Mr. Kim and his son and the applicable carry over provisions.
- H. Mr. Kim's son would like some advice on whether he should contribute to a TFSA and/or an RRSP. What would you suggest he do and why?

Assignment Problem Eleven - 11
(Comprehensive Case Covering Chapters 1 to 11)
Family Information

Adam Huffer is 42 years old. His wife, Estelle Huffer is 38 years old. They have been married for 19 years. They have a daughter, Portia, who is 15 years old and in good health.

Portia, who is very precocious, began attending university on a full time basis in September, 2018. Her only income for the year is $3,400 that she earned in various part time jobs. Adam has paid her $5,400 tuition fee for the fall semester, as well as $450 for required textbooks, and $2,400 for her residence fees. As her income is less than the basic personal tax credit, she has agreed to transfer her tuition credit to her father.

Assignment Problems

Adam and Estelle's only surviving parent is Adam's father, Jack. While he does not qualify for the disability tax credit, he is dependent on Adam and Estelle because of his limited mobility. He is 69 years old and lives with them. His 2018 Net Income For Tax Purposes is equal to $12,300, including OAS payments and a small pension from a former employer. Adam claims any available personal credit for Jack.

Adam serves as a volunteer fireman. During 2018 he spent over 300 hours in this work, for which he received no compensation. Because he was convicted of arson when he was a juvenile, he feels that this volunteer work, at least partially, makes up for some of the damage he did in his teen years.

For many years, Adam has owned a small office building that he rented to the Red Cross. On January 1, 2018, he donates this building to that organization, receiving a tax receipt from them for its fair market value of $325,000. This estimated value is made up of $250,000 for the building and $75,000 for the land. Adam's capital cost for the property of $210,000 was made up of $150,000 for the building and $60,000 for the land. On January 1, 2018, the UCC of the building was $119,859. Adam would like to use the maximum amount of this credit during the current taxation year.

During 2018, Adam paid for medical and dental services as follows:

Root Canal Fee - Adam	$ 1,350
Teeth Cleaning - Adam And Estelle	360
Psychological Counseling For Portia	820
Teeth Whitening For Portia	625
Breast Enhancement Surgery For Portia	8,450
Prescription Glasses For Estelle And Portia	500
Electric Wheelchair For Jack	4,200
Total	**$16,305**

Estelle will claim the credit for qualifying medical expenses.

Adam's Employment Information

Adam works for a large Canadian public company. As CEO, his 2018 salary is $350,000, none of which is commissions. The amounts withheld by his employer during 2018 are as follows:

Registered Pension Plan Contributions*	$12,300
EI Premiums	858
CPP Contributions	2,594

*Adam's employer makes a matching contribution of $12,300.

As CEO, Adam is required to travel extensively by his employer. He uses his own vehicle for this travel. He purchased his current automobile, a BMW 750i, for $132,000 on January 1, 2018. During the year, he drove the automobile a total of 63,000 kilometers, of which 59,000 were employment related. Operating costs paid for the year totaled $11,300.

In addition to his automobile costs, his other 2018 employment related travel were as follows:

Hotels	$16,000
Food	7,200

His employer provides him with the following allowances for his travel:

Hotels And Food ($700 Per Day)	$21,000
Use Of Personal Automobile ($300 Per Week)	15,600

On a regular annual basis, Adam's employer grants him options to buy the shares in the Company at their trading value on the grant date. During 2018, he exercises options to acquire 1,000 shares at a price of $25 per share. On the exercise date the shares are trading at $28 per share. These shares paid no dividends during the year and Adam still holds the shares on December 31, 2018.

All of the family's other stock investments are owned by Estelle. As a consequence, Adam has no income other than his employment related income and income that results from his charitable donation of real property.

Estelle's Investment Information

When Estelle's father died 6 years ago, he left her with shares in several small business corporations. Prior to 2018, she had the following two dispositions of small business corporation shares:

2013 In this year she sold shares in ABC, a qualified small business corporation, for $500,000. Her adjusted cost base for these shares was $275,000, resulting in a capital gain of $225,000. The taxable amount of this gain was eliminated using the lifetime capital gains deduction.

2015 In this year she sold shares in DEF, a qualified small business corporation, for $623,000. Her adjusted cost base for these shares was $216,000, resulting in a capital gain of $407,000. Once again, the taxable amount of this gain was eliminated using the lifetime capital gains deduction.

Estelle had no other dispositions of capital assets prior to 2018.

All of Estelle's income is derived from her corporate holdings. During 2018, she received a total of $32,000 in non-eligible dividends from these corporations.

In 2018, she had the following dispositions:

- Shares of GHI, a qualified small business corporation, for $662,000. Her adjusted cost base for these shares was $360,000, resulting in a capital gain of $302,000.

- Shares of JKL, a non-qualified small business corporation, for $230,000. Her adjusted cost base for these shares was $250,000, resulting in a capital loss of $20,000.

For several years, Estelle has been carrying forward a $15,000 net capital loss. In previous years, she has chosen not to use this carry forward in order to maximize her lifetime capital gains deduction. She would like to use this deduction in 2018, regardless of whether her lifetime capital gains deduction is maximized. Estelle has never had a CNIL balance.

Required: Ignore GST/HST/PST considerations in your solution.

A. Determine Adam's Federal Tax Payable for 2018.

B. Determine Estelle's Federal Tax Payable, including alternative minimum tax for 2018.

In both Part A and Part B, indicate any carry forward amounts available at the end of 2018.

Tax Software Assignment Problems

Tax Software Assignment Problem Eleven - 1

This problem is an expansion of the Chapter 4 problem.

Mr. Buddy Musician (SIN 527-000-061) was born in Vancouver on August 28, 1950. He has spent most of his working life as a pianist and song writer. He and his family live at 111 WWW Street, Vancouver, B.C. V4H 3W4, phone (604) 111-1111.

Mr. Musician's wife, Natasha (SIN 527-000-129), was born on June 6, 1992. She and Mr. Musician have four children. Each child was born on April 1 of the following years, Linda; 2012, Larry; 2013, Donna; 2014, and Donald; 2015. Natasha's only income during 2017 is $3,000 from singing engagements.

Buddy and Natasha Musician have two adopted children. Richard (SIN 527-000-285) was born on March 15, 2000 and has income of $2,800 for the year. Due to his accelerated

Tax Software Assignment Problems

schooling, he started full time attendance at university in September of 2017 at the age of 17. His first semester tuition fee is $3,000 and he requires books with a total cost of $375. These amounts are paid by Mr. Musician.

The other adopted child, Sarah, was born on September 2, 1997, and is in full time attendance at university for all of 2017 (including a four month summer session). Her tuition is $9,600 and she requires textbooks which cost $750. These amounts are also paid by Mr. Musician. Sarah has no income during the year.

Neither Richard nor Sarah will have any income in the next three years. They both have agreed that the maximum tuition amount should be transferred to their father.

Mr. Musician's mother, Eunice, was born on April 10, 1930 and his father, Earl, was born on November 16, 1928. They both live with Mr. Musician and his wife. While his father has some mobility issues, he is not infirm. His mother is legally blind. Eunice Musician had income of $9,500 for the year, while Earl Musician had income of $7,500.

Other information concerning Mr. Musician and his family for 2017 is as follows:

1. Mr. Musician earned $16,500 for work as the house pianist at the Loose Moose Pub. His T4 showed that his employer withheld $500 for income taxes and $268.95 for EI. No CPP was withheld as he has previously filed an election to stop contributing to the CPP.

2. During the year, Mr. Musician made his annual $3,000 donation to Planned Parenthood Of Canada, a registered Canadian charity.

3. Mr. Musician has been married before to Lori Musician (SIN 527-000-319). Lori is 52 years old and lives in Fort Erie, Ontario.

4. Mr. Musician has two additional children who live with their mother, Ms. Dolly Nurse (SIN 527-000-582), in Burnaby, British Columbia. The children are Megan Nurse, aged 12 and Andrew Nurse, aged 14. Neither child has any income during 2017. While Ms. Nurse and Mr. Musician were never married, Mr. Musician acknowledges that he is the father of both children. Although Buddy has provided limited financial aid by paying their dental and medical expenses, the children are not dependent on Buddy for support.

5. Mr. Musician wishes to claim all his medical expenses on a calendar year basis. On December 2, 2017, Mr. Musician paid dental expenses to Canada Wide Dental Clinics for the following individuals:

Himself	$1,200
Natasha (wife)	700
Richard (adopted son)	800
Sarah (adopted daughter)	300
Linda (daughter)	100
Earl (father)	1,050
Lori (ex-wife)	300
Dolly Nurse (mother of two of his children)	675
Megan Nurse (daughter of Dolly Nurse)	550
Total	$5,675

6. Mr. Musician signed a contract with Fred Nesbitt on January 13, 2017 to do permanent modifications to his house. The contract was for the installation of ramps with sturdy hand railings outside his front and back doors to give his parents easier access to the house and modifications to their bathroom so they would be less likely to fall when using the shower. The contract price was $5,800. As neither of his parents has a severe and prolonged mobility impairment, these expenditures are not eligible medical expenses.

7. Mr. Musician paid four quarterly instalments of $1,000 each (total of $4,000) for 2017, as requested on his Instalment Reminders from the CRA. He paid each instalment on the due date.

8. Mr. Musician receives $6,978.87 in Old Age Security payments and $5,500 in Canada Pension Plan "retirement benefit" payments over 12 months. There was no tax shown as withheld on his T4A(OAS) or his T4A(P).

9. Mr. Musician builds a state-of-the-art home theatre in a new extension of his home. In order to finance it, he sells stock in his RRSP and withdraws the funds from his RRSP. His T4RSP showed $52,000 in withdrawals from the House of Rock Bank (Box 22) and total tax of $15,600 deducted from these payments.

10. Several of Mr. Musician's songs, including his outstanding hit, "Drop Kick Me Jesus Through The Goal Posts Of Life", have provided him with substantial royalty payments over the years. In 2017, the Never Say Die Record Company paid him $78,000 in royalty payments. No T5 was issued by the Company.

11. In order to ensure the financial security of his family, Mr. Musician decided to return to songwriting in earnest. On November 1, 2017, he rented a small, quiet studio for $700 a month and purchased a Roland electric piano for $7,750 that was delivered there. He does not plan to use the space or piano for personal enjoyment, only for composing.

12. The previous year, on January 2, 2016, Mr. Musician elected not to make any further CPP contributions on his self-employed income.

13. Mr. Musician is required by a court order to pay spousal support of $400 per month to his former spouse, Lori Musician. Mr. Musician made spousal support payments of $4,800 during 2017.

14. Mr. Musician is required by a court order to make child support payments of $350 per month for his two children, Megan and Andrew Nurse. A total of $4,200 was paid during the year.

15. Mr. Musician made contributions to the Federal Liberal Party in the amount of $610 during the year.

16. Mr. Musician made a $5,000 contribution to his TFSA during the year. Thanks to the excellent investing advice of his gardener, the balance in his TFSA account has grown to more than $150,000 by the end of the year.

Required: With the objective of minimizing Mr. Musician's Tax Payable, prepare Mr. Musician's 2017 income tax return using the ProFile tax software program assuming Natasha does not file a tax return. List any assumptions you have made, and any notes and tax planning issues you feel should be placed in the file.

Tax Software Assignment Problem Eleven - 2

This problem is an expansion of the Chapter 4 problem.

George Pharmacy is a pharmaceutical salesman who has been very successful at his job in the last few years. Unfortunately, his family life has not been very happy. Three years ago, his only child, Anna, was driving a car that was hit by a drunk driver. She and her husband were killed and their 14 year old son, Kevin, was blinded in the accident. He also suffered extensive injuries to his jaw that have required major and prolonged dental work.

George and his wife, Valerie, adopted Kevin. Valerie quit her part-time job to care for him. She also cares for her mother, Joan Drugstore who lives with them. Joan suffers from dementia, Parkinson's and severe depression. The family doctor has signed a letter stating that she is dependent on George and Valerie because of her impairments. Joan does not meet the residency requirements necessary to qualify for Canadian Old Age Security payments.

Valerie's parents separated two years ago in Scotland after her father, David Drugstore, suffered enormous losses in the stock market. They were forced to sell their home and David moved to Chile. David phones periodically to request that money be deposited in his on-line bank account.

George's brother, Martin, completed an alcohol rehabilitation program after being fired for drinking on the job. He is also living with George and Valerie while he is enrolled as a full time student at Western University. George is paying his tuition and Martin has agreed to transfer any available education related amounts to George. Although Martin plans to file his 2017 tax return, he has not done so yet.

Kevin is taking several undergraduate psychology courses at Western University. After hearing a talk given by an expert blind echolocator, i.e., one who uses sound to locate objects, his goal is to become a researcher at the Brain and Mind Institute and study the use of echolocation.

Other information concerning George for 2017 is given on the following pages.

Required: Prepare the 2017 income tax return of George Pharmacy using the ProFile tax software program assuming Valerie does not file a tax return. List any assumptions you have made, and any notes and tax planning issues you feel should be placed in the file. Ignore HST implications in your solution by assuming that George does not qualify for the GST/HST rebate.

Personal Information	Taxpayer
Title	Mr.
First Name	George
Last Name	Pharmacy
SIN	527-000-509
Date of birth (Y/M/D)	1953-07-02
Marital Status	Married
Canadian citizen?	Yes
Provide information to Elections Canada?	Yes
Own foreign property of more than $100,000 Canadian?	No

Taxpayer's Address

123 ZZZ Street, London, Ontario N0Z 0Z0	
Phone number (519) 111-1111	

Family Members	Spouse	Child	Mother-In-Law
First Name	Valerie	Kevin	Joan
Last Name	Pharmacy	Pharmacy	Drugstore
SIN	527-000-483	527-000-517	None
Date of birth (Y/M/D)	1952-12-30	2001-10-17	1932-02-24
Net income	$6,520 in CPP	Nil	$500

Family Members	Father-In-Law	Brother
First Name	David	Martin
Last Name	Drugstore	Pharmacy
SIN	None	527-000-533
Date of birth (Y/M/D)	1933-01-12	1970-06-02
Net income	Nil	$8,300

During September, David was arrested in Chile. Valerie had to spend three weeks in Chile and $2,000 in bribes before she could get him released from jail. George had to pay Nannies On Call $3,500 for in-home help to take care of Kevin while she was gone.

T2202A - (Martin)	Box	Amount
Tuition fees - for Martin Pharmacy (brother)	A	8,000
Number of months in school - part-time	B	0
Number of months in school - full-time	C	8

T2202A - (Kevin)	Box	Amount
Tuition fees - for Kevin	A	3,600
Number of months in school - part-time	B	8
Number of months in school - full-time	C	0

Donor	Charitable Donation Receipts	Am't
Valerie	Mothers Against Drunk Drivers (MADD)	1,000
George	Canadian Institute For The Blind (CNIB)	3,000

T4	Box	Amount
Issuer - Mega Pharma Inc.		
Employment income	14	378,000.00
Employee's CPP contributions	16	2,564.10
Employee's EI premiums	18	836.19
Income tax deducted	22	114,000.00
Employment commissions	42	82,000.00
Charitable donations	46	400.00

During 2017, Mega reimbursed George $3,788 for meals and entertainment with clients, $2,268 for hotels and $4,925 for airline tickets.

In addition to George's salary, he also earns commissions. His employer requires him to have an office in his home and has signed the form T2200 each year to this effect.

During 2017, George purchased a new computer and software that will be used solely in his home office for employment related uses. The computer cost $3,600 and the various software programs cost $1,250.

House Costs	
Area of home used for home office (square feet)	650
Total area of home (square feet)	5,000
Telephone line including high speed internet connection	620
Hydro	3,200
Insurance - House	4,000
Maintenance and repairs	3,800
Mortgage interest	6,200
Mortgage life insurance premiums	400
Property taxes	6,700

(Y/M/D)	Patient	Medical Expenses	Description	Am't
2017-12-31	George	Johnson Inc.	Out of Canada insurance	731.00
2017-08-31	George	Dr. Smith	Dental fees	155.40
2017-09-19	George	Optician	Prescription glasses	109.00
2017-11-07	Valerie	Pharmacy	Prescription	66.84
2017-06-07	Joan	Dr. Wong	Psychiatric counseling	2,050.00
2017-03-22	David	Tropical Disease Centre	Prescription	390.00
2017-12-20	Martin	Dr. Walker	Group therapy	6,000.00
2017-10-01	Kevin	Dr. Takarabe	Orthodontics and Dental	30,000.00

George paid $800 for the care and feeding of Kevin's seeing eye dog, Isis, during 2017.

During 2017, George purchased a new computer and software that will be used solely in his home office for employment related uses. The computer cost $3,600 and the various software programs cost $1,250.

Real Estate Rental - Commercial Property	Amount
Address - 888 YYZ Drive, Toronto, Ontario M0M 0M0	
Year of purchase	2013
Gross rents	16,000
Property taxes	5,128
Insurance	1,890
Interest on mortgage	3,175
Payment on principal	2,200
Furnace repairs	550
Maintenance contract	3,469
Building purchased for $120,100 - UCC beginning of year	107,441
Fixtures purchased for $8,500 - UCC beginning of year	4,651

The building and fixtures were purchased on August 28, 2013. At the time the building and fixtures were being used as a drugstore and Mr. Pharmacy has retained the same tenant.

At the beginning of 2017, George had a net capital loss carry forward of $10,500 from the sale of shares in 2016. He had not disposed of any capital assets prior to 2016.

Asset Dispositions	Asset 1	Asset 2	Asset 3
Description	Molson Inc. shares	Imperial Oil shares	Sailboat
Number of units	150	387	N/A
Year of acquisition	2014	2015	2015
Date of disposition	February 14	June 6	October 1
Proceeds of disposition	37,000	9,600	74,000
Adjusted cost base	27,600	12,100	72,000
Outlays and expenses	35	29	N/A

Asset Dispositions	Asset 4	Asset 5	Asset 6
Description	Motorcycle	Painting	Coin collection
Year of acquisition	2017	2010	2014
Date of disposition	November 17	August 28	March 24
Proceeds of disposition	14,000	1,100	700
Adjusted cost base	21,000	450	1,800
Outlays and expenses	N/A	N/A	N/A

George knows he should have been contributing to various savings plans over the years, but his increasing number of needy dependants required he spend all of his take home pay to support them and he has contributed to none. It was only in 2017 that his compensation had increased enough so that he had sufficient funds to consider savings plans.

His daughter had made contributions totalling more than $10,000 to an RESP for Kevin prior to her death, but George has made no RESP contributions to the plan since then.

Tax Software Assignment Problem Eleven - 3

This problem is an expansion of the Chapter 4 problem.

Information Related To Chapter 4 Material

Seymour Career and Mary Career are your tax clients. They have been married for two years. Mary has progressed quickly in MoreCorp, the large, publicly traded firm she is working for due to her strong tax and accounting background. Her firm has an excellent health and dental plan that reimburses 100 percent of all medical and dental expenses.

Personal Information	Taxpayer	Spouse
Title	Ms.	Mr.
First Name	Mary	Seymour
Last Name	Career	Career
SIN	527-000-129	527-000-079
Date of birth (Y/M/D)	1979-12-08	1958-01-29
Marital status	Married	Married
Canadian citizen?	Yes	Yes
Provide information to Elections Canada?	Yes	Yes
Own foreign property of more than $100,000 Cdn?	No	No

Taxpayer's Address
123 ABC Street, Saint John, N.B.   E0E 0E0
Phone number (506) 111-1111
Spouse's address same as taxpayer? Yes

Dependant	Child
First Name	William
Last Name	Career
SIN	527-000-319
Date of Birth (Y/M/D)	2010-02-24
Net Income	Nil

T4 - Mary	Box	Amount
Issuer - MoreCorp		
Employment Income	14	152,866.08
Employee's CPP Contributions	16	2,564.10
Employee's EI Premiums	18	836.19
RPP Contributions	20	Nil
Income Tax Deducted	22	48,665.11
Charitable Donations	46	1,000.00

Donor	Charitable Donation Receipts	Amount
Seymour	Canadian Cancer Foundation	500
Seymour	Salvation Army	250

Information Related To Chapter 6 Material

Tax Software Note To create a return for Seymour that is coupled to Mary's, hit the F5 key with Mary's return open.

Seymour earns business income writing and editing instruction manuals on a contract basis. He has six different clients and operates under the business name Crystal Clear Communications from an office in their home. One of his clients issues him a T4A for the work that he has done for them.

During the year, Seymour is a part time student at Dalhousie University for 3 months. He is enrolled in the musicology program.

T2202A - Seymour	Box	Amount
Tuition fees	A	2,200
Number of months in school - part-time	B	3
Number of months in school - full-time	C	0

T4A - Seymour	Box	Amount
Issuer - 3065 Canada Inc.		
Fee For Services (Professional)	48	20,000.00

Business or Professional Income - Seymour	
Revenues without T4A	41,603.17
T4A's issued (see T4A information)	20,000.00
Membership dues - Business Writers Association	231.00
Business insurance	126.16
Bank service charges	156.20
Cell phone air time	485.27
Postage and courier charges	110.00
Supplies	2,982.17
Separate business phone line charge	577.86
Fees for accounting and tax advice	500.00
Air fare (business travel)	526.97
Hotels (business travel)	1,240.91
Meals when traveling on business	607.14
Meals and drinks when entertaining clients	887.12
UCC of furniture - beginning of year	2,254.94
UCC of computer application software - beginning of year	219.15
UCC of computer hardware (Class 50) - beginning of year	426.00
Application software purchased May 12, 2017	525.00
Laptop computer purchased May 12, 2017	2,048.00

The mortgagee of Seymour's house, the Royal Bank, does not require life insurance.

House Costs	
Area of home used for business (square feet)	160
Total area of home (square feet)	1,500
Gas for heating	1,712.86
Hydro	1,641.18
Insurance - house	757.55
Snow plowing contract	440.00
Installation of new gas furnace	3,675.00
Painting of house interior	2,548.05
Mortgage interest paid to Royal Bank	8,456.22
Mortgage life insurance premiums	375.00
Mortgage principal paid	1,279.58
Property taxes	2,533.01
Interest on late property taxes	122.52

Tax Software Note   As the problem requires that you ignore GST/HST implications, enter all motor vehicle expenses as non-eligible for GST or HST.

Tax Software Assignment Problems

Car Costs - Seymour	
Description - Subaru, cost = $35,000, bought 2014-02-15	
January 1 odometer	89,726
December 31 odometer	124,701
Business kilometers driven	8,412
Parking	321.71
Gas	2,582.12
Maintenance and repairs	458.63
Car insurance	779.00
Licence and registration fees	49.87
Interest on 4 year car loan granted on purchase date	597.89
UCC of Class 10.1 - beginning of year	15,470.00

Information Related To Chapter 7 Material

Seymour was previously married and has a 19 year old daughter from the previous marriage. As part of the property settlement, he received the house that he and his family had lived in. Since Mary already owned a much nicer home, he moved in with her when they were married in 2015 and rented out the property.

Seymour believed that in June he had paid an income tax instalment of $2,400 for 2017, but could find no record of it. You call the CRA and find that the June payment was towards his 2016 tax liability. Seymour had tax owing of more than $10,000 for 2016 and has not completely paid off the liability yet. He has paid no instalments for 2017.

Mary also paid no instalments for 2017. She has received tax refunds in the last two years.

During 2015, one of his clients convinced Seymour to take out a demand loan to purchase shares in the public company, EEE Art Films Ltd. for $37,000. Later that year, the company's president was indicted for fraud. In 2016, Seymour sold his shares for $2,000 and used the proceeds to pay down his demand loan. During 2017, Seymour did not have sufficient funds to pay off the demand loan, but managed to reduce the principal by $10,000.

The interest and penalties paid by Seymour during 2017 were as follows:

Interest on credit cards for business expenses	$ 627.27
Interest on loan to buy laptop and software	104.24
Interest on loan to make 2016 RRSP contribution	162.15
Interest on loan to purchase EEE Art Films securities	1,372.52
Interest on late payment of 2016 income tax	233.72
Interest on insufficient tax instalments for 2016	52.81
Interest on late GST/HST payments	212.82
Penalty for late filing of 2016 tax return	303.92
Total	$3,069.45

Mary has invested in the stock market over the years and has done well. Seymour holds no securities outside of his RRSP during 2017. Mary has received her T3 and T5 information slips from her stockbroker and bank. The interest from the TD Bank is from a joint chequing account in the name of both Mary and Seymour.

Tax Software Note By inputting the joint T5 on Mary's return, the T5 information will appear on Seymour's Statement Of Investment Income (Schedule 4), but not on his T5 slip screen.

T5	Box	Slip 1	Slip 2
Issuer		Power Corp.	TD Bank
Recipient (Input both on Mary's return)		Mary	Joint 50% each
Actual amount of eligible dividends	24	950.00	
Taxable amount of eligible dividends	25	1,311.00	
Interest from Canadian sources	13		236.11

T3	Box	Amount
Issuer - TD Asset Management		
Recipient - Mary Career		
Foreign country - United States		
Foreign non-business income (Canadian dollars)	25	1,553.10
Foreign income tax paid - investment (Canadian dollars)	34	37.00
Other income - investment	26	214.50
Actual amount of eligible dividends	49	346.00
Taxable amount of eligible dividends	50	477.48

Real Estate Rental - Seymour	Amount
Address - 555 LLL Street, Moncton, NB, E0E 0E0	
Gross rents	12,000.00
Property taxes	3,610.00
Insurance	650.00
Interest on mortgage	4,207.25
Payment on principal	1,511.92
Wiring and furnace repairs	2,282.71
Snow removal and landscaping annual contract	1,070.00
Building purchased May 1, 2004 for $150,000 - UCC beginning of year	150,000.00
Appliances purchased June 6, 2015 for $1,700 - UCC beginning of year	1,350.00

Information Related To Chapter 8 Material

When Mary's grandmother died in 2015, she inherited some pieces of jewelry, as well as a dining room set and a chandelier. Since the jewelry is not suited to Mary's relaxed style of dress, she sold some pieces during 2017. She replaced the dining room set and chandelier and sold them separately to two colleagues at work.

Mary has purchased Extreme Wi-Fi Technologies stock over the years. Her transactions in this stock are as follows:

Acquisition Date	Shares Purchased (Sold)	Cost Per Share	Total Cost
April 1, 2015	1,500	$ 2	$ 3,000
October 1, 2015	2,000	12	24,000
April 1, 2016	(1,000)	?	
June 1, 2016	400	25	10,000
January 6, 2017	(800)	?	
February 1, 2017	800	20	16,000
March 14, 2017	(600)	?	

Tax Software Assignment Problems

Mary Career provides you with the following information about her sales of securities and other items.

Asset Dispositions	Disposition 1	Disposition 2	Disposition 3
(All owned by Mary) Description	Extreme Wi-Fi Technologies	Extreme Wi-Fi Technologies	Fidelity Small Cap Fund
Number of units	800	600	258.92
Year of acquisition	2015	2015	2015
Date of disposition	January 6	March 14	February 17
Proceeds of disposition	11,806	13,465	2,982.31
Adjusted cost base	?	?	5,300.33
Outlays and expenses	29	29	Nil

Asset Dispositions	Disposition 4	Disposition 5	Disposition 6
Description	Diamond Pendant	Gold Ring	Pearl Brooch
Year of acquisition	2015	2015	2015
Date of disposition	July 20	July 20	July 20
Proceeds of disposition	4,000	750	1,300
FMV at grandmother's death	5,800	600	850

Asset Dispositions	Disposition 7	Disposition 8
Description	Dining room set	Crystal Chandelier
Year of acquisition	2015	2015
Date of disposition	July 20	July 20
Proceeds of disposition	200	1,500
FMV at grandmother's death	3,000	800

Information Related To Chapter 9 Material

Seymour has made all of the required payments to his ex-wife Monica DeWitch (SIN 527-000-186) in 2017. In your files, you have noted that his 2014 divorce agreement requires Seymour to pay spousal support to his ex-wife of $200 per month. He also pays her child support of $250 per month for his 19 year old daughter, Faith.

Mary tells you that her parents have established an RESP for William in 2017, and are the sole contributors. They have contributed $300 in lieu of Christmas and birthday presents.

Mary has learned that Seymour's mother purchased a Guaranteed Investment Certificate (GIC) in William's name in 2017. The GIC paid interest of $120 in 2017 which Seymour had spent without advising her. She expects a T5 to be issued in William's name.

Mary registered William for art classes at the Da Vinci Institute on Saturdays. She provides you with the following receipts:

Child	Child Related Expenses (Organization or Name and SIN)	No. of weeks	Amount
William	No Worries Childcare (after school and summer)		3,100
William	Da Vinci Institute	16	1,000

On December 23, 2017, you receive a call from Mary Career with the terrible news that Seymour has just suffered a massive heart attack and died. Mary, his executor, inherits all of his assets except for the rental property and appliances in Moncton which he has left to his daughter, Faith. Assume the transfer of the property and appliances takes place in 2017.

As Seymour was thinking of selling the property, he had it appraised in early December. The appraisal valued the land at $60,000, the building at $180,000, and the appliances at $700. Seymour had purchased the property on May 1, 2004 for $195,000 (land of $45,000 and building of $150,000) and lived in it until his marriage to Mary in 2015.

Tax Software Notes   On Seymour's "Info" page, input his date of death. Answer No to the question "Is this an Early Filed ...?". On Mary's return, check that her marital status has been changed to widowed and the date of change is included.

Answer Yes on the Info page on Seymour's return to the question "Did you dispose of a property ...?"

Complete the T2091, Designation Of Property As A Principal Residence for Seymour's Moncton property and S3PrincipalResidenceDetail.

Information Related To Chapter 10 Material

On January 10, 2018, you receive a phone call from Mary Career. She has just received a T4RSP in the mail which shows that Seymour had withdrawn virtually all the funds from his RRSP without her knowledge. She knows this could substantially increase Seymour's tax liability and is very concerned. At the moment, she cannot find any trace of the funds that were withdrawn.

Her stockbroker has told her that a spousal contribution can be made to her RRSP to utilize Seymour's unused contribution room. She would like you to calculate the maximum RRSP contribution that can be deducted on Seymour's return so that she can contribute that amount to her RRSP and have the RRSP receipt issued with Seymour's name as the contributor.

She would also like you to calculate the maximum RRSP contribution that can be deducted on her own return for 2017 and 2018. Since Mary has received more than $1 million in life insurance benefits, she will make the maximum RRSP contributions for Seymour and herself that you have calculated immediately (before the end of February, 2018).

She provides you with the following T4RSP and RRSP receipt for the contributions that she has already made, as well as information related to her and Seymour's RRSP limits.

RRSP information - Mary	(Y/M/D)	Amount
Issuer of receipt - TD Asset Management	2017-12-10	5,400
Issuer of receipt - TD Asset Management	2018-01-05	16,800
Contributions made prior to 2018/03/02 and not deducted		Nil
Unused deduction room at the end of 2016		14,091
Earned income for 2016		180,000

T4RSP - Seymour	Box	Amount
Issuer of receipt - Royal Bank		
Withdrawal payments (in amounts of < $5,000 each)	22	126,000
Income tax deducted	30	12,600

RRSP information - Seymour	(Y/M/D)	Amount
Issuer of receipt - TD Asset Management		Maximum ?
Contributions made prior to 2018/03/02 and not deducted		Nil
Unused deduction room at the end of 2016		19,762
Earned income for 2016		45,000

Information Related To Chapter 11 Material

In checking Seymour's file, you find he has a net capital loss carry forward of $17,500 [(1/2)($35,000)] from the sale of his EEE Art Films Ltd shares in 2016. Mary has informed you that she has made all of the RRSP contributions as you had calculated.

On February 14, 2018, you receive a call from a very upset Mary Career. She has just received an amended T4. The original T4 had not included information on the stock options in her employer, MoreCorp (a public company), that she had exercised.

Mary had options to purchase 500 shares of MoreCorp at $42 per share. When she received the options, the shares were trading at $40 per share. On December 20, 2017, when the shares were trading at $125 per share, she exercised her options for 200 shares. She left verbal instructions for MoreCorp to immediately donate all of the shares to Tax Behind Bars, a Canadian registered charity whose volunteers provide extensive tax education to inmates in prisons across Canada.

Unfortunately for Mary, the employee she had given the donation instructions to was fired for falsifying her credentials so the donation was not done and she did not receive a 2017 charitable donation receipt.

Amended T4 - Mary	Box	Original Am't	Amended Am't
Issuer - MoreCorp			
Employment income	14	152,866.08	169,466.08
Employee's CPP contributions	16	2,564.10	2,564.10
Employee's EI premiums	18	836.19	836.19
RPP contributions	20	Nil	Nil
Income tax deducted	22	48,665.11	48,665.11
Stock option deduction 110(1)(d)	39	Nil	8,300.00
Charitable donations	46	1,000.00	1,000.00

Required: With the objective of minimizing the tax liability for the family, prepare Mary's 2017 income tax return and Seymour's final 2017 return. List any assumptions you have made and provide any explanatory notes and tax planning issues you feel should be placed in the files. Include in your solution Mary's maximum RRSP deduction for 2018.

CHAPTER 12

Taxable Income And Tax Payable For Corporations

Note On Current Developments

Small Business Deduction

For many years, the small business deduction reduced the Federal tax rate on the qualifying income of Canadian Controlled Private Companies (CCPCs) to 11 percent. In 2016, the deduction was increased, resulting in a federal rate on qualifying income of 10.5 percent, with further rate reductions scheduled for 2017 and 2018.

However, the government concluded that they could not afford the reductions scheduled for 2017 and 2018, resulting in a cancellation of these changes. This resulted in the relevant rate remaining at 10.5 percent for 2017 and, as originally proposed, for subsequent years.

It appears that the government has changed its mind on this issue. Through increases in the small business deduction, the Federal Small Business rate has been reduced to 10 percent for 2018, with a further reduction to 9 percent scheduled for 2019.

We would note that these current and planned reductions have been accompanied by a tightening of some of the rules related to private corporations in general. This combination indicates that the government, while discouraging some types of tax planning involving private corporations, is committed to supporting small businesses.

Tax Planning By Private Corporations

Income Sprinkling

The current government is convinced that some private corporations are being used in an offensive manner to sprinkle income to various related parties. As discussed briefly in Chapter 1, income splitting is one of the most powerful weapons in a tax planner's arsenal. While the government finds the use of income splitting to be appropriate in certain situations (e.g., spousal RRSPs and pension income splitting), it believes that abusive use of income sprinkling creates an unfair element in our taxation system. This reflects the fact that the more sophisticated forms of income splitting are only available to wealthy Canadians.

Note On Current Developments

The government's approach to dealing with this problem was to significantly expand the coverage of the Tax On Split Income (TOSI). As this tax is related directly to individuals and involves business entities other than corporations, the changes in the TOSI were covered in Chapter 11. We will not provide additional direct coverage of the TOSI in this or subsequent Chapters. However, we will refer to this tax as required in material that deals with other types of business entities (partnership and trusts).

Private Companies Holding Passive Investments

It is not uncommon for a private corporation to be sufficiently successful that it is producing income that is larger than current consumption needs of the owner, in some cases significantly larger. Given the desire to avoid taxation at the individual level, such owners will often invest this excess in passive investments to be held in the corporation. There are, in fact, many private companies that are holding millions of dollars in passive investments that have nothing to do with the corporation's business.

With respect to the income on passive investments held by companies eligible for the small business deduction, there is no real issue. As we will find in Chapter 13, such passive income is taxed at very high rates, in some cases higher rates than would be applicable to the individual owner if the income was received directly outside of a corporation.

The problem is the source of funds to make the passive investments. A simple example will serve to illustrate the issue.

EXAMPLE   Sam and Ira Johnston are brothers, both of whom have employment income in excess of $250,000. Any additional income that they receive personally will be taxed at a combined federal/provincial rate of 52 percent.

They both have a business which produces $200,000 in business income, none of which is required to meet their families' financial needs. Sam's business is a proprietorship while Ira's business is operated inside a private company. On its active business income, Ira's private company is taxed at a combined federal/provincial rate of 15 percent.

ANALYSIS   The amounts of after tax business income retained by the two brothers would be as follows:

	Sam	Ira
Before Tax Business Income	$200,000	$200,000
Tax Payable On Additional Income		
Sam At 52 Percent	(104,000)	
Ira At 15 Percent		(30,000)
After Tax Retention	$ 96,000	$170,000

Ira's corporation has $74,000 ($170,000 - $96,000) more in funds available for acquiring passive investments as compared to Sam's proprietorship. While subsequent earnings on Ira's investments will be taxed at corporate rates similar to those applicable to Sam, over time Ira will accumulate a much larger investment portfolio. This is viewed by the government as an unfair situation.

As you will learn later in this Chapter, the small business deduction is only available on the first $500,000 of active business income. To deal with the problem identified in the preceding example, legislation has been prepared that will reduce this $500,000 total for CCPCs that have high levels of passive investment income. This new legislation will not be in effect until 2019.

The legislation is very complex and difficult to understand. Given this, and the fact that all of our examples and problems are based on 2018, we will not provide coverage of these provisions until the next edition of this text. In our opinion, providing such coverage would only serve to confuse students.

Computation Of Net Income

12-1.   The day-to-day records of most corporations are kept in terms of accounting proce-dures and policies that are normally referred to as Generally Accepted Accounting Principles (GAAP). As noted in Chapter 6, Business Income, many of the rules for computing business income under the *Income Tax Act* are identical to those used under GAAP. However, there are a number of differences that are specifically provided for and, as a result, the first step in the computation of Taxable Income for a corporation is to convert accounting Net Income as determined under GAAP into Net Income For Tax Purposes. Only then can we move from Division B's Net Income For Tax Purposes to Division C's Taxable Income.

12-2.   In making this conversion, there are many adjustments that could be required in particular circumstances. Some adjustments are necessary because of different allocation patterns that result in timing differences between accounting and tax income. Examples of this would be differences between accounting amortization and CCA, as well as alternative approaches to the determination of pension cost deductions. Other adjustments involve permanent differences between accounting and tax amounts. An example of this type of difference would be the non-taxable one-half of capital gains. While accounting records include 100 percent of such gains, one-half of such gains will never be included in Net Income For Tax Purposes.

12-3.   As is noted in Chapter 6, a reconciliation between accounting Net Income and Net Income For Tax Purposes is a required part of the corporate tax return. The form that the CRA provides for this reconciliation is designated Schedule 1. The most common adjustments from this Schedule are listed in Figure 6-1 in Chapter 6 and that list has been duplicated as Figure 12-1 (following page) for your convenience.

12-4.   Chapter 6 on business income provided a detailed discussion of the conversion of Net Income for accounting purposes into Net Income For Tax Purposes. As that discussion is equally applicable to corporations and unincorporated businesses, it will not be repeated here. However, if you are not familiar with the material in Chapter 6, we suggest that you review it before proceeding with these Chapters on corporate taxation. Exercise Twelve-1 provides a fairly simple illustration of how this reconciliation works.

Exercise Twelve - 1

Subject: Schedule 1 Reconciliation

Available information for the S1 Company for the year includes the following:

1.   A capital asset was sold for $48,300. It had a cost of $120,700 and a net book value of $53,900. It was the last asset in its CCA class and the UCC balance in this class was $34,600 before the disposition. There were no other additions or dispo-sitions during the year.
2.   During the year, the Company acquired goodwill at a cost of $180,000. Since there was no impairment of the goodwill during the year, no write-down was required for accounting purposes.
3.   During the year, the Company expensed charitable donations of $15,000.
4.   Premium amortization on the Company's bonds payable was $4,500 for the year.

You have been asked to prepare a Schedule 1 reconciliation of accounting Net Income and Net Income For Tax Purposes. Determine the addition and/or deduction that would be made in Schedule 1 for each of the preceding items.

SOLUTION available in print and online Study Guide.

We suggest you work Self Study Problem Twelve-1 at this point.

Figure 12 - 1
Conversion Of Accounting Net Income To Net Income For Tax Purposes

Additions To Accounting Income:
- Income tax expense
- Amortization, depreciation, and depletion of tangible and intangible assets (accounting amounts)
- Recapture of CCA
- Tax reserves deducted in the prior year
- Losses on the disposition of capital assets (accounting amounts)
- Pension expense (accounting amounts)
- Scientific research expenditures (accounting amounts)
- Warranty expense (accounting amounts)
- Amortization of discount on long-term debt issued (see discussion in Chapter 7)
- Foreign tax paid (accounting amounts)
- Excess of taxable capital gains over allowable capital losses
- Interest and penalties on income tax assessments
- Non-deductible automobile costs
- 50 percent of business meals and entertainment expenses
- Club dues and cost of recreational facilities
- Non-deductible reserves (accounting amounts)
- Charitable donations
- Asset write-downs including impairment losses on intangibles
- Fines, penalties, and illegal payments

Deductions From Accounting Income:
- Capital cost allowances (CCA)
- Incorporation costs (First $3,000)
- Terminal losses
- Tax reserves claimed for the current year
- Gains on the disposition of capital assets (accounting amounts)
- Pension funding contributions
- Deductible scientific research expenditures
- Deductible warranty expenditures
- Amortization of premium on long-term debt issued
- Foreign non-business tax deduction [ITA 20 (12)]
- Allowable business investment losses
- Landscaping costs

Computation Of Taxable Income

Deductions Available To Corporations

12-5.   The reconciliation schedule illustrated in Figure 12-1 is used to establish a corporation's Net Income For Tax Purposes. When this task is completed, certain specified items are deducted from the resulting Net Income For Tax Purposes figure in order to arrive at Taxable Income. These deductions are specified in Division C of the *Income Tax Act* and the relevant items for individuals were given detailed coverage in Chapters 4 and 11. However, there are significant differences in the Division C deductions available to individuals and those available to corporations.

12-6.   With respect to the Division C items that are available to individuals, the following are not available to corporations:

- employee stock option deduction
- deduction for payments (social assistance and workers' compensation benefits)
- lump-sum payments
- lifetime capital gains deduction
- northern residents deductions

Figure 12 - 2

Conversion Of Corporate Net Income For Tax Purposes To Taxable Income

Net Income (Loss) For Tax Purposes

Less:
- Charitable donations (Limited to 75 percent of Net Income For Tax Purposes with a five year carry forward of unused amounts)
- Dividends received from taxable Canadian corporations
- Loss carry overs from subsequent or prior taxation years

Equals Taxable Income (Loss)

12-7.   A further significant difference relates to two items that, with respect to individuals, serve as a base for credits against Tax Payable. While these items are not available as a base for credits against corporate Tax Payable, they are available as deductions in the calculation of corporate Taxable Income. These items are:

Charitable Donations   Unlike the situation for individuals where charitable donations are the basis for a tax credit, corporations deduct charitable donations from Net Income For Tax Purposes in the determination of Taxable Income. While corporations have a deduction rather than a tax credit, the rules for determining which donations can be deducted by a corporation are essentially the same as the rules for determining which donations qualify for the tax credit for individuals. Further, corporations are subject to the same limits that apply to individuals, with respect to the amount that can be deducted in the current taxation year. The five year carry forward provision is also applicable to corporations. These matters are given detailed consideration in Chapters 4 and 11 and will not be repeated here.

Dividends   As noted in previous Chapters, individuals must gross up dividends received from taxable Canadian corporations by 16 percent for non-eligible dividends or 38 percent for eligible dividends. This is accompanied by a federal dividend tax credit equal to either 8/11 of the gross up or 6/11 of the gross up. There is no corresponding gross up or tax credit with respect to dividends received by a corporation. However, a corporation is permitted to deduct the full amount of such dividends in the calculation of Taxable Income. Note that, while this deduction removes dividends from Taxable Income and the Tax Payable calculation, they must be included in determining Net Income For Tax Purposes.

12-8.   In addition to the two preceding deductions, corporations are allowed to deduct loss carry overs from previous or subsequent years in the calculation of Taxable Income. Other than in situations where a corporation has been the subject of an acquisition of control (see Chapter 14), the rules related to the deduction of loss carry overs by corporations are basically the same as those applicable to individuals. These general rules are covered in Chapter 11 and will not be repeated here.

12-9.   The calculation of corporate Taxable Income is outlined in Figure 12-2.

Dividends From Other Corporations
Deduction From Taxable Income
12-10.   In the calculation of Taxable Income, ITA 112(1) permits a corporation to deduct dividends that are received from taxable Canadian corporations in the determination of Taxable Income.

12-11.   The reason for this deduction is fairly obvious. If taxes were levied on transfers of dividends between companies, it could result in taxes being repeatedly assessed on the same diminishing stream of income. That is, the paying corporation would be taxed on the income that provided the dividend and if, in addition, the receiving corporation had to include the amount received in its Taxable Income, double taxation of the same income would result. In more complex, multi-level corporate structures, this could extend to triple, quadruple, or even greater applications of tax to a single stream of income.

EXAMPLE   Mr. X owns 100 percent of the common shares of Company X, and Company X owns 100 percent of the common shares of Company Y. Both Companies pay out all of their after tax income as dividends. Company Y has income of $1,000 for the year and Company X has no income other than dividends from Company Y. Assume both Company X and Company Y are subject to a combined federal/provincial tax rate of 30 percent and Mr. X is subject to a combined federal/provincial tax rate on non-eligible dividends received of 33 percent.

ANALYSIS   A comparison of the after tax flow through, with and without the intercompany dividend deduction, would be as follows:

	No Deduction	Deduction
Company Y Income	$1,000	$1,000
Corporate Taxes At 30 Percent	(300)	(300)
Dividends To Company X	$ 700	$ 700
Corporate Taxes At 30 Percent	(210)	Nil
Dividends To Mr. X	$ 490	$ 700
Personal Taxes At 33 Percent	(162)	(231)
After Tax Retention	$ 328	$ 469

12-12.   Without the deduction, the after tax retention is only $328. This means that the total tax rate on the $1,000 of income earned by Company Y is an almost confiscatory 67.2 percent. While the application of the dividend deduction provides a more reasonable level of taxation, you should note that the combined corporate and personal tax on the $1,000 income stream is $531 ($300 + $231). This heavy level of taxation reflects the fact that, with a corporate tax rate of 30 percent, flowing income through a corporation can result in the payment of higher taxes than would be the case with the direct receipt of income. This point is discussed more fully in Chapter 13, which provides coverage of the concept of integration.

Exercise Twelve - 2

Subject: Corporate Taxable Income

The Chapman Company had Net Income For Tax Purposes for the year ending December 31, 2018 of $263,000. This amount included $14,250 in taxable capital gains, as well as $14,200 in dividends received from taxable Canadian corporations. Also during 2018, the Company made donations to registered charities of $8,600. At the beginning of the year, the Company had available a non-capital loss carry forward of $82,000, as well as a net capital loss carry forward of $18,000 [(1/2)($36,000)]. Determine the Company's minimum Taxable Income for the year ending December 31, 2018 and the amount and type of any carry forwards available at the end of the year.

SOLUTION available in print and online Study Guide.

Dividends From Untaxed Income

12-13.   While the preceding justifications for not taxing intercorporate dividends make sense in the majority of situations, problems can arise. One problem involves situations in which the corporation paying the dividend was not taxed on the funds prior to their distribution. Given the fact that, for most companies, accounting income is higher than Taxable Income, it would not be surprising to find cases where there is sufficient accounting income to warrant a dividend payment, combined with a tax loss for the period.

12-14.   In this case, there will be no taxation of the original income at the corporate level. This means that only personal taxes will be paid on the income stream and, as a consequence, the use of a corporation will result in a significantly lower level of taxation than would be the case if the income was received directly by the individual. In addition, because no tax will be assessed until the income is paid out in dividends, this situation may result in a significant deferral of the taxation that is applicable to the income stream.

Term And Other Preferred Shares

12-15.   A further problem arises when corporations attempt to achieve what is sometimes referred to as "after tax financing". Because of the favourable tax treatment given to both individual and corporate recipients of dividend income, rates that corporations will have to pay on preferred shares will sometimes be lower than rates paid on debt securities.

12-16.   For most corporations, debt securities will continue to remain attractive because the tax deductibility of interest payments provides a lower after tax cost of funds than would be the case with the use of preferred shares. However, this is not the case when the corporation is in a loss position and, as a consequence, such companies have often issued preferred shares.

12-17.   To make these preferred shares more attractive to investors, issuers add features such as redemption provisions. These features produce a preferred share that has most of the characteristics of debt. In fact, IAS 32, *Financial Instruments: Presentation*, may require that such preferred shares be treated as debt for accounting purposes.

12-18.   Despite many debt-like features, the payments made on such preferred shares are, for tax purposes, dividend income. As previously discussed, this type of income is taxed very favourably in the hands of individual investors and is not taxed at all in the hands of corporate investors.

12-19.   The loss of tax revenues on this type of security could be very high. To prevent this loss, the ITA either imposes special taxes under Part IV.1 and Part VI.1, or denies the dividend deduction to alter the treatment of dividends on these preferred shares. However, these provisions go beyond the scope of this material.

Dividends On Shares Sold For Loss (Stop Loss Rules)

12-20.   As the declaration and payment of dividends by a corporation reduces the corporation's net assets, it would be expected that the value of the shares would fall by approximately the amount of any dividend declared and paid. Given this, it would be possible for one corporation to acquire shares in another corporation at a time when it was anticipated that a dividend would be paid on the acquired shares. The dividends on these shares could be received tax free and, if the value of the shares declined when they went ex-dividend, they could be sold to create a capital loss. The following example illustrates the problem that is created by this situation:

> **EXAMPLE**   On June 30, 2018, Brian Company acquires 1,000 shares of Leader Company, a public company, at a cost of $20 per share. On July 1, 2018, the Leader Company declares and pays its regular $3 per share dividend. Because this dividend had been anticipated by the market, the price of the Leader Company stock falls $3 per share to $17 per share. On July 15, 2018, Brian Company sells all of its Leader Company shares at a price of $17 per share.

> **ANALYSIS**   In the absence of a special rule, the preceding situation would provide very favourable results for Brian Company. They would have received $3,000 in dividends which, because of the deduction for intercorporate dividends, would not be included in their Taxable Income. In addition, they would have a potentially deductible capital loss of $3,000 on the disposition of the shares.

12-21.   To prevent this from happening, ITA 112(3) and (3.01) contain "stop loss" rules applicable to shares held as capital property, and ITA 112(4) and (4.01) contain similar rules for shares held as inventory. Under these rules, any loss resulting from a disposition of shares by a corporation must be reduced by the amount of dividends received that are eligible for deduction under ITA 112(1). These rules apply if:

- the shares are held for less than one year; or
- the corporation holding the shares, along with other non-arm's length persons, owns more than 5 percent of the class of shares on which the dividend was received.

12-22.   In the preceding example, since the Brian Company held the shares for less than one year, the $3,000 capital loss would be eliminated by the $3,000 dividend received. The second condition, whether the Brian Company owns more than 5 percent of the class of shares, is not relevant given the length of time the shares were owned.

Exercise Twelve - 3

Subject: Stop Loss Rules

On June 16, 2017, Loren Ltd. acquires 1,000 of the 10,000 shares of Manon Inc. at a cost of $25.30 per share. On July 1, 2018, these shares pay a dividend of $2.16 per share. These are the only dividends that were received on these shares. Loren sells the shares on July 29, 2018 for $21.15 per share. Loren Ltd. has taxable capital gains of $50,000 in the year. What is the amount of the allowable capital loss that Loren Ltd. will include in its tax return for the taxation year ending December 31, 2018?

SOLUTION available in print and online Study Guide.

Foreign Source Dividends Received

12-23.   The situation for dividends received from non-resident corporations is more complex. The general rules are discussed in Chapter 7, which notes that foreign source dividends are included in income on a gross basis, before the deduction of any foreign taxes withheld. However, in Chapter 11 we introduced the foreign non-business tax credit provisions. These credits against federal Canadian Tax Payable are designed to compensate the recipient of foreign source non-business income for foreign taxes withheld at source, provided the income has been subject to a reasonable amount of Canadian taxation. You will recall that, in many situations, the credit against Canadian Tax Payable will be equal to the amount of foreign taxes withheld at source. Note that foreign source dividends are generally not deducted in the determination of Taxable Income (the exception to this general rule is foreign affiliate dividends which are covered in Chapter 20).

We suggest you work Self Study Problem Twelve-2 at this point.

Non-Capital Loss Carry Over For A Corporation

Additional Issues

12-24.   As the general rules for loss carry overs are the same for all taxpayers, most of the relevant material on this subject is dealt with in Chapter 11 where we discuss the determination of Taxable Income for individuals. There is, however, an additional problem in calculating the amount of the current year non-capital loss carry over for a corporation. This problem relates to the fact that dividends received from taxable Canadian corporations can be deducted by a corporation in the determination of its Taxable Income. To illustrate this problem, consider the following:

EXAMPLE During 2018 Marco Inc. has net taxable capital gains of $30,000 [(1/2)($60,000)], dividends of $25,000 received from taxable Canadian corporations, and a net business loss of $60,000. The Company also has a net capital loss carry forward of $50,000 [(1/2)($100,000)].

ANALYSIS Using the ITA 3 rules for calculating Net Income For Tax Purposes, the result would be as follows:

ITA 3(a)	Dividends Received	$25,000
ITA 3(b)	Net Taxable Capital Gains	30,000
ITA 3(c)	Subtotal	$55,000
ITA 3(d)	Net Business Loss	(60,000)
Net Income For Tax Purposes And Taxable Income		Nil

12-25.   From an intuitive point of view, it would appear that the non-capital loss for the year is $5,000, the ITA 3(c) subtotal less the net business loss. Further, as Net Income is nil, it appears that none of the net capital loss carry forward can be deducted, despite the $30,000 taxable capital gain. In addition, it does not appear that the Company will get any benefit from the potential deduction of the $25,000 in dividends that were received during the year. Fortunately, the ITA 111(8) definition of non-capital loss solves both of these problems.

An Expanded Definition

12-26.   You may recall that the ITA 111(8) definition was discussed previously in Chapter 11. In that material, we explained how the definition permits a net capital loss carry over to be deducted even in cases where current year losses result in a nil Net Income For Tax Purposes. In effect, the definition allows a net capital loss carry over to be converted to a non-capital loss carry over.

12-27.   In the Chapter 11 discussion, we were dealing only with the Taxable Income of individuals. Given this, we did not consider the additional problem that arises with the fact that dividends received by a corporation can be deducted in the calculation of corporate Taxable Income. While this was not apparent from the simplified version of the non-capital loss definition that was presented in Chapter 11, a more complete version of the ITA 111(8) definition deals with this problem. The expanded definition is as follows:

ITA 111(8) The non-capital loss of a taxpayer for a taxation year means the amount determined by the formula:

$$A - D, \text{ where}$$

A   is the amount determined by the formula:

$$E - F, \text{ where}$$

E   is the total of all amounts each of which is the taxpayer's loss for the year from an office, employment, business or property, the taxpayer's allowable business investment loss for the year, net capital loss carry overs deducted in the calculation of Taxable Income for the year (this amount cannot exceed the taxable capital gains for the year), and **dividends received from taxable Canadian corporations and deducted in computing Taxable Income**.

F   is the amount of income determined under ITA 3(c). [Sum of ITA 3(a) non-capital positive sources and ITA 3(b) net taxable capital gains, less Division B, Subdivision e deductions.]

D   is the taxpayer's farm loss for the year.

12-28.   The only difference in this definition from the one that was presented in Chapter 11 is the addition of "dividends received from taxable Canadian corporations and deducted in computing Taxable Income" in the E component. However, it is an important change in that it allows dividends that cannot be deducted because of insufficient Net Income For Tax Purposes to be added to the non-capital loss carry over balance.

Example

12-29.   All of these points can be illustrated by returning to the example presented in Paragraph 12-24. If we assume that Marco Inc. wishes to deduct the maximum amount of the net capital loss carry forward in 2018, the Net Income For Tax Purposes and Taxable Income would still be nil and the non-capital loss for the year would be calculated as follows:

Amount E:			
Net Business Loss			$ 60,000
Dividends Received And Deducted			25,000
Net Capital Loss Carry Forward Deducted			
(Limited To Net Taxable Capital Gains For The Year)			30,000
Total For Amount E			$115,000
Amount F - ITA 3(c) Income:			
Dividends Received	($25,000)		
Net Taxable Capital Gains	(30,000)	(55,000)	
Non-Capital Loss For The Year			$ 60,000
Net Capital Loss Carry Forward ($50,000 - $30,000)			$ 20,000

12-30.   Note the results of applying the non-capital loss definition. In effect, if there is not sufficient Net Income to allow their deduction in the calculation of Taxable Income, both dividends and net capital loss amounts deducted can be added to the non-capital loss carry over balance. Although subject to a 3 year carry back, 20 year carry forward limit, the loss carry over can be deducted against any type of income.

Exercise Twelve - 4

Subject: Non-Capital Loss With ABIL

For the taxation year ending December 31, 2018, Hacker Inc. has business and property income of $63,500. Also during this year, capital asset dispositions result in capital gains of $23,100 and capital losses of $38,400. The Company experiences a further loss on the arm's length sale of shares of a small business corporation in the amount of $151,500. Determine Hacker Inc.'s Net Income For Tax Purposes for 2018. Indicate the amount and type of any loss carry overs available at the end of the year.

Exercise Twelve - 5

Subject: Non-Capital Loss Carry Forward

The following information is for Loser Ltd., a Canadian public company, for the taxation year ending December 31, 2018:

Capital Gains On Capital Asset Sales	$111,000
Capital Losses On Public Company Stock Sales	84,000
Allowable Business Investment Loss	5,250
Dividends Received From Taxable Canadian Corporations	48,000
Canadian Source Interest Income	27,200
Net Business Loss	273,000

The Company has available a net capital loss carry forward of $19,000. It would like to deduct this loss during 2018. Determine the non-capital loss balance [ITA 111(8)] and net capital loss carry forward for Loser Ltd. at the end of the 2018 taxation year.

SOLUTIONS available in print and online Study Guide.

Ordering Of Taxable Income Deductions

12-31.   Chapter 11 covered the specific ordering rules in ITA 111.1 for claiming deductions in the calculation of Taxable Income. However, these rules are directed at individuals and do not apply to corporations. The *Act* does not contain an equivalent provision for corporations and, as a consequence, there is a question as to how deductions should be ordered for a corporation.

12-32.   Charitable donations in excess of 75 percent of Net Income For Tax Purposes are not deductible in the current year, but can be carried forward for five years, subject to the same 75 percent limitation in those years. As this is shorter than the carry forward period for any other type of loss, this would suggest using these amounts prior to claiming loss carry forwards. However, in reaching this conclusion, it should be noted that these donations can be deducted against any type of income.

12-33.   Turning to the deduction of loss carry overs, ITA 111(3) requires that losses within any single category must be deducted in chronological order. That is, if a corporation chooses to deduct a portion of its non-capital loss balance during the current year, the oldest losses of this type must be deducted first. However, there are no rules with respect to the order in which the individual types of loss carry forwards must be deducted.

12-34.   Farm loss carry forwards and non-capital loss carry forwards have restrictions on the time for which they are available. This would suggest that they be deducted first. However, while there is no restriction on the period of availability for capital loss carry forwards, these amounts can only be used to the extent that there are net taxable capital gains during the period.

12-35.   For a corporation that experiences only limited capital gains, these restrictions may be a more important consideration than the period of time during which the loss will be available. With the carry forward period for non-capital losses lasting 20 years, this would appear to leave plenty of time to recover this type of loss.

12-36.   An additional factor in making decisions on whether to deduct non-capital or farm losses is the period left to their expiry. Clearly, items that expire in the current year should be deducted immediately, with additional consideration given to items near the end of their carry forward period.

We suggest you work Self Study Problems Twelve-3 and 4 at this point.

Geographical Allocation Of Income

Permanent Establishments

12-37.   After Taxable Income is calculated, in order to determine the amount of provincial taxes that are payable and the province(s) to which they are due, it is necessary to allocate the income of the corporation to the various provinces. Given the variations in provincial tax rates on corporations, this can be a matter of considerable significance.

12-38.   The key concept here is the idea of a "permanent establishment". This concept is defined as follows:

> **ITR 400(2)**   Permanent establishment means a fixed place of business of the corporation, including an office, a branch, a mine, an oil well, a farm, a timberland, a factory, a workshop or a warehouse.

12-39.   This meaning has been extended to include having an agent or employee in a province, if that agent or employee has the general authority to contract for a corporation, or carries a stock of merchandise from which orders are regularly filled. The mere presence of a commission salesperson or an independent agent is not considered evidence of a permanent establishment. In addition, the presence of a controlled subsidiary in a province is not necessarily indicative of a permanent establishment.

12-40.   However, ITR 400(2)(d) indicates that where a corporation that has a permanent establishment anywhere in Canada owns land in a province, such land will be deemed to be a permanent establishment. In addition, ITR 400(2)(e) indicates that where a corporation uses substantial machinery or equipment in a particular place, that corporation shall be deemed to have a permanent establishment in that place.

Activity At Permanent Establishments

12-41.   Once the location of permanent establishments has been determined, income will be allocated on the basis of two variables. These are gross revenues from the permanent establishment, and salaries and wages paid by the establishment.

12-42.   Once these values are established, ITR 402(3) provides a formula for using these variables to allocate Taxable Income to provinces. It requires calculating, for each province, that province's gross revenues as a percentage of total corporate gross revenues, and that province's salaries and wages as a percentage of total corporate salaries and wages. A simple average of these two percentages, without regard to the relative dollar values associated with the corporate totals, is then applied to corporate Taxable Income to determine the amount of Taxable Income that will be allocated to that province.

12-43.   Note that, if the corporation has permanent establishments outside of Canada, not all of its Taxable Income will be allocated to a province. The presence of these foreign permanent establishments will be reflected in the calculation of the federal tax abatement (see Paragraph 12-46). If there are no permanent establishments outside of Canada, the federal tax abatement will be the full 10 percent, even if there is foreign investment income.

Example - Permanent Establishments

12-44.   The following example illustrates the process of allocating Taxable Income on a geographic basis:

EXAMPLE   The Linford Company has permanent establishments in Alberta, Manitoba, and Ontario. The Company's Taxable Income for the current year totaled $100,000, with gross revenues of $1,000,000 and salaries and wages of $500,000.

The following allocation of the gross revenues and the salaries and wages among the provinces occurred during the current year:

Province	Gross Revenues		Salaries And Wages	
	Amount	Percent	Amount	Percent
Alberta	$ 250,000	25.0	$100,000	20.0
Manitoba	400,000	40.0	200,000	40.0
Ontario	350,000	35.0	200,000	40.0
Totals	$1,000,000	100.0	$500,000	100.0

ANALYSIS   Using the average of the two percentages for each province, the Linford Company's Taxable Income would be allocated to the three provinces as follows:

Province	Average Percent	Taxable Income	Amount Allocated
Alberta	22.5	$100,000	$ 22,500
Manitoba	40.0	100,000	40,000
Ontario	37.5	100,000	37,500
Totals	100.0	N/A	$100,000

We suggest you work Self Study Problem Twelve-5 at this point.

Federal Tax Payable

Basic Rate

12-45.   All corporations are initially subject to the same basic tax rate. This rate is specified in ITA 123 and, for many years, has been set at 38 percent.

Federal Tax Abatement

12-46.   ITA 124(1) provides a reduction of 10 percentage points in the federal tax rate. This is normally referred to as the federal tax abatement and it is designed to leave room for the provinces to apply their respective tax rates. When deducted from the basic rate of 38 percent, this leaves a net federal rate of 28 percent.

12-47.   Note that this 10 percentage point reduction in the federal tax rate is only applicable to income earned in a Canadian jurisdiction. When a corporation has foreign operations in permanent establishments outside of Canada, less than 100 percent of its income will be allocated to the various provinces. When this is the case, the amount of abatement to be deducted is reduced by multiplying the 10 percent abatement by the total percentage of Taxable Income that was allocated to the provinces. For example, if only 80 percent of a corporation's Taxable Income was allocated to one or more provinces, the abatement would effectively be reduced to 8 percent [(10%)(80%)].

General Rate Reduction

General Rate Reduction Percentage

12-48.   In implementing changes in the federal rate on corporations, the government has decided to use a process which maintains the basic rate of 38 percent. When changes are required, the desired result is accomplished by using a "general rate reduction percentage". This percentage is applied to what is referred to as "full rate taxable income" (see explanation which follows). Since 2011, the general rate reduction percentage has been 13 percent.

12-49.   In those situations where all of a corporation's income is both allocated to a province and eligible for the general rate reduction, the corporate rate at the federal level is 15 percent:

Basic Corporate Rate	38%
Less: Federal Tax Abatement	(10%)
Balance	28%
Less: General Rate Reduction	(13%)
General Federal Corporate Rate	15%

Full Rate Taxable Income

12-50.   As noted, the "general rate reduction percentage" must be applied to "full rate taxable income". In fairly simple terms, full rate taxable income is income that does not benefit from certain other tax privileges. The most common of these privileges are the small business deduction, the manufacturing and processing profits deduction (M&P deduction), and the refundability of certain types of taxes on the investment income of private companies.

12-51.   Both the small business deduction and the M&P deduction are discussed later in this Chapter. Full Rate Taxable Income will also be considered in this Chapter, with detailed coverage beginning at Paragraph 12-141. The coverage of refundable taxes on the investment income of private companies will not be dealt with until Chapter 13.

Exercise Twelve - 6

Subject: Geographical Allocation And Federal Tax Payable

Sundown Ltd., a Canadian public company, has Taxable Income for the taxation year ending December 31, 2018 in the amount of $226,000. It has Canadian permanent establishments in Ontario and Manitoba. The Company's gross revenues for the 2018 taxation year are $2,923,000, with $1,303,000 of this accruing at the permanent establishment in Ontario, and $896,000 accruing at the permanent establishment in Manitoba. Wages and salaries total $165,000 for the year. Of this total, $52,000 is at the permanent establishment in Ontario and $94,000 is at the permanent establishment in Manitoba. Sundown has sales to the U.S. through a U.S. permanent establishment. Calculate federal Tax Payable for the taxation year ending December 31, 2018. Ignore any foreign tax implications.

SOLUTION available in print and online Study Guide.

Provincial Tax Payable

General Rules

12-52.   In calculating Tax Payable for individuals, a graduated rate structure is involved at both the federal and provincial levels. While limits on the brackets may differ from those used at the federal level, all of the provinces assess taxes on individuals using graduated rates applied to Taxable Income.

12-53.   In contrast, provincial corporate taxes are based on a flat rate applied to a Taxable Income figure. With the exception of Alberta and Quebec, the federal Taxable Income figure is used. While these two provinces collect their own corporate taxes, the Taxable Income figure that they use is normally similar to that used at the federal level.

General Rate

12-54.   As calculated in Paragraph 12-49, the general federal corporate rate is 15 percent. When the varying provincial rates are added to this percentage, Figure 12-3 (following page) shows that the general corporate tax rate ranges from a low of 26.5 percent in Ontario, to a high of 31 percent in Nova Scotia and Prince Edward Island.

Manufacturing And Processing Rate

12-55.   For many years, manufacturing and processing (M&P) income has been eligible for a tax deduction at the federal level. As discussed later in this Chapter, the deduction still exists. However, since the introduction of the general rate reduction (covered later in this Chapter), any income that qualifies for the M&P deduction also qualifies for the general rate reduction. As the M&P deduction rate is equal to the general rate reduction percentage, it is not of any benefit to corporations in terms of federal taxes payable (as will be discussed later in this Chapter, the base for the general rate reduction is reduced by amounts eligible for the M&P deduction.) As shown in Figure 12-3, the federal M&P rate (15 percent) is identical to the federal general rate (15 percent).

12-56.   This is also the situation with all but two of the provinces. At one time, there were more provinces with reduced M&P rates, but now only Ontario and Saskatchewan apply reduced rates to this type of income. Because it is still relevant in these two provinces, we provide coverage of the M&P deduction in this Chapter.

Small Business Rate

12-57.   The lowest rates in Figure 12-3 are referred to as the small business rates. As will be

Figure 12 - 3
Combined Federal/Provincial Corporate Rates - March 31, 2018

	General Rate	M&P Rate	Small Business Rate
Federal Tax Only	15.0%	15.0%	10.0%
Combined Federal/Provincial			
Alberta	27.0%	27.0%	12.0%
British Columbia	27.0%	27.0%	12.0%
Manitoba	27.0%	27.0%	10.0%
New Brunswick	29.0%	29.0%	13.0%
Newfoundland	30.0%	30.0%	13.0%
Nova Scotia	31.0%	31.0%	13.0%
Ontario	26.5%	25.0%	13.5%
Prince Edward Island	31.0%	31.0%	14.0%
Quebec	26.7%	26.7%	18.0%
Saskatchewan	27.0%	25.0%	12.0%

discussed later in this Chapter, Canadian controlled private corporations (CCPCs) are eligible for a small business deduction that lowers the federal rate to 10 percent on a limited amount of income. In general, the availability of this reduced rate is limited to the first $500,000 of active business income earned in a year.

12-58. All of the provinces, with the exception of Manitoba and Saskatchewan also apply their small business rate to the first $500,000 of active business income. Manitoba uses a reduced limit of $450,000 while Saskatchewan uses an increased limit of $600,000.

12-59. When the reduced federal and provincial rates are combined, the resulting rates range from a low of 10 percent in Manitoba, to a high of 18 percent in Quebec. You might note that the 18 percent rate for Quebec is significantly higher than the rate in other provinces. The next highest rate is 14.0 percent in Prince Edward Island.

Investment Income Rates

12-60. While this is not illustrated in Figure 12-3, different rates are applicable to certain types of investment income. We will provide coverage of these rates in Chapter 13.

Other Provincial Taxes

12-61. At one time, provincial taxes on corporate capital were fairly common. However, though some provinces levy capital taxes on specific types of entities (e.g., financial institutions), none of the provinces has a general tax on corporate capital.

12-62. Several provinces currently levy payroll taxes, often to fund the provincial health care system. For example, Ontario has a payroll tax of 1.95 percent on large amounts of salaries and wages paid.

Other Goals Of The Corporate Tax System

12-63. If raising revenues was the only goal of the corporate taxation system, there would be nothing much to discuss with respect to this matter, and there would be little need for the Chapters on corporate taxation that follow. However, in addition to raising revenues, the Canadian corporate taxation system has been structured to accomplish a number of other objectives. These include:

- **Incentives For Small Business** While there are several features of the tax system directed at encouraging small businesses, the major tax incentive for these organizations is the small business deduction.

- **Incentives For Certain Business Activities** The Canadian tax system encourages scientific research through a generous system of tax credits and a liberal policy towards deductible amounts. Tax credits are available to encourage business activities such as the employment of apprentices and the creation of child care spaces. Support is also provided to the natural resource industries through a variety of programs.

- **Incentives For Certain Regions** Certain regions of Canada are given assistance through investment tax credits and other programs.

- **Integration** One of the goals of the Canadian tax system is to keep the level of taxes paid on a given stream of income the same, regardless of whether or not a corporation is placed between the original source of the income and the ultimate recipient.

12-64. The small business deduction and the manufacturing and processing profits deduction will be examined in this Chapter. Integration will be dealt with in detail in Chapter 13. Our material on scientific research and experimental development expenditures and investment tax credits can be found in Chapter 14.

Small Business Deduction

Introduction

12-65. It has been a longstanding goal of the Canadian taxation system to provide incentives to small business. The underlying assumption is that, particularly during their formative years, these businesses need some degree of tax relief in order to allow them to accumulate the capital required for expansion. In very simplified terms, the small business deduction provides a deduction against the Tax Payable of a Canadian controlled private corporation.

12-66. The deduction was increased in 2018 to 18 percent from the previous level of 17.5 percent. A further increase in the deduction to 19 percent is scheduled for 2019.

12-67. For 2018, the federal deduction is equal to 18 percent of the first $500,000 of active business income. While most provinces use the same $500,000 limit, we have noted previously the Manitoba limit is $450,000 and the Saskatchewan limit is $600,000.

12-68. A simple example will serve to illustrate the application of this deduction.

EXAMPLE A Canadian controlled private corporation has Taxable Income of $100,000 for the year ending December 31, 2018. All of this income is earned in Canada and eligible for the small business deduction. The provincial tax rate applicable to income eligible for the small business deduction is 3 percent.

ANALYSIS The corporation's Tax Payable would be calculated as follows:

Base Amount Of Part I Tax [(38%)($100,000)]	$38,000
Federal Tax Abatement [(10%)($100,000)]	(10,000)
Small Business Deduction [(18%)($100,000)]	(18,000)
General Rate Reduction (Note)	Nil
Federal Tax Payable	$10,000
Provincial Tax Payable [(3%)($100,000)]	3,000
Total Tax Payable	$13,000

Note As explained later in this Chapter, the general rate reduction is not available on income that is eligible for the small business deduction.

12-69.   As can be seen in the example, when the small business deduction is available, it reduces the federal rate to 10 percent ($10,000 ÷ $100,000). We have also applied a provincial rate of 3 percent (roughly the average provincial rate). This produces a combined federal/provincial rate of 13 percent ($13,000 ÷ $100,000).

12-70.   The small business deduction provides a significant incentive to businesses that qualify. Only certain types of corporations qualify for this deduction and it is only available on certain amounts and types of income. The criteria for qualification can be described in non-technical terms as follows:

Type Of Corporation   The availability of the small business deduction is restricted to Canadian controlled private corporations (CCPCs).

Type Of Income   The deduction is only available on income earned in Canada that qualifies as "active business income". This would include the income of professional corporations and management companies, provided they are private and Canadian controlled. However, the income of specified investment businesses and personal services corporations (see definitions later in this Chapter) does not qualify.

Limit On Amount   The federal deduction is available on the first $500,000 of active business income earned in a year. This amount is referred to as the annual business limit and, in some circumstances, it is subject to a reduction formula.

Associated Corporations   The $500,000 annual business limit must be shared among associated corporations.

12-71.   The issues associated with these criteria are discussed in the material that follows.

Canadian Controlled Private Corporation (CCPC)

12-72.   CCPCs are defined in ITA 125(7) as private corporations that are not controlled, directly or indirectly, by one or more non-resident persons, by one or more public corporations, or a combination of non-resident persons and public corporations. In addition, corporations that have shares listed on a designated stock exchange, in or outside of Canada, do not qualify as CCPCs.

Active Business Income
The General Idea

12-73.   ITA 125(7) contains the following definition of "active business":

Active business carried on by a corporation means any business carried on by the corporation other than a specified investment business or a personal services business and includes an adventure or concern in the nature of trade.

12-74.   While the preceding defines active business, a further definition in ITA 125(7) defines income from an active business as follows:

Income of the corporation for the year from an active business means ... the income of the corporation for the year from an active business carried on by it, including any income for the year pertaining to or incident to that business, other than income for the year from a source in Canada that is a property ... [The definition goes on to cover an amount under ITA 12(10.2) that is of no interest to users of this material.]

12-75.   While this definition is not a model of clarity, it expresses the basic idea that active business income involves "doing something" to produce income. The concept excludes what is usually referred to as property income. Property income is distinguished by the fact that it generally becomes available with little or no effort on the part of the recipient (e.g., interest earned on long-term bonds).

Small Business Deduction

The Problem With Defining Property Income

12-76.   As noted, the preceding definitions of active business and active business income are largely directed towards excluding property income such as interest, dividends, and rents from eligibility for the small business deduction. The federal government does not wish to allow individuals to have access to the small business deduction by simply placing their passive investments in the shelter of a Canadian controlled private corporation. However, a blanket exclusion of property income is inappropriate since there are corporations that are "actively" involved in earning such income.

12-77.   The difficulty is in finding a way to distinguish between corporations that are simply being used as tax shelters for property or passive income, and corporations that engage in active property management. For example, if a corporation has a single residential rental property, the rents from this property would undoubtedly be viewed as passive income.

12-78.   Alternatively, a corporation that owns a chain of hotels with more than 10,000 rooms would certainly be entitled to view the rentals of these properties as an active business. The question is, at what point does the corporation cross the line between earning passive income and active business income?

12-79.   Similar, but less obvious problems arise with interest income. If a corporation has no activity other than collecting interest on term deposits, the amounts that it earns would almost certainly be viewed as passive income. Alternatively, interest earned by a company actively involved in providing mortgage financing to corporate clients could be viewed as business income. Again, a problem exists in finding the point at which a crossover is made between the two situations.

The Solution - Specified Investment Business

12-80.   The concept of a "specified investment business" provides a somewhat arbitrary solution to this problem. The term is defined in ITA 125(7) as follows:

> **Specified Investment Business** carried on by a corporation in a taxation year, means a business (other than a business carried on by a credit union or a business of leasing property other than real or immovable property) the principal purpose of which is to derive income (including interest, dividends, rents and royalties) from property but, except where the corporation was a prescribed labour-sponsored venture capital corporation at any time in the year, does not include a business carried on by the corporation in the year where
>
> (i) the corporation employs in the business throughout the year more than 5 full-time employees, or
>
> (ii) any other corporation associated with the corporation provides, in the course of carrying on an active business, managerial, administrative, financial, maintenance or other similar services to the corporation in the year and the corporation could reasonably be expected to require more than 5 full-time employees if those services had not been provided.

12-81.   As the activities of these specified investment businesses are excluded from the definition of active business, it means that income from property generated by such businesses is not eligible for the small business deduction. Stated alternatively, for corporations that are primarily engaged in earning income from property, the *Act* specifies that only those with more than five full time employees involved in earning such income are considered to be earning active business income and eligible for the small business deduction.

12-82.   While this is an arbitrary solution to the problem of distinguishing between active and passive income from a business, it does serve to resolve most of the uncertainty in this area. With respect to interpreting this rule, IT-73R6 states that "more than five full-time employees" means that at least six employees are working full business days on each working day of the year. However, this interpretation has been overturned in a Tax Court of Canada Decision (489599 B.C. Ltd. vs. The Queen).

12-83. In this decision, the court indicated that a combination of five full time employees and one part time employee would constitute "more than five full time employees". While IT-73R6 has not been revised to reflect the results in this case, the CRA has indicated that they accept this decision and will rule accordingly in future applications of the specified investment business definition.

Incidental Property Income

12-84. The definition of active business income includes incidental property income that is earned by a corporation engaged in an active business. In this regard, many corporations experience temporary excess cash balances, and these balances will usually be invested in interest bearing assets. Within reasonable limits, such interest can be included as a component of active business income. In similar fashion, revenues resulting from temporary rentals of excess space may be included in active business income.

Property Income Received From An Associated Corporation

12-85. Property income, income from a specified investment business, and non-incidental property income earned by a CCPC do not qualify for the small business deduction. However, when a corporation derives income from holding property, and the income is received from an associated company that deducted the amounts in computing active business income, ITA 129(6)(b) deems the income to be active business income to the recipient.

12-86. The logic behind this is that, while the amounts received by one of the associated companies must be considered property income, because of its legal form, the deduction by the payer corporation reduces the total active business income within the associated group.

> **EXAMPLE** Lardin Inc. is associated with Dwarm Ltd. Lardin lends $100,000 to Dwarm to use in active business activities. During the current year, Dwarm pays $6,000 of interest to Lardin.

> **ANALYSIS** Normally, Lardin could not classify the interest received as active business income. However, if Dwarm is earning active business income, the payment to Lardin reduced the amount of this income, as well as the total active business income of the associated group. In order to prevent this reduction, the recipient corporation is allowed to treat such interest as active business income.

Annual Business Limit

12-87. The federal limit on the amount of active business income that is eligible for the small business deduction is $500,000 per taxation year. As discussed in the paragraph which follows, this annual limit must be shared by associated corporations.

Allocation Among Associated Companies

12-88. In the absence of special rules, it would be very easy to avoid the annual limit that applies to the small business deduction. This could be accomplished by dividing a single corporation's activities between two separate corporations, thereby doubling up on the annual business limit of $500,000. However, the *Act* prevents this by requiring that associated companies share their annual business limit.

12-89. In some cases, association is fairly obvious. If, for example, a single individual owned all of the shares to two separate corporations, these corporations are clearly associated. However, a complete coverage of this subject becomes very complex. Because of this, we have allocated our detailed coverage of this subject to Chapter 14, Other Issues In Corporate Taxation.

12-90. While we are deferring our detailed coverage of this subject, we would note here that a group of associated companies can allocate the $500,000 limit in any manner that they wish. It can be divided equally among the group, allocated 100 percent to a single member of the group, or split in any proportions that the group chooses to use.

Calculating The Small Business Deduction

The General Formula

12-91.   After noting that to qualify for this deduction, a corporation must be a CCPC throughout the year, ITA 125(1) specifies that the deduction from federal Tax Payable is equal to 18 percent of the least of three figures (note that for ease of reference, this formula is included at the front of this text in "Rates and Other Data"):

(a) Net Canadian active business income.

(b) Taxable Income, less:

   (i)   100/28 times the ITA 126(1) credit for taxes paid on foreign non-business income, calculated without consideration of the additional refundable tax under ITA 123.3 (see Chapter 13) or the general rate reduction under ITA 123.4; and

   (ii) 4 times the ITA 126(2) credit for taxes paid on foreign business income, calculated without consideration of the general rate reduction under ITA 123.4 (see Note)

(c) The annual business limit of $500,000, less any portion allocated to associated corporations, less the reduction for large corporations.

Note   ITA 125(1)(b)(ii) actually has a more complicated calculation as follows:

... the amount determined by the formula

$$1 \div (A - B), \text{ where}$$

A is the percentage set out in paragraph 123(1)(a) [the basic federal rate of 38 percent], and

B is the percentage that is the corporation's general rate reduction percentage (as defined by section 123.4) for the taxation year [13 percent].

Given these numbers, ITA 125(1)(b)(ii) is calculated as $[1 \div (.38 - .13)] = 4$. We will use this number 4 in all of our examples and problems, without showing the complete calculation.

Constraints - Type Of Income And Annual Business Limit

12-92.   We have already noted that the deduction is only available on active business income earned in Canada, the item A constraint. We have also noted that the annual business limit of $500,000, the item C constraint, must be shared by associated companies.

Constraints - Taxable Income

12-93.   With respect to the limit which uses Taxable Income, we would note that active business income earned during the taxation year is included in Net Income For Tax Purposes. In many cases, this amount will also be included in full in Taxable Income. However, it is possible that large Division C deductions could eliminate all or part of this income from the Taxable Income total. Examples of such Division C deductions would be as follows:

- charitable donations
- non-capital loss carry overs
- farm loss carry overs

12-94.   You will notice that neither dividends nor net capital losses are included in this list. This reflects the fact that these amounts can only be deducted to the extent that either dividends or taxable capital gains are included in Net Income. Given this, they cannot serve to offset amounts of active business income that are included in Net Income For Tax Purposes.

12-95.   A simple example will illustrate the need for this Taxable Income constraint on the small business deduction:

EXAMPLE During the current year, Allard Ltd. has active business income of $123,000, taxable capital gains of $15,000, and dividends received from taxable Canadian corporations of $50,000. At the beginning of the year, Allard Ltd. has a net capital loss carry forward of $35,000 and a non-capital loss carry forward of $105,000. The Company will use the loss carry forwards to the extent possible during the current year. The calculation of Allard's Net Income For Tax Purposes and Taxable Income would be as follows:

Net Income For Tax Purposes	
($123,000 + $15,000 + $50,000)	$188,000
Dividends Received	(50,000)
Net Capital Loss Carry Forward	
(Limited To Taxable Capital Gains)	(15,000)
Subtotal (Equal To Active Business Income)	$123,000
Non-Capital Loss Carry Forward	(105,000)
Taxable Income	$ 18,000

12-96. Note that if only the net capital loss carry forward and dividends were deducted, Taxable Income would have been equal to the $123,000 in active business income. The problem is the non-capital loss carry forward. It has further reduced Taxable Income to $18,000, an amount well below the active business income.

12-97. If, in this case, the small business deduction was based on active business income, the amount would be $22,140 [(18%)($123,000)]. As this deduction is in excess of the Tax Payable on $18,000 of Taxable Income, this is not a reasonable outcome. The example clearly illustrates the need for the Taxable Income constraint on the small business deduction.

Constraints - Foreign Tax Credits

12-98. Another concern of the federal government is to ensure that the small business deduction is not provided on income that has not been taxed in Canada. To prevent this from happening, the B component of the ITA 125(1) formula reduces Taxable Income by:

- 100/28 times the ITA 126(1) credit for taxes paid on foreign non-business income, calculated without consideration of the additional refundable tax under ITA 123.3 (see Chapter 13) or the general rate reduction under ITA 123.4; and

- 4 times the ITA 126(2) credit for taxes paid on foreign business income, calculated without consideration of the general rate reduction under ITA 123.4.

12-99. The 100/28 figure is based on the notional assumption that foreign non-business income will be subject to a federal tax rate of 28 percent (i.e., if the credit is equal to the taxes paid at 28 percent, 100/28 times the credit will equal the notional amount of income received).

12-100. In similar fashion, the 4 times figure that is applicable to foreign business income is based on the notional assumption that this income will be subject to a federal tax rate of 25 (1 ÷ 4) percent.

12-101. Based on the preceding analysis, subtracting these amounts from Taxable Income has the effect of removing from this figure the amounts of foreign income on which the foreign tax credit has eliminated the Canadian taxation at the assumed rates of 28 and 25 percent. A simple example can be used to clarify this point:

EXAMPLE A corporation earns $100,000 in foreign non-business income, with $18,000 being withheld by the foreign government.

If this income had been earned in Canada, it is assumed that the tax would be $28,000 (using the notional rate on this type of income of 28 percent). Being received from a foreign source, the $28,000 in Canadian Tax Payable will be offset by the $18,000 foreign tax credit. This will leave a net Canadian Tax Payable of $10,000.

Using the foreign tax credit of $18,000 and an assumed tax rate of 28 percent, the formula removes $64,286 [(100/28)($18,000)] from Taxable Income, leaving $35,714 ($100,000 - $64,286). If we multiply this $35,714 by the notional rate of 28 percent, the result is $10,000, the amount of Canadian tax remaining after the application of the foreign tax credit. This demonstrates how the formula ensures that the small business deduction is not available on Taxable Income on which foreign tax credits have eliminated Canadian taxation.

If the foreign tax withheld and the foreign tax credit had been $28,000 [(28%)($100,000)], the formula would have removed $100,000 [(100/28)($28,000)], or all of the foreign source income.

Exercise Twelve - 7

Subject: Amount Eligible For The Small Business Deduction

Kartoom Ltd. is a CCPC throughout the year and is not associated with any other corporation. For the year ending December 31, 2018, Kartoom has Net Income For Tax Purposes of $570,000. This amount is made up of dividends from taxable Canadian corporations of $85,000, active business income of $425,000, and foreign non-business income of $60,000. The foreign income was subject to withholding in the foreign jurisdiction at a rate of 15 percent. Kartoom receives a foreign tax credit against federal Tax Payable that is equal to the amount withheld. Kartoom has a non-capital loss carry forward of $160,000 which it intends to deduct during 2018. Determine the amount eligible for the small business deduction for the year ending December 31, 2018.

SOLUTION available in print and online Study Guide.

Elimination Of Small Business Deduction For Large CCPCs

The Problem

12-102.   As the name implies, the small business deduction was designed to provide assistance to small corporations. For a variety of reasons, including the belief that such corporations have a positive impact on employment growth, and the fact that small corporations often experience financing difficulties in their formative years, the generous tax advantages provided by this deduction were thought to be appropriate.

12-103.   However, in designing the small business deduction provisions, eligibility was based on the type of income earned (active business income) and the type of corporation (CCPCs). No consideration was given to the size of the corporation's income or assets. As a consequence, under its usual provisions, some very large private corporations received the benefit of the small business deduction on amounts of active business income that were below the annual business limit. This was clearly not in keeping with the intent of this legislation.

The Solution

12-104.   To deal with this problem, there is a formula that reduces the annual business limit on the basis of the size of the CCPC's Taxable Capital Employed In Canada. As found in ITA 125(5.1), the formula for the **reduction** is as follows:

$$\textbf{Annual Business Limit REDUCTION} = A \times \frac{B}{\$11,250} \text{ where,}$$

A   is the amount of the corporation's annual business limit for the year ($500,000 or less if shared with associated corporations).

B   is 0.225 percent (.00225) of the excess of, the previous year's total Taxable Capital Employed In Canada by the corporation and its associated companies, over $10 million.

12-105.   "Taxable capital employed in Canada" is defined in ITA 181.2.   In somewhat simplified terms, it has the following meaning:

Taxable Capital Employed In Canada (TCEC)   GAAP determined debt and equity capital of the corporation, less debt and equity investments in other corporations. When not all of the corporation's Taxable Income is allocated to a province, the resulting amount is multiplied by the same percentage that is applied to the abatement in order to determine the portion of the total capital that is employed in Canada.

12-106.   The mechanics of this formula are easily understood. Note that this formula calculates the **reduction** in the annual business limit, **not** the limit after the reduction.   If a corporation has $10 million or less TCEC, B will equal nil ($10 million or less, minus the $10 million specified deduction). This means the formula amount will be nil and there will be no reduction in the corporation's annual business limit.

12-107.   When the amount of TCEC reaches $15 million, B in the formula will be equal to $11,250 [(.00225)($15,000,000 - $10,000,000)]. The annual business limit will then be multiplied by one ($11,250 ÷ $11,250) and the reduction in the annual business limit will be 100 percent of the available amount.

12-108.   Not surprisingly, a CCPC that is associated with one or more other corporations in a taxation year ending in a given calendar year will be required to take into account the TCEC of all of these firms.

Example

12-109.   The following example illustrates the reduction of the small business deduction for a large CCPC:

EXAMPLE   Largess Inc. is a CCPC with a December 31 year end. All of its income is earned in Canada, and it is not associated with any other corporation. On December 31, 2018, the following information is available:

2018 Active Business Income	$ 523,000
2018 Taxable Income	550,000
Taxable Capital Employed In Canada During 2017	13,700,000

12-110.   For the preceding year, 2017, B in the reduction formula would be equal to $8,325 [(.00225)($13,700,000 - $10,000,000)]. Using this in the ITA 125(5.1) formula would produce the following reduction in the 2018 annual business limit:

$$\$500,000 \times \frac{\$8,325}{\$11,250} = \$370,000 \text{ **Reduction**}$$

12-111.   Given this, the reduced annual business limit would be $130,000 ($500,000 - $370,000) and the small business deduction for 2018 would be 18 percent of the least of:

Active Business Income	$523,000
Taxable Income	550,000
Reduced Annual Business Limit ($500,000 - $370,000)	130,000

12-112.   The reduced annual business limit is the least of the three figures and the 2018 small business deduction would be $23,400 [(18%)($130,000)], a significant reduction from the $90,000 [(18%)($500,000)] that would have been available in the absence of the ITA 125(5.1) requirement for reducing the annual business limit for large CCPCs.

BYRD/CHEN NOTE As indicated in our introductory Note On Current Developments, the government is also concerned that the small business deduction provides eligible corporations with the ability to accumulate large amounts of passive investments. The government's solution to this is a provision that can erode the annual business limit for CCPCs with large portfolios of passive investments. This is similar to the reduction of the limit that we have discussed in the preceding section of this Chapter. As indicated in the introductory Note, this new provision does not come into effect until 2019 and, given this, we will not include coverage of this legislation in the current edition of the text.

Exercise Twelve - 8

Subject: Small Business Deduction Reduction

Largely Small Inc. is a Canadian controlled private corporation. For the year ending December 31, 2018, its Net Income For Tax Purposes is $1,233,000, all of which is active business income, except for $36,000 in foreign source non-business income. Fifteen percent of this amount was withheld in the foreign jurisdiction and the corporation receives a foreign tax credit against federal Tax Payable that is equal to the amount withheld. The corporation's only deduction in the calculation of Taxable Income is for a non-capital loss carry forward of $914,000. The corporation had Taxable Capital Employed In Canada of $11,300,000 for the year ending December 31, 2017, and $11,600,000 for the year ending December 31, 2018. It is not associated with any other corporation. Determine the amount of Largely Small Inc.'s small business deduction for the year ending December 31, 2018.

SOLUTION available in print and online Study Guide.

Personal Services Corporations

12-113.   The small business deduction represents a very significant reduction in corporate taxes and, as a consequence, taxpayers have a strong incentive to channel income into a corporation qualifying for this benefit.

12-114.   At one point in time, this could be accomplished by having an executive of a corporation resign, establish a company, and immediately have his company sign a contract with his former employer to provide the same services as the individual was previously performing as an employee. Since this new corporation could then qualify for the small business deduction, the use of such personal services corporations provided significant tax deferral and, in some cases, significant tax avoidance, for individuals such as executives, professional athletes, and entertainers.

12-115.   Under the current rules, such blatant tax avoidance schemes are no longer possible. To begin, ITA 125(7) defines a "personal services business" as follows:

... a business of providing services where

  (a) an individual who performs services on behalf of the corporation (referred to as an incorporated employee), or

  (b) any person related to the incorporated employee

is a specified shareholder of the corporation and the incorporated employee would reasonably be regarded as an officer or employee of the person or partnership to whom or to which the services were provided but for the existence of the corporation, unless

  (c) the corporation employs in the business throughout the year more than five full time employees, or

(d) the amount paid or payable to the corporation in the year for the services is received or receivable by it from a corporation with which it was associated in the year.

12-116.   In less technical language, a business is classified as a personal services business of a corporation when a "specified" shareholder, or a person related to a "specified shareholder", is providing services to another business and the individual who is performing the services can reasonably be regarded as an officer or employee of the entity for which the services are performed. As the term is used in this definition, in general, "specified shareholder" refers to an individual who owns, directly or indirectly, not less than 10 percent of the shares of any class of the corporation that is providing the services.

12-117.   Being classified as a personal service corporation is costly in terms of tax. Such a corporation is not eligible for the small business deduction or the general rate reduction. In addition, due to the fact that the maximum individual federal rate is 33 percent, these corporations are subject to an additional tax of 5 percent, resulting in an overall federal rate of 33 percent (38% - 10% + 5%) which is equal to maximum individual federal rate.

12-118.   In addition to this high rate, personal service corporations cannot deduct any expenses other than:

* salaries, wages, other remuneration, and benefits paid in the year to the individual who performed the services on behalf of the corporation; and

* other expenses that would normally be deductible against employment income, for example, travel expenses incurred to earn employment income.

12-119.   These rules serve to make the use of a personal service corporation unattractive in situations where they were used to make an executive's employment arrangements subject to lower taxes. However, athletes, entertainers and consultants may still find it attractive to incorporate. In many cases, they will qualify for the small business deduction either because they have sufficient diversity of income, or more than five full time employees. In addition, there is advantage in that all of the income of a personal services business is added to the GRIP balance (see Chapter 13), meaning that all of the income can be paid out as eligible dividends.

Professional Corporations And Management Companies

12-120.   In general terms, these two types of corporations can be described as follows:

Professional Corporations   This term is used where a corporation is established to carry on the practice of a profession specified in ITA 248(1). The ITA definition includes a corporation that carries on the professional practice of an accountant, dentist, lawyer, medical doctor, veterinarian, or chiropractor. Each province has different laws and rules as to which professions are allowed to incorporate. The incorporation of the professional practice of an engineer or architect would not meet the ITA definition.

Management Companies   This is a term that refers to corporations established to provide various management services, primarily to an unincorporated business. The unincorporated business is usually a professional practice, such as that of a doctor or dentist.

The services provided by this type of company include various personnel functions, such as payroll and accounting services, purchasing all supplies and equipment necessary to carry on the business, and providing the necessary office space required by the professional practice.

The unincorporated business pays fees to the company to cover the cost of providing management services and to provide for some income. A 15 percent markup for profit is usually allowed. The fees paid are deductible from the revenues of the professional practice. These companies are often used to transfer a portion of a professional's income to a lower income spouse or other related parties.

12-121.   Both types of companies are eligible for the small business deduction. However, the fact that medical services are exempt goods under the GST/HST legislation has made management companies unattractive for doctors and dentists. While GST/HST must be paid on services billed by the management company, these amounts cannot be recovered by medical professionals because their services are GST/HST exempt. (For coverage of GST/HST exempt services, see Chapter 21, GST/HST.) Given this situation, and the fact that professionals can incorporate, management companies for medical professionals delivering GST/HST exempt services are not as common as they once were.

Manufacturing And Processing Profits Deduction

Introduction

12-122.   Given the importance of such activity to the Canadian economy, it is not surprising that the federal government has provided tax assistance to enterprises that are involved in manufacturing and processing (M&P). As an example of this, in Chapter 5, Capital Cost Allowances, we noted that the government is providing significantly enhanced CCA rates on both buildings used for M&P and for M&P machinery and equipment.

12-123.   A more general incentive is the M&P deduction available to some corporations for their M&P profits. IT Folio S4-F15-C1, "Manufacturing and Processing", discusses the calculation of this deduction and activities that are and are not considered to be manufacturing or processing.

12-124.   As was explained previously, the rate for this deduction is the same as the percentage for the general rate reduction. Since the general rate reduction does not apply to income that is eligible for the M&P deduction, the use of the M&P deduction does not provide any direct tax benefits at the federal level. Given this situation, it would seem logical for the government to eliminate the complex legislation related to the M&P deduction. However, this has not happened. The probable explanation for this is that two provinces, Ontario and Saskatchewan, provide special treatment for income that qualifies for the federal M&P deduction. Because of this, and the special CCA rates for M&P assets, we will continue to provide some coverage of the M&P rules.

Calculating The Deduction

General Formula

12-125.   ITA 125.1 provides for a deduction from Tax Payable equal to the general rate reduction of 13 percent, times the company's M&P profits. Given that this amount is deducted from Tax Payable, it would be more consistent to refer to this "deduction" as a tax credit. However, ITA 125.1 uses the term deduction and, as a consequence, we will also use this terminology.

12-126.   While the basic idea is that the deduction is equal to the general rate reduction percentage applied to M&P profits, there are a number of other constraints on the amount that is eligible for this deduction. ITA 125.1(1) specifies that the deduction will be equal to the corporation's general rate reduction percentage multiplied by the lesser of:

A. Manufacturing and processing profits, less amounts eligible for the small business deduction; and

B. Taxable income, less the sum of:

1. the amount eligible for the small business deduction;

2. the relevant factor (see note) multiplied by the foreign tax credit for business income calculated without consideration of the general rate reduction under ITA 123.4; and

3. where the corporation is a Canadian controlled private corporation throughout the year, aggregate investment income as defined in ITA 129(4).

Note   The relevant factor is the same for both the small business deduction and the M&P deduction. While this is a simplification, we will use 4 as the relevant factor in our examples and problems (see Paragraph 12-91 for an explanation).

12-127.   Part A of this formula provides the basic limit based on the amount of M&P profits earned during the year. As will be noted subsequently, M&P profits is a technical term and must be calculated by a formula established in ITR 5200. In many cases, particularly for large public companies, this will be the factor that limits the amount of the M&P deduction.

12-128.   Like the small business deduction formula, for ease of reference, this M&P deduction formula is included at the front of this text in "Rates and Other Data".

Constraints - Small Business Deduction

12-129.   As was previously discussed, the small business deduction provides certain corporations with a deduction equal to 18 percent of the first $500,000 of their active business income. It appears that the government believes that granting both the 13 percent M&P deduction, and the 18 percent small business deduction on the same income stream would be too generous. As a consequence, any amounts of income that are eligible for the small business deduction are not eligible for the M&P deduction. In the preceding ITA 125.1(1) formula, this is accomplished by removing amounts eligible for the small business deduction from both the A and B components. Note that it is the "amount eligible" for the small business deduction that is removed, not the deduction itself.

Constraints - Taxable Income

12-130.   As was explained in our discussion of constraints on the availability of the small business deduction, the government wants to ensure that credits are not given on amounts that are not included in Taxable Income. As was the case with the active business income that is eligible for the small business deduction, M&P profits that are included in Net Income For Tax Purposes may not find their way into Taxable Income.

12-131.   This can occur when the corporation has deductions for such items as charitable donations, non-capital loss carry overs, or farm loss carry overs. For reasons that were discussed and illustrated in the discussion of the small business deduction, amounts eligible for the M&P deduction are limited by the amount of Taxable Income for the year.

Constraints - Foreign Tax Credits

12-132   As was the case with the Taxable Income constraint, the nature of the constraint created by deducting a multiple of foreign tax credits was explained in our discussion of the small business deduction. There is, however, one significant difference.

12-133.   In the ITA 125.1(1) formula for the M&P deduction, Taxable Income is reduced by a multiple of the foreign business income credit only. It is not adjusted for the foreign non-business income credit as was the case with the ITA 125(1) formula for the small business deduction. This probably reflects the fact that the M&P formula contains an extra deduction from Taxable Income for aggregate investment income, an amount that includes foreign non-business income.

Constraints - Aggregate Investment Income

12-134.   This constraint is more difficult to explain at this stage of the text. It is based on the fact that part of the federal tax paid on the "aggregate investment income" of a Canadian controlled private corporation can be refunded to the corporation. (This procedure is discussed in detail in Chapter 13.) As it would not be appropriate to provide a tax credit against taxes that are intended to be refunded, these amounts are removed from the Taxable Income that is eligible for the M&P deduction.

12-135.   In the formula in Paragraph 12-126, note the reference to "aggregate investment income as defined in ITA 129(4)". As discussed fully in Chapter 13, Taxation Of Corporate Investment Income, this somewhat unusual concept of investment income is defined as follows:

Net Taxable Capital Gains	$xxx
Property Income (Including Foreign Source)	
Interest (That Is Not Active Business Income)	xxx
Rents	xxx
Royalties	xxx
Total Positive Amounts	$xxx
Net Capital Loss Carry Overs Deducted During The Year	(xxx)
ITA 129(4) Investment Income	**$xxx**

Note that, in contrast to the usual concept of investment income, this definition does not include most dividends. Technically only dividends that are deductible in computing a corporation's Taxable Income are excluded. This calculation is included at the front of this text in "Rates and Other Data".

Eligibility

12-136. On the surface, eligibility for the M&P deduction appears to be easily determinable. Any corporation that derives 10 percent or more of its Canadian active business gross revenues from Canadian manufacturing or processing is eligible. The problem with this rule is the determination of what constitutes M&P activity.

12-137. The *Income Tax Act* does not define the terms manufacturing or processing. However, ITA 125.1(3) specifically excludes several types of activity from the designation of manufacturing or processing. These include logging, farming and fishing, construction, producing industrial minerals, and processing mineral resources.

M&P Profits Defined

12-138. We have noted that the M&P deduction is calculated by multiplying the general rate reduction percentage by "M&P profits". The determination of M&P profits is based on a fairly complex calculation that is found in ITR 5200. Given that this is largely a mechanical process and the fact that the M&P deduction no longer has an effect on the amount of federal Tax Payable, we are not providing coverage of this calculation in our text.

Exercise Twelve - 9

Subject: Amounts Eligible For Small Business and M&P Deductions

Marion Manufacturing is a Canadian controlled private corporation throughout 2018 and is not associated with any other company. It has Net Income For Tax Purposes of $462,000, a figure that includes $411,000 in manufacturing and processing profits (as per ITR 5200). The $462,000 also includes foreign source business income of $21,000 and taxable capital gains of $30,000. Because of withholding on the foreign source business income, the Company is entitled to a foreign tax credit of $3,150 [(15%)($21,000)].

The Company's only deduction in the calculation of Taxable Income is donations to registered Canadian charities in the amount of $310,000. Marion anticipates large increases in Taxable Income in the next few years.

Determine the amount of Marion's small business deduction and M&P deduction for the year ending December 31, 2018, assuming that the Company deducts all of the $310,000 of charitable donations. Do you believe that deducting all of the donations is the best alternative for Marion? Explain your conclusion.

SOLUTION available in print and online Study Guide.

General Rate Reduction - ITA 123.4(2)

Approach To Rate Reductions

12-139.   In our discussion of the basic federal tax rate for corporations, we noted that, in implementing reductions in corporate tax rates, the government has left the basic rate of 38 percent unchanged (see Paragraph 12-45). Instead of reducing the basic rate, they have created a deduction from this rate. This deduction is referred to as the "general rate reduction" percentage and the rate is 13 percent.

12-140.   While the government wished to reduce corporate tax rates through the use of this general rate reduction, they did not want it to be available on income that was already benefitting from some other tax privilege (e.g., the small business deduction). To deal with this potential problem, the government introduced the concept of Full Rate Taxable Income.

Full Rate Taxable Income

12-141.   In defining Full Rate Taxable Income, the goal was to develop a measure of income that did not benefit in a significant way from other legislative provisions. In particular, the government did not want this reduction to be applied to income that was eligible for:

- The small business deduction. This deduction is only available to CCPCs.

- The M&P deduction. This deduction is available to CCPCs, public companies, and private companies that are not Canadian controlled.

- Refundable Taxes. Refundable taxes are applicable to the investment income of CCPCs and, in some applications to the investment income of private companies that are not Canadian controlled. They are not applicable to public companies. While we need to consider the impact of refundable taxes on Full Rate Taxable Income at this point, detailed procedures related to refundable taxes are discussed in Chapter 13.

12-142.   Since the availability of the relevant benefits depends on the type of company, we will have to give separate attention to the calculation of the Full Rate Taxable Income of CCPCs, and to the Full Rate Taxable Income of companies that are not CCPCs (public companies and private companies that are not Canadian controlled).

Application To Companies Other Than CCPCs

12-143.   For these companies, the only adjustment to Taxable Income that is required to determine Full Rate Taxable Income is the removal of income eligible for the M&P deduction. Given this, for companies other than CCPCs, Full Rate Taxable Income is defined as follows:

Regular Taxable Income	$x,xxx
Income Eligible For The M&P Deduction	(xxx)
Full Rate Taxable Income	$x,xxx

12-144.   A simple example will serve to illustrate the relevant calculations:

EXAMPLE   For the year ending December 31, 2018, Daren Ltd., a Canadian public company, has Taxable Income equal to $100,000, with $40,000 of this amount eligible for the M&P deduction.

ANALYSIS   Full Rate Taxable Income is equal to $60,000 ($100,000 - $40,000). Given this, total federal Tax Payable for Daren Ltd. would be calculated as follows:

Base Amount Of Part I Tax [(38%)($100,000)]	$38,000
Federal Tax Abatement [(10%)($100,000)]	(10,000)
M&P Deduction [(13%)($40,000)]	(5,200)
General Rate Reduction [(13%)($100,000 - $40,000)]	(7,800)
Federal Tax Payable	$15,000

12-145.   For a corporation with income consisting entirely of M&P profits, there is no general rate reduction as there is no Full Rate Taxable Income. This is illustrated by revising the example in Paragraph 12-144:

> **EXAMPLE - Revised**   Assume that the $100,000 in Taxable Income of Daren Ltd. was generated solely by M&P activities.

> **ANALYSIS**   Total federal Tax Payable for Daren Ltd. would be calculated as follows:

Base Amount Of Part I Tax [(38%)($100,000)]	$38,000
Federal Tax Abatement [(10%)($100,000)]	(10,000)
M&P Deduction [(13%)($100,000)]	(13,000)
General Rate Reduction [(13%)($100,000 - $100,000)]	Nil
Federal Tax Payable	$15,000

12-146.   This calculation illustrates the fact that the overall federal rate on income that is eligible for the M&P deduction is 15 percent. This is, of course, identical to the overall rate on income that is eligible for the general rate reduction, illustrating the fact that the M&P deduction is no longer advantageous at the federal level.

Exercise Twelve - 10

Subject: Federal Tax Payable For A Public Company

For the year ending December 31, 2018, Marchand Inc., a Canadian public company, has Taxable Income of $320,000. Of this total, $180,000 qualifies for the M&P deduction. Calculate Marchand's federal Tax Payable for the year ending December 31, 2018. Include in your solution any M&P deduction available.

SOLUTION available in print and online Study Guide.

Application To CCPCs

12-147.   Not surprisingly, the calculation of Full Rate Taxable Income for a CCPC is somewhat more complex than it is for a public company. As we have noted, in addition to the M&P deduction, these companies may benefit from the small business deduction and the refundable tax provisions on investment income.

12-148.   Given the potential presence of these additional tax privileges, Full Rate Taxable Income for a CCPC is defined as follows:

Taxable Income, reduced by:

1.   Income eligible for the small business deduction.

2.   Income eligible for the M&P deduction.

3.   The corporation's aggregate investment income for the year as defined in ITA 129(4). [This is to remove income that will benefit from refundable taxes when it is distributed by the corporation. These taxes are explained in Chapter 13.]

12-149.   The definition of aggregate investment income in ITA 129(4) was discussed in the coverage of the M&P deduction (see Paragraph 12-135). It includes both foreign and Canadian amounts of net taxable capital gains, interest, rents, and royalties, but not dividends that are deductible in computing Taxable Income. The balance is reduced by net capital loss carry overs deducted during the year.

12-150.   As is covered in Chapter 13, a portion of the Part I tax paid by CCPCs on their aggregate investment income is refunded when dividends are paid. Because of this refund, aggregate investment income is already taxed advantageously when it is flowed through a CCPC. Given this, it does not receive the benefit of the general rate reduction.

12-151.   The following example illustrates the application of the general rate reduction rules to a CCPC with no investment income.

EXAMPLE For the year ending December 31, 2018, Zaptek Ltd., a CCPC, has $200,000 in Taxable Income. This amount is made up entirely of active business income earned in Canada, none of which relates to M&P activity. Zaptek is associated with another company and, as per the agreement with that company, Zaptek is entitled to $100,000 of the annual business limit.

ANALYSIS The federal Tax Payable for Zaptek Ltd. would be calculated as follows:

Base Amount Of Part I Tax [(38%)($200,000)]	$76,000
Federal Tax Abatement [(10%)($200,000)]	(20,000)
Small Business Deduction [(18%)($100,000)]	(18,000)
General Rate Reduction [(13%)($200,000 - $100,000)]	(13,000)
Federal Tax Payable	$25,000

12-152.   The overall rate of federal tax in this example is 12.5 percent ($25,000 ÷ $200,000). This reflects a combination of a rate of 10% (38% - 10% - 18%) on the $100,000 of income that was eligible for the small business deduction, and a rate of 15% (38% - 10% - 13%) on income that was not eligible for this deduction.

Exercise Twelve - 11

Subject: Federal Tax Payable For A CCPC

Redux Ltd. is a Canadian controlled private corporation. For the year ending December 31, 2018, the Company has Taxable Income of $200,000, all of which is active business income. Of this amount, $145,000 results from M&P activity. As it is associated with two other corporations, its share of the annual business limit is $140,000. Determine the Company's federal Tax Payable for the year ending December 31, 2018. Include in your solution any M&P deduction available.

SOLUTION available in print and online Study Guide.

We suggest you work Self Study Problems Twelve-6, 7, 8, and 9 at this point.

Foreign Tax Credits For Corporations

Introduction

12-153.   The foreign tax credits that are available to individuals earning foreign business or non-business income are discussed in detail in Chapter 11. Under rules that are very similar to those applicable to individuals, corporations are also allowed to use foreign taxes paid on business and non-business income as credits against Canadian Tax Payable. While the rules are similar to those for individuals, there are differences that will be discussed here. IT Folio S5-F2-C1, "Foreign Tax Credit" gives interpretations with respect to some of the most commonly encountered requirements contained in these foreign tax credit provisions.

Calculation Of Foreign Tax Credits

Foreign Non-Business (Property) And Business Tax Credits

12-154.   The formula that limits the Canadian tax credit for foreign taxes paid on foreign source non-business income is as follows:

The **Foreign Non-Business Income Tax Credit** is the lesser of:

- The tax paid to the foreign government (for corporations, there is no 15 percent limit on the foreign non-business taxes paid by a corporation); and

- An amount determined by the following formula:

$$\left[\frac{\text{Foreign Non} - \text{Business Income}}{\text{Adjusted Division B Income}}\right][\text{Tax Otherwise Payable}]$$

12-155. The meaning of "Adjusted Division B Income" and "Tax Otherwise Payable" are explained beginning at Paragraph 12-158. Both of the foreign tax credit formulae are included at the front of this text in "Rates and Other Data".

12-156. The formula that limits the amount of foreign business income taxes paid that can be used as a foreign tax credit is as follows:

The **Foreign Business Income Tax Credit** is the least of:

- The tax paid to the foreign government

- An amount determined by the following formula:

$$\left[\frac{\text{Foreign Business Income}}{\text{Adjusted Division B Income}}\right][\text{Tax Otherwise Payable}]$$

- Tax Otherwise Payable for the year, less any foreign tax credit taken on non-business income under ITA 126(1).

12-157. As was the case with individuals, there is an additional factor to consider in the case of foreign business income tax credits. This is the "Tax Otherwise Payable", reduced by any foreign non-business income tax credit deducted under ITA 126(1).

Adjusted Division B Income

12-158. While the general descriptions in the formulae (e.g., Adjusted Division B Income and Tax Otherwise Payable) are the same as those applicable to individuals, their meaning is somewhat different. More specifically, for a corporation, "Adjusted Division B Income" is determined as follows:

Division B Income (Net Income For Tax Purposes)	$x,xxx
Net Capital Loss Carry Overs Deducted Under ITA 111(1)(b)	(xxx)
Taxable Dividends Deducted Under ITA 112	(xxx)
Dividends From A Foreign Affiliate Deductible Under ITA 113	(xxx)
Adjusted Division B Income	$x,xxx

Tax Otherwise Payable

12-159. The following table compares the components included in the calculation of Tax Otherwise Payable for foreign non-business tax credits with those used to calculate foreign business tax credits.

Tax Otherwise Payable Components	Non-Business	Business
Base Amount Of Part I Tax (38%)	Yes	Yes
Plus: Additional Refundable Tax (ART) On Investment Income Of CCPC (See Chapter 13)	Yes	No
Minus: Federal Tax Abatement	Yes	No
Minus: General Rate Reduction	Yes	Yes

12-160. "Tax Otherwise Payable" is a particularly confusing term as its calculation is different for individuals and corporations. As shown in the table, adding to the confusion is the fact that its components differ depending on whether it is being used to calculate foreign non-business tax credits or foreign business tax credits for corporations.

12-161.   You will recall that the purpose of the 10 percent federal tax abatement is to leave room for the provinces to tax corporations. It is deducted in the formula for determining foreign non-business tax credits because non-business income will, in general, be taxed in a province. As a consequence, it is appropriate to deduct this abatement in determining the limit on the foreign non-business tax credit.

12-162.   In contrast, in the calculation of the foreign business income tax credit, "Tax Other-wise Payable" is not reduced by the 10 percent federal tax abatement, reflecting the fact that foreign business income will not be taxed in a province. Also different is the fact that this calculation of "Tax Otherwise Payable" does not include the additional refundable tax on investment income under ITA 123.3. (See Chapter 13.)

12-163.   You may recall that the foreign tax credit constraint in the small business deduction calculation uses foreign tax credit amounts that do not consider the general rate reduction (see Paragraph 12-98). The reason for this is a potentially circular calculation. Since the general rate reduction amount uses the amount eligible for the small business deduction and the small business deduction calculation uses the foreign tax credits, these amounts cannot all be calculated at the same time. As a result, the foreign tax credits used in calculating the small business deduction may not be equal to the actual foreign tax credits.

Foreign Tax Credit Carry Overs

12-164.   Unlike the situation with individuals, where the amount of foreign taxes that can be used as a credit is limited to 15 percent of the foreign source non-business income, the only limit for a corporation is the limit that is found in the second component of the formula. If the actual amount of foreign taxes paid is greater than this limit, there is no carry over of the excess as a tax credit. However, as was noted in Chapter 11, unclaimed amounts can be deducted under ITA 20(12) in the determination of Net Income For Tax Purposes.

12-165.   Unlike the case with foreign non-business income taxes paid in excess of amounts used as tax credits, unused foreign business taxes paid can be carried over as a tax credit to the 3 preceding taxation years or the 10 subsequent taxation years. In calculating the allowable tax credit for such carry overs, these unused amounts will be added to the foreign tax paid factor in the calculation of the foreign business income tax credit.

Exercise Twelve - 12

Subject: Foreign Tax Credits

Internat Inc. is a Canadian public company. For the year ending December 31, 2018, it has Net Income For Tax Purposes of $146,000, including foreign business income of $20,000. The foreign government withheld $3,000 in taxes on this income, resulting in a net remittance of $17,000. None of the Company's income involves manufac-turing and processing and, based on the ITR 402(3) formula, 88 percent of the Company's income was allocated to a province. In calculating Taxable Income, the Company deducts $30,000 in dividends received from taxable Canadian companies, a non-capital loss carry forward of $75,000, and a net capital loss carry forward of $25,000. Determine the Company's Part I Tax Payable for the year ending December 31, 2018. Include in your answer any carry overs available at the end of the year.

SOLUTION available in print and online Study Guide.

We suggest you work Self Study Problem Twelve-10 at this point.

Additional Supplementary Self Study Problems Are Available Online.

Key Terms Used In This Chapter

12-166.   The following is a list of the key terms used in this Chapter. These terms, and their meanings, are compiled in the Glossary located at the back of the Study Guide.

Active Business
Active Business Income
Adjusted Active Business Income
Allowable Business Investment Loss
Allowable Capital Loss
Annual Business Limit
Associated Corporations
Business Income
Business Investment Loss
Canadian Controlled Private Corporation
Carry Over
CCPC
Common Shares
Corporation
Designated Stock Exchange
Disposition
Federal Tax Abatement
Foreign Taxes Paid Credit
Full Rate Taxable Income
GAAP
General Rate Reduction

Loss Carry Back
Loss Carry Forward
Manufacturing And Processing Profits
   Deduction (M&P Deduction)
Net Business Income
Net Capital Loss
Non-Capital Loss
Ordering Rule
Permanent Establishment
Personal Services Business
Preferred Shares
Private Corporation
Professional Corporation
Property Income
Public Corporation
Small Business Deduction
Specified Investment Business
Stop Loss Rules
Taxable Capital Employed In Canada
Term Preferred Shares

References

12-167.   For more detailed study of the material in this Chapter, we refer you to the following:

ITA 89(1)	Definitions (Private Corporation And Public Corporation)
ITA 110	Deductions Permitted
ITA 111	Losses Deductible
ITA 112	Deduction Of Taxable Dividends Received By Corporations Resident In Canada
ITA 113	Deduction In Respect Of Dividend Received From Foreign Affiliate
ITA 123	Basic Part I Rate For Corporations
ITA 123.3	Additional Refundable Tax On CCPC's Investment Income
ITA 123.4(2)	General Deduction From Tax
ITA 124	Federal Abatement
ITA 125	Small Business Deduction
ITA 125.1(1)	Manufacturing And Processing Profits Deductions
S4-F15-C1	Manufacturing And Processing
S5-F2-C1	Foreign Tax Credit
IT-67R3	Taxable Dividends From Corporations Resident In Canada
IT-73R6	The Small Business Deduction
IT-177R2	Permanent Establishment Of A Corporation In A Province (Consolidated)
IT-189R2	Corporations Used By Practising Members Of Professions
IT-206R	Separate Businesses
IT-232R3	Losses — Their Deductibility In The Loss Year Or In Other Years
IT-391R	Status Of Corporations
IT-458R2	Canadian Controlled Private Corporation

Problems For Self Study (Online)

To provide practice in problem solving, there are Self Study and Supplementary Self Study problems available on MyLab Accounting.

Within the text we have provided an indication of when it would be appropriate to work each Self Study problem. The detailed solutions for Self Study problems can be found in the print and online Study Guide.

We provide the Supplementary Self Study problems for those who would like additional practice in problem solving. The detailed solutions for the Supplementary Self Study problems are available online, not in the Study Guide.

The .PDF file "Self Study Problems for Volume 2" on MyLab contains the following for Chapter 12:

- 10 Self Study problems,
- 5 Supplementary Self Study problems, and
- detailed solutions for the Supplementary Self Study problems.

Assignment Problems

(The solutions for these problems are only available in
the solutions manual that has been provided to your instructor.)

Assignment Problem Twelve - 1

(Net Income For Tax Purposes)

Jaxtor Inc. is a Canadian public company that uses a December 31 taxation year. As a public company it must provided financial statements based on generally accepted accounting principles. For the year ending December 31, 2018, these financial statements show an accounting Net Income of $543,267.

In order to assist in preparing the Company's 2018 tax return, the following additional information is available.

1. The Company's financial statements disclosed interest on the Company's bonds payable of $12,460. This included discount amortization of $460.

2. The financial statements show a charge for amortization of $62,500. Maximum CCA on these assets, which the Company intends to deduct, would be $71,300. This does not include any CCA on Class 14.1 assets.

3. During 2018, as part of a business combination transaction, the Company acquired goodwill of $189,000. The Company's accountant found that there was no impairment of this amount during 2018.

4. During 2018, the Company sold temporary investments for $13,450. The adjusted cost base of these investments was $9,980.

5. During 2018, the Company donated a Class 10 depreciable asset to a registered charity. It received a charitable donations receipt for the $132,000 fair market value of the asset. The asset had a capital cost of $117,000 and a net book value in the accounting records of $105,300. The UCC balance in Class 10 was $94,670. Other assets remained in Class 10.

6. At the beginning of 2018, the Company had a liability for estimated warranties of $6,240. During the year, warranty costs were incurred in the amount of $5,650 and, at the end of the year, the remaining warranty liability was estimated to be $4,890.

7. During the year, the Company disposed of Class 8 depreciable assets with a capital cost of $79,000 and a net book value of $68,000 for cash proceeds of $71,000. At the beginning of the current year, the UCC balance in Class 8 was $66,720. These were the last assets in Class 8 and they were not replaced prior to the end of the year.

Required: For each of the preceding pieces of information, indicate the adjustment(s) that would be required to convert the Company's $543,267 accounting Net Income to minimum Net Income For Tax Purposes. Explanations for the adjustments are not required and no calculation of the total Net Income For Tax Purposes is required.

Assignment Problem Twelve - 2
(Corporate Taxable Income)

Cabrera Digital is a Canadian public company. It has always used a taxation year that ends on December 31. During the year ending December 31, 2018, it had operating revenues of $1,234,000 and operating expenses of $962,000, resulting in an operating income $272,000.

Also during 2018, it received the following dividends:

- Non-Eligible Dividends From 100 Percent Owned Subsidiary $23,600
- Eligible Dividends From Canadian Public Companies   61,300

The Company's only other property income was a $312,000 capital gain on a holding of temporary investments. Because of this very fortunate investment result, the Company decides to make a $241,000 donation to a registered Canadian charity. No other capital gains are anticipated in the foreseeable future.

At the beginning of the year ending December 31, 2018, the Company had the following carry forward balances:

- Net Capital Losses $262,000
- Non-Capital Losses   193,000

Required: Calculate the minimum Net Income For Tax Purposes and Taxable Income for Cabrera Digital for the year ending December 31, 2018. Indicate the amount and type of any carry forwards that are available at the end of that year.

Assignment Problem Twelve - 3
(Corporate Net And Taxable Income)

Vertin Ltd. is a Canadian public company that has always used a December 31 year end. However, as December is a very busy time for their business activities, it has requested a change in their taxation year end to July 31, a date at which their business activity is at the low point for the year. They have presented this situation to the CRA and the Department has accepted their request for the change.

The change will be implemented during 2018, resulting in a short fiscal period ending July 31, 2018. The Company's Income Statement, prepared in accordance with generally accepted accounting principles, for the period January 1, 2018 through July 31, 2018 is as follows:

Vertin Ltd.
Income Statement
7 Month Period Ending July 31, 2018

Sales (All Within Canada)		$1,796,600
Cost Of Sales		(973,400)
Gross Margin		$ 823,200
Other Expenses (Excluding Taxes):		
Wages And Salaries	($108,200)	
Cost Of Sales	(194,200)	
Amortization	(97,600)	
Rent	(113,400)	
Interest Expense	(13,200)	
Foreign Exchange Loss	(7,600)	
Travel And Promotion	(86,300)	
Bad Debt Expense	(6,200)	
Warranty Expense	(7,400)	
Charitable Donations	(8,100)	
Other Operating Expenses	(51,200)	(693,400)
Operating Income		$ 129,800
Gain On Sale Of Investments		7,800
Income Before Taxes		$ 137,600

Other Information:

1. Wages and salaries includes a $28,000 bonus to Vertin Ltd.'s CEO. Because she antici-pates retiring at the end of 2019, this bonus will not be paid until January, 2020.

2. In determining the Cost Of Sales, the Company deducted a $23,400 reserve for inventory obsolescence.

3. Amortization is on a Class 1 building, Class 8 furniture and fixtures, and Class 10 delivery vehicles. The following information is relevant for the determination of CCA for the 7 month period ending July 31, 2018:

   Building   The January 1, 2018 UCC for the building was $872,000. During 2018, the Company spent $42,000 on improved flooring in all areas of the property. The building was not a new building when it was acquired.

   Furniture And Fixtures   The January 1, 2018 UCC balance for Class 8 was $285,000. During 2018, new furniture was acquired at a cost of $40,600. Old furni-ture with a capital cost of $28,200 was sold for $17,600.

   Delivery Vehicles   On January 1, 2018, the Class 10 UCC balance was $198,300. There were no additions or disposals in this Class during the 7 month period ending July 31, 2018.

4. The interest expense relates to a line of credit that was used to finance seasonal fluctua-tions in inventory.

5. The foreign exchange loss resulted from financing costs related to the purchase of merchandise in the United Kingdom.

6. The travel and promotion expense consisted of the following items:

Business Meals And Entertainment	$32,400
Hotels And Airfare	41,800
Golf Club Memberships	12,100
Total Travel And Promotion Expense	$86,300

7. For accounting purposes, the Company establishes a warranty reserve based on estimated costs. On January 1, 2018, the reserve balance was $8,200. On July 31, 2018, a new reserve was established at $7,400.

8. The accounting gain on the sale of investments is equal to the capital gain for tax purposes.

9. During the period January 1, 2018 through July 31, 2018, the Company declared and paid dividends of $31,400.

10. On January 1, 2018, the Company has available a $24,600 non-capital loss carry forward and a $7,200 [(1/2)($14,400)] net capital loss carry forward.

Required: Calculate the minimum Net Income For Tax Purposes and Taxable Income for Vertin Ltd. for the 7 month period ending July 31, 2018. Indicate the amount and type of any carry forwards that will be available for use in future years.

Assignment Problem Twelve - 4
(Corporate Loss Carry Forwards)

The following information relates to the operations of Notem Inc. for the taxation year ended December 31, 2018 (all amounts are based on the relevant tax rules):

Net Business Loss	$141,800
Dividends From Taxable Canadian Corporations	33,500
Taxable Capital Gains	9,600
Allowable Capital Losses	4,425
Charitable Donations	5,400

At the beginning of the taxation year, the Company had a carry forward of unused charitable donations of $1,350 from the previous year, and a net capital loss carry forward of $10,500 [(1/2)($21,000)].

It is the policy of the Company to minimize net capital loss balances prior to using any other type of carry over balance.

Required: Calculate the corporation's minimum Net Income For Tax Purposes and Taxable Income for its 2018 taxation year. Indicate any balances available for carry forward to subsequent years.

Assignment Problem Twelve - 5
(Corporate Loss Carry Forwards - 4 Years)

Lisgar Ltd. is a Canadian controlled private corporation. It began operations on January 1, 2015.

For the first four years of operations, the Company had Net Income (Loss) determined using generally accepted accounting principles, charitable donations, capital gains (losses) and dividends received as follows:

	Accounting Income (Loss)	Charitable Donations	Capital Gains (Losses) (Note 1)	Dividends (Note 2)
2015	$165,000	$4,100	$26,000	$17,100
2016	(263,000)	7,800	(13,500)	28,900
2017	127,000	5,600	18,400	27,600
2018	(62,100)	3,400	3,700	15,100

Note 1   All of these gains were on the sale of common shares. The accounting gains and losses are the same amounts as the capital gains and losses for tax purposes.

Note 2   All of the dividends are received from taxable Canadian corporations.

It is the policy of the Company to deduct charitable donations prior to any loss carry overs.

They also have a policy of minimizing non-capital loss carry overs, as opposed to net capital loss carry overs.

Required: For each of the four years 2015 through 2018, provide the following information:

- The minimum Net Income For Tax Purposes and Taxable Income that would be reported for Lisgar Ltd. Indicate the amount and type of any current year losses that are available for carry back or carry forward.

- The amended figures for any years to which losses are carried back.

- An analysis of the amount and type of carry forwards that would be available at the end of the year.

Assignment Problem Twelve - 6
(Corporate Loss Carry Forwards - 4 Years)

Metronet Inc. is a Canadian public company with a December 31 year end. It commenced operations in 2015 and has had mixed results since that time. In terms of its business income (loss), the results, determined using the relevant tax legislation, were as follows:

	2015	2016	2017	2018
Net Business Income (Loss)	$233,500	$34,000	($163,000)	$57,000

Other Information:

1. In each of the years 2015 through 2018, Metronet receives dividends from taxable Canadian companies of $13,500.

2. In 2015, Metronet made charitable donations of $4,800, followed by a donation of $15,600 in 2016. The donations declined to $7,400 in 2017. No contributions were made in 2018.

3. In 2015, Metronet realized a capital loss of $24,600, followed by a $45,600 capital gain in 2016. In 2017, there was a capital loss of $48,400. Things improved in 2018, during which Metronet realized a $33,200 capital gain.

It is the policy of the Company to minimize its net capital loss carry forward balance, prior to minimizing other types of carry forwards.

Required: For each of the four years 2015 through 2018, provide the following information:

- The minimum Net Income For Tax Purposes and Taxable Income that would be reported for Metronet Inc. Indicate the amount and type of any current year losses that are available for carry back or carry forward.

- The amended figures for any years to which losses are carried back.

- An analysis of the amount and type of carry forwards that would be available at the end of the year.

Assignment Problem Twelve - 7
(Geographical Allocation Of Income)

Geotech Inc. has permanent establishments in British Columbia, Alberta, Saskatchewan, and the United States. During the current year, the company had total wages and salaries of $1,472,000 and gross revenues of $4,620,000. These were distributed among the provinces where the Company has operations in the following manner:

Province	Wages And Salaries Accrued	Gross Revenues
British Columbia	$ 309,120	$1,155,000
Alberta	559,360	1,570,800
Saskatchewan	220,800	877,800
United States	382,720	1,016,400
Total	$1,472,000	$4,620,000

For the current taxation year, the Company's Taxable Income totaled $1,127,000.

Required: Calculate the amount of the Geotech Inc.'s Taxable Income for the current year that would be allocated to each province and the United States. Any percentages used in your calculations should be rounded to one decimal place. Ignore any foreign tax implications.

Assignment Problem Twelve - 8
(Part I Tax With Reduced SBD)

Jordu Inc. is a large Canadian controlled private corporation (CCPC). For the taxation year ending December 31, 2017, the Company, along with its associated companies, had a combined Taxable Capital Employed In Canada of $13,246,900. The corresponding figure for 2018 is $14,126,384.

Gross revenues for 2018 totaled $3,460,000, with 28 percent of this amount generated in Ontario, 63 percent in British Columbia, and the remainder coming from outside of Canada. The revenues were earned in a country where Kalec has a permanent establishment. Wages and salaries for this period totaled $1,250,000, all of which were paid in British Columbia.

Taxable Income for the 2018 tax year was determined to be $1,265,000, with all but $130,000 of this total consisting of Canadian active business income. The $130,000 is foreign business income. The foreign jurisdiction withheld $19,500 in tax, remitting the remaining $110,500 to Jordu.

Jordu Inc. is required to share its small business deduction with three other associated companies. The four companies split the annual business limit equally.

Assume that Jordu's tax credit will be equal to the amount of foreign taxes paid.

Required: Calculate Jordu's minimum federal Part I Tax Payable for the year ending December 31, 2018.

Assignment Problem Twelve - 9
(Corporate Tax Payable)

For the taxation year ending December 31, 2018, Lorne Inc., a Canadian controlled private company, has Net Income For Tax Purposes of $410,500. This is made up of $312,400 of active business income and $98,100 of dividends from various Canadian public companies. It has been determined that $211,300 of the active business income qualifies as manufacturing and processing profits.

During 2018, the Company makes donations to registered charities totaling $31,400.

At the beginning of 2018, the Company has a non-capital loss carry forward of $29,300. It intends to deduct all of this carry forward during 2018.

Lorne Inc. is associated with three other CCPCs. The companies have agreed that each company will claim one-quarter of the annual business limit.

Required: Determine the minimum Taxable Income and Part I federal Tax Payable for Lorne Inc. for the year ending December 31, 2018. Show all calculations, whether or not they are necessary to the final solution. As the corporation operates in a province that has a reduced tax rate for M&P activity, a separate calculation of the federal M&P deduction is required.

Assignment Problem Twelve - 10
(Comprehensive Corporate Tax Payable)

For the year ending December 31, 2018, Mamora Ltd. had accounting income before taxes of $914,000. Mamora is a Canadian controlled private company throughout 2018.

Other Information related to the Company's 2018 taxation year is as follows:

1. The accounting income figure included a deduction for Amortization Expense of $405,525.

2. On January 1, 2018, Mamora Ltd. had the following UCC balances:

Class 1	$1,050,000
Class 8	1,460,000
Class 10	142,000
Class 13	175,000

    The Class 1 balance relates to a single building acquired at a cost of $1,650,000. It is estimated that the cost of land included in this amount is $350,000. In June, 2018, this building is sold for $1,725,000, including an estimated value for the land of $375,000. In accounting records this real property was carried at $1,550,000, a net book value for the building of $1,200,000, plus $350,000 for the land. As a result of this sale, a gain of $175,000 was included in the accounting income figure.

    The old building is replaced on February 15, 2018 with a new building acquired at a cost of $2,100,000, of which $400,000 is allocated to land. The building is used 95 percent for manufacturing and processing activity and it is allocated to a separate Class 1.

    During 2018, Class 8 assets are acquired at a cost of $150,000. There are no dispositions of Class 8 assets during the year.

    As the Company has decided to lease all of its vehicles in the future, all of the assets in Class 10 are sold during the year. The capital cost of these assets was $285,000 and the proceeds of disposition amounted to $122,000 with no asset disposed of for more than its capital cost. The net book value of these assets was $185,000, resulting in a loss of $63,000 being included in accounting income.

    The Class 13 balance relates to a single lease that commenced on January 1, 2013. The lease has an initial term of 6 years, with an option to renew for 4 years. Expenditures on this leasehold were $250,000 in 2013 and $60,000 in 2017. There were no further expenditures in 2018. The write-off of these expenditures for accounting purposes is included in the Amortization Expense figure that was deducted in the determination of accounting income.

    It is the policy of Mamora to deduct maximum CCA in each year.

3. The accounting income figure included a Gain On The Sale Of Vacant Land of $75,000. This land had been acquired several years ago for $620,000. While the Company had intended to construct a new building on this site, they had concluded that their current operations did not justify this investment. Given this, the land was sold for $695,000. The buyer provided a 2018 payment of $295,000, with the balance due in four annual payments of $100,000 each, beginning on December 31, 2019.

4. The Company spent $23,000 during the year on landscaping for its new building. While this was treated as an asset for accounting purposes, Mamora did not amortize the balance as it believed the work had an unlimited life.

5. Using the formula found in the *Income Tax Regulations*, 88 percent of Mamora's income has been allocated to provinces.

6. Mamora's accounting income includes foreign business income of $15,300. This amount is net of withholdings in the foreign jurisdiction in the amount of $2,700.

7. As the Company expects to issue more shares during 2019, it made a number of amendments to its articles of incorporation. The legal costs for these changes were $21,000. They have been deducted in the determination of accounting income.

8. Other amounts deducted in the determination of accounting income are as follows:

Bond discount amortization	$ 4,600
Donations to registered charities	12,500
Interest on late income tax instalments	1,400
Interest on late municipal tax payments	625

9. Accounting income was reduced by $42,000 for the cost of business meals and entertainment. In addition, a deduction of $23,000 was made for the cost of a membership in a golf club for the president of the Company. She uses the club only for entertaining business clients.

10. Mamora Ltd. is associated with several other CCPCs. Mamora's share of the group's annual business limit for 2018 is $175,000.

11. At the beginning of 2018, Mamora had a net capital loss carry forward of $210,000, as well as a non-capital loss carry forward of $95,000.

12. For 2018, Mamora has active business income in Canada of $976,380, $425,000 of which results from M&P activity.

13. Mamora's accounting income includes dividends from taxable Canadian corporations in the amount of $52,000.

Required:

A. Calculate the minimum Net Income For Tax Purposes for Mamora Ltd. for 2018. In addition, calculate the UCC balance on January 1, 2019 for each class of assets. Ignore the possibility of using the replacement property election.

B. Calculate the minimum Taxable Income for Mamora Ltd. for 2018. Indicate the amount, and type, of any carry overs that are available at the end of the year.

C. Calculate the minimum federal Part I Tax Payable for Mamora Ltd. for 2018. As the corporation operates in provinces that have a reduced tax rate for M&P activity, a separate calculation of the federal M&P deduction is required. Assume that the foreign tax credit for foreign business income is equal to the foreign taxes withheld.

CHAPTER 13

Taxation Of Corporate Investment Income

Note On Current Developments

As was discussed more extensively in a note at the beginning of Chapter 12, the government is concerned about the accumulation of passive investments resulting from the retention of the after tax income of private corporations. As a reflection of this concern, legislation related to the income on such passive investments was introduced in the 2018 budget. In simple terms, when such passive income exceeds $50,000 per year, there will generally be a reduction in the annual business limit that is available to Canadian Controlled Private Corporations (CCPCs). This is accompanied by changes in the Refundable Dividend Tax On Hand (RDTOH) procedures.

As indicated in the note to Chapter 12, these changes do not become effective until taxation years beginning after 2018. Given that in this edition of the text, all of our problems are based on 2018 taxation years, we will not provide coverage of this new legislation until the next edition.

Integration

The Basic Concept

13-1.   In designing a system for assessing taxes on business income, there are two theories or perspectives as to the appropriate treatment of corporations. These two perspectives are referred to as the entity view and the integration view. They can be described as follows:

Entity View   The entity view holds that corporations have a perpetual life of their own, that they are independent of their shareholders, and that they are legal entities. As such, they should pay tax separately on their earnings.

Integration View   Under the integration approach to the taxation of business income, corporations are viewed as simply the legal form through which one or more individuals (shareholders) carry on business. Therefore, business income that flows through a corporation to an individual should not be taxed differently, in total, from business income earned directly by that individual as a proprietor or partner.

13-2.   In practice, we find a variety of relationships between corporations and their shareholders. Given this situation, it would not be reasonable to apply either of these views to all Canadian corporations. For large corporations, where the shares are widely held and publicly traded, the entity view seems appropriate:

- Management of the corporation is separate from its ownership, with income allocation and distribution decisions being made without directly consulting the shareholders.

- Not all corporate profits are paid out to the shareholders.

- Some of the amounts distributed are paid to foreign shareholders, subject only to the non-resident withholding tax.

13-3.   In this type of situation, the entity view's treatment of the corporation as a separate taxable unit appears to be an equitable way to tax business income.

13-4.   This would not be the case for small corporations where the shares are privately held, either by a single individual or a small group of related individuals. With these owner managed businesses, the affairs of the shareholders and the business are closely related. Tax planning decisions involving salaries, dividends, or capital gains affect both personal and corporate taxes and the line between the corporation and its owners is often faint. This would lead to the conclusion that the taxation of business income in these situations should not be influenced by the presence of the corporation. This conclusion is consistent with the integration view of business income taxation.

13-5.   In a strict legal sense, the *Income Tax Act* reflects the entity view in that corporations are considered to be taxable units that are separate from their owners. Both the corporation and the owners are subject to taxation and this, in effect, involves double taxation of the income earned initially by the corporation. In the absence of special provisions, there would be a significantly higher level of taxation on income earned by a corporation and paid out as dividends, than there would be on income earned directly, either through a proprietorship or partnership.

13-6.   Fortunately, there are special provisions that mitigate the effects of both the corporation and its shareholders being treated as taxable entities. The most important of these provisions is the dividend tax credit that is available to individuals who have received dividends from taxable Canadian corporations.

AN IMPORTANT NOTE An understanding of dividend gross up and tax credit procedures is essential to the material which follows in this Chapter and Chapters 14, 15, and 16. If you do not fully understand these procedures, you should review the material on dividends that is found in Chapter 7.

Dividend Gross Up And Tax Credit Procedures
Eligible Dividends

13-7.   You may recall from Chapter 7 that ITA 89(1) defines eligible dividends as any taxable dividend that is designated as such by the company paying the dividend (designation procedures are covered later in this Chapter). Dividends that are designated as eligible are grossed up by 38 percent and receive a federal dividend tax credit equal to 6/11 of the 38 percent gross up. As was discussed in Chapter 7, the application of these rates will result in a more favourable result than would be the case if the rates applicable to non-eligible dividends were used. The term eligible dividends refers to the fact that such dividends are eligible for this "enhanced" dividend tax credit procedure.

13-8.   With the exception of capital dividends, all types of dividends may be designated as eligible dividends. This includes the cash and stock dividends that were discussed in Chapter 7, as well as the various types of deemed dividends that will be introduced in Chapter 14 (e.g., ITA 84(3) dividend on redemption of shares).

Non-Eligible Dividends

13-9. It is common terminology to refer to dividends that have not been designated as eligible, as non-eligible dividends, and this is the term we use. (Unfortunately, the term used in tax returns is "other than eligible" dividends which can cause confusion.) These non-eligible dividends are grossed up by 16 percent and receive a federal dividend tax credit of 8/11 of the 16 percent gross up.

13-10. Any dividend that has not been designated as eligible will be considered to be non-eligible. This includes cash dividends, stock dividends, dividends in kind, and the various types of deemed dividends that are discussed in Chapter 14. Note, however, as capital dividends are not taxable dividends, they do not qualify for either the dividend gross up procedure or the tax credit procedure.

Who Can Declare Eligible Dividends?

13-11. Legislation specifies the conditions necessary for a corporation to designate a dividend payment as being eligible for the enhanced dividend tax credit procedures. While we could discuss this legislation at this point, it will be much easier to understand after you have covered this Chapter's material on the taxation of corporate investment income. Given this, we will provide a short summary here to help you understand the following material, but defer our major coverage of the designation of eligible dividends until the end of this Chapter.

13-12. The reason for the enhanced dividend tax credit procedures for eligible dividends is to provide better integration for corporate income that is subject to the general corporate tax rate and that does not benefit from preferential tax treatment (e.g., the small business deduction). Given this, we will find that most of the taxable dividends paid by large public companies can be designated as eligible.

13-13. In contrast, the income of a CCPC may benefit from the small business deduction that was discussed in Chapter 12, or refundable taxes that will be discussed at a later point in this Chapter. Because of these provisions, the income of a CCPC may be taxed at very favourable rates. Given this, a significant amount of the dividends paid by most CCPCs cannot be designated as eligible.

13-14. It would be very convenient to have a rule that says that taxable dividends paid by non-CCPCs are eligible dividends, while dividends paid by CCPCs are non-eligible. Unfortunately, as explained at the end of this Chapter, this simple dichotomy does not work because:

- some CCPCs may have a portion of their income taxed at full rates (e.g., active business income in excess of the annual business limit of $500,000), and

- some non-CCPCs may have a portion of their income taxed at favourable rates (e.g., a CCPC that goes public with a retained earnings balance that contains amounts that benefited from the small business deduction).

Integration And Business Income

Required Corporate Rates And Provincial Dividend Tax Credits

13-15. In Chapter 7 we noted that the goal of integration is to ensure that, if an individual chooses to channel an income stream through a corporation, he will retain the same after tax amount of funds that he would have retained if he had received the income directly. Stated alternatively, integration procedures are directed at equating the amount of taxes paid by an individual on the direct receipt of income, with the combined corporate/individual taxes that would be paid if that same stream of income was channeled through a corporation.

13-16. In Chapter 7, we also demonstrated that, for integration to work, certain assumptions were required with respect to both the combined federal/provincial tax rate on corporations and the combined federal/provincial dividend tax credit. As noted in that chapter and summarized in Figure 13-1 (following page), those assumptions are as follows:

Figure 13 - 1
Corporate Rates And Dividend Tax Credits Required For Integration

Type Of Dividends	Required Corporate Combined Tax Rate	Required Provincial Dividend Tax Credit
Eligible (38% Gross Up)	27.54%	5/11 ≈ 45.5%
Non-Eligible (16% Gross Up)	13.79%	3/11 ≈ 27.3%

Corporate Federal/Provincial Tax Rate   For integration to work perfectly, the corporate rate must be such that the dividend gross up percent must restore the after tax corporate amount to the pre corporate tax amount. The relevant rates are as follows:

- For eligible dividends which have a 38 percent gross up, the required rate is 27.54 percent. For example, $10,000 of corporate income would result in corporate taxes of $2,754 and an after tax amount of $7,246 ($10,000 - $2,754). When the $7,246 is grossed up by 38 percent, the result is the original $10,000 [($7,246)(1.38)] of corporate earnings.

- For non-eligible dividends which have a 16 percent gross up, the required rate is 13.79 percent. For example, $10,000 of corporate income would result in corporate taxes of $1,379 and an after tax amount of $8,621 ($10,000 - $1,379). When the $8,621 is grossed up by 16 percent, the result is the original $10,000 [($8,621)(1.16)] of corporate earnings.

If the provincial dividend tax credit is at the level required for integration, combined corporate tax rates above 27.54 percent (for eligible dividends) and 13.79 percent (for non-eligible dividends) will result in higher taxation on income flowed through a corporation. This type of situation is referred to as under integration.

Provincial Dividend Tax Credit   For the total taxes on income flowed through a corporation to be equal to taxes that would be paid on the direct receipt of income, there must be a credit against personal taxes that is equal to the taxes paid at the corporate level. As you can see in our examples of the required rates for perfect integration, when the corporate tax rate is the one required for perfect integration, the gross up will be equal to the corporate taxes paid. Putting these two facts together leads to the conclusion that the combined dividend tax credit must be equal to the gross up of dividends received. The required rates are as follows:

- For eligible dividends, the federal dividend tax credit is equal to 6/11 of the gross up (54.5%). This means that, for the combined credit to equal the gross up, the provincial credit must be equal to 5/11 (45.5 percent) of the gross up.

- For non-eligible dividends, the federal dividend tax credit is equal to 8/11 of the gross up (72.7%). This means that, for the combined credit to equal the gross up, the provincial credit must be equal to 3/11 of the gross up (27.3 percent).

If the corporate tax rate is at the level required for integration, provincial dividend tax credits below these rates will result in under integration, (i.e., additional taxation because a corporation is used).

These required tax and dividend credit rates are summarized in Figure 13-1.

Actual Corporate Tax Rates
13-17.   For eligible dividends, integration requires a federal/provincial tax rate on corporations of 27.54 percent. For 2018, actual rates for the public companies that pay the majority of such dividends range from 26.5 percent to 31 percent (see Chapter 12). For public companies, with the range of actual rates fairly close to 27.54 percent, integration is working reasonably well, with modest amounts of over or under integration in specific provinces.

13-18.   For non-eligible dividends, integration requires a federal/provincial tax rate on corporations of 13.79 percent. For 2018, actual rates on income that is eligible for the small business deduction range from 10 percent to 18 percent. As noted in Chapter 12, the high 18 percent rate is for Quebec and it is significantly out of line, with the next highest rate at 15 percent. This means that, with the exception of Quebec, all of the other combined rates are fairly close to 13.79 percent. As a result, in general, integration is working reasonably well for corporations that are paying non-eligible dividends from active business income.

13-19.   As we shall see later in this Chapter, integration does not work for CCPCs that are earning investment income. Such income is not eligible for either the general rate reduction or the small business deduction and is subject to a further federal tax at a rate of 10-2/3 percent. When the federal rate of 38-2/3 percent (38% - 10% + 10-2/3%) is combined with provincial rates ranging from 11.5 percent to 16 percent, overall rates on investment income range from just over 50 percent to nearly 55 percent.

13-20.   While integration would clearly not work with overall corporate rates at this level, we will find that the effect of these rates is mitigated by the fact that a substantial portion of these taxes are refunded to the corporation when the investment income is paid out to shareholders as dividends.

Actual Provincial Dividend Tax Credits

13-21.   With respect to eligible dividends, for integration to work, the provincial dividend tax credit has to be equal to 5/11 (45.5%) of the gross up. As noted in Chapter 7, actual provincial dividend tax credit rates on eligible dividends range from 18.2 to 47.1 percent of the gross up, with an average of 33.5 percent. While some of the rates are above the required 45.5 percent, on average, the provincial credits are too low for effective integration.

13-22.   For non-eligible dividends, integration requires a provincial dividend tax credit equal to 3/11 (27.3%) of the gross up. Also as noted in Chapter 7, actual provincial dividend tax credit rates on non-eligible dividends range from 5.5 to 50.4 percent of the gross up, with an average of 21.7 percent. Once again, while some of the rates are above the required 27.3 percent, on average, the provincial credits are too low for effective integration. The results for both types of dividends make it clear that effectiveness of integration depends heavily on the province in which the recipient of the dividend resides.

Alternative Calculations For Dividend Tax Credits

13-23.   Note that, while federal legislation calculates the dividend tax credit as a fraction of the gross up, you often see this credit expressed as a percentage of dividends received, or a percentage of the grossed up amount of the dividends.

13-24.   Because our focus is largely on federal legislation, we will generally present dividend tax credits as a fraction of the gross up. However, if needed, it is quite simple to convert different approaches to a uniform base. For example, if an eligible dividend of $100 is paid, the federal dividend tax credit of $20.73 can be calculated as:

- 6/11 (54.55%) of the $38 [(38%)($100)] gross up. (Which is our standard approach.)
- 20.73 percent of the $100 in dividends received, or
- 15.02 percent of the $138 of grossed up dividends.

Exercise Thirteen - 1

Subject: Integration (Non-Eligible Dividends)

Jan Teason has a business that she estimates will produce income of $100,000 during the taxation year ending December 31, 2018. If she incorporates this business, all of the income would be eligible for the small business deduction and any dividends paid will be non-eligible. In the province where she lives, such corporate income is taxed at a combined federal/provincial rate of 15 percent. Ms. Teason has other income sources that place her in a combined federal/provincial tax bracket of 45 percent. In her province, the provincial dividend tax credit on non-eligible dividends is equal to 30 percent of the gross up. Would Ms. Teason save taxes if she was to channel this source of income through a corporation? Explain your result.

Exercise Thirteen - 2

Subject: Integration (Eligible Dividends)

John Horst has a business that he estimates will produce income of $100,000 during the taxation year ending December 31, 2018. Because he controls another corporation that fully utilizes $500,000 of its small business deduction, if he incorporates this business, none of this income will be eligible for the small business deduction and any dividends paid would be designated eligible. In the province where he lives, such corporate income is taxed at a combined federal/provincial rate of 30 percent. Mr. Horst has other income sources that place him in a combined federal/provincial tax bracket of 42 percent. In his province, the provincial dividend tax credit on eligible dividends is equal to 28 percent of the gross up. Would Mr. Horst save taxes if he was to channel this source of income through a corporation? Explain your result.

SOLUTIONS available in print and online Study Guide.

We suggest you work Self Study Problem Thirteen-1 at this point.

Refundable Taxes On Investment Income

Meaning Of Aggregate Investment Income

13-25.   In the following material on refundable taxes, we will be using the term "aggregate investment income". For purposes of determining the amount of refundable taxes available, this term is defined in ITA 129(4) and has a very specific definition. You may recall that we provided this definition in Chapter 12 and it is also included at the front of this text in "Rates And Other Data". It is provided again here for your convenience.

ITA 129(4) Aggregate Investment Income

Net Taxable Capital Gains	$xxx
Interest	xxx
Rents	xxx
Royalties	xxx
Total Positive Amounts	$xxx
Net Capital Loss Carry Overs Deducted During The Year	(xxx)
ITA 129(4) Aggregate Investment Income	$xxx

13-26.   Note carefully the differences between this "aggregate investment income" and what we normally think of as property or investment income. Unlike the normal definition of property or investment income, this concept includes net taxable capital gains for the current year, reduced by net capital loss carry overs deducted during the year.

13-27.   The other difference between aggregate investment income and the usual definition of investment income is that it excludes most dividends from other Canadian corporations. This reflects the fact that dividends from Canadian corporations generally flow through a corporation without being subject to Part I corporate taxes. You should also note that aggregate investment income includes income from both Canadian and foreign sources.

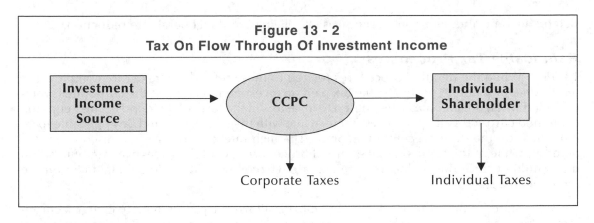

Figure 13 - 2
Tax On Flow Through Of Investment Income

Basic Concepts

The Problem

13-28.   As shown in Figure 13-2, when income is flowed through a corporation, it is subject to two levels of taxation. It is taxed first at the corporate level and, if the after tax corporate amount is distributed to the individual shareholder, it will be taxed again in the hands of that individual. If we assume that the corporate tax rate on the investment income of a CCPC is 52 percent and that the individual shareholder is taxed at a rate of 39 percent on non-eligible dividends received, the overall rate of taxation on investment income flowed through a corporation would be 70.7 percent [52% + (1 - 52%)(39%)].

13-29.   This is significantly higher than the maximum federal/provincial tax rate on Canadian individuals of 54 percent. Such a large difference is clearly not consistent with the concept of integration. Given this, it was necessary to find some method of providing tax relief for shareholders of CCPCs earning investment income.

The Solution

13-30.   The most obvious solution to this problem would be to lower the rate of corporate taxation on the investment income of a CCPC. For example, if the corporate rate was lowered to 22 percent, the overall rate on the flow through of income would be taxed at 0.524 percent [22% + (1 - 22%)(39%)]. This is within the range of rates that are applied to high net worth individuals who receive business or property income directly.

13-31.   The problem with this solution is that it would provide for a significant deferral of taxes on investment income. If an individual received the investment income directly, the full amount of taxes must be paid when the income is earned. In contrast, when a corporation is used, only the first, or corporate level, of taxation is assessed when the income is earned. If the after tax amount is left in the corporation, the assessment of the individual level of tax can be deferred indefinitely.

13-32.   For higher income individuals who do not require their investment income for current expenditures, this would present an outstanding opportunity for tax deferral, as well as the accumulation of large portfolios of passive investments. This would be the case whenever the corporate tax rate on investment income is below the rate applicable to the individual on the direct receipt of income.

13-33.   Given the opportunity for tax deferral that would result from the use of lower corporate tax rates, it is not surprising that a different solution to the problem of excessive tax rates on the flow through of a CCPC's investment income has been adopted. This solution involves leaving the corporate tax rate at a high level, but having a portion of the tax being designated as refundable. The refund of this portion of the corporate tax occurs when the income is distributed in the form of dividends that will be subject to the second level of taxation in the hands of the shareholders.

13-34.   Consistent with this concept of keeping the basic rate high on the aggregate investment income of a CCPC, this type of income is excluded from the definition of Full Rate

Taxable Income and, as a consequence, is not eligible for the general rate reduction.

Refundable Tax Procedures

13-35.   While the detailed procedures related to these refundable taxes are complex, the basic concept is not. A portion of the tax paid on investment income at the corporate level is refunded when the income is distributed to investors in the form of dividends. This keeps the combined corporate and personal tax rate in line with the rate that would be applicable to an individual on the direct receipt of income. The high rate of corporate tax discourages tax deferral, while at the same time, the refund procedures avoid the excessive rate of taxation that would occur if this high corporate tax rate was combined with individual taxes on the same income stream.

13-36.   Stated simply, the use of a refundable tax allows the government to charge a corporate tax rate that is high enough to remove much of the incentive for accumulating investment income in a corporation and, at the same time, provides a reasonable overall rate of taxation when the income is flowed through the corporation and taxed in the hands of the individual shareholder.

13-37.   In implementing this refundable tax approach, the *Income Tax Act* designates three different components of total taxes paid that can be refunded on the payment of dividends. They can be described as follows:

Ordinary Part I Tax   At this point, you should be familiar with the calculation of the regular Part I tax that is assessed on the Taxable Income of a corporation. A portion of this tax, conceptually the portion of the Part I tax that is applicable to investment income, will be designated as refundable on the payment of dividends. Note the fact that a portion of the Part I tax being designated as refundable does not change, in any way, the manner in which the Part I tax is calculated.

Additional Refundable Tax On Investment Income (ART)   The Additional Refundable Tax On Investment Income, a Part I tax, was introduced in order to ensure that the combined federal/provincial tax on investment income was sufficiently high that it would discourage the use of a corporation to defer taxes. To achieve this objective, this combined tax rate had to be at a level that was higher than the rate applicable to high net worth individuals. Since it was introduced until 2016, it was applied at a rate of 6-2/3 percent, resulting in a federal rate on investment income of 34-2/3 percent (38% - 10% + 6-2/3%). The combined federal/provincial results were rates of between 46-1/6 percent (34-2/3% + 11.5%) and 50-2/3 percent (34-2/3% + 16%).

As you are likely aware, for 2016 and subsequent years, the maximum federal rate applicable to individuals has been increased from 29 percent to 33 percent. This has resulted in the maximum combined federal/provincial rate on individuals increasing to between 48 and 54 percent. Given these increases, it would appear that a 6-2/3 percent ART would not be adequate to discourage using a corporation to defer taxes on investment income. Reflecting this view, the government increased the ART rate for 2016 and subsequent years from 6-2/3 percent to 10-2/3 percent, the same 4 percentage point increase that was applied to the maximum federal rate for individuals. The result is combined federal/provincial rates on the investment income of CCPCs ranging from 50-1/6 percent to 54-2/3 percent.

Part IV Tax   Even with the Part I refundable tax and ART in place, there is still the possibility of using a related group of corporations to defer taxation on investment income. For many years, the Part IV tax was assessed at 33-1/3 percent of certain intercorporate dividends received. In conjunction with the increase in the maximum rate applicable to individuals, this rate has been increased to 38-1/3 percent for 2016 and subsequent years. Eligible dividends are generally taxed at a lower effective rate of tax than regular income. As a result, the increase in the Part IV tax rate was 5 percentage points and not 4 to compensate for this.

13-38.   In dealing with this material, we will first consider the issues involved with a single corporation. In these single corporation situations, only the refundable Part I tax and the additional refundable tax on investment income will be considered.

Refundable Part I Tax On Investment Income

Additional Refundable Tax On Investment Income (ART)

Basic Calculations

13-39.   As was noted previously, tax legislation contains a refundable tax on the investment income of a Canadian controlled private corporation (CCPC). This additional refundable tax (ART) is assessed under ITA 123.3 (the definition is available at the front of this text in "Rates And Other Data"). The amount payable is equal to 10-2/3 percent of the lesser of:

- the corporation's "aggregate investment income" for the year [as defined in ITA 129(4)]; and

- the amount, if any, by which the corporation's Taxable Income for the year exceeds the amount that is eligible for the small business deduction.

13-40.   The basic objective of this tax is to make it less attractive to shelter investment income within a corporate structure in order to defer full taxation of the amounts earned. When this additional 10-2/3 percent is added to the usual rates applicable to a CCPC's investment income, the combined rate is in the 50-1/6 to 54-2/3 percent range. This is made up of 38-2/3 percent at the federal level (38% - 10% + 10-2/3%), plus 11.5 percent to 16 percent at the provincial level. As noted in Paragraph 13-37, the combined federal/provincial maximum rates on individuals range from 48 to 54 percent.

13-41.   This means that, with the addition of the ART, rates on the investment income of a CCPC will generally be higher than the rates applicable to an individual receiving the same income. Given this, there is little or no incentive to use a corporation to defer taxation on this type of income.

13-42.   As described in Paragraph 13-39, the ART is based on the lesser of aggregate investment income and the amount of Taxable Income that is not eligible for the small business deduction. The reason for the latter limit is to ensure that such deductions as charitable donations or non-capital loss carry overs have not totally or partially eliminated the investment income from the amount flowing through to Taxable Income. The goal is to prevent the ART from being inappropriately applied to active business income.

Exercise Thirteen - 3

Subject: Additional Refundable Tax On Investment Income

Zircon Inc. is a CCPC with a December 31 year end. Zircon is not associated with any other company. For the 2018 taxation year, its Net Income For Tax Purposes is equal to $281,000. This is made up of active business income of $198,000, dividends from taxable Canadian corporations of $22,000, taxable capital gains of $46,000 and interest income on long-term investments of $15,000. The Company has available a net capital loss carry forward of $26,000 [(1/2)($52,000)] and a non-capital loss carry forward of $23,000. The Company intends to deduct both of these carry forwards in the 2018 taxation year. Determine Zircon's Taxable Income and its additional refundable tax on investment income for the 2018 taxation year.

SOLUTION available in print and online Study Guide.

ART And Foreign Tax Credit Calculations

13-43.   As discussed in Chapter 12, the use of foreign taxes paid as credits against Canadian Tax Payable is limited by a formula that includes the "tax otherwise payable". In the case of foreign taxes paid on non-business income, the "tax otherwise payable" in the formula adds the ART that is assessed under ITA 123.3.

13-44.   This creates a potential problem in that the calculation of the ART includes the amount eligible for the small business deduction. Since one of the factors limiting the small business deduction [ITA 125(1)(b)] is Taxable Income reduced by 100/28 of the foreign non-business income tax credit and 4 times the foreign business income tax credit, this could have created an insolvable circular calculation.

13-45.   As is explained in Chapter 12, there is a similar circularity issue involving the general rate reduction under ITA 123.4. The calculation of this amount also requires knowing the amount of income that is eligible for the small business deduction.

13-46.   To avoid both of these problems, for the purposes of calculating the small business deduction, ITA 125(1)(b)(i) permits the foreign tax credit for taxes paid on foreign non-business income to be calculated using a "tax otherwise payable" figure that does not include the ART under ITA 123.3 or the general rate reduction. ITA 125(1)(b)(ii) permits the foreign tax credit for taxes paid on foreign business income to be calculated using a "tax otherwise payable" figure that does not include the general rate reduction.

13-47.   This means that in situations where the small business deduction, foreign tax credits, and the ART are involved, the following procedures should be used:

1. Calculate the foreign non-business tax credit using a "tax otherwise payable" figure that excludes both ITA 123.3 (ART) and ITA 123.4 (general rate reduction). This initial version of the foreign non-business tax credit will be used only for the purpose of determining the small business deduction, with the actual credit available calculated after the ITA 123.3 and 123.4 amounts have been determined.

2. Calculate the foreign business tax credit using a "tax otherwise payable" figure that excludes ITA 123.4 (as business income is involved, ITA 123.3 is excluded by definition). However, this credit is limited by the amount of tax otherwise payable, reduced by the foreign non-business tax credit. As a consequence, it will be necessary to calculate an initial version of this foreign business tax credit, using the initial version of the foreign non-business tax credit. This initial version will be used only for the purpose of determining the small business deduction and the M&P deduction.

3. Calculate the amount eligible for the small business deduction and M&P deduction using the numbers determined in steps 1 and 2.

4. Using the amount eligible for the small business deduction and the M&P deduction determined in step 3, calculate the ART and the general rate reduction.

5. Calculate the actual foreign non-business tax credit using a "tax otherwise payable" figure that includes the ART and the general rate reduction determined in step 4.

6. Calculate the actual foreign business tax credit using the actual foreign non-business tax credit determined in step 5 and the general rate reduction from step 4.

Problem One: Excessive Tax Rates On The Flow Through Of A CCPC's Investment Income

13-48.   With the addition of the 10-2/3 percent ART on the investment income of a Canadian controlled private corporation, this investment income is taxed at a combined federal/provincial rate ranging from 50-1/6 percent to 54-2/3 percent (see Paragraph 13-40).

13-49.   All of these combined rates are far higher than the 13.79 percent rate required for perfect integration (the 13.79 percent rate for non-eligible dividends is used as the investment income of a CCPC cannot be used as a basis for paying eligible dividends). In the absence of some type of relieving mechanism, the objective of integrating corporate and individual tax rates would not be met.

13-50. The problem of excessive rates of tax on investment income flowed through a corporation was discussed previously in Paragraph 13-28. This is a more complete example:

EXAMPLE Mr. Monroe has investments that generate interest income of $100,000 per year. He is personally subject to a combined federal/provincial tax rate of 49 percent. The dividend tax credit for non-eligible dividends in his province of residence is equal to 3/11 of the gross up. Calculate the amount of cash Mr. Monroe will retain from this investment income under the following alternative assumptions:

Case A He receives the $100,000 in interest income directly.

Case B Mr. Monroe is the sole shareholder of a Canadian controlled private corporation that earns the $100,000 of investment income. The corporation is subject to a combined federal/provincial tax rate, including the ITA 123.3 tax on investment income, of 54 percent. The corporation pays out all of its after tax earnings as non-eligible dividends, resulting in a dividend to Mr. Monroe of $46,000. Ignore any refund of Part I tax paid.

13-51. The calculations comparing the investment income if it was received directly (Case A) and if it was earned through a corporation (Case B), are as follows:

Case A - Investment Income Received Directly

Investment Income - Direct Receipt	$100,000
Personal Tax At 49 Percent	(49,000)
After Tax Cash Retained Without Corporation	**$ 51,000**

Case B - Investment Income Flowed Through Corporation
Assume No Refundable Part I Tax

Corporate Investment Income	$100,000
Corporate Tax At 54 Percent (Includes The ART)	(54,000)
Non-Eligible Dividends Paid To Mr. Monroe	**$ 46,000**

Non-Eligible Dividends Received	$ 46,000
Gross Up Of 16 Percent	7,360
Personal Taxable Income	$ 53,360
Personal Tax Rate	49%
Tax Payable Before Dividend Tax Credit	$ 26,146
Dividend Tax Credit [(8/11 + 3/11)(Gross Up)]	(7,360)
Personal Tax Payable With Corporation	**$ 18,786**

Non-Eligible Dividends Received	$ 46,000
Personal Tax Payable	(18,786)
After Tax Cash Retained With Corporation	**$ 27,214**

Savings - Direct Receipt

Income Received Directly	$ 51,000
Income Flowed Through Corporation	(27,214)
Net Savings On Direct Receipt	**$ 23,786**

13-52.   The results show that, in the absence of the refundable component of Part I tax, interest income flowed through a corporation is subject to an effective tax rate of nearly 73 percent [($100,000 - $27,214) ÷ $100,000]. This is significantly higher than the 49 percent rate that is applicable to the direct receipt of the investment income, an outcome that would represent a major failure in the government's attempt to achieve integration.

13-53.   Before leaving this example you should note that, with the inclusion of the ART on investment income, there is no deferral advantage associated with using a corporation in this example. The corporate taxes alone are $54,000, well in excess of the $49,000 that would be paid if Mr. Monroe had received the income directly.

13-54.   We have noted that the range of rates on investment income received by a CCPC is from 50-1/6 percent to 54-2/3 percent. This compares to a current range of maximum individual tax rates of 48 to 54 percent. This means that, even with the increase in the ART rate, there will still be some provinces where there is a deferral advantage resulting from leaving investment income in a CCPC. However, in the absence of the increase in the ART rate, such situations would be much more common and involve significantly larger amounts of deferral.

Solution To Problem One: Refundable Portion Of Part I Tax
Basic Concepts
13-55.   The preceding example makes it clear that taxes on investment income earned by a CCPC and flowed through to its shareholders are potentially much higher than would be the case if the shareholders received the income directly. This major imperfection in the system of integration results from a federal/provincial tax rate on the investment income of CCPCs that is between 50-1/6 and 54-2/3 percent.

13-56.   In those cases where the income is retained in the corporation, this is an equitable arrangement in that this high rate discourages the use of a CCPC to temporarily shelter passive income from a portion of the taxes that would be assessed on the direct receipt of the income by the individual. However, when the investment income is flowed through a CCPC and paid as dividends, the result is not consistent with the government's desire to tax CCPCs under the integration view of corporate taxation.

13-57.   As noted previously, the government could have dealt with this problem by reducing the corporate tax rate on the investment income of CCPCs. However, this would have allowed the owners of CCPCs to defer personal taxes on this income by leaving the investment income in the corporation. To avoid this, the refundable tax approach is used.

13-58.   Under this approach, the investment income of Canadian controlled private corporations is taxed at the usual high rates, including the ART on investment income. However, when the corporation distributes its after tax income in the form of dividends, a part of this tax is refunded. The refund is based on the amount of dividends paid by the corporation, with the refund being equal to 38-1/3 percent of dividends paid.

Concepts Illustrated
13-59.   For integration to work perfectly on non-eligible dividend payments, the overall corporate tax rate has to equal 13.79 percent (see Paragraph 13-16). In order to give you a better understanding of how the concepts associated with the refund of Part I tax work, we will use an example based on a pre-dividend refund tax rate that will provide a 13.79 percent tax rate after the refund has contributed to the total dividend. While we will not go through the calculation of this rate, the required rate is 46.837 percent, including the 10-2/3 percent ART. You should note that this rate is lower than any of the relevant combined federal/provincial rates that are currently available.

13-60.   With the initial corporate tax rate at 46.837 percent, a refund is necessary to reduce the rate to the required 13.79 percent. The rate that is specified in ITA 129(1) is 38-1/3 percent of the total dividend paid. As we will discuss later, this refund is limited by the corporation's balance in its Refundable Dividend Tax On Hand account.

13-61.   The following example, involving perfect integration, will illustrate the rates that we have just presented.

EXAMPLE   Ms. Banardi has investments that generate interest income of $100,000 per year. You have been asked to advise her as to whether there would be any benefits associated with transferring these investments to her wholly owned Canadian controlled private corporation. Ms. Banardi is personally subject to a combined federal/provincial tax rate of 49 percent. The dividend tax credit in her province of residence is equal to 3/11 of the gross up. Her corporation would be taxed on this income at a combined federal/provincial rate of 46.837 percent, including the ART on investment income.

13-62.   The calculations comparing the after tax investment income if it was earned in a corporation and if it was received directly, are as follows:

After Tax Retention - Use Of A Corporation

Corporate Investment Income	$100,000
Corporate Tax At 46.837 Percent (Includes The ART)	(46,837)
After Tax Income	$ 53,163
Dividend Refund (See Analysis)	33,047
Non-Eligible Dividends Paid To Ms. Banardi	$ 86,210

ANALYSIS   In this somewhat academic example of the dividend refund mechanism, we assume that all of the corporation's after tax income will be paid out as dividends. Given this, a bit of algebra is needed to determine the total dividend, and in the process, the amount of the refund. Specifically, we need to solve the following simple equation:

$$X = \$53,163 + [(38\text{-}1/3\%)(X)]$$
$$X - [(38\text{-}1/3\%)(X)] = \$53,163$$
$$[(61\text{-}2/3\%)(X)] = \$53,163$$
$$X = \$86,210$$

Where X = The total dividend, including the refund.

This provides a dividend refund of $33,047 ($86,210 - $53,163), an amount that is equal to 38-1/3 percent of $86,210.

In this example, we have provided a complete illustration of the conversion of available after tax income to a dividend that includes a refund equal to 38-1/3 percent of the total dividend. In future examples, we will use a condensed version of this process to do a direct calculation of the amount of the refund. The formula for the refund is as follows:

Refund = [(After Tax Funds Available ÷ .61667) - After Tax Funds Available]

Applying this to the current example gives the same result that was achieved by the more detailed calculation:

$$\$33,047 = [(\$53,163 \div .61667) - \$53,163]$$

Note that, at this point, the total corporate tax paid is equal to $13,790 ($100,000 - $86,210). This reflects the 13.79 percent rate ($13,790 ÷ $100,000) that is required for perfect integration.

The assumption that all after tax income will be paid out as dividends is not consistent with the real world approach in which the amount of the dividend is determined by a variety of factors (e.g., availability of cash or alternative investment opportunities) and very rarely, if ever, equals the after tax income plus the dividend refund.

Calculation of the after tax amounts retained follows:

Non-Eligible Dividends Received	$ 86,210
Gross Up Of 16 Percent	13,790
Personal Taxable Income	$100,000
Personal Tax Rate	49%
Tax Payable Before Dividend Tax Credit	$ 49,000
Dividend Tax Credit [(8/11 + 3/11)(Gross Up)]	(13,790)
Personal Tax Payable With Corporation	**$ 35,210**
Non-Eligible Dividends Received	$ 86,210
Personal Tax Payable	(35,210)
After Tax Cash Retained With Corporation	**$ 51,000**

After Tax Retention - Direct Receipt

Investment Income - Direct Receipt	$100,000
Personal Tax At 49 Percent	(49,000)
After Tax Cash Retained Without Corporation	**$ 51,000**

13-63. While this example provides equal amounts of after tax cash, without regard to whether the income is flowed through a corporation or received directly, it is not a realistic example. The combined federal/provincial rates on the investment income of CCPCs range from 50-1/6 to 54-2/3 percent. All of these rates are higher than the 46,837 percent rate used in our example. In addition, as we shall see in the next section of this Chapter, the amount of the refund is limited by the balance in the Refundable Dividend Tax On Hand (RDTOH). We have not taken that into consideration in this Example. If we had, the dividend refund in this example would be limited to $30,677 [(30-2/3%)($100,000)].

Use Of Other Rates In Refundable Part I Tax Example

13-64. In this example, we will use a corporate tax rate of 54-2/3 percent. This will illustrate that, when realistic corporate tax rates are used, using a CCPC to hold assets earning investment income will result in a lower after tax return than holding the investments directly. The information for this example is as follows:

EXAMPLE Mr. Leoni has investments that generate interest income of $100,000 per year. He has over $250,000 in other income and is subject to a combined federal/provincial tax rate of 51 percent. The provincial dividend tax credit is equal to 3/11 of the gross up. Mr. Leoni is the sole shareholder of a CCPC and is considering the transfer of these investments to his corporation. His corporation would be taxed on this income at a combined federal/provincial rate of 54-2/3 percent, including the ART on investment income (38% - 10% + 10-2/3% + 16%).

13-65. The calculations comparing the after tax investment income if it was earned through a corporation and if it was received directly, are as follows:

After Tax Retention - Use Of A Corporation

Corporate Investment Income	$100,000
Corporate Tax At 54-2/3 Percent (Includes The ART)	(54,667)
After Tax Income	$ 45,333
Dividend Refund [($45,333 ÷ .61667) - $45,333]	28,180
Non-Eligible Dividends Paid To Mr. Leoni	**$ 73,513**

Non-Eligible Dividends Received	$ 73,513
Gross Up Of 16 Percent	11,762
Personal Taxable Income	$ 85,275
Personal Tax Rate	51%
Tax Payable Before Dividend Tax Credit	$ 43,490
Dividend Tax Credit [(8/11 + 3/11)($11,762)]	(11,762)
Personal Tax Payable With Corporation	$ 31,728
Non-Eligible Dividends Received	$ 73,513
Personal Tax Payable	(31,728)
After Tax Cash Retained With Corporation	$ 41,785

After Tax Retention - Direct Receipt

Investment Income - Direct Receipt	$100,000
Personal Tax At 51 Percent	(51,000)
After Tax Cash Retained Without Corporation	$ 49,000

13-66.   There are two things that should be noted here. First, when a 54-2/3 percent corporate tax rate is used, the taxes of $54,667 at the corporate level are significantly higher than the $51,000 that would have been paid if Mr. Leoni had received the income directly. While there are some combinations of provincial corporate and provincial individual tax rates that would provide for some deferral of taxes at the corporate level, that is clearly not the case with the rates used here.

13-67.   With respect to the after tax flow through of investment income, using a corporation is clearly not a good idea. Mr. Leoni has $7,215 ($49,000 - $41,785) less after tax cash, as compared to the amount he would have retained on direct receipt of the $100,000 income. While this difference is particularly large when a 54-2/3 percent corporate tax rate is used, the basic result would be the same when any of the other available corporate tax rates are used. As a result, using a corporation would almost always produce less after tax cash.

Exercise Thirteen - 4

Subject: Flow Through Of Investment Income

Ms. Shelly Nicastro has investments that generate interest income of $100,000 per year. Due to her employment income, she is in the top tax bracket, with a combined federal/provincial rate of 51 percent. She is considering the transfer of these investments to her CCPC which would be subject to a tax rate on investment income of 52 percent (including the ART). The dividend tax credit in her province is equal to 30 percent of the gross up. Any dividends paid by the CCPC out of investment income will be non-eligible. Advise her as to whether there would be any tax benefits associated with this transfer.

SOLUTION available in print and online Study Guide.

Refundable Part IV Tax On Dividends Received

Problem Two: Use Of Multi-Level Affiliations To Defer Taxes On Investment Income

13-68.   In the preceding section, we demonstrated how refund procedures applicable to Part I tax payable are used to lower the overall rate of taxation on the investment income of a

Refundable Part IV Tax On Dividends Received

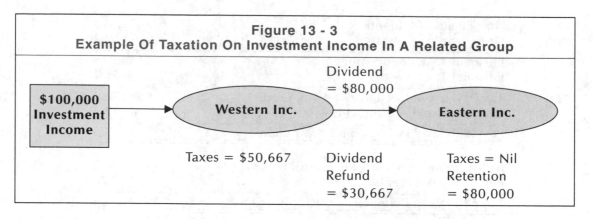

Figure 13 - 3
Example Of Taxation On Investment Income In A Related Group

CCPC, while at the same time preventing the use of a corporation to defer a portion of the overall taxation on such income. While varying provincial tax rates on corporations and individuals prevent these procedures from providing perfect results, they appear to produce results that come close to achieving the goal of integration of personal and corporate taxes.

13-69.   The situation becomes more complex when a group of related companies is involved. The refundable tax procedures that were previously described are not effective in preventing tax deferral in this case. As a result, there is a need for additional procedures.

EXAMPLE   Eastern Inc. has a 100 percent owned subsidiary, Western Ltd. Both Companies are Canadian controlled private corporations and have a December 31 year end. During the current year, Western has income of $100,000, made up entirely of interest and taxable capital gains. Assume that the combined federal/provincial tax rate for both Companies is 50-2/3 percent, including the ART. Western pays out all of its after tax income in dividends to Eastern Inc. This situation is illustrated in Figure 13-3.

ANALYSIS   On receipt of the $100,000 of investment income, Western would pay taxes of $50,667 [($100,000)(50-2/3%)]. However, when the remaining $49,333 is paid out in dividends, a dividend refund of $30,667 (38-1/3% of the $80,000 total dividend) becomes available, resulting in a total dividend of $80,000 as shown in the following calculation:

Investment Income Of Western	$100,000
Corporate Tax At 50-2/3 Percent (Includes The ART)	(50,667)
Income Before Dividends	$ 49,333
Dividend Refund [($49,333 ÷ .61667) - $49,333]	30,667
Dividends Paid To Eastern	$ 80,000

As the dividends from Western will be received tax free by Eastern, they will have after tax retention of $80,000. Unless Eastern pays out taxable dividends to its individual shareholders, no additional Part I tax will be assessed. This means that, in the absence of additional procedures, there could be a significant deferral of taxes on investment income resulting from the use of two related corporations.

Solution To Problem Two: Refundable Part IV Tax
Corporations Subject To Part IV Tax

13-70.   To eliminate this potential flaw in integration, a Part IV tax is assessed on dividends received by a private corporation from certain other types of corporations. Note that this tax is assessed without regard to whether or not the private corporation is Canadian controlled.

13-71.   In general, only private corporations are liable for Part IV tax. However, there remains the possibility that a company that is controlled largely for the benefit of an individual, or a related group of individuals, might use a small issue of shares to the public in order to avoid this tax. Such corporations are referred to as "subject corporations" and they are defined in ITA 186(3) as follows:

> **Subject Corporation** means a corporation (other than a private corporation) resident in Canada and controlled, whether because of a beneficial interest in one or more trusts or otherwise, by or for the benefit of an individual (other than a trust) or a related group of individuals (other than trusts).

13-72.   ITA 186(1) indicates that, for purposes of Part IV tax, subject corporations will be treated as private corporations. This means that both private corporations, as well as those public corporations that fall within the definition of subject corporations, will be liable for the payment of Part IV tax. In this Chapter, any subsequent references to private corporations should be considered to include subject corporations.

Rates

13-73.   For 2016 and subsequent years, the Part IV rate is 38-1/3 percent. It is applicable to portfolio dividends as well as some dividends from connected corporations (both of these terms will be subsequently explained). The rate at which this tax is refunded is the same as the rate for refunds of Part I tax. Both refunds are at a rate of 38-1/3 percent of the total dividend.

Applicable Dividends

13-74.   The Part IV tax is only applicable to certain types of dividends received by private corporations. Specifically, Part IV tax is payable on dividends received by private corporations in the following circumstances:

- A dividend is received from an unconnected company that is deductible in the calculation of the recipient's Taxable Income. While the *Income Tax Act* refers to such dividends as "assessable dividends", it is a common practice to refer to such dividends as "portfolio dividends", a practice we will follow in the remainder of this text.

- The dividend is received from a connected company that, as a result of making the dividend payment, received a dividend refund.

13-75.   Each of these types of dividends will be given attention in the material which follows.

Part IV Tax On Portfolio Dividends Received
Portfolio Dividends And Connected Corporations Defined

13-76.   A portfolio dividend is defined as a dividend received by a private corporation from a corporation to which it is not connected, and that is deductible in the determination of the private corporation's Taxable Income. As with many *Income Tax Act* terms, the definition of a portfolio dividend includes another term which requires definition. This term is "connected corporation" and the definition is found in ITA 186(4). Under this definition, a connected corporation is either:

- a controlled corporation, where control represents ownership of more than 50 percent of the voting shares by any combination of the other corporation and persons with whom it does not deal at arm's length, or

- a corporation in which the other corporation owns more than 10 percent of the voting shares, and more than 10 percent of the fair market value of all of the issued shares of the corporation.

13-77.   Given the definition of connected corporation, a 10 percent shareholding test is generally used to determine whether the dividends received are portfolio dividends or dividends from a connected corporation.

> **EXAMPLE**   A dividend is received on an investment made by a private company in 500 shares of a large publicly traded company that has 15 million shares outstanding.

> **ANALYSIS**   The 500 shares would be significantly less than 10 percent of the total shares outstanding and would not constitute control of the company. As a

Refundable Part IV Tax On Dividends Received

consequence, the dividends would be considered portfolio dividends and the Part IV tax would be applicable.

Portfolio Dividends And Integration

13-78.   The tax policy issue with respect to portfolio dividends relates to integration. If such dividends are received by an individual, they are normally subject to taxation. For example, assume that an individual receives $100,000 in dividends. This individual is subject to a combined federal/provincial marginal rate of 45 percent and lives in a province with a dividend tax credit equal to 5/11 of the eligible dividend gross up and 3/11 of the non-eligible dividend gross up. The resulting Tax Payable would be calculated as follows:

	Eligible Dividends	Non-Eligible Dividends
Dividends Received	$100,000	$100,000
Gross Up Of 38 or 16 Percent	38,000	16,000
Taxable Income	$138,000	$116,000
Personal Tax Rate	45%	45%
Tax Payable Before Dividend Tax Credit	$ 62,100	$ 52,200
Dividend Tax Credit:		
[(6/11 + 5/11)(Gross Up)]	(38,000)	
[(8/11 + 3/11)(Gross Up)]		(16,000)
Personal Tax Payable	$ 24,100	$ 36,200

13-79.   As an alternative, consider what would happen if the same $100,000 in dividends had been received by a corporation. Under the general rules for intercorporate dividends, the $100,000 would be deductible in the calculation of the corporation's Taxable Income, resulting in no Part I tax at the corporate level. While tax will ultimately be paid when the corporation distributes this income to its shareholders, there is a potential for significant deferral of taxes until such time as this corporation distributes the income as dividends.

13-80.   In order to correct this flaw in the corporate tax integration system, Part IV tax is applied as follows:

Part IV Tax - Portfolio Dividends   When a private corporation receives a dividend on shares that are being held as a portfolio investment, the recipient company is liable for a Part IV tax of 38-1/3 percent of the dividends received. This Part IV tax is refundable, on the basis of 38-1/3 percent of dividends paid, when such dividends are passed on to the shareholders of the recipient corporation.

13-81.   We can see the reasoning behind the rate of this tax by referring back to the preceding example in Paragraph 13-78. You will notice that the effective tax rate on the eligible dividends received by the individual is 24.1 percent ($24,100 ÷ $100,000). By charging a Part IV tax of 38-1/3 percent at the corporate level, the tax paid by the corporation is in excess of the 24.1 percent effective tax rate that would apply to eligible dividends received by an individual with a tax rate of 45 percent. This makes it unattractive to use a private corporation as a shelter to defer the payment of taxes on dividend income. Again, however, by making the tax refundable, it allows the dividends to flow through the recipient corporation without assessing an unreasonable level of taxation on the income flowed through a corporation.

Dividends From A Connected Corporation

The Investment Income Problem

13-82.   It is the intent of the government to allow a Canadian controlled private corporation to be used to defer taxes on active business income. Earning such income entitles the corporation to the use of the small business deduction and this, in most situations, provides a rate of corporate taxation that will effectively defer taxes on income left in the corporation. To the extent that a connected corporation is paying dividends out of such income, there will be no dividend refund and no Part IV tax to be paid by the recipient corporation. This maintains the tax deferral on active business income as it moves between corporations.

13-83.   However, when the connected corporation is a private company (whether or not it is Canadian controlled) and the dividends are paid out of investment income, a problem arises. This problem was illustrated by the example presented in Paragraph 13-69.

13-84.   In that example, Western paid an $80,000 dividend to Eastern, a payment that included a $30,667 refund of taxes previously paid by Western. Under the general rules for dividends, the $80,000 dividend paid by Western would be included in the calculation of Eastern's Net Income For Tax Purposes and deducted in the determination of its Taxable Income, with the net result that no Part I taxes would be paid on the $80,000. This would, in effect, allow retention of 80 percent of the investment income within the corporate group, a result that is contrary to the general concept of integration.

The Solution

13-85.   In order to correct this situation, a second application of Part IV tax is as follows:

Part IV Tax - Connected Companies   When a private corporation receives dividends from a connected private corporation that has received a dividend refund under ITA 129(1) as a result of paying the dividends, the recipient company is liable for a Part IV tax equal to its share of the refund received by the paying corporation. If the dividend paid is eligible for a full 38-1/3 percent of the dividend paid, the Part IV tax can also be expressed as 38-1/3 percent of the dividends received.

However, the payor corporation may be earning both active business income and investment income. In such situations, if dividends reflect a distribution of both types of income, the dividend refund will not be at the full 38-1/3 percent rate. (See the Paragraph 13-93 example.) This is why the Part IV tax on dividends received from a connected corporation is expressed in terms of the recipient's share of the refund received by the paying corporation, not in terms of a specific rate.

As was the case with the Part IV tax on portfolio dividends, this Part IV tax is refundable on the basis of 38-1/3 percent of dividends paid by the assessed corporation.

Example Of Connected Corporation Dividends

13-86.   Returning to the example presented in Paragraph 13-69, you will recall that Western has $100,000 in investment income and pays maximum dividends of $80,000 to Eastern. When the Part IV tax is taken into consideration, the tax consequences for the two companies are as follows:

Investment Income Received By Western	$100,000
Corporate Tax At 50-2/3 Percent (Including The ART)	(50,667)
Income Before Dividends	$ 49,333
Dividend Refund [($49,333 ÷ .61667) - $49,333]	**30,667**
Dividends Paid To Eastern	$ 80,000
Investment Income (Dividends Received From Western)	$80,000
Part IV Tax Payable (100% Of Western's Refund*)	**(30,667)**
Income Retained By Eastern	$49,333

*Because all of Western's income was from investments, Western's dividend refund is the full 38-1/3 percent of dividends paid. This means that Eastern's Part IV tax can also be calculated as 38-1/3% of the $80,000 in dividends received from Western.

13-87.   As this simple example shows, after the application of the Part IV tax, the amount retained in Eastern is the same $49,333 that was retained in Western. This retention reflects a tax rate on the amount retained within the corporate group of 50-2/3 percent [($100,000 - $49,333) ÷ $100,000], about the same rate that would be paid by an individual taxpayer in the maximum federal/provincial tax bracket on the direct receipt of the $100,000 in investment income. Clearly, the application of Part IV tax has served to maintain integration in situations involving connected companies.

13-88.   If Eastern decides to distribute the retained income to its shareholders, the results would be as follows:

Income Retained By Eastern	$49,333
Dividend Refund [($49,333 ÷ .61667) - $49,333]	**30,667**
Non-Eligible Dividend To Shareholders	$80,000

13-89.   In effect, the $100,000 of investment income has passed through two corporations and into the hands of individual shareholders, subject to corporate taxes of only 20 percent. This has been accomplished, despite the fact that the initial level of corporate taxation was sufficiently high to discourage allocating investment income to a multi-level corporate structure.

13-90.   Note, however, the effective corporate tax rate in this example is only 20 percent. It is for this reason that the aggregate investment income of a CCPC is subtracted in the determination of Full Rate Taxable Income. This, in turn, means that the dividends paid out by Eastern will not be eligible dividends. The applicable gross up will only be 16 percent and the federal dividend tax credit will be 8/11 of the gross up.

Applicability

13-91.   We would remind you again that the Part IV tax on dividends from a connected company is only applicable when the paying corporation has received a dividend refund. This means that dividends paid out of a corporation's aggregate investment income or paid out of portfolio dividends received will be subject to Part IV tax. If the paying corporation was earning only active business income, no refund would be available when this after tax income was paid out as dividends. As a consequence, no Part IV tax would be assessed on the corporation receiving the dividend.

13-92.   This result is consistent with the goals of integration in that, when a corporation is earning active business income that is taxed at the low small business rate, tax deferral is permitted on income that is retained in the corporation, and not paid out as dividends.

Dividends Paid Out Of Mixed Income Of A Connected Corporation

13-93.   In many cases, a corporation will be earning both investment income and active business income. This will result in a situation, unlike the example previously presented, where some part of the dividends paid by the corporation will be eligible for a refund, and the remainder will not. In this type of situation, the Part IV tax will not be equal to 38-1/3 percent of the dividends received. An example will make this point clear:

EXAMPLE   Lower Ltd. declares and pays a dividend of $45,000. As a result of paying this dividend, the Company receives a dividend refund equal to $9,000 or 20 percent of the dividend (the limiting factor would be the RDTOH balance as explained in the next section). Upper Inc. owns 60 percent of the outstanding shares of Lower Ltd. and receives dividends of $27,000.

ANALYSIS   In this case, the dividend refund is clearly less than 38-1/3 percent of the dividends paid, indicating that Lower's income is made up of a combination of investment income and other income. In this more realistic situation, the Part IV Tax Payable by Upper will be based on Upper's 60 percent share of the $9,000 dividend refund of Lower that resulted from paying the dividend. Upper's Part IV tax would be $5,400 [(60%)($9,000)].

Exercise Thirteen - 5

Subject: Part IV Tax

Opal Ltd., a Canadian controlled private corporation, received the following amounts of dividends during the year ending December 31, 2018:

Dividends On Various Portfolio Investments	$14,000
Dividends From Emerald Inc. [(100%)($41,500)]	41,500
Dividends From Ruby Inc. [(30%)($60,000)]	18,000

Opal Ltd. owns 100 percent of the voting shares of Emerald Inc. and 30 percent of the voting shares of Ruby Inc. The fair market value of the Ruby Inc. shares is equal to 30 percent of the fair market value of all Ruby Inc. shares. As a result of paying the $60,000 dividend, Ruby Inc. received a dividend refund of $15,000. Emerald Inc. received no dividend refund for its dividend payment.

Determine the amount of Part IV Tax Payable by Opal Ltd. as a result of receiving these dividends.

SOLUTION available in print and online Study Guide.

Other Part IV Tax Considerations

13-94.   The preceding material has dealt with the basic features of the Part IV tax on dividends received by private corporations. There are a few additional points to be made. First, you should note what kinds of dividends are not subject to Part IV tax. For a private or a subject company, the only dividends, besides capital dividends, that will not be subject to Part IV tax are those received from a connected corporation that does not get a dividend refund as a result of paying the dividend.

13-95.   A second point is that ITA 186(1)(c) and (d) allows a corporation to use unabsorbed non-capital losses to reduce any Part IV tax. The Part IV tax otherwise payable can be reduced by 38-1/3 percent of any non-capital or farm losses claimed for this purpose. However, if this option is chosen, the corporation has effectively used a possible permanent reduction in future taxes to acquire a reduction of Tax Payable that could otherwise ultimately be refunded. This would only make sense in situations where the non-capital loss carry forward was about to expire, or where the company did not expect to have Taxable Income in the carry forward period. With the non-capital loss carry forward period set at 20 years, this is unlikely to be a very useful strategy.

Refundable Dividend Tax On Hand (RDTOH)

Basic Concepts

A Tracking Mechanism

13-96.   In the simple examples we used to illustrate refundable taxes, it was easy to see the direct connection between the amounts of investment income and the amount of the refund that could be made on the payment of dividends. In the real world, such direct relationships do not exist.

13-97.   Corporations usually earn a combination of investment and business income, they seldom pay out all of their earnings in the form of dividends, and there are usually lags between the period in which income is earned and the period in which dividends are paid. As a consequence, some mechanism is needed to keep track of amounts of taxes that have been paid that are eligible for the refund treatment. This mechanism is the Refundable Dividend Tax On Hand account (RDTOH).

General Overview

13-98.   The RDTOH will normally start with an opening balance, reflecting amounts carried over from the previous year. There is no conversion of amounts accumulated at rates other than the current rates. One common point of confusion is that the RDTOH balance at the end of a taxation year is calculated without deducting the dividend refund for that year. As a result, any dividend refund for the preceding year must be deducted from the RDTOH carried forward from the preceding year in order to calculate the opening RDTOH.

13-99.   This balance will be increased by the payment of the various types of refundable taxes. In somewhat simplified terms (which will be explained in the following material), these additions will be:

- The refundable portion of Part I tax paid, calculated as 30-2/3 percent of aggregate investment income (there are a number of technical complications here).

- Part IV tax on dividends received, calculated at a rate of 38-1/3 percent of portfolio dividends, plus an amount equal to the recipient's share of the dividend refund received by a connected corporation paying dividends.

13-100.   The dividend refund for the current year will be limited by the balance in this account. That is, the dividend refund for the current year will be equal to the lesser of the balance in the RDTOH at the end of the year, and 38-1/3 percent of the taxable dividends paid for the year. These concepts will be presented in a more technical form in the following material.

RDTOH - General Definition

13-101.   ITA 129(3) defines the RDTOH at the end of a taxation year as the aggregate of four items. The first three are additions and can be described as follows:

ITA 129(3)(a)   Refundable Part I tax for the year.

ITA 129(3)(b)   The total of the taxes under Part IV for the year.

ITA 129(3)(c)   The corporation's RDTOH at the end of the preceding year.

13-102.   The fourth item, the corporation's dividend refund for its preceding taxation year, is subtracted under **ITA 129(3)(d)**. This complete definition is available at the front of this text in "Rates And Other Data".

13-103.   The only one of these four items that requires further elaboration is ITA 129(3)(a), the refundable portion of Part I tax for the year.

Refundable Portion Of Part I Tax Payable

The Problem

13-104.   The situation here is made complex by the fact that in calculating a corporation's Part I tax payable, there is no segregation of taxes on investment income from taxes on other types of income. This means that there is no direct measure of what portion of the regular Part I tax payable should be refunded. To deal with this situation, the RDTOH definition limits this addition to the refundable balance as the least of three amounts. These are specified under ITA 129(3)(a)(i), (ii), and (iii).

Investment Income Constraint - ITA 129(3)(a)(i)

13-105.   The basic amount of Part I tax that should be considered refundable is based on the amount of investment income for the year:

ITA 129(3)(a)(i)   the amount determined by the formula

$$A - B, \text{where}$$

A   is 30-2/3 percent of the corporation's aggregate investment income for the year, and

B   is the amount, if any, by which the foreign non-business income tax credit exceeds 8 percent of its foreign investment income for the year.

13-106.   Aggregate investment income is as defined in ITA 129(4). As indicated previously, aggregate investment income is the sum of:

• Net taxable capital gains for the year, reduced by any net capital loss carry overs deducted during the year.

• Income from property, reduced by any property losses. Dividends that are deductible in computing the corporation's Taxable Income are excluded.

13-107.   These amounts do not include interest or rents that are incidental to the corporation's efforts to produce active business income. As noted in Chapter 12, these amounts would be considered active business income. Note, however, the definition does include both Canadian and foreign sources of the types of income listed.

13-108.   If the corporation has no foreign source investment income, the ITA 129(3)(a)(i) amount is simply 30-2/3 percent of aggregate investment income. The RDTOH legislation is based on the assumption that the federal/provincial rate on investment income, before the dividend refund, is 50-2/3 percent. This assumption is within the range of current federal/provincial rates on the investment income of private companies (as noted in Paragraph 13-48, these rates range from 50-1/6 percent to 54-2/3 percent).

13-109.   With respect to foreign non-business income, the RDTOH legislation is based on the assumption that the Canadian tax rate on this foreign income is 38-2/3 percent (38% - 10% + 10-2/3%). Reflecting this assumption, the B component in the ITA 129(3)(a)(i) formula subtracts any amount of foreign tax credit that is in excess of 8 percent of foreign investment income for the year.

13-110.   The basic idea here is that a foreign tax credit of 8 percent will reduce the Canadian taxes paid to 30-2/3 percent (38-2/3% - 8% = 30-2/3 percent, the rate applicable to the refund). If the foreign tax credit exceeds 8 percent of the foreign investment income, the Canadian taxes paid would be less than the potential refund of 30-2/3 percent. In other words, without the 8 percent subtraction, the Canadian government would be providing a refund that is larger than the amount of Canadian tax paid on the foreign investment income.

> **EXAMPLE**   A CCPC earns $50,000 in foreign investment income. The government in the foreign jurisdiction withholds 15 percent of this amount and, as a consequence, the company receives a foreign non-business tax credit of $7,500.
>
> **ANALYSIS**   At the assumed rate of 38-2/3 percent, Canadian tax on this income would be $11,833 [(38-2/3%)($50,000) - $7,500]. This results in a Canadian tax rate on this income of only 23.7 percent ($11,833 ÷ $50,000). Without some type of adjustment, the refundable taxes on this $50,000 of income would be at a rate of 30-2/3% and would equal $15,333 [(30-2/3%)($50,000)], $3,500 more than the $11,833 in Canadian taxes that would be paid. This is clearly not appropriate.
>
> To correct this situation, the excess of the foreign non-business income tax credit over 8 percent of the foreign investment income is subtracted from the 30-2/3 percent refund on the foreign investment income. The 8 percent reflects the difference between the notional rate of 38-2/3 percent and the refund rate of 30-2/3 percent.
>
> In our example, the calculations would be as follows:

30-2/3 Percent Of Foreign Investment Income		$15,333
Deduct Excess Of:		
Foreign Non-Business Tax Credit	($7,500)	
Over 8% Of Foreign Investment Income		
[(8%)($50,000)]	4,000	(3,500)
ITA 129(3)(a)(i)		**$11,833**

This procedure has, in effect, reduced the amount of the refund to $11,833. As calculated at the beginning of this analysis, this is equal to the notional amount of Canadian taxes paid on the foreign investment income.

Taxable Income Constraint - ITA 129(3)(a)(ii)

13-111.   A further problem with respect to determining the refundable portion of Part I tax payable is that the corporation's Taxable Income may include amounts that are not taxed at full corporate rates (e.g., amounts eligible for the small business deduction). Further, Taxable Income may be reduced by such items as non-capital loss carry overs to a level that is less than the amount of investment income on which ITA 129(3)(a)(i) would provide a refund. To deal with this, the refundable portion of the Part I tax is limited as follows:

ITA 129(3)(a)(ii)   30-2/3 percent of the amount, if any, by which the corporation's taxable income for the year exceeds the total of:

A   the amount eligible for the small business deduction;

B   (100 ÷ 38-2/3) of the tax credit for foreign non-business income; and

C   4 times the tax credit for foreign business income.

13-112.   Component B is designed to remove foreign investment income that is not taxed because of the foreign non-business tax credit. The elimination is based on the assumption that it is taxed at a notional rate of 38-2/3 percent (38-2/3 ÷ 100). In similar fashion, Component C is designed to remove foreign business income that is not taxed because of the foreign business income tax credit. The elimination here is based on the assumption that this type of income is taxed at a notional rate of 25 percent (1 ÷ 4). The factor of 4 in Component C is actually the result of a more complex calculation. See Chapter 12, Paragraph 12-91 for details of this calculation explained in the context of the small business deduction formula.

Tax Payable Constraint - ITA 129(3)(a)(iii)

13-113.   A final issue here relates to the fact that the dividend refund could exceed the corporation's actual Tax Payable for the year. This could happen if, for example, the company had large amounts of tax credits for scientific research and experimental development. To deal with this issue, the refundable portion of Part I tax paid is limited as follows:

ITA 129(3)(a)(iii)   the corporation's Federal tax for the year payable under this Part (Part I).

Formula For Part I Tax Addition To RDTOH

13-114. To summarize, the addition to the RDTOH for Part I tax (also available in the front of this text under "Rates And Other Data") is the least of:

ITA 129(3)(a)(i)   30-2/3 percent of aggregate investment income, reduced by the excess, if any, of foreign non-business income tax credits over 8 percent of foreign investment income.

ITA 129(3)(a)(ii)   30-2/3 percent of the amount, if any, by which Taxable Income exceeds the sum of:

- the amount eligible for the small business deduction,
- (100 ÷ 38-2/3) of the foreign non-business tax credit, and
- 4 times the foreign business tax credit.

ITA 129(3)(a)(iii)   Part I tax payable.

The Dividend Refund

13-115.   While in theory, dividend refunds should only be available when dividends are paid out of investment income, corporate tax legislation does not provide a basis for tracking the income source of a particular dividend payment. As a consequence, a dividend refund is available on any taxable dividend that is paid by the corporation as long as there is a balance in the RDTOH. Given this, the dividend refund will be equal to the lesser of:

- the balance in the RDTOH account at the end of the year; and
- 38-1/3 percent of all taxable dividends paid during the year.
    (**Byrd & Chen Note**: Since both 38-1/3 percent and 38-2/3 percent are used in

various corporate tax calculations, we would advise readers to be sure they understand the appropriate use of each as the two numbers are easy to confuse.)

Example Of RDTOH Calculations

13-116.   The following simplified example illustrates the refundable tax calculations.   In the separate Study Guide which accompanies this text, there is a completed corporate tax return in Chapter 13 which includes an additional illustration of the RDTOH account.

EXAMPLE   Fortune Ltd. is a Canadian controlled private corporation. Based on the formula in ITR 402(3), 90 percent of the Company's income is earned in a province. The following information is available for the year ending December 31, 2018:

Canadian Source Investment Income	
(Includes $25,000 In Taxable Capital Gains)	$100,000
Gross Foreign Non-Business Income (15 Percent Withheld)	20,000
Gross Foreign Business Income (15 Percent Withheld)	10,000
Active Business Income (No Associated Companies)	150,000
Portfolio Dividends Received	30,000
Net Income For Tax Purposes	$310,000
Portfolio Dividends	(30,000)
Net Capital Loss Carry Forward Deducted	(15,000)
Taxable Income	$265,000

RDTOH - December 31, 2017	$110,000
Dividend Refund For 2017	20,000
Taxable Dividends Paid During 2018	40,000

ANALYSIS   The Part I Tax Payable would be calculated as follows:

Base Amount Of Part I Tax [(38%)($265,000)]	$100,700
Federal Tax Abatement [(10%)(90%)($265,000)]	(23,850)
Small Business Deduction (Note 1)	(27,000)
ART (Note 2)	11,200
General Rate Reduction (Note 3)	(1,300)
Foreign Non-Business Tax Credit (Note 1)	(3,000)
Foreign Business Tax Credit (Note 1)	(1,500)
Part I Tax Payable	$ 55,250

Note 1   In order to simplify the calculation of the small business deduction, the foreign tax credits are assumed to be equal to the amounts withheld (15 percent). Additional calculations would be required to support this conclusion.

The small business deduction would be equal to 18 percent of the least of:

1.	Active Business Income	$150,000
2.	Taxable Income	$265,000
	Deduct:	
	[(100/28)($3,000 Foreign Non-Business Tax Credit)]	(10,714)
	[(4)($1,500 Foreign Business Tax Credit)]	(6,000)
	Adjusted Taxable Income	$248,286
3.	Annual Business Limit	$500,000

The small business deduction is $27,000 [(18%)($150,000)].

Note 2 The Additional Refundable Tax (ART) is equal to 10-2/3 percent of the lesser of:

- Aggregate Investment Income, calculated as follows:

Canadian Source Investment Income	$100,000
Gross Foreign Non-Business Income	20,000
Net Capital Loss Carry Forward Deducted	(15,000)
Aggregate Investment Income	$105,000

- An amount calculated as follows:

Taxable Income	$265,000
Amount Eligible For the Small Business Deduction	(150,000)
Balance	$115,000

This results in an ART equal to $11,200 [(10-2/3%)($105,000)].

Note 3 The general rate reduction would be calculated as follows:

Taxable Income	$265,000
Amount Eligible For Small Business Deduction (Note 1)	(150,000)
Aggregate Investment Income	(105,000)
Full Rate Taxable Income (= Foreign Business Income)	$ 10,000
Rate	13%
General Rate Reduction	$ 1,300

13-117. Based on the preceding information, the refundable portion of Part I tax would be the least of the following three amounts:

30-2/3% Of Aggregate Investment Income [(30-2/3%)($105,000)]		$ 32,200
Deduct Excess Of:		
Foreign Non-Business Tax Credit	($3,000)	
Over 8% Of Foreign Investment Income [(8%)($20,000)]	1,600	(1,400)
Amount Under ITA 129(3)(a)(i)		**$ 30,800**

Taxable Income		$265,000
Deduct:		
Amount Eligible For Small Business Deduction	($150,000)	
[(100 ÷ 38-2/3)($3,000 Foreign Non-Business Tax Credit)]	(7,759)	
[(4)($1,500 Foreign Business Tax Credit)]	(6,000)	(163,759)
Total		$101,241
Rate		30-2/3%
Amount Under ITA 129(3)(a)(ii)		**$ 31,047**

Amount Under ITA 129(3)(a)(iii) = Part I Tax Payable	**$ 55,250**

The refundable portion of Part I tax is equal to $30,800, which is the least of the preceding three amounts.

13-118.   The Part IV tax would be $11,500, 38-1/3 percent of the $30,000 in portfolio dividends received. Given this, the balance in the RDTOH account at the end of the year is as follows:

RDTOH - End Of Preceding Year (Given)	$110,000	
Less: Dividend Refund For Preceding Year (Given)	(20,000)	$ 90,000
Refundable Portion Of Part I Tax	$ 30,800	
Part IV Tax Payable [(38-1/3%)($30,000)]	11,500	42,300
RDTOH - December 31, 2018		$132,300

13-119.   The dividend refund for the year would be $24,865, the lesser of:

- 38-1/3 Percent Of Taxable Dividends Paid [(38-1/3%)($40,000)] = $15,333
- RDTOH Balance - December 31, 2018 = $132,300

13-120.   Using the preceding information, the total federal Tax Payable for Fortune Ltd. is calculated as follows:

Part I Tax Payable	$55,250
Part IV Tax Payable	11,500
Dividend Refund	(15,333)
Federal Tax Payable	$51,417

Exercise Thirteen - 6

Subject: Refundable Part I Tax

Debut Inc. is a Canadian controlled private corporation. During the taxation year ending December 31, 2018, Debut Inc. has the following amounts of property income:

Dividends From Portfolio Investments	$22,000
Foreign Non-Business Income (Net Of 5 Percent Withholding)	14,250
Capital Gains	38,250
Net Rental Income	6,500
Interest Income On Ten Year Bond	9,200

The Company's Net Income For Tax Purposes is $121,825. The only deductions in the calculation of Taxable Income are the dividends on portfolio investments and a net capital loss carry forward of $9,000 [(1/2)($18,000)]. A $9,000 small business deduction and a foreign tax credit of $750 served to reduce Tax Payable. Assume that the Company's Part I Tax Payable has been correctly determined to be $20,036 Determine the refundable amount of Part I tax for 2018.

Exercise Thirteen - 7

Subject: Dividend Refund

Quan Imports Ltd. is a Canadian controlled private corporation with a December 31 year end. On December 31, 2017, it had an RDTOH balance of $12,500. As a result of paying dividends in 2017, the Company received a dividend refund of $2,300. During 2018, Quan Import's only income is $24,000 in taxable capital gains and $6,000 in dividends received from an investment in Royal Bank shares. During 2018, the Company declares and pays a $15,000 dividend on its common shares. Determine the Company's dividend refund for 2018.

SOLUTIONS available in print and online Study Guide.

Working Through Large Corporate Tax Problems

13-121.   At this point we have completed our general coverage of Taxable Income and Tax Payable for corporations. As we are sure you are aware, there are a great many concepts and procedures involved in this process. While we have illustrated the concepts and procedures in individual examples, we have not provided a comprehensive example that encompasses all of these items.

13-122.   You will find, however, that several of the Self Study and Assignment Problems involve fairly comprehensive calculations of corporate Taxable Income and Tax Payable. Given the complexity of these problems, it is useful to have a systematic approach to dealing with this type of problem. To fill that need, we would suggest you approach the required calculations in the following order (we are assuming that only federal taxes are being calculated as this is generally the case with the problem material in this text):

- Net Income For Tax Purposes. Depending on the problem, this may require converting an accounting Net Income figure into the required tax figure.
- Taxable Income. This would include making deductions for charitable donations, dividends from taxable Canadian corporations, and loss carry overs.
- Basic federal Part I Tax Payable at the 38 percent rate.
- Federal tax abatement. If there is foreign business income, this may require a calculation of the amounts that are to be allocated to Canadian provinces.
- If the corporation is a CCPC:
    - Small business deduction (without consideration of the general rate reduction or the ART in the foreign income tax credit constraints).
    - Aggregate investment income.
    - Additional refundable tax on investment income (ART). Note that this is an addition to Part I Tax Payable, not a deduction.
- Manufacturing and processing profits deduction (without consideration of the general rate reduction in the foreign income tax credit constraints).
- General rate reduction.
- Foreign non-business income tax credit.
- Foreign business income tax credit.
- If the corporation is a CCPC or other private corporation:
    - Part IV tax payable.
    - Refundable portion of Part I tax (for CCPCs only, not other private corporations).
    - Balance in the refundable dividend tax on hand account (RDTOH).
    - Dividend refund.

> **We suggest you work Self Study Problems Thirteen-2 and 3 at this point.**

Designation Of Eligible Dividends

Basic Concepts

The Problem

13-123.   Integration relies largely on the dividend gross up/tax credit mechanism to ensure that flowing an income source through a corporation does not result in significantly different overall amounts of tax, when compared to the amount of tax that would be paid by an individual receiving the income directly. In designing this mechanism, the gross up and credit amounts must use an assumed corporate tax rate. For this to work perfectly, thousands of different gross up and credit amounts would have to be used to reflect the many real world tax rates that are applicable to different corporations.

13-124.   This is obviously not a practical solution. However, it is equally obvious that the use of a single assumed corporate tax rate would result in significant under integration (more tax being paid when a corporation is used because the assumed rate is above actual tax rates), or over integration (less tax being paid when a corporation is used because the assumed rate is below actual tax rates).

The Solution

13-125.   In general, public corporations pay tax at much higher rates that those that apply to CCPCs earning active business income. In somewhat simplified terms, dividends paid from the more heavily taxed income of public corporations can be designated as "eligible" dividends as they are eligible for the enhanced gross up/tax credit procedures. In contrast, dividends paid out of the active business income of CCPCs are considered to be non-eligible and subject to different gross up and tax credit procedures that result in a higher effective rate of tax. As previously described, these procedures and the assumed rates are as follows:

Eligible Dividends   These dividends are assumed to be paid out of what is referred to as "full rate taxable income". They are subject to a gross up of 38 percent and receive a federal dividend tax credit equal to 6/11 of the gross up. These amounts are based on the assumption that the combined federal/provincial tax rate on the dividend paying corporation is 27.54 percent. For integration to work perfectly, a provincial dividend tax credit of 5/11 of the gross up is required.

Non-Eligible Dividends   These dividends are assumed to be paid out of the active business income of CCPCs. They are subject to a gross up of 16 percent and receive a federal dividend tax credit equal to 8/11 of the gross up. These amounts are based on the assumption that the combined federal/provincial tax rate on the dividend paying corporation is 13.79 percent. For integration to work perfectly, a provincial dividend tax credit of 3/11 of the gross up is required.

Implementing The Solution

13-126.   As eligible dividends are taxed more favourably than non-eligible dividends, it is necessary to have a procedure for determining the type of dividend that has been received by an investor. A simple solution to this problem would have been to classify dividends paid by public corporations as eligible dividends (these corporations are generally subject to full corporate rates) and dividends paid by CCPCs as non-eligible dividends (these corporations usually get either the small business deduction or benefit from refundable taxes). However, public corporations may have income that has been taxed at low rates and, somewhat more commonly, CCPCs may have income that has been taxed at full corporate rates.

13-127.   Given this situation, the system has different procedures for CCPCs and non-CCPCs:

CCPCs It is assumed that, in general, dividends paid by CCPCs are non-eligible. However, to track components of their income that have been taxed at full corporate rates, CCPCs have a notional account referred to as a General Rate Income Pool (GRIP). The balance in this account is available to pay eligible dividends.

Non-CCPCs   In general, non-CCPCs are comprised of public companies and private companies that are not Canadian controlled. For these companies, it is assumed that, in general, dividends paid are eligible. However, to track components of their income that have been taxed at low rates, they have to use a notional account referred to as a Low Rate Income Pool (LRIP). The balance in this account must be reduced to nil by the payment of non-eligible dividends prior to the payment of eligible dividends.

13-128.   We will provide a separate discussion of both procedures in the following material.

CCPCs And Their GRIP

Default Treatment

13-129. While individual CCPCs may have some amount of full rate taxable income, most of the income earned by such corporations will benefit either from the small business deduction or the refund procedures applicable to distributed investment income. Given this, the majority of dividends paid by most CCPCs will be non-eligible. For these corporations, the default assumption is that their dividends will be so classified.

13-130. However, it is still necessary to deal with the fact that, to the extent that a CCPC has full rate taxable income or has received eligible dividends, its dividends should benefit from the eligible dividend procedures. The mechanism to provide for this is the General Rate Income Pool (GRIP).

General Rate Income Pool (GRIP)

13-131. The General Rate Income Pool is a notional account that is designed to track amounts of a CCPC's income that qualify as a basis for paying eligible dividends. As noted in the previous section, the default treatment for CCPC dividends is to classify them as non-eligible. However, to the extent that there is a balance in the GRIP account of the corporation, CCPC dividends paid can be designated as eligible.

13-132. The GRIP balance is defined in ITA 89(1). It is a very complex definition that consists of an A component and a B component. The content of the B component involves such things as loss carry overs and other future events that may influence the current year. The application of this component goes beyond the scope of this text and will be given no consideration in any of our material. The A component is defined as follows (also available at the front of this text in "Rates And Other Data"):

$$A = C + D + E + F - G, \text{ where}$$

C is the CCPC's GRIP at the end of the preceding taxation year.

D is 72 percent of the CCPC's adjusted taxable income for the year.
Adjusted Taxable Income is regular Taxable Income, reduced by the amount eligible for the small business deduction and the lesser of the CCPC's aggregate investment income and its Taxable Income for the year.

E is the amount of eligible dividends received by the CCPC during the year.

F involves a group of technical additions related to becoming a CCPC, amalgamations, and wind-ups.

G is the amount of eligible dividends paid during the **preceding** year, less the amount of any Excessive Eligible Dividend Designation (EEDD) made during the preceding year (see Paragraph 13-139).

13-133. Several comments on this formula are relevant at this point:

- The D component calculates a Taxable Income that is adjusted to eliminate the types of income for which CCPCs receive favourable tax treatment. As dividends are paid out of after tax funds, the residual income is multiplied by 72 percent, reflecting a notional federal/provincial tax rate of 28 percent.

- If a CCPC receives eligible dividends, the addition in E allows these dividends to retain that status on their flow through to the shareholders of the CCPC.

- Note that the balance is reduced, not by eligible dividends paid in the current year, but by eligible dividends paid in the preceding year.

13-134. A simple example will illustrate these provisions:

EXAMPLE Norgrave Ltd., a CCPC, had no GRIP balance at the end of 2016. During 2017, the Company received eligible dividends of $106,600 and designated $25,000 of its dividends paid as eligible. At the end of 2017, Norgrave has a GRIP of $106,600.

For 2018, Norgrave has Taxable Income of $225,000. This amount includes aggregate investment income of $55,000. In addition, the Company receives eligible dividends during the year of $50,000.

In determining 2018 Tax Payable, the Company has a small business deduction of $27,000 [(18%)($150,000)]. During 2018, Norgrave pays dividends of $40,000, with $20,000 of this amount being designated as eligible.

ANALYSIS The 2018 ending balance in GRIP will be calculated as follows:

C - GRIP Balance At End Of 2017		$106,600
D - Taxable Income	$225,000	
Amount Eligible For The Small		
Business Deduction	(150,000)	
Aggregate Investment Income		
(Less Than Taxable Income)	(55,000)	
Adjusted Taxable Income	$ 20,000	
Rate	72%	14,400
E - Eligible Dividends Received		50,000
G - Eligible Dividends Designated in 2017		(25,000)
GRIP At End Of 2018		$146,000

The eligible dividends paid during 2018 will be deducted from the GRIP in 2019.

Exercise Thirteen - 8

Subject: GRIP Balance

Lanson Inc., a CCPC, had no GRIP balance at its year end on December 31, 2016. During 2017, the Company received eligible dividends of $365,000 and designated $140,000 of its $165,000 in dividends paid as eligible. At the end of 2017, Lanson has a GRIP of $365,000.

For 2018, Lanson has Taxable Income of $960,000. This amount includes net taxable capital gains of $65,000, mortgage interest received of $23,000, and a net capital loss carry forward deduction of $14,000. In addition, the Company receives eligible dividends during the year of $85,000. In determining 2018 Tax Payable, the Company has a small business deduction of $40,500. During 2018, Lanson pays dividends of $78,000, with $42,000 of this amount being designated as eligible. Determine the Company's GRIP balance at the end of 2018.

SOLUTION available in print and online Study Guide.

Non-CCPCs And Their LRIP
Low Rate Income Pool (LRIP)
13-135.   For non-CCPCs, their income will generally be taxed at full corporate rates. This means that, in general, their dividends can be designated as eligible. However, in some situations, a non-CCPC may have balances that have not been taxed at full corporate rates. This could include amounts of income retained by a CCPC before it became a public company, as well as non-eligible dividends received from a CCPC.

13-136.   Such balances will be allocated to a notional account referred to as a Low Rate Income Pool (LRIP). This account, defined in ITA 89(1), is similar to the GRIP account in that it

Designation Of Eligible Dividends

is used to track certain types of income. However, the two accounts serve very different purposes:

- The GRIP account is used to track balances that can be used by a CCPC as the basis for designating eligible dividends. To the extent that a GRIP balance is present, CCPC dividends can be designated as eligible until such time as the balance is exhausted. Note, however, the presence of a GRIP balance does not require that dividends be designated as eligible. Designation as eligible is at the discretion of the corporation.

- The LRIP account is used to track balances that have not been subject to full corporate tax rates. When an LRIP balance is present, any dividends paid by the corporation will be considered non-eligible. Stated alternatively, a corporation with a positive LRIP balance cannot designate any of its dividends as eligible until the LRIP balance is exhausted. In this situation, the corporation has no discretion.

13-137.   The definition of the LRIP balance, as found in ITA 89(1) is as follows:

$$(A + B + C + D + E + F) - (G + H), \text{where}$$

A   is the non-CCPCs LRIP at the end of the preceding year.
B   is the amount of non-eligible dividends received by the non-CCPC from a corporation resident in Canada.
C   is a group of technical additions related to corporate reorganizations.
D   is an adjustment for a non-CCPC that was a CCPC in some preceding year.
E   is an adjustment for a non-CCPC that was a credit union in some preceding year.
F   is an adjustment for a non-CCPC that was an investment company in some preceding year.

G   is the amount of taxable dividends, other than eligible dividends, paid by the non-CCPC during the year.

H   is the amount of any EEDD made by the non-CCPC during the year.

13-138.   A simple example will serve to illustrate this definition.

EXAMPLE   At the end of 2017, Ovamp Ltd. has an LRIP balance of $450,000. During 2018, the Company receives non-eligible dividends from a CCPC in the amount of $225,000. During 2018, the Company pays dividends of $360,000.

ANALYSIS   Given the presence of a positive LRIP balance in excess of the total dividends paid, none of the Ovamp dividends could be designated eligible.

Part III.1 Tax On Excessive Eligible Dividend Designations
Calculation
13-139.   The enhanced dividend tax credit procedures are available on any dividend that the paying corporation has designated as eligible. This raises the possibility that a corporation might designate a dividend as eligible under circumstances where such a designation is not appropriate (e.g., a CCPC designating a dividend as eligible when it has no balance in its GRIP at the end of the year). To discourage this, the government has introduced a Part III.1 tax on what is referred to as an Excessive Eligible Dividend Designation (EEDD).

13-140.   If the EEDD is inadvertent, the Part III.1 tax is equal to 20 percent of the excess amount. In these circumstances, Part III.1 provides for an election that will allow the taxpayer to effectively undo the designation.

13-141.   If the CRA concludes that the EEDD reflects an attempt to artificially manipulate either a GRIP or an LRIP, the Part III.1 tax rate goes to 30 percent. In addition, there are two other consequences:

- The tax applies to the entire dividend, not just the EEDD.
- No election is available to undo the excessive election.

13-142.   In order to appropriately track all dividend payments, any resident Canadian corporation that pays a taxable dividend is required to file a return for the year under Part III.1.

13-143.   ITA 89(1) defines EEDD differently for CCPCs and non-CCPCs. These definitions will be considered separately in the following material.

EEDD For A CCPC

13-144.   If a CCPC designates an amount of eligible dividends that is in excess of its GRIP at the end of the year, it will be considered an EEDD and be subject to Part III.1 tax.

> **EXAMPLE** At its December 31, 2017 year end, Sandem Inc., a CCPC, has a GRIP of $45,000. It paid no dividends in 2017. During 2018, the Company pays dividends of $100,000, of which $60,000 are designated as eligible. There are no additions to the Company's GRIP during 2018.

> **ANALYSIS** The Company has an EEDD of $15,000 ($60,000 - $45,000). Provided the CRA believes that this was an inadvertent result, this amount will be subject to a Part III.1 tax of 20 percent on the excess of $15,000. There is also the possibility of electing to have the EEDD treated as a non-eligible dividend.

> If the CRA concludes that the EEDD was a deliberate attempt to manipulate the Company's GRIP, an additional 10 percent is added to the Part III.1 tax. In addition, the applicable 30 percent tax is assessed on the entire eligible amount of $60,000, not just the $15,000 EEDD amount and no election is available to undo the excessive election.

EEDD For A Non-CCPC

13-145.   In somewhat simplified terms, an EEDD for a non-CCPC is equal to the lesser of its eligible dividends paid and its LRIP at the time the dividend is paid. For example, if a non-CCPC paid an eligible dividend of $50,000 at a point in time that its LRIP was equal to $40,000, the EEDD would be $40,000. Note that, unlike the situation with EEDDs for CCPCs, where the amount is based on the end of year balance of the GRIP, the EEDD for a non-CCPC is based on the balance of the LRIP at the point in time when the eligible dividend is paid.

13-146.   A simple example will illustrate these provisions:

> **EXAMPLE** Victor Ltd., a Canadian public company, receives $42,000 in non-eligible dividends from a CCPC on June 15, 2018. Its LRIP has a balance of nil prior to this. On September 23, 2018, Victor pays dividends of $100,000, with $30,000 of this amount being designated as eligible.

> **ANALYSIS** As at September 23, 2018, the balance in the LRIP would be $42,000. The lesser of this amount and the eligible dividend would be $30,000 and this would be the amount of the EEDD.

> This result seems somewhat counter-intuitive in that a non-eligible dividend was paid in an amount sufficient to eliminate the LRIP. However, the legislation is clear that the LRIP is measured at a particular point in time and, if an eligible dividend is paid when there is a positive balance in this account, it creates an EEDD. We would note that this situation could have been avoided had the non-eligible dividend been paid before, even by one day, the payment of the eligible dividend.

> Provided there were no further dividend transactions, the LRIP balance at the end of the year would be nil as the payment of $70,000 in non-eligible dividends would have eliminated the $42,000 balance created by the non-eligible dividends received.

> With respect to the Part III.1 tax, a tax of 20 percent would normally be assessed on the EEDD of $30,000. However, if the CRA concludes that a deliberate attempt to manipulate the LRIP was involved, the tax rate will be increased to 30 percent.

A Final Word On Eligible Dividends

13-147.   You should be aware that the preceding is a fairly simplified version of the provisions related to eligible dividends and their designation. The complete legislation is far more complex, dealing with a number of transitional situations, changes in a corporation's classification, as well as problems associated with corporate reorganizations. However, we feel that this version of the material is appropriate for an introductory text in taxation.

We suggest you work Self Study Problems Thirteen-4, 5, 6, and 7 at this point.

Additional Supplementary Self Study Problems Are Available Online.

Key Terms Used In This Chapter

13-148.   The following is a list of the key terms used in this Chapter. These terms, and their meanings, are compiled in the Glossary located at the back of the Study Guide.

Additional Refundable Tax
  On Investment Income (ART)
Aggregate Investment Income
ART
Canadian Controlled Private Corporation
CCPC
Connected Corporation
Dividend Gross Up
Dividend Tax Credit
Dividends
Eligible Dividends
Excessive Eligible Dividend
  Designation (EEDD)

General Rate Income Pool (GRIP)
Integration
Low Rate Income Pool (LRIP)
Over Integration
Part IV Tax
Portfolio Dividend
Private Corporation
Public Corporation
RDTOH
Refundable Dividend Tax On Hand
Refundable Part I Tax
Subject Corporation
Under Integration

References

13-149.   For more detailed study of the material in this Chapter, we refer you to the following:

ITA 82(1)	Taxable Dividends Received
ITA 89(1)	Definitions (Canadian Corporations, GRIP, LRIP, and EEDD)
ITA 123.3	Refundable Tax On CCPC's Investment Income
ITA 123.4	General Rate Reduction
ITA 129(1)	Dividend Refund To Private Corporation
ITA 129(3)	Definition Of Refundable Dividend Tax On Hand
ITA 129(4)	Aggregate Investment Income
ITA 185.1	Tax On Excessive Eligible Dividend Designations
ITA 185.2	Election To Treat Excessive Eligible Dividend As An Ordinary Dividend
ITA 186	Part IV Tax
IT-67R3	Taxable Dividends From Corporations Resident In Canada
IT-243R4	Dividend Refund To Private Corporations
IT-269R4	Part IV Tax On Taxable Dividends Received By a Private Corporation Or A Subject Corporation
IT-391R	Status Of Corporations
IT-458R2	Canadian Controlled Private Corporation

Sample Corporate Tax Return For Chapter 13

The Sample Tax Return for this Chapter can be found in the print and online Study Guide.

Problems For Self Study (Online)

To provide practice in problem solving, there are Self Study and Supplementary Self Study problems available on MyLab Accounting.

Within the text we have provided an indication of when it would be appropriate to work each Self Study problem. The detailed solutions for Self Study problems can be found in the print and online Study Guide.

We provide the Supplementary Self Study problems for those who would like additional practice in problem solving. The detailed solutions for the Supplementary Self Study problems are available online, not in the Study Guide.

The .PDF file "Self Study Problems for Volume 2" on MyLab contains the following for Chapter 13:

- 7 Self Study problems,
- 4 Supplementary Self Study problems, and
- detailed solutions for the Supplementary Self Study problems.

Assignment Problems

(The solutions for these problems are only available in
the solutions manual that has been provided to your instructor.)

Assignment Problem Thirteen - 1
(Integration Example)

Assume the following with respect to the shareholder of a CCPC who is an individual.

- The corporation's business income for the year is $225,000.
- Any dividends paid are non-eligible dividends.
- The individual's marginal federal tax rate is 29 percent and his marginal provincial tax rate is 16 percent.
- The provincial dividend tax credit on non-eligible dividends is equal to 35 percent of the gross up.
- The combined federal and provincial corporate tax rate on business income is 13.7931 percent.

Required: Indicate, using these assumptions, whether integration is working perfectly. If your answer is no, briefly explain why this is the case.

Assignment Problem Thirteen - 2
(Part I and Part IV Refundable Taxes)

Burton Investments Ltd. is a Canadian controlled private corporation that sells office supplies. It owns 52 percent of the outstanding shares of Puligny Inc. On December 15, 2018, Puligny Inc. declared and paid a dividend of $122,000, of which Burton Investments Ltd. received $63,440 (52 percent). As a result of paying the $122,000 dividend, Puligny Inc. received a dividend refund in the amount of $12,500.

Other 2018 income that was reported by Burton Investments consisted of the following amounts:

Capital Gain	$18,000
Dividends From Bank Of Montreal Common Shares	13,480
Interest	1,150

The capital gain was on the sale of land that had been used as an auxiliary parking lot, but was no longer needed.

Burton's office supply business is seasonal and, as a consequence, temporary cash balances must be set aside for the purchase of inventories during the busy parts of the year. All of the $1,150 in interest was earned on such temporary cash balances.

At the end of 2017, the Company's Refundable Dividend Tax On Hand balance was $22,346. The 2017 dividend refund was $7,920.

The Company's Taxable Income for the year ending December 31, 2018 was $62,800. No foreign income was included in this total. Assume the Part I Tax Payable for the year ending December 31, 2018 was correctly calculated as $12,560. Because of its association with Puligny Inc., its share of the annual business limit on income eligible for the small business deduction is $40,000. Burton's active business income is more than its share of the annual business limit.

Burton Investments paid taxable dividends of $22,500 in 2018.

Required: For the taxation year ending December 31, 2018, determine the Part IV and refundable Part I taxes that will be payable by Burton Investments Ltd. In addition, determine the balance in the Refundable Dividend Tax On Hand account at December 31, 2018, and any dividend refund available.

Assignment Problem Thirteen - 3
(Part I And Part IV Refundable Taxes, GRIP)

Radco Inc. is a Canadian controlled private corporation with a December 31 year end. The various components of its Net Income For Tax Purposes are as follows:

• Active Business Income (Note 1)	$823,462
• Taxable Capital Gains	161,576
• Canadian Source Interest From Long-Term Investments	71,345
• Dividends (Note 2)	614,292

Note 1 As determined under ITR 5200, $624,560 of this total qualified as M&P profits. As these amounts are allocated to a province which has a special rate for M&P profits, the company calculates the federal M&P deduction.

Note 2 The total dividend figure is made up of the following amounts:

Eligible Dividends From Canadian Public Companies	$123,470
Non-Eligible Dividends From Nad Ltd. (Note 3)	279,217
Non-Eligible Dividends From Jad Ltd. (Note 3)	211,605
Total Dividends	$614,292

Note 3 Radco owns 100 percent of the shares of Nad Ltd. As a result of paying this dividend, Nad Ltd. received a dividend refund of $57,236. Radco owns 40 percent of Jad Ltd. Jad Ltd. did not receive a refund as a result of paying these dividends.

Additional Information

1. On September 12, 2018, Radco paid taxable dividends to its shareholders totaling $186,780. Of this total, $63,567 was designated as eligible.

2. At the beginning of 2018, Radco has a net capital loss carry forward $172,400 [(1/2)($344,800)]. In addition, there is a non-capital loss carry forward of $18,263. The Company would like to deduct as much as possible of these carry forwards during 2018.

3. Radco is associated with both Nad Ltd. and Jad Ltd. The Companies have agreed that Nad and Jad will each receive $150,000 of the small business deduction's annual business limit. The remaining $200,000 is allocated to Radco.

4. At December 31, 2017, Radco had a RDTOH balance of $19,742 and a GRIP balance of $32,476. During 2017, the Company paid taxable dividends of $30,000, $12,000 of which were designated as eligible. As a result of paying the dividends, Radco received a dividend refund of $10,000.

5. Using the formula found in ITR402(3), 90 percent of Radco's Taxable Income has been allocated to the provinces.

Required: Show all of the calculations used to provide the following required information, including those for which the result is nil.

For Radco Inc.'s 2018 taxation year, calculate the following items:

A. Part I federal Tax Payable.
B. Part IV Tax Payable.
C. The balance in the Refundable Dividend Tax On Hand account on December 31, 2018.
D. The balance in the GRIP account on December 31, 2018.
E. The dividend refund, if any.
F. Total federal Tax Payable (net of any dividend refund).

Assignment Problem Thirteen - 4
(Comprehensive Corporate Tax Payable With CCA)

Oland Ltd. is a Canadian controlled private corporation with a December 31 year end. For the year ending December 31, 2018, the Income Statement of the Company, prepared in accordance with generally accepted accounting principles, is as follows:

Revenues		$1,561,472
Expenses:		
Cost Of Goods Sold	($776,257)	
Selling And Administrative Costs	(394,672)	
Amortization Expense	(125,489)	
Charitable Donations	(27,000)	(1,323,418)
Operating Income		$ 238,054
Gain On Sale Of Property	$153,600	
Loss On Sale Of Vehicles	(55,000)	
Gain On Sale Of Investments	11,000	
Dividends Received (See Note)	123,400	233,000
Net Income Before Taxes		$ 471,054

Note   The components of the dividends received are as follows:

Eligible Dividends From Canadian Public Companies	$ 62,300
Non-Eligible Dividends From 80 Percent Owned Subsidiary	
(The Subsidiary Received A Refund Of $15,000	
As A Result Of Paying The Dividend)	48,000
Non-Eligible Dividends From Wholly Owned Subsidiary	
(No Dividend Refund)	13,100
Total Dividends Received	$123,400

Oland is associated with both of these companies. The two subsidiaries have each been allocated $125,000 of the small business deduction's annual business limit. The remaining $250,000 has been allocated to Oland.

Other Information:

1. Selling And Administrative Costs include $22,490 in business meals and entertainment.

2. During 2018, Oland Ltd. acquired a competing business at a price that included goodwill of $110,400. For accounting purposes, there is no impairment or write-down of the goodwill in 2018.

3. Selling And Administrative Costs includes bond discount amortization of $3,850.

4. Selling And Administrative Costs includes interest on late income tax instalments of $1,240 and on late municipal tax payments of $625.

5. Selling And Administrative Costs include membership fees for several employees in a local golf and country club. These fees total $7,285.

6. As the Company expects to issue more shares during 2018, it made a number of amendments to its articles of incorporation and included the legal costs in Selling And Administrative Costs. These costs totalled $11,482.

7. On January 1, 2018, the Company had the following UCC balances:

Class 1	$582,652
Class 8	575,267
Class 10	75,348
Class 13	88,600
Class 14.1	Nil

The Class 1 balance relates to a single real property acquired in 2000 at a cost of $750,000. It is estimated that the value of the land at this time was $50,000. On February 1, 2018, this property is sold for $850,000. It is estimated that, at this time, the value of the land has increased to $80,000. In the accounting records, this real property was carried at $696,400, $646,400 for the building and $50,000 for the land.

The old building is replaced on February 15, 2018 with a new building acquired at a cost of $923,000 of which $86,000 is allocated to land. As the building is used more than 90 percent for non-residential purposes, it qualifies for the special 6 percent CCA rate. In order to use this rate, the building is put into a separate CCA class. No elections are made with respect to the replacement of the building.

During 2018, Class 8 assets were acquired at a cost of $226,000. Class 8 assets with a capital cost of $185,000 were sold for $210,000. These Class 8 assets were paintings by Canadian artists and each was sold for an amount in excess of its cost. The accountant had not amortized them for accounting purposes as he could not determine an estimated useful life. Class 8 contains a large number of assets at the end of 2018.

As the Company has decided to lease all of its vehicles in the future, all of the assets in Class 10 are sold during the year. The capital cost of these assets was $142,000 and the proceeds of disposition amounted to $43,000. The net book value of these assets was $98,000.

The Class 13 balance relates to a single lease that commenced on January 1, 2013. The lease has an initial term of seven years, with two successive options to renew for three years each. At the inception of the lease, the Company spent $110,000 on leasehold improvements. On January 1, 2015, an additional $44,800 was spent on further improvements.

8. It is Oland's policy to deduct maximum amounts of CCA.

9. During 2018, Oland spends $18,500 landscaping the grounds of its new building. For accounting purposes this was treated as an asset. However, the Company will not amortize this balance as it believes the work has an unlimited life.

10. Investments were sold during the year for $126,000. The adjusted cost base of these investments was $115,000.

11. On December 31, 2017, the Company had a balance in its Refundable Dividend Tax On Hand account of $52,460. The Company claimed a dividend refund of $12,800 in its 2017 corporate tax return.

12. At the end of 2017, Oland has a GRIP balance of $162,345. During 2017, the Company designated $12,350 of its dividends paid as eligible.

13. During 2018, Oland paid $42,300 in dividends. Of this total, $26,300 were designated as eligible.

14. At the beginning of 2018, Oland had a $23,000 net capital loss carry forward [(1/2)($46,000)]. It also had a non-capital loss carry forward of $36,400. The Company would like to deduct as much as possible of these two carry overs during 2018.

15. All of Oland's Taxable Income will be allocated to a province.

16. It has been determined that Oland has $300,289 of active business income. Of this total, $43,000 results from manufacturing and processing activity. Because of special rates in the province in which it operates, Oland makes a separate calculation of the manufacturing and processing deduction.

Required: Show all of the calculations used to provide the following required information, including those for which the result is nil.

A. Determine Oland's minimum Net Income For Tax Purposes and Taxable Income for the year ending December 31, 2018. Include in your solution the January 1, 2019 UCC balance for each CCA class.

B. Determine Oland's Part I federal Tax Payable for the year ending December 31, 2018.

C. Determine the December 31, 2018 balance in Oland's Refundable Dividend Tax On Hand account.

D. Determine Oland's minimum federal Tax Payable for the year ending December 31, 2018. This should include both Part I and Part IV Tax Payable, net of any dividend refund.

E. Determine the December 31, 2018 balance in Oland's GRIP.

Assignment Problem Thirteen - 5
(Comprehensive Corporate Tax Payable)

Fancom Inc. is an Alberta corporation that qualifies as a Canadian controlled private company. For the taxation year ending December 31, 2018, the components of its Net Income For Tax Purposes and Taxable Income are as follows:

Active Business Income (Note 1)	$328,000
Gross Foreign Business Income	40,800
Gross Foreign Non-Business Income	31,200
Interest On Long-Term Investments	49,900
Taxable Capital Gains [(1/2)($33,000)]	16,500
Eligible Dividends Received On Portfolio Investment	21,000
Net Income For Tax Purposes	**$487,400**
Eligible Dividends Received	(21,000)
Charitable Contributions	(86,400)
Net Capital Loss Carry Forward Deducted	(13,900)
Non-Capital Loss Carry Forward Deducted	(263,000)
Taxable Income	**$103,100**

Note 1 As determined by the *Income Tax Regulations*, $152,000 of this active business income was manufacturing and processing profits.

Note 2   Foreign jurisdictions withheld $6,120 from the foreign business income and $7,800 from the foreign non-business income.

Other Information:

1.   During the year ending December 31, 2018, Fancom used its existing cash resources to pay taxable dividends of $223,200. Of this total, $49,300 were designated as eligible.

2.   As of December 31, 2017, Fancom Inc. has a GRIP of $49,360. During 2017, the Company designated $18,700 of its dividends paid as eligible.

3.   As of December 31, 2017, the balance in Fancom's RDTOH account was $27,400. A dividend refund of $13,400 was claimed in the 2017 corporate tax return.

4.   As determined by the *Income Tax Regulations*, 85 percent of Fancom's Taxable Income can be allocated to a Canadian province.

Required: Show all of the calculations used to provide the following required information, including those for which the result is nil.

A.   Calculate Fancom's Part IV Tax Payable for the year ending December 31, 2018.

B.   Assume that the foreign business and non-business tax credits are equal to the foreign taxes withheld. Calculate Fancom's minimum Part I Tax Payable for the year ending December 31, 2018. As the corporation operates in a province that has a reduced rate for M&P activity, a separate calculation of the federal M&P deduction is required.

C.   Assume the foreign business and non-business tax credits are equal to the foreign taxes withheld. Calculate Fancom's dividend refund for the year ending December 31, 2018.

D.   Determine the December 31, 2018 balance in Fancom's GRIP account.

Assignment Problem Thirteen - 6
(Comprehensive Corporate Tax Payable)

Ferris Ltd. is a Canadian controlled private corporation. For the year ending December 31, 2018, its accounting Net Income Before Taxes, as determined under generally accepted accounting principles, was $600,600. Other information for the 2018 fiscal year follows.

1.   The Company's amortization expense was $711,200. Maximum deductible CCA for the year was $946,000. It is the Company's policy to always deduct maximum available CCA.

2.   The Company's revenues included foreign source non-business income of $22,100 (Canadian dollars). This was the amount that was received after the withholding of $3,900 (15 percent of the gross amount) by the foreign tax authorities.

3.   Ferris sold depreciable assets for $582,000. These assets had an original cost of $510,000 and a net book value of $435,000. They were Class 8 assets and, at the beginning of 2018, the UCC balance in this class was $442,000. No Class 8 assets were purchased during the year. The Company has numerous assets left in this class at the end of the year.

4.   During the year, the Company had the following amounts of Canadian source investment income:

Interest On Long-Term Investments	$31,600
Taxable Capital Gains On Sale Of Depreciable Assets	36,000
Eligible Dividends On Bank of Nova Scotia Shares	14,200

5. During the year, the Company begins selling a product on which they provide a 10 year warranty. At the end of the year, they established a warranty reserve of $25,000 to reflect the expected costs of providing warranty services. No costs were incurred in 2018.

6. The Company spent $66,400 on business meals and entertainment.

7. It has been determined that Ferris has active business income of $277,100 for the year. Included in this amount were manufacturing and processing profits, as determined by the *Income Tax Regulations*, of $188,300.

8. During the year ending December 31, 2018, the Company used its existing cash resources to pay taxable dividends of $274,000. Of this total, $20,800 were designated as eligible.

9. As of December 31, 2017, Ferris Ltd. has a GRIP of $17,300. During 2017, the Company designated all of the $8,100 in taxable dividends paid as eligible.

10. As of December 31, 2017, the balance in Ferris's RDTOH account was $21,700. A dividend refund of $2,700 was claimed in the 2017 corporate tax return.

11. The Company has available a non-capital loss carry forward of $267,300 and a net capital loss carry forward of $24,800 [(1/2)($49,600)]. Management has indicated that they would like to deduct as much of these amounts as possible in the 2018 tax return.

Required: Show all of the calculations used to provide the following required information, including those for which the result is nil.

A. Calculate Ferris's minimum Net Income For Tax Purposes and Taxable Income for the year ending December 31, 2018.

B. Calculate Ferris's Part IV Tax Payable for the year ending December 31, 2018.

C. Assume the foreign non-business tax credit is equal to the foreign tax withheld. Calculate Ferris's Part I federal Tax Payable for the year ending December 31, 2018. As the corporation operates in a province that has a reduced rate for M&P activity, a separate calculation of the federal M&P deduction is required.

D. Assume the foreign non-business tax credit is equal to the foreign tax withheld. Calculate Ferris's dividend refund for the year ending December 31, 2018.

E. Determine the December 31, 2018 balance in Ferris's GRIP account.

F. Do not assume the foreign non-business tax credit is equal to the foreign tax withheld, but assume that any excess of foreign tax withheld over the federal foreign tax credit will be applied against the provincial tax liability. Using the amounts calculated in Part C, compare your results under this new scenario with the Part C calculation of Part I Tax Payable. As part of your solution, provide a detailed calculation of the small business deduction, the ITA 123.3 refundable tax (ART) and the foreign tax credit available to Ferris for the year ending December 31, 2018.

G. Assume that any excess of foreign tax withheld over the federal foreign tax credit cannot be applied against the provincial tax liability. Comment on any tax planning issues that should be reviewed because of this change in assumption.

Assignment Problem Thirteen - 7
(Comprehensive Tax Payable)

Industco Inc. is a Canadian controlled private corporation. It uses a taxation year that ends on December 31. It keeps its records in accordance with generally accepted accounting principles. For the year ending December 31, 2018, the Company's condensed Income Statement, is as follows:

Operating Revenues In Canada		$2,846,000
Operating Expenses In Canada		(1,905,000)
Operating Income In Canada		$ 941,000
Other Income Items:		
Eligible Portfolio Dividends	$ 52,000	
Foreign Non-Business Income		
(Net Of 15 Percent Withholding)	25,500	
Foreign Business Income		
(Net Of 10 Percent Withholding)	45,000	
Canadian Source Interest	26,000	
Gain On Sale Of Class 8 Assets	225,000	373,500
Accounting Income Before Taxes		$1,314,500

Other information related to operating expenses follows.

Amortization And CCA   The operating income figure was reduced by a charge for amortization of $623,000.

At the beginning of 2018, the company has a balance in Class 1 of $1,000,000. The only asset in the Class is the Company's headquarters building. The Company has owned this building since 2001.

In general, other property is leased. However, in February, 2018, a policy change results in the acquisition of a new building at a cost of $650,000, of which $125,000 is allocated to the land on which the building is situated. The building is used 100 percent for non-residential purposes and is allocated to a separate Class 1. One-half of the non-residential use is for manufacturing and processing.

The January 1, 2018 balance in Class 8 was $4,200,000. During 2018, there were additions to this class in the total amount of $700,000. Also, Class 8 assets with a cost of $400,000 were sold for proceeds of $550,000. The net book value of these assets in the accounting records was $325,000. There were numerous assets remaining in the class at the end of the 2018 taxation year.

At the beginning of 2018, the UCC in Class 10 was $800,000, reflecting the Company's fleet of trucks. As the Company is changing to a policy of leasing its trucks, all of these trucks were sold during the year for $687,000. The capital cost of the trucks was $1,200,000 and their net book value in the accounting records was equal to the sale proceeds of $687,000.

Landscaping   The Company spent $95,000 on landscaping for its main office building. This amount was recorded as an asset in the accounting records and, because the work has an unlimited life, no amortization was recorded on this asset.

Advertising   The Company spent $17,000 on advertisements in *Fortune* Magazine, a U.S. based publication. Over 90 percent of the magazine's non-advertising content is original editorial content. The advertisements were designed to promote sales in Canadian cities located on the U.S. border.

Travel And Entertainment   Included in the travel costs deducted in 2018 was $12,000 for airline tickets and $41,400 for business meals and entertainment.

The Company paid, and deducted for accounting purposes, a $2,500 initiation fee for a corporate membership in the Highland Golf And Country Club.

Taxes On Vacant Land   The Company paid, and deducted, property taxes of $15,000 on vacant land that is being held for possible future expansion of its head-quarters site.

Other Information

1. Industco Inc. declared and paid taxable dividends of $83,000 during 2018. Of this total, $54,000 was designated as eligible.

2. It has been determined that 92 percent of Industco's Taxable Income can be allocated to a province.

3. The December 31, 2017 balance in Industco's Refundable dividend Tax On Hand account was $111,000. The dividend refund for the year ending December 31, 2017 was $33,000.

4. At the end of 2017, Industco Inc. has a GRIP balance of $98,000. During 2017, the company designated $64,000 of its dividends paid as eligible.

5. Industco Inc. is associated with two other Canadian controlled private corporations. Industco has been allocated $125,000 of the annual business limit.

6. Assume that the foreign tax credits for the foreign non-business and foreign business income are equal to the amounts withheld.

7. Industco's Canadian active business income is equal to its net business income for tax purposes. One-half of this Canadian active business income results from manufacturing and processing activity.

8. At the beginning of 2018, Industco has a net capital loss carry forward of $42,000 and a non-capital loss carry forward $18,000. The Company intends to deduct the maximum amount of these carry forwards during 2018.

Required: Determine the following amounts. You should show all of the calculations required to provide these amounts, even when the result of the calculations is nil.

A. Industco's Net Income For Tax Purposes and Taxable Income for the year ending December 31, 2018. As the Company's active business income is based on its net business income for tax purposes, a separate calculation of this component of Net Income For Tax Purposes is required.

B. Industco's minimum federal Part I Tax Payable for the year ending December 31, 2018.

C. The December 31, 2018 balance in Industco's Refundable Dividend Tax On Hand account.

D. Industco's dividend refund for the year ending December 31, 2018.

E. Industco's minimum federal Tax Payable for the year ending December 31, 2018. This should include both Part I and Part IV Tax Payable, net of any dividend refund. As the corporation operates in a province that has a reduced tax rate for manufacturing and processing activity, a separate calculation of the federal M&P deduction is required.

F. Determine the December 31, 2018 balance in Industco's GRIP.

Assignment Problem Thirteen - 8
(Comprehensive Corporate Tax Payable)

Angie's Amazing Getups Incorporated is a Canadian controlled private corporation with a head office in London, Ontario. The company is a manufacturer of high end custom costumes and makeup used in movie and theatre productions with sales in Canada and the U.S.

The company started in business in 2015 when the sole shareholder, Angela Q. Snodgrass, was photographed by the paparazzi after a particularly enthusiastic night of partying. When Angela saw herself on the front page of every tabloid newspaper the next day, she knew that fame was not for her. Since Angela was a highly trained clothing designer and makeup artist, she felt she would be able to use those skills to start her own business and keep out of the limelight.

Assignment Problems

In November, 2018, after discovering that her bookkeeper, Ponzi Madoff, had been defrauding her, Angela fired him and took over the bookkeeping responsibilities herself, despite having a limited knowledge of accounting. She has produced the following Income Statement and miscellaneous financial information for the year ended December 31, 2018 and needs your help.

Angie's Amazing Getups Incorporated
Income Statement
Year Ending December 31, 2018

Sales		$7,578,903
Cost Of Goods Sold		(5,468,752)
Gross profit		$2,110,151
Expenses:		
General And Administrative Expenses	($852,000)	
Amortization Expense	(550,000)	
Interest	(8,500)	(1,410,500)
Operating Income		$ 699,651
Other Income:		
Loss On Disposal Of Limited Life Licence		(17,000)
Interest Income		110,532
Income Before Income Taxes		$ 793,183
Income Taxes		
Current	($182,000)	
Future	(35,000)	(217,000)
Net Income		$ 576,183

During your review of Angela's work and last year's tax return for the corporation, you have made the following notes.

1. In the accounting records, the Allowance For Doubtful Accounts was $25,000 at December 31, 2018, and $20,000 at December 31, 2017. During 2018, the company had actual write-offs of $11,750. As a result, the accounting Bad Debt Expense was $16,750. This amount is included in General and Administrative Expenses on the Income Statement.

   A review of the listing of receivables (for tax purposes), indicates that the actual items that may be uncollectible total $15,000 at December 31, 2018. In 2017, the company deducted a reserve for bad debts of $13,000 for tax purposes.

2. General And Administrative Expenses include:

Donations To Registered Charities	$ 27,000
Accrued Bonuses - Accrued September 1, 2018, Paid June 15, 2019	78,000
Meals And Entertainment Costs:	
$1,000 Per Month For Premium Membership At Golf Club For Angie	12,000
$200 Per Month For Memberships At Golf Club For Salespeople	2,400
$32,000 For Meals While Entertaining Clients	32,000
$5,000 In Food Costs For Angie's Personal Chef For Her Meals At Home	5,000
$6,000 For Annual Summer BBQ For All Staff	6,000
Sponsorship Of Various Theatre Productions That Use Angie's Costumes	100,000
Advertising In A U.S. Theatre Magazine Directed At U.S. Clients	15,000
New Software Purchased October 1, 2018	
($13,000 For Applications And $25,000 For Systems)	38,000
Accounting And Legal Fees For Amended Articles Of Incorporation	6,000
Costs To Attend Annual Convention Of Costume Designers Held In Thailand	17,000

3. Interest Expense consists of the following:

Interest Expense - Operations	$5,000
Penalty And Interest For Late And Insufficient Instalment Payments	2,000
Interest On Late Payment Of Municipal Property Taxes	1,500

4. Travel costs (included in General and Administrative costs) include both air travel and travel reimbursement to employees for business travel. The company policy is to reimburse employees $0.59 per kilometer for the business use of their automobiles. During the year, seven employees each drove 4,000 kilometers on employment related activities and one employee drove 7,500 kilometers. None of the kilometer based allowances are required to be included in the income of the employees.

5. Maximum CCA has always been taken on all assets. The undepreciated capital cost balances at January 1, 2018 were as follows:

Class 1 (4%)	$650,000
Class 8	95,000
Class 10.1	17,850
Class 14	68,000
Class 14.1	Nil
Class 44	65,000
Class 53	135,000

6. During 2018, a limited life licence to produce costumes based on a popular theme park was sold for $63,000. The original cost of this licence was $95,000 and its net book value at the time of sale was $80,000. The licence was the only asset in Class 14.

7. Purchases and sales of equipment and other capital assets made during 2018 were as follows (note: some items are discussed in other sections of this problem). All amounts were capitalized for accounting purposes:

   a. The company purchased land and constructed a new building on it during the year. The building will be used 95% for manufacturing and processing. The cost of the land was $350,000, and the building cost $475,000 to construct.
   b. The company purchased a new set of furniture for the reception area for $1,200.
   c. Some outdated desks used by the finance department with a cost of $5,000 were sold for proceeds of $3,500.
   d. Landscaping of the grounds around the new building cost $35,000. This amount was capitalized for accounting purposes.
   e. A company car for use by the president of the company was purchased for $90,000. This car replaced the only other existing company car, which was purchased in 2016 for $95,000. The old car was sold for $60,000.
   f. A fence around the new building, high enough to prevent the paparazzi from taking pictures of Angela while she was at the office cost $52,000.

8. The company sold some shares that had been purchased several years ago. The capital gain on these shares was $152,708. Angela didn't know how to account for this, so she credited the entire amount to retained earnings.

9. Included in the financial statement income is income earned in the United States. The amounts reported in the financial statements are net of the tax paid, because Angela was unsure of the appropriate accounting treatment. All amounts are reported in Canadian dollars. The foreign income consisted of:

   a. Foreign business income of $70,000. US tax returns have been filed, and the US taxes paid on this amount totals $6,000.
   b. Foreign portfolio dividend income of $15,000. Foreign taxes of $2,000 have been paid on this dividend income.

10. The Investment Income account balance on the Income Statement consists of the foreign dividend income (point 10) and the following Canadian source investment income:

Interest on long term investments	$ 56,532
Eligible dividends on bank shares	$ 16,000
Non-eligible dividend from Snodgrass Ltd.	$ 25,000

Angie's Amazing Getups Incorporated owns 8 percent of the shares of Snodgrass Ltd., a very profitable CCPC owned by Angela's mother. Snodgrass Ltd. received no dividend refund from the payment of dividends in 2018.

11. Except for the investment income noted in points 10 and 11, and any additional investment income you may calculate, all income is Canadian Active Business Income.

12. Included in the income of the company are manufacturing and processing profits. It has been determined that manufacturing and processing profits as determined under the Income Tax Regulations are $65,000.

13. The corporation has permanent establishments in Ontario and the United States. Its gross revenue and salary and wages information is as follows:

	Gross Revenue	Salary and Wages
Ontario	73.8%	89.1%
United States	26.2%	10.9%

14. As Angela did not know how to deal with the dividends paid to her personally by Angie's Amazing Getups Incorporated, she included them in General And Administrative Expenses. A total of $60,000 in non-eligible dividends were paid to her during 2018.

15. The balances in the tax accounts on December 31, 2017 were as follows:

Charitable donation carry forward	$ 3,500
Non-capital loss carry forward	52,500
Net capital loss carry forward [(1/2)($17,666)]	8,833
Refundable dividend tax on hand	40,500
Dividend refund for 2017	9,500
GRIP	76,500

None of the dividends paid in 2017 were designated eligible.

Required: Show all of the calculations used to provide the following required information, including those for which the result is nil. Ignore GST/HST/PST implications.

Determine Angie's Amazing Getups Incorporated's:

A. Minimum Net Income For Tax Purposes and Taxable Income for the year ending December 31, 2018.

B. Part I Tax Payable for the year ending December 31, 2018. Any percentages used in your calculations should be rounded to one decimal point. For the purposes of dealing with any foreign tax credits that the company is eligible for, assume that the foreign tax credit is equal to the foreign tax paid when determining the amount of the small business deduction and the manufacturing and processing profits deduction.

C. December 31, 2018 balance in the Refundable Dividend Tax On Hand account.

D. Minimum federal Tax Payable for the year ending December 31, 2018. This should include both Part I and Part IV Tax Payable, net of any dividend refund. Actual foreign tax credits should be calculated in order to determine the final balance of taxes owing by the company.

E. December 31, 2018 balance in the GRIP account.

CHAPTER 14

Other Issues In Corporate Taxation

Introduction

14-1. Chapters 12 and 13 dealt with basic issues associated with the determination of Taxable Income and Tax Payable for a corporation. Specifically, Chapter 12 described the basic adjustments associated with converting Net Income For Tax Purposes to corporate Taxable Income. This was followed by consideration of how this Taxable Income is allocated to individual provinces for the determination of provincial Tax Payable. With respect to Tax Payable, Chapter 12 dealt with the rates applicable to corporations, the small business deduction, the M&P deduction, foreign tax credits, and the general rate reduction.

14-2. After a fairly detailed discussion of the concept of integration, Chapter 13 focused on taxation of investment income earned by Canadian controlled and other private corporations. This Chapter concluded with coverage of the designation of eligible dividends for both public companies and Canadian controlled private corporations.

14-3. In presenting the material in Chapters 12 and 13, we focused on what we view as basic issues, skipping over some of the more technical considerations related to the determination of corporate Taxable Income and corporate Tax Payable. This was done in the belief that avoiding the more technical considerations would enhance your understanding of the basic procedures associated with these determinations.

14-4. In this Chapter 14, we are turning our attention to these technical issues. In this Chapter we will provide coverage of:

- the acquisition of control rules;
- the associated company rules;
- investment tax credits;
- tax basis shareholders' equity; and
- distributions of corporate surplus, including capital dividends and deemed dividends.

Acquisition Of Control Rules

Economic Background

14-5. Over a period of years, some corporations may experience sufficiently large losses that they have no hope of recovering their economic health. While they may have accumulated large amounts of net capital or non-capital loss carry forwards, they have no real prospect of being able to use these amounts. Such companies can become attractive takeover targets for profitable corporations, provided they can structure their business to make use of the tax benefits associated with these losses. For example, if a profitable company can acquire a company for $100,000 that has $1,000,000 in loss carry forwards that can be utilized in the future, it is clearly a bargain for the purchaser. Further, if the acquiree cannot make use of the losses, receiving the $100,000 may be a better alternative than declaring bankruptcy.

14-6. This situation is of concern to the government in that there are billions of dollars of such benefits available in the economy at any point in time. If access to these benefits was relatively trouble-free, the cost to the government could be enormous. As a consequence, the government has enacted legislation which significantly restricts the use of loss carry forwards in situations where there has been an acquisition of control.

Acquisition Of Control Legislation

14-7. ITA 111(4) through 111(5.5) contain rules that are applicable when there has been an acquisition of control by a person or group of persons. IT-302R3, which deals with the losses of a corporation, indicates that control requires ownership of shares that carry with them the right to elect a majority of the board of directors.

14-8A. An acquisition of control most commonly occurs when a majority shareholder sells his shares to an arm's length person. However, it can also occur through the redemption of shares. For example, if Ms. A owns 75 percent of AB Ltd. and Ms. B, an unrelated person, owns the other 25 percent, there would be an acquisition of control by Ms. B if AB Ltd. was to redeem all of Ms. A's shares.

14-8B. In recent years, several new anti-avoidance rules designed to address loss trading among trusts (ITA 251.2) and using de facto control to avoid the acquisition of control rules (ITA 256.1). The complexity of these rules is beyond the scope of this general text. We would also notes that the *Income Tax Act* now refers to acquisition of control situations as "loss restriction events".

Deemed Year End

14-9. To prevent losses from being used prior to the end of the taxation year in which the acquisition of control took place, ITA 249(4) requires that the corporation have a deemed year end on the day preceding an acquisition of control.

14-10. If the acquisition of control occurs prior to the corporation's normal year end, a short fiscal period will be created. For example, if the corporation's normal year end was December 31, and the acquisition of control took place on February 1, 2018, the deemed year end would create a fiscal year with only one month (January 1, 2018 through January 31, 2018). Further, if the corporation retains its old year end after the acquisition of control, there will be a second short fiscal year that runs from February 1, 2018 through December 31, 2018.

14-11. Note, however, ITA 249(4) allows the corporation to change its year end when there is an acquisition of control. This means that the corporation could have avoided a second short fiscal period by establishing January 31 as the new year end. This means that the first fiscal year after the acquisition of control will end on January 31, 2019.

14-12. The extra year end is of importance in that the non-capital losses that may be available after the acquisition of control are time limited. In our example, the deemed year end creates, in effect, an extra year end that shortens the period during which time-limited losses can be used. However, with a 20 year carry forward period for non-capital losses, this is unlikely to be an important consideration.

14-13. Other implications of such short fiscal periods include the need to base CCA calculations on a fraction of the year, the need to prorate the annual business limit for the small business deduction, as well as the usual year end procedures such as inclusions of reserves.

Restrictions On The Use Of Charitable Donations

14-14.   ITA 110.1(1.2) places two restrictions on the deduction of charitable donations:

- Undeducted amounts that are present at the time of the acquisition of control cannot be carried forward to taxation years subsequent to that date.

- No deduction is available on a gift made subsequent to the acquisition of control if the gifted property was acquired prior to the acquisition date in anticipation of the acquisition of control.

14-15.   An example of the latter restriction would be a situation where an individual, who does not have sufficient tax payable to use a credit on the donation of a particular property, transfers that property to a corporation he controls, with the expectation that he will sell the shares in the corporation and the corporation will make the donation and take the deduction.

Restrictions On The Use Of Losses

General Rules

14-16.   The acquisition of control rules apply to any losses that have not been deducted at the deemed year end. This would include losses that have been carried forward from prior years, as well as any additional losses that accrue in the taxation year which is created by the deemed year end.

14-17.   As will be explained later, the losses in this deemed taxation year may be increased by provisions that require the recognition of unrealized losses on capital assets. They can also be reduced by gains resulting from an election to have one or more deemed dispositions.

Capital Losses

14-18.   The acquisition of control rules are particularly harsh in their treatment of net capital losses. ITA 111(4)(a) indicates that any net capital losses that are present at the deemed year end are simply lost. They cannot be carried forward to future years and, as a consequence, they will be of no benefit to the corporation subsequent to the acquisition of control. Note that this would include any unused Allowable Business Investment Losses that are present at the deemed year end.

14-19.   In addition, if there are capital gains in the three years before the deemed year end, ITA 111(4)(b) prevents net capital losses from years subsequent to the deemed year end from being carried back to those years.

Non-Capital Losses

14-20.   While non-capital losses can be carried forward, they too are subject to restrictions. These restrictions, found in ITA 111(5), are that:

- after the acquisition of control has taken place, the corporation must continue to carry on the business in which the loss occurred;
- there must be a reasonable expectation of profit in that business; and
- the losses can only be applied against future income generated by the same, or a similar business.

14-21.   A brief example can be used to illustrate these provisions:

EXAMPLE   Bostox Ltd. operates two separate lines of business, manufacturing cameras and the sale of specialty food products. During the year ending December 31, 2017, the camera business experienced a loss for tax purposes of $5 million, while the food specialty products operation had business income for tax purposes of nil. The $5 million loss could not be carried back and, as a result, it became a loss carry forward. On January 1, 2018, Bostox Ltd. is acquired by another company. During the year ending December 31, 2018, the camera business lost an additional $1 million, while the food products business earned $7 million.

ANALYSIS If there was no acquisition of control, both the current 2018 loss of $1 million and the $5 million loss carry forward resulting from the camera business could be deducted against the income of the specialty food products business. This would have resulted in a 2018 Taxable Income of $1 million ($7 million profit on food products, offset by a current loss of $1 million on cameras and a non-capital loss carry forward of $5 million).

However, with the acquisition of control at the beginning of 2018, the loss carry forward can only be used against profits produced by the camera business. This means that none of the loss carry forward can be deducted in 2018, but the $1 million 2018 camera business loss can be netted against the $7 million food products income, resulting in a 2018 Taxable Income of $6 million. The $5 million loss carry forward will still be available, but can only be applied against future camera business income.

Exercise Fourteen - 1

Subject: Acquisition Of Control

India Inc. operates two separate lines of business, one of which sells fountain pens, while the other provides professional accounting services. In its first year of operations ending on December 31, 2017, the pen business had a loss of $192,000, and the accounting business had income of $57,000, resulting in a Net Income For Tax Purposes and Taxable Income of nil. This leaves a non-capital loss carry forward of $135,000. For the taxation year ending December 31, 2018, the pen business had income of $42,000, and the accounting business had income of $247,000, resulting in a Net Income For Tax Purposes of $289,000.

Determine the minimum Taxable Income for 2018 assuming (1) that there was no acquisition of control in either year and (2) that there was an acquisition of control on January 1, 2018. The Company has no deductions from Net Income For Tax Purposes other than possible loss carry forwards from 2017.

SOLUTION available in print and online Study Guide.

Unrecognized Losses At Deemed Year End
The Problem
14-22.   As previously indicated, the acquisition of control restrictions apply to losses that accrue in the taxation year that has been created by the deemed year end. As there has been a deemed year end, there may be a loss from normal operations for the fiscal period that has ended. In addition, there may be losses resulting from actual dispositions of capital assets during the period.

14-23.   However, the acquisition of control rules are also concerned with accrued losses that have not been recognized at the deemed year end. The problem is that, if such accrued losses are realized after that time, they will not be subject to the acquisition of control restrictions.

EXAMPLE A corporation owned a parcel of land with an adjusted cost base of $200,000 and a fair market value of $150,000. If the land was to be disposed of subsequent to the acquisition of control, the result would be a deductible capital loss. This could be viewed as a way of avoiding the restrictions imposed by the acquisition of control rules.

Special Rules
14-24.   In recognition of this problem, the acquisition of control rules require a number of special procedures at the deemed year end. They are as follows:

Non-Depreciable Capital Property   ITA 111(4)(c) requires that non-depreciable capital property be written down to its fair market value, if that value is below its adjusted cost base. ITA 111(4)(d) requires that the amount of the write-down be treated as a capital loss. The new lower value becomes the adjusted cost base of the property. The resulting allowable capital loss can be applied against available taxable capital gains, or carried back. However, if it is not used at the deemed year end, or in the three year carry back period, it is lost forever.

Depreciable Capital Property   ITA 111(5.1) requires that depreciable capital property be written down to its fair market value, if that value is below the UCC. The write-down amount is treated as CCA to be deducted in the deemed taxation year. This will reduce the income for that period and, in some cases, create or increase the loss for that year. For capital gains purposes, the property will retain the original capital cost.

Accounts Receivable   ITA 111(5.3) does not permit the deduction of a reserve for doubtful accounts under ITA 20(1)(l). Rather, amounts must be written off as specific bad debts on the basis of the largest possible amount. If a doubtful account is not written off at the time an acquisition of control occurs, no deduction is available if the account subsequently becomes uncollectible. This procedure will generally result in a larger deduction and will reduce income, increase a loss, or create a loss in the deemed taxation year.

Exercise Fourteen - 2

Subject: Write-Downs At Deemed Year End

On November 15 of the current year, Parkat Ltd. acquires control of Sparkat Ltd. On November 14, Sparkat Ltd. has the following assets:

• Land with an adjusted cost base of $293,000 and a fair market value of $215,000.

• Class 8 depreciable assets with a capital cost of $416,000, a UCC balance of $276,000 and a fair market value of $184,000.

Indicate the tax consequences of the procedures that will be applied to these assets in the deemed year end that results from the acquisition of control.

SOLUTION available in print and online Study Guide.

Deemed Disposition Election
The Problem
14-25.   The requirement that non-depreciable capital property be written down to fair market value at the deemed year end is particularly onerous in that the resulting capital losses may simply disappear. To offset the harshness of this requirement, ITA 111(4)(e) allows the corporation to elect, at the time of the deemed year end, to have a deemed disposition/reacquisition of any depreciable or non-depreciable capital property on which there is an accrued gain or recapture of CCA. This election can be used to trigger capital gains that will offset either unused losses of the current period or unused loss carry forwards from earlier periods.

14-26.   The election can also be used to trigger recapture which can absorb non-capital losses from the current or previous years. This is a less important application in most situations as non-capital losses do not disappear at the deemed year end. However, as noted in Paragraph 14-20, there are restrictions on the use of such losses after the deemed year end. Given this, it may be desirable to minimize non-capital loss carry forwards when an acquisition of control occurs.

Procedures

14-27.   The elected value, which will serve as the deemed proceeds of disposition, cannot exceed the fair market value of the asset at the time of the deemed disposition. The minimum value for the election is the adjusted cost base or capital cost of the property. The elected value can be any amount between this minimum and maximum. This means that, in the case of property on which CCA has been taken, any election that will create a capital gain will also create recapture of CCA.

14-28.   If the corporation has net capital losses and there are non-depreciable properties with accrued gains, this election is clearly desirable in that it will generate capital gains, which can be used to offset the net capital losses that would disappear as a result of the acquisition of control.

14-29.   The situation is less clear cut when the gains are on depreciable capital property. While the deemed disposition will create the needed capital gains, it will generally result in recapture of CCA. This may or may not be a desirable situation.

Example

14-30.   The following example will illustrate the procedures associated with the ITA 111(4)(e) deemed disposition election:

> **EXAMPLE**   Burkey Ltd. has a December 31 year end. On June 1, 2018, a new investor acquires control of the Company. While its basic operations have been profitable for many years, it has a net capital loss carry forward of $200,000 [(1/2)($400,000)]. On May 31, 2018, the Company has non-depreciable capital assets with a fair market value of $800,000 and an adjusted cost base of $500,000. Its depreciable capital assets have a fair market value of $1,200,000, a capital cost of $1,100,000, and a UCC of $600,000.

> **ANALYSIS**   The ITA 111(4)(e) election is clearly desirable with respect to the non-depreciable capital property. It generates a taxable capital gain of $150,000 [(1/2)($800,000 - $500,000)]. Deducting a $150,000 carry forward against this 2018 gain will use up $150,000 of the net capital loss. This will leave an unused amount of $50,000 ($200,000 - $150,000).

> Using the ITA 111(4)(e) election on the depreciable capital property will create a $50,000 [(1/2)($1,200,000 - $1,100,000)] taxable capital gain. Deducting a $50,000 loss carry forward against this amount will use up the remaining $50,000 of the net capital loss balance. However, the election will also create recaptured CCA of $500,000 ($1,100,000 - $600,000), an amount on which it appears that tax would have to be currently paid. Given that, in the absence of this election, taxation on the recapture could be deferred indefinitely, the election may not be desirable with respect to the depreciable capital property. One other factor that should be considered is that the election would result in increased CCA in the future.

Adjusted Cost Base After Election

14-31.   In addition to serving as the deemed proceeds of disposition, the elected value also becomes the adjusted cost base or capital cost of the asset on which the election was made. If the elections were made at fair market value on both properties in the preceding example, the new adjusted cost base of the non-depreciable assets would be $800,000, while the capital cost of the depreciable assets would be $1,200,000.

14-32.   However, if the $1,200,000 value was allowed to be used for CCA purposes, the Company would be able to deduct 100 percent of the $100,000 difference between the $1,200,000 elected value and the old capital cost of $1,100,000, despite the fact that they have, in effect, paid tax on only one-half of this amount.

14-33.   To prevent this from happening, ITA 13(7)(f) specifies that, when an election is made under ITA 111(4)(e), the new capital cost of the property for CCA purposes only, is equal to the original capital cost of the asset, plus one-half of the excess of the elected value over the asset's original capital cost. In the example in Paragraph 14-30, this value would be $1,150,000 [$1,100,000 + (1/2)($1,200,000 - $1,100,000)]. You might recall that other paragraphs in ITA 13(7) contain the same rule for both non-arm's length transfers of depreciable property and for some changes in use.

14-34. Future CCA would be based on this $1,150,000 figure and, in addition, if the assets were sold for more than $1,150,000, the new capital cost of $1,150,000 would be subtracted from the UCC to determine any recapture. However, any future capital gain would be based on the new adjusted cost base of $1,200,000.

Exercise Fourteen - 3

Subject: Election On Acquisition Of Control

Means Ltd. has a December 31 year end. On May 1, 2018, all of the Company's shares are acquired by a new owner. For the period January 1, 2018 through April 30, 2018, the Company has an operating loss of $45,000. On April 30, 2018, the Company has available a net capital loss carry forward of $110,000 [(1/2)($220,000)]. Also at that time, the Company has the following assets:

Asset Type	Adjusted Cost Base Or Capital Cost	UCC	Fair Market Value
Non-Depreciable	$500,000	N/A	$650,000
Depreciable	400,000	350,000	500,000

Advise the Company with respect to the most appropriate elections to be made prior to the acquisition of control and explain your results.

SOLUTION available in print and online Study Guide.

We suggest you work Self Study Problems Fourteen-1 and 2 at this point.

Associated Companies

The Problem

14-35. In the absence of special rules, it would be very easy to avoid the annual limit that applies to the small business deduction. This could be accomplished by dividing a single corporation's activities between two separate corporations, thereby doubling up on the annual business limit of $500,000. However, as was noted in Chapter 12, the *Act* makes this more difficult by requiring that associated companies share their annual business limit.

14-36. For example, assume that Mr. Robards owns all of the outstanding voting shares of both the Mark Company and the Grand Company. These two Companies would be considered to be associated and, as a consequence, would have to share the $500,000 annual business limit. As was indicated in Chapter 12, they can elect to allocate the annual limit in any proportion they wish, provided the total does not exceed $500,000. If the Mark Company has active business income and the Grand Company does not, it would be most advantageous to allocate the entire annual limit to the Mark Company, so that it could claim the maximum small business deduction.

14-37. The preceding example is very clear cut and results in an allocation of the small business deduction that reflects the goals of the relevant legislation. However, with a deduction that can be worth $90,000 [(18%)($500,000)] per year in federal tax alone, there is a significant incentive to develop arrangements that will avoid the intent of the legislation. Correspondingly, there is a need to have legislation that is sophisticated enough to frustrate these arrangements. As a consequence, the identification of associated companies can be very complex.

Definitions

Related Persons

14-38A.   ITA 251 provides definitions of related persons. The legislation for identifying associated companies makes much use of these definitions. Given this, working with the associated companies rules requires an understanding of the related persons rules. Note, however, you are dealing with two different concepts. ITA 251 deals with all classes of related taxpayers, while ITA 256 deals only with corporations. Further, even with corporations, the terms related and associated have different meanings.

14-38B.   The more important of the related persons definitions are as follows:

ITA 251(2)(a) - Related Persons   With respect to individuals, Paragraph (a) notes that individuals are related if they are connected by blood relationship, marriage, common-law partnership, or adoption. Various other Subsections in ITA 251 and 252 elaborate on this statement to point out that all of the following individuals would be "related" to the taxpayer:

- Parents and grandparents, as well as parents and grandparents of the taxpayer's spouse or common-law partner.
- The taxpayer's spouse or common-law partner, as well as the spouse or common-law partner's siblings and their spouses and common-law partners.
- Siblings of the taxpayer, as well as spouses or common-law partners of the taxpayer's siblings.
- Children, including those that are adopted, or born outside of marriage. Also included here would be spouses and common-law partners of children and children of the taxpayer's spouse or common-law partner.

ITA 251(2)(b) indicates that a corporation is related to:
- a person who controls it, if it is controlled by one person;
- a person who is a member of a related group that controls it; or
- any person related to a person who controls it or who is related to a member of a related group that controls it.

ITA 251(2)(c) indicates that two corporations are related if:
- they are controlled by the same person or group of persons;
- each of the corporations is controlled by one person and the person who controls one of the corporations is related to the person who controls the other corporation;
- one of the corporations is controlled by one person and that person is related to any member of a related group that controls the other corporation;
- one of the corporations is controlled by one person and that person is related to each member of an unrelated group that controls the other corporation;
- any member of a related group that controls one of the corporations is related to each member of an unrelated group that controls the other corporation; or
- each member of an unrelated group that controls one of the corporations is related to at least one member of an unrelated group that controls the other corporation.

Associated Companies

14-38C.   The definitions that relate directly to identification of associated companies are found in the ITA 256. The more important of these are as follows:

ITA 256(1.1) - Specified Class, Shares Of   In simplified terms, this definition refers to non-voting shares that have a fixed dividend rate and redemption amount. Such shares are commonly referred to as preferred shares.

ITA 256(1.2)(a) - Definition Of Group   For purposes of defining associated companies, a group is two or more persons, each of whom owns shares in the corporation in question. A related group involves a group of persons, each member of which is related to every other member. ITA 251(4) notes that a related group is a group of persons, each member of which is related to every other member. An unrelated group is any group, other than a related group.

ITA 256(1.2)(c) - Control   The definition of associated corporations also involves the concept of control. For purposes of determining association, a corporation is deemed to be controlled by another corporation, a person, or a group of persons, if the corporation, person, or group of persons owns either:

- shares (common and/or preferred) of capital stock with a fair market value of more than 50 percent of all issued and outstanding shares of capital stock; or

- common shares with a fair market value of more than 50 percent of all issued and outstanding common shares.

This definition is based on legal control. Control can also be "Control In Fact" as described in ITA 256(5.1) or control through other corporations as described in ITA 256(6.1) and 256(6.2).

Deeming Rules   The most relevant deeming rules can be described as follows:

- **ITA 256(1.2)(d) - Holding Companies**   This provision indicates that where shares of a corporation are held by another corporation, a shareholder of the holding corporation is deemed to own the shares of the held corporation in proportion to his interest in the holding corporation. Similar provisions apply to shares held by partnerships and trusts. Note, however, if a holding corporation holds a controlling interest in an investee, the holding corporation is considered to control all of the shares held by that investee.

- **ITA 256(1.3) - Children Under 18**   This provision requires that shares of a corporation owned by a child under the age of 18 be deemed to be owned by a parent of the child for the purpose of determining whether the corporation is associated with any other corporation that is controlled by that parent or a group that includes that parent.

- **ITA 256(1.4) - Rights And Options**   This provision requires that rights to acquire shares be treated as though they were exercised for purposes of determining associated companies. This Subsection also indicates that, where a person has a right to require a shareholder to redeem, cancel, or acquire its own shares, for purposes of determining association, the corporation is deemed to have carried out the redemption, cancellation, or acquisition.

- **ITA 256(1.5) - Person Related To Himself, Herself, Or Itself**   This provision indicates that, where a person owns shares in two or more corporations, the person shall as shareholder of one of the corporations be deemed to be related to himself, herself or itself as shareholder of each of the other corporations.

ITA 256(2) - Association Through A Third Corporation   This provision indicates that two corporations, both of which are associated with a third corporation, are deemed to be associated with each other. This Subsection also includes an election that can mitigate this rule. The third corporation can elect to not be associated with the other two corporations. A consequence of this is that the third corporation's annual business limit will be set at nil. However, the election will allow the other two corporations to be exempt from the association rules under ITA 256(2).

14-39.   Given these definitions and rules, we are now in a position to look at the definition of associated companies as it is found in ITA 256(1).

Examples - Associated Corporation Rules

14-40.   The preceding definitions are essential to the understanding of the associated corporation rules found in ITA 256(1). This Subsection contains five Paragraphs designated (a) through (e), with each Paragraph describing a relationship involving association. These five Paragraphs will be given individual attention in the material that follows.

14-41. The first of these paragraphs indicates that one corporation is associated with another in a taxation year if, at any time in the year;

> **ITA 256(1)(a)** one of the corporations controlled, directly or indirectly in any manner whatever, the other.

14-42. This type of association can be illustrated by the situation shown in Figure 14-1 in which A Company owns 75 percent of the outstanding voting shares of B Company. In this situation, Company A and Company B are associated by virtue of ITA 256(1)(a).

14-43. The second Paragraph in ITA 256(1) indicates that one corporation is associated with another in a taxation year if, at any time in the year;

> **ITA 256(1)(b)** both of the corporations were controlled, directly or indirectly in any manner whatever, by the same person or group of persons.

Figure 14 - 1   [ITA 256(1)(a)]

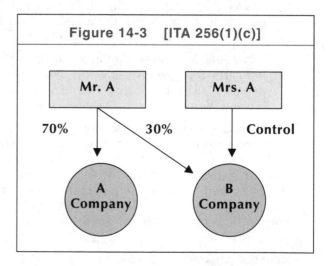

Figure 14 - 2   [ITA 256(1)(b)]

14-44. This type of association can be illustrated by the situation shown in Figure 14-2. In this situation, Mr. A owns 75 percent of the voting shares of both A Company and B Company. As a consequence, these two Companies are associated by virtue of ITA 256(1)(b), in that they are both controlled by the same person.

14-45. The third Paragraph in ITA 256(1) indicates that one corporation is associated with another in a taxation year if, at any time in the year;

> **ITA 256(1)(c)** each of the corporations was controlled, directly or indirectly in any manner whatever, by a person and the person who so controlled one of the corporations was related to the person who so controlled the other and either of those persons owned, in respect of each corporation, not less than 25 percent of the issued shares of any class, other than a specified class, of the capital stock thereof.

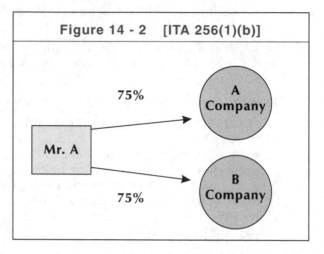

Figure 14-3   [ITA 256(1)(c)]

14-46. This type of association can be illustrated by the situation shown in Figure 14-3. In this situation, Mr. A owns 70 percent of the voting shares of A Company and his spouse, Mrs. A, owns 70 percent of the voting shares of B Company. In addition, Mr. A owns not less than 25 percent of the shares of B Company. Provided that the B Company shares owned by Mr. A are not of a specified class, Companies A and B are associated under ITA 256(1)(c). As the required cross ownership can be in either direction, the two Companies would also be associated if the cross ownership was by Mrs. A in A Company.

14-47. The fourth Paragraph in ITA 256(1) indicates that one corporation is associated with another in a taxation year if, at any time in the year;

ITA 256(1)(d) One of the corporations was controlled, directly or indirectly in any manner whatever, by a person and that person was related to each member of a group of persons that so controlled the other corporation, and that person owned, in respect of the other corporation, not less than 25 percent of the issued shares of any class, other than a specified class, of the capital stock thereof.

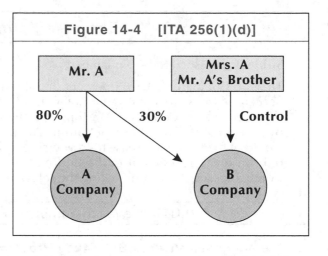

Figure 14-4 [ITA 256(1)(d)]

14-48. This type of association can be illustrated by the situation in Figure 14-4. In this situation, Mr. A owns 80 percent of the voting shares of A Company, while Mrs. A and Mr. A's brother each own 35 percent (70 percent in total) of the voting shares of B Company. This means that Mr. A is related to each member of a group that controls B Company. Mr. A also has the required cross ownership, in that he owns 30 percent of the shares of B Company. Provided that the shares of B Company owned by Mr. A are not of a specified class, A Company and B Company are associated by virtue of ITA 256(1)(d). Note that, under ITA 256(1)(d), the cross ownership has to be by Mr. A in B Company. If the cross ownership was in the other direction (e.g., Mrs. A owns 30 percent of A Company), the two Companies would not be associated under ITA 256(1)(d).

14-49. The final Paragraph in ITA 256(1) indicates that one corporation is associated with another in a taxation year if, at any time in the year;

ITA 256(1)(e) Each of the corporations was controlled, directly or indirectly in any manner whatever, by a related group and each of the members of one of the related groups was related to all of the members of the other related group, and one or more persons who were members of both related groups, either alone or together, owned, in respect of each corporation, not less than 25 percent of the issued shares of any class, other than a specified class, of the capital stock thereof.

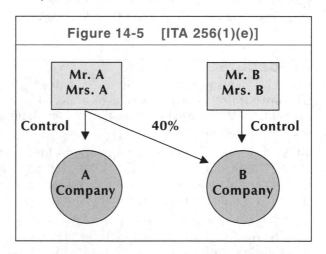

Figure 14-5 [ITA 256(1)(e)]

14-50. This type of association can be illustrated by the situation in Figure 14-5. Mr. and Mrs. A are a related group that control A Company, and Mr. and Mrs. B are a related group that control B Company. If we assume that Mrs. B is Mr. A's sister, then each member of one related group is related to all of the members of the other related group. Mr. and Mrs. A each own 50 percent of the voting shares of A Company, Mr. and Mrs. B each own 30 percent of the voting shares of B Company. Mr. A owns the remaining 40 percent of the voting shares of B Company. In this situation, A Company and B Company are associated under ITA 256(1)(e). Once again, Mr. A's cross ownership has to be shares other than those of a specified class. However, if A Company shares were available, the cross ownership could be in the other direction (e.g., Mrs. B owns not less than 25 percent of A Company).

Exercise Fourteen - 4

Subject: Associated Companies

The Top Company owns 65 percent of the shares of Middle Company, as well as 10 percent of the shares of Bottom Company. Middle Company owns 35 percent of the shares of Bottom Company. Mr. Top, who owns all of the shares of Top Company, also owns 5 percent of the shares of Bottom Company and has options in those shares that would, if exercised, increase his ownership by another 10 percent. Mr. Top's 12 year old son owns 15 percent of the Bottom Company shares. Indicate which of these Companies are associated, citing the relevant provisions of the *Income Tax Act*.

SOLUTION available in print and online Study Guide.

We suggest you work Self Study Problems Fourteen-3 and 4 at this point.

Investment Tax Credits

Background

14-51.   In terms of directing economic incentives to specific regions or types of activities, investment tax credits are a very effective tax policy tool. They can be used to provide tax reductions that are very specifically targeted (e.g., scientific research expenditures). In addition, by making some of them refundable, they can even provide benefits for enterprises with no Tax Payable.

14-52.   Despite their advantages in terms of targeting benefits, the use of investment tax credits has declined over the last 10 to 20 years. At one time, they were applicable to large classes of assets in broadly defined regions of Canada. At present, their use is confined to specific targeted areas. The ones that we will discuss in this Chapter are credits for salaries of eligible apprentices, current expenditures for scientific research, and the cost of qualified property.

Procedures

14-53.   Investment tax credits are tax incentives that are available to Canadian taxpayers who are earning business income or undertaking scientific research and experimental development. With some exceptions, they are available on the same terms for corporations as they are for individuals.

14-54.   In general terms, the procedures for investment tax credits, which are contained in ITA 127(5) through ITA 127.1(4), allow the taxpayer to deduct a specified percentage of the cost of certain types of current and capital expenditures from federal Tax Payable. The credits provide for a direct reduction in the amount of tax that is payable.

14-55.   When capital expenditures are involved, the amount of the investment tax credit must be removed from the capital cost of the asset, so that only the net capital cost is deductible through capital cost allowances (CCA). The legislation is such that the deduction from capital cost occurs in the taxation year following the year in which credit is claimed.

14-56.   The capital cost must also be reduced by any government or non-government assistance received or receivable for the property, such as grants or subsidies. However, the reduction for these other types of assistance is made in the year in which the assistance is received or receivable.

14-57.   When the investment tax credits are earned by making deductible current expenditures, the credits will be added to income in the following year.

14-58.   In effect, the tax mechanism that is involved with investment tax credits is that the enterprise gives up $1 of current or future tax deductions, in return for a $1 reduction in the amount of Tax Payable. This is clearly beneficial in that the cost of losing a $1 deduction is only $1 multiplied by the company's tax rate, a figure that could be below $0.15. By contrast, $1 of reduced tax payable is a cash flow savings of $1.

Eligible Expenditures

14-59. To provide a general picture of the applicability of investment tax credits, brief descriptions are provided of expenditures that qualify for these credits:

Salaries And Wages Of An Eligible Apprentice   An eligible apprentice is defined in ITA 127(9) and can be described as follows:

> **Eligible apprentice** means an individual who is employed in Canada in a prescribed trade (a trade currently listed as a "Red Seal Trade") in the first two years of their apprenticeship contract. This contract must be registered with a federal, provincial or territorial government under an apprenticeship program designed to certify or license individuals in the trade.

Qualified Property is defined in ITA 127(9) with further elaboration provided in ITR 4600 and 4601. As presented in this material, qualified property must be newly acquired primarily for use in Canada, and it must be available for use in specified activities. These activities include manufacturing and processing, logging, farming or fishing, and storing grain.

Qualified Scientific Research And Experimental Development (SR&ED) Expenditures includes current expenditures for basic or applied research, and for the development of new products and processes. (Capital expenditures do not qualify for SR&ED credits.) The rules related to SR&ED expenditures are extremely complex and the application of these rules goes beyond the scope of this introductory text. As a result, we provide only very limited coverage of this topic and do not include coverage of what qualifies as SR&ED expenditures.

Rates
General
14-60. Current rates for the investment tax credits that we have described are as follows:

Type Of Expenditure	Rate
Salaries And Wages Of Eligible Apprentices	
(Limited To The First $20,000 Of Salaries And Wages For Each Apprentice)	10%
Qualified Property	
In Atlantic Provinces And Gaspe Peninsula	10%
Prescribed Offshore Regions (East Coast)	10%
Rest Of Canada	Nil
Scientific Research And Experimental Development	
Incurred By Any Taxpayer	15%
Incurred By CCPCs (See Paragraph 14-61)	35%

Exercise Fourteen - 5

Subject: Investment Tax Credit Procedures

During 2018, Colus Inc. pays salaries to five eligible apprentices totalling $125,000 ($25,000 per apprentice). In addition, it acquires $3,000,000 in Class 53 assets on which a 10 percent investment tax credit is available. Describe the 2018 and 2019 tax consequences associated with making these expenditures and claiming the related investment tax credits. Include in your solution the CCA for 2018 and 2019.

SOLUTION available in print and online Study Guide.

Special Rate On SR&ED Expenditures By CCPCs

14-61.   With respect to the 35 percent rate for SR&ED expenditures, this overall rate results from providing an additional 20 percent for some expenditures made by a corporation that is a CCPC throughout a taxation year under ITA 127(10.1).

14-62.   Assuming that the corporation is not associated with any other corporations, the amount on which this 35 percent rate is applicable is limited by ITA 127(10.2) as follows:

Annual Expenditure Limit = ($8 million – 10A) x [($40 million – B) ÷ $40 million]

Where

A   is the greater of $500,000 and the corporation's Taxable Income for the preceding taxation year.

B   is nil if the corporation's Taxable Capital Employed In Canada for the preceding taxation year is $10 million or less. If it exceeds $10 million, B is equal to the lesser of $40 million and the amount by which the Taxable Capital Employed In Canada exceeds $10 million.

14-63.   If a CCPC has previous year Taxable Income that is less than $500,000 and previous year Taxable Capital Employed In Canada of less than $10 million, the limit on which the 35 percent investment tax credit will be applicable is $3 million. However, the formula contains two factors which will serve to limit this amount:

- If the CCPC's Taxable Income for the preceding year exceeds $500,000, the limit will be reduced by $10 for every $1 of the excess. The limit will be completely eliminated when the Taxable Income for the previous year reaches $800,000 [$8,000,000 - (10)($800,000) = Nil].

- If the CCPC's Taxable Capital Employed In Canada for the preceding year exceeds $10 million, the limit will be reduced by $3 for every $40 of the excess. It will be completely eliminated when the Taxable Capital Employed In Canada for the preceding year reaches $50 million as shown in the following calculation:

$$[\$3 \text{ Million}]\left[\frac{\$40 \text{ Million} - (\$50 \text{ Million} - \$10 \text{ Million})}{\$40 \text{ Million}}\right] = \text{Nil}$$

Exercise Fourteen - 6

Subject: SR&ED Credits For CCPCs

Anfax has been a CCPC since it began operations and has a taxation year ending on December 31.   It had Taxable Income of $560,000 for 2017 and $500,000 for 2018. Its Taxable Capital Employed In Canada equaled $12,500,000 for 2017 and $11,500,000 for 2018. Determine its annual SR & ED expenditure limit for 2018.

SOLUTION available in print and online Study Guide.

Refundable Investment Tax Credits

General Rules - 40 Percent Refund

14-64.   A problem with tax credits is that, in general, they have value only when the taxpayer has a tax liability. To deal with this problem, some tax credits are "refundable". What this means is that, when a taxpayer has earned a tax credit and does not have sufficient Tax Payable to use it in full, the government will pay ("refund") all or part of the unused amount to the taxpayer. We have encountered this type of situation previously for individuals with respect to the refundable medical expense supplement tax credit (see Chapter 4).

14-65.   A refund can be made for up to 40 percent of the investment tax credits earned by a taxpayer, provided the taxpayer is:

- an individual;
- a "qualifying corporation", which is a Canadian controlled private corporation throughout the year with Taxable Income in the previous year, less an adjustment for Taxable Capital Employed In Canada (which is the same as the one illustrated in Paragraph 14-63), that is $500,000 or less before loss carry backs; or
- a trust where each beneficiary is an individual or a qualifying corporation.

14-66.   This means that if an individual had $1,000,000 in SR&ED current expenditures, he would be eligible for a $150,000 [(15%)($1,000,000)] investment tax credit. If the individual did not have sufficient Tax Payable in the current year or the three previous years to use this credit, there would be a refund (payment) of up to $60,000 [(40%)($150,000)].

Additional Refund - 100 Percent Refund
14-67.   In the case of a qualifying corporation, additional amounts are refundable. To the extent that current SR&ED expenditures are eligible for the 35 percent investment tax credit, the resulting credit is eligible for a 100 percent refund. This means that a qualifying corporation that spends $3,000,000 on current SR&ED expenditures is eligible for a refund payment of up to $1,050,000 [(35%)($3,000,000)] from the government (qualifying corporations are described in Paragraph 14-65).

14-68.   The 100 percent refund is only available on the first $3,000,000 of expenditures that qualify for the 35 percent investment tax credit. We would remind you that capital expenditures do not qualify for SR&ED credits.

Carry Overs Of Investment Tax Credits
14-69.   Under the definition of investment tax credit in ITA 127(9), unused investment tax credits may be carried back for up to 3 years and forward for 20 years. A taxpayer is required to claim all other available tax credits before calculating and claiming the investment tax credit for the year. Also, a taxpayer must reduce, to the fullest extent possible, federal Tax Payable for the current year before using investment tax credits to reduce previous years' federal Tax Payable.

Exercise Fourteen - 7

Subject: Refundable Investment Tax Credits

Sci-Tech Inc. has made a number of expenditures that qualify for investment tax credits. They have invested $123,000 in Qualified Property in Nova Scotia. In addition, they have $1,200,000 in current expenditures for scientific research and experimental development. The Company is a Canadian controlled private corporation and, for the previous taxation year, has Taxable Income of $176,000 and Taxable Capital Employed In Canada of $6,000,000. The Company has no Tax Payable for the current year or the three previous years.

Determine the amount of the refund that Sci-Tech will receive as a result of earning these investment tax credits and any available carry forwards. Include in your answer any other tax consequences of these investment tax credits.

SOLUTION available in print and online Study Guide.

We suggest you work Self Study Problem Fourteen-5 at this point.

Effect Of Acquisition Of Control On Investment Tax Credits
14-70.   As was the case with companies having accumulated loss carry forwards, the government is concerned about the large amount of unused investment tax credits that are being

carried forward in the tax records of Canadian corporations. The carry forwards reflect the fact that these corporations have experienced losses and, as a consequence, have not had a tax liability to which the non-refundable credits could be applied.

14-71.   While the government does not object to these credits being used against Tax Payable resulting from improved profitability for the corporations that have experienced losses, there is concern that these loss corporations will be acquired by profitable corporations in order to make use of these credits. As a consequence, there are acquisition of control rules that apply to the carry forward of investment tax credits.

14-72.   These rules are found in ITA 127(9.1) and (9.2). Their effect was described in the cancelled IT-151R5, Scientific Research and Experimental Development Expenditures as follows:

> If control of a corporation has been acquired ... subsection 127(9) may apply to restrict the availability of the corporation's investment tax credits. In general, these provisions limit the application of investment tax credits to the tax on the income from a particular business carried on by the corporation before the acquisition of control or any other business substantially all the income of which is from the sale, leasing, rental, or development of properties or the rendering of services similar to those of the particular business carried on by the corporation before the acquisition of control.

14-73.   As you can see, the effect of these provisions is to treat investment tax credits in a manner similar to the treatment of non-capital loss carry forwards when there is an acquisition of control.

Tax Basis Shareholders' Equity

Shareholders' Equity Under GAAP

14-74.   In this Chapter, we will be considering various distributions to shareholders. In order to comprehend this material, some understanding of the tax basis components of shareholders' equity is required.

14-75.   You should be familiar with the components of Shareholders' Equity as they appear in a Balance Sheet prepared using generally accepted accounting principles (GAAP). The two basic components of the total balance disclosed are:

Contributed Capital   This is the amount that has been paid by investors in return for shares issued. In jurisdictions where par value shares can still be used, this balance may be divided into par value amounts and an excess over par amount, commonly designated contributed surplus.

Earned Capital (Retained Earnings)   This component reflects amounts that have been earned by the corporation and retained in the business. While this balance is sometimes referred to as earned surplus, the more common designation is retained earnings. In some situations, part of this balance may be designated as reserves.

14-76.   This segregation into contributed and earned capital is based on the general legal requirement that dividends cannot be paid out of contributed capital. By using this disclosure, investors are informed as to the legal basis for payment of dividends by the corporation. However, this legal basis may not be supported by the cash resources that would be needed to, in fact, pay cash dividends.

Paid Up Capital (Tax Basis Contributed Capital)

14-77.   ITA 89(1) defines paid up capital, normally referred to as "PUC". This Subsection indicates that the amount should be calculated without reference to the *Income Tax Act*, telling us that PUC should be based on legal stated capital as determined under the legislation governing the particular corporation (*Canada Business Corporations Act* or relevant provincial legislation). As contributed capital under GAAP is also based on legal stated capital, the initial PUC for shares issued will generally be equal to contributed capital under GAAP. However, as will be discussed in this and subsequent Chapters, there will be adjustments to PUC that have no equivalent adjustment under GAAP.

14-78.   PUC is applied on an average per share basis to each class of shares. This means, for example, that if a corporation issues 100,000 shares to one individual at $10 per share and, at a later point in time, issues an additional 100,000 shares of the same class to a different individual at $15 per share, the per share PUC will be $12.50 for all of the shares of that class. Stated alternatively, all shares of a particular class will have the same per share PUC value.

14-79.   Note the difference between the PUC value per share and the adjusted cost base (ACB) of a share. The ACB of a share is the average cost of the shares held by a particular shareholder. In the example in Paragraph 14-78, the taxpayer acquiring the first issue has an adjusted cost base of $10 per share, while the purchaser of the second issue has an adjusted cost base of $15 per share.

14-80.   The importance of PUC lies in the fact that it is a capital contribution and does not reflect accumulated earnings of the corporation. Because of this, it can be distributed to shareholders as a return of capital (subject to any restrictions imposed by corporate law), without tax consequences for either the corporation, or the shareholder. This may not be the case, however, when capital distributions are made to shareholders of public corporations.

Exercise Fourteen - 8

Subject: Determination Of PUC And Adjusted Cost Base

Halide Ltd. has one class of shares. The Company issued its first 100,000 shares at a price of $1.10 each. Two years later, an additional 50,000 shares were issued for $1.35 per share. During the current year, a further 30,000 shares were issued for $1.82 per share. One of the investors in the Company acquired 2,400 shares of the first group of shares issued, and an additional 3,850 shares from the most recent issue. Determine the adjusted cost base per share, as well as the total PUC of this investor's shares.

SOLUTION available in print and online Study Guide.

Tax Basis Retained Earnings
Amount
14-81.   The situation with respect to Retained Earnings is much more complex. To begin, we will be dealing with a different total for tax purposes. As you are aware, there are significant differences between accounting Net Income and Net Income For Tax Purposes.

14-82.   While the accounting literature defines accounting/tax differences as temporary differences with reference to Balance Sheet accounts (e.g., the difference between the Net Book Value and the UCC of a depreciable asset), most of these Balance Sheet differences are created by Income Statement differences (e.g., the difference between Amortization Expense and CCA). As a result, total Retained Earnings as determined under GAAP will, in most cases, be a significantly different number than the corresponding tax figure.

14-83.   A further point here relates to terminology. In general, the term Retained Earnings has replaced Earned Surplus in accounting literature and in published financial statements. However, the term surplus is still alive and well in tax work. As evidence, we would note that the *Income Tax Act* contains only 11 references to Retained Earnings, in contrast to 206 references to Surplus.

Basic Components
14-84.   Moving beyond the differences in the total amount, we encounter further problems in relating tax and GAAP figures. Under GAAP, Retained Earnings is often a single

homogeneous balance. While some companies still segregate parts of this balance into reserves, such components have no formal meaning beyond assisting with disclosure.

14-85.   In contrast, the corresponding tax balance has four components, each with a well defined role in tax work. The four components are as follows:

- Capital Dividend Account (private companies only)
- Post-1971 Undistributed Surplus
- Pre-1972 Undistributed Surplus (no longer covered in this text)
- Pre-1972 Capital Surplus On Hand (no longer covered in this text)

14-86.   The Capital Dividend Account is only available to private companies. It is discussed in detail in this Chapter beginning at Paragraph 14-90.

14-87.   "Post-1971 Undistributed Surplus" tracks the earnings retained after 1971 that do not have any special tax status.

14-88.   In Chapter 8 we noted that, prior to 1972, capital gains were not subject to tax in Canada. The 1972 introduction of capital gains taxation resulted in the need to have a complex set of transitional rules to avoid taxation of gains accrued prior to that date. Although at one time these rules were very important, with the passage of time this is no longer the case.

14-89.   "Pre-1972 Undistributed Surplus" is simply earnings that accrued prior to 1972 that are retained in the corporation. The "Pre-1972 Capital Surplus On Hand" tracks capital gains and losses that accrued prior to 1972, but were realized after 1971. Such transactions are no longer of sufficient importance to warrant coverage in a general text such as this.

Capital Dividend Account (CDA)
Objective
14-90.   The objective of the Capital Dividend Account (CDA) is to track items that can be distributed on a tax free basis to the shareholders of the corporation. While a number of different items can be included in this account, the reason for its use can best be understood in the context of capital gains.

> **EXAMPLE**   During 2015, Uval Ltd. acquires land at a cost of $150,000. During 2018, the land is sold for $190,000, resulting in a capital gain of $40,000 ($190,000 - $150,000).

> **ANALYSIS**   It is the intent of tax legislation to assess tax on only one-half of capital gains. This means that Uval will have a taxable capital gain of $20,000 [(1/2)($40,000)]. However, the remaining $20,000 is still being held by the corporation. While the goal of tax legislation is not to have taxes assessed on this balance, in the absence of some special provision, its distribution would be subject to tax in the hands of the recipient shareholders.

14-91.   The CDA provides the required relief in this situation. The untaxed balance of $20,000 will be added to the CDA. This balance can then be used to pay a capital dividend, a special type of dividend that can be distributed tax free to the shareholders of the corporation. Such dividends will be discussed in more detail at a later point in this chapter.

14-92.   While this analysis would appear to be relevant to all types of corporations, only private corporations can have a CDA. Note, however, the use of this account is available to private corporations, without regard to whether they are Canadian controlled.

Procedures
14-93.   As indicated in the preceding section, there are a number of different items that can be allocated to the capital dividend account. The complete definition of these items is found in ITA 89(1) and is very complex. Without becoming involved in some of the more complex issues found in that Subsection, the basic components of the CDA are as follows:

Capital Dividends Received   Capital dividends received from other corporations are added to the CDA. This preserves the tax free status of non-taxable amounts that pass through more than one corporation.

Capital Gains   The non-taxable portion of realized net capital gains are accumulated in the CDA account, with this balance being reduced by the non-deductible portion of realized capital losses (this would include 100 percent of the gain on publicly traded shares that have been gifted to a registered Canadian charity).

Note that this component of the CDA cannot become negative and reduce the aggregate amount of the other CDA components, like capital dividends received.

EXAMPLE   In 2013, a resident private corporation realizes a capital loss of $15,000, the non-deductible portion of which is $7,500. In 2015, it realizes a capital gain of $10,000, the non-taxable portion of which is $5,000. In 2018, it receives a capital dividend of $1,000.

ANALYSIS   While the net of the capital gains component of the CDA is a negative amount of $2,500, the balance of this component in the CDA would be nil. The overall balance in the CDA is $1,000 (the capital dividend received).

Life Insurance Proceeds   Life insurance proceeds received by the corporation are added to the account, net of the adjusted cost base of the policy. This can be an important addition when the company insures the life of one or more of its shareholders. This is a common procedure in owner-managed businesses, where life insurance proceeds are sometimes used to finance the buyout of the shares from the estate of a deceased shareholder.

Capital Dividends Paid   The account is reduced by capital dividends paid. As will be discussed in Paragraph 14-109, an ITA 83(2) election is required.

Exercise Fourteen - 9

Subject: Capital Dividend Account

The following transactions involve the Knerd Corporation's capital dividend account:

- In 2016, they sold land with an adjusted cost base of $86,000, for cash of $108,000.

- During the year ending December 31, 2017, the Company received a capital dividend of $8,200.

- On July 15, 2018, they sold goodwill for proceeds of $43,000. The goodwill had been internally developed and was not reflected in the Company's records. On January 1, 2018, there was a nil balance in the Company's Class 14.1 UCC.

- On October 31, 2018, the Company paid an ITA 83(2) capital dividend of $16,000. The appropriate election was made.

Determine the balance in the capital dividend account at December 31, 2018.

SOLUTION available in print and online Study Guide.

We suggest you work Self Study Problems Fourteen-6 and 7 at this point.

Distributions Of Corporate Surplus

Introduction

14-94.   Corporate surplus, generally referred to by accountants as Retained Earnings, forms the basis for various distributions to shareholders of a corporation. This happens most commonly through the cash dividends that are paid by most Canadian companies. Less commonly, we encounter stock dividends and dividends in kind (distributions of corporate assets other than cash).

14-95.   These fairly routine types of dividends were given coverage in Chapter 7 in our material on property income. However, they will be reviewed at this point as an introduction to the various types of deemed dividends that are under consideration here. We will also give further attention to ITA 83(2) capital dividends.

14-96.   In addition to these various types of actual dividends, several types of deemed dividends can occur. The specific types of deemed dividends that will be covered in this section of Chapter 14 are as follows:

- ITA 84(1) Deemed Dividend on Increase of PUC
- ITA 84(2) Deemed Dividend on Winding Up or Reorganization of a Business
- ITA 84(3) Deemed Dividend on Redemption, Acquisition, or Cancellation of Shares
- ITA 84(4) and (4.1) Deemed Dividend on Reduction of PUC

14-97.   With the exception of capital dividends, all of the dividends considered here are subject to taxes when they are actually received or deemed to be received by an individual. This means that, provided they are received from a taxable Canadian corporation, they will generally be subject to the dividend gross up and tax credit procedures. In those situations where they are designated as such by the payor, they will be treated as eligible dividends.

14-98.   When such dividends are received by a corporation, rather than by an individual, there will be no gross up of the amount, nor any credit against corporate tax payable. The recipient corporation will include only the amount received in their Net Income For Tax Purposes. Further, this amount will generally be deducted in the determination of Taxable Income.

Regular Cash Dividends

14-99.   Regular cash dividends are paid out of a corporation's unrestricted surplus balances. The payment of cash dividends serves to reduce these balances. Unlike the payment of interest on debt, the payment of cash dividends does not create a tax deduction for the corporation. In effect, they are paid out of after tax funds.

14-100.   If cash dividends are received by an individual or a trust, they are subject to the usual gross up and tax credit procedures. In contrast, if they are paid to another corporation, they are included in the corporation's Net Income For Tax Purposes, but deducted in the determination of the corporation's Taxable Income.

14-101.   A further point here relates to the accounting treatment of dividends on certain types of preferred shares. IAS 32, *Financial Instruments - Presentation*, recommends that shares which require mandatory redemption by the issuer be classified as liabilities. Consistent with this, the dividend payments on these shares must be disclosed as interest, resulting in the amount of the distribution being deducted in the determination of accounting net income.

14-102.   To date, this treatment has not been recognized by the CRA. From a tax point of view, the dividends paid on preferred shares with mandatory redemption provisions will be given the same treatment as any other dividend. This means that, even if the GAAP based financial statements of the enterprise present preferred dividends as interest expense, they will not be deductible to the paying corporation. This difference will require adjustment in converting accounting income to a corporation's Net Income For Tax Purposes.

Stock Dividends

14-103.   From an accounting perspective, a stock dividend is a pro rata distribution of new shares to the existing shareholder group of the corporation, normally accompanied by a capitalization of Retained Earnings equal to the fair market value of the shares issued.

> **EXAMPLE**   Jessica Rabin owns 100 shares of Fergis Ltd. She acquired these shares several years ago for $2,500 ($25 per share). On January 1, 2018, the Shareholders' Equity of Fergis Ltd. is as follows:

No Par Common Stock (1,000,000 Shares)	$ 7,500,000
Retained Earnings	12,500,000
Total Shareholders' Equity	$20,000,000

On December 31, 2018, the publicly traded shares of Fergis have a fair market value of $30 per share. On this date, the Company declares a 10 percent stock dividend (100,000 shares). This dividend is not designated as eligible.

> **ANALYSIS - Fergis Ltd.**   At the time of the stock dividend, Fergis would transfer an amount equal to the $3,000,000 [($30)(10%)(1,000,000)] fair market value of these shares from Retained Earnings to the contributed capital account. Subsequent to this transfer, the Shareholders' Equity of Fergis would be as follows:

No Par Common Stock (1,100,000 Shares)	$10,500,000
Retained Earnings ($12,500,000 - $3,000,000)	9,500,000
Total Shareholders' Equity	$20,000,000

From a tax point of view, the $3,000,000 increase in contributed capital would generally be an increase in PUC, reflecting an increase in the amount that could be distributed to the shareholders of the company on a tax free basis.

> **ANALYSIS - Jessica Rabin**   As a result of the stock dividend, she will receive 10 shares [(10%)(100)] of stock worth $300 [(10)($30)]. This dividend will be taxable to the extent that it reflects an increase in PUC. Provided the increase in the Fergis Ltd. PUC is equal to the $3,000,000 increase in Contributed Capital (the usual case), Jessica will have a dividend of $300 [($3,000,000)(100 ÷ 1,000,000)]. This non-eligible dividend will be grossed up to a taxable amount of $348 [($300)(116%)].

> With respect to the adjusted cost base of the new shares, ITA 52(3) will deem her to have acquired 10 additional shares at a cost of $300. With this addition, the average per share adjusted cost base would be $25.45 [($2,500 + $300) ÷ 110].

> **Note On PUC**   In most accounting and tax texts, the usual procedure is to transfer an amount equal to the fair market value of the dividend shares issued to Retained Earnings. However, this may not be the case. In some provinces, the amount of legal stated capital to be assigned to the dividend shares is discretionary. If the assigned amount is a value that is lower than fair market value, the corresponding transfer to PUC will be lower. This results in a lower taxable value for the stock dividend and a smaller addition to the adjusted cost base of the shares.

14-104.   These stock dividend rules create an unfortunate situation for the taxpayer. An individual receiving stock dividends will require a cash outflow (taxes on the dividend received) with no corresponding cash inflows (the dividends are not received in cash). This approach to the taxation of stock dividends serves to significantly discourage their use in Canada, particularly in the case of large publicly traded companies.

14-105.   As noted, however, it is possible for a company to issue shares with a legal stated capital and a PUC that is less than fair market value. When this is the case, the negative tax effect that was described in the preceding paragraph can be reduced.

Exercise Fourteen - 10

Subject: Stock Dividends

On June 30, 2018, the Shareholders' Equity of Sturgis Inc. is as follows:

Common Stock (23,400 Shares Outstanding)	$351,000
Retained Earnings	462,000
Total Shareholders' Equity	$813,000

On this date, the Company declares a 5 percent stock dividend. This dividend is not designated as eligible. At this time, the shares are trading at $25 per share. The Company increases its PUC by the fair market value of the new shares issued.

Jean Tessier is holding 1,000 of the Sturgis shares which he acquired several years ago at a cost of $18 per share. Determine the effect of this transaction on Jean's 2018 Net Income For Tax Purposes and 2018 federal Tax Payable. In addition, determine the adjusted cost base per share of his Sturgis Inc. holding.

SOLUTION available in print and online Study Guide.

Dividends In Kind

14-106.   While somewhat unusual, corporations do sometimes declare dividends that are payable in assets other than cash, or the corporation's own shares. An example of this might be a situation in which a corporation has a major holding of another corporation's shares and wishes to dispose of them. If the block is large, sale on the open market could significantly depress the proceeds received. A possible alternative is to distribute the shares on a pro rata basis to the corporation's existing shareholders.

14-107.   From the point of view of the corporation, the dividend is treated as a disposition of the distributed property. Under ITA 52(2), the proceeds of disposition will be deemed to be the fair market value of the property distributed. Depending on the type of property, this could result in a capital gain, capital loss, recapture or terminal loss for the corporation.

14-108.   Also under ITA 52(2), the shareholders are deemed to have acquired the assets at their fair market value. This amount is considered to be a taxable dividend subject to the usual gross up and tax credit procedures for eligible and non-eligible dividends.

> **EXAMPLE**   Hold Ltd. owns shares in Bold Inc. These shares have an adjusted cost base of $800,000 and a fair market value of $3,500,000. Hold Ltd. decides to distribute the Bold Inc. shares as a dividend in kind to its shareholders, all of whom are individuals.
>
> **ANALYSIS**   The tax consequences of this dividend are as follows:
>
> * Based on deemed proceeds of $3,500,000, Hold Ltd. will have a taxable capital gain of $1,350,000 [(1/2)($3,500,000 - $800,000)].
>
> * Hold Ltd. will have declared a dividend of $3,500,000.
>
> * The shareholders will have received a taxable dividend of $3,500,000, subject to either the eligible or non-eligible dividend gross up and tax credit procedures.
>
> * The adjusted cost base of the Bold Inc. shares to the Hold Ltd. shareholders will be $3,500,000.

Exercise Fourteen - 11

Subject: Dividends In Kind

Sandrine Cloutier owns 15 percent of the 500,000 outstanding shares of Cloutier Ltd. Cloutier Ltd. owns 150,000 shares of Botan Inc. The Botan Inc. shares were acquired at a cost of $42 per share and have a current fair market value of $51 per share. On June 30, 2018, Cloutier Ltd. declares a non-eligible dividend involving the distribution of all of the Botan shares on a pro rata basis to its existing shareholders.

Determine the effect of the payment of this dividend on Cloutier Ltd.'s 2018 Net Income For Tax Purposes. In addition, determine the effect of the payment of this dividend on Sandrine Cloutier's 2018 Net Income For Tax Purposes and 2018 federal Tax Payable.

SOLUTION available in print and online Study Guide.

Capital Dividends Under ITA 83(2)

14-109.   As we have previously indicated, the balance in the capital dividend account reflects amounts that can be distributed on a tax free basis to the shareholders of the private corporation. However, this tax free status does not happen automatically. When a corporation makes a distribution, an amount not in excess of the balance in the capital dividend account can be designated as a capital dividend. This is accomplished through an election under ITA 83(2), using Form T2054. Note that, provided there is a balance in the capital dividend account, this election can be made both for regular and for deemed dividends.

14-110.   Distributing a capital dividend reduces the balance in the capital dividend account. It will be received by the taxpayer, whether the taxpayer is a corporation, a trust or an individual, on a tax free basis with no reduction in the adjusted cost base of their shares. You will also recall that, if the recipient of the capital dividend is a private corporation, the amount of the dividend will be added to the recipient corporation's capital dividend account.

14-111.   If an election is made to pay a capital dividend in excess of the balance in the capital dividend account, a tax equal to 60 percent of the excess will be assessed under ITA 184(2) of the *Income Tax Act*. This will not affect the tax free nature of the dividend to the recipient.

14-112.   In some circumstances, an excess election can occur inadvertently. For example, the non-taxable portion of a capital gain may be added to the capital dividend account and, at a subsequent point in time, a reassessment will cause the capital gain to be recharacterized as business, rather than capital. This in turn means that the capital dividend account will be reduced through the reassessment process. If this happens, ITA 184(3) and 184(4) contain provisions that allow for a revision of the election in order to avoid the 60 percent penalty.

14-113.   As a final point, the fact that capital dividends are not taxable dividends means that they are not subject to the dividend gross up and tax credit procedures. In turn, this means that they cannot be classified as either eligible or non-eligible dividends under any circumstances.

Deemed Dividends Under ITA 84(1) - Increase In PUC
General Rules
14-114.   ITA 84(1) dividends involve a situation where there has been an increase in the corporation's PUC, accompanied by a smaller increase in the net assets of the corporation. This would include situations where the increase in PUC is accompanied by no increase in the net assets of the corporation.

14-115.   The most common example of this type of deemed dividend would involve situations where a corporation issues shares to settle a debt obligation that has a carrying value that is smaller than the fair market value of the shares.

EXAMPLE   A corporation issues shares with a PUC of $500,000 to a creditor, in settlement of debt with a carrying value of $450,000. Because of a decline in interest rates since the debt was issued, the $500,000 reflects the market value of the debt.

ANALYSIS   This transaction would result in an ITA 84(1) deemed dividend of $50,000 ($500,000 - $450,000).

14-116.   The reason for treating this $50,000 as a form of income to the shareholders is that it represents an increase in the amount that can be distributed to them on a tax free basis. As a group, their economic position has clearly been improved as a result of this transaction.

14-117.   It is important to note that, because the extra $50,000 in PUC will be allocated to all of the shareholders of the particular class, a corresponding treatment will be given to the deemed dividend. That is, the $50,000 dividend will be allocated on a pro rata basis to all of the shareholders of the class, not just the new shareholder who acquired his shares by giving up $450,000 in debt securities.

14-118.   In order to provide equity in this situation, the amount assessed as a dividend will be added to the adjusted cost base of the shares. For the new shareholder, his share of the $50,000 ITA 84(1) deemed dividend is added to the adjusted cost base of the shares that were issued to him, resulting in an adjusted cost base for these shares of $450,000 plus his share of the deemed dividend. Note that this will not be the PUC of these shares, since PUC is calculated as an average value for all of the outstanding shares on a class by class basis.

EXAMPLE   Lantin Inc. has 250,000 shares outstanding at the beginning of the current year. These shares were sold for $12 each, resulting in a PUC of $3,000,000. Jeanne Moreau owns 25,000 of these shares which she acquired at the time of their issue for $12 each.

During the current year, the company issues 50,000 new shares with a market value of $750,000 ($15 per share) in order to retire debt with a carrying value of $675,000.

Shortly after the 50,000 new shares were issued, Ms. Moreau sells her 25,000 shares for $450,000 ($18 per share).

ANALYSIS   The ITA 84(1) deemed dividend will be calculated as follows:

PUC Of New Shares [(50,000)($15)]	$750,000
Increase In Net Assets (Carrying Value Of Debt Retired)	(675,000)
ITA 84(1) Deemed Dividend	$ 75,000

This would be allocated to all of the outstanding shares in the amount of $0.25 ($75,000 ÷ 300,000) per share. This would be a taxable dividend, subject to either the eligible or non-eligible dividend gross up and tax credit procedures.

With respect to Ms. Moreau's holding, this $0.25 per share dividend would increase her per share adjusted cost base to $12.25 ($12.00 + $0.25). Given this, the tax consequences of her sale would be calculated as follows:

Proceeds Of Disposition [(25,000)($18)]	$450,000
Adjusted Cost Base [(25,000)($12.25)]	(306,250)
Capital Gain	$143,750
Inclusion Rate	1/2
Taxable Capital Gain	$ 71,875

Exercise Fourteen - 12

Subject: ITA 84(1) Deemed Dividends

At the beginning of the current year, Unilev Inc. has 126,000 shares of common stock outstanding. The shares were originally issued at $10.50 per share for total proceeds of $1,323,000, with this amount constituting the PUC. During the current year, a creditor holding $450,000 of the Company's debt agrees to accept 40,000 newly issued common shares of the Company in exchange for settlement of the debt obligation. At the time of this exchange, the shares are trading at $12.70 per share.

Subsequent to the exchange, Mr. Uni, who had purchased 5,000 Unilev Inc. shares at the time of their original issue, sells the shares for $13.42 per share.

Describe the tax consequence(s) to all of the shareholders of Unilev Inc. as a result of the exchange of debt for common shares. In addition, describe the tax consequences to Mr. Uni resulting from the sale of his Unilev Inc. shares.

SOLUTION available in print and online Study Guide.

Excluded Transactions

14-119. There are a number of transactions involving increases in PUC that are specifically excluded from the ITA 84(1) deemed dividend treatment. The most important of these are:

- **Stock Dividends** While there will be an increase in PUC in excess of the increase in net assets when a stock dividend is declared, such dividends are not considered to be an ITA 84(1) deemed dividend. Rather, they are taxed under ITA 82(1) as regular dividends. From the point of view of the recipient of the dividend, this distinction is of no consequence.

- **Shifts Between Classes** When the PUC of one class of shares is decreased and, at the same time, the PUC of a different class is increased by a corresponding amount, there is no ITA 84(1) deemed dividend.

- **Conversion Of Contributed Surplus** In situations where the consideration received for shares issued is in excess of the amount added to PUC, for tax purposes a contributed surplus balance is created. This contributed surplus balance can generally be converted to PUC, without the increase in PUC being treated as a deemed dividend under ITA 84(1).

Deemed Dividends Under ITA 84(2) - On Winding-Up

14-120. When there is a winding-up of a Canadian corporation under the provisions of ITA 88(2), the corporate assets will be sold and the liabilities, including taxes on the various types of income created by the sale of the assets, will be paid. The remaining cash will then be distributed to the shareholders of the corporation. Subsequent to this distribution, the shares of the corporation will be canceled. This process is covered in detail in Chapter 17.

14-121. In this Chapter, we would note that ITA 84(2) indicates that the excess of the fair market value of the amount distributed over the PUC of the shares that are canceled is considered to be a deemed dividend. While ITA 84(2) defines this entire amount as a deemed dividend, some components of this total are, in effect, redefined under ITA 88(2)(b). Specifically, ITA 88(2)(b) indicates that the ITA 84(2) dividend will be dealt with as follows:

Capital Dividend To the extent that the corporation has a balance in its capital dividend account, ITA 88(2)(b) indicates that this amount of the distribution will be considered a separate dividend, which will be received on a tax free basis under ITA 83(2). As was noted in our discussion of capital dividends, this treatment will only apply if an appropriate election is made.

Distribution Of Pre-1972 Capital Surplus On Hand   As mentioned previously in this Chapter, the importance of Pre-1972 Capital Surplus On Hand has diminished greatly over time and is no longer of importance to most users of a general text such as this. However we would point out here that if the corporation has pre-1972 Capital Surplus On Hand, the distribution of this amount will be deemed not to be a dividend.

Taxable Dividend   Any remaining distribution will be treated as a taxable dividend under ITA 84(2), subject to either the eligible or non-eligible dividend gross up and tax credit procedures.

14-122.   To illustrate these provisions, consider the following:

EXAMPLE   After selling its assets and paying all of its liabilities, a corporation has cash of $1,200,000 available for distribution to its only shareholder. The PUC of the company's shares is $100,000 and this is also their adjusted cost base. The balance in the capital dividend account is $175,000. The company makes the appropriate election to have the distribution of the $175,000 treated as a capital dividend under ITA 83(2).

ANALYSIS   The analysis of the $1,200,000 distribution would be as follows:

Cash Distributed	$1,200,000
PUC Of Shares	(100,000)
ITA 84(2) Deemed Dividend	$1,100,000
ITA 83(2) Capital Dividend	(175,000)
ITA 88(2)(b) Taxable Dividend	$ 925,000

Depending on whether or not the $925,000 wind-up dividend, or some portion of it, is designated as eligible, it would be subject to either the eligible or non-eligible dividend gross up and tax credit procedures.

14-123.   From the point of view of the shareholder, there has been a disposition of his shares, an event that requires the determination of a capital gain or loss. In the absence of a mitigating provision, this capital gain or loss would be calculated using the $1,200,000 as the proceeds of disposition, an approach that would double count $1,100,000 of this amount as both a deemed dividend and a capital gain or loss.

14-124.   Fortunately, this problem is resolved by the ITA 54 definition of "proceeds of disposition". This definition indicates that, to the extent that an amount received is considered to be a deemed dividend under ITA 84(2), it is excluded from the proceeds of disposition. This means that the capital gain on the disposition of the shares in the example would be calculated as follows:

Cash Distributed	$1,200,000
Less: ITA 84(2) Deemed Dividend	(1,100,000)
ITA 54 Proceeds Of Disposition	$ 100,000
Adjusted Cost Base	(100,000)
Capital Gain	Nil

Exercise Fourteen - 13

Subject: ITA 84(2) Deemed Dividends

After selling its assets and paying all of its liabilities, a corporation has cash of $2,350,000 available for distribution to its only shareholder. The corporation was established 20 years ago with an investment of $250,000. This figure is both the PUC and the adjusted cost base of the shares. The balance in the capital dividend account is $340,000 and the company makes the appropriate election to have the distribution of this amount be treated as a capital dividend under ITA 83(2). What are the tax consequences of distributing the $2,350,000 to the corporation's only shareholder?

SOLUTION available in print and online Study Guide.

Deemed Dividends Under ITA 84(3) - On Redemption, Acquisition, Or Cancellation Of Shares

14-125. An ITA 84(3) deemed dividend occurs most commonly when a corporation redeems some of its outstanding shares. Such dividends can also occur when the corporation acquires or cancels some of its outstanding shares. To the extent that the redemption amount paid by the corporation exceeds the PUC of the shares redeemed, a deemed dividend is assessed under ITA 84(3).

14-126. For the corporation, this is a distribution of their unrestricted surplus balance. From the point of view of the person receiving the redemption proceeds, the deemed dividend component of the proceeds will be treated as an ordinary taxable dividend, subject to either the eligible or non-eligible dividend gross up and tax credit procedures.

14-127. However, there is a problem here. As a redemption of shares is also a disposition of the redeemed shares, the proceeds of redemption will also be used as the proceeds of disposition. As was the case with the ITA 84(2) deemed dividends on winding up, this creates the possibility that some amount of the proceeds will be double counted as both a deemed dividend and a capital gain.

14-128. The solution to this problem is similar to the one we described in our discussion of ITA 84(2) deemed dividends. The ITA 54 definition of proceeds of disposition excludes any amounts received that are deemed to be ITA 84(3) dividends.

> **EXAMPLE** Mr. Jonas owns all of the preferred shares of Jonas Ltd. They were issued with a PUC of $75,000. However, their adjusted cost base to Mr. Jonas is $25,000. They are redeemed by the corporation for $200,000.
>
> **ANALYSIS** The analysis of this transaction is as follows:

Cash Distributed	$200,000
PUC Of Shares Redeemed	(75,000)
ITA 84(3) Deemed Dividend	**$125,000**

This deemed dividend would be subject to either the eligible or non-eligible dividend gross up and tax credit procedures.

The capital gain on the disposition would be calculated as follows:

Proceeds Of Redemption	$200,000
Less: ITA 84(3) Deemed Dividend	(125,000)
ITA 54 Proceeds Of Disposition	$ 75,000
Adjusted Cost Base	(25,000)
Capital Gain (PUC - ACB)	$ 50,000
Inclusion Rate	1/2
Taxable Capital Gain	**$ 25,000**

We would note that, in situations where the PUC and adjusted cost base are equal, these calculations will result in no capital gain or loss. If the PUC exceeds the adjusted cost base, the result will be a capital gain. Alternatively, if the PUC is less than the adjusted cost base, a capital loss will result from the disposition. Note that, if the individual shareholder receiving redemption proceeds is affiliated with the corporation, any capital loss arising on the disposition will be disallowed.

Distributions Of Corporate Surplus

Exercise Fourteen - 14

Subject: ITA 84(3) Deemed Dividends

When first incorporated, Tandy Ltd. issued 233,000 common shares in return for $1,922,250 in cash ($8.25 per share). All of the shares were issued to Ms. Jessy Tandy, the founder of the Company. Except for 15,000 shares, she is still holding all of the originally issued shares. The 15,000 shares were sold to Ms. Tandy's brother, Jesuiah, for $7.90 per share, the estimated market value of the shares at that time. Because of ongoing difficulties between the two siblings, Ms. Tandy has arranged for Tandy Ltd. to redeem all of her brother's shares at a price of $11.75 per share during the current year. Any dividends resulting from the redemption will be non-eligible. Determine the tax consequences of this redemption to Ms. Tandy and Jesuiah.

SOLUTION available in print and online Study Guide.

Deemed Dividends Under ITA 84(4) And ITA 84(4.1)

14-129.   This type of dividend is not as common as the other deemed dividends we have discussed. It arises when a corporation resident in Canada distributes a part of its invested capital to its shareholders, without redeeming or canceling any of its shares. It might occur, for example, if a corporation divested itself of a major division and did not wish to reinvest the proceeds from the sale in other corporate assets. In this type of situation, the proceeds may be distributed to shareholders. Such distributions are commonly referred to as liquidating dividends.

14-130.   In order to make all, or part, of the distribution tax free, it is usually accompanied by a reduction in PUC. For a non-public company, if the reduction in PUC is equal to the amount distributed, no ITA 84(1) dividend arises. However, if the distribution exceeds the PUC reduction, an ITA 84(4) deemed dividend is created. Note that ITA 84(4.1) contains a different set of rules for public companies. Under these alternative rules, a deemed dividend can arise, even if the distribution does not exceed the PUC reduction.

> **EXAMPLE** Jong Ltd., a CCPC, has shares with a PUC of $5,000,000 and a nil balance in its capital dividend account. As it has disposed of a major division for cash, it will distribute $1,000,000 to its shareholders. In order to limit the tax effects of this distribution, the PUC of the shares will be reduced by $700,000.

> **ANALYSIS** Under ITA 84(4), $700,000 of the total distribution will be a tax free distribution of PUC. The remaining $300,000 is treated as a deemed dividend, subject to the usual gross up and tax credit procedures. The adjusted cost base of the shares would be reduced by $700,000, the amount of the tax free distribution to shareholders. However, there would be no reduction in the adjusted cost base for the $300,000 distribution as it would be subject to tax as a deemed dividend.

14-131.   ITA 84(4.1) provides a different rule that overrides ITA 84(4) in the case of public companies. For these companies, if a payment is made to shareholders in conjunction with a reduction of PUC that is not part of a reorganization of the corporation's business or its capital, and there is no redemption, acquisition, or cancellation of shares, the entire distribution is generally treated as a deemed dividend. Note that ITA 84(3) would be applicable if there was a redemption, acquisition, or cancellation of shares.

14-132.   With respect to our example, this means that, if Jong Ltd. is a public company, the entire $1,000,000 distribution will be considered to be a deemed dividend under ITA 84(4.1). As the $1,000,000 amount will be subject to tax, the adjusted cost base of the shares will not be reduced by this distribution.

14-133.   There is an exception to this general rule for public corporations. If the payment can reasonably be considered to be derived from a transaction that is outside the ordinary course of business for the corporation, it can be considered a tax free return of capital to the extent that it is accompanied by a PUC reduction.

14-134.   An example of this would be where the company disposes of a business unit of the corporation and does not wish to reinvest the proceeds in some other line of business activity. The distribution would have to be made within 24 months of the occurrence of the non-ordinary transaction and the exception would only apply to the first such payment made. If there is more than one payment, the second and any subsequent payments would come under the general ITA 84(4.1) deemed dividend rule.

Exercise Fourteen - 15

Subject: ITA 84(4) Deemed Dividends

Mr. Jondo owns all of the outstanding shares of Jondo Ltd., a CCPC. The shares have a PUC of $450,000 and an adjusted cost base of $625,000. Because it has recently consolidated its operations, Jondo Ltd. pays a liquidating dividend of $330,000, accompanied by a PUC reduction of $225,000. What are the tax consequences of this distribution to Mr. Jondo?

SOLUTION available in print and online Study Guide.

We suggest you work Self Study Problem Fourteen-8 at this point.

Additional Supplementary Self Study Problems Are Available Online.

Key Terms Used In This Chapter

14-135.   The following is a list of the key terms used in this Chapter. These terms, and their meanings, are compiled in the Glossary located at the back of the Study Guide.

Acquisition Of Control	Liquidating Dividend
Annual Business Limit	Paid Up Capital
Apprenticeship Job Creation Tax Credit	Preferred Shares
Associated Corporations	PUC
Capital Dividend	Qualified Property
Capital Dividend Account	Qualifying Corporation
CCPC	Redemption Of Shares
Common Shares	Refundable Investment Tax Credit
Contributed Capital	Related Persons
Control [ITA 256(1.2)(c)]	Retained Earnings
Corporation	Scientific Research And
Deemed Dividends	Experimental Development (SR&ED)
Deemed Disposition	Shareholders' Equity
Dividends	Specified Class ITA 256(1.1)
Dividends In Kind	Specified Shareholder ITA 248(1)
Earned Capital	Stock Dividend
Earned Surplus	Taxable Capital Employed In Canada
Group Of Persons	Winding-Up Of A Canadian Corporation
Investment Tax Credit	

References

14-136.   For more detailed study of the material in this Chapter, we refer you to the following:

ITA 52(2)	Cost Of Property Received As Dividend In Kind
ITA 52(3)	Cost Of Stock Dividends
ITA 82(1)	Taxable Dividends Received
ITA 83(2)	Capital Dividend
ITA 84	Deemed Dividend
ITA 88(2)	Winding Up Of A Canadian Corporation
ITA 127(5) to 127.1(4)	Investment Tax Credits
ITA 249(4)	Year End On Change In Control
ITA 251	Arm's Length
ITA 256	Associated Corporations
ITR 4600	Investment Tax Credit - Qualified Property
ITR 4601	Investment Tax Credit - Qualified Transportation Equipment
ITR 4602	Certified Property
IC 78-4R3	Investment Tax Credit Rates
S1-F5-C1	Related Persons And Dealing At Arm's Length
S3-F2-C1	Capital Dividends
IT-64R4	Corporations: Association And Control (Consolidated)
IT-149R4	Winding Up Dividend
IT-302R3	Losses Of A Corporation
IT-463R2	Paid-Up Capital

Problems For Self Study (Online)

To provide practice in problem solving, there are Self Study and Supplementary Self Study problems available on MyLab Accounting.

Within the text we have provided an indication of when it would be appropriate to work each Self Study problem. The detailed solutions for Self Study problems can be found in the print and online Study Guide.

We provide the Supplementary Self Study problems for those who would like additional practice in problem solving. The detailed solutions for the Supplementary Self Study problems are available online, not in the Study Guide.

The .PDF file "Self Study Problems for Volume 2" on MyLab contains the following for Chapter 14:

- 8 Self Study problems,
- 5 Supplementary Self Study problems, and
- detailed solutions for the Supplementary Self Study problems.

Assignment Problems

(The solutions for these problems are only available in
the solutions manual that has been provided to your instructor.)

Assignment Problem Fourteen - 1

(Acquisition Of Control Rules - Losses)

For many years, Janice Virtue had been a professor of Business Ethics in the Faculty of Business at a major Canadian university. In 2016, while continuing to teach one section of Business Ethics, she established Virtue Ltd. (VL) in order to market her numerous publications and online courses involving the application of ethical principles to business situations.

While the company experienced a net operating loss of $128,000 in the fiscal period ending December 31, 2016, VL experienced rapidly increasing sales during 2017. Because Janice believed the improvement was indicative of the success to come, VL moved to larger premises which were purchased for $423,000. Of this total, $100,000 related to the land, with the remaining $323,000 allocated to the building. Because the building was to be used exclusively for non-residential purposes, it was allocated to a separate Class 1. In selling the previous premises in 2017, VL experienced an allowable capital loss on the land of $36,000. The building was sold at its UCC value.

The Net Income For Tax Purposes of VL for the year ending December 31, 2017, after deducting CCA on the Class 1 building, was $16,000. VL realized no capital gains during the year.

In early 2018, a joint CRA/RCMP operation found that Janice was the mastermind and guiding force behind a network of illegal aliens working throughout Canada. They were selling stolen weapons and preparing thousands of tax returns with large fictitious charitable donations. The fee for the tax return preparation was always paid for in cash which was not reported to the CRA.

Various charges were laid and, while Janice remains free on bail, a court date has been set for September.

By May, 2018, Janice's lawyer indicated that it is likely that she will be convicted on multiple charges and will spend a significant amount of time in prison. She has also been advised by her employer that her contract to teach Business Ethics will not be renewed in the fall.

Given these circumstances, Janice decides to sell her VL shares. She finds a corporate buyer who is willing to acquire the shares on June 1, 2018. This buyer, Peerzon Books, is a large publicly traded Canadian company. The VL assets include the copyrights to all of her publications. While sales of these publications have fallen off precipitously in 2018, Peerzon believes its crack marketing team will be able to put the proper spin on Janice's life experiences and sales will take off.

As this acquisition of control resulted in a deemed year end, VL prepared an Income Statement for the period January 1, 2018 through May 31, 2018. This short fiscal period statement showed an additional business loss of $34,000 for this period. There were, however, no further capital losses.

On May 31, 2018, the values of the Company's assets were as follows:

Asset	Cost	UCC	Fair Market Value
Temporary Investments	$ 32,000	N/A	$ 7,000
Accounts Receivable	123,000	N/A	110,000
Land	100,000	N/A	115,000
Building	323,000	$313,310	352,000
Equipment	46,000	33,120	5,000
Vehicles (Class 10)	36,000	21,420	25,000
Copyrights	Nil	Nil	42,000

VL will make all possible elections to minimize any net capital and non-capital loss balances.

Shortly after taking over VL, Peerzon Books decided that some of the extra space in VL's facilities could be used for manufacturing electronic reading devices. VL's income (loss) from the two separate businesses for the period June 1 through December 31, 2018, and for the 2019 taxation year was as follows:

Business	June 1 to Dec. 31, 2018	2019 Year
Electronic Reading Devices	$123,000	($ 26,000)
Janice's Publications	(53,000)	185,000

Required:

A. Determine the amount of the non-capital loss balance that will be carried forward after the acquisition of control by Peerzon Books, and calculate the amount of the net capital losses that will be lost as a result of this change in ownership, if any.

B. Indicate the maximum amount of the non-capital loss carry forward that can be used during the period June 1 through December 31, 2018, and the amount remaining at December 31, 2018.

C. Indicate the maximum amount of the non-capital loss carry forward that can be used during 2019, and the amount remaining at December 31, 2019.

Assignment Problem Fourteen - 2
(Acquisition Of Control Rules)

Boudin Inc. was incorporated 10 years ago in New Brunswick. At its formation, all of the shares were issued to Andre Boudin. The Company's business involved the distribution of health food products throughout the Maritime provinces. The Company's taxation year ends on December 31.

The Company operated successfully for a number of years. However, late in 2015, a local newspaper found that many of the claims made by the products that they distributed were either misleading or false. Widespread publication of this information resulted in a steep decline in the sales of Boudin Inc.

Because of this the Company had an operating loss of $42,000 in 2016 and $123,000 in 2017. In addition, there was a 2017 allowable capital loss of $32,000 on the disposal of some temporary investments.

In early 2018, seeing no real hope for a return to profitable operations, Mr. Boudin begins a search for a buyer for his Company's shares. On May 1, 2018, all of the shares are sold to Healthy Bites Ltd., a manufacturer of health food products. This Company hopes to be able to revive the fortunes of Boudin Inc.

For the period January 1, 2018 through April 30, 2018, Boudin Inc. experienced a business loss of $48,000. This figure includes a write-down of inventories to their fair market values on April 30, 2018, and a deduction for uncollectible receivables, calculated as per the provisions of ITA 111(5.3). It does not include any taxable capital gains, allowable capital losses, Allowable Business Investment Losses, or property losses.

On April 30, 2018, Boudin Inc.'s assets had the following values:

Asset	Cost	UCC	Fair Market Value
Long-Term Investments*	$ 47,000	N/A	$ 82,000
Land	207,000	N/A	305,000
Building	465,000	$360,000	485,000
Equipment	350,000	190,000	150,000

*Healthy Bites intends to sell these investments as soon as possible.

Required:

A. Indicate the amount of any non-capital and net capital loss carry forwards that would remain after the May 1, 2018 acquisition of control, using the assumption that Healthy Bites Ltd. elects to have a deemed disposition of all eligible assets at their fair market values.

B. If Healthy Bites Ltd. decides to only use the election(s) required to eliminate those losses that would expire at the acquisition of control, indicate the assets on which the elections should be made, and the amounts that should be elected.

C. Advise Healthy Bits Ltd. as to which course of action (Part A or B) they should take.

Assignment Problem Fourteen - 3
(Associated Companies)

The following situations are **independent** of each other. All of the corporations involved are Canadian controlled private corporations and have only one class of shares.

A. Barton Ltd. owns 51 percent of the shares of Norton Inc.

B. Thomas Boulding owns 60 percent of the shares of Boulding Ltd. and 70 percent of the shares of Boulding Inc.

C. Mary Cunningham and Brenda Parton each own 50 percent of the shares of Elm Ltd. In addition, they each own 50 percent of the shares of Maple Inc. Mary and Brenda are not related.

D. Alice Fielding owns 100 percent of the shares of Fielding Inc. and 40 percent of the shares of Lawson Ltd. Betty Falcon owns 100 percent of the shares of Falcon Inc. and 40 percent of the shares of Lawson Ltd. Alice is the sister of Betty's husband. The remaining 20 percent of the shares of Lawson Ltd. are owned by unrelated parties.

E. Michael Forbes owns 70 percent of the shares of Forbes Ltd. and 30 percent of the shares of Malcom Inc. Forbes Ltd. also owns 30 percent of the shares of Malcom Inc.

F. Richard Barnes, Susan Firth, and Terry Anson each own one-third of the shares of Rastau Ltd. In addition, Richard and Susan each own 50 percent of the shares of Sucrol Inc.

Required: For each of the preceding situations, indicate whether the corporations are associated and explain your conclusion with reference to the *Income Tax Act*. In order to assist you in answering this question, we have provided you with the content of ITA 256(1).

> **ITA 256(1) Associated corporations** — For the purposes of this Act, one corporation is associated with another in a taxation year if, at any time in the year,
>
> (a) one of the corporations controlled, directly or indirectly in any manner whatever, the other;
> (b) both of the corporations were controlled, directly or indirectly in any manner whatever, by the same person or group of persons;
> (c) each of the corporations was controlled, directly or indirectly in any manner whatever, by a person and the person who so controlled one of the corporations was related to the person who so controlled the other, and either of those persons owned, in respect of each corporation, not less than 25% of the issued shares of any class, other than a specified class, of the capital stock thereof;
> (d) one of the corporations was controlled, directly or indirectly in any manner whatever, by a person and that person was related to each member of a group of persons that so controlled the other corporation, and that person owned, in respect of the other corporation, not less than 25% of the issued shares of any class, other than a specified class, of the capital stock thereof; or
> (e) each of the corporations was controlled, directly or indirectly in any manner whatever, by a related group and each of the members of one of the related groups was related to all of the members of the other related group, and one or more persons who were members of both related groups, either alone or together, owned, in respect of each corporation, not less than 25% of the issued shares of any class, other than a specified class, of the capital stock thereof.

Assignment Problem Fourteen - 4
(Associated Companies)

Each of the following is an **independent** Case involving the ownership of voting shares of Canadian controlled private corporations. All of the corporations have taxation years that end on December 31 and have only one class of shares.

A. Mr. Bond owns 55 percent of Sarnen Inc. Sarnen Inc. owns 40 percent of Barxo Ltd. Mr. Bond also owns 14 percent of Hax Ltd., which in turn owns 54 percent of the shares of Barxo Ltd. Mr. Bond's 10 year old daughter owns 6 percent of the shares of Barxo Ltd.

B. Mr. Jones, Mr. Knight, and Mr. Long are three unrelated individuals.

- Mr. Jones owns 50 percent of the shares of Anix Inc. and 25 percent of the shares of Brex Ltd.
- Mr. Knight owns 50 percent of the shares of Brex Ltd.
- Mr. Long owns 50 percent of the shares of Anix Inc. and 25 percent of the shares of Brex Ltd.

C. Sam Scully owns 60 percent of Scully Inc. His sister, Susan Wilson, owns 80 percent of Wilson Ltd. and 30 percent of Scully Inc. Sam Scully also owns 10 percent of Wilson Ltd.

D. Joan and Sarah Lartch are sisters. Joan owns 100 percent of the shares of JL Inc. and 31 percent of the shares of Meadow Ltd. Her sister Sarah owns 60 percent of the shares of SL Inc., with the remaining 40 percent of the shares held by her mother. Sarah also owns 39 percent of the shares of Meadow Ltd. The remaining shares of Meadow Ltd. are held by an unrelated party.

E. John and May Carp each own 30 percent of the shares of Jomay Inc. Serge and Beth Carp each own 45 percent of the shares of Besa Ltd. John and Serge Carp are brothers. Beth Carp owns 40 percent of the shares of Jomay Inc. and May Carp owns 10 percent of the shares of Besa Ltd.

Required: For each of the preceding Cases, determine whether the corporations are associated. Support your conclusions with references to specific provisions of ITA 256. In order to assist you in answering this question, we have provided you with the content of ITA 256(1).

> **ITA 256(1) Associated corporations** — For the purposes of this Act, one corporation is associated with another in a taxation year if, at any time in the year,
>
> (a) one of the corporations controlled, directly or indirectly in any manner whatever, the other;
>
> (b) both of the corporations were controlled, directly or indirectly in any manner whatever, by the same person or group of persons;
>
> (c) each of the corporations was controlled, directly or indirectly in any manner whatever, by a person and the person who so controlled one of the corporations was related to the person who so controlled the other, and either of those persons owned, in respect of each corporation, not less than 25% of the issued shares of any class, other than a specified class, of the capital stock thereof;
>
> (d) one of the corporations was controlled, directly or indirectly in any manner whatever, by a person and that person was related to each member of a group of persons that so controlled the other corporation, and that person owned, in respect of the other corporation, not less than 25% of the issued shares of any class, other than a specified class, of the capital stock thereof; or
>
> (e) each of the corporations was controlled, directly or indirectly in any manner whatever, by a related group and each of the members of one of the related groups was related to all of the members of the other related group, and one or more persons who were members of both related groups, either alone or together, owned, in respect of each corporation, not less than 25% of the issued shares of any class, other than a specified class, of the capital stock thereof.

Assignment Problem Fourteen - 5
(Investment Tax Credits)
The following three independent cases involve the tax procedures associated with various types of investment tax credits.

Case A
In 2017, Baron Inc. employed 22 eligible apprentices. The total amount paid to these individuals is $458,000. Ten of the apprentices are paid $17,000 for the year, with the remaining twelve each being paid $24,000.

Also during 2017, the Company acquires $850,000 in Class 53 assets on which a 10 percent investment tax credit is available.

Required: Describe the 2017 and 2018 tax consequences associated with making these expenditures and claiming the related investment tax credits. Include in your solution the CCA for 2017 and 2018.

Case B

Since its incorporation several years ago, Aria Inc. has been a Canadian controlled private corporation. Selected information for the taxation years 2017 and 2018 is as follows:

	2017	2018
Taxable Income	$ 425,000	$ 511,000
Taxable Capital Employed In Canada	10,800,000	11,200,000

Required: Determine Aria's SR&ED annual expenditure limit for the 2018 taxation year.

Case C

Sylman Ltd. has qualified as a Canadian controlled private company since its incorporation. During 2017 it had Taxable Income of $17,000. The corresponding figure for 2018 is $4,000. The Company has no Tax Payable for the taxation year ending December 31, 2018, or for any of the three preceding years.

Despite its very low income figures, the Company has Taxable Capital Employed in Canada for 2017 of $14,700,000. The corresponding figure for 2018 is $14,482,000.

During 2018, the Company has made a number of expenditures that qualify for investment tax credits:

- $106,000 for qualified expenditures in the Atlantic Provinces.
- $2,700,000 in current expenditures for SR&ED.

Required: Determine the amount of the refund that Sylman Ltd. will receive as a result of earning these investment tax credits and any available carry forwards. Include in your answer any other tax consequences of these investment tax credits.

Assignment Problem Fourteen - 6
(Capital Dividend Account)

Since its incorporation in 2007, Park Inc. has qualified as a Canadian controlled private corporation. During the period since incorporation and until December 31, 2018, the Company has had the following transactions that might involve the capital dividend account.

1. In 2009, the Company sold a depreciable asset with a capital cost of $225,000. It was the last asset in its class and the balance in the Class at the time of the sale was $129,600. The proceeds from the sale were $275,000. No assets were added to the Class during 2009.

2. In 2011, the Company received a capital dividend of $46,000.

3. In 2012, the Company received life insurance proceeds, net of the adjusted cost base of the policy, in the amount of $27,500.

4. In 2013, the Company paid a capital dividend of $38,000 and eligible dividends of $19,000. The required election was made.

5. In 2013, the Company sold a parcel of land for $100,000. The adjusted cost base of this land was $145,000.

6. In January 2018, Park acquired all of the shares of a small incorporated business at a cost of $850,000. This total cost was allocated as follows:

Non-Depreciable Assets	$150,000
Depreciable Assets (See Note)	500,000
Goodwill	200,000
Total Cost	$850,000

Note   The capital cost of the non-depreciable assets to the acquired business was $100,000. The capital cost of the depreciable assets was $450,000 and their UCC was $375,000. The goodwill was internally generated and was not reflected on the books of the acquired business. Park does not use a rollover provision to transfer the assets.

While Park intended to integrate this business into its other operations, they received an unsolicited offer to purchase the shares of this business for $965,000. Finding this offer too attractive to resist, it was accepted and the business was sold on October 1, 2018. On January 1, 2018, Park had no UCC balance in Class 14.1. The total proceeds were allocated as follows:

Non-Depreciable Assets	$175,000
Depreciable Assets	550,000
Goodwill	240,000
Total Proceeds	$965,000

7. In 2018, the Company received a capital dividend of $17,800. They paid a capital dividend of $21,600 and eligible dividends of $8,000. The required election was made.

Required: Determine the balance in the Company's capital dividend account as of December 31, 2018.

Assignment Problem Fourteen - 7
(Corporate Surplus Distributions)

Groman Ltd. is a Canadian controlled private corporation whose shareholders are all individuals. On December 31 of the current year, the Company's condensed Balance Sheet is as follows:

Total Assets		$62,000
Liabilities		$22,000
Shareholders' Equity:		
500 Preferred Shares (Paid Up Capital)	$11,000	
600 Common Shares (Paid Up Capital)	15,600	
Retained Earnings	13,400	40,000
Total Equities		$62,000

Any dividends paid or deemed to be paid by Groman Ltd. would be non-eligible.

Required: Discuss the tax consequences of each of the following **independent** transactions. Tax consequences would include the increase or decrease in the individual shareholder's Taxable Income, any change in the adjusted cost base and/or PUC of any shares that are still in the hands of the individual shareholder after the described transaction(s), and any federal dividend tax credits that result from the described transaction(s).

A. (i) A long-term debtholder has agreed to convert $10,000 of his debt to 500 Preferred Shares, with a Paid Up Capital (PUC) of $11,000. This conversion does not qualify for the ITA 51 rollover that is described in Chapter 17 of the text.

 (ii) After the conversion described in A(i), a different shareholder, with 250 Preferred Shares, sold them for $5,500 in an arm's length transaction. His shares cost $4,100 a number of years ago.

B. The Company declared and distributed a 5 percent stock dividend on the Common Shares. An addition of $780 was made to Paid Up Capital, with Retained Earnings reduced accordingly.

C. In return for assets with a fair market value of $17,500, the Company issued a demand note for $12,000 and 250 fully paid Preferred Shares having a per share Paid Up Capital equal to those currently outstanding.

D. An investor owns 100 of the Common Shares. They were purchased at a price of $15 per share. The Company redeems these shares at a price of $32 per share.

Assignment Problem Fourteen - 8

(Comprehensive Corporate Tax Payable, Associated Companies, and ITCs)

Meredith Markby Corporation (MMC) was incorporated on January 1, 2013 and is involved in the sale and manufacture of high tech detection equipment used by police forces across the country. Meredith Markby, the controlling shareholder, is a woman who is fascinated by detective shows on TV, but she doesn't know much about tax or accounting. She has asked you for assistance in preparing the corporate income tax return for 2018. The company is a CCPC throughout the 2018 fiscal year.

Meredith has prepared the following income statement for the company:

Meredith Markby Corporation
Income Statement
For the year ended December 31, 2018

Sales		$17,338,000
Expenses:		
Salaries And Wages	($5,758,000)	
Advertising And Promotion	(253,500)	
Amortization Expense	(905,875)	
Bad Debt Expense*	(54,700)	
Dividends Paid To Shareholders	(235,000)	
Office Expenses	(418,975)	
Penalty And Interest On 2016 Income Taxes	(3,500)	
Cost Of Goods Sold	(9,000,000)	(16,629,550)
Other Income And Expenses:		
Investment Income - Canadian Source	$ 271,650	
Net Foreign Dividend Income	25,000	
Rental Income From Alan Markby Limited	150,000	
Income Tax Refund From 2017	131,000	
U.S. Income Tax Paid	(87,000)	
Gain On Sale Of License	575,000	
Gain On Disposal Of Equipment	20,000	1,085,650
Net Income		**$ 1,794,100**

*The accounting and tax figures for Bad Debt Expense are the same.

Additional information follows:

1. The company declared and paid dividends of $505,000 during the year. Prior to paying the dividend, the company filed an election under ITA 83(2) to designate the balance in the capital dividend account at December 31, 2018, as a capital dividend. The remaining portion of the payment was designated as an eligible dividend for 2018.

2. The following information from the working paper file will be useful in determining the balance in the capital dividend account:

2013 - Sold a depreciable capital asset with a capital cost of $97,000 for proceeds of $127,000.

2014 - Capital dividend of $25,000 received from investment in Meredith's father's corporation. The Company discontinued operations shortly after his death and was wound up.

2015 - Capital dividend of $15,000 paid to Meredith.

2016 - Sold a non-depreciable capital asset with an ACB of $21,000 for proceeds of $15,000.

2016 - Life insurance proceeds of $70,000 received by MMC on death of Meredith's father, a key employee of MMC. The adjusted cost base of his policy was $20,000.

3. The company has sales in the Canadian provinces of Ontario, BC, Manitoba, and Saskatchewan. They also have U.S. sales in the state of Michigan. The head office and manufacturing operations are in Ontario. There are employees in all provinces and states where the company has sales who have general authority to contract on behalf of the employer. However, the company has warehouses in Ontario and Michigan only. All Canadian customers are serviced through the Ontario office and warehouse. Sales, salaries and wages in Canadian dollars for these five locations are:

	Salaries	Sales
Ontario	$4,724,000	$ 7,137,000
BC	615,000	3,657,000
Manitoba	177,000	2,958,000
Saskatchewan	127,000	2,546,000
Michigan	115,000	1,040,000
Total	$5,758,000	$17,338,000

4. The December 31, 2017 balance in the Refundable Dividend Tax on Hand account was $156,000. The dividend refund for 2017 was $42,000. All the dividends paid in 2017 were designated as eligible dividends. These totaled $126,000.

5. At the end of 2017, MMC has a GRIP of $165,000.

6. Meredith Markby owns 70% of the voting shares of MMC and her husband owns 20%. Their 6 year old daughter, Suzie owns the final 10%. Meredith has indicated to you that she is concerned that the corporation may be considered to be associated with one or both of the following two corporations:

   a. Alan Markby Limited is owned 100% by Meredith's husband, and has taxable and active business income of $92,000. MMC rents Alan Markby Limited property at an annual cost equal to $150,000. This is fair market rent for the property. Alan Markby Limited has only active business income.

   b. Jordan's Murder Mystery Shows Incorporated is owned 100% by Meredith's sister's husband. This company has taxable income of $452,000 in 2018.

   Meredith is willing to allocate up to $100,000 of the annual business limit to any associated company or companies. None of the companies (including MMC) has Taxable Capital Employed in Canada for 2017 or 2018 in excess of $10,000,000.

7. Included in the financial statement income is business income earned in the United States. This foreign income totals $538,000. U.S. tax returns have been filed, and the U.S. tax paid on this amount totals $87,000. All amounts are in Canadian dollars.

8. The company also has foreign portfolio dividend income of $37,000. $12,000 in foreign taxes has been paid on this dividend income. All amounts are in Canadian dollars. The amount was reported net of the tax paid as Net Foreign Dividend Income in the financial statements, because Meredith was unsure of the appropriate accounting treatment.

9. The following are the opening balances in undepreciated capital cost:

Class 8 - Equipment $2,631,250
Class 1 - New building used 98% for manufacturing,
    acquired in 2016 $4,897,532
Class 1 - Used office building - acquired in 2013 $653,246
Class 10 - Delivery Vehicles $358,000
Class 14.1   Nil

10. During the year, the company had the following additions and disposals of capital assets:

a. Sold equipment for $100,000. The original cost of the equipment was $150,000. Its net book value at December 31, 2017 was $80,000.
b. Purchased Class 8 assets costing $45,000.
c. Added a new delivery vehicle to their fleet at a cost of $75,000.

11. The advertising and promotion line of the Income Statement includes the following items:

a. $40,000 in clothing worn by Meredith and Alan on sales calls to demonstrate the ability of the product manufactured by the company to assist in crime solving efforts.
b. $32,000 in meals for Meredith, Alan and Suzie. These meals were necessary because Meredith has no time to cook for her family since she is busy running the business.
c. $120,000 for meals for the sales staff of the company while on sales calls outside of the town where the head office is located.
d. $15,000 golf club membership fee, plus $5,000 for business meals at the golf club.
e. $2,500 for sponsoring the local police hockey team in the international police hockey tournament.
f. $7,000 donation to registered charities supported by the family.

12. Included in the income of the company are manufacturing and processing profits. It has been determined that manufacturing and processing profits as determined under the Income Tax Regulations are $535,000.

13. Canadian source investment income totals $271,650, and includes the following:

Interest on long term investments $ 67,000
Capital gain on sale of shares*   186,000
Eligible dividends on bank shares   18,000
Interest on surplus cash in checking account   650

*The capital gain on the sale of shares is equal to the accounting gain.

14. The company has a net capital loss carryforward of $137,000 [(1/2)($274,000)].

15. During 2018, the company hired 5 apprentices. The amount paid to each apprentice during the year was $27,000. The apprentices began work on May 1, 2018, and worked for MMC for the remainder of the year. These apprentices work in "Red Seal Trades", and the contracts are registered with the Federal government.

16. The company filed its tax return late for 2016. As a result, penalties and interest were assessed, and paid of $3,500. This amount has been deducted in determining income for 2018.

17. During 2018, MMC sold an unlimited life licence to produce and sell one of their products in Europe, for $600,000. Legal fees associated with the sale of this license were $25,000. The net proceeds of $575,000 are included in the income statement as Other Income. The product had been developed internally and the associated costs were written off as incurred.

Required: Show all of the calculations used to provide the following required information, including those for which the result is nil.

A. Determine Meredith Markby Corporation's minimum Net Income For Tax Purposes and Taxable Income for the year ending December 31, 2018. In the determination of Net Income for Tax Purposes, explain why any amounts were irrelevant.

B. Determine Meredith Markby Corporation's Part I Tax Payable for the year ending December 31, 2018. Any percentages used in your calculations should be rounded to one decimal point. For the purposes of dealing with any Foreign Tax Credits that the company is eligible for, assume that the Foreign Tax Credit is equal to the foreign tax paid when determining the amount of the small business deduction, the manufacturing and processing profits deduction and the general rate reduction. For inclusion in total Tax Payable, complete the full foreign tax credit using the figures you determined for the small business deduction, the manufacturing and processing profits deduction and the general rate reduction.

C. Determine the December 31, 2018 balance in Meredith Markby Corporation's Capital Dividend Account prior to the payment of the capital dividend for 2018.

D. Determine the December 31, 2018 balance in the Meredith Markby Corporation's Refundable Dividend Tax On Hand account.

E. Determine Meredith Markby Corporation's minimum federal Tax Payable for the year ending December 31, 2018. This should include both Part I and Part IV Tax Payable, net of any dividend refund.

F. Determine the December 31, 2018 balance in Meredith Markby Corporation's GRIP.

Tax Software Assignment Problem

Tax Software Assignment Problem Fourteen - 1

Note The following problem contains 2017 (not 2018) information as the current Profile software release does not support fiscal periods ending after April 30, 2018. Shortly after the first filing version of the 2018 Intuit ProFile software is available in January, 2019, the updated 2018 version of this problem will be available on MyLab at:

www.pearsoncanada.ca/byrdchen/ctp2019

RadionFaux Industries Ltd. (RIL) is a Canadian controlled private corporation, located at 123 ABC Street in Ottawa, Ontario K4E 1A1. Its Ontario Corporation tax account number is 1234567. Its phone number is (613) 111-1111. It was incorporated on February 24, 1990 in Ottawa.

The government's Crown Copyright no longer permits us to use fake Business Numbers in software problems. To reduce the number of ProFile's error messages because of this, enter NR (for not registered) in the Business Number field.

The Company has 1,000 shares of common stock issued and outstanding, all of which are held by Margaret Ottawa (SIN 527-000-301).

Ms. Ottawa, the president and director of the Company, is the person who should be contacted with respect to matters concerning the Company's books and records. She is the authorized person as well as the signing officer.

RIL is a retailer of pet supplies. All of its sales occur within Canada. It has net assets of $235,000 on December 31, 2017. This includes a few investments that Ms. Ottawa inherited from her father two years earlier.

RIL owns all of the 500 common shares of OttawaFaux Inc., which holds most of the investments Ms. Ottawa inherited from her father. The common shares have a book value of $1,200,000. OttawaFaux Inc. has the same location and phone number as RadionFaux Industries Ltd. OttawaFaux Inc. has a December 31 fiscal year end. Enter NR (for not registered) in the Business Number field for OttawaFaux Inc.

OttawaFaux Inc. is also involved in earning active business income through the breeding and sale of championship dogs. It has total assets of $2,000,000 and total revenues for 2017 of $200,000. Its Taxable Capital Employed In Canada as at December 31, 2016 was $350,000.

As at December 31, 2016, the following information applied to RIL:

Taxable Capital Employed In Canada	$328,000
RDTOH	5,200
Dividends Declared And Paid During 2016	Nil
GRIP Balance	11,750
Capital Dividend Account Balance	6,000

RIL does not use International Financial Reporting Standards (IFRS). For the taxation year ending December 31, 2017, RIL's Income Statement, before any deduction for income taxes, was as follows:

Sales Revenues	$580,000
Interest On Long-Term Debt	27,500
Interest Received On Foreign Bank Account (Note 1)	18,000
Eligible Dividends On Royal Bank Shares	17,500
Non-Eligible Dividends From OttawaFaux Inc. (Note 2)	42,000
Gain On Sale Of Shares (Note 3)	27,000
Total Revenues	**$712,000**
Cost Of Goods Sold	$208,000
Amortization Expense	122,000
Other Operating Expenses	147,000
Total Expenses (Excluding Taxes)	**$477,000**
Net Income (Before Taxes)	**$235,000**

Note 1 This interest is net of $2,000 in taxes withheld in Ireland.

Note 2 As a result of paying this $42,000 in dividends to RIL, OttawaFaux Inc. received a dividend refund of $14,000.

Note 3 On March 23, 2017, RIL sold 2,700 shares of Canadian Imperial Bank of Commerce. The common shares had cost $118,800 on June 6, 2014 and were sold for net proceeds of $145,800.

Other Information:

1. Expenses include a deduction for charitable donations to the Ottawa Civic Hospital in the amount of $5,000.

2. RIL's Expenses include penalties of $3,500 resulting from a judgment in the Tax Court Of Canada.

3. RIL reimbursed Ms. Ottawa $34,000 for business meals and entertainment for clients and suppliers during the year.

4. During the year, RIL incurred $20,000 in landscaping costs. For accounting purposes these are being treated as a capital asset, to be amortized using the straight-line method over 10 years. The related amortization is included in the Amortization Expense shown on the Income Statement.

5. The opening UCC balances were $246,000 for Class 1, $135,000 for Class 8 and $90,000 for Class 10. The only fixed asset disposition during the year was the sale of a delivery truck. The truck had cost $35,000 and was sold for its net book value of $12,000. The only fixed asset acquisition was $52,000 in office furniture.

6. During 2017, RIL paid taxable dividends of $92,000. Of these dividends, $25,000 was designated as eligible. On September 1, 2017, RIL also elects to pay the maximum capital dividend allowable.

7. RIL allocates $60,000 of the annual business limit to OttawaFaux Inc. This is $5,000 more than OttawaFaux Inc. can utilize in 2017, but RIL cannot use the excess.

8. RIL paid quarterly income tax instalments of $8,000 each on the 15th of March, June, September and December during 2017.

9. RIL has a website describing the products it carries, but no income is generated from the website.

Required: Prepare the federal corporate tax return for RIL for the 2017 taxation year using the ProFile T2 corporate software program. On the ProFile schedule titled "Info", the Filing question "Complete return from GIFI?" is answered Yes by default, click No. Ignore the GIFI requirements except as follows:

On GIFI Schedule 125:
- Input the total revenues less the Gain On Sale Of Shares ($685,000) on the line "Total Sales Of Goods And Services" (Code 8000).
- Choose "Realized gains / losses on sale of investments" (Code 8211) from the drop down menu under Code 8089 and input the Gain On Sale Of Shares.
- Choose "Purchases / cost of materials" (Code 8320) from the drop down menu under Cost of Sales and input the Cost of Goods Sold.
- Choose "Amortization of tangible assets" (Code 8670) from the drop down menu under Operating Expenses and input the amortization expense.
- Choose "Other expenses" (Code 9270) from the drop down menu under Operating Expenses and Other Operating Expenses.

On GIFI Schedule 100:
- Input the Net Income figure as "Cash and deposits" (Code 1000) in order to make the total assets equal to the total liabilities and equity.

Although this will not properly complete the GIFI statements, it will eliminate the warning messages that would otherwise be generated when the Net Income figure and Amortization Expense are input on Schedule 1. These GIFI entries will have no effect on the calculations in the tax return.

In addition, to prevent audit warnings, S141, "Notes Checklist", has to be completed. Assume there are no notes to the financial statements and answer "No" to any other relevant questions.

CHAPTER 15

Corporate Taxation And Management Decisions

The Decision To Incorporate

Basic Tax Considerations

Deferral And Reduction

15-1.   One of the more important decisions facing the owner of a business is deciding whether or not the business should be incorporated.   There are, of course, a number of non-tax considerations involved in this decision and these factors will be reviewed in this Chapter. At this point, however, we are concerned with the influence of corporate taxation on this decision.

15-2.   The decision to incorporate, from both a legal and a tax point of view, has the effect of separating the business from its owners. This means that, in order for incorporated business income to be made available to the owner, it must go through two levels of taxation. First, the amount of Tax Payable applicable to the corporation will be determined. Then, when any after tax amounts are distributed to the owner, additional personal taxes will be payable on the amounts received.

15-3.   This dual system of taxation may or may not be advantageous to the owner of the business. In terms of the types of tax advantage that can result from an individual incorporating business income, there are two possibilities:

Tax Reduction   In some situations, the total taxes that would be paid at the combined corporate and personal level will be less when the business is incorporated than would be the case if the individual had earned the business income directly as an individual proprietor.

Tax Deferral   As was noted in Paragraph 15-2, getting income from its source through a corporation and into the hands of a shareholder involves two levels of taxation. If the shareholder does not require all available income for his personal needs, after tax funds can be left in the corporation, resulting in a postponement of the second level of taxation. If the rate at which the corporation is taxed is lower than the rate at which the individual would be taxed on the direct receipt of the income, the use of a corporation provides tax deferral.

15-4.   As you probably discerned while proceeding through the earlier chapters on corporate taxation, whether the presence of a corporation will provide a deferral or reduction of taxes depends on both the type of corporation and the type of income that is being earned by that business entity. An additional important factor, as will be discussed in this Chapter, is the province in which the individual and the corporation pay income taxes.

15-5.   This means that there is no one answer to the question of whether incorporation will provide tax reduction and/or tax deferral. Given this, we will devote a major section of this Chapter to examining the various possible combinations of income types and corporate classifications in order to provide you with a general understanding of the availability of these two tax features. This material begins in Paragraph 15-12.

Using Imperfections In The Integration System

15-6.   We have previously noted that the integration provisions that are contained in Canadian tax legislation are based on the assumption that certain corporate and personal tax rates prevail. Even at the federal level, actual corporate tax rates vary from the notional rates required for effective integration.

15-7.   In addition, there are significant variations in the corporate tax rates used by the provinces. This means that it is unlikely that the combined federal/provincial rate in any given province will be equal to the notional combined rates assumed in the integration model. As it may be possible to use incorporation to take advantage of these imperfections in the integration system, it is important for you to understand how the imperfections can influence the decision to incorporate. We will provide a section which deals with this issue, beginning in Paragraph 15-58.

Income Splitting

15-8.   Even in situations where the use of a corporation neither reduces, nor defers significant amounts of taxes for a single individual, incorporation may be attractive to a family or other related group of individuals. In a typical family situation, it is fairly common to find some individuals earning amounts far in excess of the amount required to put them in the maximum personal tax bracket while, at the same time, other members of the group have incomes that leave them in a lower bracket or free of taxes altogether.

15-9.   As was discussed in Chapter 1, if some method can be found to redistribute the aggregate family or group income from high income to low income individuals, the tax savings can be significant. While we did not discuss this in Chapter 1, using a corporation can be one of the most effective approaches to achieving income splitting goals. Given this, we will provide a section which deals with this possibility beginning in Paragraph 15-89. You should note, however, that the newly introduced rules for the Tax On Split Income (TOSI) have made using a private corporation for income splitting much more difficult. (See coverage in Chapter 11.)

Other Advantages And Disadvantages

Advantages

15-10.   Other advantages that are normally associated with the use of a corporation are as follows:

Limited Liability   Because a corporation is a separate legal entity, the shareholders' liability to creditors is limited to the amount that they have invested. That is, creditors of the corporation can look only to the assets of the corporation for satisfaction of their claims. However, for smaller corporations, obtaining significant amounts of financing will almost always require the owners to provide personal guarantees on any loans, making this advantage somewhat illusory for this type of company. Note, however, limited liability may still be important for a smaller corporation if it is exposed to significant product or environmental claims.

Lifetime Capital Gains Deduction   Individuals who dispose of the shares of a qualified small business corporation are eligible to claim the lifetime capital gains deduction ($848,252 for 2018). To qualify, a business must be a Canadian controlled private corporation with substantially all of the fair market value of its assets (at least 90 percent) used in an active business carried on primarily in Canada (at least 50 percent) at the time of disposition. In addition, no one other than the seller, or related persons, can own the shares during the 24 months preceding the sale. During this 24 month period, more than 50 percent of the fair market value of the assets must have been used in active business carried on primarily in Canada. For a more complete discussion of this provision, see Chapter 11.

Flexibility On Timing, Type And Distribution Of Income   In the case of a corporation with a single shareholder, the owner can determine when his compensation will be paid and the form that it will take (e.g., salary vs. dividends). As mentioned previously, he may also be able to use the corporate form to split income with family members.

Foreign Taxes   Foreign estate taxes can often be avoided by placing foreign property in a Canadian corporation.

Estate Planning   A corporation can be used in estate planning, particularly with respect to freezing the asset values of an estate (see Chapter 19).

Disadvantages

15-11.   Disadvantages that are normally associated with incorporation include the following:

Use Of Losses   An individual can deduct business and unrestricted farm losses against any other source of income, including employment and property income. If the business or farm is incorporated, such losses can only be deducted against past or future corporate income. The corporation's losses belong to the corporation and cannot be used to offset income earned by the individual shareholder. This is of particular importance to operations that are just getting started as they will frequently experience significant losses in their formative years.

Tax Credits   A corporation is not eligible for personal tax credits, such as the basic personal, tuition fee, age, pension, and disability tax credits.

Charitable Donations   Charitable donations provide the basis for a tax credit for individuals, largely at 29 or 33 percent at the federal level. In contrast, they are a deduction in calculating Taxable Income for a corporation. In general, this deduction will not be as valuable as the tax credit that an individual would receive for donations.

Additional Maintenance Costs   The legal, accounting, and other costs associated with maintaining a business operation will be significantly higher in the case of a corporation (e.g., the cost of filing a corporate tax return on an annual basis).

Winding Up Procedures   The complications associated with the termination of an incorporated business will be greater than would usually be the case with a proprietorship or partnership. In addition, there may be adverse tax effects on winding up.

We suggest you work Self Study Problems Fifteen-1 and 2 at this point.

Tax Reduction And Deferral

Approach

15-12.   As we have noted, whether the use of a corporation will result in a reduction or deferral of taxes will depend on the type of income being earned, as well as the type of corporation. In this section, we will examine this issue by using a basic example to consider this issue in the following situations:

- A public corporation.

- A CCPC earning active business income that is eligible for the small business deduction, and business and property income that is not eligible for the small business deduction.

- A CCPC earning investment income (net taxable capital gains and other property income, excluding dividends).

- A CCPC earning both eligible and non-eligible dividend income.

15-13.   These cases should serve to provide you with a good understanding of the ability of incorporation to provide either tax reductions or tax deferral for an individual taxpayer under current rates of corporation taxation.

15-14.   To assist you in understanding this material (which is covered in detail in Chapter 13), we remind you that eligible dividends include:

- Designated dividends paid by CCPCs with a positive General Rate Income Pool (GRIP) at the end of the taxation year in which the dividend is paid.

- Designated dividends paid by non-CCPCs that do not have a positive Low Rate Income Pool (LRIP) balance at the time the dividend is paid.

Basic Example
Data On The Individual Taxpayer

15-15.   In order to consider the various results that can be achieved by incorporating a source of income, we will use a simple example in which an individual, Mr. Renaud, has access to $100,000 in income that he can either receive directly or channel through a corporation. We will assume that, before any consideration of this additional $100,000, Mr. Renaud has sufficient Taxable Income to place him in the maximum federal tax bracket of 33 percent (amounts over $205,842 for 2018).   The Tax Payable on his other income is sufficient to absorb all of his personal and other tax credits.

15-16.   To illustrate the effects of incorporating different types of income, several cases will be presented with varying assumptions as to the source of this income and the type of corporation that will be established.   However, before turning to these cases, we will give consideration to the various personal and corporate tax rates that will be used.

Personal Tax Rates And Tax Payable

15-17.   In these examples, we will assume that Mr. Renaud lives in a province where the maximum provincial tax rate on individuals is 16 percent. As all of Mr. Renaud's additional income will be subject to this maximum rate, his combined federal/provincial marginal rate will be 49 (33 + 16) percent. The 16 percent provincial rate that we are using is just below the 2018 average for the various provinces. However, it is significantly below the maximum rate of 21 percent.

15-18.   This 49 percent rate is applicable to the direct receipt of income. This means that, if Mr. Renaud receives the $100,000 in income without channeling it through a corporation, taxes of $49,000 will be paid and $51,000 will be retained.

15-19.   If the income is channeled through a corporation, the situation becomes more complex. Taxes must be paid at the corporate level, leaving only part of the total income available for distribution to shareholders. When this after tax amount is distributed to the shareholders, the amount of dividends received must be grossed up, with this amount providing a basis for a credit against Tax Payable. The amounts involved will depend on whether the dividends are non-eligible (e.g., paid by a CCPC out of income that has benefited from the small business deduction), or eligible (e.g. paid by a non-CCPC out of fully taxed income):

Non-Eligible Dividends These dividends are grossed up by 16 percent and benefit from a federal dividend tax credit of 8/11 of the gross up. We will assume that Mr.

Renaud lives in a province where the dividend tax credit on non-eligible dividends is 22 percent of the dividend gross up (the 2018 average for the 10 provinces).

Eligible Dividends These dividends are grossed up by 38 percent and benefit from a federal dividend tax credit of 6/11 of the gross up. We will assume that Mr. Renaud lives in a province where the dividend tax credit on eligible dividends is 34 percent of the dividend gross up (the 2018 average for the 10 provinces).

15-20. Using these gross up and tax credit amounts, the rates applicable to Mr. Renaud on eligible and non-eligible dividends can be calculated as follows:

Personal Tax On Dividends	Non-Eligible Dividends	Eligible Dividends
Provincial Dividend Tax Credit	22.0%	34.0%
Dividends Received	100.0%	100.0%
Gross Up	16.0%	38.0%
Taxable Dividends	116.0%	138.0%
Times The Combined Federal/Provincial Tax Rate	49.0%	49.0%
Equals: Combined Federal/Provincial		
Tax Rate On Dividends Received	56.8%	67.6%
Less: Dividend Tax Credit [(8/11 + 22%)(16%)]	(15.2%)	
Less: Dividend Tax Credit [(6/11 + 34%)(38%)]		(33.6%)
Effective Personal Tax Rate On Dividends Received	41.6%	34.0%

15-21. For use in our examples, we will round the non-eligible rate to 42 percent. For eligible dividends, we will use 34 percent.

Corporate Tax Rates

15-22. In making the required calculations, we will use the corporate federal tax rates that apply for the 2018 calendar year. With respect to provincial rates, we will use 3 percent for income eligible for the small business deduction and 13 percent for other income. Both of these rates are close to the average rates applicable in the 10 provinces. When these provincial rates are added to the corresponding federal rates, the combined rates are 13 percent (10% + 3%) for income eligible for the small business deduction and 28 percent (15% + 13%) for other income. The following table provides the rates that will be used in our examples:

General Part I Tax Rate	38%
Federal Tax Abatement	10%
General Rate Reduction (GRR)	13%
Refundable Tax On Investment Income Of A CCPC (ART)	10-2/3%
Federal Small Business Deduction	18%
Provincial Tax Rates	
Income Eligible For Federal Small Business Deduction	3%
Income Not Eligible For Federal Small Business Deduction	13%
Refundable Portion Of Part I Tax On Investment Income	30-2/3%
Refundable Part IV Tax	38-1/3%

15-23. Note that the general rate reduction is not applicable to income that benefits from either the small business deduction or the M&P deduction. In addition, it is not applicable to aggregate investment income of a CCPC which attracts the 10-2/3 percent Additional Refundable Tax (ART).

15-24. We will apply this basic information, in a number of different situations, in order to examine the question of whether the incorporation of $100,000 in income will serve to either reduce or defer taxes for an individual taxpayer.

Public Corporation
M&P Deduction
15-25.   As discussed in Chapter 12, both the M&P deduction and the GRR are at the same rate. As these two provisions cannot be used simultaneously, the effective federal tax rate will not be altered by the use of the M&P deduction. Given this, we will not give separate attention to situations where a public corporation is earning income that is eligible for the M&P deduction. Keep in mind, however, that companies will continue to make the M&P calculation in those provinces where there is a favourable provincial rate for this type of income.

General Results
15-26.   With only $100,000 of income, there is no possibility that Mr. Renaud would be in a position to establish a public company. However, this case does serve to illustrate a simple calculation of corporate taxes. In addition, this same tax calculation would apply to a CCPC on amounts of active business income in excess of the CCPC's allocated annual business limit.

15-27.   As discussed in Chapter 13, dividends paid by non-CCPCs, a category that includes public companies, will generally be designated as eligible. There will be situations, however, where a public corporation has an LRIP. While this raises the possibility that at least some of the dividends paid by such a company would be non-eligible, we do not feel that this situation is of sufficient importance that an illustration of the tax reduction and deferral results is warranted. It should be fairly obvious to you that for non-eligible dividends, the tax reduction results would be significantly worse than those illustrated in the following calculations.

Public Corporation	
Federal Tax [(38%)($100,000)]	$38,000
Federal Tax Abatement [(10%)($100,000)]	(10,000)
General Rate Reduction [(13%)($100,000)]	(13,000)
Federal Tax Payable	$15,000
Provincial Tax Payable [(13%)($100,000)]	13,000
Corporate Tax Payable	$28,000
Corporate Business Income	$100,000
Corporate Tax Payable	(28,000)
Maximum Eligible Dividend Payable	$ 72,000
Personal Tax On Eligible Dividends [(34%)($72,000)]	(24,480)
Income Retained By The Individual	$ 47,520
After Tax Retention - With Corporation	$ 47,520
After Tax Retention - Without Corporation	(51,000)
Advantage (Disadvantage) With Corporation	($ 3,480)

Analysis
15-28.   If the $100,000 had been received directly, $51,000 [($100,000)(1 - .49)] would be retained, an amount greater than the $47,520 that is retained when the $100,000 is flowed through a public corporation. In terms of total taxes, incorporation is clearly not desirable.

15-29.   However, there is a deferral of tax on income that is left within the corporation. Taxes at the corporate level are $28,000, significantly less than the $49,000 that would be paid on the direct receipt of income. There is some question as to whether this amount of deferral would justify the payment of an additional $3,480 in taxes.

15-30.   More to the point is that, in real world terms, deferral is not an issue for shareholders of publicly traded companies. In the case of private corporations with a single shareholder or a small shareholder group, these individuals can control the extent to which their corporation distributes resources. If they do not have an immediate need for funds, tax deferral can be achieved by leaving resources in their corporation.

15-31.   This is not the case with large publicly traded companies. Their dividend decisions are based on a large number of factors, including corporate cash needs and the maximization of share values. The cash flow needs of individual shareholders would rarely be at the top of this list.

Integration And Eligible Dividends

15-32.   The preceding example is based on the public corporation paying eligible dividends. The government's stated goal in bringing in the eligible dividends legislation was to improve integration by lowering the total corporate and personal taxes paid on income flowed through a public company. The calculations in Paragraph 15-27 make it clear that, at current corporate tax rates, this stated goal has not been achieved.

15-33.   As discussed in Chapter 7, the gross up and tax credit procedures on eligible dividends are based on a notional corporate tax rate of 27.54 percent. As the combined federal/provincial rates for 2018 average 28 percent, which is close to the required rate for integration to be effective, corporate tax rates are not the main problem.

15-34.   The problem is with the dividend tax credit rates. Effective integration requires the combined federal/provincial tax credit to be equal to the gross up. This means that, given the federal rate of 6/11, the provincial dividend tax credit would have to be 5/11 or 45.5 percent. In actual fact, most of the provincial dividend tax credit rates are below this level, ranging from a low of 18.2 percent to a high of 47.1 percent.

Exercise Fifteen - 1

Subject: Eligible Dividends And Integration

Ms. Jennifer Ashley is the owner of a number of successful CCPCs. For 2018, she has sufficient income that any additional personal income will be taxed at a combined federal/provincial rate of 45 percent. She lives in a province where the provincial tax credit on eligible dividends is equal to 47.1 percent of the gross up. Ms. Ashley has made an investment in a business venture that she anticipates will generate $100,000 of active business income during the coming year. If she retains personal ownership of this investment, she will retain $55,000 [($100,000)(1 - 45%)] after taxes. If she transfers this investment to a new private corporation, it would not be allocated any amount of the small business deduction and its income would be taxed at a combined federal/provincial rate of 26.5 percent (15% + 11.5%). She has asked your advice as to whether she should retain the investment personally, or transfer it to a new corporation. Provide the information required by Ms. Ashley.

SOLUTION available in print and online Study Guide.

CCPC - Active Business Income

General Results

15-35.   A CCPC can be subject to two different tax rates on its active business income. A low rate is available on up to $500,000 of income that is eligible for the small business deduction, with a higher tax rate assessed on income that is not eligible for this valuable deduction. With respect to the provinces, there is a similar dual rate system. In addition, we will have to take into consideration the fact that dividends that have been paid out of income that has benefited from the small business deduction cannot be designated as eligible dividends.

15-36.   We will continue to use the Mr. Renaud example from Paragraph 15-15 to illustrate the tax consequences of applying these two rates. While using the basic data from this example, we will consider two different cases:

Case One   In Case One, we will assume that the corporate income is eligible for the small business deduction. This means that dividends that are received by Mr. Renaud will be non-eligible and subject to tax at a rate of 42 percent (see Paragraph 15-21).

Case Two   In Case Two, we will assume that none of the corporate income is eligible for the small business deduction (the full amount has been allocated to an associated corporation). This means that the dividends that are received by Mr. Renaud can be designated as eligible and subject to tax at a rate of 34 percent. You will note that the results in this case are identical to those for a public corporation (see Paragraph 15-27).

Active Business Income Of CCPC	Case One SBD Deduction	Case Two No SBD
Federal Tax [(38%)($100,000)]	$ 38,000	$ 38,000
Federal Tax Abatement [(10%)($100,000)]	(10,000)	(10,000)
Small Business Deduction [(18%)($100,000)]	(18,000)	N/A
General Rate Reduction [(13%)($100,000)]	N/A	(13,000)
Federal Tax Payable	$ 10,000	$ 15,000
Provincial Tax Payable:		
At 3 Percent	3,000	N/A
At 13 Percent	N/A	13,000
Corporate Tax Payable	$ 13,000	$ 28,000
Corporate Business Income	$100,000	$100,000
Corporate Tax Payable	(13,000)	(28,000)
Maximum Dividend Payable	$ 87,000	$ 72,000
Personal Tax At 42 Percent (Non-Eligible)	(36,540)	N/A
Personal Tax At 34 Percent (Eligible)	N/A	(24,480)
Income Retained By The Individual	$ 50,460	$ 47,520
After Tax Retention - With Corporation	$ 50,460	$ 47,520
After Tax Retention - Without Corporation	(51,000)	(51,000)
Advantage (Disadvantage) With Corporation	($ 540)	($ 3,480)

Analysis

15-37.   As can be seen in the preceding table, there is a disadvantage for income flowed through a corporation, even when that income is eligible for the small business deduction. In the absence of the small business deduction, the corporate choice results in a $3,480 disadvantage.

15-38.   In both cases the use of a corporation results in deferral of taxes. In the small business deduction case the corporate taxes are only $13,000, as compared to $49,000 when the income is received directly. When this significant amount of deferral is combined with the small tax disadvantage associated with this alternative, using the corporate route when the small business deduction is available seems advantageous. Note, however, the benefit of the deferral can only be achieved if the funds are left in the corporation.

15-39.   The situation is less clear when the small business deduction is not available. As corporate taxes are only $28,000, well below the $49,000 that would be paid on direct receipt of income, there is significant deferral. However, the price that is paid for this is $3,480 in extra taxes to be paid when the income is distributed by the corporation. If Mr. Renaud is in a position to leave the funds in the corporation for some length of time, it seems likely that he would find this to be a worthwhile trade off.

15-40.   A further point related to tax deferral is sometimes overlooked. Any income that is left in the corporation should not be left idle. If it is not needed in the principal activities, it is likely that it will be invested in assets that will produce investment income. If this income is taxed as investment income, the result will be prepayment of taxes at the corporate level. This will be illustrated in a later example when we look at the taxation of investment income received by a Canadian controlled private corporation.

Exercise Fifteen - 2

Subject: Incorporation Of Active Business Income

Keith Slater has an unincorporated business that he anticipates will have active business income of $126,000 for the taxation year ending December 31, 2018. He has employment income in excess of $300,000, with additional amounts subject to a provincial tax rate of 16 percent. The provincial dividend tax credit is equal to 3/11 of the dividend gross up for non-eligible dividends. Also in his province of residence, the corporate tax rate is 4 percent on income eligible for the small business deduction and 12 percent on other income. Mr. Slater has asked your advice as to whether he should incorporate this business. Advise him with respect to any tax deferral that could be available on income left in the corporation and on any tax savings that could be available if all of the income is paid out as dividends.

SOLUTION available in print and online Study Guide.

"Bonusing Down" Active Business Income

15-41.   A traditional tax planning technique for owners of CCPCs that have active business income in excess of their annual business limit is to "bonus down". As our example has shown, income that is eligible for the small business deduction benefits from significant tax deferral, as well as a modest tax savings. In contrast, if a CCPC's Taxable Income does not benefit from the small business deduction, the after tax retention of this excess income will be lower than that from direct receipt of the income. As shown in Paragraph 15-36, the after tax retention on $100,000 of income that is not eligible for the small business deduction is $3,480 less than if the income is received directly.

15-42.   When it is likely that a CCPC will have Taxable Income in excess of its annual business limit ($500,000 if there are no associated companies), the simple solution is for the owner of the CCPC to pay himself sufficient additional salary that the corporation's Taxable Income will be reduced to the amount of income that is eligible for the small business deduction.

> **EXAMPLE**   In our example, if Mr. Renaud had a CCPC with active business income of $600,000, paying additional salary of $100,000 would result in after tax retention of $51,000 on receipt of this salary. This, of course, is $3,480 higher than the $47,520 that would be paid if the $100,000 ($600,000 - $500,000) that is not eligible for the small business deduction was taxed at the corporate level, with the residual amount being paid to Mr. Renaud as eligible dividends.

15-43.   Tax practitioners sometimes find it difficult to convince some individuals that bonusing down is a good idea. The problem is that bonusing down involves paying taxes out of the owner-manager's personal funds. It is not uncommon to encounter individuals who, even in situations where there is a clear cut tax advantage to using this procedure, will simply refuse to make the required salary payments. While this is usually not a rational decision, it appears to reflect a greater level of comfort for an owner-manager when he does not have to pay the taxes directly out of his personal assets.

Electing Out Of The Small Business Deduction

15-44.   ITA 89(11) allows a CCPC to make an election not to be a CCPC. A related provision, ITA 89(12), allows a corporation to revoke the ITA 89(11) election and return to being a CCPC. Note that the use of either of these provisions creates a deemed year end. In some circumstances, this may have adverse tax consequences (e.g., shortened loss carry forward periods).

15-45.   The good news is that making this election will allow the corporation to designate its dividends as eligible. The bad news is that it will lose the small business deduction. While there may be some situations where this election may be useful, the fact that it appears to have a significant tax cost would suggest that its application would be rare.

CCPC - Investment Income Other Than Dividends

15-46.   As was discussed in Chapter 13, the aggregate investment income of a CCPC is taxed at full corporate rates. Neither the small business deduction nor the general rate reduction is available to offset these rates. In addition, there is an additional refundable tax under ITA 123.3 (the ART) equal to 10-2/3 percent of investment income.

15-47.   To offset this high level of taxation, a dividend refund is available at a rate of 38-1/3 percent of dividends paid.   Note, however, investment income that is eligible for a refund does not add to the corporation's GRIP balance. This means that it does not contribute to the corporation's ability to pay dividends that are eligible for the enhanced gross up and tax credit procedures.

15-48.   Continuing our Mr. Renaud example from Paragraph 15-15, after tax retention on $100,000 of investment income received by a CCPC, compared to the direct receipt of investment income, would be as follows:

Investment Income Of CCPC

Federal Tax [(38%)($100,000)]	$ 38,000
Additional Refundable Tax [(10-2/3%)($100,000)]	10,667
Federal Tax Abatement [(10%)($100,000)]	(10,000)
Federal Tax Payable	$ 38,667
Provincial Tax Payable [(13%)($100,000)]	13,000
Corporate Tax Payable	$ 51,667
RDTOH Balance [(30-2/3%)($100,000)]	$ 30,667
Corporate Investment Income	$100,000
Corporate Tax Payable	(51,667)
Net Corporate Income Before Dividend Refund	$ 48,333
Dividend Refund (See Note)	30,044
Maximum Dividend Payable	$ 78,377
Personal Tax On Non-Eligible Dividends At 42 Percent	(32,918)
Income Retained By The Individual	$ 45,459
After Tax Retention - With Corporation	$ 45,459
After Tax Retention - Without Corporation	(51,000)
Advantage (Disadvantage) With Corporation	($ 5,541)

Note   The dividend refund is the lesser of the balance in the RDTOH account and 38-1/3 percent of taxable dividends paid. The available cash of $48,333 would support a dividend of $78,377 ($48,333 ÷ .61667), which includes a potential dividend refund of $30,044 [(38-1/3%)($78,377)]. This is less than the balance in the RDTOH so a dividend refund of $30,044 is available which leaves an RDTOH balance of $623.

15-49.   As the corporate taxes of $51,667 exceed $49,000 that would be paid on direct receipt of the $100,000, there is no deferral of taxes through the use of a corporation. When this is combined with the $5,541 reduction in after tax retention, it is clear that the use of a corporation in this situation would be a bad idea.

Exercise Fifteen - 3

Subject: Incorporation Of Interest Income

David Slater has investments that he anticipates will earn interest income of $126,000 for the year ending December 31, 2018.   He has employment income in excess of $300,000, with additional amounts subject to a provincial tax rate of 18 percent. The provincial dividend tax credit is equal to 3/11 of the dividend gross up for non-eligible dividends. Also in his province of residence, the corporate tax rate is 4 percent on income eligible for the small business deduction and 12 percent on other income. Mr. Slater has asked your advice as to whether he should transfer these investments to a corporation in which he would own all of the shares. Advise him with respect to any tax deferral that could be available on income left in the corporation and on any tax savings that could be available if all of the income is paid out as dividends.

SOLUTION available in print and online Study Guide.

We suggest you work Self Study Problem Fifteen-3 at this point.

CCPC - Dividend Income
Possible Sources Of Dividend Income
15-50.   A CCPC can only designate dividends as eligible to the extent that it has a balance in its GRIP.   Dividend receipts that increase this balance enable the CCPC to designate its dividends as eligible. In general, dividends received by a CCPC will be subject to Part IV tax. The exception to this is if the dividend is received from a connected company that did not claim a dividend refund as a result of paying the dividend.   Dividend income effects for a CCPC can be summarized as follows:

Eligible Dividends   Any dividends received (portfolio or connected company) that have been designated eligible will be added to the CCPC's GRIP balance. Non-eligible dividends have no effect on the CCPC's GRIP balance.

Portfolio Dividends These dividends will be subject to Part IV tax regardless of whether they are eligible or non-eligible.

Connected Company Dividends These dividends can be eligible or non-eligible and may be subject to Part IV tax depending on:

- If a dividend refund results from the dividend payment, the dividends will be subject to Part IV tax. The fact that there is a dividend refund generally means that the connected company had investment income.

- If no dividend refund results from the dividend payment, the dividends will not be subject to Part IV tax. The fact that there is no dividend refund generally means that the connected company had income that benefitted from the small business deduction.

Analysis
15-51.   Recalling that Mr. Renaud would pay taxes on eligible dividends received at a rate of 34 percent (see Paragraph 15-21), his after tax retention on the direct receipt of $100,000 of these dividends would be $66,000 [($100,000)(1 - .34)]. His rate on non-eligible dividends is 42 percent (see Paragraph 15-21) and this would result in after tax retention of $58,000 [($100,000)(1 - .42)]. A comparison of this retention with the after tax results from using a corporation, assuming the connected company paid non-eligible dividends, would be as follows:

Dividend Income Of CCPC	Eligible Portfolio Dividends	Non-Eligible Portfolio Dividends	Connected With Refund	Connected No Refund
Corporate Dividend Income	$100,000	$100,000	$100,000	$100,000
Part IV Tax Payable At 38-1/3%	(38,333)	(38,333)	(38,333)	N/A
Net Corporate Income				
Before Dividend Refund	$ 61,667	$ 61,667	$ 61,667	$100,000
Dividend Refund At 38-1/3%	38,333	38,333	38,333	N/A
Maximum Dividend Payable	$100,000	$100,000	$100,000	$100,000
Personal Tax On:				
Eligible Dividends At 34%	(34,000)			
Non-Eligible Dividends At 42%	N/A	(42,000)	(42,000)	(42,000)
Income Retained By Individual	$ 66,000	$ 58,000	$ 58,000	$ 58,000
After Tax Retention:				
With Corporation	$ 66,000	$ 58,000	$ 58,000	$ 58,000
Without Corporation	(66,000)	(58,000)	(58,000)	(58,000)
Advantage (Disadvantage)	Nil	Nil	Nil	Nil

15-52. In all cases, the dividends that can flow through to the investor total the full $100,000 that was received by the corporation. As a result, the total Tax Payable on dividends is the same whether the investment is held personally or in a corporation.

15-53. The Part IV tax does, however, influence the conclusions on tax deferral. If the dividends are subject to Part IV tax, this 38-1/3 percent tax is higher than the 34 percent tax rate on eligible dividends received by Mr. Renaud, and less than the 42 percent tax rate applicable to non-eligible dividends. As a result, there is a prepayment of taxes on eligible dividends that are flowed through a corporation.

15-54. The situation is different in the absence of a Part IV tax in that no taxes will be assessed on dividends received at the corporate level. This, of course, provides for a significant deferral of Tax Payable on dividends not subject to Part IV tax.

Conclusions On Tax Reductions And Deferrals

15-55. The results from the preceding cases can be summarized as follows:

	Corporate Taxes Before Dividend Refund	After Tax Retention On Flow Through
Public Corporation ($100,000 Of Income)		
(Paragraph 15-27):	$28,000	$47,520
CCPC ($100,000 Of Active Business Income):		
Eligible For SBD (Paragraph 15-36)	$13,000	$50,460
Not Eligible For SBD (Paragraph 15-36)	28,000	47,520
CCPC ($100,000 Of Interest Income):		
Investment Income (Paragraph 15-48)	$51,667	$45,459
CCPC ($100,000 Of Dividend Income):		
Eligible Portfolio Dividends (Paragraph 15-51)	$38,333	$66,000
Non-Eligible Portfolio Dividends (Paragraph 15-51)	38,333	58,000
Connected With Refund (Paragraph 15-51)	38,333	58,000
Connected No Refund (Paragraph 15-51)	Nil	58,000

15-56.　The conclusions reached can be summarized as follows:

Tax Reduction Available　As illustrated previously, Mr. Renaud is subject to taxes on the direct receipt of income, other than dividends, at a rate of 49 percent, while his rate on the direct receipt of dividends is 34 percent (eligible) or 42 percent (non-eligible). This means that his after tax retention resulting from the direct receipt of income would be:

- $51,000 On $100,000 Of Business Or Interest Income
- $66,000 On $100,000 Of Eligible Dividend Income
- $58,000 On $100,000 Of Non-Eligible Dividend Income

Comparing these amounts to those in the preceding table, there is no case where there is a reduction in taxes through the use of a corporation. The least unfavourable scenario is where a CCPC is earning active business income. In this case, the tax cost of $540 is relatively small.

When a public company is involved, the use of a corporation results in the payment of $3,480 more taxes and correspondingly less retention ($47,520 vs. $51,000). The same $3,480 shortfall results when a CCPC is earning active business income that is not eligible for the small business deduction. The situation is even worse for investment income earned by a CCPC. The shortfall here is $5,541 ($45,459 vs. $51,000).

In the case of dividend income received by a CCPC, the after tax results are the same whether the income is received directly or flowed through a corporation.

Tax Deferral Available　Tax deferral occurs when income is not distributed to shareholders and taxes paid at the corporate level are less than those that would be paid if the income was received directly by the shareholder. On direct receipt of relevant amounts, Mr. Renaud would pay the following amounts in income tax:

- $49,000 On $100,000 Of Business Or Interest Income
- $34,000 On $100,000 Of Eligible Dividend Income
- $42,000 On $100,000 Of Non-Eligible Dividend Income

Comparing these amounts to the corporate tax amounts in the preceding table, we find that there is tax deferral in some, but not all cases.

There is deferral in the case of public companies, with taxes on business or interest income only $28,000 at the corporate level.

The worst case scenario is when a CCPC earns interest income. Corporate taxes are $51,667, as compared to $49,000 on direct receipt of income.

In the cases where Part IV tax is applicable, the $38,333 that would be required when that tax is assessed, is larger than the $34,000 that would be paid on the direct receipt of eligible dividends, but smaller than the $42,000 that would be paid on the direct receipt of non-eligible dividends.

The most significant amounts of deferral are available to a CCPC earning active business income eligible for the small business deduction, or dividend income that is not subject to Part IV tax. In the case of income eligible for the small business deduction, taxes at the corporate level are $13,000, $36,000 less than the $49,000 that would have been paid on the direct receipt of this income.

Even if a CCPC has active business income that is not eligible for the small business deduction, taxes on $100,000 of this additional income would only be $28,000, $21,000 less than the $49,000 payable on direct receipt of this amount of income.

There is also deferral in the case of dividend income when it is not subject to Part IV tax. However, for dividends to not be subject to Part IV tax, they must be received from a connected corporation that did not receive a dividend refund as a result of their payment. This would generally involve payment from a CCPC earning business income. This means that deferral would have been available at the level of the paying corporation, without the use of an additional corporation to receive the dividends.

15-57.   These conclusions are based on assumed provincial personal and corporate tax rates as outlined previously. While the rates we have used are within the range of current actual rates, the use of other rates will produce different results. As these differences can be important, we will give some attention to this issue in the next section of this Chapter.

Exercise Fifteen - 4

Subject: Incorporation Of Interest And Dividend Income

One of your clients has asked your advice on whether he should transfer a group of investments to a new Canadian controlled private corporation that can be established to hold them. He anticipates that the transferred investments will have the following amounts of income during the 2018 taxation year:

Eligible Dividends On Portfolio Investments	$46,000
Non-Eligible Dividends From 100 Percent Owned Subsidiary	
(A Dividend Refund Of $29,000 Will Be Received by The Payor)	87,000
Interest Income	32,000

Although he has employment income of over $250,000, your client needs all of the income that is produced by these investments as he has newborn quintuplets. On additional amounts of income, your client is subject to a provincial tax rate of 18 percent. The provincial dividend tax credit is equal to 5/11 of the dividend gross up for eligible dividends and 3/11 of the dividend gross up on non-eligible dividends. The corporation will be subject to a provincial tax rate of 4.5 percent on income eligible for the small business deduction and 12 percent on other income. The corporation will make the maximum eligible dividend designation. Provide the requested advice and explain your conclusions.

Exercise Fifteen - 5

Subject: Incorporation Of Capital Gains

One of your clients has asked your advice on whether she should transfer a group of investments to a new corporation that can be established to hold them. The corporation will be a Canadian controlled private corporation and she anticipates that, during the coming year, the market value of these investments will increase by $92,000. No other income will be generated by the investments.

For the year ending December 31, 2018, your client has employment income in excess of $250,000 and will sell these investments by the end of the year to finance her trip across Canada by bicycle. None of these investments are eligible for the lifetime capital gains deduction. The corporation will be subject to a provincial tax rate of 3.5 percent on income eligible for the small business deduction and 12 percent on other income. On additional personal income, your client is subject to a provincial tax rate of 16 percent. The provincial dividend tax credit is equal to 3/11 of the dividend gross up for non-eligible dividends.

Provide the requested advice, including an explanation of your conclusions.

SOLUTIONS available in print and online Study Guide.

We suggest you work Self Study Problem Fifteen-4 at this point.

Provincial Taxes And Integration

Introduction

15-58.   We have presented a number of different cases dealing with the question of whether it is better, both in terms of tax reduction and tax deferral, for an individual to receive income directly or, alternatively, channel that income through a corporation. In doing so, we have given consideration to both the type of income being earned, and whether the corporation is eligible for the small business deduction on the income.

15-59.   The conclusions that we reached were presented in Paragraph 15-56. We found that, while there were several cases the use of a corporation provided some degree of tax deferral, there were no scenarios that provided a reduction in taxes.

15-60.   It is important to note, however, that all of our conclusions were based on calculations that used average provincial tax rates. As discussed in other Chapters of this text, there are wide variations in all of these provincial amounts. Further, these variations can provide results that are different than those summarized in Paragraphs 15-55 and 15-56. For example, if a province legislates a tax free period of time for corporations that move within its jurisdiction, this will make the use of a corporation more attractive in that province.

15-61.   This section will be concerned with how variations in provincial tax rates can influence the decision to incorporate. In doing so, we will not attempt to delineate every possible combination of rates and type of income. With 10 provinces and 3 territories, several different types of income, and various corporate, individual and dividend tax credit rates to consider, there are literally hundreds of possible combinations. Given this, our goal will be to help you understand how changes in each of the provincial rates will act to influence conclusions on the use of a corporation for tax deferral or tax reduction purposes.

Tax Deferral

15-62.   The analysis of using a corporation to provide tax deferral is very straightforward. If the combined federal/provincial tax rate on corporations is less than the combined federal/provincial tax rate on individuals, the use of a corporation provides for deferral. Some examples of this analysis are as follows:

Alberta CCPC Earning Active Business Income   The combined federal/provincial tax rate on the corporation would be 12 percent. For an Alberta resident individual in the maximum tax bracket, the combined federal/provincial rate would be 48 percent. In this case, the use of a corporation would clearly provide deferral.

Manitoba CCPC Earning Investment Income   The combined federal/provincial tax rate on the corporation would be 50.7 percent. For a Manitoba resident individual in the maximum tax bracket, the combined federal/provincial rate would be 50.4 percent. In this case, there would also be a small amount of deferral.

British Columbia Public Corporation (or CCPC Earning Over $500,000 In Active Business Income)   The combined federal/provincial tax rate on the corporation or income would be 27 percent. For a British Columbia resident individual in the maximum tax bracket, the combined federal/provincial rate would be 49.8 percent. In this case, the use of a corporation would clearly provide deferral.

15-63.   We would remind you not to look at the deferral issue in isolation from other considerations. If the income will be distributed out of the corporation in the future, both tax deferral and tax reduction must be considered. If all of the income will be distributed immediately, tax deferral is irrelevant.

Tax Reduction

Introduction

15-64.   The question of whether a corporation can be used to reduce tax involves a more complex analysis. In looking at the after tax retention when income is received directly, only the combined federal/provincial tax rate on individuals is relevant. However, in looking at after tax retention of income that is flowed through a corporation, three factors must be considered:

1. The combined federal/provincial tax rate on individuals.
2. The combined federal/provincial tax rate on corporations.
3. The combined federal/provincial dividend tax credit.

15-65.   As we will demonstrate in the next section, the first of these factors is not influential in this analysis. For any given combination of corporate tax rates and dividend tax credit rates, the conclusion on whether a corporation can be used to reduce taxes will be the same, without regard to the tax rate on individuals.

15-66.   The real determinate here is the relationship between the combined corporate tax rate and the combined dividend tax credit. As our later analysis will show, if the combined dividend tax credit exceeds the combined corporate taxes paid, the use of a corporation will reduce taxes. Alternatively, if the credit is less than the corporate taxes, direct receipt of income will be preferable.

Provincial Rates On Individuals

15-67.   Maximum combined federal/provincial tax rates on individuals range from a low of 47.5 percent in Saskatchewan to a high of 54 percent in Nova Scotia. Note, however, variations in the combined rate influence both the direct receipt of income and the amounts that are flowed through a corporation. That is, a high tax rate on individuals will reduce after tax retention on both the direct receipt of income, as well as on the after tax retention of income flowed through a corporation. Correspondingly, a low tax rate on individuals will increase both types of after tax retention.

15-68.   What this means is that, for any specific combination of corporate tax rate and dividend tax credit rate, the tax rate applicable to individuals will not alter the conclusion on whether the use of a corporation will serve to reduce taxes. While the amount of the advantage or disadvantage associated with the use of a corporation will vary with the tax rate on individuals, the conclusion on the ability of a corporation to reduce taxes will not. This is illustrated by the following example.

> **EXAMPLE**   A CCPC has $100,000 of active business income that will be taxed at a combined federal/provincial rate of 13 percent. The provincial dividend tax credit on non-eligible dividends is equal to 3/11 of the gross up. We will consider two cases, the first based on the assumption that Niko Parma is taxed at a combined federal/provincial rate of 48 percent (33% federal, plus 15% provincial), the second based on the assumption that Nela Parma is taxed at a combined federal/provincial rate of 54 percent (33% federal, plus 21% provincial).
>
> **ANALYSIS**   If the individuals received the $100,000 directly, Niko's after tax retention would be $52,000 [($100,000)(1 - .48)] and Nela's would be $46,000 [($100,000)(1 - .54)]. The after retention if the income is flowed through a corporation would be as follows:

Comparison - Rates For Individuals	Niko (48%)	Nela (54%)
Corporate Income	$100,000	$100,000
Corporate Taxes At 13 Percent	(13,000)	(13,000)
Available For Dividends	$ 87,000	$ 87,000

	Niko (48%)	Nela (54%)
Non-Eligible Dividends Received	$ 87,000	$ 87,000
Gross Up (16%)	13,920	13,920
Taxable Dividends	$100,920	$100,920
Individual Tax Rate	48%	54%
Taxes Before Dividend Tax Credit	$ 48,442	$ 54,497
Dividend Tax Credit (Equal Gross Up)	(13,920)	(13,920)
Individual Taxes	$ 34,522	$ 40,577
Dividends Received	$ 87,000	$ 87,000
Individual Taxes	(34,522)	(40,577)
After Tax Retention	$ 52,478	$ 46,423
After Tax Retention With Corporation	$ 52,478	$ 46,423
Direct Receipt Retention	(52,000)	(46,000)
Advantage With Corporation	$ 478	$ 423

15-69.   This example involves a low corporate tax rate of 13 percent, a factor that favours the use of a corporation. That is why, in this example, better after tax retention results from the use of a corporation, without regard to the individual's personal tax rate. While the amount of the advantage varies with the provincial tax rate on individuals, the conclusion that a corporation can be used to reduce taxes does not.

Provincial Dividend Tax Credit And Provincial Corporate Tax Rates

15-70.   As can be seen in the preceding example, the major determinate of whether the use of a corporation will provide tax reduction is the relationship between the combined federal and provincial taxes paid at the corporate level, and the combined federal/provincial dividend tax credit. As the federal components of these values do not vary, the provincial rates become the determining factor.

15-71.   The rules here can be stated fairly simply:

Favourable To Incorporation   If the combined federal/provincial dividend tax credit exceeds the combined taxes paid at the corporate level, the use of a corporation will reduce taxes and provide a higher level of after tax retention. This is sometimes referred to as over integration.

Unfavourable To Incorporation   If the combined federal/provincial dividend tax credit is less than the combined taxes paid at the corporate level, the use of a corporation will increase taxes and reduce the amount of after tax retention. This is sometimes referred to as under integration.

Examples - Effects Of Provincial Rates On Integration
Data

15-72.   The range of values in the 10 provinces for provincial corporate tax rates and provincial dividend tax credit rates are as follows:

Corporate Tax Rates   The provincial rates for public companies (which would also apply to CCPCs whose active business income is not eligible for the small business deduction) range from 11.5 percent to 16 percent. When these are combined with the federal rate of 15 percent, the combined rates range from 26.5 percent to 31 percent.

The provincial rates for CCPCs earning income eligible for the small business deduction range from zero percent to 8 percent. When these are combined with the federal rate of 10 percent, the combined rates range from 10 percent to 18 percent.

Dividend Tax Credit Rates   The provincial rates for eligible dividends range from 18.2 percent of the gross up to 47.1 percent of the gross up. When combined with the federal rate of 6/11 (54.5%) of the gross up, the combined rates range from 72.7 percent of the gross up to 101.6 percent of the gross up.

The provincial rates on non-eligible dividends range from 5.5 percent of the gross up to 50.4 percent. When combined with the federal rate of 8/11 (72.7%) of the gross up, the combined rates range from 78.2 percent to 123.1 percent of the gross up.

15-73.   The following two examples illustrate the effects of provincial corporate tax rates and provincial dividend tax credit rates on the after tax retention for individuals. They both use the following information:

EXAMPLE   The company has $100,000 in business income. The shareholders will be taxed at a combined federal/provincial rate of 45 percent. If the $100,000 of income is received directly by the individuals, they will retain $55,000 [($100,000)(1 - .45)].

Public Company Paying Eligible Dividends

15-74.   Dealing first with public companies that are paying eligible dividends, we will consider the following three alternative cases:

Perfect Integration   For a public company paying eligible dividends, perfect integration occurs when the combined federal/provincial tax rate on corporations is 27.53623 percent (for this example, we have rounded this to 27.536) and the dividend tax credit is equal to one (6/11 + 5/11).

Worst Case   Here we will use a combination of the highest corporate tax rate (31%) and the lowest dividend tax credit rate (72.7%).

Best Case   Here we will use a combination of the lowest corporate tax rate (26.5%) and the highest dividend tax credit rate (101.6%).

ANALYSIS   If the income is flowed through a corporation, the after tax retention under the three cases described would be as follows:

Public Company	Perfect Integration	Worst Case (31%/72.7%)	Best Case (26.5%/101.6%)
Corporate Income	$100,000	$100,000	$100,000
Corporate Taxes:			
At 27.536 Percent	(27,536)		
At 31 Percent (Worst)		(31,000)	
At 26.5 Percent (Best)			(26,500)
Available For Dividends	$ 72,464	$ 69,000	$ 73,500
Eligible Dividends Received	$ 72,464	$ 69,000	$ 73,500
Gross Up (38%)	27,536	26,220	27,930
Taxable Dividends	$100,000	$ 95,220	$101,430
Individual Tax Rate	45%	45%	45%
Taxes Before Dividend Tax Credit	$ 45,000	$ 42,849	$ 45,644
Dividend Tax Credit:			
[($27,536)(1)]	(27,536)		
[($26,220)(72.7%)] (Worst)		(19,062)	
[($27,930)(101.6%)] (Best)	N/A		(28,377)
Individual Taxes	$ 17,464	$ 23,787	$ 17,267

Public Company	Perfect Integration	Worst Case (31%/72.7%)	Best Case (26.5%/101.6%)
Eligible Dividends Received	$72,464	$69,000	$73,500
Individual Taxes	(17,464)	(23,787)	(17,267)
After Tax Retention With Corporation	$55,000	$45,213	$56,233
After Tax Retention With Corporation	$55,000	$45,213	$56,233
Direct Receipt Retention	(55,000)	(55,000)	(55,000)
Advantage (Disadvantage)	Nil	($ 9,787)	$ 1,233

ANALYSIS - Continued   This example clearly illustrates the influence of varying provincial rates for corporate taxes and dividend tax credits. The results range from a $9,787 reduction in after tax retention with the use of a corporation, to a $1,233 increase in after tax retention with the use of a corporation. Considering that only $100,000 of income was involved, this represents a significant difference in the results achieved through using a corporation.

CCPC Paying Non-Eligible Dividends

15-75.   This example calculates the after tax retention of non-eligible dividends paid by a CCPC. We will consider the following three alternative cases:

Perfect Integration   As you may recall from earlier examples in the text, for a CCPC paying non-eligible dividends, perfect integration occurs when the combined federal/provincial tax rate on corporations is 13.793 percent and the dividend tax credit is equal to one (8/11 + 3/11).

Worst Case   Here we will use a combination of the highest corporate tax rate (18%) and the lowest dividend tax credit rate (78.2%).

Best Case   Here we will use a combination of the lowest corporate tax rate (10%) and the highest dividend tax credit rate (123.1%).

CCPC - Non-Eligible Dividends	Perfect Integration	Worst Case (18%/78.2%)	Best Case (10%/123.1%)
Corporate Income	$100,000	$100,000	$100,000
Corporate Taxes:			
At 13.793 Percent	(13,793)		
At 18.5 Percent (Worst)		(18,000)	
At 10.5 Percent (Best)			(10,000)
Available For Dividends	$ 86,207	$ 82,000	$ 90,000
Non-Eligible Dividends Received	$ 86,207	$ 82,000	$ 90,000
Gross Up (16%)	13,793	13,120	14,400
Taxable Dividends	$100,000	$ 95,120	$104,400
Individual Tax Rate	45%	45%	45%
Taxes Before Dividend Tax Credit	$ 45,000	$ 42,804	$ 46,980
Dividend Tax Credit:			
[($14,530)(1)]	(13,793)		
[($13,120)(78.2%)] (Worst)		(10,260)	
[($14,400)(123.1%)] (Best)	N/A		(17,726)
Individual Taxes	$ 31,207	$ 32,544	$ 29,254

CCPC - Non-Eligible Dividends	Perfect Integration	Worst Case (18%/78.2%)	Best Case (10%/123.1%)
Non-Eligible Dividends Received	$86,207	$82,000	$90,000
Individual Taxes	(31,207)	(32,544)	(29,254)
After Tax Retention With Corporation	$55,000	$49,456	$60,746
After Tax Retention With Corporation	$55,000	$49,456	$60,746
Direct Receipt Retention	(55,000)	(55,000)	(55,000)
Advantage (Disadvantage)	Nil	($ 5,544)	$ 5,746

ANALYSIS   The results extend from a negative $5,544 in the worst case to a positive $5,746 for non-eligible dividends in the best case. This compares to a range of negative $9,787 to a positive $1,233 for eligible dividends. This comparison suggests that integration is working pretty well for non-eligible dividends, with the positive and negative results balanced over the relevant range of provincial corporate tax rates and provincial dividend tax credit rates. This is not the case for eligible dividends. In the best case scenario, there is only $1,233 in over integration. This contrasts with the very large $9,787 under integration result in the worst case scenario. This suggests that with most combinations of provincial corporate tax rates and provincial dividend tax credits, using a corporation that pays eligible dividends results in a higher tax bill for the shareholders.

Summary: Tax Deferral And Tax Reduction

15-76. The preceding examples make it clear that the province in which the corporation and the individual is taxed (which may not be the same province) is a significant factor in deciding whether the use of a corporation will be advantageous. Depending on the type of corporation and the type of income, whether tax deferral is possible depends heavily on the province in which the income is taxed. In a similar fashion, the applicable combination of corporate tax rate and dividend tax credit will determine whether the use of a corporation will serve to reduce taxes.

> **We suggest you work Self Study Problem Fifteen-5 at this point.**

Tax Free Dividends

Tax Rates On Dividends

15-77.   In this Chapter we are concerned with owner-managed businesses and these will typically be CCPCs. In most cases, the bulk of their income will either be active business income that benefits from the small business deduction or, alternatively, investment income that qualifies the corporation for a refund of taxes paid. While such corporations may have a positive GRIP account that will allow them to pay eligible dividends, most of their dividends will be non-eligible. Given this, our analysis will focus on non-eligible dividends that are subject to the gross up of 16 percent.

15-78.   For an individual in the 33 percent federal tax bracket, subject to an 18 percent provincial tax rate on Taxable Income, and living in a province where the dividend tax credit is equal to 3/11 of the gross up on non-eligible dividends and 5/11 on eligible dividends, the combined federal/provincial rate is:

- 43.2% on non-eligible dividends received [(33% + 18%)(116%) - (8/11 + 3/11)(16%)],
- 32.4% on eligible dividends received [(33% + 18%)(138%) - (6/11 + 5/11)(38%)], and
- 25.5% on capital gains [(33% + 18%)(1/2)].

15-79.   The rate on non-eligible dividends is well above that applicable to eligible dividends and capital gains. However, it is well below the maximum 51 percent rate (33% + 18%) that would be applicable to most other types of income. In addition to the fact that dividends are taxed at favourable rates, the structure of the dividend tax credit system is such that a substantial amount of dividends can be received without incurring any taxation. This very desirable result will be explained and illustrated in this section on tax free dividends.

Use Of Tax Credits

Credits In General

15-80.   For 2018, every individual has a personal credit against federal Tax Payable based on $11,809 multiplied by the 15 percent rate applicable to the lowest federal tax bracket. This means that the first $11,809 of an individual's income can be received tax free.

15-81.   Extending this analysis, it can be said that, for most types of income, the amount that can be received tax free is limited to the total tax credit base amounts available to the individual. That is, for every dollar of tax credit amount, one dollar of income can be received on a tax free basis. There are two exceptions to this:

   Dividends   An individual with only the basic personal credit of $1,771 [(15%)($11,809)] can receive tax free dividends of nearly three times the $11,809 base for this credit. More specifically, such an individual can receive $30,727 in non-eligible dividends without incurring any liability for federal tax. (See the calculations in Paragraph 15-86.) Note that, depending on the amount of the provincial dividend tax credit, this amount may or may not be totally free of provincial tax.

   Charitable Donations   The tax credit on amounts of charitable donations over $200 is based on 29 or 33 percent, rather than the 15 percent applicable to other credit amounts. Since the 33 percent rate is applicable if income is taxed at 33 percent, we will only consider the credit rate of 29 percent in this analysis. This means that a dollar of charitable donations in excess of $200 will allow an individual in the lowest tax bracket to receive $1.93 in tax free income. More specifically, a $1 contribution in excess of $200 is eligible for a tax credit of $0.29. This $0.29 would eliminate $0.29 of tax payable, the amount of tax that an individual in the lowest bracket would pay on $1.93 of income [(15%)($1.93) = $0.29]. This is unlikely to be an important exception in that it would be unusual for someone in the 15 percent federal tax bracket to be making significant charitable donations.

Special Rules For Dividends

15-82.   How can an individual receive such a large amount of dividends without paying federal tax? The answer lies in the dividend gross up and tax credit mechanism. For an individual in the lowest tax bracket, the increase in tax associated with one dollar of non-eligible dividends received compared to one dollar of interest income can be calculated as follows:

Tax Increase Per $1	Dividend	Interest
Cash Received	$1.0000	$1.0000
Gross Up At 16 Percent	.1600	N/A
Taxable Income	$1.1600	$1.0000
Federal Tax Payable At 15 Percent	$0.1740	$0.1500
Federal Dividend Tax Credit [(8/11)($0.16)]	(0.1164)	N/A
Increase In Federal Tax Payable	$0.0576	$0.1500

15-83.   For each dollar of non-eligible dividends received, an individual must add a taxable dividend of $1.16 ($1 + $0.16 gross up) to Taxable Income. For individuals in the lowest federal tax bracket, the federal tax on this amount will be $0.1740 [($1.16)(15%)]. However, there will be a federal credit against this tax payable equal to 8/11 of the gross up, or $0.1164 [(8/11)($0.16)]. This means that there is only a $0.0576 increase in federal tax for each one dollar increase in non-eligible dividends. This is in contrast to an increase in federal tax of $0.15 for each one dollar increase in interest income, i.e., a 15 percent rate of increase. As the preceding calculations demonstrate, dividend income uses up an individual's available tax credits at a much lower rate than most other types of income, i.e., a 5.76 percent rate.

15-84.   For example, one dollar of interest income will use up one dollar [($1.00)($.15 ÷ $.15)] of an individual's personal tax credit base of $11,809. In contrast, one dollar of non-eligible dividends received will use up only $0.384 of this base [($1.00)($.0576 ÷ $.15)]. This means that, in comparison with other types of income, a much larger amount of dividends can be received before an individual's tax credits are absorbed and taxes will have to be paid.

15-85.   The amount of dividends that can be received tax free by an individual with no other source of income is a function of the total amount of personal tax credits available and can, in fact, become a fairly large amount.

Tax Free Amounts For 2018

15-86.   For 2018, ignoring possible tax credits other than the basic personal and spousal, the amount of non-eligible dividends that can be received free of federal tax by a single individual, and by an individual with a dependent spouse (or eligible dependant) with no other source of income is calculated in the table which follows. Note that, in the dependent spouse case, the grossed up amount of the dividends exceeds $46,605, the top of the 15 percent federal tax bracket. This means that some of this dividend will be taxed at a higher federal rate of 20.5 percent.

	Single Individual	Dependent Spouse
Non-Eligible Dividends Received	$30,727	$50,273
Gross Up Of 16 Percent	4,916	8,044
Taxable Income	$35,643	$58,317
Taxed At 15%	(35,643)	(46,605)
Taxed At 20.5%	$ Nil	$11,712
Federal Tax At 15%	$5,346	$6,991
Federal Tax At 20.5%	Nil	2,401
Dividend Tax Credit (8/11 Of Gross Up)	(3,575)	(5,850)
Basic Personal Credit [(15%)($11,809)]	(1,771)	(1,771)
Spousal Credit [(15%)($11,809)]	N/A	(1,771)
Federal Tax Payable	Nil	Nil

Note While this is not relevant to our analysis in this section, you might wish to note that, with respect to eligible dividends, the tax free amount for a single individual would be $57,321, and $74,134 for an individual with a dependent spouse.

15-87.   There may or may not be provincial tax payable on the amounts in the preceding table. A number of provincial factors would have to be considered. These include the provincial tax rates, the provincial tax brackets, the provincial personal tax credit amounts and the provincial dividend tax credit rates.

15-88.   The alternative minimum tax is not a factor in determining the amount of non-eligible dividends that can be received on a tax free basis. As the dividend tax credit is not available in the calculation of the alternative minimum tax payable, the dividend gross up is deducted in the calculation of adjusted taxable income for alternative minimum tax purposes. Given this, the $40,000 basic exemption that is provided by the alternative minimum tax legislation, combined with the $11,809 basic personal tax credit (plus the $11,809 spousal credit in the dependent spouse example), would serve to eliminate the alternative minimum tax on the tax free non-eligible dividends calculated in Paragraph 15-86. However, alternative minimum tax may be a consideration when a large amount of eligible dividends are involved. See Chapter 11 for our coverage of alternative minimum tax.

Income Splitting

Basic Concept

15-89.   In Chapter 1 we provided a very simple example of income splitting. As illustrated in that example, if an individual can find a way to share a large block of income with related parties in lower tax brackets, the result can be a significant reduction in taxes, not just in the current year, but on an ongoing basis.

15-90.   While the examples presented earlier in this Chapter suggested that there are limits on an individual's ability to reduce or defer taxes through the use of a corporation, these examples did not take into consideration that a corporation could be used to effectively implement income splitting. This possibility is further enhanced by the fact that, as discussed in the preceding section, individuals without other sources of income can receive substantial amounts of dividends without paying any taxes at the federal level.

15-91.   Note, however, income splitting only works when the Tax On Split Income (TOSI) does not apply to the recipient of the split income. The 2018 extension of the TOSI to related adults has made it extremely difficult to effectively use a corporation in an income splitting strategy.

> **We suggest you work Self Study Problem Fifteen-6 at this point.**

Shareholder Benefits Including Loans

The Owner-Manager Environment

15-92.   Much of the material in this Chapter deals with owner managed corporations. These are typically CCPCs with either a single shareholder or a small group of shareholders. When there is a shareholder group, the group often consists of members of a single family.

15-93.   Unlike the situation with publicly traded companies, in this environment the owner-manager is subject to few constraints on the use of the corporate assets. In effect, he is in a position to provide significant benefits to himself and other related individuals.

15-94.   This situation is complicated by the fact that some things that might be considered benefits are, in fact, necessary to the operation of the business. For example, the owner-manager may need an automobile to use in carrying out the business of the corporation. If he provides himself with a $30,000 Honda, this cost would appear to be a legitimate business expense. However, if he provides himself with a $450,000 Bentley, there is some question as to whether calling on clients really requires this type of vehicle.

15-95.   As was discussed in earlier Chapters, the CRA deals with potential abuses in the area of corporate ownership and leasing of vehicles by:

- restricting the corporation's ability to deduct the costs of owning or leasing vehicles; and
- assessing taxable benefits for personal use of corporate vehicles.

15-96.   Another problem area is travel costs. Most owner-managers have legitimate reasons to travel on matters related to corporate business. However, there is always the temptation of trying to find some business reason for spending a week in a luxury resort in Phoenix. In fact, there is a thriving industry that encourages such behaviour. It is not difficult to find a 30 minute seminar on human resource management that is conveniently conducted just before the ski lifts open at Whistler.

15-97.   Unlike the situation with automobiles, there are no provisions that deal specifically with travel costs. Such costs are only subject to the general constraint that requires a business purpose for their incurrence. In addition, they must be reasonable in the circumstances. Not surprisingly, there are frequent disputes in this area.

Shareholder Benefits Other Than Loans

15-98.   ITA 15(1) deals with situations where a corporation has provided a benefit to a shareholder that does not appear to have a business purpose. Examples of this type of situation would include:

- a corporation providing a shareholder with a jet for personal use;
- a corporation building a swimming pool at a shareholder's personal residence; or
- a corporation selling assets to a shareholder at prices that are substantially below fair market value.

15-99.   When any of these events occur, the shareholder is required to include the value of these benefits or appropriations in his income. Such amounts will not be considered dividends and, as a consequence, they will not be eligible for the dividend tax credit.

15-100.   A further point here is that, when an amount is included in a shareholder's income under ITA 15(1), IT-432R2 indicates that the corporation is not allowed to deduct the amount that has been included in the shareholder's income.

> **EXAMPLE**   A corporation provides a shareholder with a $10,000 holiday trip to Italy.

> **ANALYSIS**   ITA 15(1) requires the inclusion of the $10,000 cost of the trip in the shareholder's income. Despite the fact that this amount is being taxed in the hands of the shareholder, the corporation would not be able to deduct the cost of the trip.

15-101.   It would seem clear, given this non-deductibility, that corporations should avoid providing benefits that will be assessed to shareholders under ITA 15(1).

Shareholder Loans

General Rule

15-102.   ITA 15(2) is applicable when a corporation makes a loan to a shareholder or an individual connected to, or affiliated with, a shareholder. Under ITA 15(2.1), persons are connected for this purpose if they do not deal with each other at arm's length. When such loans are made, this general rule requires that the full principal amount of the loan be included in the Net Income For Tax Purposes of the recipient of the loan (the shareholder or the person connected to the shareholder) in the taxation year in which the loan is made.

15-103.   This general rule applies without regard to the amount of interest paid on the loan. Note, however, in periods subsequent to the inclusion of the principal amount of the loan in the income of the shareholder, there is no imputed interest benefit, even in cases where the loan is on an interest free basis.

15-104.   Under this general rule, the granting of the loan to a shareholder has the same tax consequences as the payment of an equivalent amount of salary to the shareholder. However, there is an important difference. Taxes paid on salary cannot normally be recovered by repaying the salary. In contrast, when all or part of a shareholder loan that has been included in the taxpayer's income under ITA 15(2) is repaid, the amount of the repayment can be deducted from Net Income For Tax Purposes under ITA 20(1)(j).

Exceptions To The General Rule

15-105.   There are three exceptions to this general rule that are available to shareholders, without regard to whether or not they are also employees of the corporation. They can be described as follows:

> **Non-Resident Persons**   ITA 15(2.2) indicates that the general rule does not apply to indebtedness between non-resident persons. This means that, if both the corporation and the shareholder receiving the loan were non-residents, the principal amount of any loan would not have to be included in income.

> **Loans In Ordinary Course Of Business**   ITA 15(2.3) indicates that the general rule does not apply when the loan is in the ordinary course of the corporation's business. This would cover such situations as a customer, who is also a shareholder, taking

advantage of an on-going promotion by a furniture store that provides interest free loans to purchase furniture. In addition, ITA 15(2.3) notes that this would apply to loans made by a corporation that is in the business of making loans. This covers situations where, for example, an individual happens to be a shareholder of the bank that provides him with a personal loan.

Repayment Within One Year　ITA 15(2.6) indicates that the general rule does not apply when the loan is repaid within one year after the end of the taxation year of the lender or creditor in which the loan was made or the indebtedness arose. If, for example, a corporation with a June 30 year end extended a $100,000 loan to a shareholder on January 1, 2018, the $100,000 would not have to be included in income if it is repaid, in full, by June 30, 2019. Any part of the balance that is unpaid on that date would, in fact, have to be included in the taxpayer's 2018 income.

A further point with respect to this exception is that IT-119R4 indicates that this exception is not available when the repayment is part of a series of loans and repayments. The primary evidence of this type of situation would be a repayment near the end of a corporate taxation year, followed by a loan for a similar amount early in the following corporate taxation year.

15-106.　Additional exceptions to the general rule requiring the principal of shareholder loans to be included in income involve situations where the shareholder is also an employee of the corporation making the loan. These exceptions are found in ITA 15(2.4) and can be described as follows:

Not Specified Employee　ITA 15(2.4)(a) indicates that loans made to a shareholder, who is an employee, are not subject to the general rule if the shareholder is not a specified employee. This exception applies without regard to the purpose of the loan. A specified employee is one who, at any time of the year, owns 10 percent or more of any class of the shares of the corporation, or who does not deal at arm's length with the corporation. For example, an arm's length employee who owns less than 1 percent of the shares purchased through stock options.

Dwelling Loans　ITA 15(2.4)(b) indicates that loans made to a shareholder, who is an employee, or the spouse or common-law partner of the employee, to acquire a dwelling to live in are not subject to the general rule.

Stock Acquisition Loans　ITA 15(2.4)(c) indicates that loans made to a shareholder, who is an employee, to acquire shares in the lending corporation or a corporation related to the lending corporation, are not subject to the general rule.

Motor Vehicle Loans　ITA 15(2.4)(d) indicates that loans made to a shareholder, who is an employee, to acquire a motor vehicle to be used in employment duties, are not subject to the general rule.

15-107.　In order for these exceptions to apply, the following conditions must be met:

- the loan must be made to the individual because he is an employee, not because he is a shareholder [ITA 15(2.4)(e)]; and

- at the time the loan is made, bona fide arrangements must be made to repay the loan within a reasonable period of time [ITA 15(2.4)(f)].

15-108.　The first of these conditions can create significant problems for owner-managers of private corporations wishing to obtain loans from their corporations. In order to avoid having the principal amount of the loan included in Net Income For Tax Purposes, the owner-manager must demonstrate that he received the loan because of his role as an employee.

15-109.　In order to do this, the owner-manager will likely have to make similar loans available to all employees with duties similar to those of the owner-manager. That is, if the company gives the owner-manager a $100,000, low interest loan to purchase a residence, such loans would have to be made available to all employees with duties similar to those of the owner-manager. If this is not the case, the CRA is likely to conclude that the owner-manager received the loan because of his role as a shareholder.

15-110.   A further problem would arise if, as would not be uncommon in owner-managed situations, there are no other senior employees of the business, or no other employees at all. It is not clear in this case whether the owner-manager would be able to demonstrate that he received a loan in his capacity as an employee. However, the CRA will look at the loan practices of other similar corporations as an approach to making this determination.

Imputed Interest Benefit

15-111.   It was previously noted that, if the principal amount of a shareholder loan is included in the taxpayer's income, there is no imputed interest benefit related to a low rate or interest free loan. However, if the loan is exempted from the general inclusion in income rule by one of the exceptions described in Paragraphs 15-105 and 15-106, ITA 80.4(2) is applicable and a benefit may be assessed. The analogous benefit for employees, which was discussed in Chapter 3, is assessed under ITA 80.4(1).

> **EXAMPLE**   On July 1, 2018, Andros Ltd., a CCPC with a taxation year that ends on December 31, extends a $100,000 loan to its only shareholder, George Andros. The loan is interest free and, because it will be repaid in January, 2019, the $100,000 principal amount does not have to be included in his income. Assume the prescribed rate throughout 2018 is 2 percent.
>
> **ANALYSIS**   For 2018, Mr. Andros will be assessed a taxable benefit under ITA 80.4(2) equal to $1,000 [(2% - Nil)($100,000)(6/12)]. In the examples in IT-421R2, "Benefits To Individuals, Corporations, And Shareholders From Loans Or Debt", interest is calculated on the basis of the number of months the loan is outstanding. While not illustrated, calculations could also be based on the number of days the loan is outstanding. We would remind you that, if the loan proceeds are invested in income producing assets, the imputed interest that is assessed on the loan will be deductible.

15-112.   In the fairly common situation where the shareholder also works as an employee of the business, the benefit may be assessed under either ITA 80.4(1) or ITA 80.4(2). If the benefit is assessed under ITA 80.4(1), it will be classified as employment income. In contrast, if it is assessed under ITA 80.4(2), it will be considered property income. There are additional differences when the loan is made to assist an employee/shareholder with the purchase of a home.

15-113.   In the case of a home purchase loan, for the first five years the loan is outstanding, the benefit assessed to an employee under ITA 80.4(1) will use a rate no higher than the prescribed rate that prevailed when the loan was made. Should the rate go down, the employee is entitled to use the lower prescribed rate for the benefit calculation (see Chapter 3 for examples of this procedure). Alternatively, in the case of a home purchase loan to a shareholder, the ITA 80.4(2) benefit must be calculated using the actual quarterly prescribed rates that prevail over the term of the loan.

Exercise Fifteen - 6

Subject: Shareholder Loans - Car Purchase

Ms. Martha Rourke is an employee of Rourke Inc., a large private company in which her husband owns 70 percent of the outstanding shares. Ms. Rourke owns the remaining 30 percent of the shares. On July 1, 2018, she receives a $50,000 interest free loan that will be used to purchase an automobile to be used in her employment duties. The loan is to be repaid on June 30, 2022. Assume the prescribed rate for all of 2018 is 2 percent. What are the tax implications of this loan for Ms. Rourke in 2018?

SOLUTION available in print and online Study Guide.

Exercise Fifteen - 7

Subject: Shareholder Loans - Term Outstanding

On June 1, 2018, Generic Inc. loans $162,000 to its principal shareholder, Ms. Jan Fisk, in order to finance her gambling debts. Generic Inc. has a taxation year that ends on June 30. The loan is interest free. Assume that, during all periods, the relevant prescribed rate is 2 percent. What are the tax consequences to Ms. Fisk if the loan is repaid (1) on January 1, 2019 and (2) on December 31, 2019?

Exercise Fifteen - 8

Subject: Shareholder Loans - Home Purchase

On November, 1, 2018, Hasid Ltd. loans Mr. Aaron Hasid, the CEO and principal shareholder of the Company, $123,000 in order to assist in his purchase of a principal residence. The Company has a taxation year that ends on December 31. The loan does not bear interest and, during all periods, assume that the relevant prescribed rate is 2 percent. The loan is to be repaid in four equal annual instalments, the first occurring on October 31, 2019. What are the tax consequences of this loan to Mr. Hasid? State any assumptions that you have made in providing your answer.

SOLUTIONS available in print and online Study Guide.

We suggest you work Self Study Problems Fifteen-7 and 8 at this point.

Management Compensation

General Principles

Salary As The Bench Mark

15-114. The most obvious and straightforward way to compensate managers is to pay salaries. Provided they are reasonable, the amounts are a deductible expense to the corporation. At the same time, they are fully taxable to the recipient, rendering such payments neutral in terms of tax planning. For large publicly traded corporations, where the managers are not the principal owners of the business, salary is the usual starting point in negotiating management compensation. However, for some high income executives, stock based compensation may be of greater importance than salary.

15-115. Even with a public corporation, however, the tax effects of various methods of compensation should not be ignored. By paying salaries, a corporation receives a deduction from Taxable Income in the year of accrual, while the recipient employee receives an equal addition to Taxable Income in the year of payment.

15-116. Any form of compensation that creates an excess of the corporation's deductions over the employee's inclusions creates an aggregate tax savings. In addition, any form of compensation that is deductible to the corporation prior to inclusion in the income of the employee involves tax deferral. These considerations can allow for improved after tax benefits to the employee or, alternatively, a lower after tax cost to the corporation.

Tax Effective Alternatives

15-117. Some simple examples of compensation features that can be used to defer or reduce the payment of taxes are as follows:

- **Registered Pension Plans** Within prescribed limits, a corporation can deduct contributions to Registered Pension Plans in the year of contribution. These contributions will not become taxable to the employee until they are received as a pension benefit, resulting in an effective tax deferral arrangement. In addition to tax effectiveness, such plans can promote loyalty and reduce employee turnover.

- **Deferred Profit Sharing Plans**   In a fashion similar to Registered Pension Plans, amounts that are currently deductible to the corporation are deferred with respect to inclusion in the employee's Taxable Income. As with registered pension plans, these plans can also promote loyalty and reduce employee turnover.

- **Provision Of Private Health Care Plans**   The premiums paid by the corporation for such benefits as dental plans can be deducted in full by the corporation and will not be considered a taxable benefit to the employee. This can generate a significant tax savings.

- **Stock Options**   Stock options provide employees with an incentive to improve the performance of the enterprise. In addition, for CCPCs, taxation of any benefits resulting from the options is deferred until they are exercised or sold (for a full discussion of the deferral of stock option benefits, see Chapter 3). Further, the value of the employment benefit received is enhanced by the fact that, in general, one-half of the amount can be deducted in the calculation of Taxable Income.

  From the point of view of the corporation, evaluation of stock option compensation is more complex. Discouraging the use of options is the fact that no tax deduction is available for the granting of options. However, IFRS 2, *Share-Based Payment*, requires that the estimated value of options be charged to expense for accounting purposes when they are granted, despite the fact that the cost of issuing stock options is not deductible for tax purposes.

15-118.   Changes in tax legislation over the years have served to restrict the tax benefits associated with employee compensation. Perhaps most importantly, the rules related to taxable benefits on employer provided automobiles can be quite unfavourable, in some cases resulting in a taxable benefit that exceeds the value derived from having use of the vehicle. The rules related to employee fringe benefits and employee stock options were covered in Chapter 3. Chapter 10 contained coverage of deferred compensation plans and this Chapter 15 included coverage of shareholder loans.

Salary Vs. Dividends

15-119.   For large public corporations, there is little point in considering the tax benefits related to salary/dividend trade-offs. The dividend policy of public corporations is normally based on considerations that extend well beyond the compensation that is provided to the management group of the company.

15-120.   In situations where the manager of the business is also an owner, such an individual is in a position to receive compensation in the form of either salary or dividends. If there are no other owners involved in the decision, the choice is completely at the discretion of the owner-manager and tax factors will generally be an important consideration in making this decision. The choice between compensation in the form of salary or in the form of dividends, the salary vs. dividend decision, is the subject of the remainder of this Chapter.

Salary Vs. Dividends For The Owner - Manager

The Basic Trade-Off

Example - Data

15-121.   To illustrate the basic trade-off that is involved in salary vs. dividend decisions, assume that Ms. Olney owns all of the shares of a corporation that has $100,000 in Taxable Income, and that she has sufficient property income from other sources to place her in the 49 percent federal/provincial tax bracket (33% federal rate plus 16% provincial rate).

15-122.   If the full $100,000 of corporate income is paid to Ms. Olney in the form of salary, it can be deducted by the corporation and will reduce the corporation's Taxable Income to nil. This means that no Part I taxes will be paid at the corporate level. However, the $100,000 will be taxed at Ms. Olney's marginal rate of 49 percent. This means that she will pay tax of $51,000 and be left with after tax funds of $49,000.

15-123.   If no salary is paid to Ms. Olney, corporate taxes will be assessed and any remaining amount, after adjustments for any refundable taxes, will be paid in dividends. This amount will be subject to personal tax and the resulting after tax cash flow to her can be determined. These amounts, which are dependent on the type of corporation and the type of income earned, were calculated earlier in this Chapter. The results of those calculations were summarized in Paragraph 15-55. You may wish to refer to this summary as you work through the remainder of this Chapter.

Analysis Of The Example

15-124.   In looking at the question of whether or not to incorporate an income source, we looked at the possibilities for both tax deferral and tax reduction through the use of a corporation. In salary vs. dividend decisions, we are not concerned with deferral. The question we need to answer here is:

> "What is the most tax effective way to have a corporation provide its owner-manager
> with a required amount of after tax income?"

15-125.   There is, of course, no deferral available on amounts that are to be removed from the corporation.

15-126.   In comparing Ms. Olney's $51,000 retained with the various results listed in Paragraph 15-55, in all cases flowing business or property income through a corporation resulted in lower after tax retention. Even in the case of a CCPC earning income that is eligible for the small business deduction, the after tax retention was $50,460, which is lower than the $51,000 that would be retained through direct receipt of the $100,000.

15-127.   This would suggest that, in general, salary should be used. However, the preceding analysis is based on a number of assumptions with respect to provincial tax rates on personal and corporate income. In addition, other factors such as RRSP contributions, CPP contributions and payroll tax costs have been ignored. These factors will be considered in the following material.

Other Considerations

Provincial Tax Rates And Credits

15-128.   The results that were presented in Paragraph 15-55 assumed a provincial tax rate on individuals of 16 percent, a provincial dividend tax credit on non-eligible dividends equal to 22 percent of the gross up, and provincial rates on corporations for income eligible for the small business deduction and other types of income of 3 and 13 percent, respectively. While these numbers are fairly representative, they are not the only possible rates.

15-129.   In assessing the importance of these differences, you should recognize that the payment of salaries is analogous to the direct receipt of income. That is, if a corporation has $100,000 in income and pays this entire amount in salaries, there will be no corporate Tax Payable. Further, the taxes paid by the individual on the salary will be similar to the taxes that would be paid if the income were received directly. This means that the comparison of salary payments with dividends involves the same type of analysis as the comparison of the after tax retention from the direct receipt of income with the after tax retention resulting from channeling income through a corporation.

15-130.   Given this, we can discuss the effect of varying provincial tax rates on the salary vs. dividend decision by using the conclusions reached in the comparison of the direct receipt vs. flow through decisions. Direct receipt vs. flow through decisions were considered in Paragraphs 15-58 through 15-76. Applying that analysis to salary vs. dividend decisions, the following statements can be made:

Tax Rates For Individuals   In the analysis contained in Paragraphs 15-67 through 15-69, we noted that higher tax rates on individuals made the use of a corporation more attractive from the point of view of deferring taxes on income retained within the corporation. Here, however, we are concerned only with amounts that will be distributed, either in the form of dividends or in the form of salary and, as a consequence, tax deferral is not an issue. This means that the level of individual tax rates is not a major issue in this type of decision. This point is illustrated with the example found in Paragraph 15-68.

Dividend Tax Credit And Corporate Tax Rates   For integration to work, the combined federal/provincial dividend tax credit must be equal to the combined corporate taxes paid.

- **Eligible Dividends**   For eligible dividends subject to a 38 percent gross up, this would require a combined corporate tax rate of 27.54 percent and a dividend tax credit equal to the gross up. This in turn would require a provincial corporate tax rate of 12.54 percent [27.54 - (38 - 10 - 13)] and a provincial dividend tax credit of 5/11 of the gross up (1.0 - 6/11).

- **Non-Eligible Dividends**   For non-eligible dividends (the type usually paid by a CCPC) subject to a 16 percent gross up, this would require a combined corporate tax rate of 13.79 percent and a dividend tax credit equal to the gross up. This requires a provincial corporate tax rate of 3.79 percent [13.79 - (38 - 10 - 18)] and a provincial dividend tax credit equal to 3/11 of the gross up (1.0 - 8/11).

The examples in Paragraphs 15-74 and 15-75 illustrate the results of applying the current range of values for corporate tax rates and dividend tax credit rates in all of the Canadian provinces. While these examples were designed to illustrate the desirability of using a corporation, they can also be used to evaluate salary vs. dividend decisions. As noted, paying salary is, from a tax point of view, the equivalent of direct receipt of income.

Analyzing these examples in the context of salary/dividend decisions, it is clear that, in situations where the dividend tax credit exceeds the corporate taxes paid, paying dividends will result in lower taxes than would be the case with paying salary. Similarly, when the dividend tax credit is less than the corporate taxes paid, the payment of salary, all other things being equal, will result in lower taxes.

Dividend Benefit - Income Splitting

15-131.   When a corporation is used for income splitting purposes, amounts may be distributed to individuals with little or no other source of income. As was noted in Paragraph 15-86, $30,727 in non-eligible dividends can be paid to such an individual without any federal tax liability being incurred. The fact that this is a much larger amount than can be distributed tax free in any other form clearly favours the use of dividends for distributions of corporate assets in these circumstances.

15-132.   A constraint on this approach is the Tax On Split Income (TOSI). If TOSI is applicable, amounts received by a specified individual will have all of this income subject to tax at the maximum federal rate of 33 percent. This will often make it difficult to implement an income splitting strategy involving corporate dividends.

Dividend Benefit - CNIL Reduction

15-133.   An individual's Cumulative Net Investment Loss (CNIL) is the cumulative amount by which investment expenses exceed investment income since 1987 (see Chapter 11 for an explanation of this amount, as well as the general provisions of the lifetime capital gains deduction). An individual's ability to make a deduction under the provisions of the lifetime capital gains deduction is reduced, on a dollar-for-dollar basis, by the balance in the CNIL account. This means that, if an individual contemplates selling shares of a qualified small business corporation, or an interest in a qualified farm or fishing property, sensible tax planning would suggest the elimination of any CNIL balance.

15-134.   For an individual whose income is provided by his owner-managed corporation, dividends can assist with this problem. The receipt of dividends reduces the CNIL by $1.16 for each $1.00 of non-eligible dividends received. In contrast, salary payments leave this balance unchanged. Another possibility, if the corporation has an amount owing to the shareholder, is to pay interest to the shareholder on the balance outstanding. This interest would also decrease any CNIL.

Salary Benefit - Earned Income For RRSP And CPP

15-135.   One of the most attractive features of the Canadian income tax system is the fact that individuals can make deductible contributions to RRSPs. Not only are the contributions deductible at the time that they are made, once inside the plan they enjoy the tremendous benefits associated with tax free compounding over, what may be, a period of many years. Most individuals will want to take advantage of these provisions.

15-136.   Dividends do not constitute Earned Income for the purposes of determining the maximum RRSP contributions, nor do they count as pensionable earnings on which CPP contributions can be based. As a result, if the owner-manager has no other source of Earned Income (e.g., employment income from a source other than his corporation), it will be necessary for the corporation to pay salary if the individual wishes to make RRSP and CPP contributions.

15-137.   The maximum for CPP pensionable earnings for 2018 is $55,900. In order to be eligible for the maximum CPP payments at retirement, salary of at least the maximum pensionable earnings for the year should be paid. With the 2019 RRSP limit at $26,500, if the owner-manager has no other source of Earned Income, a 2018 salary of at least $147,222 will be required to make the maximum RRSP contribution for 2019 [(18%)($147,222) = $26,500]. Note that RRSP deduction room can be carried forward, but there is no equivalent carry forward for the CPP program.

Salary Benefit - Earned Income For Child Care Costs

15-138.   If an individual is in a position to deduct child care costs, they are limited to two-thirds of earned income. Salary payments would add to this limit while dividends would not. For a detailed discussion of the deductibility of child care costs, see Chapter 9.

Salary Benefit - Corporate Tax Savings Carry Over

15-139.   In a particular year, an owner-manager may wish to withdraw amounts in excess of the earnings of the corporation. If this happens, there will be no current tax savings associated with the payment of salaries, a fact that would tend to make the payment of such amounts less attractive.

15-140.   However, payment of salaries in this situation would serve to create a loss carry over and, if we assume that the loss carry over can be used in some past or future year, the corporate tax savings associated with the payment of salaries would not be lost. The savings, however, will be deferred in the case of a carry forward and this means that, to properly evaluate the payment of salaries in this situation, consideration would have to be given to the time value of money.

Salary Cost (Possible) - Provincial Payroll Taxes

15-141.   With respect to provincial payroll taxes, four provinces and two territories assess such taxes. Rates are as follows:

Manitoba (Health And Post-Secondary Education Levy) No tax on the first $1.25 million of payroll. Excess is taxed at a rate of 2.15 or 4.3 percent.

Newfoundland/Labrador (Health And Post-Secondary Education Levy)   No tax on the first $1.2 million of payroll. Excess is taxed at a rate of 2 percent.

Salary Vs. Dividends For The Owner - Manager

Ontario (Employer Health Tax) Ontario has a complex system which provides exemptions for some employers. When applicable, the tax rate ranges from 0.98 percent on Ontario payrolls totalling less than $200,000, to 1.95 percent on Ontario payrolls totalling over $400,000.

Quebec (Health Services Fund)   Quebec also has a complex system which includes exemptions for certain employers. When applicable the tax rate ranges from 1.55 percent to 4.26 percent of payroll.

Territories (Payroll Tax)   Nunavut and the Northwest territories tax all payroll at a rate of 2 percent. This tax is employee paid unlike the preceding payroll taxes listed.

Salary Costs - CPP And EI

15-142.   In our example from Paragraph 15-121, we ignored the fact that salaries cannot be paid without contributions being made to the CPP. In addition, some provinces levy a payroll tax on salaries and wages as described in the preceding paragraph. These costs can constitute a significant reduction in the after tax cash flow associated with the payment of salaries.

15-143.   With respect to CPP contributions, 2018 employee contributions are based on 4.95 percent of $55,900 (maximum pensionable earnings), less a basic exemption of $3,500. This results in a maximum employee contribution for 2018 of $2,594. The employer is required to withhold and remit this contribution from salary paid and contribute an amount that is equal to the employee's contribution. This brings the total CPP cost of paying salaries of $55,900 or more to $5,188.

15-144.   As covered in Chapter 4, if an individual pays more CPP contributions than is required, perhaps because he has changed employers, he is refunded the excess through his tax return. Form PD24, Application for a Refund of Overdeducted CPP Contributions or EI Premiums, provides a way for employers who have made excess contributions for an employee to recover the excess.

15-145.   If an owner-manager owns more than 40 percent of the voting shares of the corporation, he cannot participate in the Employment Insurance (EI) program. While generally not relevant in the situations covered here, an employee's maximum EI premium for 2018 is 1.66 percent of $51,700 (maximum insurable earnings), with no exemption, an amount of $858. The employer must contribute 1.4 times the employee's premium, an amount of $1,201. This results in a total cost of $2,059 for an employee with maximum insurable earnings in excess of $51,700.

Salary Benefit - CPP And Canada Employment Tax Credits

15-146.   While CPP is an added cost of choosing the salary alternative, the payment of these costs provides a benefit to the individual in the form of future CPP benefit payments, as well as a benefit from the CPP tax credit. You will recall from Chapter 4 that this credit is equal to 15 percent of amounts paid by the employee. This provides a maximum credit of $389 on the payment of the 2018 maximum CPP of $2,594. Note that this would not be a consideration if the individual has other sources of income which required the payment of maximum CPP.

15-147.   A further benefit of paying salary is the Canada employment credit of $179 [(15%)($1,195)] for 2018. Unless the individual has other sources of employment income in excess of the base amount for this credit, the Canada Employment credit is only available on the payment of salary by the corporation.

Example Extended

15-148.   Returning to our example of Ms. Olney from Paragraph 15-121, as the owner of 100 percent of the shares of the corporation, she is not eligible to participate in the EI program. In addition, assume the province in which she lives assesses a 2 percent payroll tax to finance its health care program and provides a provincial credit for CPP contributions at a 6 percent rate. Her corporation is a Canadian controlled private corporation and all of its $100,000 in income is eligible for the small business deduction. Given this income and the costs associated with paying salary, the maximum salary that could be paid to Ms. Olney would be $95,496, a figure that would result in no corporate Tax Payable.

Pre-Tax Corporate Income	$100,000
Employer's CPP Contribution	(2,594)
Gross Salary [($100,000 - $2,594) ÷ 1.02]	(95,496)
Payroll Tax [(2%)($95,496)]	(1,910)
Corporate Taxable Income	Nil

15-149.   If $95,496 is paid to Ms. Olney as salary, her personal taxes are as follows:

Combined Tax Before Credits [(33% + 16%)($95,496)]	$46,793
Credit For Employee's CPP Contribution	
[(15% + 6%)($2,594)]*	(**545**)
Canada Employment Credit [(15%)($1,195)]	(179)
Personal Tax Payable	$46,069

*We have assumed that Ms. Olney has sufficient property income to place her in the maximum federal tax bracket. This income would absorb other tax credits and, as a consequence, only the CPP and Canada employment credits that result from the payment of salary are included in this analysis.

15-150.   With this amount of taxes payable, Ms. Olney's after tax retention would be calculated as follows:

Salary Received	$95,496
Employee's CPP Contribution - Maximum	(2,594)
Personal Tax Payable	(46,069)
After Tax Cash Retained	$46,833

15-151.   This more realistic result provides considerably less cash than the $51,000 [($100,000)(1 - 0.49)] that was left when CPP, payroll taxes and the Canada Employment credit are ignored. Note, however, while they would not be easy to quantify, the payment of CPP does provide the owner/manager with future benefits. Using the numbers in Paragraph 15-55, this makes payment of salary, if these additional factors are considered, less desirable than dividends paid out of:

- income eligible for the small business deduction (retention was $50.460),
- business income ineligible for the small business deduction (retention was $47,520).

Exercise Fifteen - 9

Subject: Salary And Dividend Compensation

For the year ending December 31, 2018, Broadmoor Inc., a Canadian controlled private corporation has Taxable Income, before consideration of dividends or salary paid to its sole shareholder, of $550,000   All of this income is from active business activities. The cash balance of the Company, prior to any payments on the current year's taxes, is also equal to this amount. The Company makes the maximum eligible dividend designation each year. Its only shareholder, Ms. Sarah Broad, has no income other than dividends or salary paid by the corporation and has combined federal/provincial personal tax credits of $5,000.

In her province of residence, assume:

- the corporate tax rate is 4 percent on income eligible for the small business deduction and 14 percent on other income
- her combined federal/provincial Tax Payable totals $65,000 on the first $205,842 with additional amounts of income taxed at a combined federal/provincial rate of 48 percent

- the dividend tax credit is 30 percent of the gross up for all dividends
- there is no payroll tax

Determine the amount of after tax cash that Ms. Broad will retain if (1) the maximum salary is paid by the corporation out of the available cash of $550,000 and (2) the maximum amount of eligible and non-eligible dividends are paid. Ignore the required CPP contributions and the Canada employment tax credit.

SOLUTION available in print and online Study Guide.

Use Of Tax Credits

15-152.   Our example in this section has involved an individual with other sources of income that placed her in the maximum federal tax bracket. This amount of income would generally be sufficient to absorb any tax credits available to the individual. However, there may be situations where a salary vs. dividend decision is being made with respect to an individual with no other source of income. This would be a fairly common situation when a corporation is being used for income splitting purposes, or for a corporation with only a limited amount of income to distribute.

15-153.   If the individual has no other source of income and provincial tax rates favour the use of dividends, there may be a problem with the full use of available tax credits. We noted earlier in this Chapter that dividend payments use up tax credits at a much lower rate than other types of income, such as salary. If only limited amounts of income are being distributed, the use of dividends may leave a portion of the individual's tax credits unused. When this is the case, some combination of salary and dividends may provide the optimum solution.

15-154.   A further potential complication stems from the fact that provincial tax credits can only be deducted against the provincial tax liability and federal tax credits can only be deducted against the federal tax liability. In our examples and problems we have not taken this into consideration and have given a single figure for combined federal/provincial tax credits.

15-155.   In the real world, it would be possible to have a situation where an individual would have to pay some federal tax in order to use up all of their provincial tax credits, or alternatively, pay some provincial tax in order to use up all of their federal tax credits. Given this text's focus on federal income taxes, no further attention will be given to this complication of the issue.

15-156.   The following example illustrates the salary vs. dividend issue when the full utilization of tax credits is a consideration.

> **EXAMPLE**   Mr. Eric Swenson is the sole shareholder of Swenson Sweets, a Canadian controlled private corporation. The Company has a December 31 year end and, for 2018, it has Taxable Income, before consideration of salary or dividends to Mr. Swenson, of $29,500, all of which results from active business activities. This amount is available in cash, prior to the payment of any salary or dividends. Mr. Swenson has combined federal/provincial personal tax credits of $3,920.
>
> The corporation operates in a province with a corporate tax rate on active business income of a CCPC of 3 percent and no payroll taxes. The provincial tax rate on personal income is 10 percent of the first $46,605 of Taxable Income, with a provincial dividend tax credit on non-eligible dividends that is equal to 3/11 of the gross up. In solving this problem, we will ignore CPP contributions and the Canada employment tax credit.

15-157.   If the full $29,500 is paid out in salary, corporate Taxable Income would be nil and there would be no corporate tax payable. Mr. Swenson's after tax cash retention would be as follows:

Salary Received		$29,500
Personal Tax Payable		
Personal Taxes At 25% (15% + 10%)	($7,375)	
Personal Tax Credits (Given)	3,920	(3,455)
After Tax Cash Retained (All Salary)		**$26,045**

15-158.   As dividends are not tax deductible, corporate tax must be paid prior to any dividend distribution. The combined federal/provincial tax rate would be 13 percent (38% - 10% - 18% + 3%) resulting in corporate taxes of $3,835 [(13%)($29,500)]. This means that the maximum dividend that can be paid will be $25,665 ($29,500 - $3,835). The after tax retention in this case is as follows:

Non-Eligible Dividends Received	$25,665
Gross Up Of 16%	4,106
Taxable Dividends	$29,771
Personal Tax Rate	25%
Personal Tax Payable Before Tax Credits	$ 7,443
Personal Tax Credits (Given)	(3,920)
Dividend Tax Credit [(8/11 + 3/11)($4,106)]	(4,106)
Tax Payable ($583 In Unused Credits)	**Nil**

Non-Eligible Dividends Received	$25,665
Personal Taxes (See Paragraph 15-86	
- No Taxes Would Be Paid On This Amount)	Nil
After Tax Cash Retained (All Dividends)	**$25,665**

15-159.   While the low federal/provincial tax rate on corporations suggests that dividends should be the best alternative, the preceding results do not confirm this view. The problem is that dividend income absorbs available tax credits at a much lower rate than other types of income. The fact that the all dividend solution leaves $583 of unused tax credits suggests that a better solution might be to pay a lesser amount of dividends, plus sufficient salary to absorb these unused credits.

15-160.   To investigate this possibility, we need to determine the salary/dividend mix that will fully utilize all of Mr. Swenson's credits. To begin, consider what would happen when we add a $1,000 salary payment to the all dividends case. As the salary will be fully deductible, the after tax cost of making this payment is $870 [($1,000)(1.0 - 0.13)]. As a result, in this type of situation, where the goal is to distribute all of the available corporate income, dividends will only have to be reduced by this $870 per $1,000 of salary increase.

15-161.   The resulting increase in taxes payable can be calculated as follows:

Increase In Salary	$1,000.00
Decrease In Dividends	(870.00)
Decrease In Dividend Gross Up [(16%)($870)]	(139.20)
Decrease In Taxable Income	($ 9.20)
Personal Tax Rate	25%
Decrease In Tax Payable Before Dividend Tax Credit	($ 2.30)
Decrease In Dividend Tax Credit	
= Increase In Tax Payable [(8/11 + 3/11)($139.2)]	139.20
Net Increase In Personal Tax Payable	**$ 136.90**

15-162.   This analysis demonstrates that each $1,000 increase in salary results in an increase in personal Tax Payable of $136.90. Alternatively, this can be stated as an increase in personal Tax Payable of $0.1369 for every dollar of increase in salary. This means that to utilize Mr. Swenson's $583 in unused tax credits, he will have to receive salary of $4,259 ($583 ÷ $0.1369). This results in the following amount being available for dividends:

Corporate Taxable Income Pre-Salary	$29,500
Salary	(4,259)
Corporate Taxable Income	$25,241
Corporate Tax At 13%	(3,281)
Available For Dividends	$21,960

15-163.   When this dividend is paid out to Mr. Swenson, his after tax retention is as follows:

Non-Eligible Dividends Received	$21,960
Gross Up Of 16%	3,514
Taxable Dividends	$25,474
Salary	4,259
Taxable Income	$29,733
Personal Tax Rate	25%
Personal Tax Payable Before Tax Credits	$ 7,433
Personal Tax Credits (Given)	(3,920)
Dividend Tax Credit [(8/11 + 3/11)($3,514)]	(3,514)
Personal Tax Payable (Salary And Dividends)	Nil*

*$1 rounding error

Comparison	All Salary	All Dividends	Salary And Dividends
Non-Eligible Dividends Received	N/A	$25,665	$21,960
Salary Received	$29,500	N/A	4,259
Personal Tax Payable	(3,455)	Nil	Nil
After Tax Cash Retained	$26,045	$25,665	$26,219

15-164.   As shown in the preceding calculations, this mix of salary and dividends is such that it utilizes all of Mr. Swenson's tax credits and leaves Tax Payable of nil. This results in a solution that not only improves on the $25,665 that was retained in the all dividend scenario, it also improves on the $26,045 that was retained in the all salary case. It would appear to be the optimum solution for this example where only tax effects are considered.

Optimizing A Limited Payment Of Cash

15-165.   A similar analysis could be done if the corporation had limited cash. Assume that, while the corporation in the example (Paragraph 15-156) had Taxable Income of $29,500, it had only $16,000 in cash. To determine the maximum salary that can be paid (X), it is necessary to solve the following equation:

$$X = \$16,000 - [(13\%)(\$29,500 - X)]$$

$$X - 0.13X = [\$16,000 - (13\%)(\$29,500)] = \underline{\$13,983}$$

15-166.   Based on this amount of salary, the amount of after tax cash retained would be calculated as follows:

Corporate Cash Before Taxes		$16,000
Corporate Taxes [(13%)($29,500 - $13,983)]		(2,017)
Corporate Cash Available For Salary		$13,983

Salary Received		$13,983
Personal Tax Payable:		
Personal Tax On Salary [(25%)(13,983)]	($3,496)	
Personal Tax Credits (Given)	3,920	Nil
After Tax Cash Retained ($424 In Unused Credits)		$13,983

15-167.   Alternatively, if maximum dividends are paid, the amount of after tax cash retained would be calculated as follows:

Corporate Cash Before Taxes	$16,000
Corporate Taxes [(13%)($29,500)]	(3,835)
Corporate Cash Available For Dividends	$12,165

Non-Eligible Dividend Received	$12,165
Personal Taxes (See Paragraph 15-86 - No Taxes Would Be Paid)	Nil
After Tax Cash Retained	$12,165

15-168.   It is clear that the salary approach results in a considerably larger after tax retention than the dividend approach. This result would be expected given that the corporate cash was insufficient to utilize the personal tax credits in either approach.

Exercise Fifteen - 10

Subject: Salary vs. Dividends

For the year ending December 31, 2018, Mortell Inc., a Canadian controlled private corporation, has Taxable Income, before consideration of dividends or salary paid to its sole shareholder, of $198,000. The Company's cash balance is over $200,000. It is subject to a combined federal/provincial tax rate of 14 percent. Ms. Mortell, the Company's only shareholder, has employment income of $150,000 and, under normal circumstances, does not make withdrawals from the corporation. However, she needs an additional $30,000 in cash to create the home theatre of her dreams. Ms. Mortell's combined federal/provincial tax rate on additional income is 45 percent. She lives in a province where the provincial dividend tax credit is equal to 25 percent of the dividend gross up for non-eligible dividends. She has asked your advice as to whether the payment of salary or, alternatively, the payment of non-eligible dividends, would have the lowest tax cost. Provide the requested advice.

SOLUTION available in print and online Study Guide.

Exercise Fifteen - 11

Subject: Salary vs. Dividends - Limited Corporate Cash

For the year ending December 31, 2018, Fargo Ltd. has Taxable Income, before consideration of dividends or salary paid to its sole shareholder, of $21,500. The Company's cash balance, prior to the payment of any taxes for the year is $18,500. The Company's Taxable Income is subject to a combined federal/provincial tax rate of 13 percent. There is no payroll tax in this province.

Mr. Fargo, the Company's president and sole shareholder, is 71 years of age and has no other source of income (he is not eligible for OAS). He has combined federal/provincial personal tax credits of $3,950 and lives in a province that has a personal tax rate on the first $46,605 of Taxable Income equal to 10 percent. The provincial dividend tax credit is 30 percent of the gross up for non-eligible dividends.

Mr. Fargo would like to remove all of the cash from the corporation and has asked your advice as to whether it would be better to take it out in the form of all non-eligible dividends or all salary. As Mr. Fargo is over 70 years old, no CPP contributions are required. Ignore the Canada employment tax credit. Provide the requested advice.

SOLUTION available in print and online Study Guide.

Conclusion

15-169.   As the preceding discussion makes clear, the salary vs. dividend decision is complex. Determination of the total tax consequences of the two alternatives does not necessarily resolve the issue. In addition to important factors already discussed in the chapter such as income splitting and bonusing down, consideration should be given to:

- the administrative costs related to withholding and remitting income tax and CPP premiums when salary is paid
- the ability to defer personal taxation to the subsequent calendar year if the payment of salary is deferred and the corporation's year end is within 180 days of December 31
- the effect of the gross up on dividends if the OAS clawback is relevant
- if the owner-manager is applying for a mortgage or loan, it will be more advantageous to have a history of salary received rather than dividends received

15-170.   The preceding material does not give you a comprehensive approach to solving these problems on a quantitative basis. In actual fact, there are problems here that are probably not subject to quantitative solutions. For example, whether or not an individual feels a need for retirement income involves many subjective considerations. With an issue such as this, a tax advisor can only outline the various possible outcomes.

We suggest you work Self Study Problems Fifteen-9 to 11 at this point.

Additional Supplementary Self Study Problems Are Available Online.

Key Terms Used In This Chapter

15-171. The following is a list of the key terms used in this Chapter. These terms, and their meanings, are compiled in the Glossary located at the back of the Study Guide.

Active Business Income	Low Rate Income Pool (LRIP)
Aggregate Investment Income	Manufacturing And Processing
Annual Business Limit	Profits Deduction (M&P Deduction)
Bonusing Down	Over Integration
Canadian Controlled Private Corporation	Private Corporation
Charitable Donations Tax Credit	Public Corporation
Eligible Dividends	Specified Employee
Estate Planning	Tax Avoidance
General Rate Income Pool (GRIP)	Tax Deferral
Income Splitting	Tax Planning
Integration	Taxable Benefit
Lifetime Capital Gains Deduction	TOSI (Tax On Split Income)
Limited Liability	Under Integration

References

15-172. For more detailed study of the material in this Chapter, we refer you to the following:

ITA 6(1)	Amounts To Be Included As Income From Office Or Employment
ITA 15(1)	Benefit Conferred On Shareholder
ITA 15(2)	Shareholder Debt
ITA 18(1)	General Limitations (On Deductions)
ITA 20(1)(j)	Repayment Of Loan By Shareholder
ITA 67	General Limitation Re Expenses
ITA 80.4	Loans - Imputed Interest
ITA 80.5	Deemed Interest
ITA 82(1)	Taxable Dividends Received
ITA 121	Deduction For Taxable Dividends
ITA 123 To	
125.4	Rules Applicable To Corporations
ITA 146	Registered Retirement Savings Plans
ITA 147	Deferred Profit Sharing Plans
S3-F6-C1	Interest Deductibility
IT-67R3	Taxable Dividends From Corporations Resident In Canada
IT-119R4	Debts Of Shareholders And Certain Persons Connected With Shareholders
IT-124R6	Contributions To Registered Retirement Savings Plans
IT-307R4	Spouse Or Common-Law Partner Registered Retirement Savings Plans
IT-421R2	Benefits To Individuals, Corporations And Shareholders From Loans Or Debt
IT-432R2	Benefits Conferred On Shareholders
IT-487	General Limitation On Deduction Of Outlays Or Expenses

Problems For Self Study (Online)

To provide practice in problem solving, there are Self Study and Supplementary Self Study problems available on MyLab Accounting.

Within the text we have provided an indication of when it would be appropriate to work each Self Study problem. The detailed solutions for Self Study problems can be found in the print and online Study Guide.

We provide the Supplementary Self Study problems for those who would like additional practice in problem solving. The detailed solutions for the Supplementary Self Study problems are available online, not in the Study Guide.

The .PDF file "Self Study Problems for Volume 2" on MyLab contains the following for Chapter 15:

- 11 Self Study problems,
- 5 Supplementary Self Study problems, and
- detailed solutions for the Supplementary Self Study problems.

Assignment Problems

(The solutions for these problems are only available in
the solutions manual that has been provided to your instructor.)

Assignment Problem Fifteen - 1
(Advantages Of Incorporation)

Philip Caron is in his mid-fifties and he is married with two teen aged children. For over fifteen years, he has worked as an unincorporated welder. The business is currently netting approximately $250,000 per year. In recent years, Mr. Caron has been using about half of the business earnings for personal living expenses.

In the last five years, he has been refining a fork lift which can be attached to half-ton trucks. He has a product which is selling well with few malfunctions and he is in the process of patenting the design. As a result, his welding business is now predominantly manufacturing these fork lift units.

Some of his welding equipment is old and he is faced with the need to replace it. Also, he needs to acquire larger welders and pipe benders to mass manufacture the fork lift. The business expansion will require substantial capital investment for which external financing will be required.

Required: Briefly discuss whether Mr. Caron should incorporate his business.

Assignment Problem Fifteen - 2
(Example Of Integration)

One of your long-standing clients, Mr. Carson Jones, has operated a successful unincorporated business for 10 years. This business is something of a sideline for him in that he has employment and investment income of over $250,000 per year. Further, these latter sources of income are more than adequate to meet his personal needs and absorb all of his available tax credits.

However, he has an intense dislike for paying taxes, particularly since the government has increased the top federal tax rate to a near obscene (in his opinion) 33 percent. When this maximum federal rate is combined with the top rate of 20 percent in his province, the result is an overall rate of 53 percent.

Given this, he is looking for ways to save taxes. One approach that he would like to consider is transferring the income from his business, as well as a group of publicly traded securities, to a new corporation. The new corporation would be named Carjon Ltd.

He has asked your advice on this approach and, to assist you in providing this advice, he has provided you with the following relevant data:

Taxable Income of business (Active Business Income)	$115,000
Eligible portfolio dividends	133,000
Federal corporate tax rate after federal abatement	28%
Federal Small Business Deduction	18%
General Rate Reduction	13%
Provincial rate on Active Business Income of CCPCs	5%
Provincial dividend tax credits on:	
Eligible dividends	40% of dividend gross up
Non-eligible dividends	23% of dividend gross up

Required:

A. Assume no corporation is used and the income is received directly. Calculate Carson's personal Tax Payable, showing separately the Tax Payable on the active business income and the dividends.

B. Assume the income and dividends are received by Carjon Ltd. Calculate corporate Tax Payable, after tax income available for distribution, and personal taxes that would be payable on the distribution. Your calculations should show separately the Tax Payable on the active business income and any eligible or non-eligible dividends.

C. Compare the Tax Payable with and without the use of Carjon Ltd. and explain why the Tax Payable amounts are different. Advise Carson as to whether he should make the proposed transfers to a new corporation.

Assignment Problem Fifteen - 3
(Flow Through Of Interest Income)

Ms. Martha Abdul is employed by a large public company and has an annual salary of $250,000. The following facts relate to her province of residence:

- The highest marginal tax rate on individuals is 16 percent.
- The provincial dividend tax credit on non-eligible dividends is equal to 28 percent of the gross up.
- The provincial tax rate on the investment income of CCPCs is 12 percent.

Near the end of the current year, Ms. Abdul won $400,000 in the provincial lottery. As she has no current need for these funds and is not keen on investment risk, she intends to invest the full amount for one year in a debt security that pays interest at an annual rate of 3.5 percent. She will not have any other investment income during the year.

Required: Prepare calculations that will compare the after tax retention of income that will accrue to Ms. Abdul if:

A. The investment is owned by her as an individual.

B. The investment is owned by a CCPC in which she is the sole shareholder, and which pays out all available income in dividends.

Assignment Problems

Assignment Problem Fifteen - 4
(Flow Through Of Dividend Income)

Ms. Toni Naidu has $175,000 in cash that she does not currently require for personal expenses. As she has employment income of over $160,000, her marginal federal tax rate is 29 percent. At this income level, her applicable provincial rate is 16 percent. The provincial dividend tax credit for eligible dividends is 35 percent of the gross up.

In her province of residence, the combined federal/provincial rate on investment income earned by a CCPC is 49 percent. This includes the ITA 123.3 refundable tax on investment income.

Ms. Naidu would like to invest her $175,000 in preferred shares of a widely held public company. The shares pay eligible dividends of $5,250 annually on December 15. Ms. Naidu's only investment income for the year will be the $5,250 of dividends paid on these shares.

Required: Prepare calculations that will compare the after tax retention of income that will accrue to Ms. Naidu for 2018 if:

A.   The investment in preferred shares is owned by her as an individual.

B.   The investment is owned by a corporation in which she is the sole shareholder, and which pays out all available income in dividends.

Assignment Problem Fifteen - 5
(Incorporation Of Investment Income)

The following information provides tax information for the province in which Jason Tegue lives for 2018:

- The combined federal and provincial corporate tax rate on the investment income of CCPCs is 50-2/3 percent (including the ART).
- The provincial dividend tax credit on eligible dividends is equal to 40 percent of the gross up on these dividends.
- The provincial dividend tax credit on non-eligible dividends is equal to 30 percent of the gross up on these dividends.
- Provincial tax payable on an individual's first $93,208 of Taxable Income is $12,817. Amounts in excess of this are subject to provincial tax at a rate of 17.4 percent.

Jason owns the following investments, and anticipates the following Canadian source income for 2018:

	Value At 31/12/2017	Type Of Income	Expected Income For 2018
Powor Corp Bonds	$ 78,000	Interest	$ 8,600
Larch Company Shares	312,000	Dividends	17,400
Inbridge Inc. Shares	36,000	Capital Gains	6,200
Calgary Dominion Bank Shares	38,000	Dividends	3,600
Calgary Dominion Bank Shares		Capital Gains	2,800
Totals	$464,000	N/A	$38,600

Jason only invests in the shares and debt of large, publicly traded companies. He does not own more than 1 percent of the shares or debt in any of these corporations. All of the dividends received will be designated as eligible by the paying corporation.

In 2018, in addition to the above investment income, Jason expects to earn $92,000 in employment income. He has combined federal/provincial personal tax credits of $3,491. The total adjusted cost base for his investments is $450,000.

Jason asks you whether it is financially more attractive for him to have his investments owned by a corporation or to own them directly, as he currently does. Assume that he and his investments will generate the anticipated amounts of income.

Jason's lifestyle requires him to use all available income. As a consequence, he would like you to assume that, if the investments are transferred to his corporation, the corporation will pay out all available funds as dividends.

Required: Provide an appropriate analysis for Jason Tegue.

Assignment Problem Fifteen - 6
(Partner As Individual Or Corporation)

Having worked as an individual management consultant, Mellisa Fox has enjoyed a great deal of success. Her effectiveness has generated a fairly long list of potential clients who would like to use her services. Recognizing the opportunities involved in this situation, Mellisa has decided to join Consulting Unlimited (CU) as a fourth partner.

Her entrance into the partnership will be effective January 1, 2018. She is giving consideration to three different approaches, the first two of which require the establishment of a new Canadian controlled private corporation (CCPC) in which she will be the sole shareholder. If she adopts one of these alternatives, the other partners in CU have agreed to allocate 25 percent ($125,000) of the small business deduction annual limit to her corporation.

> **Alternative 1**   Her new corporation will pay corporate tax on its full share of the partnership income, with the after tax funds being paid to Mellisa as dividends.
>
> **Alternative 2**   Mellisa will receive sufficient salary from her corporation to reduce the corporation's income to its $125,000 share of the annual business limit. Corporate taxes will be paid on the remaining Taxable Income.
>
> **Alternative 3**   Mellisa will join the partnership as an individual. Her share of the partnership income will be taxed as business income.

Mellisa lives in a province where the provincial tax payable on the first $205,842 of Taxable Income is $22,150, with additional amounts being taxed at a provincial rate of 14 percent. In this province, the provincial dividend tax credit is equal to 40 percent of the gross up for eligible dividends and 30 percent of the gross up for non-eligible dividends. Mellisa's tax credits for 2018 total $4,241.

If she forms a new corporation it would be subject to a combined federal/provincial tax rate on income eligible for the small business deduction of 12.5 percent. The rate on other active business income would be 27 percent.

During the CU's taxation year ending December 31, 2018, it is expected to have Taxable Income of $930,000. All of this income will be active business income and Mellisa or her corporation will be entitled to 25 percent of the total.

Because she has no other source of income, she requires all of the income that is generated by her participation in CU.

Required: Calculate the after tax personal retention of Mellisa's share of the partnership income for each of the three approaches. Ignore CPP considerations and the Canada employment tax credit in your calculations. Which approach would you recommend? Briefly explain why this alternative is the best and any other factors she should consider.

Assignment Problem Fifteen - 7
(Shareholder Loans)

Borsa Ltd. is a Canadian controlled private corporation with a taxation year that ends on December 31. All of the Company's shares are owned by Derek Borsa. In addition to being the sole shareholder of the Company, Derek works on a full time basis in the business.

Having grown up in a relatively poor working class family, Derek has always exhibited a strong sense of social responsibility. This is reflected in the policies of his Company which provides a generous package of benefits to its employees. Included in these benefits is the provision of interest free loans to employees who have at least 12 months service. Specifically, the Company will provide an interest free loan:

• of up to $150,000 to assist an employee in acquiring a residence. The principal amount of the loan must be repaid the earlier of 5 years from the day the loan was granted and the last day of employment.

• of up to $25,000 to assist an employee in acquiring an automobile to be used in employment related activities. The principal amount of the loan must be repaid the earlier of 3 years from the day the loan was granted and the last day of employment.

Derek borrows from the Company on a regular basis for various reasons. During the year ending December 31, 2018, Derek received loan proceeds from the Company as follows:

1. On February 1, Derek borrows $50,000 to cover a medical procedure on his shoulders in the United States. Derek would have had to wait over 18 months to have this procedure done in Canada while suffering a great deal of pain. As he feels Borsa Ltd. benefits from his increased productivity after the procedure, the loan is interest free and will be repaid on September 30, 2019.

2. On April 1, Derek borrows $15,000 from the company to finance a week at a luxurious resort in British Columbia to please his new wife. The loan will be repaid on December 31, 2018. Because he does not want to appear to his employees to be taking advantage of company funds, he decides that he should pay interest at the market rate for such loans. Assume the relevant rate is currently 5 percent.

3. On June 1, Derek borrows $150,000 in order to purchase a new residence. The loan is interest free. The loan will be repaid in two annual instalments of $75,000, on February 28, 2019 and 2020. It does not qualify as a home relocation loan.

4. On August 1, Derek borrows $50,000 in order to complete the renovations and landscaping of his new residence. The loan is interest free and will be repaid on July 31, 2020.

5. On November 1, to fulfill a lifelong dream, he borrows $212,000 from the Company to purchase a Mercedes S Class sedan. As it will be used purely for personal activities, he does not qualify for the $25,000 interest free loan. The loan bears interest at an annual rate of 1 percent and will be repaid on May 1, 2021.

All repayments and interest payments are made as scheduled. In all of the years under consideration, assume the relevant prescribed rate is 2 percent.

Required:

A. Indicate the tax consequences that will accrue to Derek as a result of receiving these loans. Briefly explain your conclusions for each loan for the years it is outstanding. Base your interest calculations on the number of months the loans are outstanding.

B. Identify any tax planning issues that are associated with these loans.

Assignment Problem Fifteen - 8
(Bonusing Down)

Donat Ltd. is a Canadian controlled private corporation (CCPC) that anticipates that its Taxable Income for the taxation year ending December 31, 2018 will be $625,000. All of the Corporation's shares are owned by Martin Donat. The anticipated income figure of $625,000 is after the deduction of a $275,000 salary payment to Martin. He plans to maintain his salary at $275,000 for the next 5 years.

All of Donat Ltd. income, both in the current and in previous years, is the result of active business income. However, this is the first year that its Taxable Income has exceeded the annual business limit for the small business deduction. It has no balance in its GRIP account at the beginning of 2018.

Martin has read an article written by a financial expert which states that when the Taxable Income of a CCPC exceeds $500,000 you must "bonus down" to prevent double taxation.

He does not need any additional funds for his personal living costs currently, but plans to build his dream home in 2022. That year, he will require substantial cash for the home's construction.

In Martin's province of residence, assume:

- for 2018 that provincial corporate tax rates are 13 percent on active business income in excess of the small business deduction and 2.5 percent on active business income eligible for the small business deduction.
- for 2018 to 2022 any Taxable Income in excess of Martin's $275,000 salary will be taxed at 33 percent federally and 19 percent provincially
- for 2022 the dividend gross up will be 38 percent for eligible dividends and 16 percent for non-eligible dividends
- for 2022 the federal dividend tax credit will be 6/11 of the gross up for eligible dividends and 8/11 of the gross up for non-eligible dividends
- for 2022 the provincial dividend tax credit will be 36 percent of the gross up for eligible dividends and 20 percent of the gross up for non-eligible dividends

Required: As Martin's tax consultant would you advise him to bonus down by paying himself additional salary of $125,000 in 2018? Justify your conclusion.

Assignment Problem Fifteen - 9

(Salary Vs. Dividends - Required Amount)

Lara Collins is the sole shareholder of Collins Inc., a Canadian controlled private corporation. It uses a December 31 taxation year.

All of its income qualifies for the small business deduction. This income is allocated to a province where the provincial rate on this type of income is 3 percent.

Lara needs an additional $30,000 in cash in order to create a much needed woman cave in her basement. Collins Inc. has sufficient cash to pay either additional salary or additional dividends in order to provide the required funds. The Company has no balance in its GRIP account.

Lara's 2018 Taxable Income, before consideration of any additional payment from Collins Inc., is $93,000. This includes salary of $75,000 from Collins Inc. In the province where she is resident, the provincial tax rate on Taxable Income over $93,208 is 12 percent. The dividend tax credit for non-eligible dividends in this province is 30 percent of the dividend gross up.

Required: Determine the amount that would be required in the way of salary and in the way of dividends, in order to provide Lara with the required after tax funds of $30,000. Which alternative would have the lowest tax cost to Lara and her corporation?

Assignment Problem Fifteen - 10
(Salary Vs. Dividends - Required Amount)

Simon Fahrquest is the sole shareholder of Dawg Ltd., a very successful business that was incorporated a number of years ago. The Company has always qualified as a CCPC and uses a December 31 year end.

Simon has never been particularly fond of people, but has always loved dogs, particularly those of mixed breed. While he has no family, he currently owns 12 dogs, none of which are purebred.

While Dawg Ltd. has always been very profitable, Simon has chosen to live modestly in a dog friendly residential property that he has owned for many years. Each year, he estimates the amount of cash that he will need for his living expenses which vary year to year and looks to his corporation to provide the needed cash.

Since after meeting Simon's financial needs, Dawg Ltd. always has cash that isn't required for operations, it donates at least $100,000 per year to the Society For The Prevention Of Cruelty To Animals (SPCA), a registered charity. The donations specify that the funds must be used for the protection, maintenance, and placement of mixed breed dogs.

For 2018, Simon estimates that he will need $50,000 in after tax cash to meet his personal needs. He expects Dawg Ltd. will have Taxable Income of $350,000 before any payments to him, all of which will qualify for the small business deduction. The provincial tax rate on such income is 3 percent.

In Simon's province of residence, the provincial taxes on the first $46,605 of Taxable Income total $4,528. Additional income will be taxed at a provincial rate of 12 percent. Also in this province, the provincial dividend tax credit for non-eligible dividends is equal to 32 percent of the dividend gross up.

For the 2018 taxation year, Simon estimates that his personal tax credits will total $3,260.

Required:

A. Determine the tax cost of providing Simon with the required $50,000 in after tax cash using only salary payments.

B. Determine the tax cost of providing Simon with the required $50,000 in after tax cash using only dividend payments.

C. Given the information in this problem, do you believe that better results could be achieved with a combination of salary and dividends? Would your answer be different if Simon's personal tax credits totalled $10,000 instead of $3,260? Calculations are not required in answering this Part C.

D. Simon would like to increase his donations to the SPCA and has asked your advice on the most tax advantageous way to do this. What factors should be considered when analyzing this issue?

Ignore CPP contributions and the Canada employment credit in your solution.

CHAPTER 16

Rollovers Under Section 85

Rollovers Under Section 85

Introduction

16-1. Chapter 15 gave detailed consideration to the question of whether it would be advantageous to establish a corporation in order to reduce, defer, or redistribute the amount of Tax Payable. If the results of this analysis favour the use of a corporation, Section 85 of the *Act* provides an attractive basis for the transfer of property to the new corporation.

16-2. The problem that is involved with such a transfer is that the assets may have been owned by the transferor for some period of time. In these circumstances, it is possible that their fair market values may be well in excess of their adjusted cost base and/or their undepreciated capital cost. As a transfer by a taxpayer to a corporation would be considered a disposition by that taxpayer, the incorporation of an existing business could result in a need to include both capital gains and recapture in the transferor's Taxable Income. In a typical situation, where the owner of an operating business decides to transfer all of its assets to a newly formed corporation, the resulting tax liability could be significant.

> **EXAMPLE**   Joanne Browski has an unincorporated business that is using assets with a fair market value of $572,000. The tax values for these assets total $225,000. Ms. Browski would like to transfer these assets to a corporation and continue her operations in that legal form (note, that while we have treated the group of assets like a single asset in order to simplify this example, in actual practice, each asset would have to be treated individually).

> **ANALYSIS**   Under the general tax rules, asset dispositions must be recorded at fair market value. If this applied to Ms. Browski's transfer, the amount of taxation would be significant and could be a deterrent to the incorporation of her business.

16-3. Section 85 of the *Income Tax Act* is designed to provide relief in this type of situation. In somewhat simplified terms, it permits Ms. Browski's property to be transferred to a corporation on either a tax free basis, or with a level of taxation that is determined at her discretion. As noted in earlier Chapters, such transactions are referred to in tax work as rollovers.

16-4. Of the rollovers that are available, the content of Section 85 provide for one of the most important and widely used. In this Chapter we will provide detailed coverage of the application of this Section. Other rollovers involving corporations will be given coverage in Chapter 17.

General Rules For The Transfer

Transferor And Transferee

Transferors

16-5.   As indicated in the introduction, we are concerned here with transfers of property to a corporation at a value that can be elected by the transferor and the corporation. There are several possibilities with respect to the identity of the transferor:

- The transferor may be an **individual** who wishes to incorporate his proprietorship.
- The transferor may be a **corporation** that wishes to transfer some of its assets to a different corporation.
- The transferor may be a **trust** that wishes to transfer some of its assets to a corporation.
- The transferor may be a **partner** who wishes to incorporate his partnership interest.

16-6.   ITA 85(1) refers to taxpayers and this subsection covers the rules related to transferors who are individuals, corporations, and trusts. As partnerships are not "taxpayers" for income tax purposes, a separate ITA 85(2) provides for the transfer of partnership assets to a corporation.

Transferees

16-7.   With respect to transferees, Section 85 requires that they be taxable Canadian corporations. A "Canadian corporation" is defined in ITA 89(1) as a corporation that is currently resident in Canada and that was either incorporated in Canada, or has been a resident continuously since June 18, 1971. ITA 89(1) also defines a "taxable Canadian corporation" as a Canadian corporation that was not, by virtue of a statutory provision, exempt from taxation under Part I of the *Income Tax Act*.

Eligible Property

16-8.   Only "eligible property", the components of which are defined in ITA 85(1.1), can be transferred under Section 85. The major items listed in the Subsection include:

- both depreciable and non-depreciable capital property, generally not including real property owned by non-residents;
- Canadian resource properties;
- foreign resource properties;
- inventories, other than inventories of real property; and
- real property owned by a non-resident person and used in the year in a business carried on by that person in Canada.

16-9.   The general exclusion of real property owned by non-residents reflects the fact that this type of property is Taxable Canadian Property and gains on its disposition are subject to Canadian taxes, without regard to the residency of the seller. The exclusion is designed to prevent a non-resident who owns Canadian real estate from being able to transfer the property on a tax free basis to a corporation, and subsequently selling the shares in the corporation on a tax free basis. As explained in Chapter 20, gains on such dispositions are typically exempted from Canadian tax by international tax treaties.

16-10.   The second exclusion from assets eligible for the Section 85 rollover would be Canadian resident owned real property that constitutes an inventory. That is, if a group of real property assets is being actively traded, rather than being held for their income producing ability, they are not eligible for a tax free rollover under ITA 85.

16-11.   This latter exclusion of inventories of real property can be a particularly troublesome provision due to the fact that, in practice, some taxpayers may not be certain as to the status of their real estate holdings. If a taxpayer was to go through the Section 85 rollover procedures and then, after the fact, find that the transferred real estate holdings were considered inventory by the CRA, the tax consequences would be very severe. In this type of situation, it would be advisable to delay the transfer to the corporation until such time as any uncertainty regarding the status of the real estate could be clearly established.

Consideration To Transferor

16-12.   In return for the property transferred to the corporation, the corporation may provide various types of consideration to the transferor. The one requirement that is specified in ITA 85(1) is that some part of this consideration must consist of shares of the transferee corporation.

16-13.   The shares issued may be either preferred, common, or some combination of the two types. Further, the requirement for share consideration to be used can be satisfied by the issuance of as little as one share to the transferor. For reasons that will become evident later in this Chapter, the usual Section 85 transaction involves the use of a combination of shares and non-share consideration (e.g. cash or debt securities). In this context, the non-share consideration is usually referred to as the "boot".

16-14.   A further point here is that, without regard to the values that are elected for the exchange, the fair market value of the consideration provided to the transferor should be equal to the total fair market value of the assets transferred to the corporation. As will be discussed later in this Chapter, if these amounts are not equal, the difference may be viewed as a benefit to the transferor, or a gift to a related party.

Making The Election

16-15.   Both the transferor and the transferee corporation must elect to have the Section 85 provisions apply. This joint election is accomplished by filing Form T2057 (transfers from individuals, trusts, and corporations) or T2058 (transfers from partnerships), on or before the earliest of the dates on which the normal tax returns are due for the two taxpayers.

16-16.   A late election may be filed for up to three years after this date and, with the permission of the CRA, a late election will be accepted after the end of this three year period. Whenever there is a late election, a penalty of one-quarter of 1 percent of any capital gain or other income will be assessed for each month beyond the normal filing date. The maximum penalty is $100 per month to a maximum of $8,000.

16-17.   In making the election, it is crucial that the taxpayer list all of the properties that are to be covered. If a property is omitted from the forms, the normal rules associated with dispositions will apply. This could result in the need to recognize capital gains, recapture, or business income on the transfer, an outcome that might require needless payment of taxes.

Establishing The Transfer Price

Importance

16-18.   One of the most significant features of ITA 85 is that it provides for the transfer of various properties to a corporation at values that are jointly elected by the transferor and transferee. Careful consideration must be given to the election of an appropriate transfer price in that, in general, this elected value establishes three important values. These are:

> **Transferor**   The deemed proceeds of disposition for the property given up.

> **Transferor**   The adjusted cost base or capital cost of the consideration received from the corporation.

> **Transferee**   The tax cost of the property received by the corporation (adjusted cost base, capital cost, or UCC).

16-19.   As will be discussed at a later point in this Chapter, the elected value is also influential in determining the PUC of the newly issued shares.

Basic Rules

16-20.   While there are a number of complications associated with establishing transfer prices, the basic rules are very straightforward. The elected values cannot exceed fair market values and cannot be less than the adjusted cost base of non-depreciable assets, or the UCC of depreciable assets. As we will see in the next section, the floor elected value is also limited by the boot, or non-share consideration, received.

EXAMPLE   Mr. Thompson owns non-depreciable capital assets with a fair market value of $750,000 and an adjusted cost base of $500,000. On the transfer of these assets to a corporation, he will receive consideration with a fair market value of $750,000. However, under the provisions of ITA 85, the elected value can be any value between a floor of $500,000 and a ceiling of $750,000.

ANALYSIS   In most situations, the transferor wishes to avoid recognizing income on the transfer and, in order to do this, the elected value will be the floor of $500,000. The election of this value will have the following tax consequences for the transferor and the transferee:

• The $500,000 will be the proceeds of disposition to the transferor. As this is equal to his adjusted cost base for the assets, there will be no capital gain on the transfer.

• The adjusted cost base to the corporation will be $500,000. This means that, if the corporation were to sell the assets immediately for their fair market value of $750,000, a capital gain of $250,000 ($750,000 - $500,000) would have to be recognized. This reflects the fact that the gain on the assets at the time of transfer was only deferred, not eliminated, by the use of the ITA 85 rollover.

• While we have not specified the type of consideration that will be received by the transferor, the election of $500,000 as the transfer price means that the adjusted cost base of the consideration will be this amount. This will be less than the $750,000 fair market value of the consideration.

16-21.   You should note that this scenario raises the possibility of double taxation on the $250,000 gain. The adjusted cost base of the property transferred and the consideration received by the transferor is $500,000. If the corporation sells the assets for their fair market value of $750,000, there will be a $250,000 gain at the corporate level. If the consideration received by the transferor is in the form of shares, a sale of these shares at their fair market value of $750,000 would result in the $250,000 gain being taxed a second time at the individual level. This would suggest that, if either the assets transferred, or the consideration received by the transferor are to be sold, the election should be made at the fair market value of $750,000.

Non-Share Consideration (Boot)

16-22.   The term, "boot", is commonly used to refer to non-share consideration given to the transferor in an ITA 85 rollover. It would include cash paid to the transferor and new debt of the transferee corporation issued to the transferor. In those cases where an existing business is being transferred under these provisions, boot would include the assumption by the transferee corporation of any debt of the existing business that is being transferred.

16-23.   Other types of non-share consideration (e.g., capital assets) could be used in an ITA 85 rollover and, if this was the case, the term boot would still be appropriate. However, in almost all situations, boot is restricted to cash, new debt issued by the transferee corporation, or existing debt of the transferor assumed by the transferee corporation.

16-24.   Boot is of considerable significance in that, if the rollover is properly structured, it constitutes an amount of cash or cash equivalent that will be received by the transferor on a tax free basis. Because of this, the other basic rule on establishing a transfer price is that the elected amount cannot be less than the value of the non-share consideration provided to the transferor.

16-25. The example that was presented in Paragraph 16-20 involved non-depreciable capital assets with an adjusted cost base of $500,000 and a fair market value of $750,000. With respect to the consideration received by Mr. Thompson, assume that it is as follows:

Cash	$600,000
Shares Of Transferee Corporation	150,000
Total (Equals Fair Market Value Of Assets Transferred)	$750,000

16-26. Because the elected value cannot be below the value of the non-share consideration, the minimum elected value would be $600,000. If $600,000 was the elected value, it would result in the following tax consequences:

- The proceeds of disposition to the transferor would be $600,000, resulting in a taxable capital gain of $50,000 [(1/2)($600,000 - $500,000)].

- The adjusted cost base of the assets for the corporation would be the transfer price of $600,000. This means that if the corporation sells the assets for their fair market value of $750,000, the capital gain would be $150,000.

- The adjusted cost base of the consideration received by the transferor would be $600,000. As will be discussed at a later point, all of this amount must be allocated to the non-share consideration, leaving the share consideration with a nil adjusted cost base.

The Usual Scenario

16-27. As illustrated in the preceding example, if the boot exceeds the tax values (adjusted cost base or UCC) of the assets transferred, the result is some form of Taxable Income. As one of the usual goals in using ITA 85 is to avoid a tax liability on the transfer of assets, the normal procedure is to set the transfer price at an amount equal to the tax values of the assets and to restrict the use of boot to this value. In the example presented, this would mean using $500,000 as the elected value and paying or issuing non-share consideration in this same amount.

16-28. In addition, the fair market value of the consideration received by the transferor must be equal to the fair market value of the assets transferred to the corporation. In the example presented in Paragraph 16-20, this value is $750,000. This means that if the maximum non-share consideration of $500,000 is used, shares must be issued with a fair market value of $250,000.

16-29. If we apply this scenario to the example presented in Paragraph 16-20, the results would be as follows:

- As the proceeds of disposition would be $500,000, no capital gain would arise on the transfer to the corporation.

- The adjusted cost base to the corporation of the assets acquired will be $500,000.

- The adjusted cost base of the non-share consideration to the transferor would be $500,000. This means that the adjusted cost base of the share consideration would be nil.

16-30. There are a number of complications associated with rollovers under ITA 85 and they will be the subject of much of the remainder of this Chapter. However, the great majority of these transactions will follow the pattern illustrated in the preceding simple example.

Transfer Prices - Detailed Rules

Rules Applicable To All Assets

16-31. There are a number of rules in ITA 85 that apply to all types of property. To begin, ITA 85(1)(a) establishes that the amount elected by the taxpayer and corporation shall be deemed to be the taxpayer's proceeds of disposition, as well as the cost of the property to the corporation.

16-32.   A further general rule is as follows:

ITA 85(1)(b)   Subject to Paragraph 85(1)(c), where the amount that the taxpayer and corporation have agreed on in their election in respect of the property is less than the fair market value, at the time of the disposition, of the consideration therefor (other than any shares of the capital stock of the corporation or a right to receive any such shares) received by the taxpayer, the amount so agreed on shall, irrespective of the amount actually so agreed on by them, be deemed to be an amount equal to that fair market value;

16-33.   This establishes that the elected value cannot be less than the boot ("consideration other than shares of stock of the corporation").

16-34.   Finally, a further provision limits the elected value to the fair market value of the property transferred:

ITA 85(1)(c)   Where the amount that the taxpayer and the corporation have agreed on in their election in respect of the property is greater than the fair market value, at the time of the disposition, of the property so disposed of, the amount so agreed on shall, irrespective of the amount actually so agreed on, be deemed to be an amount equal to that fair market value;

16-35.   These general rules apply to all assets transferred, thereby establishing a range for the election. This range can be outlined as follows:

Ceiling Value   Fair market value of the assets transferred to the corporation.

Floor Value   The floor value will be equal to the greater of:

• the fair market value of the non-share consideration (boot) given to the transferor in return for the assets transferred; and

• the tax values (adjusted cost base or UCC) of the assets transferred.

16-36.   The application of the term, "tax values", in the preceding outline of the rules will vary with the type of asset involved. Attention will be given to these differences in the material which follows.

Accounts Receivable

16-37.   As was discussed in Chapter 6, when accounts receivable are transferred in conjunction with all of the other assets of a business, under the usual rules, the disposition will be treated as a capital transaction, with any resulting loss being only one-half deductible. Further, as the transferee has not included these amounts in income, no deduction can be made for bad debts. If the transferee collects less than the transfer amount, the difference must be treated as a capital loss and again, only one-half of this loss will be deductible.

16-38.   To avoid these results, the usual procedure is to use a joint election under ITA 22. This election allows any loss to be treated as a fully deductible business loss and permits the transferee to deduct bad debts after the transfer. You may recall that this election was discussed in Chapter 6. If you do not recall the application of ITA 22, you should review this material now as this election will be commonly used in the problem material in this Chapter.

16-39.   While accounts receivable can be transferred under ITA 85, taxpayers are not permitted to elect under both ITA 85 and ITA 22. In general, it will be to the advantage of the taxpayer to make the ITA 22 election and, as a result, accounts receivable will usually not be one of the assets listed in the ITA 85 election.

16-40.   Note, however, this does not prevent these assets from being transferred. Using the ITA 22 joint election, they can be transferred at fair market value, with any resulting loss being fully deductible to the transferor. The corporation will have to include the difference between the face value and the price paid in income, but any difference between the face value and the amounts collected will be 100 percent deductible.

Inventories And Non-Depreciable Capital Property

16-41.   Unlike the situation with accounts receivable, when inventories are disposed of in conjunction with the sale of a business, any difference between fair market value and cost is automatically treated as business income or loss, not as a capital gain or loss. This is specifically provided for in ITA 23, with no election being required to bring this provision into effect.

16-42.   Non-depreciable capital property of a business would include land, temporary investments, and long-term investments. As capital property is involved, any gain or loss on their disposition would be treated as a capital gain or loss.

16-43.   In making the election here, the highest value will be the fair market value of the assets transferred to the corporation. The minimum election cannot be below the amount of the boot received by the transferor. However, a further floor limit is specified for the inventories and non-depreciable capital property in ITA 85(1)(c.1) to ensure that artificial losses cannot be created. This limit is the lesser of the fair market value of the property and its tax cost. For non-depreciable capital assets, the tax cost would be the adjusted cost base of the property. For inventory, tax cost would be either cost or market, depending on how the inventory balance is carried for tax purposes.

16-44.   Putting these limits together means that the minimum elected value for the floor, as specified in ITA 85(1)(e.3), will be the greater of:

A.   The fair market value of the boot (the general floor for all assets); and

B.   The lesser of:
   • the tax cost of the property; and
   • the fair market value of the property.

16-45.   These rules can be illustrated using the three examples that follow:

	Example One	Example Two	Example Three
Fair Market Value Of Property	$15,000	$10,000	$20,000
Adjusted Cost Base	12,000	12,000	14,000
Fair Market Value Of The Boot	5,000	5,000	17,000

16-46.   In Example One, the maximum transfer value is the fair market value of $15,000 and the minimum value is the cost of $12,000. The normal election value would be $12,000. Also note that up to $12,000 of boot, an additional $7,000, could have been taken out without changing the minimum election, or creating immediate tax consequences.

16-47.   In Example Two, the $10,000 fair market value is both the floor and the ceiling. If the property is inventories, this required election will result in a fully deductible business loss of $2,000 ($12,000 - $10,000). Alternatively, if the election was made on non-depreciable capital property, the result would be an allowable capital loss of $1,000 [(1/2)($12,000 - $10,000)]. As explained beginning in Paragraph 16-50, this capital loss would be disallowed.

16-48.   In Example Three, the maximum value is again the fair market value. While the $14,000 cost is lower than the $20,000 fair market value, it is also lower than the boot. This means that, in this example, the minimum value that can be elected is the boot of $17,000. If this property is inventory, this election will result in fully taxable business income of $3,000 ($17,000 - $14,000). If the election was made on non-depreciable capital property, the result will be a taxable capital gain of $1,500 [(1/2)($17,000 - $14,000)].

16-49.   If the goal is to structure the rollover to avoid any gain on the transfer of assets, Example Three will not accomplish this objective. In order to avoid a gain, the usual procedure is to limit the non-share consideration to the minimum elected value as otherwise determined, or $14,000 in Example Three.

Exercise Sixteen - 1

Subject: Elected Value For Non-Depreciable Property

Jean Doan's unincorporated business has inventories with a fair market value of $125,000 and a tax cost of $140,000. In addition, he owns land with a fair market value of $350,000 and a tax cost of $110,000. He intends to transfer these assets to a new corporation, taking back $125,000 in cash for the inventories. For the land, he receives $150,000 in cash and $200,000 in securities. If he uses ITA 85 for the transfer, what is the possible range of values that can be elected for the two properties? Assume he elects the lowest possible value in each case. What are the tax consequences for Mr. Doan?

SOLUTION available in print and online Study Guide.

Non-Depreciable Capital Property - Disallowed Capital Losses
General Rules
16-50.   The special rules described in the following material apply only to non-depreciable capital assets. They do not apply to either inventories or depreciable capital assets as it is not possible to have capital losses on these types of assets.

16-51.   While we are discussing these rules in the material related to Section 85 rollovers, you should note that they are applicable to transfers to affiliated persons, without regard to whether Section 85 is being used. The discussion is located here because, when a non-depreciable capital asset is transferred under ITA 85, the recognition of a loss may be unavoidable because of the rules limiting the elected values. This was the case in Example Two in Paragraph 16-45.

16-52.   The basic rule applicable to these situations is found in ITA 40(2)(g), which indicates that a taxpayer's loss, to the extent that it is a "superficial loss", is deemed to be nil. As with many other concepts related to capital assets, the definition of "superficial loss" is found in ITA 54:

> **"superficial loss"** of a taxpayer means the taxpayer's loss from the disposition of a particular property where
>
> (a) during the period that begins 30 days before and ends 30 days after the disposition, the taxpayer or a person affiliated with the taxpayer acquires a property (in this definition referred to as the "substituted property") that is, or is identical to, the particular property, and
>
> (b) at the end of that period, the taxpayer or a person affiliated with the taxpayer owns or had a right to acquire the substituted property.

16-53.   Read together, these provisions deem to be nil any capital loss arising on a transfer to an affiliated person. While the allocation of the loss will depend on whether the transferor is an individual, a trust or a corporation, the denial of the loss is applicable to all taxpayers. The actual allocation of the denied loss will be dealt with after our discussion of affiliated persons.

Affiliated Persons
16-54.   The term "affiliated person" is defined in ITA 251.1(1) as follows:

A. An individual is affiliated to another individual only if that individual is his spouse or common-law partner.

B. A corporation is affiliated with:
   1. a person who controls the corporation;
   2. each member of an affiliated group of persons who controls the corporation; and
   3. the spouse or common-law partner of a person listed in (1) or (2).

C. Two corporations are affiliated if:
   1. each corporation is controlled by a person, and the person by whom one corporation is controlled is affiliated with the person by whom the other corporation is controlled;
   2. one corporation is controlled by a person, the other corporation is controlled by a group of persons, and each member of that group is affiliated with that person; or
   3. each corporation is controlled by a group of persons, and each member of each group is affiliated with at least one member of the other group.

16-55.   ITA 251.1(3) contains definitions that are required in the application of these rules. The two that are of importance here are:

Affiliated group of persons means a group of persons each member of which is affiliated with every other member.

Controlled means controlled, directly or indirectly, in any manner whatever. This definition refers to both legal control and de facto control, which does not necessarily require majority ownership of all shares.]

16-56.   As was previously noted, if a capital loss arises on a transfer to an affiliated person, it is deemed to be nil. This rule applies to all taxpayers, including individuals, trusts, and corporations. In contrast to the normal use of the term, for purposes of the affiliated person rules, the term "person" includes partnerships. You should also note that, for transfers involving ITA 85, the transferee and the transferor will almost always be affiliated (e.g., the transferor will typically control the transferee corporation).

Allocation Of Disallowed Capital Loss

16-57.   When the transferor is an individual, the disallowed loss is allocated to the adjusted cost base of the transferred property. This requirement is dictated by ITA 53(1)(f), which describes adjustments to the cost base of a transferred property.

EXAMPLE - Individual   Ms. Hannah Howard, the sole shareholder of HH Ltd., transfers land with an adjusted cost base of $50,000 and a fair market value of $40,000, to HH Ltd. The transfer is made under Section 85 at an elected value of $40,000.

ANALYSIS   The $10,000 loss ($40,000 - $50,000) on the transfer is disallowed. As the transferor is an individual, the loss will be allocated to the adjusted cost base of the land in the tax records of HH Ltd. This means that the adjusted cost base to HH Ltd. will be the same $50,000 ($40,000, plus the $10,000 loss) that was the adjusted cost base to Ms. Howard.

16-58.   When the transferor is a corporation, trust, or partnership, the allocation of the disallowed loss is covered under ITA 40(3.4). In effect, this provision keeps the loss in the tax records of the transferor, to be recognized when one of the following events occurs:

- the transferee disposes of the property to a non-affiliated person (includes deemed dispositions);
- if the transferor is a corporation,
  - it is subject to an acquisition of control; or
  - it is subject to an ITA 88(2) winding up.

EXAMPLE - Not An Individual   HC Ltd. transfers land with an adjusted cost base of $50,000 and a fair market value of $40,000 to HCSub, a corporation controlled by HC Ltd., i.e., an affiliated person. Two years later, HCSub sells the land for $35,000 to a non-affiliated person.

ANALYSIS   The $10,000 ($40,000 - $50,000) loss on the transfer to HCSub will be disallowed at the time of the transfer. However, when the land is sold by HCSub for $35,000, HC Ltd. will recognize the disallowed loss of $10,000 ($50,000 - $40,000). In addition, HCSub will recognize a $5,000 ($40,000 - $35,000) loss at the time of sale. The result is a total loss for the two companies of $15,000 ($50,000 - $35,000).

Tax Planning

16-59.   To the extent that the asset with the unrealized loss is necessary to the continued operations of the business, for example land on which the enterprise's factory is located, it makes no difference whether it is transferred under the provisions of ITA 85 or outside the election. In either case, the loss will be disallowed at the time of the transfer.

16-60.   If an asset is not essential to the operations of the corporation, a preferable course of action may be to sell it to a non-affiliated person. This will permit the immediate recognition of any loss on its disposition. However, if the asset is an integral part of the operations of the transferor this is not a viable alternative.

16-61.   The other basic point here is, that if the asset in question has an unrealized loss, there is no reason to elect to transfer it under Section 85. The objective that the taxpayer is attempting to achieve in using Section 85 is to defer the taxation of income. When losses are involved on particular assets, including those assets in the Section 85 rollover complicates the election without contributing to the taxpayer's desired goals.

Depreciable Property

General Rules

16-62.   As with other assets, the ceiling for the election is the fair market value of the asset and the general floor is the fair market value of the non-share consideration received by the transferor. However, as was the case with inventories and non-depreciable capital property, a further lower limit is specified in the *Income Tax Act*.

16-63.   ITA 85(1)(e) indicates that for depreciable property, the lower limit is the least of the UCC for the class, the fair market value of each individual property, and the cost of each individual property. This means that the overall lower limit for the election, as specified in ITA 85(1)(e.3), is the greater of:

A.   The fair market value of the boot (general floor for all assets), and

B.   The least of:

- the balance of the UCC for the class;
- the cost to the taxpayer of each individual property; and
- the fair market value of each individual property.

Examples - Elected Values

16-64.   These rules can be illustrated by the following two examples, each involving the transfer of the only asset in a CCA class:

	Example One	Example Two
Fair Market Value Of The Property	$50,000	$18,000
UCC Of Class (Last Asset In Class)	20,000	20,000
Cost Of The Property	27,000	30,000
Fair Market Value Of The Boot	15,000	15,000

Example One Analysis   In Example One, the range of the election would extend from the UCC of $20,000 as the floor to the fair market value of $50,000. Note that any election in between the UCC of $20,000 and the cost of $27,000 would result in recapture of CCA. The normal election here would be the UCC of $20,000, which results in the transferor not recognizing a capital gain or recapture of CCA. In addition, the transferor would usually take out $20,000 in boot. In Example One, $5,000 more boot could be taken out without creating immediate tax consequences.

Example Two Analysis   In Example Two, using the limits specified in ITA 85(1)(e.3) the ceiling value and the floor value would be the $18,000 fair market value of the property. With the ceiling and floor at the same value, the general rules would indicate that only this $18,000 value could be elected. In Example Two, $3,000 more boot could be taken out without creating immediate tax consequences. Since the transfer of the property removes the last asset in this CCA class, the fact that the elected value is below the UCC suggests a terminal loss. However, as will be discussed beginning in Paragraph 16-70, ITA 85 does not apply to this transfer and this terminal loss will be disallowed.

Example - Order Of Disposition

16-65.   An additional problem arises in the case of depreciable assets in situations where a number of different assets that belong to the same CCA class are being transferred at the same time. This problem can be illustrated by the following example:

> **EXAMPLE**   An individual owns two assets in a particular CCA class and the UCC for that class is $28,000. Data on the two assets is as follows:

	Asset One	Asset Two
Cost Of Asset	$15,000	$30,000
Fair Market Value	20,000	25,000

16-66.   The problem here is that the wording of the transfer price rules for depreciable assets requires the floor to be based on the least of the cost of each individual asset, fair market value of each individual asset, but UCC for the class as a whole. This determination has to be made with respect to each asset in the class, with the resulting figures summed for purposes of the election floor.

16-67.   This means that, if the general rules were applied, the floor values would be $15,000 for Asset One, plus $25,000 for Asset Two. This reflects the fact that both of these individual values are less than the $28,000 UCC for the class. However, if these values are elected, a total of $40,000 would be subtracted from the class. Since the UCC balance for the class is only $28,000, this would result in recapture of $12,000.

16-68.   To alleviate this problem, ITA 85(1)(e.1) allows an assumption that the properties are transferred one at a time. This means that for the transfer of Asset One, if the floor value of $15,000 was elected (this assumes that the non-share consideration provided to the transferor does not exceed this amount), this $15,000 would be subtracted from the UCC of $28,000.

16-69.   The resulting UCC balance would be $13,000, and when the depreciable asset rules are applied to Asset Two, this UCC balance of $13,000 would become the floor. If the taxpayer again elected to use the floor value, the $13,000 would be deducted from the UCC and this would reduce the UCC balance to nil without triggering recaptured CCA.

Exercise Sixteen - 2

Subject: Elected Value For Depreciable Property

Eric Li has two depreciable assets - a Class 1 building and a Class 10 vehicle. The assets are to be transferred to a corporation using ITA 85. Relevant information on the assets is as follows:

	Class 1	Class 10
Fair Market Value Of The Property	$475,000	$12,000
UCC Of Class (Last Asset In Class)	150,000	8,000
Cost Of The Property	220,000	28,000
Fair Market Value Of The Boot	250,000	10,000

What is the possible range of values that can be elected for the two properties? Assume he elects the lowest possible value in each case. What are the tax consequences for Mr. Li?

SOLUTION available in print and online Study Guide.

Depreciable Property - Disallowed Terminal Losses
General Rules

16-70.   In Paragraph 16-64, we noted that the terminal loss resulting from the required election on the asset in Example Two will be disallowed. More specifically, if a depreciable property with a fair market value that is less than its UCC is transferred by a person (individual, trust, or corporation) or a partnership to an affiliated person (see Paragraph 16-54), ITA 13(21.2) indicates that:

- ITA 85 does not apply;

- the proceeds of the disposition are deemed to be the UCC amount, thereby disallowing the terminal loss; and

- the transferee's capital cost for the property is deemed to be the transferor's capital cost, with the excess of that amount over the UCC of the asset deemed to be CCA deducted in previous periods.

16-71.   In Example Two from Paragraph 16-64, the property had a capital cost of $30,000, a UCC for the class of $20,000, and a fair market value of $18,000. As the $18,000 fair market value was less than the $20,000 UCC of the class, this means that ITA 85 does not apply to this transfer. In addition, ITA 13(21.2) would disallow this loss on any transfer to an affiliated person by deeming the proceeds of disposition to be equal to the UCC.

16-72.   If, however, the property is sold to the corporation for its fair market value, the property will have a deemed capital cost to the transferee of $30,000 and a UCC value of $18,000. The $2,000 disallowed loss will be deemed to be a depreciable property that is owned by the transferor. It will be allocated to the same class as the transferred property for CCA purposes and will be subject to the usual CCA procedures. However, it will be kept in a separate class so that any unamortized amount can be recognized when one of the following events occurs:

- the transferee disposes of the property to a non-affiliated person (includes deemed dispositions);
- the use of the property is changed from income earning to non-income earning;
- if the transferor is a corporation,
    - it is subject to an acquisition of control; or
    - it is subject to an ITA 88(2) winding up.

Tax Planning

16-73.   As was noted in our discussion of capital losses on transfers of non-depreciable capital property, Section 85 is normally used in order to defer the taxation of various types of income. If there is a terminal loss present on a depreciable property, ITA 85 cannot be used. This means that, if the asset is necessary to the continued operations of the business, it will be sold to the corporation at fair market value, with any terminal loss on the transaction being disallowed by ITA 13(21.2). If the asset is not necessary to the continued operations of the business, it would be preferable to sell it to a non-affiliated person.

As a consequence, no special coverage of items such as goodwill is required in this Chapter.

Summary Of Transfer Price Rules

16-74.   Figure 16-1 provides a summary of the transfer price rules that have been discussed in this section (following page).

Figure 16 - 1
Summary Of Section 85 Transfer Price Rules

	Inventory And Non-Depreciable Assets	Depreciable Assets
Ceiling (FMV Of Asset)	X	X
Floor - Greater Of:		
A. FMV Of Boot	X	X
B. Least Of:		
Tax Cost Of Asset	X	—
Cost Of Asset (Not Tax Cost)	—	X
FMV Of Asset	X	X
UCC Balance	—	X

We suggest you work Self Study Problems Sixteen-1 and 2 at this point.

Allocation Of The Elected Value

Consideration Received By The Transferor (Shareholder)

16-75.　　As noted previously, the elected value for the assets transferred is used to establish the adjusted cost base of all consideration received by the transferor. The rules for allocating this total to the various types of consideration that may be used are found in ITA 85(1)(f), (g), and (h). They involve a sequential process that can be outlined as follows:

Elected Value (Total Adjusted Cost Base Of All Consideration)	$xxx
Less: Adjusted Cost Base Of Non-Share Consideration (Fair Market Value)	(xxx)
Adjusted Cost Base Of All Shares Issued (Usually Nil)	$xxx
Less: Adjusted Cost Base Of Preferred Stock Issued	
(Usually Nil, But Limited To Fair Market Value)	(xxx)
Adjusted Cost Base Of Common Stock Issued (A Residual - Usually Nil)	$xxx

EXAMPLE　In transferring his proprietorship assets to a new corporation, Jason Browning elects a value of $972,000 for the assets transferred. As the fair market value of these assets is $1,650,000, he receives the following consideration:

- Cash of $220,000.
- Preferred shares of the new corporation with a fair market value of $345,000.
- Common shares of the new corporation with a fair market value of $1,085,000.

ANALYSIS　The $972,000 elected value would be allocated as follows:

Elected Value (Total Adjusted Cost Base Of All Consideration)	$972,000
Less: Adjusted Cost Base Of Non-Share Consideration (Fair Market Value)	(220,000)
Adjusted Cost Base Of All Shares Issued (Usually Nil)	$752,000
Less: Adjusted Cost Base Of Preferred Stock Issued	
(Usually Nil, But Limited To Fair Market Value)	(345,000)
Adjusted Cost Base Of Common Stock Issued (A Residual - Usually Nil)	$407,000

16-76.   The preceding example has been designed to illustrate the allocation of the elected value to all three types of consideration. However, in the usual ITA 85 scenario, minimum asset values will normally be elected in order to avoid the recognition of income on the transfer. Boot will then be taken out in an amount equal to these minimum values. This means that in the usual situation, non-share consideration will be equal to the elected value and, in terms of the preceding allocation process, both preferred and common shares will have an adjusted cost base of nil.

Exercise Sixteen - 3

Subject: Transfers Under Section 85 - ACB Of Consideration

Using ITA 85, Mrs. Jennifer Lee transfers non-depreciable capital property to a corporation at an elected value of $62,000. The property has an adjusted cost base of $62,000 and a fair market value of $176,000. As consideration, she receives a note for $51,000, preferred shares with a fair market value of $53,000, and common shares with a fair market value of $72,000. Indicate the adjusted cost base of the individual items of consideration received by Mrs. Lee.

SOLUTION available in print and online Study Guide.

Assets Acquired By The Corporation
General Rules
16-77.   With respect to the assets acquired by the transferee corporation, the basic rules are as follows:

Non-Depreciable Property   The elected transfer price becomes the tax cost of these assets to the corporation.

Depreciable Property   Where the transferor's capital cost exceeds the elected value for the property, ITA 85(5) requires that the capital cost to the transferee be equal to the amount that was the capital cost to the transferor. In most cases, the elected value will be equal to the transferor's UCC. ITA 85(5) requires that the difference between these two values be treated as deemed CCA. To illustrate this, consider the following asset:

Cost	$100,000
UCC	67,000
Fair Market Value	105,000
Non-Share Consideration	67,000
Elected Value	67,000

The capital cost of the asset to the transferee will be $100,000, there will be deemed CCA taken of $33,000, and future CCA will be based on the elected value of $67,000. The reason for requiring the transferee to retain the transferor's capital cost is to avoid having the transferor convert potential recaptured CCA into a capital gain, only one-half of which would be taxed.

You should also note that, in the usual situation where the transferor is not dealing at arm's length with the transferee corporation, the half year rules do not apply to the calculation of CCA by the transferee. This is the case as long as the transferor has owned the asset for at least 364 days before the end of the taxation year of the transferee in which the property was acquired, and used it as a capital property to earn business or property income.

16-78.   What these rules mean is that, in cases where the election has been made at an amount equal to the transferor's tax cost, the transferee corporation essentially assumes the tax position of the transferor.

Capital Gains On Transfers Of Depreciable Property

16-79.   The objective of using ITA 85(1) is usually to avoid tax consequences when assets are transferred to a corporation. This means that, in general, the elected values will be equal to the transferor's tax values (adjusted cost base or UCC).

16-80.   There are, however, circumstances in which the transferor may wish to generate a capital gain through the transfer of assets to a corporation. An example of this might be an individual who has large losses in the current year, or who has unused net capital or non-capital loss carry forwards that he wishes to claim.

16-81.   This creates a problem with respect to depreciable assets in that, under the general ITA 85 rules, the elected value becomes the basis for calculating future CCA amounts. An election on a depreciable asset at a value in excess of the capital cost would result in a capital gain, only one-half of which would be taxable. Under the usual disposition rules, this same excess would become part of the UCC, the basis for calculating fully deductible amounts of CCA. The following example will illustrate this problem.

> **EXAMPLE**   Jan Harding plans to transfer a depreciable asset to a Canadian controlled private corporation in which she is the only shareholder. The relevant values are as follows:
>
> | | |
> |---|---|
> | Cost | $ 80,000 |
> | Fair Market Value | 120,000 |
> | UCC | 75,000 |
> | Elected Value | 120,000 |
>
> **ANALYSIS**   The election at $120,000 would create the following amounts of income:
>
> | | |
> |---|---|
> | Recaptured CCA ($80,000 - $75,000) | $ 5,000 |
> | Taxable Capital Gain [(1/2)($120,000 - $80,000)] | 20,000 |
> | Total Income | $25,000 |

In the absence of a special rule, the cost and UCC of this asset to the corporation would be $120,000. This value would create $45,000 more CCA for the corporation than would have been available to the transferor ($120,000 - $75,000). This has been accomplished through an increase in the transferor's Taxable Income of only $25,000, clearly not an equitable situation from the point of view of the government.

16-82.   ITA 13(7)(e) acts to correct this situation. You may recall that this provision was discussed in some detail in Chapter 9. It is a general provision that applies to all non-arm's length transfers of depreciable assets, including those where ITA 85(1) has been used.

16-83.   When such transfers occur, ITA 13(7)(e) limits the capital cost of the asset for CCA purposes to the transferor's cost, plus one-half of any capital gain that results from the transfer. As applied to the example in Paragraph 16-81, the capital cost to the transferee under ITA 13(7)(e) for CCA, recapture and terminal loss purposes only, would be as follows:

Transferor's Cost		$ 80,000
Elected Transfer Price	$120,000	
Transferor's Cost	(80,000)	
Capital Gain	$ 40,000	
Taxable Portion	1/2	20,000
Capital Cost To The Transferee For CCA Purposes		$100,000

16-84.   Based on this capital cost, the increase in the CCA base to the corporation is only $25,000 ($100,000 - $75,000), the same amount the transferor recognized as income as a result of the transfer. Note, however, that for future capital gains calculations, the capital cost of the asset to the transferee is the elected value of $120,000.

Paid Up Capital (PUC) Of Shares Issued

General Rules

16-85.   Establishing the Paid Up Capital (PUC) of the shares received is important as it represents an amount that can be distributed to the shareholders as a tax free return of capital. In general, the amount of PUC for tax purposes is equal to the amount attributed to the shares under the appropriate corporate laws (legal stated capital).

16-86.   While there are some complications in those provinces that still permit the issuance of par value shares, the legal stated capital of a corporation is generally based on the fair market value of the consideration received in return for issued shares. In the case of shares issued in an ITA 85 rollover, this amount would be equal to the fair market value of the assets transferred.

16-87.   In the usual ITA 85 scenario, in order to defer taxation on the asset transfer, assets that have increased in value will be transferred at elected values that are below their respective fair market values. Again, in the usual ITA 85 scenario, the elected values will be equal to the non-share consideration, leaving the adjusted cost base of the shares issued at nil. At this point, the PUC of the shares, which is based on the fair market value of the assets transferred, will exceed the adjusted cost base of the assets by the amount of the deferred gains. If PUC was left at this value, it would provide the investor with an opportunity to distribute the deferred gains on a tax free basis. To prevent this from happening a PUC reduction is required.

Paid Up Capital Reduction

16-88.   The need for a PUC reduction, as well as the procedure for calculating the reduction can be illustrated using the following example

> **EXAMPLE**   A non-depreciable capital asset with a fair market value of $200,000 and an adjusted cost base of $150,000 is transferred under ITA 85 using an elected value of $150,000.
>
> While the usual ITA application would have the transferor receiving non-share consideration of $150,000, in order to better illustrate the mechanics of the PUC reduction, we will assume that the consideration consists of cash of $120,000 and shares with a legal stated capital of $80,000.

16-89.   If the asset had been sold to an arm's length party, the vendor would have had an immediate capital gain of $50,000 ($200,000 - $150,000). As is the intent of the legislation, these amounts of income are deferred when Section 85 is used properly. The problem is that, if the $80,000 legal stated capital of the shares issued is used as their PUC, this amount can be withdrawn from the corporation on a tax free basis. This would mean the potential capital gain could permanently escape taxation.

16-90.   Given this problem, ITA 85(2.1) requires that the PUC of issued shares be reduced by an amount equal to the total increase in legal stated capital, less any excess of the elected value over non-share consideration given. Continuing with our example, a summary of the facts and the resulting PUC reduction would be as follows:

Asset: Fair market value = $200,000, Adjusted cost base = $150,000

Consideration: Cash = $120,000, Legal stated capital of shares = $80,000

Elected Value (Total amount that can be withdrawn tax free) = $150,000

Increase In Legal Stated Capital		$80,000
Less Excess, If Any, Of:		
Total Elected Value	($150,000)	
Over The Non-Share Consideration	120,000	(30,000)
Reduction In Paid Up Capital (PUC)		**$50,000**
PUC Of Shares ($80,000 - $50,000)		**$30,000**

16-91.   It is easy to see the conceptual basis for this reduction. The amount of PUC that can be removed by the transferor on a tax free basis is reduced to $30,000, the same amount ($150,000 - $120,000) of consideration he could have received on a tax free basis at the time of the transfer. If the shares were redeemed at their fair market value of $80,000, there would be an ITA 84(3) deemed dividend of $50,000 ($80,000, less a PUC of $30,000). While the taxation of the two amounts is different, this deemed dividend is the same amount as the capital gain that would have resulted from an arm's length sale of the asset. If the non-share consideration had been equal to the elected value of $150,000 (the usual ITA 85 scenario), the PUC would be reduced to nil {$80,000 PUC - [$80,000 - ($150,000 - $150,000)]}.

16-92.   A further tax policy problem, which is not resolved by the PUC reduction, relates to the lifetime capital gains deduction. If the asset in the Paragraph 16-88 example is transferred to a corporation at an elected value of $150,000, this would be the adjusted cost base of the shares. If the shares were later sold for their fair market value of $200,000, the result would be a $50,000 capital gain which could be eligible for the lifetime capital gains deduction if they met the requirements. In effect, the use of the ITA 85(1) rollover could result in the complete elimination of tax on the $50,000 capital gain that was present on the asset prior to its transfer.

More Than One Class Of Shares

16-93.   In most Section 85 rollovers, the ITA 85(2.1) formula will reduce the PUC of all shares issued to nil. This reflects the fact that the non-share consideration taken will equal the elected value, resulting in the PUC reduction being equal to the increase in legal stated capital. If this is the case, having more than one class of shares does not create any difficulties.

16-94.   If, however, the non-share consideration is less than the elected value, the PUC reduction must be allocated to the various classes of shares. You will recall that, when we allocated the adjusted cost base, it was a sequential process (see Paragraph 16-75). The total adjusted cost base (i.e., the elected value) was allocated first to non-share consideration, then to preferred shares to the extent of their fair market value, and finally to the common shares if a residual remained.

16-95.   This is not the case with the PUC reduction. The formula in ITA 85(2.1) is such that the reduction is allocated to different classes of shares on the basis of their relative fair market values.

EXAMPLE   Joan Creek transfers non-depreciable capital assets with a fair market value of $1,600,000 to a corporation under the provisions of ITA 85(1). The elected value is equal to the $900,000 cost of the assets and, as consideration, she receives cash of $600,000, redeemable preferred shares with a fair market value of $250,000, and common shares with a fair market value of $750,000.

ANALYSIS   The total adjusted cost base for the consideration would be allocated as follows:

Paid Up Capital (PUC) Of Shares Issued

Elected Value (Total Adjusted Cost Base Of All Consideration)	$900,000
Non-Share Consideration (Fair Market Value)	(600,000)
Adjusted Cost Base Of All Shares Issued	$300,000
Less: Adjusted Cost Base Of Preferred Stock Issued	
(Limited To Fair Market Value)	(250,000)
Adjusted Cost Base Of Common Stock Issued (Residual)	$ 50,000

The PUC reduction would be calculated as follows:

Increase In Legal Stated Capital		
($250,000 + $750,000)		$1,000,000
Less Excess, If Any, Of:		
Total Elected Value	($900,000)	
Over The Non-Share Consideration	600,000	(300,000)
Reduction In PUC		$ 700,000

The PUC of the two classes of shares, reduced by a pro rata allocation of the $700,000 PUC reduction on the basis of relative fair market value, would be as follows:

$$\text{PUC Of Preferred Stock} \left[\$250,000 - \left(\frac{\$250,000}{\$1,000,000} \right)(\$700,000) \right] = \$75,000$$

$$\text{PUC Of Common Stock} \left[\$750,000 - \left(\frac{\$750,000}{\$1,000,000} \right)(\$700,000) \right] = \$225,000$$

16-96.   Note that the total PUC of the two classes is equal to $300,000 ($75,000 + $225,000). As you would expect, this is equal to the total adjusted cost base of the two classes ($250,000 + $50,000) as well as the difference between the elected value of $900,000 and the non-share consideration of $600,000. The fact that the individual amounts are different reflects the difference between the sequential allocation process for the adjusted cost base amount and the pro rata allocation of the PUC reduction.

Exercise Sixteen - 4

Subject: Transfers Under Section 85 - PUC Reduction

Using ITA 85, Mr. Rob McCleen transfers non-depreciable capital property to a corporation at an elected value of $114,000. The property has an adjusted cost base of $114,000 and a fair market value of $234,000. As consideration he receives a note for $83,000, preferred shares with a fair market value and legal stated capital of $97,000, and common shares with a fair market value and legal stated capital of $54,000. Indicate the adjusted cost base and the PUC of the preferred and common shares that were issued to Mr. McCleen.

SOLUTION available in print and online Study Guide.

We suggest you work Self Study Problem Sixteen-3 at this point.

Comprehensive Example - Section 85 Rollovers

Basic Information

16-97.   John Martin has been operating an unincorporated business. On January 1, 2018, the tax costs (UCC or adjusted cost base) and fair market values for its assets and liabilities are as follows:

	Tax Value	Fair Market Value
Cash	$ 20,000	$ 20,000
Accounts Receivable	50,000	49,000
Inventories	100,000	105,000
Prepaid Expenses	10,000	10,000
Land	50,000	70,000
Building (Capital Cost = $150,000)	110,000	140,000
Equipment (Capital Cost = $70,000)	40,000	35,000
Goodwill	Nil	50,000
Total Assets	$380,000	$479,000
Liabilities	$100,000	$100,000

Excluded Assets

16-98.   The rollover would involve a new corporation, the Martin Company, assuming all of Mr. Martin's liabilities and acquiring all of his business assets except the following:

Excluded Asset	Tax Value	Fair Market Value
Cash	$ 20,000	$ 20,000
Accounts Receivable	50,000	49,000
Prepaid Expenses	10,000	10,000
Equipment	40,000	35,000
Total Values For Excluded Assets	$120,000	$114,000

16-99.   With respect to the Cash and Prepaid Expenses, they are not eligible assets as described under ITA 85(1.1) and cannot be transferred under this rollover provision. However, as their fair market values are equal to their tax values, this is of no consequence.

16-100.   The Accounts Receivable could be transferred under ITA 85. However, the $1,000 ($50,000 - $49,000) loss would have to be treated as a capital loss, which would be disallowed as a superficial loss by ITA 40(2)(g). Further, any additional bad debts incurred by the corporation would also have to be treated as capital losses.

16-101.   The alternative is a joint election under ITA 22. This allows the $1,000 current loss to be treated as a fully deductible business loss. While the corporation will have to include this $1,000 in income, it will then be able to deduct the full amount of any additional bad debts. Taxpayers are not permitted to simultaneously use both the ITA 22 and the ITA 85 elections for their accounts receivable so we have excluded it from the ITA 85 election.

16-102.   With respect to the equipment, its fair market value is less than the UCC for the class.   In this case, ITA 13(21.2) indicates that ITA 85 does not apply and the proceeds of disposition are deemed to be the UCC amount of $40,000 thereby disallowing the terminal loss. There will be no tax consequences associated with the transfer and the corporation will retain the Mr. Martin's original capital cost of $70,000 with the difference between the capital cost and the UCC considered deemed CCA. While a terminal loss could have been recognized if the property had been transferred to an arm's length taxpayer, it would have been disallowed in this case because Mr. Martin's corporation is an affiliated person.

Implementing The Election

16-103.   Mr. Martin is interested in deferring all of the capital gains that are present on his assets and, as a consequence, he elects tax values for most of the assets that are to be transferred under ITA 85. The one exception to this is goodwill, which is transferred at a value of $1 to ensure that it is listed in the election.   In Mr. Martin's proprietorship's tax records, the proceeds of $1 will be subtracted from Class 14.1, leaving a negative balance in that Class. If there are no additions to this Class prior to the end of 2018, this amount will be treated as recapture and included in Mr. Martin's income.   The $1 will also be added to Class 14.1, restoring the balance to nil. In Martin Company's records, the $1 will be added to Class 14.1.

16-104.   Mr. Martin's total elected value of $260,001 is calculated as follows:

Tax Values Of Total Assets	$380,000
Tax Value Of Excluded Assets (Paragraph 16-98)	(120,000)
Nominal Value To Goodwill	1
Total Elected Value	$260,001

16-105.   With respect to the consideration to be given to Mr. Martin, it must equal the fair market value of the assets transferred. This amount would be $365,000 ($479,000 total, less the $114,000 fair market value of the excluded assets listed in Paragraph 16-98).

16-106.   The normal procedure would be to take back non-share consideration, in this example debt, with a fair market value equal to the elected value of $260,001, along with shares with a fair market value equal to the $104,999 ($365,000 - $260,001) excess of the fair market values of the assets transferred over their elected values. The $260,001 in debt consideration is made up of $100,000 in debt of the existing business that has been assumed by the corporation, plus $160,001 in new debt issued by the corporation.

16-107.   The ITA 85(1) election is made on an asset-by-asset basis, requiring both an elected value and specified consideration (which must include some shares) for each asset transferred. In the schedule which follows, non-share consideration is allocated to each asset up to a maximum of its elected value, with share consideration allocated to the asset to reflect the excess of the fair market value of the asset over its elected value. For example, the fair market value of the inventories is $105,000. Reflecting the fact that the elected value for this asset is its tax value of $100,000, $100,000 of non-share consideration is allocated to this asset. The $5,000 in share consideration allocated to this asset is based on the excess of its fair market value over the elected value.

		Consideration At Fair Market Value	
	Elected Value	Non-Share	Share
Inventories	$100,000	$100,000	$ 5,000
Land	50,000	50,000	20,000
Building (Capital Cost = $150,000)	110,000	110,000	30,000
Goodwill	1	1	49,999
Total Assets	$260,001	$260,001	$104,999

16-108.   In this example, the total non-share consideration is equal to the total elected value. If it were less (it cannot be more as the non-share consideration is the general floor for the values to be elected), the amount of non-share consideration allocated to some assets would be less than the full elected value.

16-109.   From the point of view of the corporation, the elected values would become the tax values to be used in subsequent periods of operation. The adjusted cost base of the shares that were issued to Mr. Martin would be determined as follows:

Total Elected Value	$260,001
Non-Share Consideration	(260,001)
Adjusted Cost Base Of Shares	**Nil**

16-110.   The initial PUC of these shares would be their legal stated capital, an amount equal to their fair market value of $104,999. However, there would be an ITA 85(2.1) reduction in this balance as follows:

Increase In Legal Stated Capital		$104,999
Less Excess, If Any, Of:		
Total Elected Value	($260,001)	
Over The Non-Share Consideration	260,001	Nil
Reduction In PUC		**$104,999**

16-111.   At this point, both the adjusted cost base and the PUC of the shares are nil ($104,999 PUC - $104,999 PUC reduction). If they were redeemed at their $104,999 fair market value, Mr. Martin would have to recognize an ITA 84(3) deemed dividend of $104,999. This deemed dividend would reduce the proceeds of disposition for capital gains purposes to nil, resulting in no capital gain on the redemption.

16-112.   Alternatively, if he were to sell the shares at their fair market value, the result would be a capital gain of $104,999. Unlike the redemption scenario which would result in the deferred gain being taxed as a dividend, a sale of shares could completely avoid taxation on the deferred gain. This would happen if the gain resulting from the sale of shares fully qualified for the lifetime capital gains deduction.

Exercise Sixteen - 5

Subject: Transfers Under Section 85 - Tax Consequences

Jasmine Wiens has operated her alternative medicine pharmacy as an unincorporated business for a number of years. The tangible assets of this business have a fair market value of $850,000 and a tax cost of $275,000. In addition to the tangible assets, because the business has been extremely profitable, Jasmine estimates that it has goodwill of $300,000, resulting in a total value for the business of $1,150,000. The total liabilities of the business amount to $83,000. As she no longer needs all of the income that the business is producing, she would like to transfer the business to a new corporation and, in order to defer taxation, she would like to use the provisions of ITA 85(1) for the transfer.

On January 20, 2018, she will make the transfer at an elected value of $275,000. The corporation will assume the $83,000 in business liabilities and, in addition, issue a note payable to Ms. Wiens in the amount of $17,000. Other consideration will be made up of redeemable preferred shares with a fair market value of $125,000 and common shares with a fair market value of $925,000. Any dividends paid by the corporation will be non-eligible. Determine the following:

1.   The adjusted cost base of each type of consideration received by Ms. Wiens.
2.   The paid up capital of each type of share issued by the new corporation.
3.   The tax consequences to Ms. Wiens of the new preferred shares being redeemed at their fair market value immediately.

SOLUTION available in print and online Study Guide.

We suggest you work Self Study Problems Sixteen-4 to Sixteen-7 at this point.

Gift To Related Party - Section 85

General Rules

16-113.   If the transferor of the assets is the only shareholder of the transferee corporation, the indirect gift rules in ITA 85(1)(e.2) are not applicable. However, Section 85 rollovers are often used for income splitting purposes, and this usually means that other members of the transferor's family will be involved as shareholders in the transferee corporation. The indirect gift rules are designed to ensure that, while other family members will be permitted to share in the future growth and income of the corporation, they are not permitted to receive a portion of the current values of the transferred assets in the form of a gift.

16-114.   ITA 85(1)(e.2) is applicable if the fair market value of the transferred property exceeds the greater of:

1.   the fair market value of all consideration received from the corporation; and
2.   the amount elected for the transfer;

and it is reasonable to regard that excess as a gift made by the taxpayer for the benefit of any related shareholder. In any situation where a party related to the transferor is a shareholder of the transferee corporation, it would be reasonable to regard the excess as a gift.

16-115.   If ITA 85(1)(e.2) is applicable, the tax consequence is that, except for purposes of determining the adjusted cost base of any shares provided to the transferor, the gift amount will be added to the elected value for the transfer to create a deemed elected value. As this deemed elected value becomes the deemed proceeds of disposition for the transferor and the deemed adjusted cost base of the property to the transferee corporation, this will usually result in a capital gain and/or business income on the rollover.

16-116.   A less direct consequence is that the fair market value of the shares held by the related person will be increased by the amount of the gift. As there will be no corresponding increase in the related person's adjusted cost base, the sale of these shares will result in a taxable capital gain.

Example

16-117.   The following example will serve to illustrate the application of ITA 85(1)(e.2).

EXAMPLE   Mr. Pohl owns a non-depreciable capital property with an adjusted cost base of $30,000. He estimated its fair market value was $130,000. A new corporation is formed with all of the common shares being issued to Mr. Pohl's adult son for $1,000 in cash. Using the provisions of ITA 85(1), Mr. Pohl then transfers his non-depreciable property to the corporation at an elected value of $30,000.

The corporation issues a $30,000 note payable and preferred shares with a fair market value and a legal stated capital of $100,000 to Mr. Pohl. By taking back $130,000 ($30,000 + $100,000) in total consideration, Mr. Pohl is filing the election on the basis that the fair market value of the non-depreciable property is also $130,000 and there is no capital gain on this transaction. However, on review, the CRA reassesses him on the basis that the actual fair market value of the property is $180,000. Mr. Pohl, after a heated exchange with his accountant, agrees to accept this value.

16-118.   Based on the reassessed value, the fair market value of the property transferred exceeds the fair market value of the consideration received as shown in the following calculation:

Fair Market Value Of Property Transferred (Reassessed Value)	$180,000
Less The Greater Of:	
• FMV Of Consideration Received = $130,000	
• Elected Amount = $30,000	(130,000)
Excess (Gift)	$ 50,000

16-119.   As Mr. Pohl's son is the only common shareholder of the new corporation, it would be reasonable to regard this $50,000 as a gift to his son. This would make ITA 85(1)(e.2) applicable to this transaction and Mr. Pohl would have a taxable capital gain determined as follows:

Deemed Elected Value = Deemed Proceeds Of Disposition	
($30,000 + $50,000 Gift)	$80,000
Adjusted Cost Base	(30,000)
Capital Gain	$50,000
Inclusion Rate	1/2
Taxable Capital Gain	$25,000

16-120.   Any CRA reassessment of the fair market values will involve specific assets. In this example, only one non-depreciable asset is involved and this means that the result will be a capital gain on that asset. If depreciable assets or inventories were involved, there could also be recapture or business income.

16-121.   We noted in Paragraph 16-115 that the ITA 85(1)(e.2) deemed elected value does not apply in determining the adjusted cost base of the shares received by the transferor. Given this, the adjusted cost base of Mr. Pohl's preferred shares would be calculated as follows:

Elected Value (Original)	$30,000
Non-Share Consideration	(30,000)
Adjusted Cost Base Of Preferred Shares	Nil

16-122.   Note, however, the deemed elected value does apply to the cost figure that is used in the following PUC reduction calculation under ITA 85(2.1). This would be relevant if there was a share redemption.

Increase In Legal Stated Capital		$100,000
Less The Excess, If Any, Of:		
Deemed Elected Value	($80,000)	
Over The Non-Share Consideration	30,000	(50,000)
PUC Reduction		$ 50,000
PUC Of Shares ($100,000 - $50,000)		$ 50,000

16-123.   The other relevant fact here is that the transferee corporation, in addition to the $1,000 invested by Mr. Pohl's son, has an asset with a fair market value of $180,000. Given this, the fair market value of the son's shares would be $51,000 ($181,000 - $30,000 - $100,000). As there has been no change in the adjusted cost base of the son's shares, a subsequent sale of the shares would result in a capital gain of $50,000 ($51,000 - $1,000).

16-124.   The actual and potential gains resulting from the application of ITA 85(1)(e.2) to this transaction are as follows:

Actual Capital Gain On Transfer	$ 50,000
Potential Gain On Mr. Pohl's Preferred Shares ($100,000 - Nil)	100,000
Potential Gain On Son's Common Shares ($51,000 - $1,000)	50,000
Total Gain	$200,000

16-125.   If Mr. Pohl had simply sold his property, the total gain would have been only $150,000 ($180,000 - $30,000), $50,000 less than the total gain in the preceding table. In effect, the $50,000 amount of the gift will be subject to double taxation.

16-126.   This example illustrates the importance of taking great care in establishing the fair market value of the property being transferred. A failure to do so can result in the double taxation that is illustrated here.

16-127.   Once that fair market value has been established, the transferor should take back a non-growth security such as preferred shares for the difference between the fair market value of the property and its tax value. Common shares can then be issued to the other family members at a nominal value. While the initial value of these shares will be nominal, it will be these shares that will have growth in value in the future.

Exercise Sixteen - 6

Subject: Gift To Related Party - Section 85

Janice Bellows establishes a new CCPC, arranging to have all of its common shares issued to her adult daughter for cash of $1,000. Ms. Bellows then transfers, using ITA 85, non-depreciable capital property with an adjusted cost base of $50,000 and an estimated fair market value of $65,000. The transfer is made at an elected value of $50,000. As consideration for this property, the corporation gives Ms. Bellows a note for $50,000 and preferred stock with a fair market value and a legal stated capital of $15,000.

A CRA reassessment of this transaction determines that the actual fair market value of the property transferred is $110,000. Ms. Bellows reluctantly accepts this value. After the reassessment, Ms. Bellows and her daughter sell their shares for their fair market value.

Taking into consideration the reassessment, describe the tax consequences of these transactions for both Ms. Bellows and her daughter. How would these tax consequences differ if Ms. Bellows had simply sold the non-depreciable capital property for its post-reassessment value of $110,000?

SOLUTION available in print and online Study Guide.

We suggest you work Self Study Problem Sixteen-8 at this point.

Excess Consideration - Section 85

Introduction

16-128.   In the previous section we considered the tax consequences of the transferor receiving consideration that is less than the fair market value of the property transferred. In situations when parties related to the transferor were also shareholders of the transferee corporation, the difference in value could be viewed as a gift to that related party. We also pointed out that the *Income Tax Act* contained provisions which, in effect, penalized the transferor for his behaviour.

16-129.   In this section we are concerned with the opposite case — situations in which the transferor receives consideration with a value in excess of the fair market value of the property being transferred. Such situations may result in the shareholder being assessed a benefit under ITA 15 (see Chapter 15, Corporate Taxation And Management Decisions, for a discussion of shareholder benefits).

16-130.   You may recall from Chapter 14 that, in transactions which result in an increase in PUC that exceeds the related increase in net assets, the excess will be treated as an ITA 84(1) deemed dividend. At first glance, that would appear to be a possibility in an excess consideration situation involving Section 85. However, that is not the case. Even if the total share consideration received by the transferor exceeds the fair market value of the assets transferred, the ITA 85(2.1) PUC reduction will prevent the PUC of the shares from exceeding the value of the transferred assets.

Shareholder Benefit - ITA 15(1)

16-131.   The following example will illustrate a situation in which the use of ITA 85(1) results in a taxable benefit to the transferor.

EXAMPLE   Ms. Sally Swit transfers non-depreciable capital property with an adjusted cost base of $65,000 and a fair market value of $150,000, to a CCPC in which she is the sole shareholder. She takes back debt with a fair market value of $120,000 and redeemable preferred shares with a fair market value and legal stated capital of $80,000. She elects to make the transfer at $150,000 (she cannot elect above the ceiling of fair market value).

ANALYSIS   The immediate tax effects of the transfer would be a taxable capital gain on the property and an ITA 15(1) shareholder benefit, calculated as follows:

Elected Value Of Property	$150,000
Adjusted Cost Base	(65,000)
Capital Gain	$ 85,000
Inclusion Rate	1/2
Taxable Capital Gain On Property	$ 42,500

Fair Market Value Of Consideration	$200,000
Fair Market Value Of The Property	(150,000)
ITA 15(1) Shareholder Benefit	$ 50,000

The total effect on Net Income For Tax Purposes is as follows:

Taxable Capital Gain	$ 42,500
Shareholder Benefit	50,000
Total Addition To Net Income For Tax Purposes	$ 92,500

Because a $50,000 benefit will be included in Ms. Swit's income as a result of a property acquisition, ITA 52(1) requires that this amount be added to the cost of the property acquired. Given this, the adjusted cost base of the preferred shares would be as follows:

Elected Value	$150,000
Fair Market Value Of Non-Share Consideration	(120,000)
Available For Shares	$ 30,000
ITA 15(1) Shareholder Benefit	50,000
Adjusted Cost Base Of Preferred Stock	$ 80,000

The ITA 85(2.1) PUC reduction for the preferred shares would be as follows:

Increase In Legal Stated Capital		$80,000
Less Excess, If Any, Of:		
Elected Value	($150,000)	
Over The Non-Share Consideration	120,000	(30,000)
Reduction In Paid Up Capital		$50,000

This would leave a PUC for the preferred shares of $30,000 ($80,000 - $50,000). As this is equal to the increase in net assets ($150,000 - $120,000), there would be no ITA 84(1) deemed dividend.

If the preferred shares were sold for their fair market value, the results would be as follows:

Proceeds Of Disposition	$80,000
Adjusted Cost Base	(80,000)
Capital Gain (Loss)	Nil

Alternatively, if the preferred shares were redeemed for their fair market value during 2018, the results would be as follows:

Redemption Proceeds	$80,000
PUC	(30,000)
ITA 84(3) Deemed Dividend (Non-Eligible)	$50,000

Proceeds Of Disposition	$80,000
Less: ITA 84(3) Deemed Dividend	(50,000)
Adjusted Proceeds Of Disposition	$30,000
Adjusted Cost Base	(80,000)
Capital Loss	($50,000)
Inclusion Rate	1/2
Allowable Capital Loss (Disallowed)	($25,000)

The non-eligible deemed dividend would be grossed up to $58,000 [(116%)($50,000)]. It would also provide a federal dividend tax credit of $5,818 [(8/11)(16%)($50,000)].

Exercise Sixteen - 7

Subject: Benefit To Transferor (Excess Consideration) - Section 85

Mr. Larry Custer uses ITA 85 to transfer non-depreciable capital property to a CCPC in which he owns 100 percent of the shares. The adjusted cost base of the property is $123,000 and he elects the fair market value of $217,000 as the transfer price. In consideration for this property, Mr. Custer receives a note for $195,000 and preferred stock with a fair market value and a legal stated capital of $75,000. Any dividends paid by the corporation will be non-eligible. What are the tax consequences for Mr. Custer if the preferred shares are (1) sold for $75,000 and (2) redeemed for $75,000 on February 14, 2018?

SOLUTION available in print and online Study Guide.

We suggest you work Self Study Problem Sixteen-9 at this point.

Dividend Stripping — ITA 84.1

Background

The General Concept

16-132.   The term dividend stripping is applied to two types of situations, depending on when the relevant shares were issued by the corporation. In simple terms, both scenarios involve an individual who is attempting to remove assets from a corporation on a tax free basis.

16-133.   Accomplishing this goal would not be a problem if the individual was willing to give up control by selling his shares to an arm's length party. However, when this is not the case and the individual retains control, the dividend stripping rules will often prevent the tax free removal of assets.

16-134.   One approach to removing assets from a corporation while still retaining control would be to pay dividends. However, dividends will be taxed in the hands of the recipient and, being a rational individual, the owner of the corporation would prefer to receive the assets on a tax free basis.

16-135.   Currently, the usual approach to accomplishing the goal of removing funds from a controlled corporation on a tax free basis is to convert what is, in effect, a dividend payment into a capital gain that would be eligible for the lifetime capital gains deduction. This is the origin of the term "dividend stripping". ITA 84.1 is a provision that is intended to thwart such efforts.

Pre-1972 Shares

16-136.   At an earlier point in time, the most important application of ITA 84.1 was to prevent the conversion of pre-1972 earnings into a pre-1972 capital gain. As we noted in Chapter 8, prior to 1972, capital gains were not subject to tax in Canada. Given this, such a conversion could have resulted in the tax free receipt of a considerable amount of assets. While such situations still arise, they are not of sufficient importance to cover in a general text such as this. As a consequence, the application of ITA 84.1 in this type of situation will not receive further attention.

Qualified Small Business Corporation Shares

16-137.   The most important current application of the dividend stripping rules from ITA 84.1 involves shares of a qualified small business corporation. The capital gains on dispositions of such shares are eligible for the lifetime capital gains deduction. This means that, if an individual can remove the retained earnings of such a corporation in the form of a capital gain, a very large amount of income can be received on a tax free basis. In general, ITA 84.1 serves to make such conversions difficult. The text and problems in this section will focus on this application of the dividend stripping rules that are found in ITA 84.1.

Applicability Of ITA 84.1

16-138.   ITA 84.1(1) specifies the conditions under which the dividend stripping rules become applicable. These conditions are as follows:

• there is a disposition by a resident Canadian taxpayer (other than a corporation) of shares of a resident Canadian corporation (the subject corporation);

• the taxpayer held the shares as capital property (i.e., the shares were held to produce income, not for resale at a profit);

• the disposition is made to a corporation with which the taxpayer does not deal at arm's length; and

• the subject corporation must be connected with the purchaser corporation after the disposition of shares (i.e., the purchaser corporation must control the subject corporation or own more than 10 percent of the voting shares and 10 percent of the fair market value of all shares).

16-139.   When these conditions are present, the provisions of ITA 84.1 will generally serve to eliminate the individual's ability to achieve their dividend stripping goals.

Dividend Stripping Example

Basic Example

16-140.   A simple example will serve to illustrate the application of ITA 84.1 to post-1971 shares. As shown in Figure 16-2 (following page), Ms. Barton is the only shareholder of Barton Industries (BI), a Canadian controlled private corporation. The Company was established in 1986 with an investment of $25,000 on the part of Ms. Barton. There has been no additional investment in the Company and, as a consequence, $25,000 is the adjusted cost base of her shares as well as their PUC. The shares have a fair market value of $900,000. Because of her

Figure 16 - 2
Application Of ITA 84.1 To Post-1971 Shares

Ms. Barton

$675,000 New Debt + Shares

100% Barton Industries
Shares - ITA 85(1)

Barton
Holdings
Ltd.

Barton Industries
PUC = $ 25,000
ACB = $ 25,000
FMV = $900,000

previous use of the lifetime capital gains deduction, Ms. Baron's available balance for the year is limited to $650,000. The shares of BI are qualified small business corporation shares. The Company has no opening balance in its GRIP account.

16-141.   Ms. Barton could, of course, make use of her lifetime capital gains deduction by selling the BI shares to an arm's length party and realizing a capital gain of $875,000 ($900,000 - $25,000). However, this approach would result in tax payable as the capital gain of $875,000 exceeds the $650,000 deduction that she has available. In addition, and perhaps more importantly, she would lose control of BI.

16-142.   Given these considerations, she chooses to transfer the BI shares to a new company, Barton Holdings Ltd. (BHL), using the provisions of ITA 85(1). Ms. Barton uses an elected value for the transfer of $675,000, in order to limit her capital gain to $650,000 ($675,000 - $25,000). She takes back $675,000 in new debt of BHL, along with the common shares of the new Company. These shares have a fair market value of $225,000 ($900,000 - $675,000) and an adjusted cost base of nil.

16-143.   Through this procedure, Ms. Barton appears to have realized the required $650,000 of the accrued capital gain on the BI shares and, at the same time, retained control of the Company. However, Ms. Barton:

- is an individual, resident in Canada;
- held the shares as capital property;
- has made a disposition of shares to a corporation with which she does not deal at arm's length; and
- has created connected corporations subsequent to the transaction since BHL owns all of the shares of BI.

16-144.   Given these facts, the dividend stripping provisions of ITA 84.1 would be applicable to this transaction.

ITA 84.1 Procedures

16-145.   The ITA 84.1 procedures begin with a reduction in the PUC of any shares of the subject corporation that are received by Ms. Barton. Note that, when both ITA 85 and ITA 84.1 are involved, the PUC reduction rules specified in ITA 84.1(1)(a) must be used. They would apply as follows in this situation.

Increase In Legal Stated Capital Of BHL Shares		$225,000
Less Excess, If Any, Of:		
PUC Of Barton Industries Shares (Note One)	($ 25,000)	
Over The Non-Share Consideration	675,000	Nil
ITA 84.1(1)(a) PUC Reduction (Note Two)		**$225,000**

Note One   This amount is technically the greater of the PUC of the subject shares and their adjusted cost base. In this example, the two amounts are equal.

Note Two   In those cases where the boot is equal to or exceeds the greater of the PUC and the adjusted cost base of the subject corporation shares, the PUC reduction will be 100 percent of the PUC of the new shares.

16-146.   This would leave the PUC of the new shares at nil ($225,000 - $225,000). Given this, the ITA 84.1(1)(b) deemed dividend would be calculated as follows:

Increase In Legal Stated Capital Of BHL Shares		$225,000
Non-Share Consideration		675,000
Total		$900,000
Less The Sum Of:		
The Greater Of The PUC And ACB Of Barton		
Industries (Subject) Shares	($ 25,000)	
PUC Reduction Under ITA 84.1(1)(a)	(225,000)	(250,000)
ITA 84.1(1)(b) Deemed Dividend (Non-Eligible)		**$650,000**

16-147.   The results from Ms. Barton's disposition of her BI shares would be as follows:

Elected Proceeds Of Disposition	$675,000
ITA 84.1(1)(b) Deemed Dividend (See Note)	(650,000)
ITA 54 Deemed Proceeds Of Disposition	$ 25,000
Adjusted Cost Base Of Barton Industries Shares	(25,000)
Capital Gain	**Nil**

Note   The definition of proceeds of disposition in ITA 54 indicates that it does not include any amount that is deemed by ITA 84.1(1) to be a dividend. In the absence of this exclusion, the deemed dividend could be taxed a second time as part of a taxable capital gain.

16-148.   As the preceding example makes clear, the effect of ITA 84.1 in this situation is to convert the $650,000 capital gain on the BI shares into an ITA 84.1 deemed dividend. This means that Ms. Barton will not be able to make use of her lifetime capital gains deduction and that she will be subject to taxation on the deemed dividend. ITA 84.1 has clearly served to make this type of transaction unattractive.

16-149.   As a final point, you should note that Ms. Barton could have achieved her goal of triggering a capital gain for purposes of the lifetime capital gains deduction. Her problem was that she also wanted to remove the gain in the form of non-share consideration. If, as an alternative, she had elected the same transfer price of $675,000, but limited the non-share consideration to the $25,000 PUC amount, she would have had her $650,000 capital gain without creating an ITA 84.1 deemed dividend. Note, however, that she does not have the $650,000 in cash. She would be holding shares with a value of $650,000 and an adjusted cost base of nil. In order to have the cash and take advantage of the lifetime capital gains deduction, she would have to sell the shares to an arms' length party and lose control of the corporation.

Exercise Sixteen - 8

Subject: Dividend Stripping

Miss Sarah Cole owns 100 percent of the outstanding shares of Cole Inc., a qualified small business corporation. The shares have a PUC and an adjusted cost base of $125,000 and a fair market value of $767,000. The Company has no balance in its GRIP account. Miss Cole uses ITA 85(1) to transfer these shares to Sarah's Holdings Ltd., at an elected value of $767,000. As consideration, she receives a note for $450,000 and preferred shares with a fair market value and a legal stated capital of $317,000. Miss Cole owns all of the shares of Sarah's Holdings Ltd. and has never made use of her lifetime capital gains deduction. What are the tax consequences of this transaction to Miss Cole?

SOLUTION available in print and online Study Guide.

We suggest you work Self Study Problem Sixteen-10 at this point.

Capital Gains Stripping — ITA 55(2)

The Problem

16-150.   A problem similar to that involved in dividend stripping arises when a corporation owns shares in a different corporation. If there is an accrued capital gain on these shares, a disposition of the shares will result in the recognition of that gain. Further, corporations are not eligible to use the lifetime capital gains deduction. This means that a disposition of the shares of the investee corporation for a gain will result in an increase in Taxable Income for the selling corporation.

16-151.   While capital gains are subject to corporate income taxes, dividends received from taxable Canadian corporations can escape corporate taxes. This means that, if the investor corporation can devise some method of disposing of its investment so that the accrued gain can be received in the form of dividends rather than as a taxable capital gain, the payment of corporate taxes can be avoided.

16-152.   In the absence of an anti-avoidance provision, this could be accomplished in a variety of ways. To illustrate this, assume the following:

- The Investee Company is a wholly owned subsidiary of the Investor Company.
- There is an accrued capital gain on the Investee Company shares.
- There is an arm's length purchaser who is prepared to buy the Investee Company shares at their fair market value.

16-153.   There are several approaches that could be used in an attempt to convert the accrued capital gain into dividends that could be received by the Investor Company on a tax free basis. The two approaches that we will consider here can be described as follows:

- **Approach One**   ITA 85(1) could be used to roll the Investee Company shares to a purchaser corporation at an elected value equal to the adjusted cost base of the Investee Company shares, resulting in no increase in Taxable Income for the Investor Company. As consideration, the purchaser corporation would issue preferred shares that are redeemable at the fair market value of the Investee Company shares. When the preferred shares are redeemed, the result will be an ITA 84(3) deemed dividend which can be received by the Investor Company on a tax free basis. Once again, it would appear that the Investor Company has disposed of the Investee Company shares without any increase in Taxable Income or Tax Payable.

- **Approach Two**   The Investee Company could assume debt equal to the accrued gain on its shares. This Company would then, using the borrowed funds, pay a dividend equal to the accrued gain. This would reduce the fair market value of the Investee Company shares by the amount of the accrued gain, leaving the Investee Company shares with a fair market value equal to their adjusted cost base. They could then be sold with no tax consequences. As the dividend would be received by the Investee Company on a tax free basis, it would appear that the Investor Company has disposed of the Investee Company shares without any increase in Taxable Income or Tax Payable.

16-154.   Such procedures are referred to as capital gains stripping, reflecting the fact that it is an attempt to "strip" out a capital gain in the form of a non-taxable, intercorporate dividend. ITA 55(2) is an anti-avoidance provision designed to prevent such conversions of capital gains to dividends by a corporation disposing of an investment in shares.

Application Of ITA 55(2)
Conditions For ITA 55(2) To Apply
16-155.   In somewhat simplified terms, the provisions of ITA 55(2) act to prevent capital gains stripping when the following conditions are present:

- An Investor Company receives dividends that are deductible in the determination of its Taxable Income as part of a transaction, or series of transactions, involving a disposition of Investee Company shares owned by the Investor Company.

- It is determined that one of the purposes of the dividend was to significantly reduce the capital gain on Investee Company shares which would have been included in the Net Income For Tax Purposes of the Investor Company, in the absence of the dividend.

- The disposition of the Investee Company shares was to an arm's length party. While we will not illustrate this in our coverage of this subject, ITA 55(2) would also be applicable if there was a significant increase in an arm's length party's interest in either the Investor Company or the Investee Company.

Application Of ITA 55(2)
16-156.   If the conditions specified in Paragraph 16-155 are present, the following rules apply to the dividend:

ITA 55(2)(a)   This provision indicates that the dividend received by the Investor Company will be deemed not to be a dividend except to the extent that the Company has a Safe Income balance (see following description). To the extent that a Safe Income balance is available, the dividend will retain its status as a dividend.

In simplified terms, Safe Income is income that has accrued after 1971 or, if the acquisition of the shares was after that date, after the date on which the shares were acquired. We would note that recent amendments to ITA 55 have made the computation of safe income considerably more complex. Coverage of these complications goes beyond the scope of this introductory text.

Note that this provision only serves to remove the dividend status from the payment received by the Investor Company. It does not indicate the tax status of the payment subsequent to its removal from the dividend category. This is accomplished using ITA 55(2)(b) or ITA 55(2)(c).

ITA 55(2)(b)   If shares are cancelled, an ITA 84(2) dividend can arise. Similarly, if shares are redeemed, an ITA 84(3) dividend can arise. If the conditions for the application of ITA 55(2) are present, ITA 55(2)(a) deems all or part of the dividend to not be a dividend and ITA 55(2)(b) deems the disallowed portion of the payment to be proceeds of disposition, except to the extent that it is otherwise included in computing such proceeds.

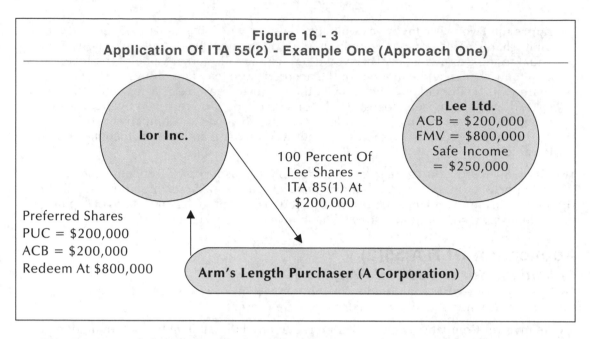

Figure 16 - 3
Application Of ITA 55(2) - Example One (Approach One)

ITA 55(2)(c)   If the conditions for the application of ITA 55 are present and ITA 55(2)(b) does not apply, the portion of the payment that is deemed not to be a dividend by ITA 55(2)(a) is deemed to be a capital gain of the Investor Company.

Capital Gains Stripping - Example One

16-157.   This first example depicts Approach One that is described in Paragraph 16-153. It is diagramed in Figure 16-3.

16-158.   In this example, ITA 85(1) is used to roll the Lee Ltd. shares into the purchaser corporation at an elected value equal to the $200,000 adjusted cost base of the shares. As consideration for the shares, Lor Inc. takes back $800,000 in redeemable preferred shares. These shares have a PUC and an adjusted cost base of $200,000.

16-159.   As you may recall from Chapter 14, a redemption is also a disposition. This requires the calculation of both a proceeds of redemption and a proceeds of disposition. Such transactions can result in an ITA 84(3) dividend, a capital gain, or both. The relevant calculations in this example are as follows:

Proceeds Of Redemption	$800,000
PUC Of Shares	(200,000)
ITA 84(3) Deemed Dividend [Absence Of ITA 55(2)]	**$600,000**
Proceeds Of Disposition	$800,000
Less The ITA 84(3) Dividend	(600,000)
Adjusted Proceeds Of Disposition	$200,000
Adjusted Cost Base	(200,000)
Capital Gain [Absence Of ITA 55(2)]	**Nil**

16-160.   in the absence of ITA 55(2), the ITA 84(3) dividend would be deducted in determining Lor's Taxable Income and Lor would have succeeded in disposing of the Lee shares for $800,000, without incurring any taxation. The provisions of ITA 55(2) will act to prevent this result from being realized.

16-161.   ITA 55(2)(a) will deem any dividend that is not from Safe Income to not be a dividend. In this example, that amount would be $350,000 ($600,000 - $250,000). While $250,000 would retain its status as an ITA 84(3) dividend, under ITA 55(2)(b), the $350,000

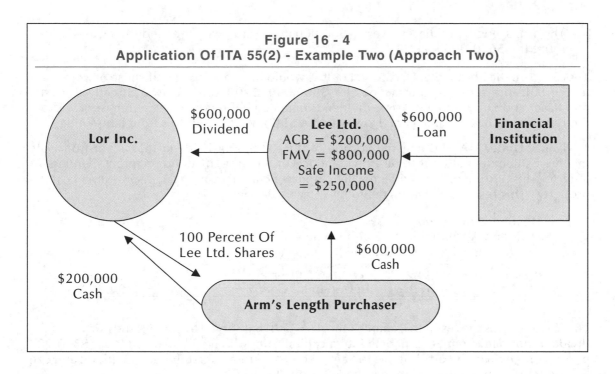

Figure 16 - 4
Application Of ITA 55(2) - Example Two (Approach Two)

would be deemed to be proceeds of disposition. As a result, the tax consequence to Lor would be calculated as follows:

Adjusted Proceeds Of Disposition	
See Calculation In Paragraph 16-159	$200,000
Deemed Proceeds Of Disposition - ITA 55(2)(b)	350,000
Total Proceeds Of Disposition	$550,000
Adjusted Cost Base	(200,000)
Capital Gain	$350,000

16-162.   As can be seen in the preceding calculation, ITA 55(2) has served to convert $350,000 of the ITA 84(3) dividend into a capital gain of $350,000. The $250,000 dividend from Safe Income can be deducted under ITA 112 in the determination of Lor's Taxable Income, resulting in no tax cost.

Capital Gains Stripping - Example Two

16-163.   This second example depicts Approach Two that is described in Paragraph 16-153. It involves the same two Companies that were used in Example One. The only difference is in the approach that they use in attempting to convert the capital gain into a tax free dividend. It is diagramed in Figure 16-4.

16-164.   In this example, Lor Inc. owns 100 percent of the shares of Lee Ltd. The shares have a fair market value of $800,000, an adjusted cost base of $200,000, and a potential capital gain of $600,000. Lee Ltd. has safe income of $250,000. An arm's length purchaser is willing to pay $800,000 for these shares. In order to implement this sale, Lor Inc. arranges the following:

- Lee Ltd. borrows $600,000 from a financial institution.

- The borrowed funds are used to pay a $600,000 tax free dividend to Lor Inc. This reduces the fair market value of Lee Ltd. to $200,000 ($800,000 - $600,000).

- Lor Inc. sells the shares to the arm's length purchaser for $200,000 in cash. As this is the adjusted cost base of the shares, there will be no capital gain.

Capital Gains Stripping — ITA 55(2)

- The arm's length purchaser invests $600,000 in Lee Ltd., with the funds being used to retire the $600,000 loan.

16-165.   In the absence of ITA 55(2), Lor Inc. would have managed to dispose of its interest in Lee Ltd. in a series of transactions for $800,000 ($200,000 received directly from the purchaser and $600,000 of tax-free dividends financed indirectly by the purchaser), without the recognition of a capital gain. However, ITA 55(2) will prevent this from happening.

16-166.   Under ITA 55(2)(a), the portion of the $600,000 dividend that is not from Safe Income will be deemed not to be a dividend to Lor Inc., the dividend recipient. Under ITA 55(2)(c), this portion of the dividend will treated as a capital gain on the disposition of capital property. This result is shown in the following calculation:

Dividends Received	$600,000
Dividend Attributable To Safe Income - Retains Status As A Dividend	(250,000)
Amount Deemed By ITA 55(2)(a) To Not Be A Dividend And By ITA 55(2)(c) To Be A Capital Gain	$350,000

16-167.   As was the result in Example One, ITA 55(2) has served to convert the portion of the dividend not paid from Safe Income into a capital gain, which will be taxed. The $250,000 portion of the dividend attributable to Safe Income will retain its status as a dividend and can be deducted in the determination of Lor's Taxable Income.

Exercise Sixteen - 9

Subject: Capital Gains Stripping

Markem Ltd. owns 100 percent of the outstanding common shares of Larkin Ltd. The shares of Larkin have an adjusted cost base of $75,000 and a fair market value of $840,000. Included in its Retained Earnings balance is $225,000 of income that has been earned since its acquisition by Markem Ltd. Markem Ltd. would like to sell its shares in Larkin Ltd. In order to implement this sale, Markem Ltd. has instructed Larkin Ltd. to borrow $750,000 from its bank, and use all of these funds to pay a dividend on the shares held by Markem Ltd. The shares are then sold to Mr. J. Leaner for $90,000. Mr. Leaner is not related to Markem Ltd. or Larkin Ltd. What are the tax consequences to Markem Ltd. of these transactions?

SOLUTION available in print and online Study Guide.

We suggest you work Self Study Problem Sixteen-11 at this point.

Additional Supplementary Self Study Problems Are Available Online.

Key Terms Used In This Chapter

16-168.   The following is a list of the key terms used in this Chapter. These terms, and their meanings, are compiled in the Glossary located at the back of the Study Guide.

Adjusted Cost Base	Non-Share Consideration
Affiliated Group Of Persons	Paid Up Capital
Affiliated Person - ITA 251.1(1)	PUC
Boot	Recapture Of CCA
Capital Cost	Rollover
Capital Gains Stripping	Safe Income
Controlled - ITA 251.1(3)	Subject Corporation
Corporation	Superficial Loss - ITA 54
Depreciable Capital Property	Taxpayer
Dividend Stripping	Terminal Loss
Eligible Capital Property	Transfer
Gift	Transferee
Individual	Transferor
Non-Depreciable Capital Property	Undepreciated Capital Cost (UCC)

References

16-169.   For more detailed study of the material in this Chapter, we would refer you to the following:

ITA 13(21.2)	Loss On Certain Transfers
ITA 15(1)	Benefits Conferred On A Shareholder
ITA 40(2)(g)	Superficial Losses
ITA 40(3.4)	Loss On Certain Properties
ITA 54	Definitions (Proceeds Of Disposition And Superficial Loss)
ITA 55(2)	Deemed Proceeds Or Capital Gain
ITA 84.1(1)	Non-Arm's Length Sale Of Shares
ITA 85	Transfer Of Property To Corporation By Shareholders
ITA 89(1)	Definitions
ITA 251.1	Affiliated Persons
IC 76-19R3	Transfer Of Property To A Corporation Under Section 85
IT-188R	Sale of Accounts Receivable
IT-291R3	Transfer Of Property To A Corporation Under Subsection 85(1)
IT-489R	Non-Arm's Length Sale Of Shares To A Corporation

\

Problems For Self Study (Online)

To provide practice in problem solving, there are Self Study and Supplementary Self Study problems available on MyLab Accounting.

Within the text we have provided an indication of when it would be appropriate to work each Self Study problem. The detailed solutions for Self Study problems can be found in the print and online Study Guide.

We provide the Supplementary Self Study problems for those who would like additional practice in problem solving. The detailed solutions for the Supplementary Self Study problems are available online, not in the Study Guide.

The .PDF file "Self Study Problems for Volume 2" on MyLab contains the following for Chapter 16:

- 11 Self Study problems,
- 6 Supplementary Self Study problems, and
- detailed solutions for the Supplementary Self Study problems.

Assignment Problems

(The solutions for these problems are only available in
the solutions manual that has been provided to your instructor.)

Assignment Problem Sixteen - 1

(Transfers To A Corporation Vs. Direct Sale)

For a number of years, Brett Manson has owned an apartment building in the city of London, Ontario. Information on its acquisition is as follows:

Acquisition Cost	$1,355,000
Estimated Cost Of The Land	(462,000)
Estimated Cost Of The Building	$ 893,000

At the beginning of the current year, values related to the property are as follows:

Estimated Fair Market Value Of Property	$1,610,000
Estimated Fair Market Value Of Land	(574,000)
Estimated Fair Market Value Of The Building	$1,036,000
UCC Of The Building	$ 685,022

At this time, Brett transfers the property to a corporation using a Section 85 rollover. The value elected for the transfer is $1,147,022 ($462,000 + $685,022). The only consideration received by Brett is common shares in the new corporation.

Later in the year, all of the common shares are sold to Jason Border, an arm's length party, for $1,610,000.

Required:

A. Describe the tax consequences for Brett of using Section 85 and selling the common shares.

B. How do these results compare with the tax consequences of simply selling the building directly to Jason Border for $1,610,000?

Assignment Problem Sixteen - 2
(Section 85 Rollovers - Short Cases)

The following **independent** cases involve transfers of assets under ITA 85.

Case One   Depreciable assets with a fair market value of $183,400 are transferred to a corporation in exchange for non-share consideration of $140,000, preferred shares with a fair market value of $22,000 and common shares with a fair market value of $21,400. The assets had a capital cost of $130,000. They were the only assets in their Class and the UCC balance in the Class was $59,904.

Case Two   Inventories of merchandise are transferred to a corporation in exchange for $93,000 in non-share consideration and $27,000 in common stock (fair market value and legal stated capital). The inventories have a cost of $87,000 and a fair market value of $120,000.

Case Three   Land is transferred to a corporation in exchange for $72,000 in non-share consideration and $751,000 in common stock (fair market value and legal stated capital). The land cost $617,000 and has a current fair market value of $823,000.

Required: For each of the three Cases provide the following information:

A. The minimum and maximum transfer prices that could be elected under the provisions of ITA 85.

B. Assuming the minimum value is elected, the amount of capital gain or business income to be included in the income of the transferor.

C. Again assuming that the minimum transfer value is elected, determine the adjusted cost base and PUC of the preferred and common stock consideration. Your answer should include the determination of any shareholder benefit under ITA 15(1) or deemed dividend under ITA 84(1) that will arise on the transfer, or explain why there is no benefit or deemed dividends.

Assignment Problem Sixteen - 3
(ACB Of Consideration And PUC)

Lily Haring has owned a depreciable property for a number of years. The property had an original capital cost of $623,000. It is the only asset in its Class and, at the present time, the UCC for the Class equals $229,663. The current fair market value of the asset is $946,000.

Lily would like to transfer this asset to a new corporation, using the provisions of Section 85(1). She is considering the following alternative consideration packages, all of which total $946,000:

Package One   Lily will take back debt with a fair market value of $229,663, along with common shares with a fair market value of $716,337.

Package Two   Lily will take back debt with a fair market value of $100,000, preferred shares with a fair market value of $100,000, and common shares with a fair market value of $746,000.

Package Three   Lily will take back debt with a fair market value of $700,000 and preferred shares with a fair market value of $246,000.

Required: For each of the three packages, determine:

• The minimum transfer value that Lily can elect and the amount and type of income that will result from electing this value.

• The adjusted cost base of each of the items of consideration received by Lily.

• The Paid Up Capital for the preferred and/or common shares issued.

Assignment Problem Sixteen - 4
(ITA 85 Transfer Of Depreciable Asset)

During the current year, Mr. Rob Banting transfers a depreciable capital property to a new corporation. Rob owns all of the shares in the new corporation and it will have a December 31 year end.

The depreciable asset was purchased several years ago for $343,000. The asset has a current fair market value of $420,000. At the time of transfer, it is the only asset in its Class and, prior to the transfer, the balance in the Class was $213,790.

Rob has been carrying forward a $52,000 capital loss on a stock sale. In order to absorb this loss, he elects to transfer the property at a value of $395,000.

As consideration, Rob takes back a note for $175,000, preferred shares with a fair market value of $90,000, and common shares with a fair market value of $155,000.

Required: Describe the income tax implications resulting from this transaction. Your answer should include both current tax implications, and the determination of values that will have future tax implications.

Assignment Problem Sixteen - 5
(Short Cases With Gift And Shareholder Benefit)

Peter Kowalski owns a rental property that was acquired years ago at a cost of $1,200,000. At the time, he estimated the value of the land to be $200,000 and the value of the building to be $1,000,000.

Peter estimates that the current value of the property is $1,500,000, with $300,000 of this amount being allocated to the land and $1,200,000 of this amount allocated to the building. As of this date, the UCC of the building is $460,800.

Peter has decided to transfer this property to a corporation using the provisions of Section 85. He is considering three possible scenarios. Consider each of the three scenarios as completely independent.

Scenario 1   Peter transfers the property to a new corporation in which he will be the sole shareholder. He has a net capital loss carryforward of $50,000. As he has no other assets with accumulated capital gains, he would like the transfer of the rental property to create a $100,000 capital gain against which he can apply his capital loss. To accomplish this, he elects a transfer value of $300,000 for the land. The elected value for the building will be $460,800. As consideration, he will receive a note payable for $760,800, and preferred shares with a legal stated capital and redemption value of $739,200.

Scenario 2   Peter transfers the property to a new corporation in which he will be the sole shareholder. The land is transferred at an elected value of $200,000 and the building is transferred at an elected value of $460,800. As consideration he will receive a note payable for $660,800, and preferred shares with a fair market value (their redemption value) of $939,200. The legal stated capital of the preferred shares will be $839,200.

Scenario 3   Peter's daughter, Stella, establishes a new corporation with an investment of $10,000 of her own money for the corporation's common shares. Peter transfers the rental property to this corporation with an elected value of $200,000 for the land and $460,800 for the building. As he would like to provide financial assistance for his daughter, in his election he claims that the fair market value of the land is $200,000, hoping that the CRA will not look at the fact that this value is too low. Based on this, he only takes back $1,400,000 in consideration, a note payable for $400,000 and preferred shares with a legal stated capital and a redemption value of $1,000,000.

On review, the CRA discovers the undervaluation and reassesses Peter on the basis that the land actually had a fair market value of $300,000. Peter does not object to this reassessment.

Required: For each of the preceding scenarios, determine for Mr. Kowalski:

- The tax consequences of the transfer for him.
- The tax cost of the land and building in the hands of the corporation.
- The adjusted cost base of the shares issued to him by the corporation.
- The PUC of the shares issued to him by the corporation.

In your solution for Scenario 3, include the effects of the CRA reassessment.

Assignment Problem Sixteen - 6

(ITA 85 Transfer With Sale/Redemption Of Shares)

Three years ago, Connie Bright acquired a commercial property consisting of land and a building at a total cost of $1,475,000. At the acquisition date, an appraisal concluded that the respective values for the two components of the property were $300,000 for the land and $1,175,000 for the building. The acquisition was facilitated by a $550,000 mortgage on the property.

During 2016 and 2017, she operated the property as a proprietorship with good success, realizing a substantial profit in each year. Given this, she would like to transfer the property to a corporation as of January 1, 2018. On that date, the relevant facts about the property are as follows:

	Land	Building
Fair Market Value	$475,000	$1,300,000
Adjusted Cost Base/Capital Cost	300,000	1,175,000
UCC	N/A	1,071,365
Mortgage Balance	N/A	525,000

Connie will elect a transfer value for the land of $475,000. The corresponding figure for the building will be $1,100,000.

The corporation will assume the $525,000 mortgage on the building and, in addition, will issue a note to Connie for $1,050,000. The corporation will also issue common shares to Connie with a fair market value of $200,000 and legal stated capital of $200,000.

The new corporation does not have a balance in its General Rate Income Pool (GRIP) account in any of the years under consideration.

Required:

A. What are the tax consequences of making this transfer at the elected value of $1,575,000 ($475,000 + $1,100,000)? Your answer should include amounts to be included in Connie's income as a result of the transfer, as well as the corporation's tax values for the assets.

B. Compute the adjusted cost base of each component of the consideration that Connie has received from the corporation.

C. Compute the PUC of the corporation's newly issued common shares.

D. What amounts would be included in Connie's Net Income For Tax Purposes if, during 2018, she sells her common shares for $400,000?

E. What amounts would be included in Connie's Net Income For Tax Purposes if, during 2018, the corporation redeems her common shares for $400,000?

Assignment Problem Sixteen - 7
(Transfers To A Corporation And Sale/Redemption Of Shares)

For a number of years, Martin Flex has owned land with a building situated on it. He has operated several different businesses from this venue.

The cost of the property for Martin was $2,800,000, with $525,000 of this amount being allocated to land and the $2,275,000 balance allocated to the building. In order to assist with the purchase of this property, Martin acquired a $1,000,000 mortgage.

He is in the process of starting a new business and would like to use the provisions of ITA 85(1) to transfer the property to a new corporation, Flexor Inc. The new corporation will have a December 31 year end.

The transfer will take place on January 1, 2018. At that time, information on the property is as follows:

• Fair Market Value Of The Land	$ 720,000
• Fair Market Value Of The Building	2,600,000
• UCC Of The Building	1,893,618
• Mortgage Balance	872,000

In implementing the ITA 85(1) rollover, Martin will elect a value of $525,000 for the land and $1,975,000 for the building. The corporation will assume the $872,000 balance on the mortgage and will issue new debt to Martin in the amount of $1,128,000. Martin will also receive common shares with a fair market value of $1,320,000. This total consideration of $3,320,000 ($872,000 + $1,128,000 + $1,320,000) is equal to the $3,320,000 ($720,000 + $2,600,000) fair market value of the land and building.

There are no additions to Flexor Inc.'s General Rate Income Pool during 2018.

Required:

A. What are the tax consequences of making this transfer at the elected value of $2,500,000 ($525,000 + $1,975,000)? Your answer should include amounts to be included in Martin's income as a result of the transfer, as well as the corporation's tax values for the assets.

B. Compute the adjusted cost base of each component of the consideration that Martin has received from the corporation.

C. Compute the PUC of the corporation's newly issued common shares.

D. What amounts would be included in Martin's Net Income For Tax Purposes if, during 2018, he sells his common shares for $1,320,000?

E. What amounts would be included in Martin's Net Income For Tax Purposes if, during 2018, the corporation redeems his common shares for $1,320,000?

Assignment Problem Sixteen - 8

(Transfers To A Corporation And Share Redemption)

Ms. Martha Fleck owns an unincorporated business that she operates out of leased premises. In order to simplify record keeping, her general accounting information is the same as that which she uses for tax purposes. On December 31, 2017, the business has the following assets and liabilities.

	Tax Value	Fair Market Value
Accounts Receivable	$132,000	$ 127,500
Inventory	261,000	312,000
Equipment (Cost = $420,000)	351,000	475,500
Goodwill	Nil	525,000
Total Assets	$744,000	$1,440,000
Liabilities	(142,500)	(142,500)
Net Assets	$601,500	$1,297,500

All of the assets of the unincorporated business will be transferred to Rollex Inc., a new corporation established for the purpose of this transfer. The Accounts Receivable have a face value of $132,000 and will be transferred using the ITA 22 joint election.

The remaining assets will be transferred under the provisions of ITA 85(1). The total consideration received by Ms. Fleck will have a value of $1,312,500 ($1,440,000 - $127,500), the fair market value of the assets other than Accounts Receivable. The consideration is made up of new debt of $112,500, assumption of the old debt of $142,500, preferred stock with a fair market value of $337,500, and common stock with a fair market value of $720,000. The new corporation does not have a balance in its General Rate Income Pool (GRIP) account in any of the years under consideration.

Ms. Fleck wishes to incorporate her business in a manner that minimizes or eliminates any tax effects resulting from the transaction.

Required: Ignore the lifetime capital gains deduction in your solution.

A. Do you agree with the decision to transfer the accounts receivable using ITA 22? Explain your conclusion and determine the tax consequences of this decision.

B. Given that Ms. Fleck wishes to minimize or eliminate current taxes, indicate the values that should be elected for each of the assets to be transferred.

C. Determine the adjusted cost base of the debt, preferred shares, and common shares that would be received by Ms. Fleck on the rollover.

D. Determine the Paid Up Capital of the common stock and preferred stock that were issued by the new corporation to Ms. Fleck.

E. Determine the tax consequences to Ms. Fleck if the preferred and common shares that she received in the rollover were immediately redeemed in January, 2018 by the new corporation at fair market values.

Assignment Problem Sixteen - 9

(Gift To Related Party - Section 85)

Ms. Martine Renaud has operated an unincorporated business for over 25 years. The business has been very successful and, on January 1, 2018, its assets and liabilities have tax values and estimated fair market values as follows:

	Tax Value	Fair Market Value
Accounts Receivable (No Reserve Taken)	$ 60,000	$ 57,000
Inventories	825,000	840,000
Depreciable Assets - CCA Class 8 (Note One)	1,725,000	1,780,000
Land	923,000	1,450,000
Building (Note Two)	1,760,000	2,436,000
Total Assets	$5,293,000	$6,563,000
Liabilities	(430,000)	(430,000)
Net Assets (Owner's Equity)	$4,863,000	$6,133,000

Note One   The capital cost of the assets in Class 8 total $1,960,000.

Note Two   The capital cost of the Building is $3,600,000.

Ms. Renaud has two daughters, Alma aged 26 and Amanda aged 28. Currently, they are both unemployed but, thanks to Ms. Renaud's generosity over the years, they both have significant assets and a comfortable lifestyle.

Ms. Renaud would like to transfer the future growth in her business to her daughters. To accomplish this, in December, 2017, she arranges for them to establish a new corporation through the investment of $10,000 each. Each daughter receives 100 common shares. The new corporation is named Almand Inc. and at this point, the corporation has no assets other than the $20,000 invested by the two daughters.

On January 1, 2018, Ms. Renaud transfers all of the assets of her unincorporated business to Almand Inc. The Accounts Receivable are transferred to the corporation using the ITA 22 joint election. The remaining assets are transferred under the provisions of ITA 85(1). The business does not have goodwill.

Ms. Renaud transfers the assets at an elected value of $5,233,000 ($5,293,000 - $60,000), the total tax value of the assets other than Accounts Receivable. Almand Inc. assumes all of the $430,000 in liabilities of Ms. Renaud's unincorporated business and issues new debt to her in the amount of $1,570,000. In addition, she receives redeemable preferred shares with a fair market value and legal stated capital of $4,506,000, a total of $6,506,000.

The CRA issues a reassessment related to the rollover transaction in November, 2018. It is based on a fair market value for the land of $1,850,000, $400,000 more than Ms. Renaud's estimate of $1,450,000. Ms. Renaud does not file an objection to the reassessment as her father, a retired appraiser, has advised her she would ultimately lose after paying outrageous accounting fees.

Required: Ignore the lifetime capital gains deduction in your solution.

A. Taking into consideration the effect of the reassessment, determine the tax consequences to Ms. Renaud that result from the transfer of her business assets to Almand Inc. Your answer should include amounts to be included in Ms. Renaud's income as a result of the transfer and the reassessment, as well as the adjusted cost base and PUC of her preferred shares.

B. Determine the tax consequence to Ms. Renaud if Almand Inc. redeems her preferred shares for $4,506,000 immediately after the reassessment.

C. Alma finds that she cannot tolerate being a 50 percent shareholder in a corporation with her sister. She sells her Almand Inc. shares to an arm's length party for $275,000 immediately after the reassessment. Determine the tax consequences of this sale for Alma.

Assignment Problem Sixteen - 10
(Excess Consideration)

For the last 10 years, Matthew Garnet has operated Garnet Enterprises as a sole proprietorship. As he no longer needs all of the income that is produced by the business, he would like to transfer the business to Garnet Ltd., a corporation in which he holds 100 percent of the outstanding common shares. This corporation will have a December 31 year end.

The transfer will take place on January 1, 2018. Mr. Garnet will use ITA 85(1) to transfer any tangible assets with fair market values in excess of their tax values (adjusted cost base or UCC). These assets, and their relevant values on the date of transfer are as follows:

	Tax Value	Fair Market Value
Depreciable Assets - CCA Class 8 (Note One)	$ 72,000	$ 106,500
Land	127,500	247,500
Building (Note Two)	414,000	648,000
Net Assets (Owner's Equity)	$613,500	$1,002,000

Note One   The capital cost of the assets in Class 8 is $130,500.

Note Two   The capital cost of the Building is $567,000.

The elected value for the Depreciable Assets and the Building will be their tax values, a total of $486,000. However, because Matthew has a net capital loss carry forward of $15,000 [(1/2)($30,000)], the Land will be transferred at an elected value of $157,500.

As consideration, Mr. Garnet will receive non-share consideration of $643,500, plus redeemable preferred shares with a legal stated capital and a fair market value of $658,500. The new corporation does not have a balance in its General Rate Income Pool (GRIP) account in any of the years under consideration.

Required: Ignore the lifetime capital gains deduction in your solution.

A. Determine the immediate tax consequences to Mr. Garnet that will result from his transfer of the Garnet Enterprises' assets to Garnet Ltd.

B. Indicate the tax values that will be recorded for the assets that are transferred to Garnet Ltd. under ITA 85(1).

C. Determine the tax consequences to Mr. Garnet if, in December, 2018:

1. He sells his shares to an arm's length party for $658,500.
2. Garnet Ltd. redeems his preferred shares for $658,500.

Assignment Problem Sixteen - 11
(Dividend Stripping)

A number of years ago, Sheila Hicks established a new corporation, Hicks Ltd., with an investment of $250,000. In return for this investment, she received 12,500 common shares in the new corporation. As Sheila, a Canadian resident, is the only shareholder, Hicks qualifies as a Canadian controlled private corporation.

The corporation has a December 31 year end.

Both the adjusted cost base and the PUC of the Hicks common shares is equal to Sheila's investment of $250,000. There have been no changes in the number of shares issued and outstanding since Hicks Ltd. was incorporated.

As the business has enjoyed great success since its inception, it is estimated that the current value of Sheila's shares is $3,200,000. As she has more than enough resources to live comfortably for the rest of her life, she would like to freeze the current value of the Hicks Ltd.'s shares and have any future increases in the Company's value accrue to her 35 year old son, Brandon Hicks.

To accomplish this goal, she will have Brandon incorporate a new company, Brandon Inc. and acquire all of its common shares with a nominal amount of his own money.

Once Brandon Inc. is incorporated in February, 2018, she will use the provisions of ITA 85(1) to transfer all of her Hicks Ltd. shares to that Company. As Hicks Ltd. is a qualified small business corporation, she would like to structure the rollover in a manner that would utilize her remaining lifetime capital gains deduction. While she has used this tax benefit in the past, for 2018, she has an unused balance of $426,000. In order to accomplish this goal, she plans to make the transfer at an elected value of $676,000 ($250,000 + $426,000), taking back an interest bearing note with a fair market value of $676,000, and retractable preferred shares with a fair market value and a PUC of $2,524,000.

Neither of the Companies would have a balance in their General Rate Income Pool (GRIP) account in any of the years under consideration.

Required:

A. Explain the tax consequences of the proposed ITA 85(1) transfer of the Hicks Ltd. shares to Brandon Inc.

B. While still accomplishing the goal of freezing her estate, indicate how Sheila could alter the rollover transaction in a manner that would reduce or eliminate the Tax Payable required under her proposed structure. Determine the tax implications that would result from this new approach.

C. As an alternative approach to using her lifetime capital gains deduction, Sheila proposes selling 2,641 Hicks Ltd. common shares to Brandon Inc. for cash. The shares would be sold for their current fair market value and this would produce, in the absence of ITA 84.1, a capital gain of just over $426,000. Explain the tax consequences of this proposed transaction.

Show all calculations required to support your answers.

Assignment Problem Sixteen - 12
(Dividend Stripping)

Daryl Foster has operated Foster's Fasteners Inc. for the last 15 years. It is a Canadian controlled private corporation that is involved in the sale of luxury hardware items. His original investment when the Company was established was $780,000. Daryl is the only shareholder and the $780,000 is both the adjusted cost base and the PUC of his shares.

As the Company has been very profitable since its inception, its shares have a current fair market value of $6,200,000.

As Daryl is nearing retirement age, he would like to extract a significant amount of funds from his corporation without incurring a great deal of taxation. He has discussed this matter with Thornton Brockton, his self-trained accountant of many years. While Thornton has never implemented such a strategy, he indicates that he has heard of a procedure called a Section 85 rollover that will allow Daryl to transfer his shares to a new corporation using an elected value that will create a capital gain of $600,000. As this is the amount of Daryl's unused lifetime capital gains deduction, Thornton advises Daryl that he can receive the original cost of his shares, plus a $600,000 capital gain on a tax free basis.

Using Section 85, Daryl will transfer all of the shares of Foster's Fasteners to Foster Investments, a new Company in which Daryl will hold all of the shares. The elected value for the transfer will be $1,380,000.

In return, Daryl will receive a non-interest bearing note for $1,380,000, plus Foster Investment shares with a redemption value of $4,820,000. Given the cash resources of Foster's Fasteners, this Company's shares should be able to pay sufficient dividends to Foster Investments to allow the payment of the note within one or two years.

Neither of the Companies have a balance in their General Rate Income Pool (GRIP) account in any of the years under consideration.

Required:

A. In the absence of ITA 84.1, indicate the tax consequences of the transfer of the shares of Foster's Fasteners to Foster Investments.

B. Determine whether ITA 84.1 would be applicable in this case. Assuming that ITA 84.1 is applicable, calculate the deemed dividend that would arise on this transfer. In addition, indicate the net economic effect that would result from this transfer combined with a redemption of the Foster Investments shares at their fair market value of $4,820,000.

Assignment Problem Sixteen - 13
(Capital Gains Strips)

From its original incorporation, Doldem Inc. has always been a Canadian controlled private corporation. For the last 5 years, it has owned 100 percent of the outstanding shares of Darco Ltd. Darco is also a Canadian controlled private corporation. The shares were acquired at a cost of $1,650,000. This is also the PUC of the Darco shares.

The Darco shares have been a very successful investment for Doldem Inc. Reflecting this, it is estimated that their fair market value on January 1, 2018 is $4,700,000. During the period during which Doldem has held the Darco shares, the subsidiary has accumulated safe income of $893,000.

Doldem does not have a balance in its RDTOH account. Neither company has a General Rate Income Pool (GRIP) balance.

Required: Indicate the amount, and type, of income that would accrue to Doldem Inc. in both of the following **independent** situations:

A. Darco Ltd. obtains a bank loan in the amount of $3,050,000 and uses all of the acquired funds to pay a dividend to Doldem Inc. Subsequent to the receipt of this dividend, Doldem Inc. sells the Darco shares to Ms. Laraz, an arm's length party, for $1,650,000.

B. Using ITA 85(1), Doldem transfers the Darco shares to Laraz Ltd., an unrelated corporation. The elected value is $1,650,000. In return for the Darco shares, Doldem receives Laraz Ltd. preferred stock with a PUC of $1,650,000 and a redemption value of $4,700,000. Immediately after the transfer, Laraz Ltd. redeems the preferred stock for $4,700,000.

CHAPTER 17

Other Rollovers And Sale Of An Incorporated Business

Introduction

17-1.   The preceding Chapter gave detailed consideration to the Section 85 rollover provisions, which provide for a tax deferred transfer of property to a corporation. In addition, Chapter 9 dealt with rollovers involving transfers to a spouse and transfers of farm property to children. There are a number of other rollover provisions in the *Act* that will be discussed in this Chapter.

17-2.   These additional rollover provisions cover share for share exchanges among corporations, share exchanges in the process of the reorganization of a corporation, amalgamations of existing corporations, the winding-up of a 90 percent or more owned subsidiary, and conversions of debt to shares. The winding-up of a Canadian corporation that is not a 90 percent owned subsidiary is also covered. This latter transaction does not involve a rollover, but is dealt with in the same Section of the *Income Tax Act* as the winding-up of a 90 percent or more owned subsidiary.

Share For Share Exchanges - ITA 85.1

Background

17-3.   ITA 85.1 provides for a rollover in which a shareholder (vendor) exchanges his shares for shares of an acquiring corporation (purchaser). When there are many diverse shareholders, a share for share exchange is easier to accomplish than a Section 85 rollover, because there is no need for each shareholder to file an election. Further, the provisions of ITA 85.1 apply automatically, unless the vendor includes any gain or loss on the transaction in his income tax return. Given these features, an ITA 85.1 exchange is an important arrangement in business combination transactions.

General Rules

17-4.   The general rules for this rollover apply automatically unless the vendor opts to include a gain or loss from the transaction in their income tax return. These general rules are as follows:

ITA 85.1(1)(a)   The vendor (acquiree) is deemed to have:

(i)   disposed of the exchanged shares for proceeds of disposition equal to their adjusted cost base.

(ii) acquired the shares of the purchaser at a cost to the vendor equal to the adjusted cost base to the vendor of the exchanged shares immediately before the exchange.

ITA 85.1(1)(b)   The cost to the purchaser (acquirer) of each of the acquired shares is deemed to be the lesser of:

(i)   its fair market value immediately before the exchange, and

(ii) its paid-up capital immediately before the exchange.

ITA 85.1(2.1)   The PUC of the purchaser shares that have been issued to the vendor is limited to the PUC of the shares given up by the vendor.

17-5.   You should note that the ITA 85.1(1)(b) provision may be problematical for the purchaser in situations where the adjusted cost base of the vendor's shares exceeds their PUC. If the shares are later sold by the purchaser, that excess of the adjusted cost base over the PUC will be subject to tax as a capital gain since the purchaser's adjusted cost base will be equal to the PUC. This would suggest that, in situations where the adjusted cost base of the shares exceeds their PUC, it might be better to use ITA 85(1) for the transfer.

Conditions For The Application Of ITA 85.1

17-6.   The conditions required for this rollover to be applicable are found in ITA 85.1(1) and (2). To begin, the vendor's shares must be held as capital property. Additional conditions for the applicability of the rollover are as follows:

ITA 85.1(2)(a)   The vendor and purchaser must be dealing with each other at arm's length.

ITA 85.1(2)(b)   The vendor, or persons with whom he does not deal at arm's length, cannot control the purchaser immediately after the exchange. Likewise, they cannot own shares having a fair market value in excess of 50 percent of the total fair market value of the purchasing corporation's outstanding shares.

ITA 85.1(2)(c)   The vendor and purchaser cannot have filed an election under ITA 85(1) with respect to the exchanged shares.

ITA 85.1(2)(d)   The vendor must not have received any consideration, other than shares of the purchaser, in return for the shares given up in the exchange.

17-7.   You should note that this last condition under ITA 85.1(2)(d) does not prevent the vendor from selling additional shares to the purchaser for non-share consideration.

Example
Application Of ITA 85.1
17-8.   A brief example will serve to illustrate the basic provisions of ITA 85.1:

EXAMPLE   Ms. Cowper is the sole shareholder of Cowper Inc., owning a total of 1,000 shares with a Paid Up Capital (PUC) and an adjusted cost base of $10,000. The shares of Cowper Inc. have a current fair market value of $125,000.

Mega Holdings Ltd. acquires these shares in return for 5,000 of its common shares. The Mega Holdings shares are currently trading at $25 per share, resulting in a total value for the 5,000 shares of $125,000.

ANALYSIS   The information in the example is presented graphically in Figure 17-1.

In the absence of the share for share exchange provisions in ITA 85.1, Ms. Cowper would have a capital gain of $115,000 ($125,000 - $10,000). However, under the rollover provisions of ITA 85.1, the following results apply:

Figure 17 - 1
ITA 85.1 Example

- Ms. Cowper is deemed to have disposed of her shares for an amount equal to the $10,000 adjusted cost base of the Cowper Inc. shares. This means that there is no capital gain on the disposition. [ITA 85.1(1)(a)(i)]

- Ms. Cowper is deemed to have acquired the shares in Mega Holdings Ltd. at a cost equal to the adjusted cost base of the Cowper Inc. shares, or $10,000. [ITA 85.1(1)(a)(ii)]

- The adjusted cost base of the Cowper shares acquired by Mega Holding Ltd. is deemed to be equal to $10,000, the lesser of their fair market value of $125,000, and their PUC of $10,000 [ITA 85.1(1)(b)]. You should note that this limit applies, even in situations where the vendor opted to forego the rollover under ITA 85.1 by including the gain in income (see Paragraph 17-9).

- The PUC of the Mega Holding Ltd. shares that have been issued to Ms. Cowper is limited to the $10,000 PUC of the Cowper shares that have been given up. [ITA 85.1(2.1)]

Opting Out Of ITA 85.1

17-9. As we have noted, ITA 85.1 applies automatically unless the vendor opts out in their income tax return. In this example, Ms. Cowper could opt out of ITA 85.1 by including the taxable capital gain of $57,500 [(1/2)($125,000 - $10,000)] in her income tax return. Note that, unlike the situation when ITA 85(1) is used in a rollover, there is no flexibility on the transfer value. With respect to the shares that are exchanged, opting out requires that 100 percent of the capital gain on the exchanged shares be included in income. This could be a problem if, for example, Ms. Cowper only wanted to recognize part of the gain on her shares.

17-10. There are two possible solutions to this problem. The transfer of Ms. Cowper's shares could be made using the provisions of ITA 85(1). This would allow the use of an elected value that would limit the amount of gain that would be recognized.

17-11. An alternative, perhaps simpler solution, would be to sell a portion of her shares to Mega Holdings for cash. This would allow the recognition of the desired amount of capital gain. The remaining shares could then be exchanged on a tax free basis under ITA 85.1.

Exercise Seventeen - 1

Subject: Share For Share Exchange

Ms. Aly Alee is the sole shareholder of Aayee Ltd., a Canadian controlled private corporation that is not a qualified small business corporation. The corporation was established several years ago by Ms. Alee with an investment of $450,000. It has identifiable net assets with a fair market value of $2,200,000. The shares of her company are acquired by a large publicly traded company, Global Outreach Inc., through the issuance of 50,000 new shares. At the time of this business combination, the Global Outreach Inc. shares are trading at $49 per share. Indicate the tax consequences of this transaction to both Ms. Alee and Global Outreach Inc.

SOLUTION available in print and online Study Guide.

ITA 85.1 In Practice

17-12.   We have illustrated ITA 85.1 using an example that involves a large public company acquiring a corporation with a single shareholder. This is not the usual application of ITA 85.1. ITA 85.1 was designed to be used in situations where a public company acquires a widely held corporation with a large number of shareholders.

17-13.   As noted in Paragraph 17-3, Section 85 can be used as an alternative to Section 85.1. However, in situations where the acquiree has a large number of shareholders, this approach would require the filing of numerous, in some cases hundreds, of separate Section 85 elections. The use of Section 85.1 avoids this by making its application automatic, unless the acquiree includes any gain or loss in income. This is a much more efficient procedure in most business combination situations.

We suggest you work Self Study Problems Seventeen-1 and 2 at this point.

Exchange Of Shares In A Reorganization - ITA 86

BYRD/CHEN NOTE   ITA 86 has been widely used in the implementation of estate freezes, a procedure used to transfer the future growth in a private corporation to the spouses, children, or other parties related to the principal shareholder of a CCPC. The 2018 expansion of the applicability of the Tax On Split Income (TOSI) has made this a much more difficult procedure to implement effectively. When the TOSI is applicable, both dividends and capital gains received as a result of this procedure will be subject to taxation at the maximum federal rate, removing most or all of the incentive for undertaking an estate freeze.

More specifically, the TOSI will always be applicable to income received by children under 18. In addition, it will be generally applicable to other related individuals unless the income they receive is an Excluded Amount. If they are 18 or over and actively involved in the business, the income can escape the TOSI as the corporation may be an Excluded Business. If they are 25 or over and own more than 10 percent of the CCPC's shares (voting and non-voting), the income can escape the TOSI as their holding will be viewed as Excluded Shares. See Chapter 11 for a more detailed discussion of these concepts.

There are other applications of ITA 86, a common one being transfers of ownership to a key employee or group of employees. In general, these other procedures will not result in the application of the TOSI.

In our coverage of ITA 86, we will assume that the TOSI is not applicable. To make this more realistic we will avoid applications involving minor children and non-voting shares. However, it is important that you recognize that the use of the Section 86 in estate freezes is limited by the possible application of the TOSI.

Application Of ITA 86(1)
Basic Procedure

17-14.   ITA 86(1) applies when there has been a reorganization involving an exchange of shares within a single corporation. In the usual application, a shareholder of a corporation exchanges shares held in at least one class of existing shares, for authorized shares in the same company, or for authorized shares in the same company combined with non-share consideration (note that the authorized shares must be of a different class than the existing shares). In effect, there is a redemption of the taxpayer's current shareholding, combined with an acquisition of a new shareholding. ITA 86(1) allows this transaction to take place without tax consequences to the taxpayer whose shares are being redeemed.

Use In Estate Freeze

17-15.   One of the most common applications of ITA 86(1) is in an estate freeze, where an owner of a business wishes to pass on the future growth of the business to adult family members who have been actively engaged in the business.

> **EXAMPLE**   A father holds all of the outstanding common shares of a corporation. These shares have a fair market value in excess of their adjusted cost base and, as a consequence, their sale or redemption would normally result in a deemed dividend and/or a capital gain or capital loss. Further, if the father continues to hold the shares, future growth in the corporation will accrue to him.

> **ANALYSIS**   To avoid this situation, the father will exchange his common shares for newly issued preferred shares of the corporation. The preferred shares will have a fixed redemption value equal to the fair market value of the common shares given up. The fact that their value is fixed will serve to freeze the value of the father's interest in the corporation. If the father wishes to retain control of the corporation, the preferred shares can be structured to provide voting rights sufficient to achieve this objective. Common shares will then be issued to a spouse, a child, or some other related person.

17-16.   As the preferred shares held by the father reflect the full fair market value of the company, the new common shares can be issued to the related person at a fairly nominal value. However, any future growth in the value of the company will accrue to these common shares. ITA 86(1) provides for the father's exchange of shares to take place on a rollover or tax free basis (see Chapter 19 for a more detailed discussion of estate freezes). Note that the ITA 86 rollover differs from the ITA 85(1) rollover in that there are no elected amounts and no election form to be filed.

Conditions For The Reorganization

General Conditions

17-17.   For the provisions of ITA 86(1) to apply, several conditions must be met.

> **Shares Must Be Capital Property**   First, the original owner's shares must be capital property to the owner. They cannot be part of an inventory of securities that is being held for trading purposes.

> **All Shares Held By Transferor In A Particular Class**   A second condition is that the transaction must result in an exchange of all of the outstanding shares of a particular class that are owned by the transferor. For example, all Class A common shares that are owned by the transferor must be exchanged for some other type of share. Note that there is no requirement that Class A common shares that are held by other shareholders be exchanged as part of the transaction. Further, it is not necessary that other classes of shares owned by the transferor be exchanged for new shares.

> **Reorganization Of Capital**   A third condition is that the share exchange must be integral to a reorganization of the capital of the corporation. This will often require that the articles of incorporation be amended to authorize any new class of shares.

> **Transferor Must Receive Shares**   A final condition is that the transferor must receive shares of the capital stock of the corporation. While this does not preclude the transferor from receiving non-share consideration, such non-share consideration should not exceed the adjusted cost base or the PUC of the shares transferred. If it does, the excess will have to be taken into income as a deemed dividend and either a taxable capital gain or an allowable capital loss.

Establishing Market Value For Preferred Shares

17-18.   In the more common applications of ITA 86(1), the new shares received by the transferor will usually be preferred shares. These shares must be designed in such a fashion as to clearly establish their fair market value. If this is not the case, a subsequent dispute with the CRA could result in some of the benefits of using ITA 86(1) being lost. Adding the following characteristics to the preferred shares will serve to establish a defensible fair market value:

- The preferred shares must be redeemable at the option of the shareholder. The CRA rigorously enforces this requirement to protect the fair market value of the preferred shares.

- The preferred shares should be entitled to a dividend at a reasonable rate. Without a reasonable dividend entitlement to the original shareholder, the incoming shareholders could benefit by receiving a disproportionate share of the corporation's future profits. However, there is no requirement for the entitlement to be cumulative.

- The corporation must guarantee that dividends will not be paid on any other class of shares, if the payment would result in the corporation having insufficient net assets to redeem the preferred shares at their specified redemption price.

- The preferred shares must become cumulative if the fair market value of the net assets of the corporation falls below the redemption value of the preferred shares, or if the corporation is unable to redeem the shares on a call for redemption.

- The preferred shares may or may not have normal voting rights. However, they should carry votes on any matter regarding the rights attached to the preferred shares.

- The preferred shares should have preference on liquidation of the corporation. While the very nature of preferred shares tends to guarantee preference, the CRA requires additional assurance that the normal provisions for such shares will not be avoided.

Procedures

General Rules

17-19.   As noted previously, an ITA 86(1) reorganization involves a redemption (disposition) of a given shareholder's holding of a particular class of shares (old shares, hereafter). In return, the shareholder acquires shares of a different class (new shares, hereafter) and, in some reorganizations, non-share consideration. ITA 86(1) specifies a number of rules that apply in such a reorganization of capital. These are as follows:

Non-Share Consideration   ITA 86(1)(a) indicates that the cost to the shareholder of this consideration is deemed to be its fair market value.

Cost Of New Shares   ITA 86(1)(b) indicates that the cost of the new shares to the shareholder is equal to the cost of the old shares, less any non-share consideration received.

Proceeds Of Redemption For Old Shares   Because there is a redemption of shares, there is the possibility of an ITA 84(3) deemed dividend. ITA 84(3)(a) defines such dividends as the excess of the "amount paid" over the PUC of the shares being redeemed. This "amount paid" clearly includes any non-share consideration and, when shares are included in the redemption payment, ITA 84(5)(d) indicates that their value is based on any increase in PUC resulting from the issuance of these shares. Putting this together leads to the conclusion that the total proceeds for the redemption will be equal to the non-share consideration plus the PUC of any new shares issued. Note that, in the usual ITA 86(1) scenario, the PUC of the new shares will often be reduced by a PUC reduction under ITA 86(2.1)(a). (See Paragraph 17-20.)

Proceeds Of Disposition For Old Shares   As the redemption of the old shares is a type of disposition, there is also the possibility of a capital gain or loss. For the purposes of determining the capital gain or loss on this disposition, ITA 86(1)(c) defines the proceeds of disposition for the old shares as being equal to the cost of the new shares (the cost of the old shares, less non-share consideration), plus any non-share consideration received by the taxpayer.

In our general discussion of ITA 84(3) redemptions in Chapter 14, we discuss the possibility that the combination of redemption procedures and disposition procedures could result in the double counting of all or part of any gain on the transaction. As we noted there, this possibility is eliminated by the fact that the ITA 54 definition of proceeds of disposition excludes ITA 84(3) dividends.

PUC Reduction Calculation

17-20.   As noted in the preceding rules, a PUC reduction may be required on the new shares. This is specified in ITA 86(2.1)(a). This reduction is calculated as follows:

Increase In Legal Stated Capital Of New Shares		$xx,xxx
Less The Excess, If Any, Of:		
PUC Of Old Shares	($x,xxx)	
Over The Non-Share Consideration	x,xxx	(x,xxx)
ITA 86(2.1)(a) PUC Reduction		$xx,xxx

17-21.   In reviewing this PUC reduction formula, note that where the non-share consideration is equal to, or greater than the PUC of the old shares, the amount subtracted from the increase in the legal stated capital of the new shares will be nil. This means that the PUC reduction will be equal to the increase in legal stated capital for the new shares. In common sense terms, if the shareholder takes back the full amount of the old PUC in the form of non-share consideration, the PUC of the new shares will be nil.

17-22.   As was the case with rollovers to a corporation under Section 85, if the PUC reduction applies to more than one class of shares, it will generally be allocated to the individual classes on the basis of the relative fair market value of each class.

Example Using ITA 86(1) In An Estate Freeze

Basic Data

17-23.   An example will serve to illustrate the ITA 86(1) procedures. You might note that the example illustrates the manner in which an ITA 86(1) reorganization of capital can be used to freeze the value of an individual's estate. The example is illustrated graphically in Figure 17-2 (following page).

EXAMPLE   Mr. David Jones owns all of the outstanding shares of Jones Inc. These common shares have an adjusted cost base of $50,000 and a paid up capital of $75,000. Because of the successful operations of the Company, the current fair market value of these common shares is $500,000.

Mr. Jones would like to have future growth in the value of the corporation accrue to his daughter, Ms. Veronica Jones. Veronica is 30 years old and has been actively and substantially involved in the business for over 5 years. To accomplish this, Mr. Jones exchanges his common shares for a $150,000 note payable from the corporation and preferred shares with a fair market value and a legal stated capital of $350,000. Common shares are purchased by Veronica Jones for $1,000. These are the only Jones Inc. common shares outstanding subsequent to these transactions.

PUC Reduction

17-24.   The first step in applying the ITA 86(1) rules in this situation would be to calculate the required PUC reduction and the resulting PUC value for the preferred shares. As the non-share consideration of $150,000 exceeds the $75,000 PUC of the shares given up, we would expect the PUC reduction formula to reduce the PUC of the preferred shares to nil. The following calculations support this expected result:

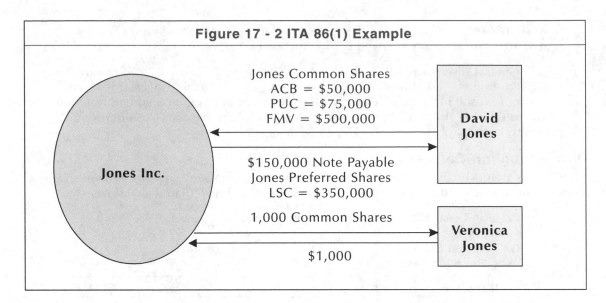

Figure 17 - 2 ITA 86(1) Example

Cost Of Non-Share Consideration (Note Payable)		$150,000

Legal Stated Capital Of Preferred Shares		$350,000
Less The Excess, If Any, Of:		
PUC Of Shares Given Up	($ 75,000)	
Over The Non-Share Consideration	150,000	Nil
ITA 86(2.1)(a) PUC Reduction		**$350,000**

Legal Stated Capital Of Preferred Shares	$350,000
ITA 86(2.1)(a) PUC Reduction	(350,000)
PUC Of Preferred Shares	**Nil**

Other Calculations

17-25.   Other required values can be calculated as follows:

Adjusted Cost Base Of Shares Given Up	$ 50,000
Non-Share Consideration	(150,000)
Adjusted Cost Base Of Preferred Shares	**Nil**

PUC Of Preferred Shares	Nil
Plus Non-Share Consideration	$150,000
Proceeds Of Redemption - ITA 84(5)(d)	$150,000
PUC Of Shares Given Up	(75,000)
ITA 84(3) Deemed Dividend	**$ 75,000**

Adjusted Cost Base Of Preferred Shares	Nil
Plus Non-Share Consideration	$150,000
Proceeds Of Disposition - ITA 86(1)(c)	$150,000
Less ITA 84(3) Deemed Dividend	(75,000)
Adjusted Proceeds Of Disposition	$ 75,000
Adjusted Cost Base Of Shares Given Up	(50,000)
Capital Gain	$ 25,000
Inclusion Rate	1/2
Taxable Capital Gain	**$ 12,500**

Economic Analysis

17-26.   The shares held by David's daughter, Veronica, will have an adjusted cost base and a PUC of $1,000 and this will also be their initial fair market value. However, if the corporation prospers, all future increases in its value will accrue to her. In other words, by exchanging his common shares for non-growth preferred shares, Mr. Jones has frozen the value of his interest in Jones Inc.

17-27.   In reviewing this example, you should note that Mr. Jones' potential gain has not disappeared. If he had simply sold his shares without the reorganization, he would have realized a gain of $450,000 ($500,000 - $50,000). As a result of the reorganization, he has recognized $100,000 ($75,000 dividend + $25,000 capital gain). This gain reflects the excess of the $150,000 non-share consideration received by Mr. Jones, over the $50,000 adjusted cost base of the original shares.

17-28.   This reorganization has left an unrecognized gain of $350,000 ($500,000 - $150,000). This gain will remain unrecognized until such time as Mr. Jones' holding of preferred shares is either redeemed or sold for its fair market value of $350,000. As these shares have a PUC of nil, a subsequent redemption would result in an ITA 84(3) deemed dividend of $350,000. As the adjusted cost base of the shares is also nil, a subsequent sale of the shares would result in a capital gain of $350,000, the taxable amount of which would be one-half, or $175,000.

17-29.   A final point here is that this example does not represent a typical ITA 86(1) estate freeze. While it does accomplish the goal of transferring future growth in the corporation to a related party, the approach used has resulted in current Tax Payable for Mr. Jones. This could have been avoided by limiting the non-share consideration to $50,000, the lesser of the $75,000 PUC and the $50,000 adjusted cost base of the old shares. It is this approach that would be used in a typical ITA 86(1) transaction.

Exercise Seventeen - 2

Subject: Exchange Of Shares In Reorganization (ACB = PUC = Boot)

Mr. Sam Samson is the sole shareholder of Samdoo Ltd. It is a Canadian controlled private corporation and its common shares have a fair market value of $2,300,000, an adjusted cost base (ACB) of $1,000,000, and a paid up capital (PUC) of $1,000,000. At this time, Samdoo Ltd. has no balance in its GRIP account. Mr. Samson exchanges all of his Samdoo Ltd. shares for cash of $1,000,000 and preferred shares that are redeemable for $1,300,000. Determine the ACB and the PUC of the redeemable preferred shares. Indicate the amount, and type, of any income that will result from this transaction.

Exercise Seventeen - 3

Subject: Exchange Of Shares In Reorganization (ACB > PUC, PUC = Boot)

Mr. Sam Samson is the sole shareholder of Samdoo Ltd. It is a Canadian controlled private corporation and its common shares have a fair market value of $2,300,000, an adjusted cost base (ACB) of $1,250,000, and a paid up capital (PUC) of $1,000,000. At this time, Samdoo Ltd. has no balance in its GRIP account. Mr. Samson exchanges all of his Samdoo Ltd. shares for cash of $1,000,000 and preferred shares that are redeemable for $1,300,000. Determine the ACB and the PUC of the redeemable preferred shares. Indicate the amount, and type, of any income that will result from this transaction.

SOLUTIONS available in print and online Study Guide.

Exercise Seventeen - 4

Subject: Exchange Of Shares In Reorganization (ACB > Boot > PUC)

Mr. Sam Samson is the sole shareholder of Samdoo Ltd. It is a Canadian controlled private corporation and its common shares have a fair market value of $2,300,000, an adjusted cost base (ACB) of $1,250,000, and a paid up capital (PUC) of $1,000,000. At this time, Samdoo Ltd. has no balance in its GRIP account. Mr. Samson exchanges all of his Samdoo Ltd. shares for cash of $1,200,000 and preferred shares that are redeemable for $1,100,000. Determine the ACB and the PUC of the redeemable preferred shares. Indicate the amount, and type, of any income that will result from this transaction.

SOLUTION available in print and online Study Guide.

We suggest your work Self Study Problem Seventeen-3 at this point.

Gift To Related Person - ITA 86(2)

Background

17-30.   ITA 86(2) contains a rule designed to prevent a taxpayer from using the reorganization of capital rollover provision to confer a benefit on a related person. This rule is applicable whenever the fair market value of the old shares exceeds the sum of the fair market value of the new shares and the fair market value of the non-share consideration received, and it is reasonable to regard all, or part, of this excess as a gift to a related person. You might wish to note that this provision is similar to the provision that is applicable when the use of an ITA 85(1) rollover involves a gift to a related person (see Chapter 16).

17-31.   In situations where ITA 86(2) applies, the rules for the reorganization of share capital are as follows:

Proceeds Of Disposition   Under ITA 86(2)(c), the proceeds of the disposition for capital gains purposes on the old shares will be equal to the lesser of:

  • the non-share consideration, ***plus the gift***; and
  • the fair market value of the old shares.

This compares to the proceeds of disposition under ITA 86(1)(c), which is equal to the cost of the new shares, plus any non-share consideration.

Capital Losses   Under ITA 86(2)(d), any capital loss resulting from the disposition of the old shares will be deemed to be nil.

Cost Of New Shares   Under ITA 86(2)(e), the cost to the taxpayer of the new shares will be equal to:

  • the cost of the old shares; less
  • the sum of the non-share consideration, ***plus the gift***.

This compares to a cost for the new shares under ITA 86(1)(b) equal to the cost of the old shares, less any non-share consideration.

17-32.   To illustrate these procedures, we will modify the example in Paragraph 17-23 by decreasing the amount of consideration received to create a $100,000 gift. The revised example is as follows:

EXAMPLE Mr. David Jones owns all of the outstanding shares of Jones Inc. These common shares have an adjusted cost base of $50,000 and a paid up capital of $75,000. Because of the successful operations of the Company, the current fair market value of these common shares is $500,000.

Mr. Jones would like to have future growth in the value of the corporation accrue to his daughter, Ms. Veronica Jones. Veronica is 30 years old and has been actively and substantially involved in the business for over 5 years. To accomplish this, Mr. Jones exchanges his common shares for a $150,000 note payable from the corporation and preferred shares with a fair market value and a legal stated capital of $250,000. Common shares are purchased by Veronica Jones for $1,000. These are the only Jones Inc. common shares outstanding subsequent to these transactions.

Calculation Of Gift

17-33. The gift involved in this approach is calculated as follows:

Fair Market Value Of Shares Given Up		$500,000
Less Fair Market Value Of Consideration:		
Non-Share Consideration	($150,000)	
Fair Market Value Of Preferred Shares	(250,000)	(400,000)
Gift		$100,000

17-34. As his daughter is the only holder of common shares, this $100,000 gift would accrue to her. As she is clearly a related person, ITA 86(2) would be applicable.

PUC Reduction

17-35. The PUC reduction and PUC of the preferred shares is calculated as follows:

Cost Of Non-Share Consideration (Note Payable)		$150,000
Legal Stated Capital Of Preferred Shares		$250,000
Less The Excess, If Any, Of:		
PUC Of Shares Given Up	($ 75,000)	
Over The Non-Share Consideration	150,000	Nil
ITA 86(2.1)(a) PUC Reduction		$250,000
Legal Stated Capital Of Preferred Shares		$250,000
ITA 86(2.1)(a) PUC Reduction		(250,000)
PUC Of Preferred Shares		Nil

Other Calculations

17-36. The remaining calculations that would be required under ITA 86(2) are as follows:

Adjusted Cost Base Of Common Shares Given Up		$ 50,000
Less:		
Non-Share Consideration	($150,000)	
Gift (See Paragraph 17-33)	(100,000)	(250,000)
Adjusted Cost Base Of Preferred Shares		Nil
PUC Of Preferred Shares		Nil
Plus Non-Share Consideration		$150,000
Proceeds Of Redemption - ITA 84(5)(d)		$150,000
PUC Of Common Shares Given Up		(75,000)
ITA 84(3) Deemed Dividend		$ 75,000

Proceeds Of Disposition Under ITA 86(2)(c) - Lesser Of:
- Fair Market Value Of Shares Given Up = $500,000
- Non-Share Consideration Plus Gift

($150,000 + $100,000) = $250,000	$250,000
Less ITA 84(3) Deemed Dividend	(75,000)
Adjusted Proceeds Of Disposition - ITA 54	$175,000
Adjusted Cost Base Of Common Shares Given Up	(50,000)
Capital Gain	$125,000
Inclusion Rate	1/2
Taxable Capital Gain	$ 62,500

17-37.   At the time of the reorganization, the potential gain on David's shares was $450,000 ($500,000 - $50,000). In the original version of this example (Paragraph 17-25), a gain of $100,000 was recognized ($75,000 + $25,000) at the time of the reorganization, leaving $350,000 of the gain deferred until David's preferred shares are redeemed or sold (the shares had a fair market value of $350,000, with both their PUC and adjusted cost base equal to nil).

17-38.   In this version of the example, the gain that is recognized at the time of the reorganization is $200,000 ($75,000 + $125,000), $100,000 larger than in the original version of the example. This reflects the fact that the amount of the gift was added to the ITA 86(2)(c) proceeds of disposition, resulting in a capital gain that is $100,000 larger. It is important to note, however, the total gain, current and deferred, is unchanged at $450,000. While the current gain is increased to $200,000, the deferred amount is reduced to $250,000 (the preferred shares have a fair market value of $250,000, with both their PUC and adjusted cost base equal to nil). While the gift resulted in current taxation which could have been deferred, it did not involve a penalty in the form of additional taxation.

17-39.   ITA 86(2) does, however, involve a penalty to his daughter Veronica. The new common shares issued to Veronica will have a fair market value equal to $101,000, the $1,000 she paid plus the $100,000 gift. The $100,000 additional value will not be reflected in the adjusted cost base of her shares and, as a consequence, this amount will be taxed when she disposes of the shares.

17-40.   In effect, the granting of the benefit has increased the amount that will be subject to taxation in the hands of Veronica by the $100,000 amount of the gift, without reducing Mr. Jones' total current and deferred income on the shares. This makes it clear that ITA 86 reorganizations should be structured in a manner that avoids such benefits being granted.

Exercise Seventeen - 5

Subject: Gift To A Related Party - ITA 86(2)

Janrev Inc. is a Canadian controlled private corporation. Its shares have a fair market value of $1,600,000 and a paid up capital (PUC) of $250,000. Ms. Jan Reviser owns 80 percent of the shares. Her shares have an adjusted cost base of $200,000. The remaining 20 percent of the shares are held by her 19 year old daughter and they have an adjusted cost base of $50,000. On May 1, 2018, Ms. Reviser exchanges all of her Janrev Inc. shares for cash of $300,000 and preferred shares that are redeemable for $800,000. At this time, Janrev has no balance in its GRIP account. Indicate the amount, and type, of any income that will result from this transaction.

SOLUTION available in print and online Study Guide.

Using ITA 86(1) - Tax Planning Considerations

General Usage

17-41. The major advantages of using ITA 86(1), as compared to using ITA 85(1), can be described as follows:

- An ITA 86(1) share reorganization may be simpler to implement than a Section 85 rollover as it does not require the use of a second corporation.
- The corporate law steps are easier, only requiring shares to be exchanged, and possibly new share classes to be formed.
- The use of ITA 86(1) does not require an election to be filed with the CRA.

17-42. The disadvantages associated with using ITA 86(1) are as follows:

- When only a single corporation is used, it is difficult to segregate investment income from active business income.
- A single corporation exposes all of the assets to any operating risk, and limited liability protection is reduced.
- In an ITA 86(1) reorganization, all of the taxpayer's shares of a particular class have to be exchanged. This can be a problem if the original shareholder wishes to retain some of the common or growth shares.
- ITA 86 does not provide the range of elected values that is available Under ITA 85(1).

17-43. It is usually possible to get around the last disadvantage by re-issuing common shares to the original shareholder after the reorganization is completed.

Use In Key Employee Successions

17-44. In addition to its use in estate freezes, an exchange of shares can be very effective when arranging for gradual succession to a key employee. For example, consider a situation where an employee has little personal equity, but has a good work record with the company and excellent owner-manager potential.

17-45. An ITA 86(1) reorganization could be used to convert common shares owned by the existing shareholder into preferred shares. The employee could then purchase the common shares over some agreed upon succession period. The annual investments in common shares would likely be modest, as most of the company's value would be reflected in the preferred shares, making the investments feasible for the incoming shareholder. The original owner could continue to be involved in the business throughout the succession years.

17-46. Eventually, when the original owner is ready to sell the preferred shares, the incoming shareholder will have the benefit of several years of management experience, and should be able to obtain funding to acquire the preferred shares from the original owner.

We suggest you work Self Study Problems Seventeen-4 and 5 at this point.

Amalgamations - ITA 87

The Nature Of An Amalgamation

17-47. ITA 87 provides for a tax deferred rollover in situations where there is an amalgamation of corporations. This may involve two independent corporations wishing to merge and continue their business affairs on a combined basis. Alternatively, associated or related corporations may amalgamate to pursue common corporate goals.

17-48. If the two corporations want to transfer their assets to a new corporation on a tax free basis, the rollover provisions of ITA 87 would apply. The following simple example will illustrate this kind of situation (illustrated in Figure 17-3, following page):

Figure 17 - 3
ITA 87 Amalgamation Example

EXAMPLE   The shareholders of Alpha Inc. have shares with an adjusted cost base of $1,000,000 and a fair market value of $5,000,000, while the shareholders of Beta Inc. have shares with an adjusted cost base of $1,700,000 and a fair market value of $5,000,000. All of the assets and liabilities (except intercompany balances) of Alpha Inc. and Beta Inc. are transferred to a new Company, Alpha-Beta Ltd. The shareholders of Alpha Inc. and Beta Inc. exchange their shares for shares in Alpha-Beta Ltd.

17-49.   In the absence of a rollover provision, the exchange of shares would be viewed as a disposition of the Alpha Inc. shares and the Beta Inc. shares, combined with an acquisition of the Alpha-Beta Ltd. shares. The fact that the share dispositions could result in taxable capital gains and the asset transfers could result in taxable capital gains and recapture, could serve to discourage the combination of the two companies.

17-50.   Fortunately, ITA 87 contains rollover provisions for both the transfer of assets to the amalgamated corporation and for the exchange of shares. The conditions necessary for this rollover to apply are as follows:

- All of the predecessor corporations must be taxable Canadian corporations.

- All shareholders of the predecessor corporations must receive shares of the amalgamated corporation due to the amalgamation.

- All of the assets and liabilities of the predecessor corporations, other than intercompany balances, must be transferred to the amalgamated corporation in the amalgamation.

- A formal amalgamation procedure, supported by the relevant corporate legislation is required. The transfer cannot simply be a normal purchase of property, or involve the distribution of assets on the winding-up of a corporation.

Position Of The Amalgamated Company

17-51.   The tax values for the amalgamated corporation's assets will simply be the sum of the tax values of the assets that were present in the records of the predecessor corporations. In addition, all types of loss carry forwards (capital, non-capital, and farm) of the predecessor corporations flow through and become available to the amalgamated corporation.

17-52.   The predecessor corporations will be deemed to have a taxation year that ends immediately before the amalgamation and, in most situations, this will result in an extra taxation year that will count towards the expiration of losses with a limited carry forward period. The amalgamated corporation is deemed to have been formed on the date of the amalgamation and may choose any year end it wishes. We would also note that, while this may not be consistent with corporate law, the *Income Tax Act* treats the amalgamated company as a brand new company and the predecessor companies as if they have come to an end.

17-53.   With respect to assets, reserves, loss carry forwards, and other tax accounts of the predecessor companies, ITA 87 provides rollover provisions as follows:

Rollover Provisions In ITA 87 Amalgamations

Item	Rollover Effect
Inventories	At Cost
Depreciable Capital Property	At UCC
Non-Depreciable Capital Property	At ACB
Reserves	Flowed Through
Non-Capital Losses	Flowed Through
Net Capital Losses	Flowed Through
Restricted Farm Losses	Flowed Through
General Rate Income Pool (GRIP) (See Note 1)	Flowed Through
Low Rate Income Pool (LRIP) (See Note 2)	Flowed Through
Capital Dividend Account (See Note 3)	Flowed Through
Refundable Dividend Tax On Hand (See Note 3)	Flowed Through

Note 1   If a CCPC is formed as the result of an amalgamation, ITA 89(5) may be applicable.   In situations where a predecessor corporation was a CCPC, this subsection provides for the flow through of its GRIP account to the amalgamated company. Where the predecessor was a non-CCPC, a notional GRIP is calculated and flows through to the amalgamated company.

Note 2   If a non-CCPC is formed as the result of an amalgamation, ITA 89(9) may be applicable. In situations where a predecessor corporation was a non-CCPC, this subsection provides for the flow through of its LRIP account to the amalgamated company. Where the predecessor was a CCPC, a notional LRIP is calculated and flowed through.

Note 3   The amalgamated company is treated as a public company if, prior to the amalgamation, any of the predecessor companies was a public company. If this is the case, the amalgamated company will no longer have access to any capital dividend accounts, or refundable dividend tax on hand accounts of the predecessor companies.

17-54.   As can be seen in the preceding table, ITA 87 basically provides for a summing of the relevant tax values of the assets of the two companies that are amalgamating. The amalgamated corporation will be liable for taxes on future recapture and capital gains on the same basis as the predecessor corporations.

17-55.   With respect to loss carry forwards, the limitations that were discussed in Chapter 14 are applicable if there is an acquisition of control. As noted, the deemed year end of the predecessor corporations will count as one year in any carry forward period. However, losses carried forward may qualify for deduction in the first taxation year of the amalgamated company.

Position Of The Shareholders

17-56.   The shareholders of the predecessor corporations are deemed to dispose of their shares for proceeds equal to the adjusted cost base of the shares, and they are deemed to acquire the shares of the amalgamated company at the same value. For these general provisions to apply, ITA 87(4) specifies the following conditions:

• The shareholders must not receive any consideration other than shares in the amalgamated company.

• The original shares must be capital property of the shareholders.

• The amalgamation must not result in a deemed gift to a person related to the shareholders.

Vertical Amalgamations

17-57.   In situations where there is a desire to combine a parent and its subsidiary, a choice of rollovers may be available. The alternative to ITA 87, "Amalgamations", is the use of ITA 88(1), "Winding-Up". However, ITA 88(1) is only applicable to situations where the parent company owns 90 percent or more of the shares of each class of capital stock of a subsidiary. In contrast, ITA 87 can be used without regard to the percentage of ownership.

Asset Bump-Ups

17-58.   You may recall from an advanced financial accounting course that the cost of acquiring a subsidiary will usually exceed both the carrying values and the sum of the fair values of the acquired identifiable assets.

> **EXAMPLE**   Placor Inc. acquires 100 percent of the outstanding voting shares of Lacee Ltd. at a cost of $1,000,000. At this time the net identifiable assets of Lacee had carrying values of $700,000 and tax values of $650,000. The fair value of these assets totaled $900,000.

17-59.   The excess of the $1,000,000 investment cost over the tax values total of $650,000 creates a problem when there is an amalgamation involving either ITA 87 or ITA 88(1). Both of these provisions transfer assets to the amalgamated company at tax values. In the absence of a special legislative provision, the $350,000 excess of the investment cost over tax values of the assets will be lost.

17-60.   Fortunately, there is a provision that provides a limited amount of relief from this adverse tax consequence. As will be discussed in our coverage of winding-up (Paragraph 17-82), ITA 88(1) provides for a "bump-up" in certain asset values to reflect the parent company's excess of its investment cost over the subsidiary's tax values.

17-61.   ITA 87 provides for the same bump-up under ITA 87(11) by referring to the ITA 88(1) provision. However, there is a difference. Under ITA 88(1), the bump-up is available in situations where the parent owns 90 percent or more of the issued shares. Under ITA 87(11), the bump-up is only available when the parent owns 100 percent of the subsidiary's issued shares. Note that no bump-up is available under either provision when the ownership percentage is less than 90 percent.

Non-Tax Considerations

17-62.   While a statutory amalgamation does not involve a new company, there are likely to be significant legal complications. Each of the predecessor companies will have contracts with employees, suppliers, and customers. While they are still legally in force, modifications may be required to make the terms more compatible throughout the organization. There may also be problems with creditors. In fact, it is not uncommon for debt covenants to have a provision requiring the approval of debt holders before an amalgamation can take place. These factors may add considerable complexity to the amalgamation process.

Amalgamations - Tax Planning Considerations

17-63.   A Section 87 amalgamation offers a number of opportunities for tax planning. Some of the possibilities include:

- The utilization of loss carry forward amounts that the predecessor corporation(s) might not be able to absorb. Note, however, that if there is an acquisition of control, the usual restrictions on the use of loss carry forwards apply.

- With respect to acquisitions of control in the amalgamation process, we would note that, if the two predecessor corporations are related, an amalgamation will not result in an acquisition of control. However, if they are not related and the shareholders of one of the predecessor companies owns the majority of the voting shares in the amalgamated company, that company will be considered to have acquired control of the other predecessor company prior to the amalgamation.

- Current year losses of one predecessor corporation can effectively be utilized against Taxable Income of the other. Note, however, that corporate law in Canada does not generally allow a corporation to amalgamate if its financial health is in question. For example, a company that is insolvent is not allowed to amalgamate with another company.

- Bringing together a profitable and an unprofitable corporation may allow for a faster write-off of capital assets (through CCA) than would otherwise be possible by the unprofitable predecessor corporation.

- The amalgamation may provide for an increase in the amount of the manufacturing and processing profits tax deduction.

17-64.   The timing of an amalgamation can be an important tax planning issue. As the amalgamation transaction results in a deemed year end, the company may have a short fiscal year for purposes of calculating CCA. In addition, outstanding reserves may have to be brought into income sooner, and the short fiscal period will count as a full year in the eligible loss carry forward years.

17-65.   For income tax instalments there is a look through provision. While the amalgamated company does not have a previous tax year on which to base instalment payments of income tax, prepayments continue to be required based on the instalment history of the predecessor corporations.

Exercise Seventeen - 6

Subject: ITA 87 Amalgamations

During its taxation year ending December 31, 2017, Downer Ltd. incurs a non-capital loss of $93,000 and a net capital loss of $150,000. Neither loss can be carried back. On January 1, 2018, using the provisions of ITA 87, the Company is amalgamated with Upton Inc., an unrelated company that also has a December 31 year end. The combined company is named Amalgo Inc. and it elects to use a December 31 year end. The terms of the amalgamation give 20,000 Amalgo Inc. shares to the Downer Ltd. shareholders and 150,000 Amalgo Inc. shares to the Upton Inc. shareholders. During the year ending December 31, 2018, Amalgo Inc. has Net Income For Tax Purposes of $1,200,000, including over $300,000 in taxable capital gains. During its 2018 taxation year, will Amalgo Inc. be able to deduct the losses incurred by Downer Ltd. prior to the amalgamation? Explain your conclusion.

SOLUTION available in print and online Study Guide.

Winding-Up Of A 90 Percent Owned Subsidiary

The Nature Of A Winding-Up

Winding-Up Of Corporations In General

17-66.   IT-126R2 states that a corporation is considered to have been "wound up" where:

(a) it has followed the procedures for winding-up and dissolution provided by the appropriate federal or provincial companies *Act* or winding-up *Act*, or

(b) it has carried out a winding-up, other than by means of the statutory procedures contemplated in (a) above, and has been dissolved under the provisions of its incorporating statute.

17-67.   In general, a winding-up operation requires that all outstanding creditor claims be satisfied and that all corporate property be distributed to the shareholders before the winding-up is undertaken. IT-126R2 also notes that, where there is substantial evidence that dissolution procedures will be completed within a short period of time, Section 88(1) can be used prior to the completion of the wind-up. Note, however, that losses cannot be accessed until the actual wind-up takes place.

17-68.   A winding-up may be undertaken for several reasons. As with amalgamations, a winding-up allows for the losses of a subsidiary to be carried over to the parent corporation. Winding-ups are also undertaken to simplify an organizational structure, or when a subsidiary is ceasing its business operations.

90 Percent Owned Subsidiary

17-69.   The two major Subsections of ITA 88 can be described as follows:

ITA 88(1)   This Subsection is a rollover provision, providing for the tax free combination of the assets of a 90 percent or more owned subsidiary with those of its parent.

ITA 88(2)   This Subsection deals with the general winding-up of corporations, other than those to which ITA 88(1) is applicable. It is not a rollover provision.

17-70.   At this point we are concerned only with the provisions contained in ITA 88(1). The content of ITA 88(2) will be considered beginning in Paragraph 17-94.

17-71.   To use the ITA 88(1) rollover, the parent corporation must own at least 90 percent of each class of the subsidiary's shares. Therefore, not all winding-ups of subsidiaries qualify for the treatment described in ITA 88(1). A winding-up involving a subsidiary where a parent corporation has control, but owns less than 90 percent of the issued shares, would be implemented under the provisions of ITA 88(2). This provision would not allow for a tax free transfer of assets.

17-72.   If the parent has the required 90 percent or more ownership, it is permitted to exchange the subsidiary's shares for the assets of the subsidiary on a tax deferred basis. This transaction is very similar to an amalgamation, as it allows the assets of the two companies to be combined without recognizing any accrued capital gains or recaptured CCA on the transfers required to effect the combination. Note that this rollover provision only applies to ITA 88(1) transactions. It does not apply when an ITA 88(2) wind-up takes place.

17-73.   As with other rollovers, there are two components to a winding-up transaction. The first is the acquisition of the subsidiary's assets by the parent and the second is the deemed disposition of the subsidiary's shares by the parent. We will now turn our attention to these components.

Acquisition Of Assets

General Rules

17-74.   In an ITA 88(1) winding-up, the subsidiary is deemed to have disposed of its assets and the parent is deemed to have acquired the assets on the following basis:

- A cost of nil in the case of Canadian or foreign resource property.

- The "cost amount" to the subsidiary in the case of other property. Cost amount is defined in ITA 248(1) as UCC for depreciable property and adjusted cost base for non-depreciable capital property.

GRIP Balances

17-75.   ITA 89(6) applies to situations in which a CCPC has wound up a subsidiary under ITA 88(1). If the subsidiary was also a CCPC, this provision provides for a flow through of the subsidiary's GRIP balance to the GRIP balance of the parent company.

17-76.   A second, much more complex provision in ITA 89(6), applies when the subsidiary is a non-CCPC. This provision attempts to measure what the subsidiary's GRIP would have been at the end of its last taxation year had it been a CCPC at that time. This amount will also be included in the parent company's GRIP.

LRIP Balances

17-77.　ITA 89(10) applies when a non-CCPC has wound up a subsidiary under ITA 88(1). If the subsidiary was also a non-CCPC, this provision provides for a flow through of the subsidiary's LRIP balance to the LRIP balance of the parent company.

17-78.　Once again, a second and much more complex provision applies when the subsidiary is a CCPC. This provision attempts to measure what the subsidiary's LRIP would have been at the end of its last taxation year had it been a non-CCPC at that time. This amount will also be transferred to the parent company's LRIP.

Deferral Of Loss Carry Forwards

17-79.　As indicated previously, an ITA 88(1) winding up is very similar to an amalgamation. There is, however, one important difference between an amalgamation under ITA 87 and the winding-up of a subsidiary under ITA 88(1) and this involves loss carry forwards.

17-80.　As is generally the case under ITA 87, non-capital losses and net capital losses of the subsidiary will be available to the parent company when ITA 88(1) is used. However, under ITA 88(1.1), they will not become available until the first taxation year of the parent that begins after the date that the winding-up period commences.

> **EXAMPLE** If a parent's fiscal year begins on February 1 and the winding-up commences on February 15, 2018, the losses of the subsidiary will not be available to the parent until its fiscal year beginning February 1, 2019.

17-81.　In those situations where the subsidiary has a different year end than the parent, subsidiary losses are deemed to have occurred in the parent's fiscal year that includes the subsidiary's year end.

> **EXAMPLE** A parent has a June 30 year end, while its subsidiary has a September 30 year end. A winding-up commences on August 15, 2018 and is completed by August 31, 2018. The subsidiary has a non-capital loss for the period that is terminated on August 31, 2018 by the winding-up.

> **ANALYSIS** The loss will be deemed to have occurred in the parent's year ending June 30, 2019. This would suggest that the loss would not expire until the parent's year ending June 30, 2039. However, ITA 88(1.1)(b) limits the carry forward period to the period that would have been available to the subsidiary if it had not been wound up. This means that, in actual fact, the loss expires on June 30, 2038. The losses of the subsidiary are not available to the parent until its fiscal year beginning on July 1, 2019.

Exercise Seventeen - 7

Subject:　Losses In A Winding-Up

Park Inc. has a September 15 year end, while its 100 percent owned subsidiary, Side Ltd., has an October 31 year end. There is a winding-up of Side Ltd., using the rollover provision found in ITA 88(1), on June 30, 2018. Side Ltd. has a non-capital loss of $50,000 for the period November 1, 2017 to June 30, 2018. What is the earliest taxation year in which the $50,000 loss can be deducted? If it is not deducted then, in what taxation year will it expire?

SOLUTION available in print and online Study Guide.

Asset Bump-Up

17-82.　As we pointed out in our discussion of amalgamations, ITA 88(1) provides for a transfer of all or part of the excess of the purchase price of a 90 percent or more owned subsidiary's shares over the tax values of the subsidiary's assets. As noted, this bump-up is also available under ITA 87 when the parent owns 100 percent of the subsidiary. Under either of these provisions, the amount of this bump-up in tax values is limited by two amounts:

Winding-Up Of A 90 Percent Owned Subsidiary

1. The basic amount of the bump-up is found in ITA 88(1)(d)(i) and (i.1). This amount is the excess of the adjusted cost base of the subsidiary shares held by the parent, over the sum of:

    - the tax values of the subsidiary's net assets at the time of the winding-up; and
    - dividends paid by the subsidiary to the parent since the time of the acquisition (including capital dividends).

2. ITA 88(1)(d)(ii) further limits the amount that can be recognized to the excess of the fair market value of the subsidiary's non-depreciable capital property over their tax values at the time the parent acquired control of the subsidiary.

17-83.   The following example will illustrate these procedures:

EXAMPLE   On December 31, 2008, ParentCo acquires 100 percent of the outstanding shares of SubCo for $5,000,000. At that time, the only non-depreciable capital property owned by SubCo was land with a fair market value of $2,000,000 and a cost of $1,000,000. Between December 31, 2008 and December 31, 2018, SubCo pays dividends of $150,000 to ParentCo. On December 31, 2018, when the tax values of SubCo's assets total $4,200,000, SubCo is absorbed in a Section 88(1) winding-up.

ANALYSIS   The amount of the available asset bump-up will be the lesser of the two amounts described in Paragraph 17-82:

Adjusted Cost Base Of SubCo Shares		$5,000,000
Tax Values Of SubCo Assets At Winding-Up	($4,200,000)	
Dividends Paid By SubCo Since Its Acquisition	(150,000)	(4,350,000)
Excess		$ 650,000

Fair Market Value Of Land At Acquisition		$2,000,000
Cost Of Land At Acquisition		(1,000,000)
Excess		$1,000,000

17-84.   In this situation, the write-up of the land is restricted to the lower figure of $650,000. As a result, the subsidiary is deemed to have disposed of the land for $1,000,000 with no gain or loss. However, the parent is deemed to have acquired the same land for $1,650,000.

Exercise Seventeen - 8

Subject: Winding-Up Of A 90 Percent Or More Owned Subsidiary

On January 1, 2014, Procul Ltd. acquired 100 percent of the outstanding shares of Lorne Inc. at a cost of $1,200,000. At this point in time, the fair market value of Lorne's identifiable net assets was $850,000, including $270,000 for the Land. The tax values of the net assets at that time totalled $410,000.

On December 31, 2018, there is a winding-up of Lorne Inc. under the provisions of ITA 88(1). Lorne Inc. has paid no dividends since its acquisition by Procul Ltd. On December 31, 2018, the condensed Balance Sheet of Lorne Inc. is as follows:

Cash	$120,000
Land - At Cost (Purchased In 2010)	140,000
Depreciable Assets - At UCC (Purchased In 2010)	240,000
Total Assets	$500,000

Liabilities	$ 75,000
Shareholders' Equity	425,000
Total Equities	$500,000

Determine the tax values that will be recorded for Lorne Inc.'s assets after they have been incorporated into the records of Procul Ltd.

SOLUTION available in print and online Study Guide.

Disposition Of Shares

17-85. The disposition of shares component of the winding-up is straightforward. In general, the parent is deemed to have disposed of its shares of the subsidiary for proceeds equal to the adjusted cost base of the shares. As an example, assume the parent had paid $4,000,000 for the subsidiary's shares. This amount would also be the deemed proceeds of the disposition and there would be no capital gain.

17-86. An exception to this general rule will arise if the tax values of the subsidiary's net assets transferred and the paid up capital of the subsidiary's shares is more than the amount paid for the shares by the parent. In this case, the deemed proceeds of disposition will be the lesser of the paid up capital and the tax values of the net assets transferred. As a result, a capital gain can arise in these situations.

> **EXAMPLE** Prawn Ltd. owns 100 percent of the outstanding shares of Shrimp Inc. The cost of these shares was $4,000,000. This subsidiary is being wound up under the provisions of ITA 88(1). At the time of the winding-up, the tax values of the subsidiary's net assets total $4,800,000 and the PUC of the subsidiary's shares is $4,500,000.

> **ANALYSIS** Given these facts, the exception applies and the deemed proceeds of disposition would be the greater of the $4,000,000 cost of the shares and $4,500,000. This latter figure is the lesser of the $4,800,000 tax value of the subsidiary's net assets and the $4,500,000 PUC of the subsidiary's shares. This gives proceeds of disposition of $4,500,000 and a capital gain of $500,000 ($4,500,000 - $4,000,000). It is expected that such gains situations would be fairly rare and, because the proceeds are defined using cost except when it is less than the alternative values, there is no possibility of a capital loss.

Tax Planning Considerations - Amalgamation Vs. Winding-Up

17-87. Figure 17-4 (following page) contains a comparison of the features of an amalgamation under ITA 87 and the winding-up of a subsidiary that is at least 90 percent owned under ITA 88(1). A discussion of several of the items follows.

17-88. A significant consideration in deciding between an amalgamation under ITA 87 and a winding-up under ITA 88(1) is the ability to recognize all or part of the excess of investment cost over tax values. In the case of an ITA 87 amalgamation, recognition is possible only in cases involving a parent and a 100 percent owned subsidiary. Under ITA 88(1), recognition can occur as long as the parent owns 90 percent or more of each class of the subsidiary's issued shares.

17-89. Under either provision, it is possible that substantial tax values will disappear in the transaction. This would suggest that, when the adjusted cost base of the parent's investment is significantly greater than the tax values of the subsidiary's net assets, it may be better to continue to operate the subsidiary as a separate legal entity.

17-90. Under the amalgamation procedures, the predecessor corporations will have a deemed year end, which will count towards the expiry of time limited non-capital loss carry forwards. However, subject to the acquisition of control rules, the amalgamated company will be able to use the losses immediately.

Winding-Up Of A 90 Percent Owned Subsidiary

Figure 17 - 4 Comparison Of Amalgamation Under ITA 87 And Winding-Up Under ITA 88(1)		
Factor	**Amalgamation - ITA 87**	**Winding-Up Of 90% Owned Subsidiary - ITA 88(1)**
Valuation of assets	Tax values of assets of predecessor corporations carried forward to amalgamated company.	Tax values of subsidiary's assets carried forward to parent.
Recognition of some of the excess of investment cost over tax values	Recognition only if 100% owned subsidiary. If 100% owned, same treatment as ITA 88(1).	Write-up allowed if excess is associated with values of non-depreciable capital property.
Capital cost allowances	Claim in last year of predecessor and first year of amalgamated corporation.	No claim by subsidiary in year of winding-up, but available to parent in year of winding-up.
Loss carry forwards	Carried forward. However, their use may be limited if the amalgamation results in an acquisition of control.	Carried forward, but only available to parent beginning in taxation year after winding-up.
Year end	Deemed year end before amalgamation, counts one year for loss carry forwards.	Year end of parent corporation continued. Subsidiary has a terminal year end that counts as one taxation year.

17-91.   In contrast, the parent company that is using ITA 88(1) to absorb a 90 percent owned subsidiary will have its usual year end. However, it will not be able to use subsidiary loss carry forwards until the first taxation year beginning subsequent to the winding-up. In addition, the wind-up will count as an additional year in the expiry of time limited loss carry forwards. The analysis of this situation may be complicated by differing year ends for the two corporations.

17-92.   In considering CCA claims, ITA 87 creates a deemed year end for both predecessor corporations, requiring them to take pro rata CCA claims for what will normally be a short fiscal period. Under the ITA 88(1) procedures, the subsidiary disposes of its assets prior to its year end and, as a consequence, there will be no claim for CCA in the subsidiary's final year. However, CCA may be claimed on these assets by the parent company, subsequent to their being acquired under the winding-up procedures.

17-93.   If the subsidiary is not 100 percent owned, ITA 88(1) cannot be used unless the minority shareholder group is at arm's length with the parent company. If the minority share- holders are at arm's length and ITA 88(1) can be used to transfer the assets belonging to the controlling interest, an application of this Subsection will generally have tax consequences for the non-controlling interest. A winding-up will require reporting of capital gains and recap- tured CCA on property distributed by the subsidiary to the minority shareholders. Further, any liquidating dividend paid to the minority shareholders will be a taxable dividend.

We suggest you work Self Study Problem Seventeen-6 at this point.

Winding-Up Of A Canadian Corporation

The Nature Of The Transaction

Wind-Up (Liquidation) Vs. Rollover

17-94.   The winding-up procedures for a Canadian corporation, as described in ITA 88(2), are applicable where a corporation is being liquidated. If, for example, owners of a corporation decide that the business is no longer viable, winding-up procedures can be used in the disposition of the corporation's assets and the distribution of the resulting proceeds to the shareholders.

17-95.   In distinguishing the winding-up of a 90 percent or more owned subsidiary from a liquidating winding-up, you should note that the liquidation of a business has quite different objectives. In the case of the winding-up of a 90 percent or more owned subsidiary, we are usually not disposing of the business but, rather, are transferring its assets to a different legal entity that is controlled by the same investor or group of investors that previously had indirect control of its operations. This explains why a rollover is available on the winding-up of a 90 percent or more owned subsidiary, and no equivalent provision is available for the winding-up when a liquidation is under way.

Distributions To Shareholders

17-96.   While a winding-up can be implemented by distributing corporate assets directly to the shareholders, it is generally simpler for the corporation to liquidate its assets, pay off its creditors, pay any taxes that are applicable at the corporate level, and distribute the after tax proceeds to the shareholders.

17-97.   The distribution to shareholders becomes a fairly complex issue when a corporation is liquidated, as the proceeds available for distribution will consist of a combination of capital being returned, earnings that can be distributed on a tax free basis, and earnings that can only be distributed in the form of taxable dividends. A further complication is that there may be a combination of eligible and non-eligible dividends.

Disposition Of An Incorporated Business

17-98.   Later in this Chapter we will discuss the transfer of an incorporated business to a different group of owners. This can be accomplished through a sale of shares or, alternatively, through a sale of the corporation's assets. If the sale of assets is the more advantageous approach, the provisions of ITA 88(2) apply. That is, the sale of assets will be followed by a winding-up, with the after tax proceeds of the winding-up being distributed to the shareholders. While the business itself will continue to operate, the assets will now be on the books of a different legal entity.

Example

Basic Data

17-99.   The ITA 88(2) procedures will be illustrated in the following example.

> **EXAMPLE**   The Marker Company, a Canadian controlled private corporation, has been in operation for 20 years. It has a May 31 year end. On June 1, 2018, the following Balance Sheet, based on tax values, has been prepared in contemplation of liquidating the Company:

The Marker Company
Balance Sheet - As At June 1, 2018 (Tax Values)

Accounts Receivable (Net Realizable Value)	$ 12,000
Refundable Dividend Tax On Hand	8,000
Land - At Cost (Note One)	250,000
Building - At UCC (Note Two)	195,000
Total Assets	$465,000

Winding-Up Of A Canadian Corporation

Liabilities	Nil
Common Stock - No Par (Note Three)	$ 10,000
Retained Earnings (Note Three)	455,000
Total Equities	$465,000

Note One   The current fair market value of the Land is $300,000.

Note Two   The cost of the Building was $320,000. Its current fair market value is $350,000.

Note Three   The paid up capital and adjusted cost base of the common shares is $10,000. The Retained Earnings includes $75,000 in the capital dividend account. The Company's GRIP balance is nil.

The assets of the Company are sold for their fair market values which total $662,000 ($12,000 + $300,000 + $350,000). The Company has no other income for the taxation year. The provincial corporate tax rates are 4.5 percent on income eligible for the small business deduction and 14 percent on other corporate income.

Cash Available For Distribution

17-100.   At the corporate level, the proceeds from the disposition of the individual assets and the related tax effects are as follows:

Asset	Proceeds	Taxable Capital Gain	Active Business Income
Accounts Receivable	$ 12,000	Nil	Nil
Land	300,000	$25,000	Nil
Building	350,000	15,000	$125,000
Totals	$662,000	$40,000	$125,000

The Tax Payable on Marker's Taxable Income of $165,000 ($40,000 + $125,000) would be calculated as follows:

Federal Tax On Active Business Income [(38% - 10% - 18%)($125,000)]	$12,500
Federal Tax On Investment Income [(38% - 10% + 10-2/3%)($40,000)]	15,467
Part I Tax Payable	$27,967
Provincial Tax On Active Business Income [(4.5%)($125,000)]	5,625
Provincial Tax On Investment Income [(14%)($40,000)]	5,600
Total Tax Payable	$39,192

17-101.   The balance in the Refundable Dividend Tax On Hand account, subsequent to the preceding dispositions, is calculated as follows:

Balance Before Dispositions (From Balance Sheet)	$ 8,000
Addition (See Note)	12,267
Balance Available	$20,267

Note   The addition to the RDTOH would be $12,267, the least of the following figures:

- 30-2/3% Of Investment Income [(30-2/3%)($40,000)] $12,267

- 30-2/3% Of Taxable Income, Less Amount Eligible For Small Business Deduction [(30-2/3%)($165,000 - $125,000)] $12,267

- Federal Part I Tax Payable $27,967

17-102.   The after tax amount of cash that is available for distribution to shareholders is calculated as follows:

Gross Proceeds	$662,000
Tax Payable	(39,192)
Refundable Dividend Tax On Hand*	20,267
Available For Distribution	$643,075

*Given the size of the gross proceeds, the balance in the RDTOH is clearly going to be less than 38-1/3 percent of the dividends that will be declared.

Distribution To Shareholders

17-103.   The balance in the capital dividend account can be distributed to the shareholders as a tax free capital dividend. This balance is calculated as follows:

Balance Before Dispositions (Balance Sheet Note Three)	$ 75,000
Disposition Of Land	25,000
Disposition Of Building	15,000
Capital Dividend Account - Ending Balance	$115,000

17-104.   Prior to the sale of assets, the Company's GRIP balance was nil. As all of the income resulting from the sale of assets was either investment income or eligible for the small business deduction, there would be no addition to the GRIP account resulting from the sale of assets. This means that all dividends paid that are subject to tax would be non-eligible. The non-eligible taxable dividend component of the total distribution to the shareholders is calculated as follows:

Total Distribution	$643,075
Paid Up Capital	(10,000)
ITA 84(2) Deemed Dividend On Winding-Up*	$633,075
Capital Dividend Account	(115,000)
Non-Eligible Dividend Subject To Tax	$518,075

*As explained in Chapter 14, in a winding up, when the total distribution to shareholders exceeds the PUC of the shares being canceled, the excess is an ITA 84(2) deemed dividend. This deemed dividend is treated first as a capital dividend, if the appropriate election is filed. Any excess is treated as an eligible or non-eligible taxable dividend.

17-105.   Treatment of the $115,000 as a capital dividend is conditional on the appropriate election being made under ITA 83(2). The remaining taxable non-eligible dividend will be grossed up to $600,967 [(116%)($518,075)]. The dividend will provide a federal dividend tax credit of $60,285 [(8/11)(16%)($518,075)].

17-106.   In the ITA 54 definition of "proceeds of disposition", Paragraph j indicates that amounts that are deemed to be a dividend under ITA 84(2) are not included in this amount. As a consequence, in determining the capital gain resulting from the distribution to the shareholders, the ITA 84(2) dividend will be subtracted as follows:

Total Distribution to Shareholders	$643,075
ITA 84(2) Deemed Dividend	(633,075)
Deemed Proceeds Of Disposition	$ 10,000
Adjusted Cost Base Of Shares	(10,000)
Capital Gain	Nil

Exercise Seventeen - 9

Subject: Winding-Up Of A Canadian Corporation

Windown Inc. is a Canadian controlled private company. After disposing of all of its assets and paying all of its liabilities, including Tax Payable resulting from the asset dispositions, the Company is left with cash of $865,000. The PUC of the Company's shares is equal to their adjusted cost base, an amount of $88,000. After the sale of assets, the Company has an RDTOH account balance of $47,000, a capital dividend account balance of $26,000, and a GRIP of nil. Determine the tax consequences to the shareholders associated with making the maximum distribution of cash to shareholders on the winding-up of Windown Inc. on June 1, 2018. Assume that appropriate elections will be made to minimize the taxes that will be paid by the shareholders.

SOLUTION available in print and online Study Guide.

We suggest you work Self Study Problem Seventeen-7 at this point.

Convertible Properties

Application

17-107.   There is one more rollover that you should be familiar with. ITA 51 contains a provision that permits a holder of shares or debt of a corporation to exchange those securities for shares of that corporation on a tax free basis. For this rollover provision to apply, the following two conditions must be met:

- The exchange must not involve any consideration other than the securities that are being exchanged.

- The exchange must not be part of a reorganization of capital or a rollover of property by shareholders to a corporation under ITA 85 or ITA 86.

17-108.   In practical terms, this provision is designed to accommodate a tax deferred conversion of debt or preferred shares of a corporation into preferred or common shares of the same corporation.

> **EXAMPLE**   An investor acquires convertible bonds with a par value of $10,000 at a price equal to par value. The bonds are convertible into 50 shares of the issuing company's common stock and, at the time of purchase, this common stock is trading at $18 per share (the conversion value of the bonds is $9,000). The bonds are converted when the common shares are trading at $22 per share.
>
> **ANALYSIS**   The conversion of the bonds is a disposition and, in the absence of a special provision, the tax consequences would be as follows:

Proceeds Of Disposition [(50)($22)]	$11,000
Adjusted Cost Base	(10,000)
Capital Gain	$1,000

17-109.   The ITA serves to provide relief in this type of situation. ITA 51(1)(c), deems such exchanges not to be a disposition. Given this deeming provision, no gain will be recognized.

17-110.   Going with this provision, ITA 51(1)(d) deems the cost of the acquired shares to be equal to the cost of the shares or debt given up. In effect, ITA 51 allows convertible securities to be converted with no immediate tax consequences. No gain or loss is recorded and the adjusted cost base of investors' securities remains unchanged.

Other Considerations

17-111. A conversion provision can assist corporations seeking to add an equity kicker to enhance the marketability of their debt or preferred shares. In addition, conversion arrangements can be used to facilitate income splitting within a corporation. Different classes of shares can be used to allow the redistribution of income and, with the ability to convert different classes of shares on a tax deferred basis, an additional element of flexibility is introduced into such arrangements.

17-112. ITA 51.1 contains a similar provision to cover situations under which bondholders of a particular company are allowed to convert their holdings into a different debt security of that company. Here again, there is a tax deferred rollover with the adjusted cost base of the old bond holding becoming the creditor's adjusted cost base for the new debt security.

17-113. We would call your attention to the fact that the accounting rules on debt that is convertible into common or preferred shares require that the proceeds from its issuance be divided between the amount paid by investors for the liability component of the financial instrument and the amount paid for the equity option (see IAS 32, *Financial Instruments: Presentation*). This important issue has not, at this point in time, been given recognition in tax legislation. For tax purposes, the full amount received for convertible debt must be allocated to the debt component of the security.

Sale Of An Incorporated Business

Alternatives

17-114. Assume that you are the sole shareholder of an incorporated business and that you have decided to dispose of your company. If the business has a value that extends beyond your personal services, it should be possible to arrange a sale of the business. In approaching the problem of selling an incorporated business, you are usually confronted with the following three alternatives:

- Sale of the individual assets of the corporation, on a piecemeal basis.
- Sale of the total net assets of the corporation, including any unrecorded intangibles such as goodwill.
- Sale of the shares of the corporation.

17-115. In the next section, consideration will be given to the advantages and disadvantages, as well as to the tax effects that are associated with each of these alternatives. However, before turning our attention to these alternatives, some attention must be given to the tax treatment of restrictive covenants.

Restrictive Covenants (a.k.a. Non-Competition Agreements)

General Rules

17-116. Restrictive covenants are arrangements under which a taxpayer agrees to have his ability to provide goods or services restricted in one or more ways. Such agreements may relate to particular products or services (e.g., the taxpayer will not provide audit services) and may refer to specific geographic areas (e.g., the taxpayer will not provide audit services in the greater Calgary area). They may or may not be limited in terms of time. It is not uncommon, particularly in the case of owner-managed businesses, for the purchaser to require the seller to sign a restrictive covenant.

17-117. ITA 56.4(2) requires that, in general, 100 percent of payments made to a taxpayer for agreeing to a restrictive covenant be included in income as an "other source" under subdivision d. Fortunately for taxpayers, ITA 56.4(3) contains three important exceptions to this general rule.

Exceptions To 100 Percent Income Inclusion

17-118. These exceptions are as follows:

ITA 56.4(3)(a) - Employment Income In cases where the payment relates to past employment with the payor, the receipt will be treated by the recipient as employment income. While 100 percent of the amount would still be subject to tax, classification as employment income would mean that it does not have to be included in the recipient's income until it is received (employment income is on a cash basis). When this exception is applicable, ITA 56.4(4)(a) allows the payor to treat the payment as wages paid or payable.

ITA 56.4(3)(b) - Class 14.1   Provided the payor and recipient file a joint election, the restrictive covenant payment can be treated as an acquisition of a Class 14.1 asset by the payor, and as Class 14.1 proceeds of disposition by the recipient.

From the point of view of the payor, this is an unfavourable treatment. Instead of being a fully deductible expense, the payment is added to Class 14.1 where it will only be deductible on a 5 percent declining balance basis.

However, from the point of view of the recipient, this is a very favourable approach. As the intangible asset that is reflected in the restrictive covenant payment will normally have a capital cost of nil, the entire proceeds of disposition will be treated as a capital gain, only one-half of which will be taxable. In the absence of this treatment, the full amount of the restrictive covenant payment would be taxable to the recipient.

ITA 56.4(3)(c) - Sale Of An Eligible Interest   An eligible interest is an interest in shares in a corporation that carries on business, or in a partnership that carries on business. In a situation where a restrictive covenant is sold in conjunction with an eligible interest, the amount received can be added to the proceeds of disposition. As was the case with the ITA 56.4(3)(b) exception, the payor and the recipient must file a joint election for this exception to apply. When this exception is applicable, ITA 56.4(4)(c) requires the purchaser to treat the payment as a cost of the purchase.

If this addition creates or increases a capital gain, only one-half of this amount will be subject to tax. Note that the application of this provision is more complex when there is more than one restrictive covenant involved in the sale of a single eligible interest.

17-119.   The first of these exceptions, treatment of the restrictive covenant payment as employment income, is not relevant to the material in this Chapter. However, the other two exceptions are very significant when a business is being sold and will be given further attention in our discussion of the alternative ways in which a business can be sold.

Sale Of Individual Assets
General Procedures
17-120.   Disposing of a business via a piece-by-piece sale of individual assets would only occur in certain situations. These could be described as follows:

- The business has not been successful in producing an adequate rate of return on the assets invested. In such situations, the most reasonable course of action may be the sale of individual assets.

- Some owner-managed businesses have income producing activities that are so closely tied to the skills of the owner/manager that the sale of the business independent of those skills would not be feasible.

17-121.   This type of disposition would only be appropriate in limited circumstances. Given that the circumstances associated with the particular business will dictate whether this approach will be used, there is no need to devote any attention to the advantages or disadvantages of this alternative.

Restrictive Covenants - Sale Of Individual Assets
17-122.   In the situations that are involved here, it is unlikely that a restrictive covenant will be used. However, if this was to occur, treatment of the amount involved as an acquisition/disposition of a Class 14.1 asset would be possible. This treatment will be discussed in the next section dealing with the sale of total assets as a going concern.

Sale Of Assets As A Going Concern

General Procedures

17-123.   In contrast to a liquidation, where the assets are sold on an individual basis, the purchaser in this situation would acquire the corporation's assets as a going concern and, in so doing, would acquire any goodwill or other intangible assets that might be associated with the enterprise.

17-124.   As was the case with the piece by piece sale of individual assets in a liquidation, the sale of all assets as a going concern may result in a combination of business income, capital gains, recapture, and terminal losses.

17-125.   In both types of asset sales, you should note that there are really two transactions involved. The first transaction involves the sale of assets and the payment of liabilities at the corporate level. Included in this process will be the determination of any tax liability resulting from the sale of the assets. At this point, the corporate assets would consist entirely of the after tax proceeds resulting from the disposition of the tangible and other assets of the corporation. In most situations, the owner will choose to distribute these assets and wind up the corporation.

17-126.   This distribution of the after tax proceeds of the sale of corporate assets is the second transaction and, in general, it will involve income tax effects for the recipient share-holders. Given this two transaction process, a complete analysis of the alternatives of selling the assets of the business versus disposing of the shares will require dealing with both taxation on the corporation as a result of disposing of the assets, and personal taxation as a result of distributing the after tax proceeds of this sale.

17-127.   In dealing with the sale of corporate assets, an understanding of the tax effects associated with such dispositions is required. These effects can be outlined as follows:

Cash   In most circumstances, the cash of the business will be retained in the business. If it is "sold", there will be no tax consequences associated with its disposition.

Accounts Receivable   In the absence of any special election, the sale of accounts receivable as a component of the sale of a business will be treated as a capital transaction. This means that any difference between the face value and the consideration received will be treated as a capital loss, only one-half of which will be deductible.

However, ITA 22 provides for a joint election to treat the sale of receivables as an income transaction. This allows the purchaser to treat any difference between the amount paid for the receivables and the amount actually collected as a bad debt expense. A more detailed description of this election is presented in Chapter 6.

Inventories   Even when inventories are sold as part of the sale of a business, any difference between the sales price and the vendor's cost will be treated as ordinary business income. This is provided for in ITA 23 and, unlike the situation with the ITA 22 treatment of receivables, no election is required. For the purchaser, the transfer price becomes the tax cost that will eventually be allocated to cost of goods sold.

Prepayments   The *Income Tax Act* does not recognize prepayments as an asset. This means that some amounts that are treated as prepayments in the accounting records have, for tax purposes, been deducted as expenses. As a result of this, when such balances are sold for their fair market value, the proceeds will be included in income.

Non-Depreciable Capital Assets   The most common non-depreciable capital assets of a business are land and investments. Depending on the amount of consideration received for these assets, the transferor will have a capital gain or loss. With respect to capital losses, they can only be deducted from capital gains.

If some of the consideration being paid for these assets is deferred, the corporation can use capital gains reserves to defer part of the applicable taxation. However, the use of this technique would require continuing the corporation through the deferral period and this may not be in keeping with the objectives of the vendor.

For the purchaser, the adjusted cost base of non-depreciable capital assets will be the purchase price, which presumably is the fair market value.

Depreciable Assets   The disposition of a depreciable asset can result in recapture, a terminal loss, or some combination of recapture and a capital gain. Unlike capital gains, recapture and terminal losses will be subject to 100 percent inclusion in, or deduction from, active business income and will be included in income eligible for the small business deduction.

As was the case with non-depreciable capital assets, if some of the consideration for these assets is not received immediately, reserves can be used to defer the taxation of capital gains.

For the purchaser, the capital cost of depreciable assets will be the purchase price, which presumably is the fair market value.

Goodwill   If goodwill is present, some amount of the consideration received for the going concern will be allocated to goodwill. Any allocated amount will be treated as proceeds of disposition for a Class 14.1 asset. As the capital cost of goodwill will most commonly be nil, when the lesser of the proceeds of disposition and the capital cost of the goodwill is subtracted from any Class 14.1 balance, it commonly results in the entire proceeds of disposition allocated to goodwill being treated as a capital gain.

The purchaser of the going concern will add the allocated cost of the goodwill to Class 14.1 where it will be subject to CCA on a 5 percent declining balance basis. The half-year rule is applicable to this Class.

Restrictive Covenants - Sale Of Total Assets
17-128.   Restrictive covenants may take one of two different forms when there is a sale of the total assets of the corporation. If it is anticipated that the corporation will continue in business, the agreement can be between the purchaser of the assets and the corporation. In contrast, if the corporation is to be liquidated, the agreement will likely be between the purchaser and the former owner(s) of the shares. It is also possible that the purchaser will require both the corporation and the former shareholders to sign a restrictive covenant.

17-129.   Whether the agreement is between the purchaser and the corporation or, alternatively, the purchaser and the shareholder(s) of the corporation, treatment of the amount as an acquisition/disposition of a Class 14.1 asset is possible. This approach is conditional on the parties being prepared to make the required joint election.

17-130.   If the election is made, the consideration given for the restrictive covenant will be treated as the proceeds of disposition of a Class 14.1 asset. As previously discussed, in most situations, this will result in the amount being treated as a capital gain.

17-131.   If the payment is eligible for the joint election and the election is made, the purchaser will treat the payment for the restrictive covenant as the acquisition cost of a Class 14.1 asset. However, if the payment is not eligible, or if no joint election is filed, ITA 56.4 provides no specific guidance for the purchaser.

17-132.   This means that the purchaser will have to apply basic principles from other Sections of the *Income Tax Act*. Without regard to the fact that the vendor will be taxed on the full amount of the payment under ITA 56.4(2), the purchaser's treatment may involve a deduction of the full amount of the payment, or an addition of the payment to one or more assets. The specific treatment by the purchaser will depend on the nature of the payment as determined under general tax principles.

Sale Of Shares
General Procedures
17-133.   In terms of accounting, legal, and tax considerations, this is the simplest way to sell a business. The calculation of the gain on the sale only requires the adjusted cost base of the

shares to be subtracted from the proceeds received from their disposition. Any resulting difference will be a capital gain or loss, and will be subject to the usual treatment accorded to share dispositions.

17-134.   In preparing for the sale of shares, a corporation will declare tax-free capital dividends to the extent of its capital dividend account and taxable dividends for any additional amount which will generate a dividend refund if there is an RDTOH balance.

Lifetime Capital Gains Deduction

17-135.   If the corporation is a "qualified small business corporation" as defined in ITA 110.6(1), the disposition of shares may qualify for the lifetime capital gains deduction. The conditions associated with the designation "qualified small business corporation" are discussed in Chapter 11. Note here, however, that this deduction is only available on the sale of shares by an individual. If the shares are sold by a corporation, this valuable deduction is not available.

Restrictive Covenants - Sale Of Shares

17-136.   In cases where a business disposition involves a sale of shares, any restrictive covenant that is required will involve an agreement between the purchaser of the shares and the vendor of the shares. In this situation the exception under ITA 56.4(3)(c) (see Paragraph 17-118) becomes important. The sale of shares would be a disposition of an eligible interest and this would allow the taxpayer receiving payment for the restrictive covenant to include it as part of the proceeds of disposition. As such, it would serve to create or increase a capital gain on the sale, only one-half of which would be taxable.

17-137.   Note that this treatment requires the vendor and purchaser to file a joint election and, if they fail to do so, the vendor will have to include the full amount of the payment in income when it is received or becomes receivable. If the election is filed, the purchaser will include the payment in the cost of his purchase. If the election is not filed, the treatment by the purchaser will require the application of general tax principles.

Evaluation Of Alternatives

Advantages Of Selling Shares

17-138.   Generally speaking, the vendor of a business will favour selling shares over selling assets. Factors favouring this alternative are as follows:

- The sale of shares offers the simplicity of a single transaction. In contrast, in a sale of assets, the vendor must deal with the legal and tax consequences arising at the corporate level. In addition, the vendor must steer the corporation through a winding-up procedure and deal with the personal tax consequences of these procedures. The greater complexity will require additional personal efforts on the part of the vendor. Also, the legal and accounting fees associated with these transactions are likely to be significant.

- Any income produced by the sale of shares will usually be reported as capital gains. At worst, only one-half of such gains are taxable. At best, the taxable gains may be reduced or eliminated through the use of the lifetime capital gains deduction. If assets are sold by the corporation, some of the resulting income could be recaptured CCA, which must be included in income in full. In addition, if capital gains arise on the sale of assets, they will be treated as investment income to the corporation and will not be eligible for the small business deduction.

- If the enterprise has an unused non-capital loss carry forward, it will still be available to the enterprise if shares are sold. Any non-capital loss carry forwards are, of course, subject to the acquisition of control rules, requiring that they be applied against income earned in the same business in which the losses were incurred. However, if the sale of assets alternative is chosen, such loss carry forward balances will be completely unavailable to the purchaser.

- When a payment for a restrictive covenant is a component of the sale of shares, the vendor may be able to treat the amount received as an addition to his proceeds of disposition, rather than an amount that has to be fully included in income. This treatment is conditional on the vendor and purchaser filing a joint election, in which case the purchaser will add the amount paid to his acquisition cost.

- A sale of assets could result in the payment of land transfer taxes that would not be applicable if shares are sold.

Advantages Of Purchasing Assets

17-139.   As just described, there are a number of advantages that can be associated with selling shares, most of them benefitting the vendor. From the point of view of the purchaser, a purchase of assets is generally more desirable than a purchase of shares. Some of the advantages of purchasing assets are as follows:

- In acquiring assets, the purchaser acquires a completely new, and usually higher, set of tax values for the assets transferred. For example, consider a depreciable asset with a capital cost of $100,000, a UCC of $40,000, and a fair market value of $400,000. If shares are acquired, the CCA deductions available to the corporation will continue to be based on $40,000 and, if the assets are subsequently disposed of, capital gains will be determined from the original capital cost of $100,000. In contrast, if the asset was purchased in an arm's length transaction for its fair market value of $400,000, this amount would be the capital cost and UCC to the purchaser. This bump-up in asset values and the availability of higher CCA claims can significantly reduce the tax liabilities of the purchaser.

- Goodwill can be recognized when assets are acquired. The CCA deductions related to Class 14.1 are not available if shares are acquired.

- In situations where the purchaser has an existing corporation, he may prefer to have that corporation acquire the assets, rather than acquiring the shares of an additional corporation and incurring the administrative costs associated with maintaining a second corporation.

- If shares are acquired, all of the assets must be acquired. In a sale of assets, redundant assets can be left out of an acquisition of assets. Note, however, if there are unwanted assets, it is fairly common for these assets to be disposed of prior to the sale of shares.

- If shares are acquired, the existing liabilities of the corporation will continue to be in place. It is possible that the purchaser can obtain financing on more favourable terms, in which case he would prefer to acquire assets.

- If shares are acquired, the purchaser may become responsible for any future tax reassessments. While this exposure could occur because the purchased corporation continues to operate, it is usually covered in the buy and sell agreement for the transaction. This agreement is normally written to protect the purchaser from future problems in this area.

- A further problem relates to potential non-tax liabilities related to product or environmental liabilities. Again, because the purchased corporation is continuing to operate, it could be responsible for such liabilities. However, this is another issue that is normally dealt with in the buy and sell agreement.

- Most of the preceding discussion has implicitly assumed that the corporation's assets have fair market values in excess of their related tax values. If this is not the case and unrealized losses are present, selling assets may be advantageous to the vendor as well as the purchaser. This is based on the fact that the vendor would prefer to have fully deductible terminal or business losses, rather than capital losses that are only one-half deductible against taxable capital gains.

Conclusion

17-140.   While each situation needs to be evaluated on the basis of the specific assets and values involved, in general, a vendor will wish to sell shares while a purchaser will wish to acquire assets. As a result, negotiations will usually involve higher prices being offered for the assets of the business than are offered for the shares of the incorporated business.

Example

17-141.   To illustrate the sale of an incorporated business, we will use the following example.

> **EXAMPLE**   Mr. O'Leary owns all of the outstanding shares of O'Leary Ltd., a Canadian controlled private corporation. Mr. O'Leary has reached retirement age and wishes to dispose of the business. He has received an offer to buy the shares for $180,000 or, alternatively, the assets of the business for $200,000. All of the liabilities of the business have been settled in preparation for the sale.
>
> The cost of Mr. O'Leary's original investment was $50,000. As no additional investment has been made, this is also his adjusted cost base and paid up capital for the outstanding shares. The provincial tax rate on business income eligible for the small business deduction is 4.5 percent. The provincial rate on all other income is 14 percent. The corporation has no balance in its RDTOH account, its capital dividend account, or its GRIP account. Mr. O'Leary is subject to a combined federal/provincial rate of 46 percent on non-dividend income and 31 percent on non-eligible dividends received.
>
> Relevant information on the assets of the business is as follows:

Asset	Cost	Fair Market Value
Cash	$ 5,000	$ 5,000
Receivables	10,000	10,000
Inventories	55,000	60,000
Land	20,000	40,000
Plant And Equipment (UCC = $45,000)	95,000	60,000
Goodwill	Nil	25,000
Total	$185,000	$200,000

Sale Of Shares For $180,000

17-142.   With respect to the sale of shares, the tax consequences are as follows:

Proceeds Of Disposition	$180,000
Adjusted Cost Base	(50,000)
Capital Gain	$130,000
Inclusion Rate	1/2
Taxable Capital Gain (For Mr. O'Leary)	$ 65,000

17-143.   At a 46 percent rate, the normal Tax Payable on this gain would be $29,900, leaving Mr. O'Leary with after tax funds of $150,100 ($180,000 - $29,900). However, it is likely that O'Leary Ltd. is a qualified small business corporation. If this is the case, the lifetime capital gains deduction could be used to eliminate all of the taxes on this disposition of shares, resulting in Mr. O'Leary retaining the entire $180,000 proceeds. Alternative minimum tax might be applicable if the capital gain is sheltered through the lifetime capital gains deduction.

Sale Of Assets For $200,000

17-144.   The tax consequences resulting from selling the assets are calculated as follows:

Account		Taxable Income
Inventories ($60,000 - $55,000)		$ 5,000
Plant And Equipment - Recaptured CCA ($60,000 - $45,000)		15,000
Active Business Income		$20,000
Taxable Capital Gains		
Land [($40,000 - $20,000)(1/2)]	$10,000	
Goodwill [(1/2)($25,000)]	12,500	22,500
Corporate Taxable Income		$42,500

17-145.   The resulting Tax Payable would be calculated as follows:

	Federal Tax On:		
	Active Business Income [(38% - 10% - 18%)($20,000)]		$ 2,000
	Investment Income [(38% - 10% + 10-2/3%)($22,500)]		8,700
Federal Part I Tax			$10,700
Provincial Tax On Active Business Income [(4.5%)($20,000)]			900
Provincial Tax On Investment Income [(14%)($22,500)]			3,150
Total Tax Payable			$14,750

17-146.   There is no opening balance in the RDTOH. The addition to the account, which will be the balance in the account is $6,900, the least of the following three figures:

• 30-2/3% Of Investment Income [(30-2/3%)($22,500)]	$ 6,900
• 30-2/3% Of Taxable Income, Less Amount Eligible For Small Business Deduction [(30-2/3%)(42,500 - $20,000)]	$ 6,900
• Federal Part I Tax Payable	$10,700

17-147.   The allocation to the capital dividend account would be as follows:

Non-Taxable Portion Of Capital Gain On:	
Land [(1/2)($20,000)]	$10,000
Goodwill [(1/2)($25,000)]	12,500
Capital Dividend Account	$22,500

17-148.   Given the preceding analysis of the liquidation of the corporate assets, the net cash retained by Mr. O'Leary after the distribution of corporate assets can be calculated as follows:

Proceeds Of Disposition - Sale Of Assets	$200,000
Corporate Tax Payable (Before Dividend Refund)	(14,750)
Dividend Refund (Note)	6,900
Funds Available for Distribution	$192,150
Paid Up Capital	(50,000)
ITA 84(2) Deemed Dividend	$142,150
Capital Dividend (Balance In Account - Election Required)	(22,500)
Deemed Taxable Dividend	$119,650
Tax Rate (On Non-Eligible Dividends Received)	31%
Personal Tax Payable On Non-Eligible Dividend	$ 37,092

Note   Technically, the dividend refund is the lesser of the $6,900 balance in the RDTOH account and 38-1/3 percent of taxable dividends paid. However, given the size of the distribution in this example, it is clear that $6,900 will be the lower figure.

17-149.   There would be no capital gain on the distribution as shown in the following:

Total Distribution	$192,150
ITA 84(2) Deemed Dividend	(142,150)
Deemed Proceeds Of Disposition	$ 50,000
Adjusted Cost Base Of The Shares	(50,000)
Capital Gain	Nil

17-150.   Based on the preceding calculations, Mr. O'Leary's after tax retention from the sale of assets would be calculated as follows:

Amount Distributed	$192,150
Tax On Deemed Dividend	(37,092)
Cash Retained	$155,058

17-151.   This amount is larger than the $150,100 that would be retained from a sale of shares if the resulting capital gain was subject to tax. However, it is significantly smaller than the $180,000 that would be retained from a sale of shares if the lifetime capital gains deduction could be used to eliminate the entire gain on the sale.

We suggest you work Self Study Problem Seventeen-8 at this point.

Additional Supplementary Self Study Problems Are Available Online.

Key Terms Used In This Chapter

17-152.   The following is a list of the key terms used in this Chapter. These terms, and their meanings, are compiled in the Glossary located at the back of the Study Guide.

Adjusted Cost Base	Parent Company
Amalgamation	Proceeds Of Disposition
Business Combination	PUC
Canadian Corporation	Qualified Small Business Corporation
Control (IAS 27)	Recapture Of CCA
Convertible Property	Redemption Of Shares
Corporation	Reorganization Of Capital (ITA 86)
Disposition	Restrictive Covenant
Exchange Of Shares In A	Rollover
Reorganization (ITA 86)	Share For Share Exchange (ITA 85.1)
Gift	Small Business Corporation
Goodwill	Subsidiary
Legal Stated Capital	Taxable Canadian Corporation
Lifetime Capital Gains Deduction	Terminal Loss
Merger	Vertical Amalgamation
Non-Share Consideration	Winding-Up Of A 90% Owned Subsidiary
Paid Up Capital	Winding-Up Of A Canadian Corporation

References

17-153.   For more detailed study of the material in this Chapter, we refer you to the following:

ITA 22	Sale Of Accounts Receivable
ITA 23	Sale Of Inventory
ITA 24	Ceasing To Carry On Business
ITA 51	Convertible Property
ITA 51.1	Conversion Of Debt Obligation
ITA 54	Definitions (Proceeds Of Disposition)
ITA 84(2)	Distribution on Winding-Up, Etc.
ITA 84(3)	Redemption Of shares
ITA 84(5)	Amount Distributed Or Paid Where A Share ...
ITA 85	Transfer Of Property To Corporation By Shareholders
ITA 85.1	Share For Share Exchange
ITA 86	Exchange Of Shares By A Shareholder In Course Of Reorganization Of Capital
ITA 87	Amalgamations
ITA 88(1)	Winding-Up (Of A 90 Percent Owned Subsidiary)
ITA 88(2)	Winding-Up Of A Canadian Corporation
ITA 110.6	Capital Gains Exemption
S4-F3-C1	Price Adjustment Clause
S4-F5-C1	Share For Share Exchange
S4-F7-C1	Amalgamations of Canadian Corporations
IT-115R2	Fractional Interest In Shares
IT-126R2	Meaning Of "Winding-Up"
IT-140R3	Buy-Sell Agreements
IT-142R3	Settlement Of Debts On The Winding-up Of A Corporation
IT-146R4	Shares Entitling Shareholders To Choose Taxable Or Capital Dividends
IT-149R4	Winding-Up Dividend
IT-188R	Sale Of Accounts Receivable
IT-243R4	Dividend Refund To Private Corporations
IT-287R2	Sale Of Inventory
IT-302R3	Losses Of A Corporation - The Effect That Acquisitions Of Control, Amalgamations, And Windings-Up Have On Their Deductibility - After January 15, 1987
IT-444R	Corporations — Involuntary Dissolutions

Problems For Self Study (Online)

To provide practice in problem solving, there are Self Study and Supplementary Self Study problems available on MyLab Accounting.

Within the text we have provided an indication of when it would be appropriate to work each Self Study problem. The detailed solutions for Self Study problems can be found in the print and online Study Guide.

We provide the Supplementary Self Study problems for those who would like additional practice in problem solving. The detailed solutions for the Supplementary Self Study problems are available online, not in the Study Guide.

The .PDF file "Self Study Problems for Volume 2" on MyLab contains the following for Chapter 17:

- 8 Self Study problems,
- 5 Supplementary Self Study problems, and
- detailed solutions for the Supplementary Self Study problems.

Assignment Problems

(The solutions for these problems are only available in
the solutions manual that has been provided to your instructor.)

Assignment Problem Seventeen - 1

(Section 85.1 Share For Share Exchange After ITA 85 Rollover)

In 2010, Sandy O'Brien opened a business, Sandy's Frames, that specialized in providing frames for high end paintings and drawings. From 2010 through 2013, he operated the business as a proprietorship. He did not incorporate as he needed all of the income produced by the business to cover his living expenses.

However, by 2013 his profits had increased to the point where he no longer needed all of the income produced by the business. Given this, he decided to incorporate.

His accountant advised him that he could avoid current taxation by using the provisions of ITA 85(1) to transfer his business assets to the new corporation. To facilitate this, on January 1, 2014, the following values were established for the assets of the business.

Tax Values Of The Business Assets	$1,820,000
Fair Market Value Of The Business Assets	$3,140,000

On this date, the assets are transferred to a new corporation, Frames Ltd., at an elected value of $1,820,000. As consideration, Sandy took back a note payable for $900,000, redeemable preferred shares with a fair market value of $920,000, and 6,950 common shares with a fair market value of $1,320,000. No other shares were issued during the years under consideration.

Over the next few years, the business continues to expand and prosper and, on January 1, 2018, he receives an offer from Conglomerate Inc., a large public company, for all of the common shares. Under terms of this offer, Sandy will give up all of the common shares of Frames Ltd. in return for a separate class of shares issued by Conglomerate Inc. These shares have a fair market value of $1,970,000. In addition, subsequent to the exchange transaction, Sandy's preferred shares will be redeemed for $920,000. Frames Ltd. does not have GRIP balance or an RDTOH balance at this time. Sandy and the controlling shareholders of Conglomerate Inc. deal with each other at arm's length.

While Sandy has been very successful with his business, he has made a number of very bad real estate investments. As a consequence, as of January 1, 2018, he has a $420,000 net capital loss carry forward.

Assume that Frames Ltd. does not meet the criteria for qualification as a small business corporation.

Required:

A. Advise Sandy with respect to the tax consequences that would arise for him from the redemption of his preferred shares and the acceptance of the offer from the public company for the exchange of shares. Your answer should consider both the application of ITA 85.1 and opting out of this provision.

B. Indicate the adjusted cost base of the Frames Inc. common shares on the books of Conglomerate Ltd.

C. Advise Sandy as to the alternative approaches that could be used to utilize his net capital loss carry forward in conjunction with the share exchange.

Assignment Problem Seventeen - 2
(ITA 85(1) and ITA 86(1) Share Exchange)

Homer Parsons opened an unincorporated retail business in 2011. This business, known as Parsons' Paranormal Services, provides services related to helping individuals make contact with dead loved ones.

Homer quickly gains a reputation for success in such matters and, by 2014, he has opened several locations in the city and retained a number of very wealthy clients. As a result, the business is producing income far in excess of his current needs. At this time, in order to defer current taxation, Homer decides to incorporate. His accountant advises him that he can do this on tax free basis by using the provisions of ITA 85(1).

On January 1, 2014, the assets of the business have tax values (adjusted cost base or UCC) which total $1,986,000. The estimated fair market value of these assets is $2,950,000. On this date the assets are transferred to a new corporation at an elected value of $1,986,000. As consideration for the business assets, Homer takes back a note payable for $1,500,000 and common shares with a fair market value of $1,450,000. The new company, named Parsons Paranormal Inc. (PPI), will have a December 31 year end.

In its corporate form, the business continues to operate very successfully and, on January 1, 2018, the assets have tax values of $7,347,000. Their fair market value total $8,450,000.

Homer has an adult son who appears to have paranormal skills superior to his own. His name is Orpheus and, since 2014, he has become increasingly active in the business. As Homer now has sufficient resources to retire comfortably, he would like to transfer the future growth of the business to Orpheus.

To accomplish this, he is going to exchange his common shares in PPI for $5,000,000 in cash, plus redeemable preferred shares with a fair market value of $3,450,000. Subsequent to this exchange, Orpheus will acquire 200 common shares in PPI at a total cost of $20,000.

PPI does not have a GRIP balance or an RDTOH balance on January 1, 2018.

Required:

A. Determine the tax consequences for Homer that will result from his exchange of shares. As part of your answer, you should indicate both the adjusted cost base and the PUC of his preferred shares.

B. Determine the tax consequences for Homer that would result from the redemption of his preferred shares on February 1, 2018 for their fair market value of $3,450,000.

Assignment Problem Seventeen - 3
(Section 86 Reorganization With Gift)

Lartex Inc. was incorporated in 2009 to produce cutting edge sports clothing. At this time, the Company issued 20,000 common shares for cash of $50 per share. Of these shares, 15,000 were purchased by Lara Text, with the remainder being purchased by Bentley Rolls, an arm's length individual who was her mentor.

In 2013, Bentley dies suddenly while running a marathon. Lara acquires the 5,000 shares that were purchased by Bentley Rolls from his estate for $90 per share. In order to finance the firm's rapidly expanding operations, the Company issues an additional 5,000 shares to Lara for the same $90 per share price.

Lara has a son, Lance Text, whose dream is to make Lartex a household name. Starting in 2014, he seeks out the most challenging and rigorous courses in the business program at his university. During the following two years, he excels at his courses, especially his tax courses which he considers the most interesting and rewarding. To encourage him in his studies, during 2016, when the estimated fair market value of a share was $100, Lara gives Lance a gift of 2,500 shares of Lartex Inc.

On January 1, 2018, the fair market value of the Lartex Inc. shares has increased to $120 per share. By this time, Lance has become increasingly active in helping her with the operations of Lartex Inc. Given this, she would like to transfer the future growth in Lartex Inc. to Lance using the provisions of ITA 86.

In order to implement this transfer, she exchanges her 22,500 shares of Lartex Inc. for a $500,000 note and redeemable preferred shares with a fair market value of $2,000,000. The only remaining common shares will be the 2,500 shares owned by Lance. At this time, the Company does not have a GRIP balance.

Required:

A. Describe the immediate tax consequences of this transaction to Lara Text, including the following:

- the amount of any gift that Lara has made to Lance;
- the PUC of the new preferred shares;
- the adjusted cost base of the new preferred shares;
- the amount of any deemed dividends arising on the exchange; and
- any capital gain or loss resulting from the exchange of the common shares.

B. Describe the tax consequences of this transaction to Lance Text.

C. Describe the tax consequences of this transaction to Lara Text that would result from the immediate redemption of her newly issued preferred shares at their fair market value of $2,000,000. Ignore the possible use of the lifetime capital gains deduction.

Assignment Problem Seventeen - 4
[ITA 86(1) And 86(2)]

Sanice Ltd. was incorporated by John San in 2007 with the investment of $850,000. In return for this investment, John San received a total of 42,500 common shares of the new corporation.

Between the date of its incorporation and January 1, 2014, no new common shares are issued by Sanice. On this date, Malcolm Shelton acquires all of the outstanding shares for $1,200,000 in cash.

By January 1, 2018, the common shares of Sanice Ltd. have increased in value to $35 per share, or a total value of $1,487,500 [($35)(42,500)]. Because of continuing health problems, Malcolm would like to retire. While he has received an offer from an arm's length party to buy the Sanice Ltd. shares for $1,487,500, Malcolm would prefer to transfer both control of the Company and future increases in its value to his 42 year old daughter, Darlene Shelton.

He is planning to apply ITA 86 to an exchange of shares and is considering two alternative scenarios for implementing this exchange.

Scenario One   Malcolm would exchange his 42,500 common shares for cash of $850,000, plus redeemable preferred shares with a legal stated capital of $637,500 and a fair market value of $637,500.

Scenario Two   Malcolm would exchange his 42,500 common shares for cash of $850,000, plus redeemable preferred shares with a legal stated capital of $437,500 and a fair market value of $437,500.

Immediately after the exchange of shares, Malcolm will have the Company issue 250 common shares at a cost of $35 per share to Darlene who will purchase these shares with funds of her own.

Sanice Ltd. is not a qualified small business corporation. The Company has a nil balance in its General Rate Income Pool (GRIP) account for all years under consideration.

Required: For each of the two suggested approaches determine:

A. The amount of the gift to a related party, if any, resulting from the exchange of shares.

B. The paid up capital of the newly issued preferred shares.

C. The adjusted cost base of the newly issued preferred shares.

D. The proceeds of redemption/disposition that Malcolm received for the old common shares of Sanice Ltd.

E. The immediate tax consequences for Malcolm of the reorganization of the capital of Sanice Ltd.

F. The tax consequences for Malcolm if the new Sanice Ltd. preferred shares are immediately redeemed for their fair market value.

Assignment Problem Seventeen - 5
[Section 87 vs. Section 88(1)]

Hubble Inc. owns 100 percent of the shares of Palomar Ltd. Hubble has decided that it does not want Palomar to continue as a separate legal entity. It has asked your assistance on whether to absorb Palomar into its operations using ITA 87 or, alternatively, ITA 88(1).

At the time of this decision, Palomar Ltd. has the following asset values:

Asset	Capital Cost	Tax Value	FMV
Equipment	$ 11,000	$ 3,300	$ 700
Land	154,000	154,000	192,000
Goodwill	Nil	Nil	22,000

There are no liabilities and no tax loss carry forwards.

Hubble acquired the shares of Palomar several years ago for $231,000. At that time, the Equipment was valued at its capital cost of $11,000 and the Land was valued at $209,000, for a total of $220,000. At that time, goodwill was estimated to be $1,000.

Palomar has paid $5,000 in dividends since its acquisition by Hubble.

Required: Outline what the tax consequences would be if:

A. Palomar was amalgamated into Hubble Inc. using Section 87.

B. Palomar was rolled into Hubble Inc. using a Section 88(1) winding-up.

Assignment Problem Seventeen - 6
(Section 88(1) Winding-Up)

In 2014, Acme Ltd. purchased all of the outstanding shares of Cross Industries for cash of $1,400,000. The assets of Cross Industries at the time of the acquisition had tax values of $1,250,000, and included a piece of land that was being held as a location for a possible second manufacturing facility. This land had been acquired in 2009 for $640,000 and, at the time Acme acquired the Cross shares, it had a fair market value of $705,000.

Acme believes that the operations of Cross Industries have become so integrated with its own, that it no longer makes sense to operate Cross as a separate entity. As a consequence, they are considering the possibility of absorbing Cross using an ITA 88(1) winding-up. At January 1, 2018, the tax values of the assets of Cross Industries total $1,270,000. The Company is still holding the land for the additional manufacturing facility and it now has a fair market value of $790,000. Cross Industries has paid Acme Ltd. dividends totaling $20,000 since its acquisition.

Required: Explain the tax implications of the proposed winding-up from the point of view of both Acme Ltd. and Cross Industries.

Assignment Problem Seventeen - 7
(Winding-Up Of A Corporation)

Hextone Ltd. is a Canadian controlled private corporation (CCPC) that has operated with great success in the action video game market for more than 20 years. The Company has a December 31 year end.

The founder and driving force behind the Company's success is Dread Hextone. As he has always been a loner with severe anger management issues, he has thought it too risky to ever marry knowing the potential for spouses to be aggravating.

Dread is 54 years old. In his family, every male has died of a stroke before reaching the age of 60. He has done a calculation which compares his anticipated expenditures during his remaining expected years of life with the resources that would result from winding up Hextone Ltd. He has concluded that these resources are more than sufficient to cover his anticipated expenditures. As the success of Hextone Ltd. is largely based on Dread's personal efforts, he would not be able to sell his shares. Given this, he intends to sell the assets of the company, followed by a wind-up and distribution of the resulting cash.

The following statement of the Company's net assets as of January 1, 2018 has been prepared:

Hextone Ltd.
Statement Of Net Assets
As At January 1, 2018

	Tax Values	Fair Market Values
Cash	$ 72,356	$ 72,356
Investments	1,728,460	2,135,450
Inventories	728,645	782,662
Land	427,400	687,300
Building	736,419	1,265,000
Total Assets	$3,693,280	$4,942,768
Liabilities	(353,260)	(353,260)
Net Assets	$3,340,020	$4,589,508

Based on tax values, the components of the net asset value balance are as follows:

Paid Up Capital	$ 850,000
Capital Dividend Account	432,470
Other Income Retained	2,057,550
Total Net Asset Balance	$3,340,020

Other Information:

1. The Building had a capital cost of $1,000,000.

2. The adjusted cost base of the common shares is equal to $850,000, their paid up capital.

3. On January 1, 2018, the Company has a balance in its General Rate Income Pool (GRIP) account of $86,400.

4. All of the assets are disposed of on January 1, 2018 at their fair market values. The corporation's liabilities are also paid on this date. The after tax proceeds from the sale are distributed to Dread on January 15, 2018.

5. The provincial tax rate for the corporation on income that qualifies for the small business deduction is 4.5 percent. On all other income, the provincial rate is 11.5 percent.

6. The January 1, 2018 balance in the Company's RDTOH account is $362,675.

7. No dividends were paid during the previous two years.

Required:

A. Calculate the amount that will be available for distribution to Dread after the liquidation.

B. Determine the components of the distribution to Dread, and the amount of taxable capital gains that will accrue to him as a result of the winding-up of Hextone Ltd. Ignore the possibility that Dread might be subject to the alternative minimum tax. Assume that appropriate elections or designations will be made to minimize the taxes that will be paid by Dread.

Assignment Problem Seventeen - 8
(Sale Of Assets vs. Shares)

Mr. Robert Niche is the president and only shareholder of Niche Inc., a Canadian controlled private corporation. The Company's fiscal year ends on December 31. Mr. Niche established the Company 15 years ago by investing $344,500 in cash. There have been no other shares issued since then.

Mr. Niche is considering selling the corporation and, in order to better evaluate this possibility, he has prepared a special Statement Of Assets. In this special statement, comparative disclosure is provided for the values included in his accounting records, values that are relevant for tax purposes, and fair market values. This statement is as follows:

Niche Inc.
Statement Of Assets As At January 1, 2018

	Accounting Net Book Value	Tax Value	Fair Market Value
Cash	$ 70,850	$ 70,850	$ 70,850
Accounts Receivable	527,800	527,800	483,925
Inventories	1,130,675	1,130,675	1,268,800
Land	261,950	261,950	526,500
Building (Note One)	699,400	610,025	2,679,300
Equipment (Note Two)	564,200	382,200	222,625
Goodwill	Nil	Nil	1,054,300
Totals	$3,254,875	$2,983,500	$6,306,300

Note One Mr. Niche built this Building on the Land for a total cost of $1,665,300.

Note Two The Equipment had a cost of $1,049,750.

At the same time that this Statement Of Assets was prepared, a similar Statement Of Equities was drawn up. This latter statement contained the following accounting and tax values:

	Accounting Book Value	Tax Value
Current Liabilities	$ 906,100	$ 906,100
Loan From Shareholder	178,750	178,750
Future Income Tax Liability	704,600	N/A
Common Stock - No Par	344,500	344,500
Capital Dividend Account	N/A	213,850
Other Income Retained	N/A	1,340,300
Retained Earnings	1,120,925	N/A
Totals	$3,254,875	$2,983,500

In addition to the information included in the preceding statements, the following other information about the Company is relevant:

- The Company has available non-capital loss carry forwards of $107,900.

- The Company has available a net capital loss carry forward of $168,545 [(1/2)($337,090)].

- Niche Inc. is subject to a provincial tax rate of 3 percent on income that qualifies for the federal small business deduction and 14 percent on income that does not qualify for this deduction.

- On December 31, 2017, the Company has no balance in either its RDTOH account or its General Rate Income Pool (GRIP) account.

- Niche Inc. shares are not qualified small business corporation shares.

Mr. Niche has received two offers for his Company, and he plans to accept one of them on January 2, 2018. The first offer involves a cash payment of $4,560,000 in return for all of the shares of the Company. Alternatively, another investor has expressed a willingness to acquire all of the assets, including goodwill, at a price equal to their fair market values. This investor would assume all of the liabilities of the corporation and has agreed to file an ITA 22 election with respect to the Accounts Receivable. If the assets are sold, it is Mr. Niche's intention to wind up the corporation.

Mr. Niche will have over $300,000 in income from other sources and, as a consequence, any income that arises on the disposition of this business will be taxed at the maximum federal rate of 33 percent, combined with a provincial rate of 18 percent. He lives in a province where the provincial dividend tax credit on eligible dividends is 5/11 of the gross up, and on non-eligible dividends is equal to 3/11 of the gross up.

Required: Determine which of the two offers Mr. Niche should accept. Ignore the possibility that Mr. Niche might be subject to the alternative minimum tax. Assume that appropriate elections or designations will be made to minimize the taxes that will be paid by Mr. Niche.

Assignment Problem Seventeen - 9
(Sale Of Assets vs. Shares)

Mr. Nathan Naper is the president and only shareholder of Nepean Ltd., a Canadian controlled private corporation. The Company's fiscal year ends on December 31. Mr. Naper established the Company 15 years ago by investing $265,000 in cash. There have been no other shares issued since then.

Mr. Naper is considering selling the corporation and, in order to better evaluate this possibility, he has prepared a special Statement Of Assets. In this special statement, comparative disclosure is provided for the values included in his accounting records, values that are relevant for tax purposes, and fair market values. This statement is as follows:

Nepean Ltd.
Statement Of Assets
As At January 1, 2018

	Accounting Net Book Value	Tax Value	Fair Market Value
Cash	$ 54,500	$ 54,500	$ 54,500
Accounts Receivable	406,000	406,000	372,250
Inventories	869,750	869,750	976,000
Land	201,500	201,500	405,000
Building (Note One)	538,000	469,250	2,061,000
Equipment (Note Two)	434,000	294,000	171,250
Goodwill	Nil	Nil	811,000
Totals	$2,503,750	$2,295,000	$4,851,000

Note One   Mr. Naper built this Building on the Land for a total cost of $1,281,000.

Note Two   The Equipment had a cost of $807,500.

At the same time that this Statement Of Assets was prepared, a similar Statement Of Equities was drawn up. This latter statement contained the following accounting and tax values:

	Accounting Book Value	Tax Value
Current Liabilities	$ 697,000	$ 697,000
Loan From Shareholder	137,500	137,500
Future Income Tax Liability	542,000	N/A
Common Stock - No Par	265,000	265,000
Capital Dividend Account	N/A	164,500
Other Income Retained	N/A	1,031,000
Retained Earnings	862,250	N/A
Totals	$2,503,750	$2,295,000

In addition to the information included in the preceding statements, the following other information about the Company is available:

- The Company has available non-capital loss carry forwards of $83,000.

- The Company has available a net capital loss carry forward of $129,650 [(1/2)($259,300)].

- Nepean Ltd. is subject to a provincial tax rate of 3 percent on income that qualifies for the federal small business deduction and 14 percent on income that does not qualify for this deduction.

- On December 31, 2017, the Company has no balance in either its RDTOH account or its General Rate Income Pool (GRIP) account.

- Nepean Ltd. is not a qualified small business corporation.

Mr. Naper has received two offers for his Company, and he plans to accept one of them on January 2, 2018. The first offer involves a cash payment of $3,508,000 in return for all of the shares of the Company. Alternatively, another investor has expressed a willingness to acquire all of the assets, including goodwill, at a price equal to their fair market values. This investor would assume all of the liabilities of the corporation and has agreed to file an ITA 22 election with respect to the Accounts Receivable. If the assets are sold, it is Mr. Naper's intention to wind up the corporation.

Mr. Naper will have over $300,000 in income from other sources and, as a consequence, any income that arises on the disposition of this business will be taxed at the maximum federal rate of 33 percent, combined with a provincial rate of 18 percent. He lives in a province where the provincial dividend tax credit on eligible dividends is 5/11 of the gross up, and on non-eligible dividends is equal to 3/11 of the gross up.

Required: Determine which of the two offers Mr. Naper should accept. Ignore the possibility that Mr. Naper might be subject to the alternative minimum tax. Assume that appropriate elections or designations will be made to minimize the taxes that will be paid by Mr. Naper.

CHAPTER 18

Partnerships

Introduction

Taxable Entities In Canada

18-1. As is noted in Chapter 1, the *Income Tax Act* (ITA) is applicable to individuals (human beings), corporations, and trusts. In the case of individuals and corporations, these taxable entities have a separate legal existence. In contrast, trusts are simply arrangements for transferring property and, as such, are not separate legal entities. Partnerships are similar to trusts in that they do not have a legal existence separate from the participating partners. More to the point here is the fact that, under the provisions of the *Income Tax Act*, partnerships are generally not defined taxable entities. An exception to this is "SIFT Partnerships" which are taxable under Part IX.1 of the *Act* (see discussion at the end of this Chapter).

18-2. The *Income Tax Act* deals with the fact that partnerships are generally not taxable entities through the use of a deeming rule. A deeming rule is a statutory fiction that requires an item or event be given a treatment for tax purposes that is not consistent with the actual legal nature of the item or event. We have encountered several such rules in previous chapters:

- A member of the Canadian armed forces is deemed to be a resident of Canada, even if he does not set foot in the country during the year.

- A change in use is deemed to be a disposition of an asset combined with its immediate re-acquisition.

- The death of an individual results in a deemed disposition of all of his capital property.

18-3. The deeming rule that is applicable to partnerships is that, for purposes of determining the income or loss of its members, such organizations are considered to be a person resident in Canada. Note that this rule applies only for the purpose of calculating the income or loss of members. It does not make a partnership a taxable entity and there is no requirement that these organizations file a separate income tax return.

18-4. In general terms, a partnership is treated as a flow-through entity. The preceding deeming rule requires that an income figure be determined at the partnership level using the usual rules for various types of income (e.g., business income, property income, capital gains). Then the income or loss of the partnership is allocated to the taxable entities (i.e., individuals, trusts, or corporations) based on the amounts agreed to in the partnership agreement, or in equal proportions in the absence of a partnership agreement. This process is illustrated in Figure 18-1 (following page).

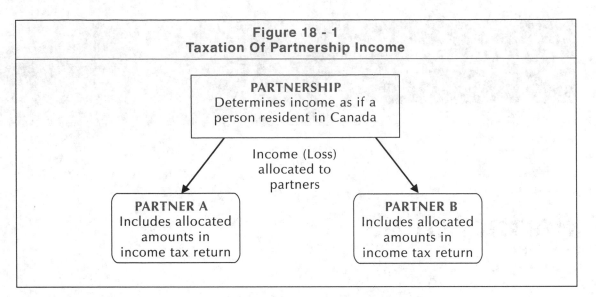

Figure 18 - 1
Taxation Of Partnership Income

PARTNERSHIP
Determines income as if a
person resident in Canada

Income (Loss)
allocated to
partners

PARTNER A
Includes allocated
amounts in
income tax return

PARTNER B
Includes allocated
amounts in
income tax return

18-5.   We would note that, while partnerships are not taxable entities under the *Income Tax Act*, they are considered taxable entities for GST purposes (see Chapter 21). This means that, in contrast with the income tax situation, a partnership must file a GST return, pay any GST owing or is entitled to receive any GST refund.

Chapter Coverage

18-6.   In this Chapter we will examine the income taxation rules that are applicable to partnerships. We will begin by defining partnerships. This will be followed by an examination of the various types of partnerships, as well as other arrangements that resemble partnerships. These other arrangements include co-ownerships, joint ventures, and syndicates. Our focus will then shift to looking at the rules for calculating income for a partnership and the process of allocating this income and other amounts to partners.

18-7.   Other issues that will be covered include:

- the determination of the adjusted cost base of a partnership interest;
- admitting and retiring partners;
- limited partnerships, limited partnership losses and the at-risk rules;
- the transfer of property between the partners and the partnership; and
- reorganizing a partnership as a new partnership, as a corporation, and as a sole proprietorship.

Partnerships Defined

The Importance Of Defining A Partnership

18-8.   The general rules for determining the income tax consequences for partnerships and their members are found in Subdivision j of Division B of Part I of the *Income Tax Act*, ITA 96 through 103. However, since these rules apply specifically to partnerships, we must first determine if we are, in fact, looking at a partnership. To do this requires a definition of a partnership.

18-9.   The importance of this definition is that it allows us to distinguish a partnership from other similar types of organizations such as syndicates, joint ventures, and co-ownership arrangements. This is necessary in that, unlike the situation for these other types of organizations, there is a separate calculation of the income of a partnership.

18-10.   As we have noted, this calculation must be carried out using the assumption that the partnership is a separate person resident in Canada. Further, as the calculation must be used for allocating income to all of the members of the partnership, partners have no flexibility with respect to the amounts to be included in their required tax returns. For example, a partner does not have the discretion to take an alternative amount of CCA on property owned by the partnership. Note, however, they do have discretion with respect to CCA on property that is used by the partnership, but owned by the partner (e.g., partial use of a personally owned automobile for partnership business).

18-11.   In contrast, if the organization is considered to be a co-ownership, syndicate, or joint venture (see Paragraph 18-24), there is no requirement for a separate calculation of income. This provides the participants with much greater flexibility in determining the tax procedures to be used. In this case, one participant could take maximum CCA, while others take a lower amount, or even none at all.

Basic Partnership Elements

18-12.   Unfortunately, there is no specific definition of a "partnership" in the *Income Tax Act*. There are several definitions of certain types of partnerships. For example, ITA 102(1) defines a "Canadian Partnership" and ITA 197(1) defines a "SIFT Partnership". However, all of these specialized definitions presume that a partnership already exists. This leaves the question of defining a partnership unanswered.

18-13.   Guidance on defining a partnership is provided in IT Folio S4-F16-C1, *What Is A Partnership?*. This Folio notes that "whether a partnership exists is a matter of fact and law". It then proceeds to discuss provincial law dealing with this issue, as well as several court cases that have bearing on this issue. What we would gather from reading through this material is that there are three basic elements that are required for an organization to be considered a partnership and these are:

1.   There must be two or more persons (individuals, corporations or trusts) involved.
2.   These persons must be carrying on a business in common.
3.   It must be the intent of the partners to carry on a business with a view to making a profit.

18-14.   Also helpful in this area, IT Folio S4-F16-C1 quotes a Supreme Court Case (Backman v. Canada, 2001 DTC 5149) which lists factors that would be viewed as providing evidence of the existence of a partnership:

• the contribution by the parties of money, property, effort, knowledge, skill or other assets to a common undertaking;
• a joint property interest in the subject matter of the adventure;
• the sharing of profits and losses;
• a mutual right of control or management of the enterprise;
• financial statements prepared as a partnership;
• bank accounts in the name of the partnership; and
• correspondence with third parties as a partnership.

18-15.   The presence of a valid partnership agreement would serve to support the view that a partnership exists. Such agreements will usually include provisions that deal with many issues, including the following:

• the initial and ongoing partner contributions and ownership percentage of each partner,
• the responsibilities of each partner and the division of work between the partners,
• how income and drawings will be allocated and how much compensation is to be paid,
• signing authority on the partnership bank accounts and required approval for purchases,
• procedures for bringing in new partners, and
• procedures to deal with the withdrawal or death of a partner, or the sale of the business.

Types Of Partnerships

General Partnerships

18-16.   A general partnership is one in which all of the partners are general partners. As defined in the *Guide For The T5013 Partnership Information Return* (T4068):

A **general partner** is a partner whose personal liability for the debts and obligations of the partnership are not limited.

18-17.   Provincial partnership law provides additional guidance on the rights, duties and obligations of general partners. These include:

- Each partner is considered to act on behalf of the partnership, which means that the actions of each partner are generally binding on the other partners.

- Partners are jointly and severally liable for partnership debt and wrongful acts of other partners. This means that a partner can be liable, together with all other partners, for unpaid partnership debt and wrongful acts of other partners.

- Property contributed to the partnership or acquired with partnership funds is considered partnership property and is to be held exclusively for partnership use.

- Partners are entitled to share equally in profits and losses, unless there is an agreement to the contrary.

- Partners are not entitled to remuneration (salary or wages) or to interest on capital contributions. As is explained later in this Chapter, any remuneration or interest on capital is treated as an income allocation and is not deductible to the partnership.

18-18.   When the term partnership is used without a qualifying adjective, the reference is normally to a general partnership.

Limited Partnerships

18-19.   A limited partnership is a partnership with at least one general partner (i.e., a partner whose liability is unrestricted) and one or more limited partners. To be considered a limited partnership, the partnership has to be registered as such under the appropriate provincial registry. In the absence of such registration, the partnership will be considered a general partnership.

18-20.   A limited partner has the same rights, duties, and obligations as a general partner with one important difference, a limited partner is only liable for partnership debt and wrongful or negligent actions of other partners to the extent of the partner's actual and promised contributions to the partnership.

> **EXAMPLE**   A limited partner contributes $1,000 and agrees to contribute a further $2,000 within a certain period of time. That partner will be potentially liable for up to $3,000 of claims against the partnership.

18-21.   It should be noted, however, that a limited partner will lose his limited liability protection, and therefore become a general partner, if he participates in the management of the partnership.

Limited Liability Partnerships (LLP)

18-22.   This form of partnership is only available to certain types of professionals as specified in provincial legislation. For example, in Ontario, only lawyers and chartered professional accountants are currently permitted to form such partnerships. In contrast, Alberta extends this legislation to include several other professional groups.

18-23.   Unlike members of limited partnerships, members of limited liability partnerships are personally liable for most types of partnership debt. There is, however, an important exception. Members of limited liability partnerships are not personally liable for obligations arising from the wrongful or negligent action of:

- their professional partners; or
- the employees, agents or representatives of the partnership who are conducting partnership business.

We suggest you work Self Study Problem Eighteen-1 at this point.

Co-Ownership, Joint Ventures, And Syndicates

Introduction

18-24.   Our major concern in this Chapter is the taxation of partnerships. However, as we have noted, there are other types of organizations that have structures similar to partnership arrangements. Co-ownership, joint ventures, and syndicates are specific types of arrangements that contain features common to partnerships. For example, each of these organizational structures requires two or more persons. This common feature is but one of several that may make it difficult to determine whether a specific arrangement is, in fact, a partnership or, alternatively, a different type of arrangement.

18-25.   As was discussed in the preceding material, the ability to distinguish these arrangements from partnerships is a critical factor in determining how a given organization will be taxed. To facilitate this process, the following material will provide additional clarification as to the nature of these other types of organizations.

Co-Ownership

18-26.   Two or more persons co-own property when they share a right of ownership in the property. For income tax purposes, the most important consideration is that profits and losses are shared in partnerships, but are typically accounted for individually by joint or co-owners.

18-27.   Two common forms of co-ownership are joint tenancy and tenancy in common. A joint tenancy is a form of property ownership where two or more joint tenants have ownership and possession of the same property. Individual interests are identical and the property cannot be sold or mortgaged without the consent of the other joint tenant(s). Spouses commonly own their principal residence and other properties in joint tenancy.

18-28.   In a tenancy in common arrangement, tenants can sell or mortgage their interests without the consent of other tenants in common. An example of a situation where a tenancy in common might be used would be the ownership of a vacation property by three brothers.

Joint Ventures

Defined

18-29.   Those of you familiar with financial reporting will recognize that some corporations are referred to as joint ventures. They are distinguished by the fact that control of the corporation is shared by two or more of the shareholders. This type of joint venture does not present any special problems in terms of tax procedures. They are subject to the same rules that are applicable to other corporate taxpayers.

18-30.   Our concern here is with unincorporated joint ventures. Like partnerships, joint ventures are not defined taxable entities under the *Income Tax Act*. Further, such arrangements are not governed by provincial legislation. However, both the *Income Tax Act* and the *Excise Tax Act* refer to joint ventures, implicitly giving recognition to this form of organization.

18-31.   The similarity of partnerships and joint ventures has led the CRA to make the following statement in 1988:

> Unlike partnerships, the concept of joint venture is not recognized by statute (i.e. provincial legislation). Although the Canadian courts have, in certain cases, recognized joint venture as being a business relationship that is distinct from partnership, in our experience, many so-called joint ventures are in fact partnerships... The CRA would rely on provincial partnership law in making such a determination.

18-32.   This would suggest that, even if participants in a joint venture call the arrangement a joint venture, if it contains the three basic partnership elements, it will be considered a partnership for tax purposes and treated accordingly.

18-33.   Despite this lack of clarity, joint ventures do appear to exist for tax purposes. Factors that have been used to distinguish this type of organization include:

- co-venturers contractually do not have the power to bind other co-venturers;
- co-venturers retain ownership of property contributed to the undertaking;
- co-venturers are not jointly and severally liable for debt of the undertaking;
- co-venturers share gross revenues, not profits; and
- while partnerships may be formed for the same purpose as a joint venture, they are usually of longer duration and involve more than a single undertaking.

Tax Procedures

18-34.   If an arrangement is considered to be a joint venture rather than a partnership, there will be no separate calculation of income at the organization level. The participants will be subject to the usual rules applicable to individuals or corporations. As we have noted, this will provide these taxable entities with greater flexibility on such issues as how much CCA can be taken for the current year.   You should note, however, since joint ventures are not a recognized entity for tax purposes, they cannot have their own fiscal period.

Syndicates

18-35.   A syndicate is generally defined as a group of persons who have agreed to pool their money or assets for some common purpose. Because a syndicate is not a legal entity, a reference to an interest in a syndicate usually means an interest in the combined assets of the syndicate members. The Canadian courts have traditionally reserved the name "syndicate" for specialized projects that are financial in nature. An example of a syndicate would be an association of insurance companies who combine forces to underwrite substantial high-risk insurance policies.

18-36.   There are no specific income tax rules that apply to syndicates. This means that, if there are any activities of the syndicate that result in assessable amounts of income, the relevant amounts will have to be allocated to the members of the syndicate.

We suggest you work Self Study Problem Eighteen-2 at this point.

Partnership Income, Losses, And Tax Credits

Introduction

18-37.   The goal of partnership taxation is to apply the income tax consequences of partnership income, losses, and tax credits to the persons who are its partners. To implement this, a two stage process is involved:

Stage 1   Determine, at the partnership level, the various components of partnership income. This requires separate calculations for business income, property income, taxable capital gains, and allowable capital losses. For most partnerships, the most important component will be net business income.

Stage 2   Allocate the amounts that were determined in Stage 1 to the members of the partnership on the basis of the provisions of the partnership agreement.

18-38.   In determining the business income component, we generally begin with the partnership's accounting figure for business income. The normal procedure is to convert this figure to Net Business Income for tax purposes. This conversion is based on a reconciliation process which is very similar to the reconciliation process that is used to determine Net Business Income For Tax Purposes (see Chapter 6). There are, however, some items that are specific to the calculation of business income for partnerships.

18-39.   Following the determination of the amount of business income to be allocated to partners, separate calculations are carried out for amounts of property income, taxable capital gains, and allowable capital losses that will be allocated to the members of the partnership.

18-40.   While it would be possible to calculate a Net Income For Tax Purposes for the partnership, this usually is not done. Such a figure has no real meaning for a non-taxable entity such as a partnership. Further, the calculation would serve no real purpose as the allocations to the partners are on a source-by-source basis. We would also note that there is no calculation of Taxable Income for a partnership. Again, as partnerships are not taxable entities, such a figure would have no real meaning.

Applicable Concepts

Taxation Year

18-41.   ITA 96(1)(a) indicates that partnership income must be calculated as if the partnership was a separate person resident in Canada. ITA 96(1)(b) follows this by indicating that this calculation should be made as if the taxation year of the partnership were its "fiscal period". The ITA 249.1(1) definition of "fiscal period" indicates that, if any member of a partnership is an individual or a professional corporation, the partnership must have a December 31 year end. Otherwise, the only restriction is that the fiscal period cannot end more than 12 months after it begins. In effect, this means that, if all of the members of a partnership are corporations (other than professional corporations), the partnership can use any year end.

18-42.   ITA 249.1(4) provides an exception to the general taxation year end rules that are described in the preceding paragraph. If the following conditions are met, the partnership can elect to use a non-calendar year as its fiscal period.

- all of the members of the partnership are individuals; and
- an election is filed with the CRA using a prescribed form (T1139) prior to the end of the partnership's first fiscal year. The complications associated with making this election are discussed in Chapter 6, Business Income.

EXAMPLE   ABC Partnership has five corporate partners, two of which are professional corporations, and one partner who is an individual. The new partnership wants to choose a March 31 fiscal year end.

ANALYSIS   The partnership must use a December 31 fiscal year end. The presence of both an individual and professional corporations as partners prevents the use of a non-calendar fiscal period under the ITA 249.1(1) definition. Similarly, the presence of corporations prevents the election of a non-calendar fiscal period under ITA 249.1(4).

18-43.   The CRA has been concerned with the ability of a corporate member of a partnership to defer taxes because it has a different year end from the partnership. Consider a partnership that has a fiscal year ending on January 31, 2018 and a corporate member with a December 31, 2018 year end. The corporation would not have to include the partnership income earned during the year ending January 31, 2018 until it files its return for the fiscal year ending December 31, 2018, despite the fact that most of that income was earned in the corporation's year ending December 31, 2017. In effect, this provides an 11 month deferral of income recognition.

18-44.   To deal with this problem, special rules are applicable in situations where a partnership has a fiscal period that ends after the taxation year end of a corporation that has a significant interest (more than 10 percent) in that partnership.

18-45.   The rules would require income adjustments similar to those required for "additional business income" which is covered in Chapter 6, Business Income.

18-46.   In the example from Paragraph 18-42, the legislation requires the corporation to include 334/365 of the partnership income for its year ending January 31, 2018 in its corporate tax return for the year ending December 31, 2017. This accrual would be deducted in the corporate taxation return for the year ending December 31, 2018, with a new accrual added for 334/365 of the partnership income for the year ending January 31, 2019.

Partnership Property

18-47.   In general, partners legally own a percentage interest in partnership property in co-ownership. The partnership cannot own property since it is not a legal entity. This creates a problem for income tax purposes because the partnership income tax rules require that the partnership determine its income or loss as if it were a separate person.

18-48.   If the partnership does not own partnership property, then gains and losses from the disposition of such property would not be considered those of the partnership. In addition, the partnership would not be able to claim CCA. The *Income Tax Act* resolves this problem with an assumption that the partnership, for income tax purposes, is considered to own partnership property.

Retention Of Income Characteristics

18-49.   Partnerships are treated as a conduit for transferring income from an originating source into the hands of the partners. Further, it is an unfiltered conduit in that the character of various types of income is not altered as it flows to the partners. If a partnership earns dividend income, capital gains, or realizes a business loss, these sources would be received as dividend income, capital gains, or business losses in the hands of the partners.

> **EXAMPLE** Partnership Deux has two equal general partners. Aside from its business income, Deux earns $50,000 of interest income and realizes a $20,000 capital gain. None of this amount is withdrawn by the two partners. Corporation Dos has two equal shareholders. It also earns $50,000 of interest income and realizes a $20,000 capital gain. The corporation does not pay out any of this amount as dividends.
>
> **ANALYSIS - Partnership** For Partnership Deux, each partner is considered to have received $25,000 [(1/2)($50,000)] of interest income and to have realized a $5,000 taxable capital gain [($20,000)(1/2)(1/2)]. Note that the income is subject to taxation, despite the fact that none of it has been withdrawn from the partnership (see next section on Accrual Basis).
>
> **ANALYSIS - Corporation**   In the case of Corporation Dos, the shareholders will not be taxed until the income is withdrawn from the corporation. The income will, however, be taxed at the corporate level on the basis of its nature (e.g., capital gains, business, or property income). When it is distributed to the shareholders, it will not retain its characteristics as capital gains, business, or property income. Rather, the entire distribution will be taxed in the hands of the shareholders as dividends.

18-50.   In addition to retaining its basic character, the originating location of each source of income is retained. If, for example, a partnership earns dividends on shares of U.S. corporations, this income would be received by the partners as foreign source dividends. Not surprisingly, the related foreign tax credits would also be flowed through to the partners.

Accrual Basis

18-51.   The partnership must calculate its net business income on an accrual basis unless its partners are professionals who can elect under ITA 34 to use the billed basis of income recognition (as noted in Chapter 6, the use of the billed basis of income recognition is being phased out). On its determination, this income is then allocated to the partners. The partners include their share of this income at the time of allocation, without regard to when the funds are withdrawn from the partnership. It is the allocation, not the receipt of the funds, which creates income for the partners that is subject to tax.

18-52.   In effect, this places the partners on an accrual basis for the determination of their individual business income amounts. While drawings of cash from the partnership reduce the partner's adjusted cost base, they will have no impact on the partner's Taxable Income or the amount of taxes the partner will be required to pay.

Exercise Eighteen - 1

Subject: Partnership Income - Accrual Basis

During the year ending December 31, 2018, PQR Partnership has business income of $55,000, capital gains of $40,000, and receives eligible dividends of $10,000. Norm Peters has a 50 percent interest in the income of this partnership. During 2018, Norm withdraws $30,000 from the partnership. Determine the tax consequences for Mr. Peters for the 2018 taxation year.

SOLUTION available in print and online Study Guide.

Calculating The Amounts To Be Allocated

Net Business Income

18-53.   For most partnerships, the major income source to be allocated is the partnership's Net Business Income. As we have noted, this is a reconciliation process which starts with accounting Net Income. Various items are then added or subtracted to arrive at the partnership's Net Business Income. A discussion of the major items in this reconciliation process follows.

Salaries Or Wages To Partners (Add Back)   Partnership agreements often provide that partners be paid salaries or wages to recognize the time they devote to partnership business. Reflecting provincial partnership legislation, the CRA does not permit the deduction of such amounts in the determination of a partnership's Net Business Income.

If salaries or wages have been deducted in determining the accounting Net Income of the partnership, they must be added back in the determination of Net Business Income for tax purposes of the partnership. While this is required in determining the total Net Business Income, it does not prevent priority allocations of this total to specific partners to reflect the work they do for the partnership. If the partnership agreement calls for such salary or wages entitlements for specific partners, the specified amounts will be allocated to those partners, with only the remaining Net Business Income allocated by some formula (e.g., a 60:40 split of the residual).

A further point here relates to whether the salaries or wages are withdrawn from the partnership. The allocated amount is included in the partner's income and added to his adjusted cost base. If, as would be the usual situation, the amounts are withdrawn from the partnership, they reduce the partner's adjusted cost base, but do not influence the partner's Net Income For Tax Purposes.

Interest On Partner Capital Contributions (Add Back)   The preceding analysis of the treatment of partner salaries is also applicable to interest on capital contributions. If the partnership agreement calls for such amounts, they cannot be deducted in the determination of the Net Business Income of the partnership.

If interest payments on partner capital contributions has been deducted in the determination of accounting Net Income, they must be added back to arrive at the partnership's total Net Business Income. If the partnership agreement indicates that such amounts be treated as a priority allocation of the partnership's total Net Business Income, they will be included in the partner's Net Income For Tax Purposes and added to his adjusted cost base. If the specified amounts are withdrawn, the withdrawal does not affect the partner's Net Income For Tax Purposes. The drawings would, however, be deducted from the partner's adjusted cost base.

EXAMPLE - Salaries And Interest On Capital Contributions   Bob and Ray are partners who share the Net Business Income of their partnership equally after a provision has been made for their salaries and Ray's interest on his capital contributions. For the year ending December 31, 2018, the Income Statement of the partnership, prepared in accordance with GAAP, is as follows:

Revenues		$135,000
Expenses:		
Cost Of Sales	($45,000)	
Salary To Bob	(30,000)	
Salary To Ray	(10,000)	
Interest On Ray's Capital Contributions	(11,000)	
Other Expenses	(10,000)	(106,000)
Accounting Income		**$ 29,000**

ANALYSIS   For tax purposes, the Net Business Income of the Bob And Ray Partnership would be calculated as follows:

Accounting Income	$29,000
Add:	
Salaries To Bob and Ray ($30,000 + $10,000)	40,000
Interest On Capital Contributions	11,000
Net Business Income	$80,000
Allocations For Salaries And Interest On	
Capital Contributions ($40,000 + $11,000)	(51,000)
Residual Net Business Income (To Be Shared Equally)	**$29,000**

This amount would be allocated to the two partners as follows:

	Bob	Ray
Priority Allocation For Salaries	$30,000	$10,000
Priority Allocation For Interest	N/A	11,000
Allocation Of Residual On Equal Basis		
[(50%)($29,000)]	14,500	14,500
Total Business Income Allocation	**$44,500**	**$35,500**

Despite the fact that the partnership agreement may refer to salaries or wages and/or for interest on capital for the partners, from a legal point of view they are allocations of Net Business Income. Given this, the usual payroll procedures (e.g., source deductions) are not required on the salaries or wages.

Drawings (Add Back)   Drawings by partners are not deductible expenses in the determination of any type of partnership income. As GAAP for partnerships is not clearly laid out, partnership drawings may or may not be deducted in the determination of accounting Net Income. To the extent they have been deducted in determining accounting income, they will have to be added back in the determination of the partnership's Net Business Income.

Dividend Income (Deduct)   Dividends received will be included in the partnership's accounting Net Income figure. These amounts will be allocated to partners as a separate source of income. This is discussed in more detail starting at Paragraph 18-57. Given this, dividends must be deducted in converting the partnership's accounting Net Income to the partnership's Net Business Income.

Charitable Donations (Add Back)   These amounts are normally deducted in the determination of a partnership's accounting Net Income. In converting this figure to Net Business Income, these amounts will have to be added back.

Donations made by a partnership that otherwise qualify as charitable donations are flowed to the partners based on their partnership agreement. Corporations are entitled to a deduction in arriving at Taxable Income, whereas individuals are entitled to a credit against Tax Payable. Donations, and the related credit or deduction, are only allocated to those partners who are partners on the last day of the partnership's year end.

Political Contributions (Add Back)   As political contributions are normally subtracted in the determination of accounting Net Income, these amounts will have to be added back to arrive at the partnership's Net Business Income.

Qualifying political contributions are allocated to each partner as per the partnership agreement. Similar to charitable donations, the allocation of the contributions and the related credit is dependent on being a partner on the last day of the partnership's year in which the political contribution was made.

Personal Expenditures (Add Back)   In some situations, a partnership may pay personal expenses of one or more partners. While these amounts may be deducted as an expense for accounting purposes, they are not deductible to the partnership in determining Net Business Income. To the extent that these amounts have been deducted in the determination of accounting Net Income, they will have to be added back in the determination of the partnership's Net Business Income.

Business Transactions With Partners (No Adjustment)   While this may not be consistent with partnership law, administrative practice of the CRA does not restrict the ability of partners to enter into legitimate business transactions with their partnerships. Examples include loans made by partners to the partnership and the renting of a partner's property to the partnership. As long as the transactions are on regular commercial terms, such transactions will be treated for tax purposes in the same manner as transactions with persons who are not partners.

In general, such transactions will not require any adjustment of the accounting Net Income to arrive at the partnership's Net Business Income.

Capital Cost Allowance   Any CCA that is deducted on partnership property must be deducted at the partnership level. As you would expect, the half-year rule, the available for use rules, the rental property restrictions, and other depreciable property rules are all applicable when determining the amount of CCA that a partnership may claim.

You should note that this requirement removes the possibility of different partners taking different amounts of CCA. If maximum CCA is deducted at the partnership level, all partners must, in effect, deduct maximum CCA.

It is not uncommon in partnership financial statements for the amortization figures to be based on the CCA amounts used for tax purposes. If this is the case, no net adjustment is required in converting accounting Net Income to the partnership's Net Business Income. However, the normal procedure, even when the amounts involved are the same, would be to add back the amortization figures used in the accounting statements, and deduct the appropriate CCA figure.

Amounts Related To Dispositions Of Capital Assets   Accounting Net Income will include 100 percent of the accounting gains and losses on dispositions of depreciable and non-depreciable capital assets. These amounts must be added back (losses) or deducted (gains) in the determination of the partnership's Net Business Income.

As net taxable capital gains will be allocated to the partners as a separate source of income, these amounts are not included in the calculation of the partnership's Net Business Income. This is discussed in more detail starting at Paragraph 18-55.

As you will recall from Chapter 5, a disposition of a depreciable capital asset can also result in recapture of CCA or terminal losses. If recapture occurs, it will be added to accounting Net Income in order to arrive at the partnership's Net Business Income. Similarly, terminal losses will be deducted.

Figure 18 - 2
Conversion - Partnership Accounting Income
To Partnership Net Business Income

Additions To Accounting Income:
- Specific To Partnerships
- Salaries of partners
- Interest on capital accounts
- Drawings of partners (if deducted)
- Personal expenditures of partners (if deducted)

- General Business (Additions)
- Amortization, depreciation, and depletion of tangible and intangible assets (Accounting amounts)
- Recapture of CCA
- Tax reserves deducted in the prior year
- Losses on the disposition of capital assets (Accounting amounts)
- Charitable donations
- Political contributions
- Interest and penalties on income tax assessments
- Non-deductible automobile costs
- Fifty percent of business meals and entertainment expenses
- Club dues and cost of recreational facilities
- Non-deductible reserves (Accounting amounts)
- Fines, penalties, and illegal payments

Deductions From Accounting Income:
- Specific To Partnerships
- None

- General Business (Deductions)
- Capital cost allowances (CCA)
- Terminal losses
- Tax reserves claimed for the current year
- Gains on the disposition of capital assets (Accounting amounts)
- Deductible warranty expenditures
- Landscaping costs
- Dividends included in accounting income
- Other property income included in accounting income

Reserves   The use of reserves is discussed in both Chapter 6 (e.g., reserve for bad debts) and Chapter 8 (e.g., capital gains reserve). These reserves are claimed by the partnership in exactly the same manner as partners, corporations, and trusts.

In general, the amounts involved in the application of reserve procedures are the same as the related amounts for accounting purposes. For example, the amount deducted for bad debts in the accounting statements is usually the same net amount that results from the application of reserve procedures in tax returns. However, the normal procedure here in determining the partnership's Net Business Income is to remove the accounting amounts and replace these amounts with the tax figures, even when the amounts are the same.

18-54.   Figure 18-2 provides a list of the more common additions and deductions that arise in the process of converting the accounting income of a partnership into Net Business Income. You will note that many of the items presented here are the same as those presented in Figure 6-3 in Chapter 6 which covers business income.

Capital Gains And Losses

18-55.   In the preceding section, we noted the need to remove any accounting gains and losses on capital asset dispositions in the determination of Net Business Income. If dispositions created recapture of CCA or terminal losses, these amounts were added or deducted in the determination of Net Business Income. However, capital gains and losses were not included.

18-56.   As you would expect, capital gain and losses are allocated to the members of the partnership to be included in their tax returns. Without going into great detail, once these amounts are allocated they are subject to the same rules that would apply if the gains and losses had resulted from dispositions by the partners themselves. One-half of the net gains will be included in Net Income For Tax Purposes. On some gains the lifetime capital gains deduction may be available and some losses may qualify as Business Investment Losses. If the partner is a private corporation, there will be an addition to the capital dividend account.

Exercise Eighteen - 2

Subject: Partnership Net Business Income

The JL Partnership has two partners. Partner J, because he is actively managing the partnership, receives an annual salary of $45,000. Because Partner L has contributed most of the capital for the business, he receives an interest allocation of $22,000. The partnership agreement calls for the remaining profits, and all other allocations, to be split 60 percent to J and 40 percent to L. The salary and interest amounts are deducted in the determination of accounting Net Income and withdrawn by the partners during the year.

During the taxation year ending December 31, 2018, the partnership's accounting Net Income is $262,000. Other relevant information is as follows:

- The accountant deducted amortization charges of $26,000. Maximum CCA is $42,000.
- Accounting Net Income includes a deduction for charitable donations of $2,500.
- Accounting Net Income includes a gain on the sale of land of $24,000.

Determine the amounts of Net Business Income that will be allocated to Partner J and Partner L for the year ending December 31, 2018.

SOLUTION available in print and online Study Guide.

Dividend Income

18-57.   As we have noted in the preceding section, dividends received by a partnership are removed in the determination of the partnership's Net Business Income. When they are allocated to the members of the partnership to be included in their tax returns, they retain their character as eligible, non-eligible or capital dividends. Their treatment subsequent to allocation will depend on the type of taxpayer involved and/or the type of dividend received:

- Partners who are individuals must gross up the dividends by either 38 percent (for eligible dividends) or 16 percent (for non-eligible dividends). The dividends are then eligible for the usual dividend tax credits.
- Dividends allocated to corporate partners will not be grossed up. One hundred percent of the amount allocated will be included in Net Income For Tax Purposes. To the extent the dividends are from taxable Canadian corporations, they can be deducted in the determination of the corporation's Taxable Income.
- Capital dividends received by the partnership are allocated as capital dividends to both individual and corporate partners, generally retaining their tax-free nature.

Foreign Source Income

18-58.   Foreign source income received by a partnership will be allocated to the partners as either business or property income. As you would expect, the amounts that will be allocated to the partners will be the pre-withholding amounts that accrued to the partnership. That is, to the extent that foreign taxes were withheld, they will be added to the amount received for purposes of allocating this income to the members of the partnership. As the pre-withholding amounts are allocated to the partners, the *Income Tax Act* allows these partners to make use of any available foreign tax credits and/or foreign tax deductions (calculation of these credits and deductions is covered in Chapters 7 and 11).

Exercise Eighteen - 3

Subject: Partnership Income Allocations

The ST Partnership has two partners who share all types of income on an equal basis. Partner S and T are both individuals. The Partnership's accounting Net Income for the year ending December 31, 2018 is $146,000. No salaries or interest payments to partners have been included in this calculation. However, the $146,000 includes $12,000 in eligible dividends, as well as a $31,000 gain on the sale of unused land. Amortization Expense deducted is equal to maximum CCA. Determine the amounts that will be included in the Net Income For Tax Purposes of Partner S and Partner T for the year ending December 31, 2018.

SOLUTION available in print and online Study Guide.

Allocations Of Related Tax Credits

18-59.   In the preceding sections, we have covered the various types of income that will be allocated to partners and the related tax credits. The type of income and expenditures that could give rise to tax credits can be summarized as follows:

- Dividend Income - tax credit is available if the partner is an individual.
- Charitable Donations - tax credit is available if the partner is an individual.
- Foreign Source Income - tax credit is available to all partners if foreign tax is withheld.
- Political Contributions - tax credit is available to all partners, but as covered in Chapter 4, the *Federal Accountability Act* bans political contributions by corporations.

Exercise Eighteen - 4

Subject: Allocations To Partners - Related Tax Credits

For the year ending December 31, 2018, the MN Partnership has correctly computed its Net Business Income to be $141,000. The partnership agreement calls for all allocations to Partner M and Partner N to be on a 50:50 basis. Partner M and N are both individuals and neither partner has Taxable Income that will be taxed federally at 33 percent. In determining the Net Business Income amount, the partnership's accountant added back $3,500 in charitable donations and $1,200 in contributions to a registered political party. In addition, $4,200 in eligible dividends received were deducted. The partners have made no charitable donations or political contributions as individuals. Determine the amount of any tax credits that the partnership will allocate to Partner M and Partner N for the year ending December 31, 2018.

SOLUTION available in print and online Study Guide.

Methods Of Allocation

18-60.   As we have seen in the preceding sections, income amounts must be allocated on a source-by-source basis. While a partnership agreement might simply state that all types of income will be allocated on the same basis, there is nothing to prevent different allocations for different sources. For example, business income could be allocated on an equal basis, with capital gains being allocated to one specific partner.

18-61.   There are many ways in which the members of a partnership may agree to allocate income or loss. These allocations may be fixed, variable, or a combination of fixed and variable elements. Factors such as the value of services provided to the partnership (a salary component), capital contributions (an interest component), and amounts of risk assumed (personal assets at risk) may be taken into consideration. Alternatively, allocations may be based upon fixed ratios determined by the partners or, in the absence of some other agreement, the equal fixed ratios that automatically apply under partnership law.

18-62. In general, the CRA will accept any income allocation agreement that is reasonable. It is possible, however, that the agreement could be constructed in a manner that would reduce or postpone taxes (e.g., an example of this would be the allocation of all partnership losses to partners with high levels of current income). In addition, an allocation could be used for income splitting purposes (e.g., allocation of large amounts of partnership income to a low-income spouse on a basis that is not consistent with his contribution of services or capital). In either of these circumstances, the CRA can apply ITA 103(1) or (1.1) to re-allocate the income on the basis that is reasonable in the circumstances.

> **We suggest you work Self Study Problems Eighteen-3 and 4 at this point.**

The Partnership Interest

The Concept

18-63. A person who is a member of a partnership has the right to participate in profits and losses of the partnership and the right to an interest in partnership property, usually on the dissolution of the partnership. Such rights, collectively referred to as a partnership interest, constitute property for income tax purposes much in the same manner as a share of capital stock of a corporation.

18-64. A partnership interest is generally considered a non-depreciable capital property and, as a consequence, a disposition of a partnership interest will usually result in a capital gain or loss.

18-65. In many cases, a partnership interest is acquired when a partnership is formed. Each member of the new organization will acquire an interest, usually through the contribution of an amount of capital that is specified in the partnership agreement.

18-66. Alternatively, a partnership interest can be acquired from an existing partnership. This type of transaction can take two forms:

- The interest can be acquired directly from a current partner or partners by purchasing their interest.

- The interest can be acquired directly from the partnership by transferring assets to this organization.

Acquiring A Partnership Interest

New Partnership

18-67. For founding members of a new partnership, establishment of the adjusted cost base (ACB) of the partnership interest is very straightforward. For each of the partners, the ACB of their interest will simply be the fair value of the assets contributed to the partnership. If the contributions involve non-monetary assets, appraisals may be required. This, however, is a practical complication that does not alter the basic concept that is involved.

Admission To Existing Partnership

18-68. From a technical point of view, partnership law provides that a partnership terminates on a change in the composition of the members (e.g., admissions or withdrawals of partners). In the discussion that follows, we assume that a partnership is not dissolved because of a change in its members. This assumption is consistent with the tax treatment of the partnership accounts. That is, tax law does not require the admission or withdrawal of a partner to be treated as a termination of the partnership, followed by the formation of a new partnership.

18-69. In those cases where a partnership interest is purchased directly from an existing partner, the procedures are very straightforward. If a person becomes a partner by acquiring another partner's interest, then cost will equal the purchase price. For example, if Mr. Davis acquires the one-third interest of Mr. Allan for $90,000, then both the cost to Mr. Davis and the proceeds of disposition to Mr. Allan would be $90,000.

18-70.   The situation becomes more complex when the partnership interest is acquired through direct payments to more than one partner.

EXAMPLE   An existing partnership has three equal partners, each of whom has made a capital contribution of $16,000. They would like to bring in a new equal partner, with each partner then having a 25 percent interest in the organization. The new partner, Mr. Zheng agrees to pay $30,000 to each of the existing partners for one-quarter of their one-third interest. Note that by selling one-quarter of their one-third interest, each partner retains a 25 percent interest [(75%)(1/3) = 25%].

Analysis   Mr. Zheng would have an ACB of $90,000, the consideration given up for the 25 percent interest.

Each of the original partners would have a capital gain calculated as follows:

Proceeds Of Disposition To Each Partner	$30,000
ACB of Part Interest [(25%)($16,000)]	(4,000)
Capital Gain For Each Partner	$26,000

18-71.   The capital accounts in the accounting records of the partnership and the partners' ACB will be as follows:

	Partner 1	Partner 2	Partner 3	Mr. Zheng
Capital Before Admitting Zheng	$16,000	$16,000	$16,000	Nil
Adjustment For Admission Of Zheng	(4,000)	(4,000)	(4,000)	$12,000
Ending Capital Accounts	$12,000	$12,000	$12,000	$12,000
ACB Of Partnership Interest	$12,000	$12,000	$12,000	$90,000

18-72.   Note that, while the accounting values for the interests of the original three partners are equal to their ACBs, this is not the case for Mr. Zheng. In contrast to his accounting value of $12,000, his ACB would be his cost of $90,000 [(3)($30,000)].

18-73.   To this point, we have only considered situations where assets were given to specific partners in return for the new partner's acquired interest. There are also situations in which the new partner makes a payment directly to the partnership in return for his interest.

18-74.   Returning to the example in Paragraph 18-70, if Mr. Zheng had paid the $90,000 directly to the partnership, there would be no tax consequences for the existing partners. No disposition of any part of their interest would have occurred and, as a consequence, no capital gain would be recorded and the ACBs of their interests would remain at $16,000. Mr. Zheng's interest would be recorded at $90,000 for both tax and accounting purposes.

Exercise Eighteen - 5

Subject: Admission Of A Partner

Alan and Balan are equal partners in the Alban Partnership. On September 1, 2018, Alan and Balan's partnership capital account balances are $48,000 each. This is also equal to the adjusted cost base of their interests. As the result of paying $40,000 to each of Alan and Balan, Caitlan is admitted as an equal partner (1/3 interest) on September 1, 2018. Calculate the tax effects of the partner admission for Alan and Balan. In addition, determine the accounting balances for each of the partner's capital accounts after the admission of Caitlan, as well as the adjusted cost base for each partner after the admission of Caitlan.

SOLUTION available in print and online Study Guide.

Adjusted Cost Base Of The Partnership Interest
Basic Concept
18-75.   As we have noted, a partnership interest is viewed in tax legislation as a non-depreciable capital asset. A discussed in Chapter 8, the adjusted cost base (ACB) of a capital property is defined in ITA 54 as its cost, plus or minus the adjustments in ITA 53.

18-76.   In the preceding section, we illustrated how the ACB of a partnership interest would be determined at the time a partnership interest is acquired.

18-77.   Subsequent to its acquisition, the partnership interest is determined by starting with the ACB of the preceding year and adjusting it for various items. The most common adjustments are for:

- current year income allocations;
- current year Drawings; and
- current year capital contributions.

18-78.   There are, however, many other possible adjustments and most of these will be covered in this section. It is important to note the importance of making these adjustments. If these adjustments were not required, any gain or loss on a subsequent sale of the partnership interest would result in these amounts becoming part of the gain or loss on the sale.

> **EXAMPLE**   John Port acquires his partnership interest for $100,000. At a later point in time, he makes an additional capital contribution of $20,000. Subsequent to making this additional contribution, he sells his interest for $150,000.

> **ANALYSIS**   As we shall note in the material which follows, John will add the $20,000 capital contribution to his adjusted cost base, resulting in a new value of $120,000 ($100,000 + $20,000). Given this, the capital gain on the disposition of the interest will be $30,000 ($150,000 - $120,000). If he had not made the required adjustment, the gain would have been $50,000 ($150,000 - $100,000).

Timing Of Adjustments
18-79.   Before proceeding to a discussion of the more common adjustments to the cost base of a partnership interest, some attention must be given to the timing of these adjustments. With respect to capital contributions and drawings, the timing is very straightforward. These adjustments are made at the time of the contribution or drawing.

18-80.   In contrast, those adjustments related to allocations of income or tax credits are not made during the period in which the income or tax credit arises. Rather, these adjustments to the ACB of a partnership interest are made on the first day of the following fiscal period. These procedures will be illustrated in the material that follows.

Adjustments For Partnership Income Components
18-81.   It would be unusual, in any given year, for the adjusted cost base of a partnership interest not to be adjusted for partnership income allocations. As this must be added on a source-by-source basis, specific sources are given separate consideration here:

> **Net Business Income**   As discussed in our section on partnership income determination, accounting Net Income must be converted to the partnership's Net Business Income. This amount is allocated to each partner on the basis of the partnership agreement. The amounts so determined will be added (Net Business Income) or subtracted (Net Business Loss) to the adjusted cost base of each partner. As noted, this increase or decrease does not occur until the first day of the following fiscal period.

> > **EXAMPLE**   Tom and Theresa begin the Double T partnership in January, 2018 and select December 31 as their year end. They each contribute $1,000 to Double T. During 2018, the partnership earns $21,000 in gross service revenue. The only expenses incurred are $6,000 in business meals and entertainment.

ANALYSIS Accounting Net Income for the partnership would be $15,000 ($21,000 - $6,000). However, Net Business Income would be $18,000, the $15,000 of accounting Net Income, plus $3,000, the non-deductible one-half of the expenses for business meals and entertainment. This means that each partner would be allocated $9,000 [(1/2)($18,000)] in business income, and each partnership interest would be increased by the same amount. While the income amounts would be included in the partners' 2018 tax return, the addition to the adjusted cost base would not be made until January 1, 2019.

Capital Gains And Losses As discussed previously, these amounts will be allocated to the partners on the basis of the partnership agreement. Once these amounts are allocated, the taxable or allowable amounts (one-half) will be included in the partner's tax returns.

Despite the fact that only one-half of these amounts will be taxable or deductible, the adjustment to the ACB of the partnership interest is for the full amount and occurs on the first day of the following fiscal period. This inclusion of the full amount provides for the non-taxable one-half of the gain to be recovered on a tax free basis if the partnership interest is sold.

EXAMPLE Weekday Partnership has four equal partners and a December 31 year end. Each partner contributed $1,950 when the partnership began on May 1, 2018. Weekday used the initial contributions of $7,800 to acquire two parcels of land. Both parcels were capital property and were sold in December, 2018. The sale of parcel A resulted in a capital gain of $5,300 and the sale of parcel B resulted in a capital loss of $700. There were no other transactions during the fiscal year.

ANALYSIS The total capital gain for each partner is $1,150 [(1/4)($5,300 − $700)]. The allocation to each partner's Net Income For Tax Purposes will be the taxable amount of $575 [(1/2)($1,150)]. However, the allocation to the partnership interest will be, as shown in the following table, the full amount of the partner's share of the capital gain.

The ACB of each partnership interest is calculated as follows:

ACB - May 1, 2018 to December 31, 2018		$1,950
Net Capital Gain Allocated:		
Capital Gain [(1/4)($5,300)]	$1,325	
Capital Loss [(1/4)($700)]	(175)	1,150
ACB Of Partnership Interest - January 1, 2019		$3,100

Dividends As previously discussed, taxable dividends earned by a partnership retain their character (i.e., eligible, non-eligible or capital) when they are allocated to the partners. In calculating the ACB of a partnership interest, a partner's share of both capital and taxable dividends is added to the ACB of his partnership interest on the first day of the following fiscal period.

EXAMPLE Fred and Barney are equal partners in Stone-Works Partnership that began operations January 1, 2018. A December 31 year end was selected. Each partner initially contributed $5,000. The only income received by the partnership was $13,000 of eligible dividends, and $4,200 of capital dividends. No amounts were withdrawn from the partnership in 2018.

ANALYSIS Each partner is required to include one-half of the taxable dividends of $13,000, plus an additional 38 percent gross-up, in his 2018 Net Income For Tax Purposes. This amounts to income of $8,970 [(50%)($13,000)(138%)]. In conjunction with this allocation, each partner would be eligible for a federal dividend tax credit of $1,347 [(50%)($13,000)(38%)(6/11)]. The capital dividends are not included in each partner's income as they are tax free. The ACB of Fred and Barney's interest would be as follows:

ACB - January 1, 2018 to December 31, 2018	$ 5,000
Allocation Of Dividends Subject To Tax [(50%)($13,000)]	6,500
Allocation Of Capital Dividends [(50%)($4,200)]	2,100
ACB Of Partnership Interest - January 1, 2019	**$13,600**

Two things should be noted in this calculation. First, for purposes of calculating the ACB of the partnership interests, no gross up is added to the dividends subject to tax. Second, the dividends are not added to the ACB until the first day of the year following their allocation to the partners.

Adjustments For Capital Contributions And Drawings

18-82.   These adjustments require little in the way of explanation:

- Net capital contributions are added to the adjusted cost base of the partner's interest.
- Drawings reduce the adjusted cost base of the partnership interest.

Note that bona fide loans by a partner to the partnership are not considered capital contributions. Similarly, loans from the partnership to a partner are not considered to be drawings.

> **EXAMPLE**   The ACB of Mr. Allan's partnership interest is $20,450 at January 1, 2018. In March, 2018, he contributes $8,200 to the partnership as a capital contribution and makes withdrawals of $2,000 in each of May, August, and November, 2018.
>
> **ANALYSIS**   The ACB of Mr. Allan's partnership interest is calculated as follows:

ACB – January 1, 2018	$20,450
Capital Contributions – March 2018	8,200
Drawings – May, August And November 2018 [($2,000)(3)]	(6,000)
ACB – December 31, 2018	**$22,650**

Charitable Donations and Political Contributions

18-83.   Amounts donated or political contributions made by a partnership in a particular year are considered donated or contributed by each partner in proportion to that partner's profit sharing ratio. As it is the partners who enjoy the benefits of making the contributions (i.e., the deductions or tax credits), such amounts reduce the ACB of a partnership interest. Note, however, this adjustment does not occur until the first day of the following fiscal period.

> **EXAMPLE**   During the taxation year ending December 31, 2018, a partnership donated $7,500 to charitable organizations. The three partners, who are all individuals, each have a one-third interest in profits. All donations are eligible for the charitable donations tax credit.
>
> **ANALYSIS**   Each of the three partners would be entitled to allocations of $2,500 towards the calculation of their individual charitable donations tax credit for 2018. As a consequence of this allocation, the ACB of each of their partnership interests would be reduced by $2,500. As we have noted, this reduction does not occur until January 1, 2019.

Negative ACB

18-84.   In general, if negative adjustments to the ACB of a capital asset exceed its cost plus any positive adjustments to the ACB, the excess must be taken into income under ITA 40(3) as a capital gain. While technically an ACB can only be positive or nil, it is common to refer to assets that have experienced such adjustments as having a negative adjusted cost base.

18-85.   This creates a problem for partnership interests in that withdrawals are deducted from the ACB of the partnership interest in the year they occur, while income allocations are only recorded on the first day of the following year. As partners usually withdraw their anticipated income allocations during the year in which they accrue, negative ACBs for partnership interests would not be unusual.

18-86.   Because of this problem, the *Income Tax Act* allows general partners to carry forward a negative ACB, without taking the capital gain into income. This deferral is applicable until the partner disposes of his interest, either through a sale or as the result of a deemed disposition at death.

> **EXAMPLE**   During 2018, in anticipation of the 2018 allocation of partnership income, a partner draws $42,000 from the partnership. For 2018, his share of partnership income is $45,000. On January 1, 2018, his partnership interest has an ACB of $25,000.

> **ANALYSIS**   On December 31, 2018, the ACB of this partnership interest would be nil and there would be an excess of drawings over the January 1, 2018 ACB of $17,000 ($25,000 - $42,000). In the absence of a special provision for partnership interests, $8,500 [(1/2)($17,000)] would have to be taken into the partner's income as a taxable capital gain. However, because of the special provision applicable to partnership interests, this will not be the case. Note that, on January 1, 2019, the ACB of this interest would be $28,000 ($25,000 - $42,000 + $45,000).

18-87.   When the disposition results from a deemed disposition at death, there are rollover provisions that allow a continued carry forward of the negative ACB when the partnership interest is bequeathed to a spouse or common-law partner, or a trust in favour of a spouse or common-law partner.

18-88.   Note that the preceding rules only apply to active general partners. In the case of limited partners (see Paragraph 18-91) or general partners who are not active in the partnership, the deferral of the gain that is implicit in carrying forward a negative ACB is not available. Such amounts must be taken into income in the year in which they occur.

Exercise Eighteen - 6

Subject: ACB Of Partnership Interest

On January 1, 2018 Raymond and Robert form the RR Partnership. The partnership has a December 31 year end. The partnership agreement provides Robert with a 40 percent share of profits and losses. Robert initially contributes $12,500 and makes a further contribution of $7,200 on June 10, 2018. He withdraws $4,000 on October 31, 2018. RR Partnership has the following sources of income for 2018:

Capital Gain On Corporate Shares	$11,600
Eligible Dividends Received From Canadian Corporations	3,100
Net Business Income	46,700

Determine the ACB of Robert's partnership interest on December 31, 2018, and at January 1, 2019. In addition, determine the amount that would be included in Robert's 2018 Net Income For Tax Purposes as a consequence of his interest in the RR Partnership.

SOLUTION available in print and online Study Guide.

Disposition Of A Partnership Interest
Sale To An Arm's Length Party
18-89.   If a partnership interest is sold to an arm's length party, the tax effects are very straightforward. The adjusted cost base of the partnership interest is subtracted from the proceeds resulting from its sale. If the result is positive, it is a capital gain, one-half of which will be taxed in the hands of the partner. Alternatively, if the result is negative, one-half of this

amount will be an allowable capital loss which can be deducted by the partner to the extent of his current year taxable capital gains. Any unused amount can be carried over to previous and subsequent years.

Withdrawal From Partnership

18-90.   When a partner withdraws from a partnership, he is essentially disposing of his interest in that partnership. While this could involve using partnership assets to buy out the partner, the more normal procedure is to have one or more of the other partners purchase the interest of the withdrawing partner.

> **EXAMPLE**   The QST Partnership has three partners who share all income amounts on an equal basis. The ACB of their partnership interests are as follows:
>
> | | |
> |---|---:|
> | Partner Q | $250,000 |
> | Partner S | 250,000 |
> | Partner T | 250,000 |
>
> Partner T has decided to retire and will withdraw from the partnership. In return for his interest, each of the remaining partners will pay him $175,000.
>
> **ANALYSIS**   Partner T will have a taxable capital gain of $50,000 [(1/2)($175,000 + $175,000 - $250,000)]. There will no immediate tax consequences to partners Q and S. However, the ACB of each of their interests will be increased to $425,000, the original $250,000, plus the additional investment of $175,000.
>
> You might wish to note that, assuming the assets of the partnership are not revalued, the accounting values for the interests of each of the remaining partners will be $375,000 [$250,000 + (1/2)($250,000)].

We suggest you work Self Study Problems Eighteen-5 and 6 at this point.

Limited Partnerships And Limited Partners

Definitions

Limited Partner

18-91.   A limited partnership is one that has at least one limited partner and one general partner. As defined in most provincial legislation, a limited partner is one whose liability for the debts of the Partnership is limited to the amount of his contribution to the Partnership, and who is not permitted to participate in the management of the Partnership. A partner whose liability is limited under partnership law is considered a limited partner for income tax purposes.

18-92.   While the term "limited partner" generally refers to a partner who is relieved of general responsibility for amounts in excess of his capital contribution, the definition also includes partners whose liability is limited by the presence of specific contractual arrangements. Examples of this type of situation include:

- guarantees that someone will acquire their partnership interest regardless of its value;
- provisions indicating that amounts a partner has agreed to contribute to the partnership may never have to be paid; and
- provisions that guarantee the partner that he will be reimbursed for any partnership losses, usually by the general partner.

18-93.   Note that members of a limited liability partnership (see Paragraph 18-22) do not fall within the definition of a limited partner. They have limited responsibility for certain types of liabilities (e.g., liabilities arising as the result of negligent action by their professional partners). However, they continue to have unlimited liability for other partnership obligations.

At-Risk Rules

Basic Concept

18-94.   Historically, limited partnership structures have been used to fund high-risk ventures that benefit from generous income tax incentives. These structures have been used with Canadian films, Canadian mining and exploration operations, scientific research and experimental development, real estate, and construction.

18-95.   General partners entice investors with limited liability protection, combined with the advantages of significant flow through of deductible losses and other tax incentives. The general partners usually do not share in the deductions, receiving their compensation through fees that are charged to the limited partners for managing the partnership.

18-96.   The at-risk rules were introduced in order to restrict the ability of certain investors in partnerships, typically limited partners, to receive tax deductions or tax credits in excess of the amount that they stand to lose on their investment. In simplified terms, the at-risk rules work to ensure that $30,000 of tax deductions are not available to a limited partner who has less than $30,000 at risk.

The At-Risk Amount

18-97.   The at-risk amount sets the annual limit on the amount of tax preferences and incentives that may flow through to limited partners. Specifically, the *Income Tax Act* provides restrictions on the allocation to limited partners of scientific research and experimental development credits, resource expenditures, investment tax credits, non-farming business losses, and property losses. Under ITA 96(2.2), the at-risk amount is calculated at the end of a partnership's fiscal period as follows:

ACB Of The Partnership Interest		$xxx
Share Of Partnership Income (But Not Losses) For The Current Period		
(Current Year Income Allocation For ACB Purposes - See Paragraph 18-98)		xxx
Subtotal		$xxx
Less:		
Amounts Owed To The Partnership	($xxx)	
Other Amounts Intended To Reduce The Investment Risk	(xxx)	(xxx)
At-Risk Amount		**$xxx**

18-98.   The addition of the share of partnership income (not losses) is intended to ensure that current year income allocations, which will not be added to the ACB of the partnership interest until the following fiscal year, are taken into consideration at the end of the current year. The amount that is added here is the same income allocation that will be added to the ACB. That is, it does not include the dividend gross up, nor is it adjusted downwards for the non-taxable portion of capital gains.

18-99.   The at-risk amount is reduced by two amounts. The first represents the outstanding balance of any amount owing by the partner to the partnership for the acquisition of the partnership interest. This amount is subtracted as it is included in the partnership interest but, prior to its actual payment, it is not really at risk.

18-100.   The second amount relates to financial incentives designed to reduce the investment risk or exposure to the limited partner. An example of this would be a promise by the general partner to acquire the partnership interest at an amount in excess of the value of the partnership interest at the option of the limited partner.

Limited Partnership Losses

18-101.   The at-risk rules limit the ability of a limited partner to utilize certain types of losses. The rules do not directly affect farm losses and capital losses since these losses carry their own restrictions. Farm losses during the current year may be limited by the restricted farm loss rules and, in addition, any carry over of such restricted farm losses can only be applied against farming income (see Chapter 6). Similarly, current year allowable capital losses are only deductible to the extent of current year taxable capital gains.

18-102. ITA 96(2.1) indicates that a partner's share of losses, other than those associated with farming or the disposition of capital assets, can be deducted to the extent of the at-risk amount. The excess is referred to as the "limited partnership loss". It is a carry forward balance that can be carried forward indefinitely and can only be claimed against future income from the partnership or increases of the at-risk amount from that same partnership. There is no carry back of limited partnership losses.

EXAMPLE On January 1, 2018, Jenny Johnson acquires a 10 percent limited partnership interest in Tax-Time, a partnership that provides tax preparation services. This interest cost her $15,000, with $6,000 paid in cash and the balance of $9,000 payable in 36 months, without interest. At December 31, 2018, Tax-Time determines that it has a $22,000 capital gain and an $111,000 business loss. Jenny is allocated 10 percent of these amounts.

ANALYSIS As a 10 percent limited partner, Jenny is allocated a portion of the business loss equal to $11,100. However, her at-risk amount restricts the business loss that Jenny may be able to use. The at-risk amount is calculated as follows:

ACB Of The Partnership Interest		$15,000
Share Of Partnership Income [(10%)($22,000 Capital Gain)]		2,200
Subtotal		$17,200
Less:		
Amounts Owed To The Partnership	($9,000)	
Other Amounts Intended To Reduce		
The Investment Risk	Nil	(9,000)
At-Risk Amount – December 31, 2018		$ 8,200

For 2018, Jenny will be able to deduct her share of the total partnership loss to the extent of her $8,200 at-risk amount. This will leave a non-deductible limited partnership loss for 2018 of $2,900 ($11,100 - $8,200). In general, Jenny will be able to use the limited partnership loss in 2019 or subsequent years if her at-risk amount increases. This may occur if she makes additional contributions, is allocated additional income from the partnership in 2019, or pays the amount owed to the partnership. It should also be noted that there are special adjustments to the ACB of a limited partner's partnership interest that are beyond the scope of this material.

Exercise Eighteen - 7

Subject: Limited Partnership Loss

During 2018, Stuart Jones acquires an interest in a mining limited partnership for $200,000. An initial $50,000 is paid immediately, with the $150,000 balance payable in eight years. The general partner has agreed to acquire Stuart's interest at any subsequent date, returning his $50,000 payment and assuming responsibility for the $150,000 payable. For 2018, the limited partnership has allocated losses of $75,000 to Stuart. How much of this loss is Stuart entitled to claim as a deduction on his 2018 tax return? What is the amount of his limited partnership loss at the end of 2018?

SOLUTION available in print and online Study Guide.

We suggest you work Self Study Problem Eighteen-7 at this point.

Transfer Of Property To And From A Partnership

Definition Of Canadian Partnership

18-103.   Since the ITA treats partners as distinct from the partnership, transferring property between the partners and the partnership may have income tax consequences. Such consequences are generally dependent on the purpose of the property transfer and whether the underlying partnership meets the ITA 102 definition of a "Canadian partnership":

> **ITA 102**   In this subdivision, "Canadian partnership" means a partnership all of the members of which were, at any time in respect of which the expression is relevant, resident in Canada.

18-104.   Whether the partnership is a general, limited, or limited liability partnership is irrelevant to the determination of its status as a Canadian partnership. In addition, the definition does not require that the partnership be formed in Canada. For example, a U.S. based partnership with all Canadian resident members would qualify.

18-105.   If the required conditions are met, the *Income Tax Act* contains rollover provisions that provide for tax deferral on such transactions. However, where the conditions are not met, the transfers will be taxed as a disposition/acquisition at fair market value.

18-106.   In covering this material on property transfers, we will first look at the rules applicable to transfers of property to and from a partnership when a rollover provision is not used. This will be followed by a discussion of some of the more commonly used partnership rollover provisions.

Transfers With No Rollover Provision

Transfers From Partners To The Partnership

18-107.   If a person transfers property to a partnership of which he is member, or to a partnership of which he becomes a member as a result of the transfer, ITA 97(1) deems the person to have disposed of the property at fair market value and the partnership to have acquired the property at the same amount.

18-108.   In general, the fair market value of the transferred asset is added to the ACB of the transferor's partnership interest. However, this addition would be reduced by any consideration given to the contributor because of his contribution. This rule is applicable without regard to whether the partnership qualifies as a Canadian partnership.

> **EXAMPLE**   Diane Jefferson is a member of CG Partnership. She is required to make an additional 2018 capital contribution to the partnership and decides to make the contribution by transferring investments that she had purchased for $10,000. At the time of the transfer, they have a fair market value of $24,000.

> **ANALYSIS**   Diane will be considered to have disposed of the investments for $24,000. This will result in a $7,000 [(1/2)($24,000 - $10,000)] taxable capital gain for 2018. Diane will also be considered to have made a $24,000 capital contribution that will increase the ACB of her partnership interest by the same amount. The partnership will be considered to have acquired the investments from Diane for $24,000.

Exercise Eighteen - 8

Subject: Transfers From Partner To Partnership (No Rollover)

Charles Woodward is one of four equal partners in LIU Partnership (LIU). During the current year, Charles contributes a tract of land to the partnership. Charles does not use a rollover provision to make the transfer. Charles acquired the land for $33,000 and, at the time of transfer, it is valued at $100,000. Describe the tax consequences to Charles and LIU in the following three situations:

    A. No consideration is received from LIU.
    B. Charles receives $25,000 in cash from LIU on the transfer.
    C. Charles receives $112,000 in cash from LIU on the transfer.

SOLUTION available in print and online Study Guide.

Transfers From The Partnership To Partners

18-109.   If a partnership transfers property to a partner, ITA 98(2) deems the partnership to have disposed of the property at fair market value and the partner to have acquired the property at the same amount. There is no requirement that the partner remains a partner after the transfer and the rule is applicable without regard to whether the partnership qualifies as a Canadian partnership. This provision is typically used when a partnership is dissolved, or when partial distributions of partnership property are made in an ongoing partnership.

> **EXAMPLE**   Bill Davis is a 40 percent partner in the FV Partnership. The partnership owns a piece of land that has an ACB of $2,900 and transfers it to Bill in June, 2018 for no consideration. The land has a fair market value of $10,000 at this time.

> **ANALYSIS**   The partnership is considered to have disposed of the land for its fair market value of $10,000, resulting in a capital gain of $7,100 ($10,000 - $2,900). Bill's share of this gain is $2,840 [(40%)($7,100)]. This amount will be allocated to Bill and, as a consequence, he will report a taxable capital gain of $1,420 [(1/2)($2,840)] in his 2018 tax return. Bill will also be considered to have acquired the land for $10,000 and to have made a withdrawal from the partnership of $10,000. The ACB of his partnership interest will be reduced by the $10,000 withdrawal and increased by the $2,840 allocation of the capital gain.

Exercise Eighteen - 9

Subject: Transfers From Partnership To Partners

Darlene is one of five equal partners in the DG Partnership. During the taxation year ending December 31, 2018, DG distributes some of its investments to each of the partners. The distributed investments have an adjusted cost base of $39,000 and, at the time of transfer, they have a fair market value of $94,000. Darlene receives one-fifth of these investments. At the time of this transfer, the adjusted cost base of Darlene's partnership interest is $30,000. What are the tax consequences to DG and Darlene with respect to this distribution? Your answer should include Darlene's adjusted cost base for the investments and the amount of her partnership interest on both December 31, 2018, and on January 1, 2019.

SOLUTION available in print and online Study Guide.

Common Partnership Rollovers
Transfers From Partners To The Partnership

18-110.   If a person transfers property to a Canadian partnership and all members of that partnership jointly elect, then property transferred to the partnership may be transferred on a rollover basis. This means that the property can be transferred at elected values (usually tax values), rather than at the fair market values that must be used in the absence of a rollover provision. This rule applies both to persons who are existing partners, as well as to persons who become partners by contributing property to the partnership.

18-111.   ITA 97(2) indicates that, for this type of transfer, the ITA 85(1) rules apply. The ITA 85(1) rules are generally applicable to transfers of property to a corporation and are discussed in detail in Chapter 16. There are, however, some differences in the application of these rules when the transfer is to a partnership. The more notable of these differences are as follows:

- Real property inventory can be transferred to a partnership, but not to a corporation.

- When a transferor takes back consideration with a value less than that of the property transferred to a corporation, it may involve a gift to a related party. In the case of transfers to a partnership, the gift portion is added to the ACB of the partnership interest. As discussed in Chapter 16, if such a transfer was made to a corporation, it would usually result in double taxation of the gifted amount.

- When a transferor receives consideration in excess of the value of the property transferred to a corporation, the excess is subject to taxation. When this happens in conjunction with a transfer of property to a partnership, the excess is generally viewed as a drawing and is not subject to taxation.

18-112.   Differences between the elected amounts and consideration other than a partnership interest affect the ACB of the partnership interest.

EXAMPLE   Janice Donovan will join the On-Off Partnership that provides interior lighting products. She plans to make an initial capital contribution of a parcel of land with an ACB of $100,000 and a fair market value of $250,000. She wishes to transfer the land at an elected value of $160,000. The existing members agree and file a joint election authorizing the transaction for $160,000. Janice has a choice between three different packages of consideration:

A. No cash.
B. Cash of $100,000.
C. Cash of $160,000.

ANALYSIS   ITA 97(2) uses the transfer limits described within ITA 85. The basic acceptable transfer range is from the land's ACB of $100,000 to its fair market value of $250,000. While not applicable in this case, the elected value is also limited to the amount of non-partnership interest consideration received. The relevant values for the three Cases are as follows:

Case	ACB Of Partnership Interest	Capital Gain
No Cash	$160,000	$60,000
Cash Of $100,000	$ 60,000	60,000
Cash Of $160,000	Nil	60,000

Exercise Eighteen - 10

Subject: Transfers From Partner To Partnership (With Rollover)

Samantha Floren is one of three equal partners in the SFL Partnership. During the current year, Samantha transfers land to the partnership as a capital contribution. She had acquired the land several years ago for $156,000. At the time of transfer, it is valued at $263,000. She would like to use any available rollover provision in order to minimize her current taxes. Assuming the appropriate rollover provision is used, what are the tax consequences of this transfer?

SOLUTION available in print and online Study Guide.

Partnership Property Transferred To A New Partnership

18-113.   A partnership may be dissolved in a number of situations. Included would be the addition or retirement of partners in cases where the partnership agreement does not provide for the continuation of the partnership. The dissolution of a partnership is considered to be a disposition of partnership property and, in the absence of a rollover provision, would result in tax consequences to the partners. However, this treatment can be avoided if the partnership property is transferred to a new partnership.

18-114.   ITA 98(6) provides automatic (i.e., no election is required) rollover treatment where all of the property of a Canadian partnership that has ceased to exist is transferred to a new Canadian partnership. A further condition is that all of the members of the new partnership must have been members of the old partnership.

18-115.   While many rollover provisions provide tax free treatment by providing for a deemed disposition at the tax cost of the property, ITA 98(6) takes a different approach. This Subsection deems the old and new partnerships to be the same entity, with the result being that there is no disposition of the property and no tax consequences to the transferor. This means that the ITA 98(6) rollover involves fewer complications than would be found in most rollover applications.

18-116.   It is important to note that, while all of the members of the new partnership have to have been members of the old partnership, not all of the members of the old partnership have to become members of the new partnership. This rollover is typically used when a partner retires.

18-117.   The retirement of a partner usually involves distributing some of the partnership property to the retiring partner. This makes it impossible to fully comply with the requirement of ITA 98(6) that all of the property of the old partnership be transferred. This problem was resolved by IT-338R2, "Partnership Interests - Effects On Adjusted Cost Base Resulting From The Admission Or Retirement Of A Partner", which states that all of the property of the old partnership is considered to mean all the property after the settlement of a retired partner's interest. While IT-338R2 has been cancelled, it appears that the CRA continues to maintain this position.

Partnership Property Transferred To A Sole Proprietorship

18-118.   This rollover, provided for in ITA 98(5) applies automatically where a Canadian partnership ceases to exist and, within three months of the cessation date, one of the partners continues to carry on the partnership business as a sole proprietor. This rollover treatment is provided for partnership property distributed to the proprietor and, in general, ensures that there are no tax consequences associated with the disposition of that proprietor's partnership interest.

18-119.   There is an exception in situations where the tax cost of partnership property received by the proprietor exceeds the ACB of his or her partnership interest. In this case, there will be a capital gain.   Alternatively, if the ACB of the proprietor's partnership interest exceeds the tax cost of partnership property received by the proprietor, the rules allow the tax cost of non-depreciable partnership property to be increased to reflect this difference. You might wish to note that this is similar to the bump that is available in amalgamations and subsidiary wind ups (see Chapter 17)

18-120.   This rollover typically applies where one of the partners in a two-person partnership retires or dies, leaving the remaining person to continue the business. As a partnership must have at least two partners, there is no possibility of the partnership continuing. Note, however, that the rollover only applies to the partner who continues the business. A retiring partner will have a disposition at fair market value with the usual tax consequences associated with such a disposition.

Partnership Property Transferred To A Corporation

18-121.   The decision to convert a partnership to a corporation, or to incorporate a partnership, generally arises when a partnership that has realized losses in its initial years becomes profitable. Prior to that time, the partnership form is useful as it allows the partners to use the partnership losses to offset their income from other sources. Once the partnership has become profitable, corporate status may be preferred because of the availability of the small business deduction, the possibility of deferring taxes on income retained within the corporation, or the desire to split income with other related persons.

18-122.   The process of incorporating a partnership on a tax deferred basis generally requires two rollovers, ITA 85(2) and ITA 85(3).   Under ITA 85(2), eligible partnership property is transferred to a taxable Canadian corporation for either shares or a combination of shares and other consideration. The transfer takes place at elected values which can include the tax cost of the property, thereby avoiding tax consequences to the partnership. This roll-over treatment is only available if the corporation and all the partners jointly elect rollover treatment.

18-123.   At this point, the partnership is holding shares in the corporation and the partners are continuing to hold their partnership interests. ITA 85(3) then provides for a transfer at tax values of the partnership's holding of the corporation's shares to the partners in return for their partnership interests. This is accompanied by a wind-up of the partnership.

18-124.   If the following conditions are met, the ITA 85(3) rollover treatment is automatic, with no election required:

- The partnership must have disposed of property to a taxable Canadian corporation under ITA 85(2).
- The partnership must be wound up within 60 days of the disposition of its property to the corporation.
- Immediately before the partnership is wound up, the only property it holds is money or property received from the corporation as a result of the application of ITA 85(2).

18-125.   The winding-up of a partnership usually requires the distribution of all partnership property, the settlement of partnership obligations, as well as certain provincial formalities such as de-registration.

18-126.   These rules are designed to provide a tax free means of incorporating a partnership. However, tax consequences may arise in two particular instances. First, ITA 85(2) only applies to "eligible property" as defined in ITA 85(1.1). The major item that would not be included in this definition would be an inventory of real property (i.e., real property held for sale rather than use). If such non-eligible property is transferred from a partnership to a corporation, the transfer will be at fair market value, resulting in the usual tax consequences.

18-127.   A second situation in which the incorporation of a partnership may result in tax consequences would arise when a partner receives consideration in excess of the ACB of his partnership interest. While this may result in a capital gain, it can be avoided with the proper use of the ITA 85(3) rollover provision.

> **EXAMPLE**   Danielle and Christine are equal partners in the Flag Partnership. The recent success of the business has led to a decision to incorporate. The only asset Flag owns is an inventory of flags that cost $50,000, but is currently worth $200,000. The ACB of each partner's partnership interest is $34,000. The corporation will issue only common shares as consideration for the acquisition of the flag inventory.
>
> **ANALYSIS**   Danielle, Christine, and the corporation will jointly elect to transfer the inventory from the Flag Partnership at its tax cost of $50,000. Flag will be deemed to have disposed of the inventory for $50,000 and the corporation will be considered to have acquired the inventory for $50,000. No tax consequences will arise on the disposition. Flag Partnership will receive common shares of the corporation that will have an ACB and PUC of $50,000. At this point, Flag Partnership owns shares of the corporation and the corporation owns the inventory.

When the Flag Partnership distributes the shares to Danielle and Christine, the following tax consequences will arise:

- The Flag Partnership will be considered to have disposed of the shares for their tax cost of $50,000, resulting in no tax consequences.

- Each partner will be considered to have acquired the shares for an amount equal to the ACB of her partnership interest ($34,000).

- Each partner will be considered to have disposed of her partnership interest for the cost of the shares acquired from the partnership ($34,000). As a result, there is no capital gain or loss.

We suggest you work Self Study Problem Eighteen-8 at this point.

Specified Investment Flow Through Partnerships

18-128.   Because partnerships are not taxable entities, income is flowed through such structures without income taxes being assessed at the partnership level. As we shall see in Chapter 19, trusts are also "flow-through" entities. That is, even though trusts are taxable entities for income tax purposes, if all of their income is distributed to beneficiaries, no taxes will be paid at the trust level.

18-129.   At one point in time, this flow-through feature of partnerships and trusts resulted in the conversion of a large number of business entities into publicly traded partnerships and trusts. As the government viewed this development as a significant form of tax avoidance, legislation was put in place which designated most of these publicly traded entities as specified investment flow through partnerships and trusts (SIFTs). The legislation was such that it made SIFTs sufficiently unattractive that, with the exception of real estate investment trusts, they have largely disappeared. Given this, we do not provide coverage of this subject in *Canadian Tax Principles*, except in Chapter 7, Property Income, where we have limited coverage of real estate income trusts (REITs).

Additional Supplementary Self Study Problems Are Available Online.

Key Terms Used In This Chapter

18-130.   The following is a list of the key terms used in this Chapter. These terms, and their meanings, are compiled in the Glossary located at the back of the Study Guide.

At-Risk Amount	Limited Liability Partnership
At-Risk Rules	Limited Partner
Canadian Partnership	Limited Partnership
Co-Ownership	Limited Partnership Loss
Deeming Rule	"Negative" Adjusted Cost Base
General Partner	Partner
General Partnership	Partnership
Joint Tenancy	Partnership Interest
Joint Venture	Syndicates
Limited Liability	Tenancy In Common

References

18-131.   For more detailed study of the material in this Chapter, we refer you to the following:

ITA 40(3)   Negative ACB
ITA 53(1)(e)   Addition To Cost Base Of An Interest In A Partnership
ITA 53(2)(c)   Deduction From Cost Base Of An Interest In A Partnership
ITA 85(2)   Transfer Of Property To Corporation From Partnership
ITA 85(3)   Where Partnership Wound Up
ITA 96   General Rules (Partnerships And Their Members)
ITA 97   Contribution Of Property To Partnership
ITA 98   Disposition Of Partnership Property
ITA 99   Fiscal Period Of Terminated Partnership
ITA 100   Disposition Of An Interest in a Partnership
ITA 102   Definition Of "Canadian Partnership"
ITA 103   Agreement To Share Income

S4-F16-C1   What Is A Partnership?

IT-81R   Partnerships - Income Of Non-Resident Partners
IT-231R2   Partnerships - Partners Not Dealing At Arm's Length
IT-242R   Retired Partners
IT-278R2   Death Of A Partner Or Of A Retired Partner
IT-378R   Winding Up Of A Partnership
IT-413R   Election By Members Of A Partnership Under Subsection 97(2)
IT-457R   Election By Professionals To Exclude Work In Progress From Income
IT-471R   Merger Of Partnerships

T4068   Guide for the T5013 Partnership Information Return

Problems For Self Study (Online)

To provide practice in problem solving, there are Self Study and Supplementary Self Study problems available on MyLab Accounting.

Within the text we have provided an indication of when it would be appropriate to work each Self Study problem. The detailed solutions for Self Study problems can be found in the print and online Study Guide.

We provide the Supplementary Self Study problems for those who would like additional practice in problem solving. The detailed solutions for the Supplementary Self Study problems are available online, not in the Study Guide.

The .PDF file "Self Study Problems for Volume 2" on MyLab contains the following for Chapter 18:

- 8 Self Study problems,
- 4 Supplementary Self Study problems, and
- detailed solutions for the Supplementary Self Study problems.

Assignment Problems

(The solutions for these problems are only available in
the solutions manual that has been provided to your instructor.)

Assignment Problem Eighteen - 1
(Existence Of Partnership)

Barry and Lance Booker are brothers who live in the same New Brunswick community. Barry is an accountant who specializes in advising small businesses. Lance has held various jobs in restaurants over the last few years. However, he is currently between jobs.

As a result of information he has accumulated while working with his accounting clients, Barry has started a new business involving catering services. To this end, he has acquired a building, furniture, and equipment. He has also registered the business and opened up a bank account under his own name. Barry spends a few hours each day managing the business.

As he is aware of Lance's financial difficulties, he has decided to treat his brother as a partner in this business, sharing profits on a 50:50 basis when filing their annual income tax returns. There is no formal partnership agreement.

Required: In the following two **independent** Cases, determine whether a partnership exists.

A. Lance's involvement with the business consists of helping Barry pick out furniture and equipment and occasionally taking messages when Barry is out of town. It appears that the business will be consistently profitable.

B. Lance does all the accounting, payroll and invoicing for the business. He also does most of the ordering and is responsible for paying the suppliers. While it is unlikely that the business will be profitable in its first year of operation, Barry expects it to experience profitability in subsequent years.

Assignment Problem Eighteen - 2
(Existence Of Partnership)

Mr. Poliacik joined Mr. Ewing's practice by entering into a business association with Mr. Ewing. They operated under the name " Ewing/Poliacik". Mr. Poliacik made no capital contribution on joining.

Both individuals were lawyers. Mr. Poliacik's specialty was litigation. Mr. Ewing was involved in non-litigation matters.

An agreement was signed, but it never referred to the individuals as partners or the association as a partnership. When asked why they did not refer to themselves as partners, Mr. Poliacik stated that they did not know each other well enough to accept the risks of partnership. The agreement stated that all fees billed by each individual belonged to that individual.

Both parties agreed to open a combined general and trust bank account. Both parties had signing authority on the general account, although Mr. Poliacik's authority was limited to client disbursements only. Mr. Ewing had sole signing authority on the trust account. The accounts did not indicate that they were registered to a partnership.

Mr. Poliacik's fees were to be split based on a graduated scale. The first $100,000 was to be split 50:50, then 60:40 on the next $25,000, 80:20 on the next $25,000 and 90:10 thereafter. The larger percentage went to Mr. Poliacik. In addition, Mr. Poliacik was entitled to 10 percent of fees billed by Mr. Ewing to clients introduced by Mr. Poliacik.

Mr. Ewing agreed to be 100 percent liable for office expenses and bookkeeping services. Mr. Poliacik's share of the office operating expenses was $62,500 in the first year. This amount would be adjusted in the future as the expenses increased. Mr. Poliacik was not entitled to the 10 percent finder's fee from Mr. Ewing until his share of the annual expenses had been paid.

Mr. Poliacik was responsible for making his own CPP contributions and professional insurance. He will register for GST as an individual and his personal income tax return will not include a separate calculation of partnership income.

The combined business was not registered for GST purposes. There were no filings with the law society indicating that Mr. Poliacik and Mr. Ewing were partners.

Required: Determine whether the business association is a partnership.

Assignment Problem Eighteen - 3
(Partnership Vs. Joint Venture)

Chantale Bergeron is a real estate agent who had dreamed of becoming a real estate developer for a long time. In 2015, she received a substantial inheritance and purchased a tract of land with the intention of developing a group of residential lots. She paid $1,200,000 for the land which she had secretly learned from contacts would soon be adjacent to a new highway exit.

As Chantale had spent her inheritance purchasing the land and had no track record in the development business, she had difficulty in finding financing for the required $700,000 in site servicing costs. She finally located a developer, Elise Ltd. who was willing to provide the required $700,000 on an interest free basis in return for 40 percent of the profit resulting from the sale of the lots.

By December 31, 2018, it was estimated that the land's fair market value had increased to $2,000,000 because of the opening of the highway exit. During 2019, the sites are developed, with the servicing costs coming in at the estimated $700,000. All of the lots are sold prior to December 31, 2019 for total proceeds of $3,700,000.

> **Case A** On December 31, 2018, Chantale and Elise Ltd. enter into a joint venture agreement. Chantale transfers the land to Elise Ltd. At the end of 2019, Elise Ltd. provides Chantale with 60 percent of the profits resulting from the development and the sale of the lots.

> **Case B** On December 31, 2018, Chantale and Elise Ltd. form a partnership to develop the lots. Chantale transfers the land to the partnership using the ITA 97(2) rollover provision to defer the gain on the transfer. The partnership agreement specifies that Chantale is entitled to all of the deferred gain on the land transfer at December 31, 2018, as well as 60 percent of the profits resulting from the sale of the lots.

Required:

A. Calculate the amount that will be added to Chantale's Net Income For Tax Purposes in 2018 and 2019 for Case A and Case B and compare the results.

B. Assume that the Case B approach is used. Calculate the adjusted cost base of the partnership interest for both Chantale and Elise Ltd. on December 31, 2019 and January 1, 2020.

Assignment Problem Eighteen - 4
(Partnership Income Allocation)

Saul and Samuel Brock are brothers and Chartered Public Accountants with significant experience in tax work. Until 2018, they have worked separately. However, they have decided that working together would produce synergies that would increase their aggregate income. Given this, as of January 1, 2018, they initiate the Brock and Brock Partnership.

Saul will be entitled to a salary of $72,000 per year, while Samuel's salary will be $48,000. In addition, Samuel will receive interest at 6 percent on his average capital balance for the year. All of these amounts were withdrawn from the partnership prior to December 31, 2018. Neither brother has Taxable Income that will be taxed federally at 33 percent in 2018.

The components of their partnership agreement dealing with income allocation are as follows:

Business Income After the allocation of priority amounts for salaries and interest on capital contributions, any remaining business income will be allocated 60 percent to Saul and 40 percent to Samuel.

Capital Gains As Samuel has contributed the majority of capital to the partnership, he will be entitled to all capital gains that are recognized by the partnership.

Dividends Any dividends received by the partnership will be split equally between the two partners.

For the year ending December 31, 2018, their GAAP based financial statements indicate that they had net business income of $649,522. Other information related to this result is as follows:

• Salaries to Saul and Samuel of $120,000 ($72,000 + $48,000) were deducted.

• Interest on Samuel's capital contribution of $4,800 was deducted.

• Business meals of $18,976 were deducted.

• Amortization expense of $31,632 was deducted.

• Charitable contributions of $4,520 were deducted.

Other Information

1. For tax purposes, the brothers intend to deduct maximum CCA for 2018. This amount has been calculated to be $38,597.

2. The partnership has 2018 gains on the sale of shares held as temporary investments in the amount of $16,164.

3. The partnership receives $10,462 in eligible dividends during 2018.

4. The charitable contributions will be allocated equally between the two brothers.

Required:

A. Calculate the amounts of income from the partnership that would be included in the Net Income For Tax Purposes of each of the two brothers.

B. Indicate the amount of any federal tax credits that each of the two brothers would be entitled to as a result of allocations made by the partnership at December 31, 2018.

Assignment Problem Eighteen - 5
(Partnership Income And ACB)

On January 1, 2018, a partnership is formed between two divorce lawyers who have, for a number of years, practiced individually. Each partner contributes $70,000.

During 2018, each partner is allocated a salary of $125,000, as well as interest on their beginning of the year capital balances at an annual rate of 5 percent. These amounts are withdrawn during the year. Any Net Business Income that remains after the priority allocations for salaries and interest will be split 50:50 by the two partners.

For the year ending December 31, 2018, their bookkeeper has prepared the following financial statements for the partnership. No amortization was deducted in preparing these statements.

Settlements Unlimited
Balance Sheet
As At December 31, 2018

Cash	$ 45,189
Accounts Receivable	186,485
Work In Progress	232,814
Furniture And Fixtures	56,581
Computer Hardware (At Cost)	17,608
Computer Applications Software (At Cost)	13,440
Total Assets	**$552,117**
Accounts Payable	$109,872
Initial Partner Capital	140,000
Income For The Period	302,245
Total Equities	**$552,117**

Settlements Unlimited
Income Statement
For The Year Ending December 31, 2018

Revenues	$682,946
Meals And Entertainment	$ 23,334
Office Supplies	12,382
Partners' Salaries	250,000
Interest On Capital Contributions	7,000
Rent	46,440
Salaries	41,545
Total Expenses	$380,701
Income For The Period (Accounting Values)	**$302,245**

The work in progress represents work done by the lawyers at their standard charge rate that has not been billed to clients at the year end.

Required:

A. The lawyers have come to you to determine the minimum amount that they must include in their 2018 tax returns as business income from the partnership.

B. Compute the ACB of each partner's partnership interest at December 31, 2018 and January 1, 2019.

Your answers should ignore GST and PST considerations.

Assignment Problem Eighteen - 6
(Partnership Income And Sale Of Partnership Interest)

Jason and Joey Blake are brothers and lawyers. While they have worked independently for several years, on January 1, 2017, they have decided to form a partnership. On January 1, 2017, they each make a capital contribution of $350,000 in cash. Because Jason's experience is in a more lucrative area of law, he is to receive 60 percent of all partnership income, with Joey receiving the remaining 40 percent. Capital gains realized by the partnership, dividends received by the partnership and charitable donations will be shared equally.

During the partnership taxation year ending December 31, 2017, the partnership has net business income for tax purposes of $335,000. The partnership had no capital gains or losses or dividend income during 2017. The partnership made no charitable donations in 2017. During this taxation year, Jason withdrew $130,000, while Joey withdrew $102,000.

The partnership's 2018 Income Statement, prepared in accordance with generally accepted accounting principles, is as follows:

Income Statement
Joey And Jason Blake Partnership
Year Ending December 31, 2018

Revenues (Note 1)		$823,000
Operating Expenses:		
Rent	($95,000)	
Amortization Expense (Note 2)	(22,000)	
Office Salaries	(46,000)	
General Office Costs	(42,000)	
Meals And Entertainment	(16,000)	
Charitable Donations	(12,000)	(233,000)
Operating Income		$590,000
Other Income:		
Gain On Sale Of Investments (Note 3)	$26,000	
Eligible Dividends Received From Canadian Corporations	22,000	48,000
Net Income		$638,000

Note 1   The revenues in the accounting based Income Statement include $105,000 in unbilled work in progress. There was no unbilled work in progress at the end of the previous year. The brothers will use the ITA 34 election to record the partnership income on a billed basis.

Note 2   Maximum 2018 CCA, which the partners intend to deduct, is $35,000.

Note 3   The gain resulted from the sale of temporary investments. The investments had an adjusted cost base of $57,000 and were sold for $83,000.

During 2018, Jason had drawings of $310,000 while Joey had drawings of $242,000.

During 2018, Jason's only income was from the partnership. Other than credits related to partnership allocations, Jason's only tax credit was his basic personal credit.

On January 1, 2019, Jason sells his interest in the partnership to an arm's length individual for $643,000.

Required: Calculate Jason's federal Tax Payable for the year ending December 31, 2018. In addition, determine the taxable capital gain or allowable capital loss that would result from Jason's sale of his partnership interest. Ignore any CPP implications with respect to self-employment income.

Assignment Problem Eighteen - 7
(Withdrawal Of A Partner)

Tammy, Loretta, and Crystal formed a partnership on January 1, 2016. The partnership is organized to provide a variety of consulting services to a broad range of clients. Each partner makes an initial capital contribution of $270,000. The partners agree to use a December 31 year end.

The partnership agreement contains the following provisions with respect to the allocation of items to individual partners:

1. Both net business income and charitable contributions will be shared equally by the three partners.

2. Any capital gains realized by the partnership will be allocated on a 50:50 basis to Crystal and Loretta.

3. All of the eligible dividends received by the partnership will be allocated to Tammy.

During the period January 1, 2016 through December 31, 2018, the partnership operates successfully. The following information related to that period:

- The partnership earned net business income of $315,000.

- Amounts not included in the net business income figure were as follows:

  - The partnership received eligible dividends totaling $6,300.
  - The partnership realized a $24,800 capital gain.
  - The partnership made charitable donations only in 2018. The total amount involved was $9,900.

- Withdrawals from the partnership were as follows:

  - Tammy - $149,000
  - Crystal - $306,000
  - Loretta - $72,000

- Additional capital was required to expand the operations of the office and, as a consequence, each partner contributed an additional $104,000 in cash.

Near the end of 2018, after a number of heated arguments with Tammy and Crystal regarding the types of clients the partnership was servicing, Loretta decides to withdraw from the partnership effective January 1, 2019. After some negotiations, each of the other partners agree to pay her $210,000 in cash for one-half of her interest in the partnership, a total of $420,000. The payments are made on February 1, 2019. The partnership has net business income of $27,600 during January, 2019.

Loretta incurred legal and accounting fees in conjunction with this withdrawal transaction totaling $2,300.

Required:

A. Calculate the adjusted cost base of Loretta's partnership interest as of January 1, 2019.

B. Determine the amount of Loretta's gain or loss on the disposition of his partnership interest. Explain how this amount, and any other amounts related to the partnership, will be taxed in her hands during 2019.

C. Indicate how the adjusted cost base of each partner's interest will be affected by the withdrawal of Loretta from the partnership.

Assignment Problem Eighteen - 8
(Limited Partnership)

On January 1, 2018, Jerry Adverse purchases a 25 percent interest in income and losses of the Precipice Enterprises Partnership for $200,000. Of this total, $120,000 is paid immediately, with the remaining $80,000 due on January 1, 2019. The partnership has a December 31 year end.

The general partner of the Precipice Enterprises Partnership has agreed to buy back Jerry's interest for $100,000, without regard to its fair market value on the buy back date. However, the agreement expires on January 1, 2020.

During the year ending December 31, 2018, the Precipice Enterprises Partnership records a net business loss of $1,200,000. Also during the year, the partnership has an $80,000 capital gain.

For the year ending December 31, 2019, the Precipice Enterprises Partnership has a further net business loss of $225,000. There are no other sources of income during this year.

Jerry does not ask the general partner to buy back his interest during the year ending December 31, 2019. As a consequence, the agreement expires on January 1, 2020.

During 2020, the Precipice Enterprises Partnership has net business income of $50,000.

Jerry has sufficient other sources of income to absorb any deductible losses generated by the partnership.

Required: For each of 2018, 2019 and 2020, calculate the following amounts related to Jerry's interest in the Precipice Enterprises Partnership:

- The adjusted cost base at the end of the year.
- The at-risk amount.
- The limited partnership income (loss) for the year.
- The deductible income (loss) for the year.
- The limited partnership loss carry forward at the end of the year.

Assignment Problem Eighteen - 9
(Partnership Winding-Up & Transfer To Corporation)

The Jones, Haggard, and Twitty Partnership was formed several years ago by Conway Jones, George Haggard, and Merle Twitty. To establish the partnership, each of the individuals invested $450,000 in cash. They prepared a standard partnership agreement which indicated that all income and losses would be shared on an equal basis. The partnership has a December 31 taxation year.

On January 1, 2018, the adjusted cost base of the three partnership interests are as follows:

Conway Jones	$ 880,000
George Haggard	698,000
Merle Twitty	567,000
Total	$2,145,000

The total tax cost of the partnership assets is $2,145,000, the same amount as the adjusted cost base of the partnership interests. On January 2, 2018, the net assets of the partnership are transferred to a corporation using the provisions of ITA 85(2). The elected values are equal to the tax costs of the individual assets and liabilities.

Through the use of an appraiser, it has been established that the fair market value of the partnership is $2,925,000. Using this value, the corporation provides the following consideration to the partnership:

Cash	$ 900,000
Preferred Shares (At Fair Market Value)	675,000
Common Shares (At Fair Market Value)	1,350,000
Total Consideration	**$2,925,000**

The partnership will be liquidated within 60 days of the ITA 85(2) rollover and property received from the corporation by the partnership will be transferred to the three partners in accordance with ITA 85(3). Under the terms of the partnership agreement, they receive the following amounts:

	Jones	Haggard	Twitty	Total
Cash	$ 465,000	$ 283,000	$ 152,000	$ 900,000
Preferred Shares	225,000	225,000	225,000	675,000
Common Shares	450,000	450,000	450,000	1,350,000
Total	**$1,140,000**	**$ 958,000**	**$ 827,000**	**$2,925,000**

Required:

A. Determine the adjusted cost base of each of the assets received by the partners as a result of the transfer of partnership assets to the corporation.

B. Calculate the capital gain or loss for each partner resulting from the transfer of the consideration received by the partnership to the partners in return for the partnership interest.

Assignment Problem Eighteen - 10
(Additional Business Income)

Note This problem involves knowledge of "additional business income" when the election of a non-calendar fiscal period is made. This material is covered in Chapter 6 of the text.

On April 1, 2015, Craig Cardinal and Don Kvill formed a partnership to teach small craft flying lessons. They elected to use a March 31 fiscal year end, to coincide with the end of the winter aircraft maintenance program and the beginning of the summer training schedule. The two partners share equally in the profits of the partnership.

In the partnership income calculation for their 2016 tax returns, the "additional business income" was calculated to be $42,200. During the year ending March 31, 2017, the partnership earned Taxable Income of $64,000 and the partners withdrew $26,000 each.

From April 1, 2017 to March 31, 2018, the partnership earned Taxable Income of $58,000 and the partners withdrew $20,000 each.

Required: Determine the minimum amount of partnership income that Craig Cardinal and Don Kvill will have to include in their personal tax returns for the years 2017 and 2018.

CHAPTER 19

Trusts And Estate Planning

A Note On Recent Changes

Testamentary Trusts

As of January 1, 2016, a number of major changes in trust legislation become effective. These changes are far reaching and will have a significant impact on tax planning, particularly the planning related to deceased individuals and their estates.

While it will be difficult for you to understand these changes prior to studying the material in this Chapter, we believe that it will be useful for you to have an overview of the general nature of these changes. You should not be concerned at this stage if you do not completely understand this overview material.

A testamentary trust is a trust that arises on, and as a consequence of, the death of an individual. Prior to 2016, such trusts benefitted from a number of special rules that are not available to inter vivos trusts (a trust established by an individual during their lifetime) such as:

- The ability to calculate Tax Payable using the graduated rate schedule that is available to individuals, rather than having Tax Payable calculated using the maximum rate on all income.
- The ability to use a non-calendar fiscal period.
- Classification as a personal trust without regard to the circumstances in which the beneficial interest was acquired.
- Exemption from the requirement to make instalment payments.
- Use of the $40,000 exemption in calculating alternative minimum tax.

As of January 1, 2016, these special rules are no longer available to most testamentary trusts. From a tax point of view, there is now no significant difference in the rules applicable to testamentary trusts and those applicable to inter vivos trusts.

The most important change here was the elimination of graduated rate taxation for testamentary trusts. The ability to take advantage of the lower rates in the tax bracket schedule was a key factor in tax planning for estates. The elimination of this benefit significantly alters the contours of the estate planning landscape.

Graduated Rate Estates

Some relief is available in those situations where the assets in an individual's estate are not yet distributed and remain under the administration of an executor. The government has provided relief through the use of Graduated Rate Estates (GREs, hereafter). As the name implies, these entities can continue to use graduated rates for up to 36 months subsequent to an individual's death. The material which follows will define and explain the use of GREs.

Tax On Split Income (TOSI)

Our material on the TOSI is found in Chapter 11. As was noted in that Chapter, the 2018 expansion of the applicability of this provision has created a much more complicated environment for tax planning. We also noted that complete coverage of the TOSI legislation is beyond the scope of a general text such as this. In paper, the legislation for the TOSI stretches over 23 pages. To cover this material comprehensively would required a full Chapter. We did not provided this coverage in Chapter 11.

Specifically, we did not deal with the application of the TOSI to income that trusts provide to their beneficiaries. Given this, we will not deal with the application of the TOSI in this Chapter which provides general coverage of trusts. While we will note situations in which the tax might be applicable, we will not extend our examples to provide calculations of this tax.

You should not let our approach mislead you as to the importance of the TOSI to trusts. As was the case with the just discussed changes to testamentary trusts, the expansion of the TOSI coverage has significantly altered the tax planning possibilities of using trusts with related parties.

Introduction

19-1.   As is noted in Chapter 1, the *Income Tax Act* recognizes three groups of taxpayers: individuals, corporations, and trusts. In previous Chapters we have given detailed consideration to the determination of Taxable Income and Tax Payable for both individuals and corporations. In this Chapter, we will turn our attention to how this process works in the case of trusts.

19-2.   Also in Chapter 1, we provide a brief introduction to tax planning, providing general descriptions of tax avoidance, tax deferral, and income splitting. In this Chapter we will find that trusts are one of the most powerful weapons in the tax planner's arsenal. They can provide a convenient and cost effective mechanism for splitting large amounts of property income among family members. Trusts can also be used to access the deferral and income splitting opportunities that are present in estate freeze transactions. In addition, they can play a significant role in many other tax and business planning arrangements.

19-3.   While trusts remain a very powerful tax planning tool, as was noted in our introductory note regarding 2016 changes, their effectiveness in estate planning has been greatly reduced by the elimination of graduated rates for most testamentary trusts.

19-4.   A further problem is that dealing with trusts requires an understanding of many legal issues that cannot be handled effectively by tax advisors alone. Further, legal advice in the area of trusts can be very expensive, with charges of $500 per hour or more being common for expert advice. When combined with an accountant's fees (which can vary greatly depending on the accountant), the costs to create and maintain a trust can be prohibitive. Since normally, the settlor (creator) of a trust doesn't personally benefit financially from creating a trust, this makes the high cost of a trust even less acceptable to the settlor.

19-5.   We have previously encountered trusts in this text. In Chapter 7, which deals with property income, we indicated that most mutual funds are organized as trusts. Also in that Chapter, we noted the use of real estate investment trusts (REITs). In Chapter 10, when we considered various types of retirement savings arrangements, we noted that most of these arrangements involve the use of trusts. Registered Pension Plans, Registered Retirement Savings Plans, Registered Retirement Income Funds, and Deferred Profit Sharing Plans, all involve assets being contributed to a trust.

19-6.   In this Chapter, we will not revisit the types of trusts that were considered in earlier Chapters. Rather, our focus in this Chapter will be on personal trusts that have been

Figure 19 - 1   Personal Trust Participants

established by individuals as a part of a tax or estate planning scenario. This will include both trusts established during the lifetime of an individual, as well as trusts that arise as a consequence of the death of an individual. While trusts can be very important in tax planning arrangements that involve private corporations, we will not deal with this subject. The complexities involved in such arrangements go beyond the scope of this text.

19-7.   In our material in this Chapter on estate planning we will give specific attention to the use of trusts. In addition, due to the importance of this subject, we will expand our coverage of estate planning to issues that go beyond the use of trusts. Particular attention will be given to general coverage of estate freeze transactions.

Basic Concepts

What Is A Trust?

Legal Perspective

19-8.   From a legal perspective, a personal trust is a relationship that arises when a settlor transfers property to a trustee to hold and administer for the exclusive benefit of the beneficiaries. This relationship is depicted in Figure 19-1.

19-9.   The settlor is the person who sets up the trust and makes the initial transfer of property to the trustee. The trustee is the individual or institution that holds formal legal title to that property, while the beneficiaries are persons who will benefit from the property that is held by the trustee. The beneficiaries can have an interest in the income from the property, the capital value of the property, or both.

19-10.   While each of these roles is separate in terms of its function in the trust arrangement, it is possible for more than one of the roles to be played by a single individual. A common example of this would be a father who is the settlor of a trust in favour of his children, but also serves as one of the trustees who holds the trust assets.

19-11.   A basic feature of trust arrangements is the separation of the legal and beneficial ownership of the transferred property. Outside of trust arrangements, the legal owner of a property is normally entitled to any benefits associated with owning the property. This is not the case here. While the trustee holds legal title to the property, all of the benefits will accrue to the persons who are specified as the beneficiaries of the trust.

19-12.   A trust is not, from a legal perspective, a separate entity. A trust cannot own property, cannot enter into contracts, and cannot be a defendant or plaintiff in a legal action. With respect to the transferred property, these rights and obligations belong to the trustee(s). We would note that you should not confuse trusts with a "trust company". Trust companies are, in fact, separate legal entities that are involved in the management of trusts.

19-13.   Trusts are subject to provincial legislation and, as a consequence, the detailed rules will vary from province to province. One point to note, however, is that it is generally difficult to vary or revoke a trust. This is of particular importance in the case of deceased individuals. While the content of a will can be challenged by a disgruntled beneficiary and its intentions altered by a surviving spouse, this is a much more difficult process when assets are placed in a trust.

Tax Perspective

19-14.   Consistent with the legal perspective of trusts, the T4013 Trust Guide defines a trust as a binding obligation enforceable by law when undertaken.   This definition also notes that it may be created by a person (either verbally or in writing), a court order, or by a statute.

19-15.   While trusts do not exist as a legal entity separate from the trustees, income tax legislation does, in fact, treat trusts as a separate taxable entity, resulting in the need to file a separate tax return (T3) for each trust. This is established in the *Income Tax Act* as follows:

> **ITA 104(2)**   A trust shall, for the purposes of this Act, and without affecting the liability of the trustee or legal representative for that person's own income tax, be deemed to be in respect of the trust property an individual, ...

19-16.   This provision means that, in general, a trust will be taxed in the same manner as individuals. However, there are numerous special rules applicable to these entities. For example, most trusts cannot use the graduated rates (15 percent to 33 percent) that are available to individuals. However, each trust will have to determine a Net Income For Tax Purposes, a Taxable Income, and calculate a separate Tax Payable.

Trusts And Estates

19-17.   When an individual dies, there is a deemed disposition of all of his capital property. Property will be deemed to have been acquired at its fair market value on the date of death by various entities as per his will or, if there is no will, under the terms of provincial legislation. As discussed in Chapter 9, this deemed disposition will often have significant consequences on the calculation of Tax Payable in the final tax return of the decedent, i.e., deceased individual.

19-18.   In this context, dictionaries define the term "estate" as the property of a deceased individual. This meaning is very clearly a reference to all of the property of the deceased individual and this, in effect, means that an individual can only have one estate.

19-19.   In the great majority of cases, the estate property will pass to a beneficiary or beneficiaries immediately and will not require much attention from either tax advisors or lawyers. For example, Mom dies, leaving all of her property, which consists of a savings account and a principal residence, both of which are jointly held with Dad, to Dad. We do not need to give any attention to this type of situation.

19-20.   However, some estates, particularly those of wealthier Canadians, can have many different types of property. This can include, publicly traded securities, shares of private companies, rental properties, business assets, and foreign investments. In such cases, there may be a considerable period of time between the date on which the individual dies and the date on which all the assets, or the proceeds from the disposition from the assets, is transferred to his beneficiaries. During this period, the estate assets, which are being administered by an executor, can produce income. When this happens, the executor of the estate will have to file a T3 return which includes this income.

19-21.   As reflected in the following provision, the *Income Tax Act* has traditionally viewed the terms estate and trust as pretty much interchangeable:

> **ITA 104(1)**   In this Act, a reference to a trust or estate (in this subdivision referred to as a "trust") shall, ...

19-22.   As long as testamentary trusts were able to use graduated rates in determining their Tax Payable, using the two terms interchangeably did not present a problem. While deciding to tax the income of testamentary trusts in general at the maximum rate, the government also concluded that it would be appropriate to continue the use of graduated rates for income that accrues during the period of time that the estate assets have not yet been distributed.

19-23.   To implement this latter goal, the government introduced the concept of a Graduated Rate Estate (GRE). While we will give more attention to this concept at a later point in this chapter, you should be aware that GREs can only be used for assets that are still held in the estate and administered by an executor prior to their distribution to beneficiaries.

Establishing A Trust

Three Certainties

19-24.   The trusts that we are dealing with in this Chapter are established by words that are set out in a trust agreement. While some provinces allow, under limited circumstances, the use of oral trust agreements, this is rarely a wise course of action. Even if such agreements are accepted for legal purposes, the CRA tends to be skeptical of such agreements and may take the position that no trust exists.

19-25.   In deciding whether or not a trust has, in fact, been created, it is important to look at what the courts have referred to as the three certainties. These can be described as follows:

Certainty Of Intention   The person creating the trust must intend to create the trust and that intention must be clear to outside observers. This is usually accomplished by preparing a written document establishing the trust.

Certainty Of Property   The property that is to be held in the trust must be known with certainty at the time the trust is created. This is usually accomplished by specifying the property in the trust document.

Certainty Of Beneficiaries   The persons who will benefit from the trust property must be known with certainty at the time the trust is created. This is usually accomplished by specifying these persons in the trust document. Note that these persons must either be named as persons (e.g., Ms. Sally Phar) or be part of an identifiable class (e.g., my children). When a class designation is used, it must refer to a clearly identifiable group of persons. For example, designating "friends" as beneficiaries would not create an identifiable group.

19-26.   In addition to establishing the facts required by the three certainties criteria, there must be an actual transfer of the trust property to the trustee. Until this transfer is completed, the trust does not exist.

Importance Of Proper Documentation

19-27.   Care must be taken to ensure that all of the necessary actions to create a trust have been carried out effectively. If one or more of the required elements is missing, the tax consequences can be significant. For example, if an individual attempted to establish a trust to split income with his adult children, a failure to complete all of the requirements necessary to that process could result in his being taxed on the income, rather than having it taxed in the hands of his adult children. This could result in the payment of a significant amount of additional tax.

Exercise Nineteen - 1

Subject: Establishing A Trust

In each of the following Cases, an individual is attempting to establish a trust. For each of these Cases, indicate whether the attempt has been successful.   Explain your conclusion.

Case A   Jack Black sends a cheque to his sister to be used for the education of her two children.

Case B   Jane Folsem transfers property to a trustee, specifying that the income from the property should be distributed to her friends.

Case C   Robert Jones transfers property to a trustee, specifying that the income from the property should be distributed to his children.

Case D   Suzanne Bush has signed an agreement that specifies that she will transfer her securities portfolio to a trustee, with the income to be distributed to her spouse.

SOLUTION available in print and online Study Guide.

Returns And Payments - Trusts

19-28.   Because they are considered by the government to be taxable entities, trusts must file tax returns. As discussed in Chapter 2, Procedures and Administration, the trust tax return (T3 return) must be filed within 90 days of a trust's year end. With respect to the payment of taxes, the tax payable on trust income is due no later than 90 days after a trust's year end. We also noted in Chapter 2 that, while there is a legislative requirement that most trusts make instalment payments, the CRA has waived this requirement on an administrative basis in the past. It appears that this practice will continue in the future.

19-29.   With respect to penalties and interest related to late filing or late payment of taxes, the rules for trusts are the same as those that are applicable to individuals.

Non-Tax Reasons For Using Trusts

19-30.   In this Chapter we are largely concerned with the tax planning uses of trusts. However, it is important to note that trusts have non-tax uses which, in some situations, may be more important than the tax features of the particular arrangement. Some of these non-tax uses are as follows:

Administration Of Assets   A trust can be used to separate the administration of assets from the receipt of benefits. For example, an individual with extensive invest-ment knowledge might have assets transferred to a trust for his spouse at the time of his death. The goal here could be to provide professional management of the assets for the benefit of a spouse with only limited knowledge of investments.

Protection From Creditors   An individual proprietor of a business might place some of his personal assets in a trust in order to protect them from claims by the creditors of the business. However, if this transfer is made when the individual is experiencing financial difficulties with his business, there are provisions in bankruptcy and other legislation which may undo the transfer.

Privacy   If assets are bequeathed in a will, they will be subject to probate, the results of which are available to the public. This is not the case with assets that are in a trust when an individual dies.

Avoiding Changes In Beneficiaries   If a father places assets in a trust for the benefit of his minor children, it ensures that these children will be the ultimate beneficiaries of the property. In contrast, if, as is common, his will bequeaths his assets to his wife with the intention that his children will be the ultimate beneficiaries of his property, his wife has no legal obligation to carry out this intention. This can be a particularly important issue if the surviving spouse remarries and other children become part of her family.

19-31.   While there are additional examples of non-tax uses of trusts, the preceding should serve to give you some idea of the versatility of trust arrangements.

Classification Of Trusts

Introduction

19-32.   The CRA's *Trust Guide* lists 32 different types of trusts, largely based on definitions that are included in the *Income Tax Act*. Understanding the meaning of the terms on this CRA list is complicated by the fact that some of the listed items are, in fact, a sub-classification of other items included on the list (e.g., an alter ego trust is a type of personal trust). A further roadblock to understanding the classification of trusts is that trusts are also classified in popular usage in terms of their goals or objectives. Such terms as "family trusts" and "spend-thrift trusts" are commonly used, despite the fact that they have no real meaning in terms of tax legislation.

19-33.   In this material, we will not provide a comprehensive classification of trusts, nor will we attempt to provide definitions for all of the terms that are applied to trusts in tax legislation and general practice. As indicated in the introduction to this Chapter, our coverage is limited to trusts that have been established by individuals as part of a tax or estate planning scenario. As all of these trusts fall within the classification of personal trusts, we will begin by considering this category.

Personal Trusts
General Definition
19-34. The *Income Tax Act* contains the following definition of a personal trust:

ITA 248(1) Personal Trust means

(a) a graduated rate estate, or

(b) a trust in which no beneficial interest was acquired for consideration payable directly or indirectly to
    (i) the trust, or
    (ii) any person or partnership that has made a contribution to the trust by way of transfer, assignment or other disposition of property;

19-35. The basic idea here is that a personal trust is one which was not acquired for consideration paid to the trust or to any person that has contributed to the trust. An exception is made for graduated rate estates. Prior to 2016, this exception applied to all testamentary trusts.

19-36. The importance of this inclusion for Graduated Rate Estates is that personal trusts can pay taxes on income amounts received by the trust at the trust level. The after tax amounts can then be distributed on a tax free basis to the beneficiaries of the trust.

Testamentary Vs. Inter Vivos Trusts
19-37. All personal trusts can be classified as either testamentary or inter vivos. With respect to testamentary trusts, they are defined as follows:

ITA 108(1) Testamentary Trust in a taxation year means a trust that arose on and as a consequence of the death of an individual, other than ...

19-38. This same Subsection of the *Income Tax Act* provides a related definition of an inter vivos trust:

ITA 108(1) Inter Vivos Trust means a trust other than a testamentary trust.

19-39. Within each of these classifications, there are various subclassifications. In this Chapter, we will deal with three types of testamentary trusts and four types of inter vivos trusts. The types that we will cover are outlined in Figure 19-2:

Figure 19 - 2 Classification Of Personal Trusts	
Testamentary	**Inter Vivos**
Graduated Rate Estate	Spousal Or Common-Law Partner
Spousal Or Common-Law Partner	Alter Ego
Other Beneficiaries	Joint Spousal Or Common-Law Partner
	Family

Testamentary Trusts
Graduated Rate Estate
19-40. As discussed in the note at the beginning of this Chapter, prior to 2016, testamentary trusts enjoyed a number of special rules which were not available to inter vivos trusts such as:

- The ability to calculate Tax Payable using the graduated rate schedule that is available to individuals, rather than having Tax Payable calculated using the maximum rate on all income.
- The ability to use a non-calendar fiscal period.

- Classification as a personal trust without regard to the circumstances in which the beneficial interest was acquired.
- Exemption from the requirement to make instalment payments.
- Use of the $40,000 exemption in calculating alternative minimum tax.
- Extended periods for refunds, reassessment, and filing of objections.
- The ability to make investment tax credits available to their beneficiaries for computing their Tax Payable.

19-41.   The government concluded that these provisions were, in many situations, overly generous. Reflecting this view, as of January 1, 2016 these special rules are no longer generally available for testamentary trusts.

19-42.   An exception to this is the Graduated Rate Estate (GRE). These are defined in ITA 248(1) as follows:

> **ITA 248(1)   graduated rate estate**, of an individual at any time, means the estate that arose on and as a consequence of the individual's death if
>
> (a) that time is no more than 36 months after the death,
> (b) the estate is at that time a testamentary trust,
> (c) the individual's Social Insurance Number (or if the individual had not, before the death, been assigned a Social Insurance Number, such other information as is acceptable to the Minister) is provided in the estate's return of income under Part I for the taxation year that includes that time and for each of its earlier taxation years that ended after 2015,
> (d) the estate designates itself as the graduated rate estate of the individual in its return of income under Part I for its first taxation year that ends after 2015, and
> (e) no other estate designates itself as the graduated rate estate of the individual in a return of income under Part I for a taxation year that ends after 2015;

19-43.   While it is not perfectly clear from this definition, a GRE is only applicable to estate assets that have not been transferred to a beneficiary, either individual beneficiaries or testamentary trust beneficiaries. Stated alternatively, only if the estate has assets that are still under the administration of an executor can it be designated as a GRE.

> **EXAMPLE 1**   Gary Crotty dies on November 1, 2018. His estate (all of his property at death) consists entirely of publicly traded securities that are, under the terms of his will, immediately transferred to a spousal trust.
>
> **ANALYSIS - Example 1**   No GRE can be designated in this case because none of the decedent's assets remain under the administration of his executor.
>
> **EXAMPLE 2**   Lizabeth Jerrard dies on November 1, 2018. Her will requires that all of her estate be transferred to a spousal trust. Her estate consists of a large number of investments in real estate and CCPC shares, some of which will take considerable time to dispose of or transfer. As of December 31, 2021, some of the estate assets are still under the administration of the executor.
>
> **ANALYSIS - Example 2**   The executor will be required to file a T3 for the income accruing on these assets. In the first return, which can have a year end no later than October 31, 2019, the estate can be designated a GRE. As long as the estate assets remain under the administration of the executor, this designation can be used in the T3s filed within 36 months of her death. On December 31, 2021, even if there still undistributed estate assets, there will be a deemed year end. In that return and any subsequent to that date, the estate will be taxed as an ordinary testamentary trust, with all of its income subject to the maximum 33 percent rate. Note that, if the required transfer of all assets to the spousal trust had occurred prior to November 1, 2021, the estate would have lost its GRE status at that date.

19-44.   Two points are relevant here:

- Because GREs are included in the definition of a personal trust, its income can be taxed in the trust. The GRE can then distribute the after tax amounts to income beneficiaries on a tax free basis.

- If some of an estate's assets are distributed to beneficiaries, the portion that remains under the administration of an executor can be designated as a GRE.

Spousal Or Common-Law Partner Trust

19-45. This category of trust is not defined in the *Income Tax Act*. Rather, it is a term that is used when a trust is established for a spouse or common-law partner. As shown in Figure 19-2, such trusts can either be an inter vivos trust established by a living person or, alternatively, a testamentary trust that is established when an individual dies. A spousal or common-law partner testamentary trust can never be designated a graduated rate estate.

19-46. As will be discussed when we present material on the taxation of trusts, if a trust meets certain conditions, the *Income Tax Act* allows a settlor to transfer property into a trust without incurring any taxation on the property dispositions. The relevant rollover provisions are found in ITA 73(1.01) for inter vivos trusts, and in ITA 70(6) for testamentary trusts. When these provisions are used, the resulting trust is usually referred to as a qualifying spousal or qualifying common-law partner trust.

Other Beneficiaries

19-47. Although listed in Figure 19-2 as a type of trust, it represents a testamentary trust that is not a spousal or common-law partner trust. Common other beneficiaries would be the decedent's children or other close relatives of the decedent. Such trusts can never be designated a graduated rate estate.

Inter Vivos Trusts

Spousal Or Common-Law Partner Trust

19-48. As noted in Paragraph 19-45, spousal or common-law partner trusts can be established as testamentary trusts on the death of the settlor or, alternatively, as inter vivos trusts by a living individual.

Alter Ego Trust

19-49. An alter ego trust is an inter vivos trust created by an individual who is 65 years of age or older with himself as the sole beneficiary during his lifetime. As was the case with spousal or common-law partner trusts, if certain conditions are met, the *Income Tax Act* contains a rollover provision that allows property to be transferred into or out of the trust on a tax free basis.

Joint Spousal Or Common-Law Partner Trust

19-50. A joint spousal or joint common-law partner trust is an inter vivos trust created by an individual who is 65 years of age or older. Similar to the alter ego trust, this type of trust is created with the individual and his spouse or common-law partner as the sole beneficiaries during their lifetimes. Also similar to the alter ego trust scenario, if certain conditions are met, there is a rollover provision in the *Income Tax Act* that allows property to be transferred into the trust on a tax free basis.

Family Trust

19-51. While the term family trust is not always used in a consistent manner, it generally refers to a trust that has been established by an individual for the benefit of family members. While a family trust could be a testamentary trust, the term is usually used in reference to an inter vivos trust. The most common goal of this type of trust is income splitting. We would note that the extension of the TOSI to related adults has placed significant constraints on using trusts for this purpose.

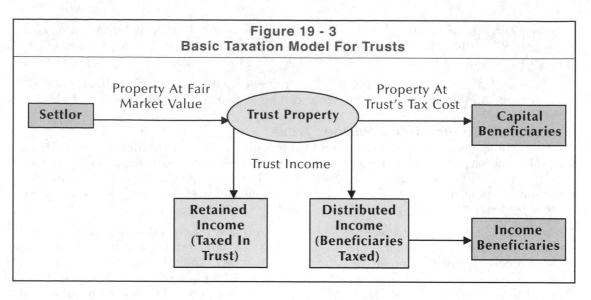

Figure 19 - 3
Basic Taxation Model For Trusts

Taxation Of Trusts

Taxation Year

19-52.   Inter vivos trusts have always been required to use the calendar year as their taxation year. In contrast, prior to 2016, testamentary trusts were allowed to use a non-calendar fiscal year. As of 2016, testamentary trusts have, in general, lost this right.

19-53.   The exception to this is Graduated Rate Estates (GREs). As long as estate assets are under the administration of an executor and have not been distributed to beneficiaries, GREs can use a non-calendar fiscal period for up to 36 months subsequent to the decedent's date of death.

The Basic Taxation Model

19-54.   While there are many variations that depend on the particular type of trust we are dealing with, as well as complications associated with the measurement of trust Taxable Income and Tax Payable, the basic model for the taxation of trusts is as shown in Figure 19-3. There are three features of this basic model that should be noted:

Settlor's Transfer Of Property To The Trust   When property is transferred to a trust by a settlor, it generally results in a disposition for tax purposes. In the usual situation, these dispositions are deemed to occur at fair market value, triggering various tax consequences (e.g., capital gains, recapture, or terminal losses). There are, however, some important rollover provisions for property transferred into a trust. These are discussed beginning in Paragraph 19-56.

Transfers Of Trust Property To Beneficiaries   If trust property is transferred to a capital beneficiary, ITA 107(2) provides a rollover provision that allows the property to be transferred at the tax cost to the trust. The proceeds of disposition to the trust and the cost to the beneficiary will be equal to the tax cost that is recorded in the trust. For exceptions to this general provision, see Rollovers To Beneficiaries beginning in Paragraph 19-69.

Income From The Trust Property   Once property has been transferred to the trust, income will begin to accrue to the trust. It is fundamental to most of the tax planning uses of trusts that income earned in the trust can be deducted by the trust from Net Income For Tax Purposes of the trust to the extent that it is either distributed to beneficiaries or they are entitled to enforce payment. We will find that in many situations, trusts will distribute all of their income, resulting in no Tax Payable at the trust level.

Any income that a trust does not distribute to beneficiaries will be taxed in the trust. Subsequent distribution of this income is on a tax free basis. At this point you should note that there is a very important difference in the calculation of Tax Payable for a testamentary trust that is designated as a graduated rate estate, and the calculation of Tax Payable for other personal trusts. As the name implies, graduated rate estates can use the schedule of graduated rates that is applicable to individuals. In contrast, most other personal trusts will have all of their income taxed at the maximum rate of 33 percent.

19-55.   While it is not illustrated in Figure 19-3, there is a special anti-avoidance rule that is designed to prevent extended deferral of the potential tax on capital gains. This rule requires a deemed disposition of capital assets after they have been held in the trust for 21 years and will be discussed in detail beginning in Paragraph 19-75.

Exercise Nineteen - 2

Subject: Basic Taxation Of Trusts

On January 1, 2018, Joanne March transfers debt securities with a fair market value of $220,000 to a newly established inter vivos trust for which her 28 year old daughter, Jocelyn, is the only beneficiary. The cost of these securities to Joanne March was $200,000. During 2018, the securities earn and receive interest of $15,000, all of which is distributed to Jocelyn. On January 1, 2019, the securities are transferred to Jocelyn in satisfaction of her capital interest in the trust. At this time, the fair market value of the securities has increased to $230,000. Jocelyn sells all of the securities for $230,000 on January 5, 2019. Joanne is not a trustee of the inter vivos trust.

Indicate the tax consequences for Joanne, Jocelyn, and the trust, in each of the years 2018 and 2019.

SOLUTION available in print and online Study Guide.

Rollovers To A Trust

Introduction
19-56.   The general taxation model for trusts requires that contributions to the trust be recorded at fair market value, often resulting in a significant tax cost for the contributor. However, as we noted in our material on the classification of trusts, spousal or common-law partner trusts, alter ego trusts, and joint spousal or common-law partner trusts can make such transfers on a rollover basis, provided certain specific conditions are met.

19-57.   In this section we are concerned with the conditions that qualify these three special types of trusts for the tax free rollover of contributions. When the trust qualifies, the rollover is accomplished by deeming the property to have been disposed of by the settlor at either its adjusted cost base (non-depreciable capital property) or its UCC (depreciable capital property), resulting in no tax consequences for the settlor at the time of transfer. The trust is deemed to have acquired the property at a value equal to the proceeds of disposition to the settlor. In the case of depreciable property, the trust retains the settlor's original capital cost for purposes of determining recapture of CCA.

19-58.   We will revisit these three types of trusts in our later section on tax planning. At that point we will discuss how these trusts can be used to reduce or defer taxes.

Qualifying Spousal Or Qualifying Common-Law Partner Trust
19-59.   You may recall from Chapter 9 that ITA 73(1.01) contains a rollover provision that allows a living individual to transfer capital property to a spouse or common-law partner without tax consequences. ITA 70(6) provides for a similar rollover for the capital property of a deceased individual.

19-60.   While we did not discuss this in Chapter 9, these rollovers apply whether the transfer is directly to the spouse or common-law partner or, alternatively, to a trust in favour of a spouse or common-law partner. However, in the case of a transfer to a trust, the trust arrangement must meet certain conditions in order to qualify for the rollover. When it meets these conditions, it is commonly referred to as a qualifying spousal or common-law partner trust.

19-61.   With respect to inter vivos spousal or common-law partner trusts, the conditions for qualifying for the rollover are as follows:

ITA 73(1.01)(c)(i)   The individual's spouse or common-law partner is entitled to receive all of the income of the trust that arises before the spouse's or common-law partner's death and no person except the spouse or common-law partner may, before the spouse's or common-law partner's death, receive or otherwise obtain the use of any of the income or capital of the trust.

19-62.   A similar provision provides the rollover conditions for testamentary spousal or common-law partner trusts:

ITA 70(6)(b)   A trust, created by the taxpayer's will, that was resident in Canada immediately after the time the property vested indefeasibly in the trust and under which

(i)   the taxpayer's spouse or common-law partner is entitled to receive all of the income of the trust that arises before the spouse's or common-law partner's death, and

(ii) no person except the spouse or common-law partner may, before the spouse's or common-law partner's death, receive or otherwise obtain the use of any of the income or capital of the trust.

19-63.   When these conditions are met, any property that is contributed to the trust, either by a living spouse or common-law partner, or as the result of the spouse or common-law partner's death, will be transferred at tax cost. For non-depreciable capital property, this value is the transferor's adjusted cost base. For depreciable property, the transfer is at the transferor's UCC amount. However, for purposes of determining recaptured CCA, the transferor's original capital cost is deemed to be the transferee's capital cost.

19-64.   While these rollover provisions are, in general, a desirable way to avoid paying taxes on transfers to a spousal or common-law partner trust, there may be circumstances where the taxpayer would prefer a transfer at fair market value. For example, if the settlor of the trust has unused capital loss carry forwards or property that is eligible for the lifetime capital gains deduction, he might wish to trigger capital gains in order to absorb these amounts. Fortunately, the settlor has the choice of electing out of the rollover provisions. For inter vivos transfers, the election is under ITA 73(1). For testamentary transfers the election that can be made by the settlor's legal representative is under ITA 70(6.2).

Exercise Nineteen - 3

Subject: Transfer To Spousal Trust

Louise died late this year, and bequeathed a group of common stocks to a qualifying spousal trust created in her will. Louise is survived by her husband who is to receive the stocks from the trust three years after her death if they have not been sold. The stocks have an adjusted cost base of $60,000 and were valued at $90,000 on the date of her death. Determine the tax consequences of the transfer, including the adjusted cost base for the stocks in the trust and in her husband's hands if they are transferred.

SOLUTION available in print and online Study Guide.

Alter Ego Trust

19-65.   An alter ego trust is an inter vivos trust established by a settlor who is 65 years of age or older at the time the trust is settled. To qualify for a tax free rollover of assets to the trust, the

Income Tax Act specifies the following conditions:

> **ITA 73(1.01)(c)(ii)**   The individual is entitled to receive all of the income of the trust that arises before the individual's death and no person except the individual may, before the individual's death, receive or otherwise obtain the use of any of the income or capital of the trust.

19-66.   As was the case with the spousal or common-law partner trust, an individual can elect out of this rollover, choosing to have the transfer to the trust take place at fair market value.

Joint Spousal Or Joint Common-Law Partner Trust

19-67.   Like an alter ego trust, a joint spousal or common-law partner trust is an inter vivos trust established by a settlor who is 65 years of age or older at the time the trust is settled. The difference in this case is that both the settlor and his spouse or common-law partner are beneficiaries of the trust. More specifically, to qualify for the tax free rollover of assets to the trust, the *Income Tax Act* specifies the following conditions:

> **ITA 73(1.01)(c)(iii)** either
>
> (A) the individual or the individual's spouse is, in combination with the other, entitled to receive all of the income of the trust that arises before the later of the death of the individual and the death of the spouse and no other person may, before the later of those deaths, receive or otherwise obtain the use of any of the income or capital of the trust, or
>
> (B) the individual or the individual's common-law partner is, in combination with the other, entitled to receive all of the income of the trust that arises before the later of the death of the individual and the death of the common-law partner and no other person may, before the later of those deaths, receive or otherwise obtain the use of any of the income or capital of the trust.

19-68.   As was the case with the alter ego trust, an individual can elect out of this rollover, choosing to have the transfer to the trust take place at fair market value.

Exercise Nineteen - 4

Subject: Transfers To Trusts

An individual has common shares with a cost of $1,000 and a current fair market value of $1,600. Seven Scenarios are presented for the transfer of these shares by the settlor to a trust. For each Scenario, indicate the tax consequences to the settlor at the time of transfer, as well as the adjusted cost base of the property within the trust.

Scenario 1:	Transfer to inter vivos trust for adult child.
Scenario 2:	Transfer to inter vivos trust for minor child.
Scenario 3:	Transfer to testamentary trust for friend.
Scenario 4:	Transfer to inter vivos qualifying spousal trust.
Scenario 5:	Transfer to testamentary qualifying spousal trust.
Scenario 6:	Transfer to joint spousal trust.
Scenario 7:	Transfer to alter ego trust.

SOLUTION available in print and online Study Guide.

Rollovers To Capital Beneficiaries
General Rule

19-69.   As is the case with transfers by a settlor into a trust, the transfer of assets to a capital beneficiary is a disposition. However, for many trusts ITA 107(2) provides a tax free rollover for these transfers. The rollover is accomplished by deeming the property to have been disposed of by the trust at either its adjusted cost base (non-depreciable capital property) or its UCC (depreciable property).

19-70.   The beneficiary is deemed to have acquired the property at a value equal to the cost amount to the trust, resulting in no tax consequences at the time of transfer to the beneficiary. In the case of depreciable property, the beneficiary retains the capital cost of the property to the trust for purposes of determining subsequent recapture of CCA.

Exceptions

19-71.   The logic of the preceding rule is based on the fact that the transfer of assets into the trust was, in terms of the beneficial interest in the assets, a transfer of the assets to the beneficiaries. Provided that tax was assessed on the transfer into the trust, it would not be equitable to assess tax again when the asset is legally transferred to the beneficiaries.

19-72.   We have noted, however, that with certain types of trusts, the transfer from the settlor to the trust is not a taxable transaction. Specifically, qualifying spousal or common-law partner trusts, alter ego trusts, and joint spousal or common-law partner trusts can use a rollover provision to transfer assets into a trust. Since no tax was assessed on the transfer into these trusts, it would not seem equitable to allow the assets to be transferred to all beneficiaries on a rollover basis.

19-73.   Tax legislation agrees with this view. The ITA 107(2) rollover does not apply in the following cases:

- if property is transferred out of an **alter ego** trust to anyone other than the settlor,

- if property is transferred out of a **joint spousal** or common-law partner trust to anyone other than the settlor or the spouse or common-law partner, and

- if property is transferred out of a **qualifying spousal** or common-law partner trust to anyone other than a spouse or common-law partner.

19-74.   When the ITA 107(2) rollover provision does not apply, the transfer of assets from the trust to a capital beneficiary will be recorded at the fair market value of the transferred assets. This will generally result in tax consequences for the trust.

***

We suggest you work Self Study Problem Nineteen-1 at this point.

***

21 Year Deemed Disposition Rule

19-75.   Trust arrangements ordinarily allow capital gains on trust assets to accumulate without tax consequences for extended periods of time. Unless the capital assets are sold or distributed by the trust, accrued gains will not attract any taxes and the assets can be left in a trust for periods that exceed the life of the individual establishing the trust.

19-76.   In order to place limits on this deferral process, ITA 104(4)(b) requires that there be a deemed disposition and reacquisition of trust capital property every 21 years. The disposition is deemed to be at fair market value, resulting in the recognition of any accrued gains on the assets. In the case of depreciable assets, if the deemed proceeds are less than the original capital cost, the original value is retained for purposes of determining recapture.

19-77.   This rule is generally applicable only to personal trusts and does not apply to trusts such as employee benefit plans or registered education savings plans. Further, the rules are modified in the case of qualifying spousal or common-law partner trusts, alter ego trusts, and joint spousal or common-law partner trusts.

Other Deemed Dispositions

19-78.   For qualifying spousal or common-law partner trusts, a deemed disposition occurs with the death of the spouse or common-law partner. In the case of alter ego trusts, the death of the settlor is the event that triggers a deemed disposition. Finally, with joint spousal or common-law partner trusts, the deemed disposition occurs only at the later of the death of the settlor or the death of the spouse or common-law partner.

Net Income For Tax Purposes Of A Trust

Basic Rules

19-79.   The overriding principle in determining the Net Income For Tax Purposes of a trust results from the statement in ITA 104(2) that a trust should be treated as an individual. This means that the general rules used by individuals, as modified by trust legislation, are applicable in computing a trust's Net Income For Tax Purposes.

19-80.   Capital gains and losses are realized on the disposition of capital assets. Also, in the calculation of Net Income For Tax Purposes, any taxable dividends that are not allocated to beneficiaries are grossed up as they would be for individuals. Finally, deductions are allowed for non-capital, net capital, and certain other types of loss carry overs.

19-81.   There are, however, additional items that must be added or deducted in calculating the Net Income For Tax Purposes of a trust. These items can be described as follows:

Amounts Paid Or Payable To Beneficiaries   As was noted in our description of the basic trust taxation model, a trust can deduct amounts that are paid or payable to one or more beneficiaries. This is usually the most important of the adjustments to the trust's income in that, in many cases, all of the trust's income will be allocated to beneficiaries. Because of the importance of this deduction, it will be the subject of a separate section of this Chapter beginning in Paragraph 19-93.

Trustee's Or Executor's Fees   Any amounts paid that are related to earning trust income, or that are paid to an executor or trustee whose principal business includes the provision of such services, are deductible to the trust.

Amounts Paid By The Trust And Allocated To The Income Of A Beneficiary   A trust can make payments to third parties to provide goods or services to beneficiaries. The CRA considers such amounts to be another way of paying income to beneficiaries and, as a consequence, such amounts are deductible to the trust and included in the income of the beneficiaries.

Income Allocated To A Preferred Beneficiary   As will be discussed beginning in Paragraph 19-83, trusts can allocate income to a preferred beneficiary while retaining the income in the trust. While such retained income would normally be taxed in the trust, because it is being taxed in the hands of a beneficiary, it can be deducted from the income of the trust.

Amounts Deemed Not Paid   A trust can designate amounts to be deemed not paid when they are, in fact, paid or payable to beneficiaries. This means that the trust will include these amounts in its own Net Income For Tax Purposes and the beneficiaries will be able to receive these amounts on a tax free basis. The reasons for doing this are discussed beginning in Paragraph 19-86.

Amounts Retained For Beneficiary Under 21 Years Of Age   Provided the eventual payment is not subject to any future condition, amounts that are held in trust for a beneficiary who is under 21 at the end of the year can be deducted by the trust and taxed in the hands of the beneficiary. (See Paragraph 19-90.)

19-82.   While positive amounts of all types of income can be allocated to beneficiaries, losses cannot be. If a trust has a disposition that results in a capital loss, or other activities that result in a non-capital loss, such losses must be used within the trust, either as a carry back to a previous year, or as a carry forward to a subsequent year. Note, however, that if the trust distributes capital assets with accrued losses, the fact that the transfer to a beneficiary is usually at the trust's tax cost means that such accrued losses can, in effect, be transferred to a beneficiary.

Preferred Beneficiary Election

19-83.   Normally a trust can only deduct amounts that are paid or payable to a beneficiary. An exception to this can arise if a joint election is made by a trust and a beneficiary. Under this preferred beneficiary election, the beneficiary will be taxed on amounts that remain in the trust [ITA 104(14)], and the trust can deduct these amounts [ITA 104(12)].

19-84.   The preferred beneficiary election is only available if:

- the beneficiary is claiming the disability tax credit; or
- the beneficiary is 18 years of age or older, is claimed by another individual as a dependant, and does not have income that exceeds the base for the beneficiary's personal tax credit.
- In addition, the beneficiary must be the settlor of the trust, the spouse or former spouse of the settlor of the trust, or the child, grandchild, or great grandchild of the settlor of the trust, or the child, grandchild, or great grandchild of the spouse of the settlor of the trust.

19-85.   This election is normally used in situations where it is desirable to have income taxed in the hands of a low income individual without actually giving that individual full access to the funds. An example of this would be a mentally disabled child with no other source of income, but lacking in the ability to deal responsibly with financial matters.

Amounts Deemed Not Paid

19-86.   Amounts paid or payable to a beneficiary are normally deducted by the trust and included in the income of the beneficiary. However, ITA 104(13.1) permits a trust to designate all or part of its income for a year as "not to have been paid" or "not to have become payable". The amounts so designated are not included in the beneficiaries' Net Income and are not deducted in computing the Net Income of the trust. As a result, the amounts are taxed in the trust and can be distributed tax free. This designation is only available to trusts that are resident in Canada throughout the taxation year and are subject to Part I tax.

19-87.   Prior to 2016, when testamentary trusts had general access to graduated rates, this provision could be used advantageously when the trust had a lower marginal tax rate than the beneficiary. Except for graduated rate estates (GREs), this can no longer occur as other testamentary trusts are generally taxed at the maximum federal rate of 33 percent.

19-88.   Prior to 2016, the amount deemed not paid provision could be used to avoid the instalment requirements that could be applicable to beneficiaries. While administratively the CRA no longer charges interest on late or insufficient instalments, instalments are required for all trusts other than graduated rate estates.

19-89.   As previously noted, a trust cannot allocate losses to beneficiaries. This means that the only way that an unused current year trust loss can be utilized is through a carry over to another year. With many trusts, this cannot happen under normal circumstances because they are legally required to distribute all of their income to beneficiaries, resulting in a nil Net Income For Tax Purposes. A solution to this problem is to designate sufficient income as having not been paid to absorb the loss carry forward. This can satisfy the legal requirement to distribute the income, while simultaneously creating sufficient Net Income For Tax Purposes to absorb the loss carry forward. Although this feature is still available, the 2016 changes in trust legislation restrict the application of this provision so it can only be used to eliminate losses in the trust. It cannot be used to create a positive amount of income in the trust.

Amounts Retained For A Beneficiary Under 21 Years Of Age

19-90.   If benefits are actually paid to a minor beneficiary, the amounts can clearly be deducted by the trust. However, an adult settlor may decide that it would be better for the income to be held in trust until the beneficiary reaches some specified age. Provided the beneficiary has not reached 21 years of age prior to the end of the year, ITA 104(18) deems amounts that are retained to have become payable during the year. This means that the trust will be able to deduct the amount retained and the beneficiary will be subject to taxes on it.

19-91.   To qualify for this treatment, the amounts must be vested with the beneficiary and there cannot be any future condition that would prevent payment. When these amounts are eventually distributed, they will be received by the beneficiary on a tax free basis.

Taxable Income Of A Trust

19-92. Once the Net Income For Tax Purposes of a trust is determined, calculation of Taxable Income involves the same deductions that would be available to individuals. Provided there is a positive Net Income For Tax Purposes, the trust can deduct non-capital losses of other years, net capital losses of other years, and farming and fishing losses of other years. The carry over periods for these losses that are applicable to individuals are equally applicable to trusts. Note that the ability to deduct net capital losses and restricted farm losses is dependent on having taxable capital gains or farm income included in the trust's Net Income For Tax Purposes for the current year.

Exercise Nineteen - 5

Subject: Trust Net And Taxable Income

During the current year, the Jordan family trust, an inter vivos trust, has business income of $220,000. Of this amount, $50,000 is retained in the trust, with a joint election being made to have this amount taxed in the hands of a beneficiary who qualifies for the disability tax credit. This beneficiary has no other income. The remaining $170,000 is distributed to the other beneficiaries of the trust.

At the beginning of the current year, the trust had a business loss carry forward of $35,000. In order to make use of this loss, the trust designates an amount of $35,000 under ITA 104(13.1) as not having been paid during the year.

Determine the trust's Net Income For Tax Purposes and Taxable Income for the current year. Briefly explain why the trust would make the preferred beneficiary election and designate amounts not paid that were paid.

SOLUTION available in print and online Study Guide.

Income Allocations To Beneficiaries

General Rules

19-93. Since a trust is a separate taxable entity, any income that is earned by trust assets will initially accrue to the trust. As we have noted, however, any income that is allocated to a beneficiary can be deducted in the calculation of the trust's Net Income For Tax Purposes. Correspondingly, the amount deducted by the trust must generally be included in the Net Income For Tax Purposes of the relevant beneficiary. In effect, when trust income is allocated to a beneficiary, the obligation to pay taxes on that income is transferred from the trust to the beneficiary.

19-94. We have also noted that a trust can make payments to third parties for goods or services that will be provided to a beneficiary. These can include such expenses as day care, tuition, and medical fees. These amounts are deductible by the trust as allocations to beneficiaries, but will be considered income paid or payable to the beneficiaries.

19-95. For a trust to be able to deduct amounts that will be distributed to beneficiaries, the amounts must be paid or payable. While it is easy to determine whether an amount has been paid, questions often arise in determining whether or not an amount is payable to a beneficiary. ITA 104(24) provides that:

> ... an amount is deemed not to have become payable to a beneficiary in a taxation year unless it was paid in the year to the beneficiary or the beneficiary was entitled in the year to enforce payment of it.

19-96.   Issuing a promissory note or a cheque payable to the beneficiary for the share of the trust income will usually fulfill the payable requirement. The CRA expands the definition of payable in IT-286R2 by stating that an amount is not considered to be payable in any of the following circumstances:

- A beneficiary can only enforce payment of an amount of income by forcing the trustee to wind up the trust.
- The beneficiary's right to income is subject to the approval of a third party.
- Payment of income is at the trustee's discretion and this provision has not been exercised.
- The beneficiary has the power to amend the trust deed and must do so to cause the income to be payable.

Discretionary And Non-Discretionary Distributions

19-97.   Both testamentary and inter vivos trusts can be set up as either discretionary or non-discretionary trusts. A discretionary trust is one in which the trustees are given the power to decide the amounts that will be allocated to each of the beneficiaries, usually on an annual basis.

19-98.   In many cases, this discretionary power will apply only to annual income distributions. However, the trust could be structured to provide discretion on both income and capital distributions, or to capital distributions only. The trustees may also be given the power to control the timing of distributions to beneficiaries.

19-99.   When discretionary trusts are used, it is important that only the amounts allocated to beneficiaries are considered to be paid or payable. If, for example, a trustee's exercise of discretion requires the approval of a third party, IT-286R2 would indicate that the amounts are not payable. This would result in the trust not being able to deduct the allocated amounts.

19-100.   A non-discretionary trust is one in which the amounts and timing of allocations to income and capital beneficiaries are specified in the trust agreement. In some cases, the trust agreement may have a combination of discretionary and non-discretionary provisions.

Flow Through Provisions
General Applicability

19-101.   Income that is paid out to beneficiaries through a trust is deemed to be property income unless there is a rule that says otherwise. Fortunately, there is a flow through rule that allows certain types of income paid out of a trust to retain the same tax characteristics as when it was earned in the personal trust. The most significant types of income covered by this flow through rule are capital gains, taxable dividends and capital dividends. Note that business income is not covered by the flow through rule. When business income is paid to beneficiaries, it is considered to be property income.

19-102.   These flow through rules are an important feature of personal trusts in that capital gains and dividends, especially capital dividends, are taxed much more favourably than other types of income. Since property income is fully taxed at an individual's regular rates, in the absence of such a flow through rule, in many instances the use of trusts would be much less attractive.

Dividends

19-103.   If either eligible or non-eligible dividends from taxable Canadian corporations are received by a trust and distributed to beneficiaries of the trust, the beneficiaries will use the same gross up and tax credit procedures that would be applicable had they received the dividends directly. At the trust level, these amounts will not be grossed up and the amount received and distributed will be deducted in the determination of the trust's Net Income.

19-104.   In contrast, if either eligible or non-eligible dividends from taxable Canadian corporations are retained in the trust, the grossed up amount of these dividends will be included in the trust's Net Income For Tax Purposes. Consistent with this, the trust will be able to deduct the appropriate dividend tax credit when it determines its Tax Payable for the year. Since capital dividends are tax free, they would have no effect on the trust's Tax Payable.

Capital Gains

19-105. Under trust law, capital gains that are realized in the trusts are considered to be an addition to capital and, in the absence of a special provision in the trust agreement, would not be payable to income beneficiaries. However, tax legislation views one-half of capital gains as a taxable amount. As a consequence, if this amount is not paid out to beneficiaries, it will be taxed in the hands of the trust. The remaining one-half of the capital gain will become part of the trust's capital and can be paid to beneficiaries on a tax free basis at any point in time.

19-106. If the trust pays out the full amount of the capital gain, the flow through rule means that one-half of this amount will be included in the recipient's income as a taxable capital gain. The remaining one-half is received as a tax free distribution of capital.

19-107. It is important to note that the capital gains that we are discussing here are those that result from dispositions of trust property within the trust. As covered in Paragraph 19-69, if the trust distributes capital assets on which there are accrued capital gains, ITA 107(2) deems the transfer to be at the trust's tax cost resulting in no tax consequences to the trust. The accrued gains will not be subject to tax until the recipient beneficiary chooses to dispose of the assets that they have received.

Tax On Split Income (TOSI)

19-108. As discussed in Chapter 11, as of 2018, individuals of any age may receive income that is subject to the TOSI. If the TOSI is applicable, tax will be assessed at the maximum federal rate of 33 percent on all such amounts, with the only available tax credits being the dividend tax credit and credits for foreign taxes assessed on foreign source income. We will not repeat the discussion of the applicability of TOSI in this Chapter.

19-109. However, the TOSI is very relevant in this Chapter because, if the trust earns income that would have been subject to the TOSI if it had been received directly by a beneficiary, it will also be subject to the TOSI if the trust distributes the income to that beneficiary. In other words, it will retain its character when it flows through the trust. Because of this, the income will be subject to the TOSI at 33 percent, the same rate that would be applicable to the trust.

Exercise Nineteen - 6

Subject: Flow Through To Beneficiaries

During 2018, the Ho family trust received eligible dividends from publicly traded Canadian corporations in the amount of $100,000. In addition, it received non-eligible dividends from the family owned Canadian controlled private corporation in the amount of $30,000. Its only other source of income was a capital gain of $20,000 on a disposition of investments in publicly traded equity securities.

The only beneficiary of the trust is the family's 19 year old son, Bryan Ho. Bryan is actively engaged in the private corporation on regular and continuous basis and, as a consequence, the TOSI is not applicable to the income that he receives from the trust.

During the current year, $60,000 of the eligible dividends from public companies, all of the non-eligible dividends from the family's private company, and all of the $20,000 capital gain were paid to Bryan.

Indicate the tax effects of these transactions on the Net Income For Tax Purposes for both the trust and for Bryan.

SOLUTION available in print and online Study Guide.

Business Income, CCA, Recapture, And Terminal Losses

19-110.   Under trust law, the amount of income that may be distributed to beneficiaries should be determined after providing for amortization expense calculated using methods similar to those specified under generally accepted accounting principles. While this could create a difference between a trust's accounting Net Income and its Net Income For Tax Purposes, this problem is resolved by most trustees by setting accounting amortization expense equal to maximum CCA.

19-111.   Business income must be calculated at the trust level, prior to allocation to the beneficiaries. This calculation would include the CCA deduction, as well as any recapture or terminal losses that might arise during the year. As noted, the flow through rule for trusts does not cover business income. This means that any business income allocated to beneficiaries is distributed to them as property income. If this was not the case, business income flowed through a trust could create a liability for CPP and GST/HST which would complicate matters for many beneficiaries.

Exercise Nineteen - 7

Subject: CCA And Recapture On Trust Assets

The Husak family trust has only one beneficiary, Martin Husak, the 32 year old son of the settlor, Dimitri Husak. Martin is actively engaged in the private corporation on regular and continuous basis and, as a consequence, the TOSI is not applicable to any income that he receives from the trust

It is an inter vivos trust and its only asset is a rental property with a fair market value equal to its capital cost. The trust is required to distribute all of its income to Martin. During the year ending December 31, 2018 the property will have net rental income, before the deduction of CCA, of $32,000. Maximum CCA for the year will be $26,000.

Dimitri is considering having the trust sell the rental property at the end of 2018. If that is done, there will be recapture of CCA of $65,000. He has asked you to compare the tax consequences for both Martin and the trust if (1) the sale takes place in December, 2018 and (2) the trust continues to hold the property.

SOLUTION available in print and online Study Guide.

Principal Residence Exemption

19-112.   Prior to 2017, a residence held in a trust that was ordinarily inhabited by a beneficiary of the trust, or by a spouse or common-law partner, former spouse or common-law partner, or a child of a beneficiary, was eligible for the principal residence exemption (see Chapter 8). This is no longer the case. For years ending after 2016, only alter ego trusts, joint partner trusts, spousal or common-law partner trusts, qualified disability trusts, or a qualifying trust for a minor child will be able to use this exemption to eliminate or reduce any capital gain resulting from the sale of a residence held in the trust. If such gains arise in other types of trusts, they will be subject to the usual capital gains taxation.

Tax Payable Of Personal Trusts

Calculation Of Basic Amount

General Approach

19-113.   In keeping with the previously expressed idea that trusts are to be taxed in the same manner as individuals, the Tax Payable for a trust is calculated using the rates applicable to individuals. However, how these rates will be applied differs, depending on whether the trust is an inter vivos trust or a regular testamentary trust, or, alternatively, a graduated rate estate. These differences will be discussed in the material that follows.

Graduated Rate Estates

19-114. As discussed previously, in the first T3 filed subsequent to an individual's death, trust assets that are still under the administration of an executor can be designated a Graduated Rate Estate. You will recall that this designation can remain in effect for up to 36 months subsequent to the death of the individual.

19-115. The major benefit resulting from this designation is that, during the period in which the designation is in effect, the trust can calculate Tax Payable using the graduated rate schedule that is applicable to individuals. As described in Chapter 4, for 2018, the federal tax rates range from 15 percent on the first $46,605 of Taxable Income to 33 percent on amounts in excess of $205,842.

Inter Vivos Trusts And Regular Testamentary Trusts

19-116. Under ITA 122(1), all of the income of an inter vivos trust is assessed tax at the highest rate applicable to individuals. Since 2016, this rate has been 33 percent.

19-117. Prior to 2016, all testamentary trusts used the same schedule of graduated rates and income brackets that was applicable to individuals. However, due to the major overhaul of taxation for testamentary trusts, beginning in 2016 testamentary trusts other than graduated rate estates and qualified disability trusts will have all of their taxable income subject to the maximum tax rate of 33 percent. This means that inter vivos trusts and regular testamentary trusts are now taxed in a similar manner.

Multiple Testamentary Trusts

19-118. Prior to 2016, it was not uncommon for an individual to establish multiple testamentary trusts, usually on the basis of a separate trust for each beneficiary of the individual's estate. This could be very advantageous in that there could be multiple applications of the graduated rate structure. For example, if there were three different testamentary trusts, each trust could benefit from the lowest rate of 15 percent.

19-119. This tax advantage is no longer available. In general, testamentary trusts will have all of their income taxed at the maximum 33 percent federal rate. While a Graduated Rate Estate can still use graduated rates, there can only be one such trust and its life is limited to 36 months.

Tainted Testamentary Trusts

19-120. Contributions by living persons to an existing testamentary trust can cause that trust to become tainted and lose its testamentary status. It will then be treated as an inter vivos trust. Given the 2016 changes in trust legislation, this no longer has significant tax effects except with respect to Graduated Rate Estates. The only property that can be included in a Graduated Rate Estate is the property that was owned by the decedent at the time of death. It would not be possible to make additions to this balance.

Other Tax Payable Considerations

Availability Of Tax Credits

19-121. While, in principle, trusts are to be taxed in the same manner as individuals, there are obvious differences between a legally constructed entity and a living, breathing human being. These differences are reflected in the fact that trusts are not eligible for many of the tax credits that are available to individuals.

19-122. To begin, ITA 122(1.1) specifically prohibits a trust from claiming any of the credits listed under ITA 118 (personal tax credits). Further, most of the other credits listed in ITA 118.1 through 118.9 are clearly directed at individuals (e.g., a trust is not likely to have medical expenses). However, some tax credits are available to trusts, generally on the same basis as they are available to individuals. These include:

- donations and gifts (As is the case with individuals, there is a credit of 15 percent on the first $200 of donations and either 29 percent or 33 percent on additional amounts.)
- eligible and non-eligible dividend tax credits
- foreign tax credits
- investment tax credits

Alternative Minimum Tax

19-123.   As is the case with individuals, trusts are subject to the alternative minimum tax legislation. However, there is one important difference. With the exception of Graduated Rate Estates, the exemption with respect to the first $40,000 of income is not available to trusts.

Tax Free Dividends

19-124.   Because dividends use up available tax credits at a much slower pace than other types of income, individuals can receive a substantial amount of dividends on a tax free basis. As explained in Chapter 15, this only works when income is taxed at the two lowest federal rates of 15 percent and 20.5 percent. As we have indicated, both inter vivos and most testamentary trusts are taxed at 33 percent on all of their income. When this is the case, the trust cannot receive any dividends on a tax free basis.

19-125.   However, Graduated Rate Estates can receive tax free dividends. For example, if such a trust has no other source of income, it can receive up to $33,890 in eligible dividends without paying any taxes.

Exercise Nineteen - 8

Subject: Tax Payable On Trust Dividends

A trust receives $100,000 in eligible dividends. This is the trust's only income for the current year. The only beneficiary of the trust is the settlor's 32 year old son. The son has no income other than that provided by the trust and no tax credits other than his basic personal credit and credits related to any trust income. Ignoring any alternative minimum tax implications, determine the Taxable Income and federal Tax Payable for both the trust and beneficiary under the following alternative assumptions:

A. The trust is a Graduated Rate Estate and it distributes all of the dividends to the beneficiary. Assume that the TOSI would not be applicable to the dividends received by the settlor's son.

B. The trust is a Graduated Rate Estate and it does not distribute any of the dividends to the beneficiary.

C. The trust is an inter vivos trust and does not distribute any of the dividends to the beneficiary.

SOLUTION available in print and online Study Guide.

We suggest you work Self Study Problems Nineteen-2, 3, and 4 at this point.

Income Attribution - Trusts

General Rules

19-126.   We introduced the income attribution rules for individuals in Chapter 9. Briefly summarized, they are as follows:

Transfer To A Spouse Or Common-Law Partner Under ITA 74.1(1), if property is transferred to a spouse or common-law partner for consideration that is less than fair market value, income earned by this property while it is held by that person, as well as any capital gain resulting from a disposition of the property by the transferee, will be attributed back to the transferor. These rules also apply, without regard to the value of the consideration, when the transferor does not elect out of the ITA 73 rollover provision.

Transfer To A Related Minor Under ITA 74.1(2), if property is transferred to a related individual under the age of 18 for consideration that is less than fair market value, income earned by this property while it is held by the minor will be attributed back to the transferor until the year the individual is 18 or older. Capital gains on a subsequent sale of the property will not be attributed back to the transferor.

19-127. While we did not discuss this point in Chapter 9, these rules are equally applicable when there is a transfer to an inter vivos trust where a spouse, common-law partner, or a related minor is a beneficiary. As was the case with individuals, these rules apply to any transfer where the consideration is less than the fair market value of the property transferred.

19-128. You should note that attribution does not occur at the time the assets are transferred to a trust in which a spouse, common-law partner, or related minor is a beneficiary. Rather, attribution occurs when income from those assets is allocated to one of these individuals. If the trust chooses to be taxed on the income before allocation, or if the income is allocated to individuals other than a spouse, common-law partner, or related minor, income will generally not be attributed to the transferor. In addition, income attribution stops at the death of the settlor.

Exercise Nineteen - 9

Subject: Income Attribution - Trusts

Last year, Trevor Carlisle transferred to a family trust, for no consideration, bonds that pay interest of $27,000 per annum. The beneficiaries of the trust are Trevor's spouse, Carmen, and their two children, Mitch (16 years old) and Rhonda (22 years old). The beneficiaries have no income other than that from the trust. The trust income and capital gains are allocated equally, and are payable to each beneficiary during the year. Total interest income earned by the trust during the year was $27,000. As well, a capital gain of $6,000 was realized on the trust's disposition of one of the bonds that Trevor transferred into the trust. Determine the Taxable Income of each beneficiary and calculate any effect the trust income will have on the Taxable Income of Trevor. How would your answer change if Trevor died on January 1 of the current year?

Ignore the possibility that some of the income received by the beneficiaries will be subject to the TOSI.

SOLUTION available in print and online Study Guide.

We suggest you work Self Study Problems Nineteen-5 and 6 at this point.

Attribution To Settlor (Reversionary Trust)

19-129. There is a further form of income attribution that is unique to trust situations. Both income from holding the transferred property and capital gains from the disposition of the transferred property will be attributed back to the settlor if a trust meets the conditions specified in ITA 75(2).

19-130. ITA 75(2) is applicable, without regard to the identity of the beneficiaries of the trust, if any one of the following conditions is satisfied:

1. The transferred property can revert to the settlor at a later point in time. In this situation, the trust is commonly referred to as a reversionary trust.

2. The transferred property will pass to persons to be determined by the settlor at a later point in time. This requirement prevents the settlor from adding additional beneficiaries, or classes of beneficiaries, subsequent to the creation of the trust.

3. The transferred property cannot be disposed of except with the settlor's consent or in accordance with the settlor's direction.

19-131.   The safest way to deal with the second condition is to not have the settlor act as a trustee. If that is not a practical alternative, it would be prudent to have at least three trustees and have majority approval of decisions. If the settlor is one of two trustees or, if decisions require unanimous approval by all trustees including the settlor, ITA 75(2) may apply.

Purchase Or Sale Of An Interest In A Trust

Income Interest

19-132.   An income interest in a trust is the right of a beneficiary under the trust to receive all or part of the income from the trust. The purchaser of an income interest in a trust will have a cost equal to the fair market value of the consideration given for that interest. This cost can be deducted against amounts of trust income that would otherwise be included in the individual's Taxable Income. Any portion of the cost that is not deducted against income from the trust in the current year can be carried forward for deduction against allocated trust income in subsequent years. When income allocations have reduced the cost of the interest to nil, subsequent receipts of income will be fully taxable.

19-133.   From the point of view of the vendor of an income interest, the proceeds of disposition will be equal to the fair market value of the consideration received. If the cost of the income interest (often nil) is different than the proceeds received, there will be a gain or loss on the disposition. As an income interest is not a capital asset, the gain or loss on its disposition will be treated as a fully taxable or deductible property income or loss.

Capital Interest

19-134.   As defined in ITA 108(1), a capital interest is all of the rights of a beneficiary of a trust, other than an income interest. As the name implies, a capital interest is a capital asset and any gain or loss on its disposition will be treated as a capital gain or loss.

19-135.   When a capital interest in a trust is purchased, the adjusted cost base is equal to the fair market value of the consideration given. This amount will be reduced by future distributions of assets from the trust. As we have noted, ITA 107(2) generally provides for a tax free rollover of assets from a trust to a beneficiary.

19-136.   If a beneficiary sells a capital interest in a trust, the proceeds of disposition will equal the fair market value of the consideration received. Unless the taxpayer has purchased the capital interest, its adjusted cost base will be nil. This means that the entire proceeds of disposition could be a capital gain. However, to determine the gain on a disposition of a capital interest in a trust resident in Canada, ITA 107(1)(a) defines the adjusted cost base to be the greater of:

- the adjusted cost base as usually determined, and
- the "cost amount" to the beneficiary.

19-137.   ITA 108(1) defines this cost amount as the beneficiary's proportionate interest in the net assets of the trust at their carrying value to the trust. This prevents the beneficiary from being taxed on the cost amount of the trust's assets, an amount that could be received on a tax free basis as a distribution from the trust. Capital losses on capital interest dispositions are determined in the usual manner. Since the adjusted cost base is usually nil, such losses are uncommon.

Exercise Nineteen - 10

Subject: Sale Of A Capital Interest

The Jardhu family trust was established when the father transferred publicly traded securities with a cost of $120,000 and a fair market value of $250,000 into the trust. The beneficiaries of the trust are the father's two sons, Sam, aged 25 and Mehrdad, aged 27. They have an equal interest in the income and capital of the trust.

At the beginning of the current year, Mehrdad sells his capital interest in the trust to Sam. There have been no capital distributions from the trust. At the time of the sale, the fair market value of the securities in the trust is $380,000. Based on this, the transfer price for the capital interest is $190,000 [(1/2)($380,000)]. Determine the tax consequences of this transaction to each of the two brothers.

SOLUTION available in print and online Study Guide.

Tax Planning

Family Trusts

Defined

19-138.   As we have noted, the term family trust is not defined in the *Income Tax Act*. Rather, it is a term that is used in practice to refer to a personal trust that has been established with members of the settlor's family as beneficiaries. These trusts can either be inter vivos trusts established during the settlor's lifetime or, alternatively, testamentary trusts created when the settlor dies. The provisions of these trusts often contain a fixed arrangement for the payments to beneficiaries. However, in some cases they are established with the payments to the beneficiaries left to the discretion of the trustees.

19-139.   While family trusts can be used for a variety of purposes, the most common objective of these trusts is income splitting. This process was introduced in Chapter 1, with further elaboration on the role of corporate structures in income splitting discussed in Chapter 15. In this Chapter we will give attention to income splitting in the context of family trusts. As we have noted, the expansion of the TOSI to related adults makes it much more difficult to implement effective income splitting strategies.

Discretionary Trusts

19-140.   As we have noted, a family trust is usually established for income splitting purposes, typically by a wealthy individual with children or other family members who are in low tax brackets. Such individuals commonly have difficulty deciding which of their family members are, and will continue to be, the most deserving. A solution to this problem is the use of a discretionary trust.

19-141.   The provisions of discretionary trusts leave the amount and/or timing of payments to beneficiaries at the discretion of the trustees. This means that, if a particular beneficiary neglects his family duties on a regular basis, or appears to be profligate in his spending habits, his share of the income can be reduced, eliminated, or delayed to a later date. Tax planners like to point out that this provides the settlor with great flexibility. A less charitable view of the settlor's objectives is that this type of arrangement provides for continued control over the behaviour of family members (e.g., if a child fails to show up for family dinners, he can be reminded that his receipts from the family trust are discretionary).

19-142.   It is important to note that the settlor of the trust cannot be in a position of unilateral control over the amount and timing of the discretionary distributions, particularly if he is also one of the beneficiaries. If the settlor is in a position of control, the provisions of ITA 75(2) (see Paragraph 19-130) may be applicable, resulting in all of the income being attributed back to him. The usual way to avoid this problem is to have at least three trustees, with the amount of the discretionary distributions determined by majority rule. The CRA has indicated that, for this approach to be effective, the settlor cannot be a required part of the majority.

Income Splitting

19-143.   If a family trust is set up properly, the potential tax savings from income splitting can be significant. The following table compares the federal Tax Payable on eligible dividends of $57,321 received by:

- A father who is subject to the maximum federal tax rate of 33 percent.

- His adult daughter with no other source of income. Assume that any income distributed to this related person will not be subject to the TOSI.

19-144.   The required calculations follow. Note that, given the amounts and type of income involved in this example, the application of the alternative minimum tax (AMT) reduces the amount of the tax savings to some degree.

	Father	Daughter	AMT (Daughter)
Eligible Dividends Received	$57,321	$57,321	$57,321
Gross Up At 38 Percent	21,782	21,782	N/A For AMT
Taxable Dividends/Income	$79,103	$79,103	$57,791
Federal Tax			
[(33%)($79,103)]	$26,104		
[(15%)($46,605) + (20.5%)($32,498)]		$13,653	
[(15%)($57,321 - $40,000 Exemption)]			$ 2,598
Federal Dividend Tax Credit			
[(54.55%)($21,782)] (Note 1)	(11,882)	(11,882)	N/A For AMT
Basic Personal Credit (Note 2)	N/A	(1,771)	(1,771)
Federal Tax Payable/AMT	$14,222	Nil	$ 827

Note 1   We have rounded 6/11 to 54.55 percent in order to avoid rounding problems.

Note 2   Since the father would have other income against which he could apply his basic personal credit, it has not been taken into consideration in the preceding calculations.

19-145.   This example is rigged to use the maximum of tax-free eligible dividends that can be paid to an individual with only the basic personal tax credit. As shown in the preceding calculations, this serves to reduce the daughter's regular Tax Payable to nil. However, AMT will be payable, resulting in a net tax savings through the use of a family trust in the amount of $13,395 ($14,222 - $827). The corresponding savings in provincial taxes would increase this amount significantly. Note that this tax savings would be available for each beneficiary if there were multiple beneficiaries. Of equal importance is the fact that this is not a one-time event. These tax savings can be accomplished on an annual basis as long as the beneficiaries have no other source of income.

19-146.   You should note that, in situations where the relevant family member will be subject to the TOSI, it would be difficult, if not impossible to achieve substantial tax savings through the use of this tax planning vehicle.

Exercise Nineteen - 11

Subject: Family Trusts

Sarah Block is holding debt securities which produce interest income of $110,000 per year. She has other sources of income in excess of $250,000. She has two children. Her daughter, Jerri, is 22 years old and currently has no income that is subject to tax.

Jerri's only tax credit is the basic personal credit. Sarah's son, Mark, is 26 years old. He is married and his wife has no income of her own. Mark has annual net rental income of $48,000.

The trust will be required to distribute all of its income on an annual basis. Determine the savings in federal taxes that could be achieved by transferring the debt securities to a family trust with her two children as equal income beneficiaries.

Assume that Mark's only tax credits are the basic personal credit and the spousal credit and that none of the income received by the beneficiaries will be subject to the TOSI.

SOLUTION available in print and online Study Guide.

Qualifying Spousal Or Common-Law Partner Trusts

19-147.   As is discussed in Chapter 9, a rollover of assets to a spouse can be accomplished without the use of a trust. In the case of a living individual, the rollover is provided for under ITA 73(1) and (1.01), while for a deceased individual, the enabling provision is ITA 70(6). This makes it clear that a trust is not required to implement a tax free transfer of property for the benefit of a spouse. Why then are we concerned with qualifying spousal or common-law partner trusts? There are essentially two important reasons:

1. A trust can provide for the appropriate management of the transferred assets, particularly when these assets include an active business. In many cases, the spouse or common-law partner of a settlor may have no experience in the management of assets and, in such situations, the trust document can ensure that professional management is used. If the assets were simply transferred to the spouse or common-law partner, the use of such management would be left to the discretion and control of the transferee.

2. Also of importance is that the use of a trust can ensure that the assets are distributed in the manner desired by the settlor. While qualification requires that the transferred assets must "vest indefeasibly" with the spouse or common-law partner, the trust document can specify who the assets should be distributed to after the spouse or common-law partner dies. This could ensure, for example, that the assets are ultimately distributed only to the settlor's children if the spouse or common-law partner was to remarry.

Alter Ego Trusts

19-148.   The most commonly cited reason for using an alter ego trust is that the trust property will not be included in the settlor's estate and, as a consequence, will not be subject to probate procedures (probate is a court process that proves the authenticity and validity of a will). There are a number of advantages associated with avoiding probate:

*   The probate fees can be high. In Ontario, for example, they are equal to 0.5 percent on the first $50,000 of the fair market value of the estate, plus 1.5 percent of the excess, with no upper limit. On a $10 million estate these fees would total almost $150,000, a payment that can be completely eliminated with the use of an alter ego trust.

*   The probate process can be time consuming. This can create difficulties for the management of an active business, as well as liquidity problems for the estate.

*   When assets such as real estate are held in more than one jurisdiction (e.g., Canada and the U.S.), the probate procedures must be undertaken in multiple jurisdictions.

*   Once probated, a will is in the public domain. For a nominal fee, any interested individual can obtain a copy, with the possibility that this will invade the privacy of surviving family members.

19-149.   While this point has not been widely discussed in the literature that we have seen on this subject, an additional tax feature involved in establishing an alter ego trust is the possibility of establishing the trust in a low tax rate province. When there is a deemed disposition at death or on emigration, the taxation will occur in the province where the trust is resident. Given that, for 2018, the combined federal/provincial rate on individuals ranges from 47.5 in Saskatchewan, to 54 percent in Nova Scotia, this 6.5 percentage point difference makes the province of residence of the trust a significant tax planning issue.

19-150.   We would also note that there is a significant non-tax reason for using an alter ego trust. From a legal point of view, it is much easier to challenge the validity of a will than it is to challenge the validity of a trust. Courts can be asked to consider moral obligations to family members in distributing the assets of an estate. With a trust, there is no will to challenge.

Joint Spousal Or Joint Common-Law Partner Trusts

19-151.   A joint spousal or joint common-law partner trust has the same tax characteristics as an alter ego trust. The basic difference is that these trusts are established to hold the combined assets of both an individual and his spouse or common-law partner. Given this, their tax planning features are largely the same as those discussed for alter ego trusts in the preceding Paragraphs.

Estate Planning

Non-Tax Considerations

19-152.   The subject of estate planning is complex and involves considerations that go well beyond the scope of this text. In fact, appropriate planning for a large estate will often involve lawyers, investment advisors, accountants, and tax advisors. Indeed, it may even be necessary to have religious advisors or psychological counselors participate in order to deal with some of the moral or emotional issues that are involved.

19-153.   The following points are among the more important non-tax considerations in planning an estate:

Intent Of The Testator   The foremost goal of estate planning is to ensure that the wishes of the testator (a person who has died and left a will) are carried out. This will involve ensuring that the assets left by the testator are distributed at the appropriate times and to the specified beneficiaries. The primary document for ensuring that the intent of the testator is fulfilled is, of course, the will.

Preparation Of A Final Will   The major document in the estate planning process is the final will. It should be carefully prepared to provide detailed instructions for the disposition of assets, investment decisions to be made, and the extent to which trusts will be used. An executor should be named to administer the estate, and the will should be reviewed periodically to ensure that it reflects the testator's current wishes and family status.

Preparation Of A Living Will   Equally important to the preparation of a final will, a living will provides detailed instructions regarding investments and other personal decisions in the event of physical or mental incapacity at any point in a person's life-time. A power of attorney is similar, except that it does not require the individual to be mentally or physically incapacitated in order to be used.

Ensuring Liquidity   A plan should be established to provide for liquidity at the time of death. Major expenses, often including funeral expenses and income taxes, will arise at this time. Funds needed for these payments should be available, or adequate life insurance should be arranged in advance, to avoid the need for emergency sales of capital assets to raise the necessary cash.

Simplicity   While the disposition of a large estate will rarely be simple, effective estate planning should ensure that the plan can be understood by the testator and all beneficiaries of legal age. In addition, any actions that can reduce the cost and complexity of administering the estate should be considered. This might involve disposing of investments in non-public shares, or repatriating assets that are located in foreign countries that might become subject to foreign taxation.

Avoidance Of Family Disputes   Unfortunately, disputes among beneficiaries are a common part of estate settlement procedures. If equitable treatment of beneficiaries is a goal of the testator, efforts should be made to ensure that all beneficiaries believe that they have been treated in an equitable manner. If the testator wants to distribute assets in a fashion that could be viewed as inequitable by any of the interested parties, care should be taken to make this intention unequivocal.

Expediting The Transition   The procedures required in the settlement of an estate should be designed to expedite the process. A long settlement period can increase uncertainties related to the value of assets, add to the complications associated with the required distribution of the assets, and prolong the frustration of the beneficiaries.

Tax Considerations

19-154.   In addition to the preceding non-tax considerations, estate planning must also consider various tax factors. Fundamental tax planning goals for all taxpayers apply equally to estate planning. Briefly, these goals involve the legal and orderly arrangement of one's affairs, before the time of a transaction or event, to reduce and defer income taxes.

19-155.   In effective estate planning, the overriding income tax goals are to defer and minimize tax payments. Several important issues should be considered in dealing with this objective. These can be described as follows:

Prior To Death   Planning should attempt to minimize taxes for the individual in the years prior to death. If the individual earns income that is not required in these years, attempts should be made to defer the payment of tax and transfer the before-tax income to the ultimate beneficiaries. The use of a discretionary trust can assist in achieving this goal.

Year Of Death   Planning should attempt to minimize income taxes payable in the year of death. Deemed dispositions will occur at death and, in addition, amounts in certain types of deferred income plans usually must be included in the taxpayer's final return. Relief can be achieved through tax deferred rollovers to a spouse and transfers of certain types of property (e.g., farm property) to children or grandchildren. The will can also contain instructions to ensure that the maximum RRSP contribution is made to the spouse's RRSP within the deadline.

Income Splitting   Effective planning should allow income splitting among family members who are in lower tax brackets. This can be accomplished by the appropriate splitting of income (e.g., paying salaries and wages for services rendered) and distributing property among beneficiaries throughout a taxpayer's lifetime, recognizing the limitations imposed by the TOSI.

Foreign Jurisdictions   Planning should normally attempt to minimize taxes that will be incurred in foreign jurisdictions. This is especially true for jurisdictions with significant estate taxes as such taxes are generally not eligible for foreign tax credits or deduction in Canada. To the extent that it is consistent with the individual's investment plans and the residence of intended beneficiaries, holdings of foreign assets at death, or distributions to beneficiaries in foreign locations, should usually be avoided by residents of Canada. Minimizing foreign investments will also simplify the administration of an estate.

Administration Period   Planning should minimize taxes payable while the estate is being administered. Discretion provided to trustees in distributing the income of an inter vivos trust may assist in achieving this goal.

19-156.   Most of the tax procedures related to these issues have already been introduced.

We have discussed spouse and common-law partner rollovers in previous Chapters and the use of trusts was covered earlier in this Chapter. An important aspect of estate planning that requires additional consideration is the estate freeze. Procedures to be used in these arrangements are outlined in the material that follows.

Estate Freeze

Objectives Of An Estate Freeze

19-157.   The objective of an estate freeze is, as the name implies, to freeze the value of the estate for tax purposes at a particular point in time. Typically, arrangements are made for all future appreciation to accrue to related parties such as a spouse, children, or grandchildren.

> **EXAMPLE**   Mr. Chisholm is a wealthy and successful entrepreneur who has a wife and two young children. He owns a variety of capital assets that are producing Taxable Income and appreciating in value. He has several objectives in creating his estate plan:
>
> - During the remainder of his life, Mr. Chisholm would like to transfer all or part of his Taxable Income to a group of individuals and charities who will ultimately be the beneficiaries of his estate.
>
> - Mr. Chisholm would like to freeze the tax values of his assets and allow future growth to accrue to the intended family members.
>
> - Since the current fair market value of his assets exceeds their tax cost, Mr. Chisholm would like to avoid any immediate taxation resulting from a disposition of these assets with accrued gains.
>
> - Mr. Chisholm would like the transfer of future growth in asset values to accrue so that his beneficiaries will not be subject to taxation in the year of the estate freeze, in any intervening years, or in the year of his death.
>
> - Mr. Chisholm wants to retain the right to the current value of the property at the time of the estate freeze. In addition, he wishes to retain control of the use of the property until his death.

19-158.   This example will be used as a basis for discussing a variety of techniques that can be used to freeze an estate's value. Some of these techniques will achieve all of Mr. Chisholm's goals, while others will only succeed in achieving one or two of them.

Techniques Not Involving Rollovers

Gifts

19-159.   Mr. Chisholm can freeze the value of his estate without using rollover provisions. The most straightforward technique is to simply give property to his prospective beneficiaries. While this would accomplish the goal of transferring future growth in the estate to the beneficiaries, unless the transfer was to a spouse or common-law partner, this approach would have the serious drawback of attracting immediate taxation on any difference between the fair market value of the assets and Mr. Chisholm's tax cost.

19-160.   In addition, if the person receiving the gift is a spouse or minor child, income attribution rules could apply after the gift is made. Further drawbacks are the fact that Mr. Chisholm would lose control over the assets and that certain income received by related persons may be subject to the TOSI.

19-161.   While gifts result in a loss of control, Mr. Chisholm may want to accelerate his donations to registered charities. The value of the tax credit associated with such gifts can more than offset any income arising as the result of such distributions. In particular, if a gift is made of shares listed on a designated stock exchange, the capital gains inclusion rate is reduced to nil (See Chapter 11).

Instalment Sales

19-162.   Mr. Chisholm could freeze the value of the estate by selling the assets to the intended family members on an instalment basis. Capital gains could be deferred until payment is received, but the gains would need to be reported over the next 5 years based on the capital gains reserve calculations (10 years if a farm or fishing property is involved).

19-163.   To avoid income attribution and inadequate consideration problems, the sale should be made at fair market value. However, if the intended family members do not have sufficient assets to make the purchase, this may not be a feasible solution. A further problem is that Mr. Chisholm would lose control over the property.

Establishing A Trust

19-164.   An estate freeze can also be accomplished by setting up a trust in favour of one or more beneficiaries. Here again, this will transfer income and future growth from Mr. Chisholm's hands to the trust. The trust can be structured so that he retains some control over the assets in the trust.

19-165.   The problem with this arrangement is that, except in the case of a qualifying spouse or common-law partner trust, a joint spousal or common-law partner trust, or an alter ego trust, there is no rollover provision that provides for tax deferred transfers of assets to a trust. As a result, if the trust is set up for beneficiaries other than Mr. Chisholm or his spouse, Mr. Chisholm will incur taxation on any capital gains accrued at the time of the transfer. As well, any dividends received from a private corporation by related beneficiaries may be subject to the TOSI, whether the shares are held directly or through a trust.

Use Of A Holding Company

19-166.   Mr. Chisholm could transfer assets to a holding company in which intended family members have a substantial equity interest, without using a rollover provision. This will freeze the value of his estate and, if the assets transferred have fair market values that are equal to or less than their adjusted cost base, it can be an effective vehicle for realizing losses. However, without the use of a rollover provision, such as that found in ITA 85, any capital gains or recapture amounts that have accrued to the time of the transfer will become subject to immediate taxation.

Section 86 Share Exchange

Nature Of The Exchange

19-167.   Chapter 17 provided an overview of ITA 86 which applies to the exchange of shares by a shareholder in the course of a reorganization of capital. In certain situations, a share exchange constitutes the best solution to the estate freeze problem. Specifically, this rollover is most appropriate in a situation that involves an individual who is the sole owner of a successful private corporation.

19-168.   By exchanging common shares for preferred shares that have equal value, the owner will, in effect, eliminate his participation in the future growth of the company. At the same time, common shares can be issued to intended family members or a discretionary family trust created for their benefit. These new shareholders can participate in the company's future income and any growth in the value of its assets.

Example

19-169.   While detailed consideration was given to ITA 86 rollovers in Chapter 17, the following simple example will serve to review these procedures.

> **EXAMPLE**   Over her lifetime, Mrs. Hadley has been the sole owner and driving force behind Hadley Inc., a manufacturing business located in Alberta. At the end of the current year, the condensed Balance Sheet of this Company was as follows:

Estate Freeze

Hadley Inc.
Balance Sheet

Net Identifiable Assets	$10,000,000
Common Stock (No Par - 1,000 Shares)	$ 2,000,000
Retained Earnings	8,000,000
Total Shareholders' Equity	$10,000,000

On the basis of an independent appraisal, the fair market value of this business was established at $15,000,000. Mrs. Hadley has a husband and three adult children and would like them to share equally in her estate. The $2,000,000 Common Stock account is both the adjusted cost base and the PUC of her shares.

19-170.   Under ITA 86, Mrs. Hadley can exchange, on a tax deferred basis, her common shares that have an adjusted cost base of $2 million (also the amount of contributed capital and PUC) for preferred shares with a redemption value of $15 million (the fair market value of the business). These preferred shares would have no participation in the future growth of the Company and, as a result, Mrs. Hadley has effectively frozen the value of her estate.

19-171.   If Mrs. Hadley wishes to retain control of the Company, the preferred shares can be established as the only outstanding voting shares. While this share exchange will be free of any capital gains taxation, Mrs. Hadley's adjusted cost base and PUC for the new preferred shares remains at the former common share value of $2 million. If the preferred shares are sold for their market value of $15 million, a $13 million capital gain will result ($15 million - $2 million). Alternatively, if the shares are redeemed for $15 million by the Company, there will be a $13 million taxable dividend under ITA 84(3).

19-172.   The tax cost basis for the identifiable assets owned by the Company has not been altered by the share exchange transaction.

19-173.   At this point, the redemption value of Mrs. Hadley's preferred shares represents the entire fair market value of the business and, as a consequence, the value of any common shares issued will not exceed the amount contributed by the investors. This means that such shares can be issued for a nominal value, without any appearance that the purchasers are indirectly receiving a gift from Mrs. Hadley. Thus, 1,000 common shares could be issued to Mrs. Hadley's intended family members at $10 per share as follows:

Spouse (250 Shares At $10)	$ 2,500
Child One (250 Shares At $10)	2,500
Child Two (250 Shares At $10)	2,500
Child Three (250 Shares At $10)	2,500
Total Common Stock Contributed	$10,000

19-174.   These common shares would benefit from the future income and growth in asset values that may be experienced by Hadley Inc.

19-175.   Prior to 2018, this Section 86 rollover would have provided an ideal solution to the estate freeze problem. It did, in fact, transfer all future growth in the estate into the hands of intended beneficiaries with no immediate tax effects on the individual making the transfer. However, there is a problem in that, with the new TOSI rules in place, income received by the family members is likely to be taxed at the maximum federal rate of 33 percent.

Rollover Provisions - Section 85 vs. Section 86

19-176.   A Section 85 rollover of property to a holding corporation can also be used to implement an estate freeze. The rollover provisions of ITA 85 were given full consideration in Chapter 16, and will not be repeated here.

19-177. In comparing the use of ITA 85 and ITA 86, you should note that Section 85 can be used in a broader variety of circumstances than is the case with Section 86. More specifically, Section 86 deals only with exchanges of shares in the course of the reorganization of an existing corporation. This means that Section 86 can only be used in situations where the assets involved in the estate freeze are shares of a corporation. Section 85 would have to be used if the estate consists of other types of property.

19-178. When Section 86 can be used, it is an easier procedure to implement. Unlike Section 85, which requires a formal election to be made and either an existing corporation or the formation of a new corporation, Section 86 applies automatically once the required conditions are met. By using a Section 86 reorganization, the savings in legal and accounting fees can be significant. The many complexities involved in effecting an estate freeze using rollovers make it difficult to comment on the relative desirability of Sections 85 and 86 for estate freezes in general terms.

SIFT Partnerships And Trusts

19-179. As was noted in Chapter 18, legislation has served to largely eliminate SIFT partnerships and trusts. Given this, we do not provide coverage of this subject in *Canadian Tax Principles*, except in Chapter 7, Property Income, where we have limited coverage of real estate income trusts (REITs).

Additional Supplementary Self Study Problems Are Available Online.

Key Terms Used In This Chapter

19-180. The following is a list of the key terms used in this Chapter. These terms, and their meanings, are compiled in the Glossary located at the back of the Study Guide.

Alter Ego Trust	Preferred Beneficiary
Beneficiary	Preferred Beneficiary Election
Capital Interest (In A Trust)	Qualifying Spousal or
Discretionary Trust	Common-Law Partner Trust
Estate	Reorganization Of Capital (ITA 86)
Estate Freeze	Reversionary Trust
Executor	Rollover
Family Trust	Settlor
Graduated Rate Estate	Split Income
Income Attribution	Spousal Or Common-Law Partner Trust
Income Interest (In A Trust)	Tax Planning
Income Splitting	Testamentary Trust
Inter Vivos Trust	Trust
Joint Spousal Or Common-Law	Trustee
Partner Trust	Twenty-One (21) Year
Non-Discretionary Trust	Deemed Disposition Rule
Personal Trust	Will

References

19-181.   For more detailed study of the material in this Chapter, we would refer you to the following:

ITA 70(6)	Transfers To Spousal Trusts On Death
ITA 73(1)	Inter-Vivos Transfers To Spousal Trusts
ITA 74.1 to 74.5	Attribution Rules
ITA 75(2)	Trust (Attribution To Settlor)
ITA 85(1)	Transfer Of Property To Corporation By Shareholders
ITA 86(1)	Exchange Of Shares By A Shareholder In Course Of Reorganization Of Capital
ITA 104 to 108	Trusts And Their Beneficiaries
ITA 122	Tax Payable By Inter Vivos Trust
ITA 122.1	Definitions (SIFT Trusts)
ITA 197	Tax On SIFT Partnership
IC-76-19R3	Transfer Of Property To A Corporation Under Section 85
S6-F1-C1	Residence Of A Trust Or Estate
S6-F2-C1	Disposition Of An Income Interest In A Trust
IT-209R	Inter-Vivos Gifts Of Capital Property To Individuals Directly Or Through Trusts
IT-286R2	Trusts - Amount Payable
IT-291R3	Transfer Of Property To A Corporation Under Subsection 85(1)
IT-305R4	Testamentary Spouse Trusts
IT-342R	Trusts - Income Payable To Beneficiaries
IT-369R	Attribution Of Trust Income To Settlor
IT-381R3	Trusts - Capital Gains And Losses And The Flow-Through Of Taxable Capital Gains To Beneficiaries
IT-394R2	Preferred Beneficiary Election
IT-406R2	Tax Payable By An Inter Vivos Trust
IT-465R	Non-Resident Beneficiaries Of Trusts
IT-510	Transfers and Loans of Property Made After May 22, 1985 to a Related Minor
IT-511R	Interspousal And Certain Other Transfers And Loans Of Property
IT-524	Trusts - Flow Through Of Taxable Dividends To A Beneficiary After 1987
T4013	Trust Guide

Problems For Self Study (Online)

To provide practice in problem solving, there are Self Study and Supplementary Self Study problems available on MyLab Accounting.

Within the text we have provided an indication of when it would be appropriate to work each Self Study problem. The detailed solutions for Self Study problems can be found in the print and online Study Guide.

We provide the Supplementary Self Study problems for those who would like additional practice in problem solving. The detailed solutions for the Supplementary Self Study problems are available online, not in the Study Guide.

The .PDF file "Self Study Problems for Volume 2" on MyLab contains the following for Chapter 19:

- 6 Self Study problems,
- 2 Supplementary Self Study problems, and
- detailed solutions for the Supplementary Self Study problems.

Assignment Problems

(The solutions for these problems are only available in
the solutions manual that has been provided to your instructor.)

Assignment Problem Nineteen - 1

(Property Transfer To And From A Trust)

Each of the following independent Cases involve transfers of property to trusts by a settlor for no consideration. Three of the Cases also involve capital distributions from trusts to capital beneficiaries.

A. A gift of non-depreciable capital property is made to a qualifying spousal inter vivos trust. The adjusted cost base of the property to the settlor was $45,700. At the time of the transfer the fair market value of the property is $51,000. At a later point in time, the property is transferred to the spouse. At this time the fair market value of the property is $49,200.

B. A gift of depreciable capital property (a rare violin) is made to an inter vivos trust in favour of the settlor's adult children. The capital cost of the violin to the settlor, a world renowned violinist was $125,000. On the date of the gift, the UCC was $72,000 and the fair market value was $155,000.

C. A transfer of a piece of vacant land is made to a qualifying spousal testamentary trust. The cost of the land for the deceased spouse was $200,000, and the fair market value on the date of the transfer to the trust is $225,500. At the time of his death, the decedent had a large net capital loss carry forward of $78,000.

D. A depreciable property is transferred to an inter vivos trust in favour of the settlor's adult children. The capital cost of the property is $17,600 and its UCC is $9,100. It is the last asset in its class. At the time of the transfer, the fair market value of the property is $5,000.

E. A gift of non-depreciable capital property is made to an inter vivos trust in favour of the settlor's adult children. The adjusted cost base of the property to the settlor was $36,900. Its fair market value on the date of the gift is $40,200. At a later point in time, when the fair market value of the property is $51,700, the property is transferred to the children.

F. A non-depreciable capital property is transferred to an alter ego trust. The cost of the capital property to the settlor was $101,500. On the date of the transfer, the estimated fair market value is $92,300. At a later point in time, when the estimated fair market value of the property has increased to $100,000, the property is transferred back to the settlor.

Assignment Problems

Required: For each Case indicate:

1.   The tax consequences to the settlor that result from the transfer of the property to the trust assuming the transfer price is chosen to optimize the tax position of the settlor.

2.   The tax value(s) for the transferred property that will be recorded by the trust.

3.   In those cases where property is transferred to a beneficiary, the tax consequences to the trust and the tax value(s) that will be recorded by the beneficiary.

Assignment Problem Nineteen - 2
(Inter Vivos Trusts - Income Attribution)

In the process of planning an estate freeze, Glen Marx intends to transfer a large group of publicly traded common stocks to a trust. The terms of this trust will require that, on an annual basis, 50 percent of the income of the trust be distributed to his wife, Greta Petrov, with the remaining 50 percent split equally between their son, Sergey and daughter, Anastasia. Sergey is 23 years old and has employment income of over $35,000 per year. Anastasia is 19 years old and has employment income of over $25,000 per year.

The trust's income will consist of interest, dividends, and capital gains.

The terms of the trust require that all of the trust's assets be distributed 15 years subsequent to the date on which it was established. This distribution will use the same allocation that is used for annual distributions.

Required:

A.   Identify the type of trust that is being used.

B.   How should the trust's year end date be chosen?

C.   Indicate the persons that will have to include the trust's income in their Net Income For Tax Purposes. Would your answer change if Anastasia was 17 years of age? If so, explain how.

D.   Explain how your answer to Part C would change if Mr. Marx forms the trust by the settlement of a nominal amount of cash. Mr. Marx then lends money to the trust to purchase the portfolio investments from him at their fair market value. Assume:

1.   the loan is an interest free loan;
2.   the trust pays interest at the prescribed rate on the loan.

E.   Would the taxation of the trust income change if Mr. Marx and Mrs. Petrov were living separately because of a marriage breakdown? Explain your conclusion.

Assignment Problem Nineteen - 3
(Trusts And Income Splitting)

Hannah Brood is an engineer with 2018 employment income of $235,000. In addition, she has holdings of debt securities that produce a total of $65,000 in interest during 2018.

She has a 19 year old son from her first marriage. The son's name is Harvey Rosen and he is enrolled as a freshman at a Canadian university. It is Harvey's life-long dream to be an accounting professor. Given this, he anticipates that he will be enrolled in university programs for at least 8 more years. Hannah expects that the cost of his living expenses, tuition, and books will be about $55,000 per year during this period. Harvey's father disappeared without a trace when Harvey was born and has never paid any child support.

While she has had three other marriages, she eventually found married life very dreary and is now separated from her most recent husband. However, she still loves children. To satisfy this maternal need, she arranged to have another child with sperm donated by her gay brother-in-law. This child is now a 1 year old named Carl Brood. Currently, Carl is cared for by a nanny who is paid $17,000 per year. When Carl reaches 4 years of age, Hannah intends to send him to a private school. She anticipates that the cost of the private school will be similar to the cost of the nanny.

Hannah does not anticipate that either child will have significant income until they complete university.

Hannah would like to transfer the debt securities to a trust for her children. As her employment income is more than sufficient for her needs, she hopes to use the trust to split income both currently and in future years. She has indicated that, while she wants to support her children fully, she does not want the trust to provide them with any direct payments until they are 30 years old. Until then, she wants the trust to pay for their care, education, and other direct expenses.

Required: Outline how a trust might be used to split income with Hannah's children. Ignore the possibility that some of the trust's distributions might be subject to the TOSI.

Assignment Problem Nineteen - 4
(Graduated Rate Estates - Tax Minimization)

After a long battle with cancer, Mr. Thomas Holt died on March 3, 2017. His will specifies that all of the considerable assets in his estate are to be transferred to a testamentary trust.

Because of difficulties with locating some of Mr. Holt's assets, the transfer to a trust has not been implemented prior to December 31, 2017. Given this, the executor of his estate files a T3 tax return for the period ending December 31, 2017. This return designates Mr. Holt's estate as a Graduated Rate Estate (GRE).

Due to administrative delays of various sorts, Mr. Holt's assets remain under the administration of the executor at December 31, 2018. Because of this, the executor files a T3 return for the GRE for the year ending December 31, 2018.

The beneficiaries of the trust are Mr. Holt's wife, Renfrew Holt. She is a very successful trial lawyer with an annual income in excess of $275,000. Their 22 year old daughter Roxanne has struggled, for several years, to have a career as a folk singer. She has not enjoyed much success and, as a consequence, she has no Taxable Income for 2018.

In his will, Mr. Holt included a provision which allowed income distributions to these beneficiaries during the period that his estate is being administered by an executor. While the provision allows for distributions to either beneficiary, the timing and amounts are at the discretion of the executor.

For the year ending on December 31, 2018, the GRE had the following income receipts:

Interest	$43,000
Eligible Dividends Received From Canadian Corporations	31,200
Total Income	$74,200

Required:

A. With a view to minimizing total Tax Payable for the GRE and the beneficiaries, determine the amounts and type of income that should be distributed to each beneficiary for 2018.

B. Using the allocations you determined in Part A, calculate the total federal Tax Payable for the GRE and Roxanne Holt for the year ending on December 31, 2018. In addition, indicate any additional taxes that would be paid by Renfrew Holt for 2018 as the result of the GRE distributions.

Ignore the possibility that some of the trust's distributions might be subject to the TOSI.

Assignment Problem Nineteen - 5
(Inter Vivos Trusts - Tax Payable)

During 2016, Valerie Larson's parents both died when their private jet was hit by a drone while circling the Toronto Island airport. As an only child, Valerie inherited a substantial estate.

Her parents had transformed the family construction business from a one man operation (her father) into a very successful online market place for quality construction services. Valerie and her two sons, Louis and Gabriel had worked for the Canadian controlled private company, Larson Services Inc. (LS) all their working lives.

Valerie decided to transfer the investments she inherited into a trust with her two sons as beneficiaries. The fiscal year of the trust ends on December 31, and Ms. Larson has no beneficial interest in either the income or capital of the trust. As the president of LS, her compensation is more than adequate for her financial needs.

Louis is aged 30, while Gabriel is 25. The terms of the trust specify that Louis is to receive 10 percent of all of the income of the trust, while Gabriel is to receive 50 percent of this income. The reason for the difference in percentages is that Louis is addicted to opioids. After the death of his grandparents, he turned to street drugs to help cope with his grief. Louis is in a long term treatment program for his addiction and he is making impressive progress.

The undistributed income is to accumulate within the trust, to be paid out to Louis when his doctors tell Valerie his addiction is under control.

The income figures for the year ending on December 31, 2018, are as follows:

Non-Eligible Dividends Received From LS	$450,000
Interest Income On Corporate Bonds	37,000
Revenues From Rental Property	205,000
Cash Expenses On Rental Property	125,350

During 2018, the rental property was sold. The property consisted of an apartment building and the land on which it was located, all of which was transferred into the trust when Valerie inherited it. The relevant information related to the disposition is as follows:

	Building	Land
Proceeds Of Disposition	$3,200,000	$728,000
Undepreciated Capital Cost	1,881,600	N/A
Capital Cost/Adjusted Cost Base	2,000,000	500,000

This is the first disposition of capital property by the trust since its establishment.

Required:

A. Calculate the Taxable Income of the trust for the year ending December 31, 2018. In addition, calculate the increase in Taxable Income resulting from being beneficiaries of the trust for Louis and Gabriel for the same period.

B. Calculate the federal Tax Payable for the trust, for the year ending December 31, 2018.

Assignment Problem Nineteen - 6

(Graduated Rate Estates - Transfers and Tax Payable)

Rhett Buttler died on March 22, 2017. The assets in his estate are to be transferred to a testamentary trust whose beneficiaries are his wife Scarlett and their adult, transgender son/daughter Ashley.

The executor of Rhett's estate missed a curve while driving his Maserati very fast. He survived the car crash with extensive physical damage, but with minor impairment to his mind. As a consequence of the accident he was not able to fully perform his executor duties for an extended period of time. As a result, on March 21, 2019, the assets of the estate are still under his administration.

The executor had filed a T3 return for the non-calendar fiscal year ending March 21, 2018, designating the estate as a Graduated Rate Estate (GRE).

For the fiscal year ended March 21, 2019, the GRE has the following:

Business Income	$50,000
Interest	7,500
Non-Eligible Dividends Received From CCPC	125,000
Rent Receipts	30,000
Rental Operating Expenses	15,000
CCA On Rental Property	5,000

As he had anticipated difficulties in settling his estate, Rhett's will indicated that the executor should make distributions of his estate's income until such time as the assets are transferred to the testamentary trust. All distributions are to be made on the last day of the fiscal period of the GRE, i.e., on March 21, 2019 for the second fiscal year.

Assume his will contained the following instructions:

Alternative One   One-half of any dividend income is to be retained in the GRE. The remaining one-half of the dividend income, as well as all of the other net income is to be paid 60 percent to Scarlett and 40 percent to Ashley.

Alternative Two   All of the GRE's income will be allocated to Scarlett and Ashley on a 60 percent and 40 percent basis.

Scarlett and Ashley have no other sources of income. They have no personal tax credits under ITA 118 other than their basic personal credit and any credits that may arise from income allocations from the GRE.

Required:

A. For each of the alternatives, calculate Taxable Income and federal Tax Payable for the fiscal year ending March 21, 2019 for the GRE.

B. For each of the alternatives, calculate Taxable Income and federal Tax Payable for Scarlett and Ashley for the year ending December 31, 2019.

C. Compare the amount of federal Tax Payable under each of the two alternatives and explain the difference.

Assume that the tax rates and tax brackets for 2019 are the same as those for 2018. Also, assume that none of the trust's distributions will be subject to the TOSI.

Assignment Problems

Assignment Problem Nineteen - 7
(Graduated Rate Estates - Transfers and Tax Payable)

Martha Dagger was killed in a paragliding accident on March 15, 2018. Her will requires that all of the property in her estate be transferred to a testamentary trust. The beneficiaries of the trust will be her 22 year old daughter, Sharon Dagger and her 14 year old son, Morris Dagger. Because of complications related to transferring the assets to the trust, on December 31, 2018, the estate assets are still under the administration of her executor.

The executor files a T3 tax return for the fiscal period ending on December 31, 2018 designating Martha's estate as a Graduated Rate Estate (GRE). While the executor could have chosen a non-calendar taxation year, he decided to use December 31 as the year end for the GRE.

Information on the property owned by Martha at her death is as follows:

	Tax Cost	Fair Market Value March 15, 2018
Shares In Deadly Dagger Inc. (a CCPC)	$ 897,000	$1,472,000
Corporate Debt Securities	478,000	456,000
Rental Property		
Land	562,000	864,000
Building (Cost = $1,740,000)	1,390,374	2,476,000

Deadly Dagger Inc. is a qualified small business corporation. Martha has available a lifetime capital gains deduction of $250,000 [(1/2)($500,000)] and no CNIL.

Martha's will specifies that 70 percent of any income that accrues in her estate prior to the estate assets being transferred to the testamentary trust be distributed on the basis of 40 percent to Sharon and 30 percent to Morris. The remaining 30 percent will be allowed to accumulate in the GRE.

Between March 15, 2018 and December 31, 2018, the following income and expense amounts were recorded by the GRE:

Non-Eligible Dividends Received		$124,000
Interest On Corporate Debt Securities		31,650
Net Rental Income:		
Rental Revenues	$251,600	
Rental Expenses Other Than CCA	(172,940)	
CCA Claimed	(55,615)	23,045
Total Income		**$178,695**

Required:

A. Determine the increase in Martha's 2018 Taxable Income that will result from her death.

B. For the fiscal period ending on December 31, 2018, determine the Taxable Income for the GRE and the total Taxable Income allocated to each beneficiary.

C. Calculate the federal Tax Payable for the GRE for the fiscal period ending on December 31, 2018.

Assignment Problem Nineteen - 8
(Estate Freeze)

Mr. and Mrs. Zahar own a very lucrative company, Zeus Goose Ltd. The fair market value of the common shares is $5,000,000 and they have a nominal cost base and paid up capital.

The Zahar's want to set up an estate freeze to pass on future growth of the Company to their three children, all of whom are in their twenties. Mr. and Mrs. Zahar are in their early fifties and want to continue to control the Company for many years. While they have obtained information on how a corporate reorganization can be used to effect an estate freeze, they would also like to investigate the use of trusts in their estate planning.

Required: Outline important issues that should be considered by Mr. and Mrs. Zahar if they are to use trusts in an estate freeze.

Ignore the possibility that some of the trust's distributions might be subject to the TOSI.

Assignment Problem Nineteen - 9
(Estate Planning)

One of your clients, Daniel Loh has read several articles describing the tax advantages of charitable donations. Mr. Loh is 73 years old and has had a very successful career in business in Canada. As a consequence, he owns a wide variety of investments in publicly traded securities and private company shares, as well as real estate in Canada and Singapore. You estimate that his assets have a current value in excess of $15 million.

Due to a car accident in Singapore that disfigured him horribly and made him a recluse, he has never married and has no friends or living relatives. When he dies, he intends to leave all of his assets to a group of his favourite charities.

As he has never spent any time on estate planning, he has asked you to help him understand the issues and give him suggestions of what he should consider.

Required: Write a brief report providing the advice requested by your client.

CHAPTER 20

International Issues In Taxation

Introduction

Subjects Covered

20-1.   This Chapter 20 is something of a potpourri of issues that are loosely related by their association with transactions and events that extend beyond Canada's borders. In some cases, we are dealing with the application of Canadian tax law to transactions and events that occur outside of Canada. In other cases, we are concerned only with the fact that individual taxable entities are moving between Canada and other jurisdictions. Some of these transactions and events relate to taxation that is associated with the laws that exist in jurisdictions outside of Canada.

20-2.   In dealing with the diverse nature of the material covered, we have organized this Chapter as follows:

Residence   While some of the material related to residence involve international issues, these issues were covered in our comprehensive coverage of residence in Chapter 1.

Taxation Of Canadian Source Income Earned By Non-Residents   While the basic approach to the assessment of income tax in Canada is to assess tax on Canadian residents, under certain circumstances, non-residents can be required to pay Canadian income taxes. Depending on the type of income, the tax may be assessed under Part I, Part XIII, or other Parts of the *Income Tax Act*. Detailed consideration will be given to Part I and Part XIII tax as they are the most commonly applied provisions.

Immigration And Emigration   We touched on this subject in Chapter 8 when we covered the deemed disposition of most capital assets when an individual emigrates from Canada. In this Chapter, we will consider some of the other complications associated with leaving Canada, as well as tax considerations related to immigration.

Taxation Of Foreign Source Income Earned By Residents   This material begins by discussing the reporting requirements applicable to Canadian residents who have foreign investments. This is followed by material dealing with resident taxpayers who have the following types of income:

- foreign source employment income;
- foreign source income from unincorporated businesses;
- foreign source interest income; and
- capital gains resulting from the disposition of foreign assets.

The remainder of the chapter provides limited coverage of dividend income received by Canadian residents from non-resident entities. This would include material on foreign affiliates, controlled foreign affiliates, and foreign accrual property income (FAPI). Some of this material is extremely difficult to understand and because of this, some instructors may choose not to include it in their courses.

The Role of International Tax Treaties

20-3.   Tax treaties are entered into between countries for the purpose of facilitating cross-border trade and investment by removing income tax obstacles. For example, a Canadian resident employed in the U.S. is potentially subject to Canadian tax under the residence approach. In the absence of a treaty, he could also be subject to U.S. tax on the same income under the source approach. This would, of course, create a significant impediment to cross-border employment.

20-4.   In addition to dealing with double taxation problems such as this, treaties also provide income tax certainty, prevent discrimination, ensure a proper division of cross-border revenues, and provide an information-sharing mechanism for the purposes of administration and enforcement of each country's tax laws.

20-5.   In cases where there are conflicts, Canada's tax treaties generally override the *Income Tax Act*. This override occurs through legislation that implements the tax treaty, as well as specific provisions of the *Income Tax Act* that recognize the priority given to the tax treaty. For example, ITA 2(3) requires a U.S. resident to pay Canadian tax on employment income earned in Canada. The tax treaty, on the other hand, may, in specific circumstances, state that such income is only taxable in the U.S. In such cases, the inconsistency is resolved through the application of the tax treaty with the result that no Canadian tax is payable by the U.S. resident.

Part I Tax On Non-Residents

Introduction

Applicability

20-6.   As covered in Chapter 1 in our material on residence, ITA 2(1) states that Canadian taxes are payable by residents of Canada on their world wide taxable income for a taxation year. While this statement makes it clear that Canadian residents are responsible for paying Canadian income taxes, it does not address the question of whether non-residents are responsible for such taxes.

20-7.   Also as mentioned in Chapter 1, ITA 2(3) specifies that non-residents are responsible for Canadian Part I tax (tax assessed on Taxable Income) on certain types of income. As listed in that subsection, non-residents are responsible for:

- income earned while carrying on a business in Canada;
- employment income earned in Canada; and
- gains and losses resulting from dispositions of Taxable Canadian Property.

20-8.   In this Chapter we will give attention to the assessment of Canadian Part I tax on non-residents in situations where they have any of these three types of income. As part of this discussion, we will provide coverage of the provisions of the U.S./Canada tax treaty that relate to such situations. Coverage of other international tax treaties goes beyond the scope of this text.

20-9.   You will note that ITA 2(3) covers business income, employment income, and capital gains on Taxable Canadian Property, but this subsection does not refer to property income.

Further there is no reference to pension income, management fees, or capital gains on Canadian property other than those items that are classified as Taxable Canadian Property. This means that, in general, non-residents are not responsible for paying Part I tax on these types of Canadian source income.

20-10. However, this is not the end of the story. When these other types of income are from a Canadian source and are earned by non-residents, a separate Part XIII tax is applicable. The application of this tax will be covered beginning in Paragraph 20-31.

Filing Requirements

20-11. In those situations where a non-resident has Tax Payable under Part I, a Canadian income tax return is required (see T4058, *Non-Residents And Income Tax*). The normal filing dates for individuals and corporations are applicable in such situations. No Canadian income tax return is required if there is no Part I Tax Payable.

Taxable Income

20-12. As some of the items that must be included in a Canadian income tax return by non-residents are exempted by various international tax treaties, such amounts can be deducted in determining Taxable Income. In addition, under ITA 115(1), non-residents will also be able to deduct Canadian employment losses, Canadian business losses, various types of loss carry overs, Canadian stock option benefits, Canadian dividends received (corporations only), and charitable donations (corporations only).

20-13. If 90 percent or more (substantially all) of the taxpayer's worldwide income is included in their Part I tax return, the other Taxable Income deductions that are available to residents, such as the lifetime capital gains deduction, become available to non-residents.

Tax Payable

20-14. Unless the non-resident's Part I return includes 90 percent or more of their worldwide income, ITA 118.94 prohibits the use of the majority of non-refundable tax credits. However, the following credits will be available to non-resident filers who are individuals if they have any amount of Canadian source income included in their Part I return.

- EI and CPP tax credits
- charitable donations tax credit
- disability tax credit (for taxpayer only)
- tuition tax credit
- interest on Canadian student loans tax credit

Carrying on Business in Canada

General Rules

20-15. As we have noted, non-residents are subject to Part I tax in Canada on income from businesses carried on in Canada. The rules for calculating business income discussed in Chapter 6 are generally applicable to non-residents. However, for non-residents, ITA 253 expands the concept of a business by deeming non-residents to be carrying on a business with respect to certain activities such as:

- Producing, growing, mining, creating, manufacturing, fabricating, improving, packing, preserving, or constructing, in whole or in part, anything in Canada.

- Soliciting orders or offering anything for sale in Canada through an agent or servant, whether the contract or transaction is to be completed inside or outside Canada.

- Disposing of certain property, such as real property inventory situated in Canada, including an interest in, or option on, such real property.

20-16. These rules are intended to ensure that certain Canadian activities that are connected to the non-resident's foreign business, are potentially taxable in Canada as business income. Without these rules, it could be questionable whether the non-resident person would be considered to be carrying on a business in Canada.

EXAMPLE   A U.S. business sends sales representatives to Canada to solicit orders. If the sales contracts can only be finalized in the U.S., under the general rules applicable to business income, it could be argued that no business was carried on in Canada. However, ITA 253 makes it clear that the soliciting of orders in Canada is carrying on business in Canada, without regard to where the contracts are finalized.

Canada/U.S. Tax Treaty On Business Income

20-17.   The treaty allows Canada to tax the business income of U.S. residents, provided that business is operated in Canada through what is referred to as a permanent establishment.

20-18.   Article V of the Canada/U.S. tax treaty defines a "permanent establishment" as a fixed place of business through which the business of a non-resident is wholly or partly carried on. The treaty provides additional clarification by adding that fixed places of business include a place of management, a branch, an office, a factory, a workshop, a mine, an oil or gas well, a quarry or other place of extraction of natural resources. Additional rules provide permanent establishment status only if certain conditions are met (e.g., most construction projects are only considered permanent establishments if they last for more than twelve months).

20-19.   The treaty specifically excludes facilities from being considered a fixed place of business if they are used exclusively for certain activities. These activities include:

• use of facilities solely for storage, display, or delivery of goods;
• maintenance of a stock of goods or merchandise for storage, display, or delivery;
• maintenance of a fixed place of business solely for purchasing goods or merchandise, or for collecting information; or
• maintenance of a fixed place of business solely for the purpose of carrying on any other activity of a preparatory or auxiliary character.

20-20.   The tax treaty also deems certain persons to be permanent establishments of a non-resident. Two examples of this are as follows:

• An agent who acts on behalf of a non-resident enterprise and who is authorized to conclude contracts in the name of that enterprise, is considered a permanent establishment.

• An individual who acts on behalf of a business and meets both a physical presence test (183 days or more in any 12 month period beginning or ending in the year) and a gross revenue test (that more than 50% of the gross active business revenues of the U.S. business are from services performed by that individual during the period the individual is in Canada), is considered a permanent establishment.

Exercise Twenty - 1

Subject: Carrying On Business In Canada

In each of the following Cases, determine whether Jazzco, a U.S. corporation, is taxable in Canada:

Case 1   Jazzco, a U.S. corporation, is the parent company of Bluesco, a company incorporated in Ontario. Jazzco produces and sells Jazz CDs, while Bluesco produces and sells Blues CDs. Jazzco sells CDs to Bluesco, who in turn sells them in Canada.

Case 2   Jazzco sets up a factory in Toronto where they produce CDs for the Canadian market. The CDs are sold exclusively to an independent Canadian franchise retail outlet at a 50 percent mark-up.

Case 3   Jazzco manufactures Jazz CDs in the U.S. Jazzco ships CDs to a warehouse located in Calgary that they have rented on a five year lease. Jazzco has employed an individual in Calgary to sell the CDs throughout western Canada. The employee, however, is not allowed to conclude contracts without approval by the U.S. office.

Case 4   Assume the same facts as in Case 3, except that the employee has the authority to conclude contracts on behalf of the employer.

Case 5   Assume the same facts as in Case 3, except that the employee has an office in the warehouse premises where he solicits orders.

SOLUTION available in print and online Study Guide.

Canadian Source Employment Income
General Rules
20-21.   As noted, under ITA 2(3), non-resident individuals are subject to Part I tax on Canadian source employment income. For this purpose, net employment is calculated using the same rules that are applicable to residents earning Canadian source employment income. These rules were covered in Chapter 3.

20-22.   In addition to this provision, ITA 115(2) deems certain non-resident individuals to be employed in Canada, even when the work is not carried on in this country. Such individuals include:

- Individuals who have become residents of another country and continue to receive employment remuneration from a resident Canadian source, provided a tax treaty exempts that remuneration from taxation in the foreign country.

- Non-resident individuals who have received signing bonuses and other similar amounts that relate to services to be performed in Canada, in situations where the resident Canadian employer is entitled to deduct the amounts in computing Canadian Income.

20-23.   The basic idea behind these provisions is that, if payments are made to a non-resident that are deductible to a Canadian resident, the payments will be taxed in Canada if they are not taxed in the other country. Note, however, that employee remuneration is generally exempted from Canadian taxation if it is subject to tax by the foreign country.

Canada/U.S. Tax Treaty On Employment Income
20-24.   In general, a source country has the right to tax the employment income of non-residents when it is earned within its borders. This view is reflected in ITA 2(3) which assesses Part I tax on Canadian source employment income earned by non-residents. However, the Canada/U.S. tax treaty contains two special rules which create exceptions to this general approach.

$10,000 Rule   Under this rule if, during a calendar year, a U.S. resident earns employment income in Canada that is $10,000 or less in Canadian dollars, then the income is taxable only in the U.S.

183 Day Rule   This rule exempts Canadian source employment income from Canadian taxation, provided it is earned by a U.S. resident who was physically present in Canada for no more than 183 days during any twelve month period commencing or ending in the calendar year. This exemption is conditional on employment income not being paid by an employer with a permanent establishment in Canada who would be able to deduct the amount paid from their Canadian Income. Stated alternatively, if the employment income exceeds $10,000 and is deductible in Canada, it will be taxed in Canada, even if the employee is present in Canada for less than 183 days during the year.

20-25.   It is important not to confuse the 183 day period in the treaty with the 183 day sojourner rule for determining residence. (See Chapter 1.) While the treaty rule applies to any physical presence in Canada, the sojourner rule applies to temporary visits or stays. Daily commutes to Canada from the U.S. for employment purposes would count towards the 183 days in the treaty rule, but not towards the 183 days in the sojourner rule.

Exercise Twenty - 2

Subject: Non-Resident Employment In Canada

Dawn Johnson is employed by Alberta Oil Ltd. as an oil well technician in Edmonton. She has accepted a transfer to the Egyptian offices of the Company for three years beginning January 1, 2018. Dawn severs her residential ties to Canada on December 31, 2017 and takes up residence in Egypt. Alberta Oil continues to pay her salary. Although the government of Egypt would normally tax such salary, the tax treaty between Canada and Egypt exempts the salary from tax in Egypt. Is Dawn required to pay Canadian tax on the salary paid to her by Alberta Oil? Justify your conclusion.

Exercise Twenty - 3

Subject: Non-Resident Employment In Canada - Canada/U.S. Tax Treaty

In each of the following Cases, determine whether the employment income is taxable in Canada:

Case 1   David resides in the state of Washington. He accepted temporary employment as a technician with a Canadian company to do service calls in the Vancouver area for four months beginning September 1, 2018. The Canadian employer agreed to pay him $2,800 Canadian per month. David remained a non-resident of Canada throughout his Canadian employment.

Case 2   Assume the same facts as in Case 1, except the employer was resident in Washington and did not have a permanent establishment in Canada.

Case 3   Sandra resides in Detroit, Michigan and has commuted daily to a full-time job in Windsor, Ontario for the last three years. In 2018, she spent 238 days at her job in Canada. She works for the municipality of Windsor and earned $50,000 Canadian in employment income. Sandra is a U.S. resident throughout the year.

SOLUTIONS available in print and online Study Guide.

Dispositions of Taxable Canadian Property

General Rules

20-26.   As we have previously noted, under ITA 2(3), non-residents are taxable on gains resulting from dispositions of Taxable Canadian Property. The general rules for dealing with capital gains and losses were covered in detail in Chapter 8. While we only considered their application to Canadian residents in that Chapter, these rules are equally applicable to non-residents.

20-27.   As defined in ITA 248(1), the main categories of Taxable Canadian Property are as follows:

- Real property situated in Canada.
- Certain capital property or inventories of a business carried on in Canada.
- A share of an unlisted corporation, an interest in a partnership, or an interest in a trust if, at any time within the preceding 60 months, more than 50 percent of the fair market value of the share or interest was derived from certain properties including Canadian real property, Canadian resource properties and timber resource properties.
- A share of a listed corporation only if, at any time within the preceding 60 months, at least 25 percent of the issued shares of any class were owned by the non-resident taxpayer and/or non-arm's length persons, and more than 50 percent of the shares' fair market value was derived from certain properties including Canadian real property, Canadian resource properties and timber resource properties.

Compliance Certificates

20-28.   There are, of course, problems related to having a non-resident comply with Canadian tax rules related to dispositions of Taxable Canadian Property. To deal with this, ITA 116 requires a non-resident, who anticipates a disposal of Taxable Canadian Property, to file Form T2062, "Request by a Non-Resident of Canada for a Certificate of Compliance Related to the Disposition of Taxable Canadian Property". This form, which must be filed within 10 days of the planned disposition, must be accompanied by a payment of 25 percent of the anticipated capital gain on the disposition (some types of security are acceptable). When these conditions are met, a certificate of compliance will be issued. There is a penalty for disposing of a Taxable Canadian Property without obtaining a compliance certificate.

20-29.   As Canadian tax authorities are still dealing with a non-resident, this procedure does not ensure compliance. What serves to ensure that Canadian taxes will be paid is a requirement that, if the non-resident seller does not acquire a compliance certificate, the purchaser (usually a Canadian resident) is responsible for the 25 percent payment on behalf of the non-resident. Note, however, that ITA 116(5) provides an exception to this if, after reasonable enquiry the purchaser had no reason to believe that the seller was not resident in Canada.

Canada/U.S. Tax Treaty On Taxable Canadian Property Dispositions

20-30.   While the general rule in ITA 2(3) indicates that non-residents are taxable on gains resulting from dispositions of Taxable Canadian Property, it is necessary to examine the Canada/U.S. tax treaty to see if any of its provisions override this general rule. The treaty acts to limit Canadian taxation on U.S. residents to gains arising from only the following specific types of Taxable Canadian Property:

- real property situated in Canada;
- property forming part of a permanent establishment of the non-resident in Canada; and
- investments such as shares of corporations resident in Canada and interests in partnerships and trusts where the value of those investments is primarily attributable to real property situated in Canada.

Exercise Twenty - 4

Subject: Dispositions Of Taxable Canadian Property
In each of the following Cases the individual is a U.S. resident who is disposing of a property. Determine whether any gain on the disposition is taxable under Part I in Canada.

Case 1   In 2018, Nancy Gordon disposed of shares of a widely held Canadian public company that she acquired in 2015. Nancy never owned more than one-quarter of one percent of the outstanding shares of this company. The company's assets consist entirely of real estate situated in Canada.

Case 2   In 2013, Joe Nesbitt acquired a condo in Whistler that he rented to Canadian residents. He sold the condo in 2018 at a considerable gain. Joe never occupied the condo.

Case 3   Assume the same facts as in Case 2, except that Joe incorporates a private corporation under British Columbia legislation solely to acquire the condo. At a later point in time, Joe sells the shares at a considerable gain.

Case 4   Assume the same facts as in Case 3, except the corporation is created under Washington state legislation.

SOLUTION available in print and online Study Guide.

We suggest you work Self Study Problem Twenty-1 at this point.

Part XIII Tax On Non-Residents

Introduction

Applicability

20-31.   In the preceding section of this Chapter, we dealt with the application of Part I tax to certain specific types of income earned by non-residents. As noted in Paragraph 20-10, this leaves many other types of Canadian source income that are not subject to Part I tax in the hands of non-residents.

20-32.   The Part XIII tax is designed to correct this situation. ITA 212 provides a long list of income types to which this tax is applicable. While most of the items on the list fall into the property income category, there are other items such as pension benefits. Notably absent, however, are taxable capital gains on assets other than Taxable Canadian Property. Capital gains on dispositions of other Canadian assets are not taxed in the hands of non-residents, either under Part I or Part XIII.

20-33.   Three other points are relevant here:

• Part XIII tax is an alternative to Part I tax. There are no situations in which both taxes would be applied to a single income source.

• Non-residents are not required to file a Canadian tax return for income that is subject to Part XIII tax.

• In general, it is the resident payer who is responsible for withholding the Part XIII tax from payment(s) being made to the non-resident, as well as remitting the withheld amounts to the CRA. The payer is also responsible for filing an information return (NR4) indicating the amounts withheld.

20-34.   As indicated, Part XIII tax applies to a long list of income types. However, in the following material, we will limit our coverage to interest, royalties, rents, dividends, and pension benefits earned or accruing to non-residents.

The Nature Of Part XIII Tax

20-35.   This is a very different type of tax than that which is assessed under Part I. Under Part I, the relevant tax rate is applied to Taxable Income, a figure that is made up of components which are calculated on a net basis. For example, interest revenues are only included after any related expenses are deducted. In contrast, the Part XIII tax is assessed on the gross amount of income received.

> **EXAMPLE**   Ms. Johnson borrows $100,000 to invest in high yield bonds. During the current year, they produce interest income of $9,000, while the interest costs for the borrowing amount to $4,000.

> **ANALYSIS**   If Ms. Johnson was a Canadian resident being taxed under Part I of the *Income Tax Act*, the applicable tax rate would be applied to $5,000 ($9,000 - $4,000). In contrast, if Ms. Johnson was a non-resident being taxed under Part XIII, the Part XIII withholding rate would be applied to the $9,000 in interest received.

Rates

20-36.   The Part XIII rate that is specified in ITA 212(1) is 25 percent for all types of income listed in ITA 212. However, this rate is rarely applied when the recipient of the income is resident in a country with which Canada has a tax treaty. All of these treaties have provisions which, while allowing the applicability of the Part XIII tax, modify the rate. This is further complicated by the fact that the rate modifications vary between the various types of income subject to the Part XIII tax.

20-37.   Comprehensive treatment of the various rates that are applicable under Canada's many international tax treaties would not be appropriate in a general text such as this. However, because it would appear to be the most important of these treaties, attention will be given to the rates that are applicable under the Canada/U.S. tax treaty.

Interest Payments
Part XIII Rules
20-38.   ITA 212(1)(b) assesses Part XIII tax on only two types of interest. These are as follows:

Participating Debt Interest   Participating debt interest is defined in ITA 212(3) as interest that is dependent on the use of property (e.g., royalties), or that is calculated by reference to revenue, cash flow, or profit. What is being described here is amounts that, while they may be called interest, are more like business income. They are not based on a principal sum and the passage of time.

Interest Paid To Non-Arm's Length Non-Residents, unless the interest is **Fully Exempt Interest**. Fully exempt interest is defined in ITA 212(3) as interest paid or payable on certain types of government issued or guaranteed debt (e.g., debt issued by the government of Canada or a province).

20-39.   Another way of stating this would be to note that Part XIII tax only applies to:

- arm's length arrangements when the interest payments are related to "participating debt", and
- non-arm's length arrangements if the interest is not fully exempt.

Canada/U.S. Tax Treaty On Interest Payments
20-40.   When it is established that Part XIII tax is applicable, it is then necessary to consult the relevant international tax treaty to determine whether Canada has the right to tax such amounts. For U.S. residents, the Canada/U.S. tax treaty states the following:

Article XI   Interest arising in a Contracting State and beneficially owned by a resident of the other Contracting State may be taxed only in that other State.

20-41.   This means that, with respect to interest paid to U.S. residents, Canada does not have the right to withhold taxes under Part XIII. Residents of the U.S. are exempt from the Part XIII tax, even in the situations described in Paragraph 20-38.

Exercise Twenty - 5

Subject: Interest Payments To Non-Residents

In each of the following Cases, determine whether the interest payments made to non-residents are subject to Part XIII withholding tax, and if so, at what rate.

Case 1   Jason, a resident of a country that does not have a tax treaty with Canada, earned $3,000 in interest from a term deposit in a Canadian bank during 2018.

Case 2   Janice, a resident of a country that does not have a tax treaty with Canada, earned interest of $1,800 on Government Of Canada bonds during 2018.

Case 3   Julian, a resident of Ottawa, acquired a vacation property in a country that does not have a tax treaty with Canada. The property is mortgaged with a bank in the foreign country. Julian paid $12,000 in interest to the foreign bank in 2018.

Case 4   Jasmine, a resident of Manitoba, paid $5,000 in interest on a loan from her brother, a resident of Ohio during 2018.

SOLUTION available in print and online Study Guide.

Dividend Payments

Part XIII Rules

20-42.   Most types of dividends are subject to the 25 percent Part XIII tax. This includes capital dividends, despite the fact that they are not subject to tax when received by Canadian residents.

Canada/U.S. Tax Treaty On Dividend Payments

20-43.   While there is nothing in the Canada/U.S. tax treaty to prevent the application of this tax to U.S. residents, the treaty serves to reduce the applicable rate. In this case, there are two different reduced rates, depending on the percentage of the dividend paying corporation that is owned by the non-resident recipient.

> **5 Percent Rate**   If the U.S. resident recipient is a corporation and owns 10 percent or more of the voting shares of the resident Canadian company that is paying the dividend, the applicable rate is only 5 percent. This 5 percent rate for inter-corporate dividends reflects a view that dividend payments between parent companies and their subsidiaries should be less heavily taxed to encourage international trade and investment.

> **15 Percent Rate**   Other dividends paid by resident Canadian companies to shareholders who are U.S. residents are subject to the Part XIII withholding tax at a reduced rate of 15 percent.

Royalty Payments

Part XIII Rules

20-44.   Royalties paid or credited to non-residents by a person resident in Canada are generally subject to a 25 percent Part XIII withholding tax under ITA 212(1)(d). Specifically excluded under Canadian legislation are payments for copyright use, payments made under cost-sharing arrangements where the costs are shared with non-residents, and arm's length payments made that are deductible under Part I against business income earned outside Canada.

Canada/U.S. Tax Treaty On Royalty Payments

20-45.   The Canada/U.S. tax treaty, in general, allows the imposition of Part XIII tax on royalties. However, it is at a reduced rate of 10 percent.   The treaty further provides that copyright and computer software royalties are not taxable by the source country.

Rental Income

Part XIII Rules

20-46.   The situation with rent payments is more complex. While ITA 212(1)(d) lists rents as one of the items subject to Part XIII tax, the *Income Tax Act* is designed to give priority to Part I tax over Part XIII tax. However, as we have noted in our discussion of the small business deduction, a taxpayer's rental activities may be so extensive that they can be considered a business. If this is the case, the non-resident taxpayer will be earning business income which will be subject to Part I tax in Canada. If this is the case, the taxpayer will have to file an income tax return including these amounts. However, there will then be no requirement to pay Part XIII tax on the rental revenues.

An Important Election For Rental Income Of Non-Residents

20-47.   If the non-resident is not carrying on a rental business in Canada, Part XIII tax is applicable. This creates a significant problem in that the Part XIII tax is applied to gross rental revenues, a figure that will usually be much larger than net rental income.

EXAMPLE   Marcia Dorne, a resident of a non-treaty country, owns a rental property in Canada. The gross rent on this property is $120,000 for the year and is paid monthly at a rate of $10,000. The property is so heavily financed that net rental income, as determined by the Part I rules, is $12,000 for the year before CCA of $11,000.

ANALYSIS   In the absence of an alternative approach, Marcia would be subject to Part XIII tax of $30,000 [(25%)($120,000)].

20-48.   Fortunately, there is an alternative approach. Under ITA 216, Marcia can elect to pay taxes under Part I, rather than under Part XIII. In the preceding example, this election would result in Part I taxes being paid on the net rental income of $1,000 ($12,000 - $11,000 CCA). If Marcia had no other source of Canadian income, this $1,000 would be taxed at the lowest federal rate of 15 percent and, when combined with the 48 percent federal surtax on income not earned in a province, the total Part I tax would be $222 [(15%)($1,000)(148%)]. This is well below the $30,000 that would be assessed under Part XIII.

20-49.   With respect to this election, two other points are worth noting:

- In general, this election can only be made in situations where the rental property is real property located in Canada.

- If a non-resident taxpayer makes this election, they will file a separate return including only the revenues and expenses related to their rental property. They cannot make any deductions from Net Income in the determination of Taxable Income and they cannot deduct any of the ITA 118 personal tax credits.

Solution To The Cash Flow Problem

20-50.   Unfortunately, use of the ITA 216 election to pay under Part I tax does not relieve the payer from the requirement to withhold Part XIII tax. This will, in many cases, create a significant tax flow problem for the non-resident landlord. Consider the example from Paragraph 20-47. The person paying the rent would have to withhold a total of $30,000 from the payments made to Marcia Dorne. As a result, she would have a negative cash flow of $18,000 [($120,000 - $30,000) - ($120,000 - $12,000)]. While the withheld Part XIII tax would eventually be refunded, there is a significant outflow of cash during the rental period.

20-51.   Fortunately, there is a solution to this problem. A non-resident taxpayer can file Form NR6, "Undertaking to File an Income Tax Return by a Non-Resident Receiving Rent from Real Property or Receiving a Timber Royalty". If this undertaking is filed, the payer can base the required withholding on 25 percent of the estimated net rental income before the deduction of CCA. In our Paragraph 20-47 example, the Part XIII withholding would be reduced from $2,500 per month [(25%)($10,000)] to $250 per month [(25%)(1/12)($12,000)]. Any difference between this amount and the actual net rental income, including any available deduction for CCA, would be claimed when Marcia Dorne's Part I tax return is filed.

Canada/U.S. Tax Treaty On Rental Income

20-52.   The Canada/U.S. tax treaty allows the imposition of Part XIII tax to rental income. When the rental property is real property, the statutory Part XIII rate of 25 percent is applicable. However, where the rental property is something other than real property in Canada (e.g. equipment or machinery), the Canada/U.S. tax treaty reduces the Part XIII withholding rate from 25 to 10 percent.

Exercise Twenty - 6

Subject: Rental Payments To Non-Residents

In each of the following Cases, determine how the rental payments made to non-residents will be taxed by Canada. In addition, indicate whether an election to pay Part I tax is available and whether the election would be desirable.

Case 1   Rentco is a U.S. corporation with worldwide rental facilities dedicated to various equipment rentals. Rentco has offices in Saskatchewan, where it rents out farming equipment.

Case 2   In 2015, Jack Foster, a U.S. resident, acquired a hunting and fishing lodge in northern Ontario that he rents out. In 2018, he rented the lodge to Canadian residents exclusively. Jack received $42,000 in gross rents and estimates that expenses, including CCA, totaled $14,000.

Case 3   Assume the same facts as in Case 2, with one additional consideration. Jack acquired three motor boats in 2016, which he rented to guests of the lodge. In 2018, he received $8,000 in gross boat rents and estimates boat related expenses of $7,000.

SOLUTION available in print and online Study Guide.

Pension Payments And Other Retirement Related Benefits
Part XIII Rules
20-53.   Amounts received by non-residents as pension or other retirement related benefits are generally subject to tax under Part XIII. This would include OAS payments, CPP payments, death benefits, certain retiring allowances, as well as payments from RRSPs, RRIFs, and DPSPs. Payments from TFSAs are not considered pension payments, but there are special rules for individuals who own TFSAs and become non-resident.

20-54.   There are some exceptions under Canadian legislation that are designed to ensure that a non-resident will only be taxed on amounts that would have been taxable had the non-resident been resident in Canada at the time the benefits were earned. For example, a non-resident may receive a pension from a former Canadian employer, most of which relates to years in which the person was non-resident and worked outside Canada. Part XIII may exempt the part of the pension that relates to employment outside Canada.

An Important Election For Pension Income Of Non-Residents
20-55.   The non-resident recipient of Canadian pension income can elect under ITA 217 to be taxed under Part I of the *Income Tax Act*, rather than under Part XIII. Unlike the ITA 216 election for rental income, this alternative requires the reporting of all Canadian sourced income, not just Canadian pension income, but it allows non-residents to claim deductions and credits normally given to Canadian residents. More detailed information is available on the CRA website in T4145, "Electing Under Section 217 of the *Income Tax Act*".

20-56.   For a low income individual, choosing to use the ITA 217 election can provide a significant advantage in that it will allow the individual to make use of some of the tax credits that are available under Part I. However, for high income individuals, the Part XIII rate is likely to be lower than the rate that would be applicable under Part I of the *Act*. In most cases, this will more than offset the loss of tax credits.

Canada/U.S. Tax Treaty On Pension Payments And Benefits
20-57.   The Canada/U.S. tax treaty permits the application of Part XIII tax to pension or other retirement related benefits paid to U.S. residents. As usual, the treaty acts to reduce the applicable Part XIII rate, in this case to 15 percent. However, this rate is only available on benefits that are periodic payments. If the benefit is a lump-sum payment (e.g., a retiring

allowance), the statutory Part XIII rate of 25 percent must be used.

20-58.   Payments from OAS, CPP and QPP are generally subject to Part XIII tax and eligible for the optional Part I treatment discussed in Paragraph 20-55. However, with respect to OAS and CPP payments made to a resident of the U.S., the treaty specifies that these will only be taxed in the U.S. There will be no withholding or filing requirements on these amounts.

20-59.   Two other important provisions under the U.S./Canada treaty can be described as follows:

Contributions To Local Plans By Non-Residents   The treaty allows deductions for contributions by non-residents to "qualifying retirement plans" that are located in the other country. This means that U.S. residents who contribute to a qualifying Canadian plan can deduct their contributions from Canadian income and, alternatively, Canadian residents who contribute to a U.S. plan can deduct their contributions from U.S. income. Two points are relevant here:

- For U.S. residents working in Canada, qualifying retirement plans include RPPs, DPSPs, and group RRSPs. Individual RRSPs do not qualify.

- Deductions for contributions to Canadian plans are limited by the available RRSP contribution room.

Contributions and Accruing Benefits By Residents   The second provision relates to ongoing contributions and benefits accruing under a pension plan in the country in which the individual is resident. Contributions to such plans are deductible in the other country, but benefits accruing would not be taxable. For example, if a U.S. resident employed in Canada continued to make contributions to a U.S. plan, the U.S. contributions would be deductible against Canadian employment income. However, any pension benefits that accrued would not be taxable in Canada.

Shareholder Loans To Non-Residents

20-60.   In Chapter 15, we gave attention to the rules associated with shareholder loans. It was noted that, in general, the principal of such loans had to be included in a taxpayer's Net Income For Tax Purposes. There are a number of exceptions to this rule. However, in situations where the principal is not included, there is still a taxable benefit to the shareholder if the interest rate on the loan was less than the prescribed rate.

20-61.   As non-residents are generally not required to file a Part I tax return, corporate loans to non-resident shareholders would be exempt from these rules in terms of the application of Part I tax. However, ITA 214(3)(a) indicates that if ITA 15 of the *Income Tax Act* (Benefit Conferred On Shareholder) would require an amount to be included in income, that amount will be viewed as a dividend paid to the non-resident shareholder, resulting in the application of Part XIII tax. A refund of the Part XIII tax will become available when the loan is repaid.

20-62.   Such loans to non-resident shareholders escape this treatment if they are repaid within one year of the end of the taxation year in which the loan is provided. If the principal is not included in income and the interest rate on the loan is less than the prescribed rate, a benefit will be calculated in the same manner as the interest benefit on such loans when they are made to a resident shareholder. However, when a non-resident is involved, this benefit will be treated as a dividend subject to Part XIII tax.

We suggest you work Self Study Problem Twenty-2 at this point.

Immigration And Emigration

Entering Canada - Immigration

Deemed Disposition/Reacquisition

20-63.   The rules related to entering Canada are found in ITA 128.1(1). Paragraph (b) of this subsection indicates that, with certain exceptions, a taxpayer is deemed to have disposed of all of their property immediately before entering Canada for proceeds equal to fair market value. Paragraph (c) calls for a deemed reacquisition of the property at the same fair market value figure.

20-64.   This process establishes a new cost basis for the taxpayer's property, as at the time of entering Canada. The goal here is to avoid having Canadian taxation apply to gains that accrued prior to the individual's immigration.

> **EXAMPLE** An individual enters Canada with securities that cost $100,000 and have a current fair market value of $150,000.

> **ANALYSIS** In the absence of the ITA 128.1(1)(b) and (c) deeming provisions, a subsequent sale of these securities for $150,000 would result in the $50,000 accrued gain being taxed in Canada, despite the fact that it accrued prior to the individual becoming a Canadian resident.

20-65.   The properties that are excluded from the deemed disposition/reacquisition are listed in ITA 128.1(1)(b). In general, these are items that would already have been subject to tax in Canada if the taxpayer was a non-resident. They include:

- Taxable Canadian Property.
- Inventories and certain other capital assets of a business carried on in Canada.
- **"Excluded Right or Interest"**   This concept is defined in ITA 128.1(10). The definition includes RPP balances, RRSP balances, DPSP balances, stock options, death benefits, retiring allowances, as well as other rights of individuals in trusts or other similar arrangements.

Departures From Canada - Emigration

Deemed Disposition On Leaving Canada

20-66.   As was noted in Chapter 8, when a taxpayer leaves Canada, ITA 128.1(4)(b) calls for a deemed disposition of all property owned at the time of departure. The disposition is deemed to occur at fair market value (see Paragraph 20-69 for treatment under the Canada/U.S. tax treaty). If the taxpayer is an individual, certain types of property are exempted from this deemed disposition rule. The major categories of exempted property are:

- Real property situated in Canada, Canadian resource properties, and timber resource properties.
- Property of a business carried on in Canada through a permanent establishment. This would include capital property and inventories.
- Excluded rights or interests of the taxpayer as described in Paragraph 20-65.

Exercise Twenty - 7

Subject: Emigration

Ms. Gloria Martell owns publicly traded securities with an adjusted cost base of $28,000 and a fair market value of $49,000.   During the current year, she permanently departs from Canada still owning the shares.   What would be the tax consequences of her departure, if any, with respect to these securities?

SOLUTION available in print and online Study Guide.

Exercise Twenty - 8

Subject: Emigration

Mr. Harrison Chrysler owns a rental property in Nanaimo, B.C. with a capital cost of $190,000 and a fair market value of $295,000. The land values included in these figures are $45,000 and $62,000, respectively. The UCC of the building is $82,600. During the current year, Mr. Chrysler permanently departs from Canada. What are the current and possible future tax consequences of his departure with respect to this rental property?

SOLUTION available in print and online Study Guide.

Problems With The Current System

20-67.   Taxpayer emigration is a problem area for those in charge of Canadian tax policy. To begin, Canada is significantly out of line with all of its trading partners in the manner in which it deals with the accrued capital gains of emigrants.

20-68.   As an illustration of this problem, consider Mr. Poutine, who departs from Canada at a time when he owns capital assets with an adjusted cost base of $80,000 and a fair market value of $120,000. On his departure from Canada, Mr. Poutine will be deemed to have disposed of these assets at their fair market value of $120,000, resulting in an assessment for a capital gain of $40,000. In many other countries, this would not occur. Mr. Poutine would be able to remove his assets without taxation and retain an unchanged adjusted cost base.

20-69.   The deemed disposition can result in double taxation as Mr. Poutine's new country of residence may consider his adjusted cost base to be the original value of $80,000. Fortunately, the Canada/U.S. tax treaty provides a fix for this situation. Under Article XIII(7), Mr. Poutine can elect to have a deemed disposition at fair market value for U.S. tax purposes as well as for Canadian tax assessment, but this fix is not available for all countries.

20-70.   A further problem in this area is the ability of some taxpayers to avoid the Canadian emigration tax rules, resulting in large sums of money being removed from Canada on a tax free basis. Some types of assets can be removed tax free on the assumption that they will be subject to Canadian taxation at a later point in time. This might not happen if one of Canada's bilateral tax treaties prohibits Canadian taxation after an individual has been a non-resident for a specified period of time.

20-71.   Other leakages can occur when assets are bumped up in value for foreign tax purposes, with no corresponding change in the Canadian tax base. This is essentially what happened in the Bronfman trust case, in which several billion dollars in assets were removed from Canada without being subject to Canadian income taxes on accrued gains.

Elective Dispositions

20-72.   As noted in the preceding Paragraphs, certain types of property are exempted from the deemed disposition rules. There may, however, be circumstances in which an individual wishes to override these exemptions and trigger capital gains at the time of departure. An important example of this would be farm property that qualifies for the lifetime capital gains deduction. (See Chapter 11 for details of this deduction.)

20-73.   An individual may wish to trigger income or losses on the exempted property at the time of departure for other reasons. An example of this would be an emigrant who wants to realize a loss on exempt property in order to offset a gain on non-exempt property.

20-74.   Such situations are provided for in ITA 128.1(4)(d), which allows an individual to elect to have a deemed disposition on certain types of properties that are exempt from the general deemed disposition rule. The properties on which the election can be made include real property situated in Canada, Canadian resource and timber resource properties, as well as property of a business carried on in Canada through a permanent establishment. Note that, if this election results in losses (capital or terminal), they can only be used to offset income resulting from other deemed dispositions. They cannot be applied against other sources of income, including capital gains from actual dispositions, for the taxation year.

Exercise Twenty - 9

Subject: Emigration

Ms. Gloria Lopez owns shares in a Canadian private company with an adjusted cost base of $120,000 and a fair market value of $235,000. In addition, she owns a rental property with a fair market value of $130,000 ($30,000 of this can be attributed to the land) and a cost of $220,000 ($60,000 of this can be attributed to the land). The UCC of the building is $142,000. During the current year, Ms. Lopez permanently departs from Canada. Calculate the minimum Net Income For Tax Purposes that will result from her departure with respect to the shares and the rental property.

SOLUTION available in print and online Study Guide.

Security For Departure Tax

20-75.   The preceding deemed disposition rules can be very burdensome for an emigrating individual. If the individual has substantial amounts of property on which gains have accrued, the deemed disposition rules can result in a hefty tax bill. This is further complicated by the fact that there are no proceeds of disposition to provide funds for paying this liability.

20-76.   In recognition of this problem, ITA 220(4.5) through (4.54) allow the taxpayer to provide security in lieu of paying the tax that results from the deemed dispositions. Similar provisions have been added such as ITA 220(4.6) through (4.63) for dealing with trusts distributing Taxable Canadian Property to non-residents.

20-77.   ITA 220(4.5) requires the CRA to accept "adequate security". Guidance on what constitutes adequate security is as follows:

> Bank letters of guarantee, bank letters of credit, and bonds from the Government of Canada or a province or territory of Canada are considered acceptable forms of security. Other types of security may also be acceptable, such as shares in private or publicly traded corporations, certificates in precious metals, various other marketable securities, a charge or mortgage on real property, or valuable personal property.

20-78.   If the taxpayer elects under ITA 220(4.5), interest does not accrue on the tax that has been deferred until the amount becomes unsecured. This will usually be at the time when there is an actual disposition of the property that was subject to the deemed disposition.

20-79.   A final point here is that ITA 220(4.51) creates deemed security on an amount that is the total amount of taxes under Part I that would be payable, at the highest tax rate that applies to individuals, on Taxable Income of $50,000. This amount is one-half of a $100,000 capital gain, and the effect of this provision is to exempt emigrants from the requirement to provide security on the first $100,000 in capital gains resulting from their departure.

We suggest you work Self Study Problem Twenty-3 at this point.

Unwinding A Deemed Disposition
The Problem

20-80.   A potential problem can arise when an individual departs from Canada and, at a later point in time, returns. A simple example will serve to illustrate this difficulty:

> **EXAMPLE**   John Fuller emigrates from Canada on June 1, 2018. At that time, he owns shares of a private company with a fair market value of $200,000 and an adjusted cost base of $125,000. As a result of the deemed disposition/reacquisition of these shares, he has a taxable capital gain of $37,500 [(1/2)($200,000 - $125,000)]. In 2019, he returns to Canada. At the time of immigration, he still owns the shares and their fair market value has increased to $260,000.

20-81.   In the absence of any special provision (and ignoring the deemed security rules discussed in Paragraph 20-75), Mr. Fuller's departure from Canada would cost him the taxes paid on the $37,500 taxable capital gain arising on the deemed disposition at emigration. On his return, the adjusted cost base of his property would be increased to $260,000 (deemed disposition/re-acquisition on immigration). However, the fact remains that his temporary absence has resulted in an out-of-pocket tax cost on the $37,500 taxable capital gain.

The Solution

20-82.   ITA 128.1(6) provides relief in this type of situation. With respect to Taxable Canadian Property such as Mr. Fuller's, ITA 128.1(6)(a) allows a returning individual to make an election with respect to property that was Taxable Canadian Property at the time of emigration. The effect of making this election is that the deemed disposition that was required under ITA 128.1(1)(b) at the time of departure, is reversed when the individual returns to Canada. As there is no real basis for establishing whether an emigrant will eventually return as an immigrant, ITA 128.1(6) has no influence on the tax consequences arising at the time of emigration.

20-83.   Returning to our example from Paragraph 20-80, if this election is made, the addition to Taxable Income that was assessed when Mr. Fuller left Canada would be reversed through an amended return, resulting in a refund of the taxes paid.

20-84.   As the deemed disposition at departure has been reversed, there would be no need for a disposition/reacquisition when he returns to Canada. This means that after the appropriate election and amended return are filed, Mr. Fuller would wind up in the same tax position as he was in before he departed from Canada. That is, he would own securities with an adjusted cost base of $125,000 with no net taxes paid as a result of his departure and return.

Short-Term Residents

20-85.   With the increasing presence of multi-national firms in the Canadian business environment, it has become common for executives and other employees to find themselves resident in Canada for only a small portion of their total working lives. In the absence of some special provision, the deemed disposition rules could be a significant hardship to employees who are in this position.

20-86.   For example, if Ms. Eng was transferred from Hong Kong to work in Canada for three years, she could become liable on departure for capital gains taxation on all of her capital property owned at the time that she ceases to be a resident of Canada. The liability could put a severe drain on her available liquid assets and could result in taxation on personal items such as paintings and furniture (note that, in many cases, where the individual is in the country for a limited period and working for a non-resident employer, the individual would be taxed as a resident of the foreign country, and not as a resident of Canada). This would not be an equitable situation and could discourage the free movement of employees to and from Canada.

20-87.   In recognition of the preceding problem, ITA 128.1(4)(b)(iv) provides an exception to the deemed disposition rules that applies to taxpayers who, during the ten years preceding departure, have been resident in Canada for a total of 60 months or less. For such taxpayers, the deemed disposition rules do not apply to any property that was owned immediately before the taxpayer last became resident in Canada, or was acquired by inheritance or bequest during the period after he last became resident in Canada. However, the rules still apply to property acquired other than by inheritance or bequest during the period of residency.

Exercise Twenty - 10

Subject: Short Term Residents

During 2015, Charles Brookings moves to Canada from the U.K. He has not previously lived in Canada. At this time his capital assets consist of shares in a U.K. company and a tract of vacant land in Canada which he had inherited. The shares have a fair market value of $250,000 and an adjusted cost base of $175,000. The land had a fair market value of $95,000 when he inherited it and a fair market value of $120,000 when he moves to Canada in 2015.

During 2016, he acquires shares of a Canadian public company for $75,000. During 2018, after finding Canada a tad uncivilized for his tastes, he moves back to the U.K. At this time, the shares in the U.K. company have a fair market value of $280,000, the shares of the Canadian company have a fair market value of $92,000 and the land has a fair market value of $130,000.

What are the tax consequences of his emigration from Canada?

SOLUTION available in print and online Study Guide.

Foreign Source Income Of Canadian Residents

Introduction

20-88.   It would be a fairly easy task to write an entire book on the tax issues associated with the foreign source income of Canadian residents. One version of the draft legislation on non-resident trusts and foreign investment entities ran to nearly 900 pages in its print edition. In addition to being extensive, much of this material is extremely complex, in some cases almost beyond the understanding of mere mortals. Despite this complexity, the importance of this subject mandates that we give some attention to the issues, even in an introductory text such as this. Although some aspects of foreign source income of Canadian residents are relatively straightforward, you should be aware that this material is not an adequate resource for making important decisions in this potentially complicated area.

20-89.   We will begin this section on foreign source income of residents by discussing the reporting requirements applicable to Canadian residents who have foreign investments. This will be followed by sections dealing with resident taxpayers having the following:

• foreign source employment income;
• foreign source income from unincorporated businesses;
• foreign source interest income; and
• capital gains resulting from the disposition of foreign assets.

20-90.   The issues involved for taxpayers having these types of income sources are not overly complex. However, a completely different situation arises when Canadian resident taxpayers receive income from what tax legislation refers to as non-resident entities. These entities are defined as corporations, trusts, or any other type of entity that was formed, organized, last continued under, or governed under the laws of a country, or a political subdivision of a country, other than Canada. In order to simplify our presentation of this material, we will limit our coverage of this material to non-resident corporations paying dividends to Canadian resident taxpayers.

Foreign Investment Reporting Requirements

20-91.   As you are aware, residents of Canada are liable for income taxes on their worldwide income. This means, for example, that if a Canadian resident has a bank account in England, any interest earned on that account should be reported in the taxpayer's Canadian tax return.

20-92.   There is little doubt that evasion of taxes on foreign income has been fairly common in the past. In an attempt to curtail tax evasion on foreign property and to amass information on foreign property owned by Canadians, the CRA requires the following:

> All Canadian resident taxpayers are required to file form T1135, *Foreign Income Verification Statement* if, at any time in the year the total cost amount (not fair market value) of all specified foreign property to the taxpayer was more than $100,000 in Canadian dollars.

20-93.   The T1135 offers a simplified reporting method to taxpayers whose specified foreign property totals more than $100,000, but less than $250,000 throughout the year. Rather than having to report the complete details on the T1135, the simplified method allows a taxpayer to report a single figure for the total income from all specified foreign property, as well as for the gain (loss) from the disposition of all specified foreign property for the year. For example, the taxpayer will be able to report a single figure for the total value of non-resident securities held, rather than having to report each individual security in this category.

20-94.   The T1135 form requires information on what is referred to as "specified foreign property". The more important types of specified foreign property are as follows:

- funds held outside Canada (e.g., funds in a foreign bank account);
- shares of a non-resident corporation (See Paragraph 20-97 for a streamlined option to these reporting requirements for foreign shares held in Canadian brokerage accounts);
- indebtedness owed by a non-resident;
- real property outside of Canada other than excluded property such as personal use or business use properties (See Paragraph 20-95); and
- an interest in a non-resident trust.

20-95.   Some of the common items excluded from the definition of specified foreign property are as follows:

- foreign securities held in Canadian mutual funds, or inside a registered account like an RRSP, RRIF, TFSA or RESP;
- a property used or held exclusively in carrying on an active business;
- a personal use property, such as a second home; and
- a share of the capital stock or indebtedness of a foreign affiliate.

20-96.   For taxpayers with less than $250,000 in specified foreign property, completing the simplified form (Part A of the T1135) is not particularly onerous. For taxpayers with specified foreign property equal to $250,000 or more, a great deal of additional information is required such as:

- the name of the entity holding or issuing the property, or a description of the foreign property;
- the relevant country code (for the country of residence of the bank, corporation, issuer or trust, or where the property is located);
- the maximum cost amount of the property during the year;
- the year end cost amount of the property;
- the amount of income or loss related to the property for the year; and
- any capital gain or loss realized on the disposition of the property during the year.

20-97.   Fortunately, in many, if not most cases, relief is available. To the extent specified foreign property is held in an account with a Canadian registered securities dealer or a Canadian trust company, the only requirements related to specified foreign property are reporting country-by-country aggregate values for maximum fair market value during the year, fair market value at the end of the year, income for the year, and gains or losses on dispositions during the year. For example, if an individual invests only in U.S. stocks and they are held with a Canadian registered securities dealer, the reporting requirements are greatly simplified. This is likely the situation for many of the individuals who are required to report their specified foreign property.

20-98. Substantial penalties can result from failure to comply with these reporting requirements. They range from $500 per month for up to 24 months if the failure to file is done knowingly to $1,000 per month for up to 24 months if there is a failure to comply with a demand to file the T1135. After 24 months, the penalty can become more severe, i.e., 5 percent of the cost of the foreign property.

Exercise Twenty - 11

Subject: Foreign Investment Reporting

During 2018, Simon Taylor, a Canadian resident, has a bank account at the Bank of Scotland. The balance ranged from £4,000 to £52,000 during the year and has a balance of £41,000 on December 31, 2018. Interest on the account for the year totalled £1,000. In 2017, he made a 2 year interest free loan of £145,000 to his brother-in-law who is a resident of Scotland. No formal loan agreement was involved. Assume 1£ = $1.70 for 2017 and 2018. Describe the foreign investment reporting obligations that Simon has for 2018 and provide the information required.

SOLUTION available in print and online Study Guide.

We suggest you work Self Study Problem Twenty-4 at this point.

Foreign Source Employment Income
The Problem
20-99. Individuals who are residents of Canada are taxable on employment income regardless of where the employment duties are performed. This creates a potential problem in that an individual earning employment income in a foreign country could be subject to Canadian taxes because they have retained their status as a Canadian resident and, at the same time, be subject to taxes in the foreign country because it is the source of the employment income. Tax treaties would normally be used to resolve this potential conflict.

Canada/U.S. Tax Treaty - Foreign Source Employment Income
20-100. This problem is, of course, the mirror image of the problem that arises when a U.S. resident is earning employment income while working in Canada. In our discussion of that situation (see Paragraph 20-21), we noted that, in general, the source country has the right to tax employment income. We also noted that, under the Canada/U.S. tax treaty, there were two exceptions to this rule. As applied to a situation where a Canadian resident is earning U.S. employment income, these exceptions are as follows:

$10,000 Rule Under this rule if, during a calendar year, a Canadian resident earns employment income in the U.S. that is $10,000 or less in U.S. dollars, then the income is taxable only in Canada.

183 Day Rule This rule exempts U.S. source employment income from U.S. taxation, provided it is earned by a Canadian resident who was physically present in the U.S. for no more than 183 days during any twelve month period commencing or ending in the calendar year. This exemption is conditional on employment income not being paid by an employer with a permanent establishment in the U.S. who would be able to deduct the amount paid from their U.S. Taxable Income. Stated alternatively, if the employment income exceeds $10,000 and is deductible in the U.S., it will be taxed in the U.S., even if the employee is present in the U.S. for less than 183 days during the year.

We suggest you work Self Study Problem Twenty-5 at this point.

Foreign Source Business Income (Unincorporated Sources)

The Problem

20-101.　The general rule that Canadian residents are taxable on their worldwide income would suggest that Canadian residents are taxable on foreign source business income. As was the case with foreign source employment income, this creates a potential problem in that a person earning business income in a foreign country could be subject to Canadian taxes because they have retained their status as a Canadian resident and, at the same time, be subject to taxes in the foreign country because it is the source of the business income.

20-102.　In many cases, the potential for double taxation is dealt with through international tax treaties. If this is not the case, a Canadian resident may have some amount of taxes withheld in the foreign jurisdiction. In these circumstances, Canada uses foreign tax credits to deal with the problem. While these credits were covered in detail in Chapter 11 for individuals and Chapter 12 for corporations, a simple example where the detailed calculations would have resulted in a foreign tax credit equal to the foreign tax withheld will serve to review the general approach used:

EXAMPLE　Ms. Johnson, a Canadian resident, is subject to a Canadian marginal tax rate of 45 percent on all of her worldwide income. During the current year, she earns foreign source business income of $1,000, from which the source country assesses and withholds taxes at a rate of 15 percent.

ANALYSIS　The pretax amount of foreign income would be included in Taxable Income, with the foreign taxes paid by Ms. Johnson, a Canadian resident, generating a credit against Canadian Tax Payable. Applying this to the preceding example results in the following calculations:

Foreign Business Income Received	$ 850
Foreign Tax Withheld	150
Gross Income = Taxable Income Addition	$1,000
Canadian Tax Payable [(45%)($1,000)]	$ 450
Foreign Tax Credit = Foreign Tax Withheld	(150)
Net Canadian Tax Payable	$ 300
Foreign Tax Withheld	150
Total Taxes Payable	$ 450
After Tax Retention ($1,000 - $450)	$ 550
Overall Tax Rate ($450 ÷ $1,000)	45%

As this simple example makes clear, this represents a very equitable solution to situations where foreign taxes are withheld on income that will be taxed again in Canada. The combined foreign and Canadian taxes total $450, exactly the same amount that would have been paid if Ms. Johnson had received the $1,000 in business income from a Canadian source.

Canada/U.S. Tax Treaty - Foreign Source Business Income

20-103.   As was discussed when we considered the Canadian business income of non-residents, the Canada/U.S. tax treaty indicates that business income will be taxed in the source country in those situations where the business is operated through a permanent establishment. Applying this here would mean that if a Canadian resident earns business income in the U.S. without having a permanent establishment in that country, it will be taxed in Canada, rather than in the U.S. Alternatively, if the business income is earned through a permanent establishment in the U.S., it will be taxed in that country. Any taxes withheld by the U.S. would be eligible for treatment as a foreign business tax credit. (See Chapters 11 and 12 for detailed coverage of this credit.)

Exercise Twenty - 12

Subject: Foreign Tax Credits

Jason Abernathy is a Canadian resident. During 2018, he earns $18,000 of business income through a permanent establishment located in the U.S. Income taxes of $1,800 were assessed and withheld at the source on that income. In calculating his foreign tax credit, his Adjusted Division B Income is equal to $100,000 and his Tax Otherwise Payable is equal to $21,000. All amounts are in Canadian dollars. Jason's marginal combined federal/provincial tax rate is 44 percent. Determine his after tax retention and overall tax rate on his foreign source business income.

SOLUTION available in print and online Study Guide.

Foreign Source Interest Income

The Problem

20-104.   Resident Canadian taxpayers are taxable on interest income, generally without regard to the source. As was the case with employment income, this raises the possibility of double taxation. In most cases this issue will be resolved by an international tax treaty. If the issue is not resolved by treaty, the Canadian resident would have tax deductions and/or credits based on any foreign taxes withheld.

Canada/U.S. Tax Treaty - Foreign Source Interest Income

20-105.   As noted in Paragraph 20-40, Article XI of the Canada/U.S. tax treaty indicates that interest paid to the other jurisdiction will be taxed only in that jurisdiction. This means that U.S. residents receiving interest from a Canadian source are not subject to the Canadian Part XIII tax. Correspondingly, Canadian residents receiving interest income from a U.S. source will be subject to Part I taxes only in Canada.

Foreign Source Capital Gains

The Problem

20-106.   The rules of the *Income Tax Act* relating to the calculation of capital gains and losses are generally applicable to residents of Canada on dispositions of property regardless of the location of that property. As was the case with foreign source employment and business income, dispositions of foreign property may result in potential taxation in both Canada and the foreign country. Again, the tax treaties would normally offer a way to resolve any conflicts.

Canada/U.S. Tax Treaty - Foreign Source Capital Gains

20-107.   In general, the Canada/U.S. tax treaty gives priority to tax to the vendor's country of residence. However, the treaty allows the U.S. to tax gains from the disposition of real property interests situated in the U.S., as well as gains on most types of property that are used in a permanent establishment through which a Canadian resident carries on business in the U.S.

Foreign Source Dividend Income - Problems

20-108.   Most foreign source investment income is taxed under the rules that are applicable to similar sources of income earned in Canada. An exception to this is dividends received from non-resident corporations.

20-109.   As you are aware, dividends paid to Canadian residents by taxable Canadian corporations receive very favourable tax treatment. When such dividends are received by individuals, they are subject to the gross up and tax credit procedures, a process that significantly reduces the effective tax rate on this type of income. When the recipient shareholder is a corporation, the dividends generally escape all taxation in that they can be deducted under ITA 112(1) in the calculation of Taxable Income. Both of these provisions are designed to make up for the fact that the dividends represent an income stream that has already been subject to Canadian tax at the corporate level.

20-110.   The basic problem with dividends received from a non-resident corporation is that the corporation that paid the dividends has not paid taxes in Canada. In fact, in some jurisdictions (e.g., tax havens), the corporation may not have paid any taxes whatsoever. This means that the usual reason for providing favourable treatment of dividend income is not relevant when dividends are received from a non-resident corporation.

20-111.   A further problem is that the foreign source dividends do not reflect the type of income that provided for the payment of dividends by the foreign corporation. Again, as you are aware, Canadian taxes are generally assessed differently on alternative types of income. For example, a CCPC will be taxed much more heavily on property income as compared to the taxes that would be paid on active business income. To maintain fairness in the system, provisions had to be created that reflect the different sources of income that enabled the non-resident corporation to pay dividends.

20-112.   In general, foreign source dividends must be included in a resident taxpayer's Net Income For Tax Purposes under ITA 90(1). When foreign source dividends are received by individuals, they do not get the benefit of the gross up and tax credit procedures. When they are received by corporations, they are not generally deductible under ITA 112(1).

20-113.   While the elimination of favourable tax treatment for dividends from a foreign source provides a partial solution to the problem of dividends being paid out of corporate income that has not been taxed in Canada, two significant problems remain:

1. This procedure can result in double taxation. For example, income earned by a foreign subsidiary of a Canadian corporation could be fully taxed in the foreign jurisdiction and, in the absence of the ITA 112(1) dividend deduction, it would be taxed again in Canada.

2. Under the general rules applicable to corporations, income from a non-resident corporation will not be taxed in Canada until such time as it is distributed to Canadian residents. This means that a Canadian resident can achieve significant tax deferral by placing investments in a foreign corporation, in situations where the income from the investments is not currently needed. This is particularly attractive when the non-resident corporation is located in a jurisdiction where there is little or no taxation of investment income.

20-114.   The first of these problems has been dealt with by developing the concept of a "foreign affiliate". As will be discussed in a subsequent section of this Chapter, dividends received from this type of non-resident corporation may be deductible, in whole or in part, to a recipient Canadian corporation. A partial solution to the second problem is contained in what are referred to as the Foreign Accrual Property Income (FAPI) rules. These rules apply to a subset of foreign affiliates referred to as controlled foreign affiliates.

20-115.   In the following material, we will give consideration to dividends from foreign corporations that are received by:

- individuals resident in Canada;
- Canadian corporations that are not affiliated with the foreign corporation;
- Canadian corporations that are affiliated with the foreign corporation but do not control it; and
- Canadian corporations that control the foreign corporation.

20-116.   We would remind you that our presentation of this material is at a very basic level and should be considered only as an overview of the topic and not as a guide for making real world decisions in this complex area.

Foreign Source Dividends Received By Individuals

20-117.   If a resident Canadian individual receives a dividend from a foreign corporation and there is no withholding of tax by the foreign jurisdiction, the amount received will be converted into Canadian dollars at the time that it is received. It would then be included in that individual's Net Income For Tax Purposes. It will not be grossed up and it will not generate a dividend tax credit.

20-118.   Alternatively, if there is withholding by the foreign jurisdiction, the pre-withholding amount of the dividend will be included in the individual's Net Income For Tax Purposes. To the extent that the withholding is 15 percent or less, the individual is entitled to a foreign tax credit. Any withholding in excess of 15 percent is eligible for a deduction from Net Income For Tax Purposes.

20-119.   While it would rarely be an appropriate choice, the individual would have the alternative of deducting the entire amount withheld, rather than using the eligible portion as a tax credit.

> **EXAMPLE**   During 2018, Martin Fingle is entitled to $25,000 in dividends from a foreign corporation in which he owns shares. The foreign jurisdiction withholds $5,000 (20%), providing a net receipt of $20,000. In addition to the dividend, Martin has Canadian source interest income of $65,000. He has no tax credits other than his basic personal credit and any credits related to foreign taxes withheld. He has no deductions from Net Income For Tax Purposes in determining Taxable Income.
>
> **ANALYSIS**   Martin's Taxable Income would be calculated as follows:

Interest Income	$65,000
Foreign Dividends (100%)	25,000
Excess Withholding [(20% - 15%)($25,000)]	(1,250)
Net Income For Tax Purposes And Taxable Income	$88,750

His Tax Payable would be calculated as follows:

Tax On First $46,605	$ 6,991
Tax On Next $42,145 ($88,750 - $46,605) At 20.5%	8,640
Tax Before Credits	$15,631
Personal Tax Credit	(1,771)
Part I Tax Payable Before Foreign Tax Credit	$13,860
Foreign Tax Credit (See Note)	(3,750)
Federal Tax Payable	$10,110

Note   The foreign tax credit would be the lesser of:

- Amount Withheld (Limited To 15% Of $25,000) = $3,750

- $$\left[\frac{\text{Foreign Non-Business Income}}{\text{Division B Income}}\right](\text{Tax Payable}) = \left[\frac{\$25,000}{\$88,750}\right](\$13,860) = \$3,904$$

20-120.   While Martin could have deducted all of the withheld amount, his additional tax savings from this deduction would only be $769 [(20.5%)($3,750)]. This is clearly not as desirable as the $3,750 (15 percent foreign tax credit) alternative.

We suggest you work Self Study Problem Twenty-6 at this point.

Foreign Dividends Received From Non-Affiliated Corporations

20-121.   The pre-withholding amount of a dividend received by a Canadian corporation from a foreign corporation is always included in the corporation's Net Income For Tax Purposes. As a foreign affiliate is not involved, there would be no deduction in the determination of the corporation's Taxable Income.

> **EXAMPLE** Martin Fingle Inc., a Canadian public corporation, is entitled to $25,000 in dividends from a foreign corporation in which it owns less than 1 percent of the shares. The foreign jurisdiction withholds $5,000 (20%), providing a net receipt of $20,000. The corporate tax rate on this income, after the general rate reduction, will be 25 percent (38% - 13%). Assume that Martin Fingle Inc. has no other source of income during the year.

> **ANALYSIS** The Corporation's Taxable Income will be $25,000, the pre-withholding amount of the dividend. Tax Payable, before the application of the foreign tax credit will be $6,250 [(25%)($25,000)]. As a corporation's use of foreign non-business tax credits is not limited to 15 percent, the tax credit will be $5,000, the lesser of:

> - Amount Withheld (no 15% limit) = $5,000

> - $\left[\dfrac{\text{Foreign Non - Business Income}}{\text{Division B Income}}\right](\text{Tax Payable}) = \left[\dfrac{\$25,000}{\$25,000}\right](\$6,250) = \$6,250$

Dividends Received From Non-Controlled Foreign Affiliates
Foreign Affiliate Defined

20-122.   A foreign affiliate of a Canadian taxpayer is defined in ITA 95(1) as a non-resident corporation in which that taxpayer has an equity percentage of at least 1 percent. As well, the aggregate equity percentages of the taxpayer and each person related to the taxpayer must be at least 10 percent. The ownership percentage can be established on either a direct or indirect basis, and is defined as the greatest percentage holding in any class of the non-resident corporation's capital stock.

20-123.   As an example of both the direct and indirect application of this rule, consider the following example:

> **EXAMPLE** Candoo, a resident Canadian corporation, owns 70 percent of the only class of shares of Forco One, a non-resident corporation. In turn, Forco One owns 20 percent of the only class of shares of Forco Two, a second non-resident corporation.

> **ANALYSIS** Forco One is a foreign affiliate of Candoo because of Candoo's 70 percent direct ownership. Forco Two is also a foreign affiliate of Candoo because the indirect ownership percentage is 14 percent [(70%)(20%)].

20-124.   We would also note that the ownership thresholds are applied on a shareholder by shareholder basis. A non-resident company will be a foreign affiliate of a Canadian resident, only if that resident owns directly or indirectly at least 1 percent of the shares of that non-resident company and, in addition, that resident, together with related persons, owns at least 10 percent of the shares of that non-resident company.

EXAMPLE   Carson Ltd. and Dawson Inc., two resident Canadian companies, each own 8 percent of Belgique, a non-resident corporation. While Carson Ltd. is part of a related group that controls Belgique, Dawson Inc. is not related to any of the other shareholders of Belgique.

ANALYSIS   Belgique would be a foreign affiliate of Carson Ltd. as Carson Ltd. owns more than 1 percent of the shares and, in addition, is part of a related group that owns more than 10 percent of the shares. Belgique would not be a foreign affiliate of Dawson Inc.

20-125.   A foreign affiliate may or may not be a controlled foreign affiliate. In this section we are limiting our discussion to situations where control is not present. In the next section of this chapter, we will provide limited coverage of controlled foreign affiliates. Note that the rules discussed in this section apply to all foreign affiliates, whether or not control exists.

Exercise Twenty - 13

Subject   Identifying Foreign Affiliates

Canvest is a resident Canadian corporation that has three investments in the shares of non-resident corporations. For each of the investments in non-resident corporations described below, determine whether the investee is a foreign affiliate.

Forco 1   Canvest owns 3 percent of Forco 1. A wholly-owned Canadian subsidiary of Canvest owns 8 percent of Forco 1.

Forco 2   Canvest owns 9 percent of Forco 2. Canvest is not related to any of the other shareholders of Forco 2.

Forco 3   Canvest owns 5 percent of Forco 3. The spouse of the shareholder who has a controlling interest in Canvest owns the other 95 percent of the shares of Forco 3.

SOLUTION available in print and online Study Guide.

Dividends Received From Foreign Affiliates - Basic Concepts

20-126.   We have previously noted that, in general, only dividends received from a taxable Canadian corporation can be deducted under ITA 112(1) in the determination of the Taxable Income of a resident Canadian corporation. However, ITA 113(1) provides a similar deduction for dividends received by a resident corporate shareholder from a foreign affiliate.

20-127.   Unlike the fairly straightforward application of ITA 112(1), the application of ITA 113(1) is very complex in that it is applied differently depending on the country where the foreign affiliate is located and income source from which the dividend is being paid. The ITA 113(1) rules are implemented by a process in which the foreign affiliate's Surplus balances are tracked by type of income and source country. We would remind you that the term Surplus in tax work is the equivalent of the term Retained Earnings in accounting work.

20-128.   While there are other types of surplus that determine the tax status of dividends from foreign affiliates, in this text we will only provide coverage of Exempt Surplus and Taxable Surplus. Coverage of other surplus balances goes beyond the scope of this introductory text.

20-129.   When a dividend is paid by a foreign affiliate it is assumed to come first from any Exempt Surplus balance that is available. If there is no Exempt Surplus balance, or if the dividend is larger than the Exempt Surplus balance, the required amount will then be removed from the Taxable Surplus balance.

Exempt Vs. Taxable Surplus

20-130.   The content of these surplus balances requires the allocation of income from four different sources. They are as follows:

- active business income
- investment income (e.g., interest and rents)
- capital gains on dispositions of assets used to produce active business income
- capital gains on dispositions of assets not used to produce active business income

20-131.   The situation is further complicated in that the classification of a particular type of income will depend on whether the foreign affiliate is located in country with which Canada has a tax treaty or a Tax Information Exchange Agreement (TIEA). For example, active business income is allocated to Exempt Surplus in a country where a tax treaty or TIEA is in effect. Alternatively, this type of income is allocated to Taxable Surplus in other countries.

20-132.   Based on this two-way allocation, the items included in Exempt Surplus are as follows:

- For a foreign affiliate that is located in a country with which Canada has a tax treaty or a tax information exchange agreement (TIEA):
  - Active business income
  - The taxable one-half of capital gains on dispositions of property used in producing active business income.
- For all foreign affiliates, without regard to the location of the foreign affiliate:
  - The non-taxable one-half of capital gains on dispositions of all types of capital property (except shares of other foreign affiliates).

20-133.   Using a similar approach, the items included in Taxable Surplus are as follows:

- For a foreign affiliate that is located in a country with which Canada does not have a tax treaty or a TIEA:
  - Active business income
  - The taxable one-half of capital gains on dispositions of property used in producing active business income.
- For all foreign affiliates, without regard to the location of the foreign affiliate:
  - The taxable one-half of capital gains on dispositions of capital property other than that used in producing active business income.
  - Investment income, which includes income from property and from non-active businesses.

Dividends Paid From Exempt Surplus

20-134.   When a dividend is paid from a foreign affiliate's Exempt Surplus, Canadian tax legislation, in effect, cedes all of the taxation of this income stream to the foreign jurisdiction. This is without regard to the level of local taxation in the foreign jurisdiction or amounts of tax withheld by that jurisdiction.

20-135.   In order to apply this approach, ITA 113(1)(a) allows the full amount of the foreign affiliate dividend to be deducted in the determination of the resident corporation's Taxable Income.

> **EXAMPLE**   A Canadian company receives a $90,000 dividend from a foreign affiliate. The affiliate had paid a $100,000 dividend from its exempt surplus (an after foreign taxes balance), with the foreign jurisdiction withholding $10,000 from the distribution to Canada.
>
> **ANALYSIS**   The Canadian corporation will include the pre-withholding $100,000 dividend in its Net Income For Tax Purposes, and will deduct the $100,000 included amount under ITA 113(1)(a) in the determination of Taxable Income under ITA 113(1)(a). No Canadian taxes will be paid on the dividend and, consistent with this result, no foreign tax credit will be available for the $10,000 that was withheld by the foreign jurisdiction.

Foreign Source Income Of Canadian Residents

Dividends Paid From Taxable Surplus

20-136.   With respect to foreign affiliate dividends paid from Taxable Surplus, the goal here is to apply ITA 113(1) in a manner that attempts to have the overall level of taxation, both domestic and foreign, be the equivalent of the amount of taxes that would be paid in Canada on the same stream of income. Currently this rate is equal to 25 percent.

Basic Rate (No Abatement)	38%
General Rate Reduction	(13%)
Overall Federal Rate	25%

20-137.   While this could have been accomplished using credits against Tax Payable, the government chose to do the required adjustments through deductions under ITA 113(1). Given the desire to apply an overall tax rate of 25 percent, tax amounts will have to be converted to income using a factor of 4 (1 ÷ 25%). Stated alternatively, every $1 of tax paid must be converted to Taxable Income of $4.

20-138. To achieve the desired overall tax rate of 25 percent, two adjustments are required:

ITA 113(1)(b) adjusts Taxable Income to reflect the income taxes paid in the foreign jurisdiction.

ITA 113(1)(c) adjusts Taxable Income to reflect taxes withheld by the foreign jurisdiction on payments to non-residents of that jurisdiction.

20-139.   An example will serve to illustrate these provisions.

EXAMPLE   Cancor, a taxable Canadian corporation, owns 50 percent of the outstanding shares of Forco, a corporation located in a country that does not have a tax treaty or a TIEA with Canada. All of Forco's income is from active business activities. During 2018, Forco pays dividends of $90,000. Of this total, $42,750 is received by Cancor, with $2,250 being withheld by the foreign jurisdiction. Forco is subject to a tax rate of 10 percent in the foreign jurisdiction.

ANALYSIS   Dividends paid are an after tax amount. This means that the original income stream that formed the basis for the current dividend was $100,000 [$90,000 ÷ (1 - 10%)], with taxes of $10,000 being paid prior to the dividend declaration.

Given this, Cancor's share of these taxes would be $5,000 [(1/2)($10,000)]. Taking this and the $2,250 in withholding into account, to achieve an overall tax rate of 25 percent on the original $50,000 income stream would require additional Canadian taxes as follows:

Required Total Tax [(25%)($50,000)]	$12,500
Foreign Taxes Paid By Foreign Affiliate	(5,000)
Foreign Taxes Withheld From Dividend	(2,250)
Required Additional Canadian Tax	$ 5,250

As we have noted, ITA 113(1) accomplishes this result with two adjustments. The first is related to the $5,000 in foreign tax paid. The $5,000 in taxes paid reflects, at a 25 percent rate, $20,000 ($5,000 ÷ 25%) in Taxable Income. This would suggest multiplying the foreign tax paid by 4. However, this does not take into consideration the fact that income has already been reduced by $5,000 from $50,000 to $45,000 by these taxes. Given this, ITA 113(1)(b) requires that the $5,000 in foreign taxes be multiplied by a relevant factor of 3 [(1 ÷ 25%) - 1]. This deduction equals $15,000.

In applying ITA 113(1)(c), we need to adjust for the $2,250 in taxes withheld from the dividend payment. Given this, ITA 113(1)(c) requires that this amount be multiplied by 4 (1 ÷ 25%). This results in a deduction of $9,000, reflecting the amount of income that would result in the payment of $2,250 in taxes.

Putting all of this together results in the following calculation of Tax Payable:

Net Income For Tax Purposes	$45,000
ITA 113(1)(b) Deduction For Foreign Tax Paid	(15,000)
ITA 113(1)(c) Deduction For Foreign Tax Withheld	(9,000)
Taxable Income	$21,000
Required Rate	25%
Canadian Tax Payable	$ 5,250

This, as expected, is the same amount that we calculated in the preceding table using a more intuitive approach that is not based on the ITA 113 legislation.

Dividends Received From Controlled Foreign Affiliates
Controlled Foreign Affiliate Defined

20-140.   While establishing the concept of a foreign affiliate alleviated the problem of excessive taxation on dividends received by Canadian corporations from non-resident corporations, it did not deal with the problem of using a non-resident corporation to defer Canadian taxation on property income. In order to deal with this issue, the government developed the concept of a "controlled foreign affiliate".

20-141.   In somewhat simplified terms, ITA 95(1) defines a controlled foreign affiliate of a Canadian taxpayer as a foreign affiliate of that taxpayer that is:

1.   controlled by the Canadian resident on the basis of his own shareholdings; or

2.   controlled by the Canadian resident, together with:

   • persons (residents or non-residents) who are not at arm's length with the Canadian resident;
   • up to four Canadian residents who are not related to the taxpayer (referred to as "relevant" shareholders; and
   • any other persons (residents or non-residents) who are related to the "relevant" Canadian shareholders.

EXAMPLE   Cantext, a Canadian public company, owns 11 percent of the voting shares of Fortext, a company located in Germany. Two other resident Canadian corporations, who are not related to Cantext, each own an additional 15 percent of the voting shares of Fortext. A French subsidiary of one of these other Canadian companies owns 20 percent of the voting shares of Fortext.

ANALYSIS   Fortext is a foreign affiliate of Cantext since Cantext holds more than 10 percent of the voting shares of Fortext. It is a controlled foreign affiliate in that:

   • Cantext owns 11 percent;
   • two unrelated Canadian companies (relevant shareholders) own an additional 30 percent; and
   • a company related to one of the relevant shareholders owns another 20 percent.

This gives a total holding of 61 percent, enough to provide control of Fortext. Note that Fortext is also a controlled foreign affiliate of both the other Canadian corporations.

20-142.   The significance of the controlled foreign affiliate concept is that, if an investment in a non-resident corporation falls within this definition, the Canadian shareholder must recognize its foreign accrual property income (FAPI, hereafter) prior to its actual distribution. That is, the FAPI of controlled foreign affiliates must be recorded as it is earned, rather than when it is distributed in the form of dividends.

20-143.   This provision is somewhat mitigated by the fact that Canadian residents are not required to report the FAPI of controlled foreign affiliates unless it exceeds $5,000. The $5,000 exemption figure recognizes that the calculation of FAPI is quite complex and should not be required when the amount of income is small. As FAPI income is taxed as it accrues, dividends subsequently paid out of such income are not taxable.

Foreign Accrual Property Income (FAPI)

General Rules

20-144.   In simplified terms, FAPI is the passive income of a controlled foreign affiliate. FAPI includes income from property (e.g. interest, portfolio dividends), income from non-active businesses (e.g. rental income), as well as the taxable one-half of capital gains resulting from the disposition of properties that are not used in an active business. An important distinguishing feature of this type of income is that, with the exception of rental income, its source can be easily moved from one tax jurisdiction to another.

20-145.   The property income definition for FAPI also includes income from a foreign investment business. This type of business is analogous to the specified investment business that is used in determining income eligible for the small business deduction (see Chapter 12).

20-146.   As is the case with the specified investment business rules, a foreign affiliate would be considered to be earning active business income if it either employs more than five full time employees or the equivalent of more than five full time employees, to earn income that would normally be considered property income. This "five-employee" exception is especially important in deciding whether foreign rental income is active (exempt from the FAPI rules) or passive (subject to the FAPI rules).

Taxation Of FAPI

20-147.   As noted in Paragraph 20-142, if a taxpayer has an investment in a controlled foreign affiliate, FAPI must be accrued as it is earned by that affiliate. Note that this is a separate issue from the taxation of dividends from either controlled or other foreign affiliates. We will deal with this latter issue in the next section. Not surprisingly, we will find that if dividends are paid out of FAPI income that has been accrued by a taxpayer, the dividends will not be taxed a second time when received by that investor.

> **EXAMPLE**   Paul Peterson, a Canadian resident, owns 80 percent of the shares of Tabasco Ltd., a company that is incorporated in Trinidad. During 2018, the Company has income of $100,000, all of which is earned by passive investments. No income taxes are paid on this income in Trinidad, and no dividends are paid out of this income to Mr. Peterson.
>
> **ANALYSIS**   Tabasco Ltd. is clearly a controlled foreign affiliate. Further, all of its income is from passive sources. Given this, under ITA 91(1), Mr. Peterson will have to include $80,000 [(80%)($100,000)] in his Canadian Net Income For Tax Purposes for 2018.

20-148.   The preceding example was simplified by the fact that Tabasco Ltd. was not subject to taxes in the foreign country. If it had been, the income of this controlled foreign affiliate would have been subject to double taxation. Fortunately, the *Income Tax Act* provides relief in the form of a deduction under ITA 91(4) that is designed to compensate for foreign taxes that have been paid on FAPI.

20-149.   Note that this is a deduction against income, rather than a tax credit. As illustrated in Paragraph 20-120, a deduction against income will reduce Tax Payable only by the amount of the deduction multiplied by the tax rate. This means that its value to the taxpayer is less than the amount of foreign taxes paid and, given this, it would not be equitable to set the deduction equal to those taxes.

20-150.   The ITA 91(4) deduction recognizes this difference by multiplying the foreign taxes paid on FAPI by what is referred to as a relevant tax factor (RTF, hereafter). As defined in ITA 95(1), the RTF for individuals is different than it is for corporations.

> **Canadian Resident Individual**   If the investor in the controlled foreign affiliate is an individual, the RTF is 1.9. This is based on the notional assumption that the Canadian tax rate on this income would have been about 52.63 percent if the individual had received it from a Canadian source (1 ÷ 52.63% = 1.9).

Canadian Resident Corporation If the investor in the controlled foreign affiliate is a corporation, the RTF is 4. This RTF is based on 1, divided by a notional tax rate that would have applied if the income had been received from a Canadian source (1 ÷ 25% = 4). That rate of 25 percent is 38 percent, less the General Rate Reduction of 13 percent. Note again, that because foreign income is involved, the 10 percent federal tax abatement is not deducted.

20-151. If the controlled foreign affiliate's income is taxed in the foreign jurisdiction at the notional rate applicable to the investor, the ITA 91(4) deduction will completely eliminate the FAPI. In most cases, the foreign tax rate will be below the notional rates, resulting in some FAPI being included in income. Note, however, that the ITA 91(4) deduction cannot exceed the FAPI.

EXAMPLE CONTINUED (Foreign Taxes Paid) Paul Peterson, a Canadian resident, owns 80 percent of the shares of Tabasco Ltd., a company that is incorporated in Trinidad. During 2018, the Company has income of $100,000, all of which is earned by passive investments. The Company pays Trinidadian taxes at a rate of 20 percent. No dividends are paid out of this income to Mr. Peterson.

ANALYSIS The tax consequences to Mr. Peterson would be as follows:

FAPI [(80%)($100,000)]	$80,000
Deduct Lesser Of:	
• FAPI = $80,000	
• ITA 91(4) Deduction [(1.9)(80%)(20%)($100,000)] = $30,400	(30,400)
Addition To Net Income For Tax Purposes	$49,600

Exercise Twenty - 14

Subject: FAPI

Forco is a wholly owned foreign subsidiary of Canco, a resident Canadian company. Forco earns $100,000 of investment income in 2018 and pays 18 percent in tax in the foreign jurisdiction. None of the after tax income is paid out as dividends. What is the effect of this information on Canco's 2018 Net Income For Tax Purposes?

SOLUTION available in print and online Study Guide.

Dividends From FAPI

20-152. A final problem remains when the controlled foreign affiliate subsequently distributes the FAPI to the Canadian resident shareholders as a dividend. While these dividends must be included in income, the *Income Tax Act* provides a deduction to reflect the fact that all or a part of the dividend may have already been taxed in an earlier year as FAPI.

20-153. The deduction is provided solely through ITA 91(5) in the case of individuals and a combination of ITA 91(5) and ITA 113(1)(b) in the case of corporations. The deductions are designed to eliminate taxation on previously taxed FAPI. It is equal to the lesser of the dividends received and the FAPI previously taxed to that shareholder after the ITA 91(4) deduction. Any withholding taxes on dividends paid to corporate shareholders of foreign affiliates are eligible for a deduction under ITA 113(1)(c). (See Paragraph 20-138.)

EXAMPLE CONTINUED (Dividend Paid) Paul Peterson, a Canadian resident, owns 80 percent of the shares of Tabasco Ltd., a company that is incorporated in Trinidad. During 2018, the Company has income of $100,000, all of which is earned by passive investments. The Company pays Trinidadian taxes at a rate of 20 percent. Tabasco Ltd. declares and pays dividends of $40,000 in January, 2019. There is no withholding tax on this dividend.

ANALYSIS   As shown in Paragraph 20-151, Mr. Peterson's addition to Net Income For Tax Purposes in 2018 was $49,600. The consequences of receiving the dividend in 2019 would be nil as shown in the following calculation.

Foreign Source Dividend [(80%)($40,000)]	$32,000
Deduct Lesser Of:	
• Previous FAPI After ITA 91(4) Deduction = $49,600	
• Dividend Received = $32,000	(32,000)
Addition To Net Income For Tax Purposes	Nil

Exercise Twenty - 15

Subject: Dividends From FAPI (An Extension Of Exercise Twenty - 14)

Forco is a wholly owned foreign subsidiary of Canco, a resident Canadian company. Forco earns $100,000 of investment income in 2018 and pays 18 percent in tax in the foreign jurisdiction. In 2019, Forco distributes its net after-tax FAPI of $82,000 to Canco as a dividend. Assume that there are no withholding taxes on the dividend payment. What is the effect of this information on Canco's 2019 Net Income For Tax Purposes?

SOLUTION available in print and online Study Guide.

We suggest you work Self Study Problem Twenty-7 at this point.

Additional Supplementary Self Study Problems Are Available Online.

Key Terms Used In This Chapter

20-154.   The following is a list of the key terms used in this Chapter. These terms, and their meanings, are compiled in the Glossary located at the back of the Study Guide.

Business Income	International Taxation
Capital Gain	Non-Resident
Controlled Foreign Affiliate	Permanent Establishment
Dividends	Person
Double Taxation	Resident
Employment Income	Sojourner
Exempt Surplus	Tax Haven
Foreign Accrual Property Income (FAPI)	Taxable Canadian Property
Foreign Affiliate	Taxable Surplus
Interest Income	
International Tax Treaty	
(a.k.a., International Tax Convention)	

References

20-155.   For more detailed study of the material in this Chapter, we would refer you to the following:

ITA 2(3)	Tax Payable By Non-Resident Persons
ITA 20(11)	Foreign Taxes On Income From Property Exceeding 15 Percent
ITA 90	Dividends Received From Non-Resident Corporation
ITA 91	Amounts To Be Included In Respect Of Share Of Foreign Affiliate
ITA 94	Application Of Certain Provisions To Trusts Not Resident In Canada
ITA 95	Definitions [Foreign Accrual Property Income]
ITA 113	Deduction In Respect Of Dividend Received From Foreign Affiliate
ITA 115	Non-Resident's Taxable Income In Canada
ITA 116	Disposition By Non-Resident Person Of Certain Property
ITA 118.94	Tax Payable By Non-Resident (Tax Credits)
ITA 126	Foreign Tax Credits
ITA 212	Tax On Income From Canada Of Non-Resident Persons (Section in ITA Part XIII which deals with Canadian property income of non-resident persons.)
ITA 216	Alternatives Re Rents And Timber Royalties
ITA 217	Alternative Re Canadian Benefits
ITA 248(1)	Definitions (Taxable Canadian Property)
ITA 249	Definition Of "Taxation Year"
ITA 253	Extended Meaning Of "Carrying On Business"
IC 72-17R6	Procedures Concerning The Disposition Of Taxable Canadian Property By Non-Residents Of Canada - Section 116
IC 75-6R2	Required Withholding from Amounts Paid to Non-Resident Persons Performing Services in Canada
IC 76-12R6	Applicable Rate of Part XIII Tax on Amounts Paid or Credited to Persons in Countries With Which Canada Has a Tax Convention
IC 77-16R4	Non-Resident Income Tax
S5-F2-C1	Foreign Tax Credit
IT-137R3	Additional Tax On Certain Corporations Carrying On Business In Canada
IT-173R2	Capital Gains Derived In Canada By Residents Of The United States
IT-176R2	Taxable Canadian Property - Interests In And Options On Real Property And Shares
IT-262R2	Losses Of Non-Residents And Part-Year Residents
IT-303	Know-How And Similar Payments To Non-Residents
IT-420R3	Non-Residents - Income Earned In Canada
IT-451R	Deemed Disposition And Acquisition On Ceasing To Be Or Becoming Resident In Canada
IT-465R	Non-Resident Beneficiaries Of Trusts
IT-468R	Management Or Administration Fees Paid To Non-Residents
IT-497R4	Overseas Employment Tax Credit

Problems For Self Study (Online)

To provide practice in problem solving, there are Self Study and Supplementary Self Study problems available on MyLab Accounting.

Within the text we have provided an indication of when it would be appropriate to work each Self Study problem. The detailed solutions for Self Study problems can be found in the print and online Study Guide.

We provide the Supplementary Self Study problems for those who would like additional practice in problem solving. The detailed solutions for the Supplementary Self Study problems are available online, not in the Study Guide.

The .PDF file "Self Study Problems for Volume 2" on MyLab contains the following for Chapter 20:

- 7 Self Study problems,
- 3 Supplementary Self Study problems, and
- detailed solutions for the Supplementary Self Study problems.

Assignment Problems

(The solutions for these problems are only available in
the solutions manual that has been provided to your instructor.)

Assignment Problem Twenty - 1

(Part I Tax On Non-Residents)

The following material describes six independent cases which involve U.S. citizens or U.S. companies that have some type of Canadian source income.

Case 1

Flager is a U.S. based manufacturing company. To facilitate Canadian sales, the company ships its product to a warehouse located in Moncton, New Brunswick. The warehouse is rented on a monthly basis, with a clause in the lease that allows cancellation on 90 days notice.

Flager has made an arrangement with Jack Martin to sell their products in the Maritime provinces. Jack works out of an office in his home. He does not have authority to conclude individual sales contracts without approval from the head office in the U.S.

Case 2

Flager is a U.S. based manufacturing company. To facilitate Canadian sales, the company ships its product to a warehouse located in Moncton, New Brunswick. The warehouse is rented on a monthly basis, with a clause in the lease that allows cancellation on 90 days notice.

Flager has made an arrangement with Jack Martin to sell their products in the Maritime provinces. Jack works out of a large office in the warehouse, which takes up a considerable portion of the total floor space. He has the authority to conclude individual sales contracts without approval from the U.S. head office.

Case 3

Genevieve Boulud is a U.S. citizen and a resident of that country. Because she speaks fluent French, her U.S. based employer transfers her to an affiliate's Montreal office for 4 months. She has employment income during this period of $36,000 US, all of which is paid by her U.S. employer.

Case 4

Ruby Nash is a U.S. citizen and a resident of that country. During the current year she accepts an employment contract which requires her to work in Calgary for a period of 3 months. Her salary is $11,000 Cdn per month. The contract is with a Canadian corporation that is responsible for paying the salary.

Case 5

Ada Taylor is a U.S. citizen and a resident of that country. She owns all of the shares in a U.S. based private company that was incorporated in the U.S. This corporation's only activity is buying and operating vacation rental properties in Canada. In order to support her increasingly decadent lifestyle, she sells all of the shares in this company during the current year. She realizes a gain on this sale of $250,000.

Case 6

Cynthia Edwards is a U.S. citizen and a resident of that country. She is a minority shareholder of a Canadian controlled private corporation. This corporation's only activity is buying and operating rental properties in major Canadian cities. Because of her concern about the inflated prices in both Toronto and Vancouver, she sells her shares in the company during the current year. The sale results in a total gain of $785,000.

Required: For each case, indicate whether the non-resident would be subject to Part I Canadian income tax.

Assignment Problem Twenty - 2
(Permanent Establishments)

A U.S. manufacturer of furniture is considering entering the Canadian market. The company will use one of the following approaches to expand its market in Canada:

A. Direct sales to wholesalers by full-time salespeople who report to a sales office in each of three Canadian provinces. The sales offices will co-ordinate marketing and shipping of products from two warehouses located in Canada. However, formal approval of contracts will be administered in the U.S. head office.

B. The sales offices described in Part A would be independent profit centres, with regional credit managers. The two warehouses from which orders are filled will be near the sales offices.

C. Company online sales territory would be expanded to include shipping to Canada.

D. Direct sales to wholesalers by non-exclusive agents. The agents will represent other suppliers as well.

E. Direct sales to wholesalers by full-time salespeople in each of three Canadian provinces. No sales offices will be opened, and the furniture will be shipped from a warehouse in the U.S. Shipment will be made only after a customer's credit and contract are approved by the U.S. head office.

F. Selling furniture to Canadian distributors. The distributors pay the shipping costs on the furniture from the U.S. port or border crossing closest to them.

Required: For each market expansion approach, assess whether or not the U.S. manufacturer will be deemed to have a permanent establishment in Canada. Justify your conclusion and identify any other information required to support your position.

Assignment Problem Twenty - 3
(Part XIII Tax On Non-Residents)

Each of the following independent cases involves a non-resident individual who has Canadian source income during the current year. All amounts are in Canadian dollars.

Case A

Hebert Haman is a resident of a country that does not have a tax treaty with Canada. He owns debt securities issued by a Canadian company that pay interest at a rate that is determined by the profits of the company. During the current year, he receives interest of $1,672 from this investment.

Case B

Kerri Kmetz is a resident of a country that does not have a tax treaty with Canada. During the current year, Kerri receives $6,350 in dividends from a Canadian private company. Kerri owns 20 percent of this company's voting shares.

Case C

Eddy Beale is a resident of the United States. He owns debt securities that were issued by a Canadian public company. The interest rate on the securities is determined by the level of profits earned by the company. During the current year, he receives interest of $1,865.

Case D

Tyrell Rodi is a resident of a country that does not have a tax treaty with Canada. During the current year he earns $1,562 of interest on a savings account in Canada.

Case E

Stephen Chow is a resident of a country that does not have a tax treaty with Canada. He is the owner of a vacation property on Vancouver Island that he rents to Canadian residents. His gross rents for the current year are $56,000. Expenses related to the property, including maximum CCA, are $18,000.

Required: For each of these situations, indicate how the Canadian source income would be taxed under Canadian tax legislation. Explain your conclusion.

Assignment Problem Twenty - 4
(Emigration - Tax Planning)

Harlen Holt, a resident of Nova Scotia, plans to emigrate from Canada on December 31, 2018. On that date, he will own the following assets:

Automobile   Harlen owns a BMW 750 which cost $135,000. Its fair market value on December 31, 2018 is $52,000.

RRSP   The December 31 balance in Harlen's RRSP is $973,000.

Shares In Public Companies   Harlen owns a portfolio of publicly traded shares which have a total adjusted cost base of $460,000. Their fair market value on December 31, 2018 totals $535,000.

Shares In A CCPC   Harlen is a minority shareholder of a CCPC. The CCPC owns and operates five apartment buildings. More than 80 percent of the fair market value of the shares is derived from the value of these buildings. The adjusted cost base of these shares is $287,000 and they have a December 31, 2018 fair market value of $300,000.

Residence   This property was purchased for $430,000, including $150,000 for the land. Its fair market value on December 31, 2018 is $540,000, including $200,000 for the land.

Cottage   This property was purchased for $345,000, including $95,000 for the land. Because a large nearby development has flooded the market with low price units, it has a fair market value on December 31, 2018 of $300,000, including a value for the land of $50,000. Harlen has rented out this property since its purchase and reported a small rental income every year. He has never taken CCA on the property.

Savings Account   The balance in this account is $45,600.

Required:

A. For each of the listed assets, indicate the tax consequences, including any amounts of deferred income, that would result from Harlen's emigration from Canada. Assume that he does not make any elections at the time of his move. Ignore the lifetime capital gains deduction.

B. Under ITA 128.1(4)(d), taxpayers can elect to have a deemed disposition on certain assets where a deemed disposition is not automatic. Determine if Harlen could use this election to minimize his tax obligation at the time of his departure. If he can, calculate the amount of the reduction in Net Income For Tax Purposes that would result from the use of this election.

Assignment Problem Twenty - 5
(Comprehensive Review Problem - Residency Of Individuals)

Note   This problem covers material from several other Chapters of the text.

Elaine Brock is a very successful marketing manager for a multi-national corporation based in the United States. While she has always been a Canadian resident, working out of the corporation's Toronto office, she has been offered a promotion that would require that she relocate to Tampa, Florida. As this is intended to be a permanent change, Elaine has applied for and received the documentation that will allow her to live and work in the United States. She will be moving to Tampa on July 1, 2018.

The corporation provides a $40,000 moving allowance that will be paid by the Toronto office prior to her move. While the corporation does not require documentation of this amount, Elaine estimates that she will incur $32,000 in actual moving costs.

Her common-law partner, Marion Davies, is a very popular singer and songwriter. Marion has also received documentation that will allow her to live and work in the United States. However, she is currently writing songs to complete a new album in her Toronto music studio and is not planning to join Elaine until early 2019.

The state of Florida does not assess a state income tax on its residents, largely because of the high level of tax revenues generated by Disney World. Assume that the marginal federal (U.S.) rate for Elaine would be 35 percent. This rate would only be applied to income earned in the United States.

On July 1, 2018, the date that Elaine departs for Tampa, she owns the following assets:

Description	Date Acquired	Original Cost	Fair Market Value
Registered Retirement Savings Plan	N/A	$235,000	$452,000
Canadian Paintings*	Various	125,000	232,000
Condo Residence In Toronto	2005	360,000	480,000
Huntsville Cottage	2008	225,000	175,000
Automobile	2013	85,000	62,000
Sailboat	2015	28,000	32,000
Shares In Brock Inc., A CCPC	2003	98,000	156,000
Shares In Bank Of Nova Scotia	2011	56,000	85,000

*None of the paintings had an adjusted cost base or a fair market value that was less than $1,000.

Elaine owns 100 percent of the real property. She has rented out the cottage since its purchase and reported a small rental income every year. She has never taken CCA on the property. The loss in value is related only to the land as the waterfront has been severely damaged by flooding. The value of the land has decreased from $130,000 at purchase to $80,000.

While Elaine intends to sell all of the other assets fairly soon, she plans on renting both the Toronto residence and Huntsville cottage for at least 3 years.

Required: Explain to Elaine the tax consequences of her move to the United States. Assume that:

- Elaine ceases to be a Canadian resident when she departs on July 1, 2018.
- Any additional income that Elaine earns in 2018 while a resident of Canada will be taxed in Canada at a combined federal/provincial rate of 47 percent.

In addition, advise Elaine as to any tax planning opportunities to minimize her Canadian Tax Payable for the current and future years. Ignore the lifetime capital gains deduction.

Assignment Problem Twenty - 6
(Foreign Investment Reporting Rules)

The following six Cases are independent. Each involves a Canadian taxpayer who does not hold any other foreign investments. All listed amounts are in Canadian dollars.

For each asset, indicate whether the foreign investment reporting rules are applicable.

1. A cottage in Woodstock, Vermont, purchased for $365,000, with a down payment of $65,000 and the assumption of a $400,000 mortgage. The cottage is used by the taxpayer and his extended family throughout the year.

2. A building in Canton, Ohio, with a cost of $1,560,000, is owned by a Canadian corporation. It is used exclusively to store the Company's products for distribution.

3. Shares in a U.S. public company with a cost of $286,000 and a current fair market value of $72,000. One-half of these shares were purchased in the taxpayer's Canadian brokerage trading account and the other half were purchased in the taxpayer's self-directed RRSP.

4. A U.S. bank account and a mortgage resulting from the sale of a rental property to a U.S. resident three years ago. The original amount of the mortgage was $135,000. However, the amount owing at the beginning of the current year is $68,000. The taxpayer's bank account in a U.S. bank has a balance of between $3,000 and $12,000 throughout the year.

5. A yacht with a cost of $1,300,000 which was purchased and is docked in San Diego, California. The yacht is used by a Vancouver taxpayer as a venue for her lavish parties.

6. A condo in Fort Meyers, Florida is purchased for $860,000. The condo is rented to Canadians for 9 months of the year and used by the taxpayer the remaining 3 months.

Assignment Problem Twenty - 7
(Foreign Source Investment Income And T1135)

Vickey Gateley works and resides in Niagara Falls, Ontario. A long time monarchist, she has developed a well diversified portfolio of stocks of British companies. At December 31, 2018, Ms. Gateley is holding British stocks with a cost of £800,000. She also has a British bank account with a London bank that has a balance that fluctuates between £25,000 and £50,000.

One of her boyfriends lives in Buffalo, New York. Three years ago, when she started spending many of her weekends there, she decided to purchase a condo in Buffalo. Because the building she chose had construction problems, the prices were depressed and she purchased four units for US$200,000 each. She has rented out the other three units.

During 2018, she earned the following amounts of investment income:

Dividends From British Public Corporations	
Net Of 15 Percent Withholding	£54,400
Interest On Bank Account	£ 1,300
Gross Rental Income From Rental Properties	US$86,000
Expenses Of Operating Rental Properties	US$45,000

Other Information

1. Ms. Gateley has left the interest in her British bank account and has not transferred it to Canada.

2. Ms. Gateley believes her condo units are very undervalued. Because of her concern with respect to future recapture, she does not take CCA on her rental properties.

3. The dividends from the British corporations were paid on a quarterly basis.

4. Assume that the exchange rates throughout 2018 were £1 = $1.70 and US$1 = Cdn$1.30.

Required:

A. Indicate the amounts of investment income that would be included in Ms. Gateley's 2018 Net Income For Tax Purposes, as well as any tax credits that would be available to Ms. Gateley to offset this income.

B. Is Ms. Gateley required to file a T1135? If yes, what assets have to be included? The detailed reporting needed on the assets is not required.

Assignment Problem Twenty - 8

(Foreign Source Dividends Received By An Individual)
Matthew Farcus is a Canadian resident who is employed on a full time basis in Ottawa. His net employment income for 2018 is $83,600. In addition he has the following additional sources of income for 2018:

Taxable Capital Gains	$ 6,850
Eligible Dividends From A Canadian Company	17,460
Dividends From Foreign Companies Before Foreign Tax Withheld:	
Foreign Country 1 - GB Ltd. (Before $6,500 Of Withholding)	$26,000
Foreign Country 2 - GR Ltd. (Before $1,350 Of Withholding)	13,500

He has the following deductions available in determining his 2018 Taxable Income:

Net Capital Loss Carry Forward	$13,100
Business Loss Carry Forward	9,850

His only tax credits are the basic personal credit, employment related credits, and any credits related to the dividends received.

Required: Determine Matthew's Federal Tax Payable for the year ending December 31, 2018.

Assignment Problems

Assignment Problem Twenty - 9
(Taxation Of Foreign Affiliate Dividends)

CTP is a Canadian public corporation that has acquired 15 percent of the shares of FTP, a corporation that is established in a foreign country. During the year ending December 31, 2017, FTP earns $20,000 in investment income, $70,000 from an active business and $20,000 of capital gains from the sale of investment assets.

In early 2018, FTP distributes all of its 2017 after tax income as a dividend to its shareholders. FTP has no additional income in 2018.

In both 2017 and 2018, CTP is subject to a federal tax rate of 25 percent.

The following Cases make use of the preceding information. However, the individual Cases make various additional or alternative assumptions.

Required: Provide the information that is requested in each of the following Cases.

Case 1 FTP is a non-controlled foreign affiliate of CTP. Assume that it is located in a country that does not have a tax treaty or a TIEA with Canada, that this country does not assess income taxes on corporations and does not assess withholding taxes on dividend payments to non-residents. What are the tax consequences for CTP resulting from its investment in FTP during 2017 and 2018? Include the increase in Net Income For Tax Purposes and total Taxes Payable for both years in your solution.

Case 2 Assume the same facts as in Case 1, except that FTP is a controlled foreign affiliate of CTP. How would the tax consequences for CTP differ from the tax consequences described in Case 1, for 2017 and 2018?

Case 3 Assume the same facts as in Case 1, except that FTP is not a foreign affiliate of CTP. How would the tax consequences for CTP differ from the tax consequences described in Case 1, for 2017 and 2018?

Case 4 Assume the same facts as in Case 1, except that FTP is located in a country that has a tax treaty with Canada. How would the tax consequences for CTP differ from the tax consequences described in Case 1, for 2017 and 2018?

Case 5 FTP is a non-controlled foreign affiliate of CTP. Assume that FTP is located in a country that has a tax treaty with Canada, that this country assesses income taxes on active business income at a rate of 10 percent and does not assess withholding taxes on dividend payments to non-residents. The income taxes paid by FTP in the foreign country total $7,000 [(10%)($70,000)]. What are the tax consequences for CTP resulting from its investment in FTP during 2017 and 2018?

Case 6 Assume the same facts as in Case 5, except that the foreign country levies the 10 percent income tax on all of FTP's 2017 income. This income tax would total $11,000 [(10%)($110,000)]. In addition, a further 8 percent withholding tax of $7,920 [(8%)($110,000 - $11,000)] was assessed on the dividend paid in 2018. The resulting dividend payment was $91,080 ($110,000 - $11,000 - $7,920). What are the tax consequences for CTP resulting from its investment in FTP during 2017 and 2018?

Assignment Problem Twenty - 10
(Canadian Source Income - Short Cases)
Case A

Mr. Jack Holt is an employee of Stillwell Industries, an American manufacturing Company. During the period June 15 through December 6 of the current year, Mr. Holt worked in Canada providing technical assistance to a Canadian subsidiary of Stillwell Industries. His salary was U.S. $5,500 per month. During the period that Mr. Holt was in Canada, Stillwell Industries continued to deposit his salary into his normal U.S. bank account. Both his salary for this period and all of his related travelling expenses were billed to the Canadian subsidiary.

Required: Explain Mr. Holt's tax position.

Case B

Mr. John McQueen was for many years a resident of Ontario. On his retirement ten years ago, he returned to his native Scotland and has not since returned to Canada. However, he has retained considerable investments in Canada, as follows:

- **Common Stocks** He has a large portfolio of common stocks that are registered in the name of his Toronto broker. The broker receives all dividends and periodically sends a cheque to Mr. McQueen in Scotland.

- **Mortgage Portfolio** He has a large portfolio of second mortgages. All collections on these mortgages are made by a Toronto law firm and are deposited into a Toronto bank account in the name of Mr. McQueen.

Required: Who is responsible for tax withholdings under Part XIII of the *Income Tax Act,* and on which amounts must withholdings be made?

Case C

Hotels International is a U.S. corporation with hotel properties throughout the world. It has recently developed a property in Nova Scotia that will open during the current year. A long-term management lease has been signed with Hotel Operators Ltd., a Canadian company specializing in the management of hotels. Under the terms of the lease, Hotel Operators Ltd. will pay all of the operating expenses of the hotel and, in addition, make an annual lease payment of $1,250,000 to the American owners of the new hotel.

Required: Will the U.S. corporation, Hotels International, be subject to Canadian income taxes on the annual lease payment, and, if so, to what extent?

Case D

The Maple Company, a public company resident in Canada, has 2,400,000 shares of its no par common stock outstanding. Sixty percent of these shares are owned by its American parent, the Condor Company. The remaining shares are owned by Canadian residents. In addition to the common shares, the Condor Company holds all of an outstanding issue of Maple Company debenture bonds. Two of the five directors of the Maple Company are Canadian residents, while the remaining three are residents of the United States. During the current year, the Maple Company paid a dividend of $1 per share on its common stock and interest of $900,000 on its outstanding debenture bonds.

Required: Calculate the amount of Part XIII taxes to be withheld by the Maple Company with respect to the interest and dividend payments to its American parent.

CHAPTER 21

GST/HST

Introduction

Background

Introduction Of The GST

21-1.   After significant controversy, a goods and services tax (GST, hereafter) was introduced in Canada on January 1, 1991. This broadly based, multi-stage transaction tax replaced the more narrowly focused federal sales tax on manufactured goods. The GST was originally introduced at a rate of 7 percent. However, this rate was reduced to 6 percent in 2006, with a further reduction to 5 percent on January 1, 2008. There have been no other GST rate changes implemented or proposed since that date.

21-2.   The concept underlying this tax was that it would be applied in an even-handed manner to all goods and service transactions. However, tax policy is often more influenced by political considerations than it is by economic logic. As a result, by the time the tax was actually introduced, it was burdened by a complex web of exemptions and modifications that significantly increased the cost of compliance.

21-3.   The developers of this tax also hoped that the provinces would be willing to amalgamate their provincial sales taxes with the federal GST in order to provide taxpayers with a uniform national approach to the taxation of goods and service transactions. This could have resulted in very substantial savings in both compliance costs and administrative costs. This, however, did not happen.

21-4.   Only the province of Quebec showed any early signs of cooperation in this area. The provinces of Alberta, British Columbia, and Ontario initially took legal action against the federal government, claiming that the GST was unconstitutional. In 1992, Quebec introduced the Quebec Sales Tax (QST), a similar, but not identical transaction tax. As part of this process, it was agreed that both the QST and all GST collected in Quebec would be administered by the province of Quebec.

Harmonized Sales Tax (HST)

21-5.   The GST situation did not change until 1997, when three of the Atlantic provinces, New Brunswick, Nova Scotia, and Newfoundland implemented a harmonized sales tax (HST, hereafter) that contained both a federal and a provincial tax component. In the harmonization process, these provinces eliminated their separate provincial sales taxes.

21-6.   The harmonized sales tax is, in effect, a combination of the 5 percent GST rate and a provincial rate that varies from 8 to 10 percent. This gives overall rates of 13 to 15 percent. Since its initial introduction in New Brunswick, Nova Scotia, and Newfoundland, both Ontario and Prince Edward have become participants in the system. British Columbia joined and then, after a bitterly fought referendum, returned to a GST/PST system.

21-7.   A major advantage of the HST system is that it is administered by the federal government, eliminating the need for the dual administrative system that is required in those provinces that collect both GST and PST. This does not, however, eliminate flexibility at the provincial level. This is evidenced by the differences in the provincial tax component rate, as well as by different rebates on the provincial portion of the HST for a number of items.

The Current Situation

21-8.   These developments have left Canada with a somewhat cluttered transaction tax landscape. The various arrangements are summarized in the following Figure 21-1:

Figure 21 - 1 Transaction Taxes In Canada As At January 1, 2018			
Type Of Tax	**Province**	**Rates**	**Tax Administration**
GST Only	Alberta	5% + 0%	Federal
GST and PST	British Columbia	5% + 7%	Federal and Provincial
	Manitoba	5% + 8%	Federal and Provincial
	Saskatchewan	5% + 6%	Federal and Provincial
HST	New Brunswick	15%	Federal
	Newfoundland	15%	Federal
	Nova Scotia	15%	Federal
	Ontario	13%	Federal
	Prince Edward Island	15%	Federal
GST and QST	Quebec	5% + 9.975%	Provincial

21-9.   This table illustrates some of the complexity of the current situation resulting from the use of different rates and regimes applying those rates. This is further complicated by the fact that in the HST provinces, rebates of the provincial portion of the tax are provided on some items in some provinces, but not others.

21-10.   It is obvious that the transaction tax situation in Canada is extremely complex due to the use of different systems (GST only, GST plus PST, and HST), the use of different provincial rates, and the use of different provincial rebates on various classes of goods. It is not surprising that this can result in very high compliance costs for businesses.

How This Text Deals With This Complexity

21-11.   It is clearly not appropriate in a general textbook on taxation to attempt detailed coverage of the GST and HST procedures applicable in each province. It is likely that an attempt to do this would require a completely separate third volume.

21-12.   The GST is applicable to all provinces either as a separate sales tax or as a component of HST. Fortunately, many of the provisions for the HST are identical to those for the GST. This means that, in general, the concepts and procedures involved are the same for both the GST and the HST.

21-13.   Given this situation, our discussion and examples will focus on one of two scenarios:

- Situations where only the GST is applicable. Alberta is the only province where this situation applies. However, it is also applicable in the three territorial jurisdictions.

- Situations where the HST is applicable.

21-14.   We will not use examples involving those provinces where both GST and PST are in effect, nor will attention be given to the unique situation in Quebec.

21-15.   With the exceptions of a brief Chapter 3 discussion of the GST component of employee benefits and a limited presentation on the impact of the GST on business income, all of our material on GST is included in this Chapter. This includes consideration of the Employee And Partner GST Rebate, as well as the application of GST to the purchase and sale of capital assets. We have also included GST procedures and administration in this chapter, rather than in Chapter 2.

21-16.   We view this as an extremely important subject. The great majority of businesses in Canada file GST returns. In addition, many organizations, such as charities and unincorporated businesses must file GST returns, even though they are not required to file income tax returns. Given the pervasiveness of this tax and the amounts that can be involved, it is our view that some understanding of its application is an essential component of the knowledge base of every professional accountant and businessperson.

Transaction Tax Concepts

General Description

21-17.   While taxes like the GST and HST are often referred to as commodity taxes, the title is not appropriate as the term commodity does not include services. When both goods and services are subject to a tax, what we are really concerned with is the taxation of transactions as opposed to the taxation of income.

21-18.   In both Canada and the U.S., the bulk of federal tax revenues has traditionally been generated by taxes on personal and corporate income. However, transaction taxes have been widely used in both countries at the provincial or state level. In addition, there has been a worldwide trend towards increased use of transaction taxes, with many industrialized countries now relying heavily on this type of taxation.

21-19.   Some of the factors that support the increased use of transaction taxes are as follows:

- **Simplicity**   Transaction taxes are easy to administer and collect. No forms are required from individuals paying the tax and, if the individual wishes to acquire a particular good or service, it is difficult to legally evade payment.

- **Incentives To Work**   An often cited disadvantage of income taxes is that they can discourage individual initiative to work and invest. Transaction taxes do not have this characteristic.

- **Consistency**   Transaction taxes avoid the fluctuating income and family unit problems that are associated with progressive income tax systems.

- **Keeping The Tax Revenues In Canada**   While some types of income can be moved out of Canada, resulting in the related taxes being paid in a different jurisdiction, taxes on Canadian transactions remain with Canadian taxing entities.

21-20.   Given these advantages for transaction taxes, why is income taxation still used? The answer to this question largely involves the question of fairness. In general, transaction taxes relate to consumption. When this is combined with the fact that lower income individuals usually spend a larger portion of their total income on consumption, transaction taxes are assessed at higher effective rates on individuals with lower incomes. Using more technical terminology, transaction taxes are usually regressive.

21-21.   This is in conflict with the widely held belief that fairness requires that individuals with higher incomes should have their income taxed at higher average rates. This goal is best accomplished through the continued use of a progressive income tax system.

21-22.   The federal government has compensated for the regressive nature of the GST by providing a GST tax credit that is available to low income individuals who file income tax returns. Similar provisions are available at the provincial level where HST is applicable.

21-23.   There are a number of different ways in which transaction taxes can be applied. These alternatives will be given consideration in the next section of this Chapter.

Example

21-24.   In discussing the various approaches that can be used in the application of transaction taxes, a simple example is useful. Such an example is diagramed in Figure 21-2. As can be seen in Figure 21-2, our example involves a manufacturer who produces 1,000 units of product at a cost of $4 of raw materials per unit, a total cost of $4,000. All of the 1,000 units are sold to a wholesaler for $10 per unit. The wholesaler then sells 800 of the units to a retailer for $25 per unit. The retailer, in turn, sells 500 of the units to a consumer for $50 per unit.

Figure 21 - 2
Transaction Tax Example

Cost = $4,000 → Manufacturer

[(1,000)($10)] = $10,000 → Wholesaler

[(800)($25)] = $20,000 → Retailer

[(500)($50)] = $25,000 → Consumer

Single Stage Transaction Taxes - Retail Sales Tax

21-25.   A single stage transaction tax could be applied at any level in this example. The most common type of single stage tax is applied at the consumer level. This would be the familiar retail sales tax that is collected in several Canadian provinces. For example, if the transactions depicted in Figure 21-2 took place in Manitoba, an 8 percent retail sales tax would be assessed on the $25,000 price that the retailer charged the consumer, resulting in a provincial sales tax of $2,000 being paid by the consumer.

21-26.   The consumer level is probably the most appropriate level to apply a single stage transaction tax. The tax is visible and its incidence is relatively clear. In contrast, when a wholesale or manufacturer's tax is used, complications can arise when business relationships are formed that blur the lines between the manufacturing, wholesale, and retail levels. This can occur with vertical integration, and necessitates estimates or notional values for transfers between the manufacturing, wholesale, or retail levels of an organization.

Multi-Stage Transaction Taxes - Turnover Tax

21-27.   Again referring to Figure 21-2, it would be possible to impose a multi-stage transaction tax at any combination of the various levels depicted. For example, the tax could be applied at the wholesale and retail levels, without application at the manufacturing level. Alternatively, the manufacturing and wholesale levels could be taxed without application at the retail level. An extension of this taxation to all levels is sometimes referred to as a turnover tax, with transactions being taxed at all levels in the distribution chain.

21-28.   The problem with such a turnover tax is that it involves the pyramiding of taxes when there is no credit for taxes paid earlier in the chain. For example, if there was a 5 percent turnover tax in place, the manufacturer in Figure 21-2 would charge the wholesaler $10.50 per unit. When the wholesaler applies his normal markup of 250 percent of cost ($25 ÷ $10), the price would be $26.25 per unit [($10.50)(2.5)]. Of this $26.25, $0.025 [($0.50)(5%)] would represent a tax on the tax that was charged to the wholesaler by the manufacturer. If the 5 percent tax was also applied to the transfers to the retailer and to the ultimate consumer, there would be further applications of tax on previously assessed amounts of tax. Given this pyramiding problem, turnover taxes are not widely used.

Value Added Tax (VAT)
Types
21-29.   VATs are multi-stage transaction taxes that can be assessed in two basic ways:

Accounts-Based Method   In this approach, the tax is assessed on the basis of the value added at each level of the business process. It is usually based on some type of accounting based determination of income (e.g., value added).

Invoice-Credit Method   In this approach, tax is assessed on gross sales. The taxpayer is then provided with a credit based on purchases made. No accounting based determination of income is required.

21-30.   These two approaches will be illustrated in the material which follows.

Accounts-Based VAT
21-31.   Internationally, the most common type of VAT uses the accounts-based method. Using this method, transactions are taxed at each level in the distribution chain. Using whatever rate is established, the VAT is applied to the value added by the business to goods and services, rather than to the gross sales of the business.

21-32.   If we assume a 5 percent rate of tax in the example presented in Figure 21-2, this method would require the raw materials supplier to charge tax on his sale price of $4 per unit. The manufacturer would then charge tax on the difference between the sales price of $10 per unit sold and the related input costs of $4 per unit sold. In corresponding fashion, the wholesaler would charge the 5 percent on the difference between the manufacturer's invoice of $10 per unit sold and the wholesale price of $25 per unit sold (i.e., the value added by the wholesaler). Finally, the retailer would charge the VAT on the difference between the retail price of $50 per unit sold and the wholesaler's price of $25 per unit sold. The total tax calculation is as follows:

Raw Materials [(5%)(1,000)($4)]	$ 200
Manufacturer To Wholesaler [(5%)(1,000)($10 - $4)]	300
Wholesaler To Retailer [(5%)(800)($25 - $10)]	600
Retailer To Consumer [(5%)(500)($50 - $25)]	625
Total Value Added Tax	$1,725

Invoice-Credit VAT
21-33.   This is the approach that is used in Canada for GST/HST calculations. Under this approach, each vendor charges tax on the full selling price. This tax is then offset by a credit for the tax that was paid on the costs incurred by the business (these are referred to as input tax credits).

21-34.   Continuing to assume a 5 percent rate of tax is applied to our basic example from Figure 21-2, the invoice-credit VAT calculations would be as follows:

Raw Materials Supplier

GST Collected [(5%)(1,000)($4)] (No Input Tax Credits)	$200
Net GST Payable	$200

Manufacturer

GST Collected [(5%)(1,000)($10)]	$500
GST Paid On Costs = Input Tax Credits [(5%)(1,000)($4)]	(200)
Net GST Payable	$300

Wholesaler

GST Collected [(5%)(800)($25)]	$1,000
GST Paid On Costs = Input Tax Credits [(5%)(1,000)($10)]	(500)
Net GST Payable	$ 500

Retailer

GST Collected [(5%)(500)($50)]	$1,250
GST Paid On Costs = Input Tax Credits [(5%)(800)($25)]	(1,000)
Net GST Payable	$ 250

Net Tax - Raw Materials Supplier	$ 200
Net Tax - Manufacturer	300
Net Tax - Wholesaler	500
Net Tax - Retailer	250
Total Net Tax - All Levels	$1,250

Comparison

21-35.   The overall results for the two approaches is as follows:

Total Tax - Accounts-Based VAT	$1,725
Total Net Tax - Invoice-Credit VAT	(1,250)
Difference	$ 475

21-36.   In this example, using the invoice-credit approach results in less tax being paid. The reason for this is that, when the invoice-credit approach is used, the enterprise receives tax credits for all purchases, without regard to whether or not the goods are sold. In this example, at both the wholesale and retail levels, purchases exceed sales. The tax credits are claimed from the government on units purchased, while the taxes collected are paid to the government on units sold. This means that enterprises benefit from having their purchases exceed their sales. In contrast, under an accounts-based VAT system, the tax to be paid is based on units sold and no benefit is received for taxes paid on units that are still on hand.

21-37.   In general, if purchases and sales are equal, the tax that is assessed under an invoice-credit VAT system is similar to that assessed under an accounts-based VAT system. This can be seen at the manufacturer level in our example. In the case of the manufacturer, the units purchased and sold were equal. For this enterprise, the two VAT approaches resulted in exactly the same net tax ($300).

21-38.   Given that the accounts-based VAT approach is more commonly used on a world-wide basis, there is some question as to why Canada chose to use the alternative invoice-credit approach. While background documents on the GST legislation do not provide a direct answer to this question, it would appear that the major advantage of the invoice-credit approach is that it does not rely on an accounting determination of value added. The tax is charged on all taxable goods sold, with input tax credits available for taxes paid on all expenditures for inputs used in commercial activities. The fact that there is no matching requirement avoids the controversies that can arise when various types of cost matching and allocation procedures are required.

21-39.   It can also be argued that the invoice-credit approach is more equitable as it is more closely associated with actual cash flows than would be the case with an accounts-based system. The cash required to pay transaction taxes is based on purchases, without regard to when these inputs result in sales. As the invoice-credit approach provides for credits based on purchases, it can be argued that this approach is fairer to the enterprises that are involved in the production/distribution chain.

21-40.   There is a further question of why the government chose to use a multi-stage tax, rather than implementing a less complex, single stage, federal sales tax at the retail level. An often cited reason is related to tighter administration and control. With the multi-stage approach, a vendor does not have to determine whether or not customers of particular goods and services are exempt because they are one or more steps away from the retail or final consumption level.

21-41.   An additional reason for using a multi-stage tax is that it is applied further up the distribution chain. This, of course, means that the tax revenues accrue to the government at an earlier point in time.

Exercise Twenty-One - 1

Subject: Alternative VAT Approaches

During a taxation period, Darvin Wholesalers purchased merchandise for $233,000. Merchandise sales during this period totalled $416,000 and the cost of the merchandise sold was $264,000. Ignoring all other costs incurred by Darvin and assuming a rate of 5 percent, how much tax would be paid by Darvin under an account-based VAT system and, alternatively, under an invoice-credit VAT system?

SOLUTION available in print and online Study Guide.

We suggest you work Self Study Problem Twenty-One-1 at this point.

Liability For GST/HST

Basic Charging Provision

21-42.   The basic charging provision for GST is found in the *Excise Tax Act* (ETA). It is as follows:

> **ETA 165(1)   Imposition of goods and services tax —** Subject to this Part, every recipient of a taxable supply made in Canada shall pay to Her Majesty in right of Canada tax in respect of the supply calculated at the rate of 5% on the value of the consideration for the supply. [**Byrd/Chen Note** Additional legislation changes this rate to the appropriate rate in those provinces where the HST has been adopted.]

21-43.   In order to understand this charging provision, it will be necessary to give attention to the concept of supply. We will cover this in the next section of this chapter.

21-44.   Note that the tax is assessed on the recipient of, rather than the provider of, taxable supplies. As we shall find in a later section of this Chapter, responsibility for collection of the tax is with the provider of the taxable supplies (the GST registrant).

The Concept Of Supply

21-45.   The term "goods and services tax" implies that it is a tax that is applied to goods and services or, more specifically, transactions that involve the provision of goods and services. The term that is used by the *Excise Tax Act* in referring to such transactions is "supply". This term is defined in the *Act* as follows:

> **ETA 123(1)   Supply** means the provision of property or a service in any manner, including sale, transfer, barter, exchange, licence, rental, lease, gift or disposition.

21-46.   While this definition includes most of the items that we would consider to be revenues under GAAP, it is actually a much broader term. It would include all of the following:

- the sale, rental, or transfer of goods,
- the rendering of services,
- licensing arrangements for copyrights or patents,
- the lease, sale, or other transfer of real property, and
- barter transactions or gifts.

Supply Categories

NOTE ON GST/HST DIFFERENCES   While the HST provinces use the same categories of supply that are used in the federal GST legislation, some fully taxable items are given point-of-sale rebates for the provincial component of the HST (e.g., Ontario provides an 8 percent point-of-sale HST rebate for children's clothing). In effect, purchasers pay only the federal GST rate of 5 percent on these items.

A full description of these differences for all of the HST provinces goes beyond the scope of this text. Given this, the examples that are described in the following discussion include items that fall into the fully taxable category under the federal GST legislation. Because of provincial rebates in the HST provinces, purchasers of some of these items will not pay the full HST rate.

Taxable Supplies

General Rules

21-47.   The *Excise Tax Act* defines taxable supplies as follows:

ETA 123(1)   Taxable supply means a supply that is made in the course of a commercial activity.

21-48.   Expanding on this definition, commercial activity is defined in the *Excise Tax Act* as follows:

ETA 123(1)   Commercial Activity of a person means

(a) a business carried on by the person (other than a business carried on without a reasonable expectation of profit by an individual, a personal trust or a partnership, all of the members of which are individuals), except to the extent to which the business involves the making of exempt supplies by the person,

(b) an adventure or concern of the person in the nature of trade (other than an adventure or concern engaged in without a reasonable expectation of profit by an individual, a personal trust or a partnership, all of the members of which are individuals), except to the extent to which the adventure or concern involves the making of exempt supplies by the person, [**Byrd/Chen Note** In somewhat simplified terms, an adventure or concern in the nature of trade is a one-shot business venture, as opposed to an ongoing activity.] and

(c) the making of a supply (other than an exempt supply) by the person of real property of the person, including anything done by the person in the course of or in connection with the making of the supply.

21-49.   As used here, the term business has the following meaning:

ETA 123(1)   Business includes a profession, calling, trade, manufacture or undertaking of any kind whatever, whether the activity or undertaking is engaged in for profit, and any activity engaged in on a regular or continuous basis that involves the supply of property by way of lease, licence or similar arrangement, but does not include an office or employment;

21-50.   Stated in practical, every-day language, this says that if you are providing goods or services in the course of business activity, or if you selling or leasing real property, you are providing taxable supplies unless:

- the business does not have a reasonable expectation of profit (this criterion only applies to businesses run by individuals, certain partnerships, or certain trusts);
- the supplies are exempt supplies; or
- the services are employment services.

21-51. Taxable supplies fall into two categories. The first category is supplies that we will refer to as fully taxable supplies. The second category is supplies that are zero-rated.

Fully Taxable Supplies

21-52. Fully taxable supplies are those that are taxed at the 5 percent federal GST rate or the appropriate HST rate (13 or 15 percent). Examples of fully taxable supplies include:

- transportation in Canada,
- restaurant meals and beverages,
- clothing and footwear,
- furniture,
- admissions to concerts, athletic and other events
- contractors' services,
- legal and accounting fees,
- haircuts, and
- cleaning services.

Zero-Rated Supplies

21-53. The *Excise Tax Act* provides a list of taxable supplies that are designated as zero-rated. While these supplies are said to be taxable, they are taxed at zero percent, rather than the regular GST or HST rate.

21-54. At first glance, this concept seems a bit senseless in that there is no tax charged on either zero-rated supplies or exempt supplies. However, an important difference exists. Because zero-rated supplies are considered to be taxable supplies, the providers of such supplies can recover the GST/HST paid on business purchases as input tax credits. In contrast, providers of exempt supplies are not eligible for input tax credits (see Paragraph 21-103).

21-55. In addition, as zero-rated supplies are considered taxable at a rate of zero percent, they are included in the threshold amounts for determining the filing frequency of a registrant's GST or HST returns. This is covered beginning in Paragraph 21-134.

21-56. Common items included in the category of zero-rated supplies are as follows:

- prescription drugs,
- medical devices such as wheelchairs, eye glasses, canes, hospital beds, and artificial limbs,
- basic groceries,
- most agricultural and fishing products,
- goods and services exported from Canada, and
- foreign travel and transportation services (see following Paragraph).

21-57. Some elaboration is required for the meaning of foreign travel. Surface travel by ship, bus, or train is zero-rated when the origin or termination point is outside Canada (e.g., a train trip to the U.S. is zero-rated). Domestic surface travel is fully taxable.

21-58. In the case of air travel, the GST/HST rules can be complicated. International air travel is zero-rated only when flights are deemed to be outside of continental North America, not just outside of Canada. As an example of the possible complications, this broader definition can make Canadian air travel to and from the United States fully taxable.

Exempt Supplies

21-59. As was the case with zero-rated supplies, the *Excise Tax Act* provides a list of supplies that are exempt from GST. Persons providing exempt supplies do not collect GST/HST and are not eligible for input tax credits for GST/HST paid on the related purchases. As we shall see when we discuss input tax credits, this means that suppliers of exempt supplies pay GST/HST that is not refundable to them on the fully taxable goods and services required to operate their business. As a consequence, the non-recoverable GST/HST paid is a cost of doing business that is likely to be passed on to customers in the form of higher prices.

21-60.   Some common items that are included in the category of exempt supplies are as follows:

- basic health care and dental services (which does not include cosmetic surgery),
- financial services provided to Canadian residents,
- sales of used residential housing and long-term residential rents (e.g., rentals for more than 30 days),
- most land sold by individuals where the land was not used in a business,
- educational courses leading to certificates or diplomas, tutoring for credit courses, and music lessons,
- child or personal care services, and
- a wide variety of services provided by charities, not-for-profit, and government organizations (see discussion under Specific Applications at Paragraph 21-188).

Applying the GST/HST Rate

Place Of Supply

The Problem

21-61.   The rate at which GST or HST will be applied varies from a low of 5 percent in a province where only the GST is applicable (e.g., Alberta), to a high of 15 percent under the HST regime (e.g., Nova Scotia). The size of this range makes the question of which rate should be applied to a particular supply of goods and services a significant issue.

21-62.   A further question relates to whether the tax should be assessed on the basis of the location of the registrant providing the supply or, alternatively, the location of the recipient of the supply. Prior to 2010, the place of supply rules were mostly based on the location of the supplier. The current rules rely more heavily on where the recipient is located. This means that a supplier must be able to deal with the transaction taxes in any province his goods and services are delivered to, as well as the transaction taxes in the province where he is located.

21-63.   There are, of course, many complications in the application of these rules. What follows provides only a basic overview of how these rules work.

Tangible Goods

21-64.   The rules for tangible goods are relatively straightforward. A GST registrant will calculate taxes on the basis of the rules that are in effect in the province where the goods are delivered. The following example illustrates the application of this approach.

> **EXAMPLE**   An Ontario HST registrant sells shirts online and ships them to purchasers in Ontario, Prince Edward Island, Alberta and Quebec.
>
> **ANALYSIS**   The GST/HST rate charged on the sales will vary as follows:
>
> - Ontario recipient - HST will be charged at 13 percent.
>
> - Prince Edward Island recipient - HST will be charged at 15 percent.
>
> - Alberta recipient - only GST at 5 percent will be charged.
>
> - Quebec recipient - only GST at 5 percent will be charged. This example makes the point that Quebec is using a separate transaction tax (QST), rather than harmonizing with the federal GST. If the Ontario registrant was a QST registrant as well, QST would also be charged on this sale. Note that Quebec consumers are required to voluntarily pay the relevant QST to Revenu Quebec on purchases shipped from outside Quebec that do not have QST charged. It is likely that this liability frequently remains unpaid as many Quebec consumers are unaware of this requirement.

Real Property

21-65.   As real property cannot be moved across provincial boundaries, there are few complications in this area. The GST or HST will be assessed on the basis of the rules in effect in the province where the real property is located. For example, on a taxable sale of real property in Ontario, HST is applicable at 13 percent regardless of where the vendor resides.

Services

21-66.   This area has the most complications in terms of the place of supply rules. The basic idea is that the place of supply is the province where the services are used.

EXAMPLE   A professor at a Manitoba university is also a freelance editor of a widely used accounting text. He does his editing in his office in Winnipeg. His editing fees are consistently in excess of $50,000 per year. Because of this, he is a GST registrant (Manitoba does not participate in the HST program). His work is sent to the Toronto office of the publisher and cheques for his fees are issued from that office.

ANALYSIS   As the services are "used" in Ontario, the editor would bill HST at 13 percent.

Applying The Rate

Consideration Received

21-67.   To determine the amount of GST or HST to be charged, the appropriate rate is applied to the amount of consideration received in return for the delivery of taxable supplies. In most cases, the consideration will be monetary and the amount to be recorded is obvious. If the consideration is non-monetary (e.g., a barter transaction), GST/HST is still applicable. In this case, however, an estimate will have to be made of the fair market value of the consideration received.

21-68.   The amount of consideration to be used for purposes of calculating the GST/HST includes all non-refundable federal taxes, provincial taxes other than retail sales taxes, and duties and fees that are imposed on either the supplier or recipient in respect of the property or services supplied.

Effect Of Trade-Ins

21-69.   Where a good owned by an entity that is not registered for GST/HST is traded in towards the supply of a new good, GST/HST is only required to be levied on the net amount after the trade-in. These types of transactions are most often seen in the automotive business, where used cars are traded in when purchasing a newer automobile.

EXAMPLE   John Bailey, a resident of Alberta, is acquiring a new Volvo at a cost of $52,000. He is given a trade-in allowance of $21,000 on his old vehicle.

ANALYSIS   The applicable GST would be $1,550 [(5%)($52,000 - $21,000)].

Collection And Remittance Of GST/HST

21-70.   As you are aware, income taxes are collected from the same person on whom the tax is assessed. An individual will calculate his Tax Payable by applying the appropriate rates to his Taxable Income. This same individual is also responsible for the payment of this tax.

21-71.   The situation is different with GST/HST. We noted previously that the basic GST/HST charging provision assesses the tax on the recipient of the taxable supply. However, the basic responsibility for the collection and remittance of the GST/HST falls on the provider of the taxable supply. This approach is implemented by requiring providers of taxable supplies to become GST registrants. Registration requirements are discussed in the section which follows.

21-72.   As an example of this process, consider a situation where a retailer is featuring a GST holiday.

EXAMPLE   An Alberta store advertises a GST holiday, indicating that merchandise can be purchased without paying the GST. A customer pays the marked price of $2,500 for a new freezer and no additional amount is added for GST.

ANALYSIS   From the customer's point of view, he has not paid the GST. However, the store will have to treat the $2,500 as a GST inclusive amount. For GST purposes, the $2,500 received was made up of $2,380.95 ($2,500 ÷ 105%) for the freezer and GST of $119.05 [(5%)($2,380.95)]. The store must include the GST received of $119.05 in its GST return.

21-73.   You should note that, while the vendor is responsible for the collection of GST/HST, this does not relieve the purchaser of the responsibility for payment. If a vendor fails to collect the tax, the CRA can assess the purchaser for the unremitted amount. This, however, would be a fairly rare procedure.

Registration

Meaning Of Person For GST/HST

21-74.   For GST/HST purposes, the *Excise Tax Act* defines a person as follows:

ETA 123(1)   **Person** means an individual, a partnership, a corporation, the estate of a deceased individual, a trust, or a body that is a society, union, club, association, commission or other organization of any kind.

21-75.   Note that this definition is broader than the one that is included in the *Income Tax Act*. For income tax purposes, the term "person" includes only individuals, corporations, and trusts. Of importance here is the fact that the GST definition includes unincorporated businesses, partnerships, and not-for profit organizations.

Who Must Register

Basic Requirement

21-76.   As we have previously indicated, the collection of GST/HST is administered through a registration requirement for providers of taxable supplies. This requirement is as follows:

ETA 240(1)   Every person who makes a taxable supply in Canada in the course of a commercial activity engaged in by the person in Canada is required to be registered for the purposes of this Part, except where

(a) the person is a small supplier;
(b) the only commercial activity of the person is the making of supplies of real property by way of sale otherwise than in the course of a business; or
(c) the person is a non-resident person who does not carry on any business in Canada.

21-77.   This requirement contains several terms and concepts that require further elaboration. We will deal with these items in the section which follows.

Commercial Activity - Inclusions

21-78.   ETA 240(1) requires registration only when "taxable supplies" are delivered in the course of "commercial activity". We have previously covered both of these definitions in our discussion of taxable supplies beginning in Paragraph 21-47.

21-79.   In simple terms, any person who provides non-exempt goods or services, in the course of a business activity, is required to register for the GST/HST unless that person is covered by one of the exceptions listed in ETA 240(1).

Commercial Activity - Exclusions

21-80.   There are several activities that might be considered commercial activity in a non-GST context that are excluded in the preceding definitions. For example, the following are not considered commercial activities for GST purposes:

- business activity that is carried on by an individual without a reasonable expectation of profit
- the provision of exempt supplies (e.g., child care services)
- the provision of employment services

21-81.   Registration for GST/HST is not required or permitted if a person is involved solely in an excluded activity.

Exemption For Non-Residents

21-82.   The ETA 240(1) requirement to register, in general excludes non-residents. The major exception to this would be when a non-resident person carries on business in Canada. This exception would apply, without regard to whether the business is carried on through a permanent establishment. An additional exception could arise in situations where a non-resident has registered for GST/HST on a voluntary basis.

21-83.   In general, resident is defined for GST/HST purposes in the same manner that it is defined for income tax purposes. We would refer you to Chapter 1 for a discussion of the issues associated with residence determination.

Exemption For Small Suppliers

Last Four Calendar Quarters Test (Cumulative)

21-84.   The ETA 240(1) registration requirement indicates that it is not applicable to "small suppliers". The idea here is that a small supplier is a person whose delivery of taxable supplies, including those of associated businesses, is less than $30,000 per year. This provision is intended to provide compliance relief for the operators of very small businesses.

21-85.   The basic test for qualification as a small supplier is based on calendar year quarters (i.e., January to March, April to June, July to September, and October to December). Under this test, an entity qualifies as a small supplier in the current quarter and the month following the current quarter if the entity and its associated entities did not have cumulative taxable supplies exceeding $30,000 during the four calendar quarters preceding the current quarter.

21-86.   If taxable supplies accumulate to $30,000 in any period consisting of two to four quarters (they do not have to be in the same calendar year), the entity ceases to be a small supplier at the end of the month following the quarter in which the $30,000 limit was exceeded. The deemed date of registration would be the day the first supply (sale) was made after ceasing to be a small supplier. The supplier must formally register within 29 days from the deemed registration day.

> **EXAMPLE**   Supplier A opened for business on January 1, 2018, and earned the following revenues from taxable supplies during the year:

Quarter	Months	Taxable Supplies
One	January to March	$ 7,000
Two	April to June	8,000
Three	July to September	20,000
Four	October to December	9,000
Total		$44,000

> **ANALYSIS**   Supplier A's revenues accumulate to more than $30,000 in the third quarter of 2018 ($7,000 + $8,000 + $20,000 = $35,000). This means that Supplier A is required to collect GST/HST starting on November 1, 2018, which is one month after the end of the July to September quarter. The deemed registration day is the day of the first sale on or after November 1, 2018. Formal registration is required within 29 days of the deemed registration day.

Calendar Quarter Test (> $30,000 In Single Quarter)

21-87.   An alternative to the "last four calendar quarters" test is the "calendar quarter test", where the $30,000 threshold is exceeded in a single calendar quarter. When a sale results in the $30,000 threshold being exceeded in a single quarter, the person is immediately deemed a registrant and must collect GST/HST on the supply (sale) that caused the limit to be exceeded, even though they are not yet registered. The supplier must formally register within 29 days from the deemed registration day.

> **EXAMPLE**   Supplier B started in business on January 1, 2018. The business is an art gallery and Supplier B had only two sales in 2018, one for $39,000 on May 15 and the other for $5,000 on August 28.
>
> | Quarter | Months | Taxable Supplies |
> |---------|--------|-----------------:|
> | One | January to March | Nil |
> | Two | April to June (May 15) | $39,000 |
> | Three | July to September (August 28) | 5,000 |
> | Four | October to December | Nil |
> | Total | | $44,000 |
>
> **ANALYSIS**   Supplier B would be deemed a registrant as of the May 15 sale, reflecting the fact that this single sale pushes the sales for that quarter past the $30,000 threshold amount. Starting with that sale, GST/HST should be collected on all taxable supplies made. While the collection of GST/HST is required starting on the deemed registration day, Supplier B must formally register within 29 days.

21-88.   In reviewing the two preceding examples, note that Supplier A and Supplier B each earned taxable revenue of $44,000 in the four calendar quarters for 2018. Supplier B, however, exceeded the $30,000 threshold in Quarter Two. This results in Supplier B being deemed to be registered starting with the May 15 transaction. In contrast, Supplier A will not have to start collecting GST/HST until November 1, 2018 using the last four calendar quarters test.

Exercise Twenty-One - 2

Subject: Requirement To Register

Ms. Sharon Salome and Mr. Rock Laughton begin separate businesses on April 1, 2018. The quarterly sales of taxable items for both businesses are as follows:

Calendar Quarter	Sharon Salome	Rock Laughton
April To June, 2018	$10,000	$ 8,000
July To September, 2018	4,000	13,000
October To December, 2018	35,000	4,000
January To March, 2019	40,000	17,000

At what point in time will Ms. Salome and Mr. Laughton have to begin collecting GST? At what point will they be required to register?

SOLUTION available in print and online Study Guide.

Voluntary Registration

21-89.   The small supplier exemption can represent an advantage to persons with limited commercial activity whose clients are consumers who cannot claim input tax credits. If the vendor is not registered, the goods or services can legally be sold without charging GST/HST which would result in savings for consumers that could be substantial.

21-90.   There is, however, a disadvantage to this exemption. If a person does not register, they cannot receive input tax credits for GST/HST paid. They are effectively treated as the final consumer. This means that the business must either absorb the GST/HST paid on its costs or, alternatively, pass the GST/HST paid on purchases and expenses on to its customers in the form of higher prices.

21-91.   Given this problem, voluntary registration is an alternative. Any person engaged in commercial activity in Canada can apply to be registered, even if taxable sales are less than the $30,000 small supplier threshold. In making a decision as to whether to use this option, the person must consider the value of the input tax credits that will be available. However, the person must also consider whether charging GST/HST will reduce the demand for his product or service, especially if some of the competition doesn't charge GST/HST.

Registrants Ineligible For The Small Supplier Exemption

21-92.   ETA 240 contains two other subsections which effectively prohibit the use of the small supplier exemption for certain types of suppliers. ETA 240(1.1) indicates that suppliers of taxi services must register, even if their revenues are less than $30,000 per year. By deeming the provision of commercial ride-sharing services (e.g., Uber) a taxi business, all of those drivers are required to register as well. ETA 240(2) requires registration of any non-resident who enters Canada for the purpose of making taxable supplies of admissions in respect of a place of amusement, a seminar, an activity or an event.

We suggest you work Self Study Problem Twenty-One-2 at this point.

Input Tax Credits

Vendors Of Fully Taxable And Zero-Rated Supplies

General Rules

21-93.   A GST registrant must collect and remit GST/HST on sales of fully taxable supplies. In the process of supplying these goods and services, the registrant will incur costs, some of which are likely to include GST/HST. To the extent that these costs have been incurred in commercial activity (i.e., supplying either fully taxable or zero-rated goods and services), the registrant can claim a refund of the GST/HST that has been included in these costs.

21-94.   The refunds that are available to the registrant are referred to as input tax credits. As was the case with some credits against income tax payable, input tax credits can be thought of as refundable. That is, if the available input tax credits for the period exceed the GST/HST collections for the period, the registrant can claim a GST/HST refund.

21-95.   As will be discussed in the sections which follow, the rules for claiming input tax credits vary, depending on whether the GST/HST was paid on current expenditures (e.g., purchases of merchandise inventories) or, alternatively, capital expenditures (e.g., buildings or equipment). In addition, the rules also vary with the type of capital expenditure on which the GST/HST was paid.

21-96.   It is important to note that, in claiming input tax credits there is no matching of costs and revenues. Input tax credits on inventory purchases become available at the time of purchase, not when the goods are sold and charged to income for accounting purposes. Input tax credits on capital expenditures become available when the asset is acquired, not over the useful life of the asset.

Current Expenditures

21-97.   With respect to current expenditures, if all, or substantially all (generally understood in tax work to mean 90 percent or more), of a current expenditure is related to commercial activity, then all of the GST/HST that was paid can be claimed as an input tax credit. In contrast, if 10 percent or less of an expenditure is related to commercial activity, no input tax credit can be claimed. If the percentage of the current expenditure used for commercial activity is between 10 and 90 percent, the input tax credit available is calculated by multiplying the total GST/HST paid by the percentage of commercial activity usage.

Capital Expenditures

21-98.   In line with the basic idea that input tax credits are not matched against amounts of GST/HST collected on sales, the GST/HST paid on purchases of capital assets used in commercial activities is eligible for treatment as an input tax credit at the time of purchase, regardless of when the purchases are paid for, or how they are amortized.

21-99.   In general, capital property for GST/HST purposes has the same meaning that is used for income tax purposes. However, for GST/HST purposes it can either be capital real property or capital personal property. In situations where a capital asset is used only partially for commercial activity, the approach used to calculate the available input tax credits will depend on the type of capital asset involved:

Capital Real Property (Land And Buildings)   For this type of property, the input tax credit available is in proportion to the extent to which the property is used in commercial activities. That is, if the building is used 35 percent for commercial activities, the input tax credit will be equal to 35 percent of the GST/HST paid on its acquisition. In other words, input tax credits on real property are available on a pro rata basis, with the available portion based on usage in commercial activities.

As is the case with current expenditures, if commercial usage is 10 percent or less, the purchaser cannot claim any input tax credit. Alternatively, if the usage is 90 percent or more, 100 percent of the GST/HST paid can be claimed as an input tax credit.

Capital Personal Property (Capital Property Other Than Real Property)   In order for the input tax credits to be available on capital personal property, the assets must be used "primarily" in commercial activities. In tax work, "primarily" is generally understood to be more than 50 percent. If commercial usage is 50 percent or less, none of the GST/HST paid on the capital personal property's acquisition can be claimed as an input tax credit. If commercial usage is more than 50 percent, the registrant is eligible for an input tax credit equal to 100 percent of the GST/HST paid.

Restrictions On Claiming Input Tax Credits

21-100.   As noted in previous Chapters of this text, income tax legislation restricts the deductibility of certain types of business costs. For many of these items, there is a corresponding restriction on the ability of the business to claim input tax credits for GST/HST purposes. Some of the more common restrictions are as follows:

Passenger Vehicles   No input tax credits are available for GST/HST paid on the portion of the cost or lease payment of a passenger vehicle that is in excess of the deduction limits. For 2018, these limits are $30,000 cost and $800 monthly lease payments, excluding GST/HST and PST. Also, if the vehicle is owned by a registrant who is an individual or a partnership and the vehicle is used partly for business (less than 90 percent) and partly for personal use, the input tax credit is prorated based on the annual CCA claimed.

Club Memberships   No input tax credit is allowed for GST/HST paid on membership fees or dues in any club whose main purpose is to provide dining, recreational, or sporting facilities.

Provision Of Recreational Facilities   No input tax credits are available for the GST/HST costs of providing certain types of recreational facilities to employees, owners, or related parties.

Business Meals And Entertainment   The recovery of GST/HST on deductible meals and entertainment expenses is limited to 50 percent of the amounts paid.

Personal Or Living Expenses   Input tax credits cannot be claimed on costs associated with the personal or living expenses of any employee, owner, or related individual. An exception is available when GST/HST is collected on the provision of the item to the employee, owner, or related individual.

Figure 21 - 3
Maximum Input Tax Credits

Taxable Purchase	Percentage Used In Commercial Activities = X%	Input Tax Credit
Current Expenditures* and Capital Real Property	X% ≤ 10%	Nil
	10% < X% < 90%	X%
	X% ≥ 90%	100%
Capital Personal Property (Excluding Passenger Vehicles*)	X% ≤ 50%	Nil
	X% > 50%	100%

*Special rules apply to certain items. See Paragraph 21-100.

Reasonableness   Both the nature and value of a purchase must be reasonable in relation to the commercial activities of the registrant before an input tax credit can be claimed. This is similar to the reasonableness test that is found in the *Income Tax Act*.

21-101.   Restrictions also apply to the time allowed for claiming input tax credits. For large businesses, whose sales are less than 90 percent taxable but in excess of $6 million, and listed financial institutions, the time limit is generally 2 years from the date the input tax credit was first available. For all other registrants the time limit is 4 years.

Summary Of Rules
21-102.   The rules for apportioning the maximum available input tax credits on purchases are summarized in Figure 21-3.

Vendors Of Exempt Supplies

21-103.   Vendors of exempt supplies cannot claim any GST/HST paid on purchases that relate to exempt supplies. In some situations, vendors are involved in making fully taxable or zero-rated supplies, as well as exempt supplies. Since these businesses can only recover GST/HST paid on their fully taxable or zero-rated activities, they must apportion their input tax credits on a "reasonable" basis. This applies to both current and capital expenditures that cannot be directly identified with particular exempt or taxable activities.

Accounting vs. Income Tax vs. GST/HST
Differences
21-104.   The concept of matching is integral to the determination of business income for both accounting and income tax purposes. For GST/HST purposes, the matching concept is not relevant. GST/HST is collected when taxable supplies are provided and input tax credits are refunded when the inputs for taxable supplies are purchased. No attempt is made to match the input tax credits claimed with sales of the related taxable supplies.

21-105.   Other significant differences between accounting, income tax and GST/HST procedures are as follows:

- Most accounting and income tax allocations, for example amortization or CCA, are irrelevant for GST/HST purposes. GST/HST paid on capital expenditures that are eligible for input tax credits can generally be claimed in the period in which the expenditure is made. (Differences between accounting income and income for tax purposes were discussed in Chapter 6 and would also be applicable here.)

- Many deductible expenses for income tax purposes do not affect the GST/HST payable or receivable. For example, GST/HST does not apply to employee wages, interest, property taxes, and educational services. While such costs are usually fully deductible in the calculation of Net Income For Tax Purposes, they do not require the payment of GST/HST and, as a consequence, do not generate input tax credits.

Similarities

21-106. In contrast to these differences, there are some features that are common to GST/HST and income tax calculations. For example, GST/HST is normally collected and revenue is recognized for income tax purposes when an invoice is issued for the provision of goods or services. When the invoice is paid is not a relevant consideration for either income tax or GST/HST purposes.

21-107. Similarly, if an account receivable becomes uncollectible, an adjustment is required for both income tax and GST/HST purposes. Also, as we have noted, some of the restrictions that apply in the deductibility of certain expenses for income tax purposes (e.g., 50 percent of business meals and entertainment and certain costs of owning or leasing automobiles) are also contained in the GST/HST legislation.

Financial Statement Presentation

21-108. This issue is covered in IAS No. 18, *Revenue*. This international accounting standard indicates that taxes that are to be refunded should not be included in reported revenues. There is no corresponding statement with respect to expenses. However, it would be logical to assume that any GST/HST paid that is eligible for an input tax credit would not be included in the reported expense. Note, however, that even though the revenues and expenses are reported net of GST/HST, the amounts due to and recoverable from the government must be included in the receivables and payables of the enterprise.

Example One - Fully Taxable And Zero-Rated Supplies

21-109. In this example, we will assume that the company sells only fully taxable and zero-rated supplies.

EXAMPLE Marson Ltd. is located in the province of Alberta which does not have a provincial sales tax and does not participate in the HST system. In the following Income Statement of Marson Ltd. for the year ending December 31, 2018, all of the items are recorded net of any GST collected or paid.

Sales	$9,500,000
Expenses:	
Cost Of Goods Sold	$6,500,000
Amortization Expense	900,000
Salaries And Wages	1,500,000
Other Expenses	200,000
Total Expenses Excluding GST And Income Taxes	$9,100,000
Net Income Before GST And Income Taxes	$ 400,000

Other Information:

1. Of the total Sales, $6,800,000 were fully taxable supplies. The remaining $2,700,000 ($9,500,000 - $6,800,000) were zero-rated.

2. Purchases of merchandise exceeded the Cost Of Goods Sold by $2,200,000, net of GST. All of the merchandise sold and purchased involved fully taxable supplies.

3. Of the Other Expenses, 80 percent related to fully taxable supplies, while the remaining 20 percent related to zero-rated supplies.

4. During 2018, capital expenditures totaled $7,500,000, net of GST, and the amounts have not been paid. These consisted of $5,000,000 for an office building and $2,500,000 for furniture and fixtures. The office building was used 60 percent for fully taxable supplies and 40 percent for zero-rated supplies. The furniture and fixtures were used 55 percent for fully taxable supplies and 45 percent for zero-rated supplies.

ANALYSIS   Based on this information Marson Ltd. is eligible for a GST refund calculated as follows:

GST Collected [(5%)($6,800,000)]	$340,000
Input Tax Credits:	
Purchases [(5%)($6,500,000 + $2,200,000)]	(435,000)
Amortization Expense	Nil
Salaries And Wages	Nil
Other Expenses [(5%)(80% + 20%)($200,000)]	(10,000)
Building [(5%)(60% + 40%)($5,000,000)]	(250,000)
Furniture And Fixtures [(5%)(55% + 45%)($2,500,000)]	(125,000)
GST Payable (Refund) - With Zero-Rated Supplies	($480,000)

21-110.   You will note that, while Marson Ltd. is showing a positive Net Income for accounting purposes, the Company is eligible for a GST refund. This example clearly illustrates the fact that GST reporting is not based on the matching principle. The input tax credits are available on the entire amount of capital expenditures, without regard to whether they have been paid for or amortized for accounting purposes. In addition, input tax credits are available on all of the inventory purchases, without regard to whether the merchandise has been sold.

Example Two - Fully Taxable And GST Exempt Supplies

21-111.   In this example, we have revised the Marson Ltd. example so that the Company sells fully taxable and GST exempt supplies. The revised information is repeated here for your convenience.

EXAMPLE   Marson Ltd. is located in the province of Alberta which does not have a provincial sales tax and does not participate in the HST system. In the following Income Statement of Marson Ltd. for the year ending December 31, 2018, all of the items are recorded net of any GST collected or paid.

Sales	$9,500,000
Expenses:	
Cost Of Goods Sold	$6,500,000
Amortization Expense	900,000
Salaries And Wages	1,500,000
Other Expenses	200,000
Total Expenses Excluding GST And Income Taxes	$9,100,000
Net Income Before GST And Income Taxes	$ 400,000

Other Information:

1. Of the total Sales, $6,800,000 were fully taxable supplies. The remaining $2,700,000 ($9,500,000 - $6,800,000) were GST exempt supplies.

2. Purchases of merchandise exceeded the Cost Of Goods Sold by $2,200,000, net of GST. All of the merchandise sold and purchased involved fully taxable supplies.

3. Of the Other Expenses, 80 percent related to fully taxable supplies, while the remaining 20 percent related to GST exempt supplies.

4. During 2018, capital expenditures totaled $7,500,000, net of GST, and the amounts have not been paid. These consisted of $5,000,000 for an office building and $2,500,000 for furniture and fixtures. The office building was used 60 percent for fully taxable supplies and 40 percent for GST exempt supplies. The furniture and fixtures were used 55 percent for fully taxable supplies and 45 percent for GST exempt supplies.

ANALYSIS   Based on this revised information, the GST refund for Marson Ltd. would be calculated as follows:

GST Collected [(5%)($6,800,000)]	$340,000
Input Tax Credits:	
Purchases [(5%)($6,500,000 + $2,200,000)]	(435,000)
Amortization Expense	Nil
Salaries And Wages	Nil
Other Expenses [(5%)(80% + 0%)($200,000)]	(8,000)
Building [(5%)(60% + 0%)($5,000,000)]	(150,000)
Furniture And Fixtures [(5%)(100%)($2,500,000)]	(125,000)
GST Payable (Refund) - With GST Exempt Supplies	($378,000)

21-112.   In this example, where some of the costs relate to the provision of exempt supplies, only 80 percent of the GST on Other Expenses is eligible for an input tax credit. Similarly, only 60 percent of the GST paid on the Building is eligible. However, because the Furniture And Fixtures were capital personal property and used primarily (more than 50 percent) for commercial activity, the full amount of the GST paid is eligible for an input tax credit, even though 45 percent of their usage was for the provision of GST exempt supplies.

Exercise Twenty-One - 3

Subject: HST Calculation

All of the operations of March Ltd. are located in Ontario where the relevant HST rate is 13 percent. During the current quarter, March Ltd. has taxable sales of $1,223,000 before HST. Its cost of sales for the period was $843,000 before HST and its merchandise inventories increased by $126,000, again before HST. Salaries and wages for the period totalled $87,000, interest expense was $16,000, and amortization expense was $93,000. No capital expenditures were made during the period. Determine the net HST payable or refund for the quarter.

Exercise Twenty-One - 4

Subject: HST Calculation

Ms. Marsha Stone lives and works in Nova Scotia where the relevant HST rate is 15 percent. During the current year she records accounting service revenue of $224,000. Martha has never used the ITA 34 option to record revenue on a billed basis. Rent for this period on her office premises totals $25,800 and she pays a clerical assistant an annual salary of $18,500. Her capital expenditures during the period are for new office furniture with a cost of $36,000 and computer hardware and software for $20,000. All amounts are before the addition of HST and the assets are used 100 percent for the provision of taxable supplies. She files her HST return on an annual basis. Determine the net HST payable or refund for the year.

SOLUTIONS available in print and online Study Guide.

Exercise Twenty-One - 5

Subject: Input Tax Credits On Capital Expenditures

Modam Ltd. is located in Alberta, which does not participate in the HST program and has no provincial sales tax. All of its operations are in that province. During its current quarter, Modam Ltd. purchases an office building and land for a total of $1,200,000 before GST. The Company spends an additional $226,000 (before GST) on office equipment. The building will be used 40 percent for taxable supplies and 60 percent for exempt supplies. The office equipment is to be allocated in the same ratio. For accounting purposes, the building will be amortized over 40 years, while the office equipment will be written off over 4 years. Determine the input tax credits that Modam Ltd. can claim as a result of these capital expenditures.

SOLUTION available in print and online Study Guide.

We suggest you work Self Study Problems Twenty-One-3 and 4 at this point.

Relief For Small Businesses

Quick Method Of Accounting

General Rules

21-113.   Eligible businesses, defined as businesses with annual GST/HST included taxable sales, including those of associated businesses, of $400,000 or less during the year, can elect to use the Quick Method of determining the net GST/HST remittance. Both fully taxable and zero-rated supplies are included in calculating the $400,000 threshold, while exempt supplies, supplies made outside of Canada, sales of capital real and personal property, and provincial sales taxes are excluded. In addition, businesses involved in legal, accounting and financial consulting services are not eligible for the Quick Method.

21-114.   If the Quick Method election is filed, the registrant charges GST or HST at the normal rate on taxable sales. The major advantage of this method is that the business is not required to keep detailed records of current expenditures that are eligible for input tax credits. Note, however, that when this method is used for current expenditures, the registrant can still claim input tax credits on capital expenditures. This means that there will continue to be a need to track the input tax credits on specific capital expenditures.

21-115.   In the absence of detailed records on current expenditures eligible for input tax credits, a specified percentage, the remittance rate, is applied to the GST/HST inclusive total of fully taxable sales to determine the amount of GST/HST to be remitted.

21-116.   Note that the remittance rate is not an alternative GST/HST rate. It is based on an assumed relationship between revenues subject to GST/HST and costs on which input tax credits are available. For example, the Quick Method remittance rate for service providers in Alberta is 3.6 percent. The following example illustrates (without going into the algebra that is involved) that this rate is based on the assumption that, for service providers subject only to GST, eligible costs are equal to 24.4 percent of fully taxable sales.

> **EXAMPLE**   An Alberta GST registrant who is providing fully taxable services has taxable revenues of $50,000 in its second, third and fourth quarters. Its eligible current expenditures for these quarters are $5,000 (less than 24.4% of revenues) for quarter 2, $12,200 (equal to 24.4% of revenues) for quarter 3, and $30,000 (more than 24.4% of revenues) for quarter 4.

ANALYSIS   The GST Payable calculated under the Quick Method is $1,890 [(3.6%)(105%)($50,000)]. The Quick Method results are the same for each quarter as the calculation is based on revenues and is not affected by the amount of current expenditures. GST Payable under the regular and Quick Method would be as follows:

	Quarter 2	Quarter 3	Quarter 4
GST On Revenues [(5%)($50,000)]	$2,500	$2,500	$2,500
Input Tax Credits On Costs At 5%	(250)	(610)	(1,500)
GST Payable - Regular Method	$2,250	$1,890	$1,000
GST Payable - Quick Method (Note)	(1,890)	(1,890)	(1,890)
Advantage (Disadvantage) Quick Method	$ 360	Nil	($ 890)

Note   The 1 percent credit described in Paragraph 21-121 would be claimed in the first quarter. Note that, in Quarter 3, when current expenditures are equal to the assumed 24.4 percent of fully taxable sales, the regular method and the Quick Method produce identical results. In Quarter 2, when current expenditures are below 24.4 percent, the Quick Method results in a lower amount payable. In contrast, in Quarter 4, when current expenditures exceed 24.4 percent, the Quick Method results in a higher amount payable.

More generally, when current expenditures, as a percent of fully taxable sales, are normally less than the percentage assumed in the Quick Method rate, use of the Quick Method is a desirable alternative. In contrast, when such expenditures normally exceed the assumed rate, the use of the Quick Method is not advantageous as it will result in a higher amount payable.

Quick Method Categories

21-117.   Conceptually, an equitable application of the Quick Method would require a large number of different rates in order to reflect the various cost structures that are present in different lines of business. However, this was clearly not a practical alternative, particularly since the goal of the Quick Method was simplification. Given this, the government decided to have rates for only two broad categories.

21-118.   The categories to which the two rates are applied can be described as follows:

Businesses That Resell Goods   These businesses have a lower remittance rate to reflect a higher percentage of eligible costs. In order to use these rates, the cost of goods purchased for resale (GST/HST inclusive) in the previous year must be equal to 40 percent or more of the revenue from sales of taxable supplies for that year (GST/HST inclusive). Examples of types of businesses eligible for this low rate include grocery and convenience stores, hardware stores, gas service stations, antique dealers, and clothing stores.

Service Providers   These higher rates (double the resellers') apply to service businesses such as consultants (other than financial), hair salons, restaurants, dry cleaners, travel agents, and taxi drivers. Since legal, accounting, and financial consulting businesses are not eligible for the Quick Method, they cannot use these rates.

Specific Quick Method Remittance Rates

21-119.   As noted in the introduction to this Chapter, in addition to the GST rate of 5 percent that is used in provinces that do not participate in the HST program, there are two different HST rates as of January 1, 2018:

- 13 percent in Ontario
- 15 percent in New Brunswick, Newfoundland, Nova Scotia, and Prince Edward Island

21-120.   As the Quick Method is designed to approximate the results under the regular method of calculating GST or HST, different Quick Method remittance rates are required in each of these situations. The relevant rates are as shown in Figure 21-4.

Figure 21 - 4		
Quick Method Remittance Rates As At January 1, 2018 (Excluding Quebec)		
GST/HST Rate	**Businesses That Purchase Goods For Resale**	**Service Providers**
GST Only At 5% (B.C., Alberta, Manitoba, and Saskatchewan)	1.8%	3.6%
HST At 13% (Ontario)	4.4%	8.8%
HST At 15% (Newfoundland, Nova Scotia, New Brunswick and Prince Edward Island)	5.0%	10.0%

21-121.   Two things should be noted about these rates:

1. In the application of all of the rates in Figure 21-4, there is a credit equal to 1 percent of the first $30,000 of GST/HST inclusive sales in the year ($300 maximum).

2. These are the rates that are used by a business in the specified province that has all of its activities in that province. For businesses that deliver supplies in provinces other than their province of residence, calculations can be quite a bit more complicated. The CRA provides detailed information in its guide, "Quick Method Of Accounting For GST/HST" (RC4058).

Example Of Quick Method

21-122.   As an example of the Quick Method, consider a quarterly filing office supply store, located and operating only in Alberta, with annual taxable sales of less than $400,000. Its first quarter taxable sales were $40,000, resulting in GST included sales of $42,000 [(105%)($40,000)]. Purchases of inventory totaled $26,600 before GST. Qualifying capital expenditures during the first quarter were $3,000 before GST. Under the regular method, the first quarter GST payable would be calculated as follows:

Sales [(5%)($40,000)]	$2,000
Purchases [(5%)($26,600)]	(1,330)
Capital Expenditures [(5%)($3,000)]	(150)
First Quarter GST Payable - Regular Method	$ 520

21-123.   Alternatively, the first quarter GST payable, as determined by the Quick Method, is calculated as follows:

Basic Tax [(1.8%)(105%)($40,000)]	$756
Credit On First $30,000 [(1%)($30,000)]	(300)
Subtotal	$456
Input Tax Credit On Current Expenditures	Nil
Input Tax Credits On Capital Expenditures [(5%)($3,000)]	(150)
First Quarter GST Payable - Quick Method	$306

21-124.   The Quick Method can be preferable, even if adequate data is available to make the calculations under the regular method. For example, a freelance writer, operating out of his principal residence, is not likely to have significant expenditures that qualify for input tax credits. In this case, the Quick Method may result in a smaller net GST payment than the regular calculation of actual GST collected, less input tax credits. It will certainly be less time consuming to file his GST return since input tax credit information on non-capital expenditures will not be needed.

Exercise Twenty-One - 6

Subject: Quick Method

Robbins Hardware sells only fully taxable supplies to customers in Alberta which does not participate in the HST program and has no provincial sales tax. During the first quarter of the year, the business has sales of $42,500, before the inclusion of GST. They have taxable purchases totaling $21,000 before GST. They do not make any capital expenditures during the quarter. Using the Quick Method, determine the GST that is payable for the quarter.

Exercise Twenty-One - 7

Subject: Quick Method

Guy's Boots sells only fully taxable shoes and boots to customers in Ontario where the HST rate is 13 percent. During the first quarter of the year, Guy's Boots has sales of $56,100, before HST. Current expenses, all of which were subject to HST, total $23,400 (before HST). Due to a major renovation of the store, Guy's Boots has capital expenditures of $42,000 (before HST). Compare the use of the Quick Method and the regular method for this quarter.

SOLUTIONS available in print and online Study Guide.

We suggest you work Self Study Problems Twenty-One-5 and 6 at this point.

Small Suppliers Exemption

21-125.   This is covered beginning at Paragraph 21-84 and will not be repeated here.

Streamlined Input Tax Credit Method

21-126.   A method for claiming input tax credits and rebates is available to registrants with annual GST/HST taxable sales, including those of associated businesses, of $1,000,000 or less in the preceding year. An additional requirement is that annual GST/HST taxable purchases total no more than $4,000,000.

21-127.   Rather than tracking GST/HST paid on each purchase, the streamlined method bases input tax credits on the total GST/HST inclusive amounts of fully taxable purchases. This amount would also include any non-refundable provincial sales taxes paid on taxable supplies. Once this total is established, it is multiplied by the following factor:

Factor   Applicable GST/HST Rate ÷ (100 Plus The Applicable GST/HST Rate)

Examples   The factor in Alberta would be 5/105. The factor in Ontario would be 13/113.

21-128.   The following items are excluded from the base to which the factor is applied:

- Capital expenditures for real property (these are tracked separately for input tax credit purposes).
- Purchases of zero-rated supplies, such as groceries and prescription drugs.
- Purchases of exempt supplies, such as interest payments.
- Purchases made outside Canada, which are not subject to GST/HST.
- Purchases from non-registrants.
- Refundable provincial sales taxes (only in Quebec).
- Expenses not eligible for input tax credits (e.g., 50 percent of the cost of meals and entertainment).

21-129.   There is no election required to use this method and it does not affect the calculation of the GST/HST on sales that must be remitted. The following example illustrates this method as applied in the province of New Brunswick.

> **EXAMPLE** Garth Steel Ltd. operates solely in New Brunswick and Nova Scotia. Its only activities involve the provision of fully taxable supplies. During the current year, it has current expenditures of $75,000, real property expenditures of $145,000 and expenditures for capital property other than real property of $25,000. All of these figures are before HST which was charged on all of these expenditures. In addition, the Company paid salaries of $200,000.
>
> **ANALYSIS** The Company's input tax credit for the current year would be as follows:

HST Included Amounts For Taxable Expenditures Other Than Real Property [(115%)($75,000 + $25,000 + Nil)]	$115,000
Factor (For New Brunswick and Nova Scotia)	15/115
Input Tax Credit On Taxable Expenditures	$ 15,000
Input Tax Credit On Real Property Expenditure [(15%)($145,000)]	21,750
Input Tax Credit For The Current Year	$ 36,750

21-130.   As noted, the streamlined method base only includes purchases of fully taxable goods. A further restriction on the amounts claimed is that credits can be claimed only to the extent that the purchases included in the streamlined method base are used to provide fully taxable or zero-rated goods and services. Where a supply is used to provide both taxable and exempt goods and services, the input tax credit claim must be pro-rated so that only the portion that applies to taxable goods and services is claimed.

Exercise Twenty-One - 8

Subject: Streamlined Input Tax Credit Method

Simplicity Inc. operates in Alberta where there is no provincial sales tax and no participation in the HST program. For the current year, the Company has GST inclusive sales of $315,000. It has GST inclusive purchases of merchandise and other current expenditures of $189,000. Capital expenditures consist of real property (land and a building) costing $150,000 and capital personal property totaling $50,000. These capital expenditure amounts are before the inclusion of GST. Using the streamlined method of accounting for input tax credits, determine Simplicity's GST payable or refund for the current year.

SOLUTION available in print and online Study Guide.

GST/HST Procedures And Administration

GST/HST Returns And Payments

Timing Of Liability

21-131.   In general, the supplier becomes responsible for the tax at the earliest of when the invoice for goods or services is issued, when payment is received, and when payment is due under a written agreement. Following this rule, a registrant usually becomes responsible for remitting GST/HST in the reporting period in which a customer is invoiced, even if this is not the same period in which the cash is actually received.

21-132.   Similarly, input tax credits for GST/HST payable to suppliers can be claimed in the reporting period invoices are issued, even if the supplier is paid in a later period.

Figure 21 - 5 Assigned And Optional Reporting Periods		
Threshold Amount Of Annual Taxable Supplies	Assigned Reporting Period	Optional Reporting Period
$1,500,000 Or Less	Annual	Monthly Or Quarterly
More Than $1,500,000 Up To $6,000,000	Quarterly	Monthly
More Than $6,000,000	Monthly	None

Taxation Year For GST Registrants

21-133.   Every registrant is required to have a "fiscal year" for GST/HST purposes. Normally, this fiscal year corresponds to the taxation year for income tax purposes. However, if registrants are using a non-calendar year for income tax purposes they have the option of using the calendar year or, alternatively, using their fiscal year for income tax purposes. For example, a company with a fiscal year ending on January 31, 2018 and subject to quarterly filing requirements could choose a three month reporting period ending on January 31, 2018, or a three month reporting period ending on March 31, 2018. The GST/HST fiscal year determines the reporting periods and filing deadlines for GST/HST returns.

Filing Due Date

21-134.   All businesses and organizations that are registered to collect GST/HST are required to file a GST/HST return on a periodic basis, even if there is no activity during the relevant period. The CRA's GST/HST Netfile service can be used to file GST/HST returns online. Filing frequencies for the remittance of GST/HST are determined by the total annual taxable supplies made by the registrant and its associated entities. The normal periods, along with the options that are available on an elective basis, are shown in Figure 21-5.

21-135.   A registrant may elect to have a shorter filing period than the one that is assigned for their amount of taxable supplies. This may be advantageous for registrants who normally receive a GST/HST refund, such as businesses with significant exports or zero-rated sales (e.g., pharmacies and grocery stores). On a practical note, it may be advantageous for some annual filers to choose to file quarterly as it would force the registrant to keep their records more up-to-date. This could help decrease the work and stress that some proprietors and small businesses face when they deal with their year end accounting. As discussed in the next Section, filing quarterly would also eliminate the need to calculate and pay GST instalments.

21-136.   For monthly and quarterly filers, GST/HST returns are due one month after the end of the reporting period. In general, for annual filers, GST/HST returns are due three months after the year end. There is an extension to June 15 for annual filers who are individuals with business income and a December 31 fiscal year end. This is the same filing due date applicable to income tax returns for these individuals.

Payments And Instalments

21-137.   In general, payment of amounts owing are due when the GST/HST returns are due. This is one month after the end of the reporting period for monthly and quarterly filers, and three months after the year end for annual filers. For annual filers who are individuals with a June 15 filing due date, the payment due date is April 30. This means the filing due date and payment due date are the same as is applicable to income tax payable for these individuals.

21-138.   Instalment payments are not required for monthly or quarterly filers. However, annual filers are required to make quarterly instalments if the GST/HST remitted for the previous fiscal year was $3,000 or more. Each instalment will be one-quarter of the net tax owing from the previous year. These instalments are due one month after the end of each quarter. For example, calendar year filers are required to make instalments by April 30, July

31, October 31, and January 31. For annual filers below the $3,000 threshold, the net tax is due on the GST/HST return filing due date.

Interest

21-139.   If the GST/HST return shows an amount owing and it is not paid by the due date, interest is assessed. Interest is also assessed on late or deficient instalments. The applicable rates are the same as those used for income tax purposes:

- on taxes owed to the government, the rate is the prescribed rate plus 4 percent; and
- on amounts owed to the taxpayer, the rate is the prescribed rate plus 2 percent.

21-140.   As is the case with interest on late income tax instalments, interest paid on late GST/HST payments is not deductible.

Late Filing Penalty

21-141.   The GST/HST late filing penalty is equal to one percent of the unpaid amount, plus one-quarter of one percent per month for a maximum of 12 months. Unlike the income tax situation, there is no doubling of this penalty for a second offense.

Associated Persons

21-142.   You may have noticed that there are a number of GST/HST rules that are related to the amount of supplies delivered during the period. In order to prevent the avoidance of these rules (e.g., splitting a business into two parts so that each would qualify for the Quick Method), GST/HST legislation has rules for associated persons.

21-143.   Two or more persons are associated for GST/HST purposes where there is substantial common ownership. For example, if one corporation controls another, the two corporations are associated. An association can exist between two or more corporations, between an individual and a corporation, and among an individual, partnership, trust and corporation.

21-144.   While associated persons file separate GST/HST returns, they must combine their total taxable sales of goods and services in certain situations, such as when determining:

- whether they qualify for the small supplier's exemption,
- whether they are eligible for the Quick Method of accounting,
- whether they are eligible for the streamlined method of calculating input tax credits,
- the required filing frequency of their returns (i.e., monthly, quarterly or annual).

Refunds And Rebates

21-145.   In a period during which input tax credits exceed GST/HST collections, a refund may be claimed in the GST/HST return for that period. Provided all required returns have been filed and are up to date, interest on unpaid refunds starts accruing 30 days after the later of the last day of the reporting period and the day after the registrant's return is filed.

21-146.   The *Excise Tax Act* also provides for a number of rebates of the GST/HST paid by consumers under certain circumstances. For example, if a GST/HST amount is paid in error, or by a foreign diplomat, a rebate of the GST/HST may be claimed on a General Rebate Application Form. Our coverage of the GST/HST rebate for new housing begins in Paragraph 21-167.

Books And Records

21-147.   For GST/HST purposes, every registrant must keep adequate books and records. This requirement is found in ETA 286(1). Such records must be maintained at the registrant's place of business or at the individual's residence in Canada.

21-148.   All books and records, along with the accounts and vouchers necessary to verify them, must be kept for a period of six years from the end of the last taxation year to which they relate. This is the same record retention limit that is applicable for income tax purposes.

Appeals

Informal Procedures

21-149.   As is the case with income tax disputes, the usual first step in disputing an assessment or reassessment is to contact the CRA. In many cases the proposed change or error can be corrected or resolved through telephone contact or by letter. In order to authorize a person or firm to represent a GST registrant in such disputes, a consent form must be signed and filed with the CRA.

Notice Of Objection

21-150.   If the informal contact with the CRA does not resolve the issue in question, the taxpayer should file a notice of objection. For GST/HST purposes, a formal notice of objection procedure is required.

21-151.   In GST/HST disputes, the notice of objection must be filed within 90 days of the date on the notice of assessment. Unlike the situation with income tax objections, there is no general extension of this time period for GST registrants who are individuals, nor is there any extension for individual GST registrants in the year of their death. Failure to meet the 90 day deadline may result in the taxpayer losing all rights to pursue the matter in question.

21-152.   On receiving the notice of objection, the Minister is required to reply to the GST registrant:

- vacating the assessment;
- confirming the assessment (refusing to change);
- varying the amount of the assessment; or
- reassessing.

21-153.   Unresolved objections will be subject to review by the Assistant Director of Appeals in each Tax Services Office. These reviewers are instructed to operate independently of the assessing divisions and should provide an unbiased second opinion. If the matter remains unresolved after this review, the taxpayer must either accept the Minister's assessment or, alternatively, continue to pursue the matter to a higher level of appeal. The taxpayer has the right to bypass this notice of objection procedure and appeal directly to a higher level.

21-154.   As noted in Chapter 2, in income tax disputes, the Minister cannot institute collection procedures until after the notice of objection period has expired. When dealing with GST/HST disputes, collection procedures are not delayed by the objection process. This more aggressive approach is allowed by GST/HST legislation and probably reflects the fact that the government considers GST/HST balances assessed as amounts collected in trust by the registrant on behalf of the government.

Tax Court Of Canada, Federal Court Of Appeal, And The Supreme Court Of Canada

21-155.   Procedures for handling GST/HST disputes in these courts are basically the same as the procedures for handling income tax disputes. These procedures are described in Chapter 2 and the description will not be repeated here.

General Anti-Avoidance Rule

21-156.   The GST/HST legislation includes a general anti-avoidance rule (GAAR). This rule is found under Section 274 of the *Excise Tax Act* and is very similar to the GAAR found in the *Income Tax Act*.

21-157.   While the GST/HST GAAR is intended to prevent abusive tax avoidance transactions, it is not intended to interfere with legitimate commercial transactions. If a transaction is considered by the CRA to be an avoidance transaction, the tax consequences of the transaction may be adjusted. This could involve denying an input tax credit, allocating an input tax credit to another person, or recharacterizing a payment. But, as with the application of the income tax GAAR, it does not apply if a transaction is undertaken primarily for bona fide purposes other than to obtain a GST/HST benefit.

Employee And Partner GST/HST Rebate

General Concept

21-158.   Many of the expenses employees can deduct against employment income include a GST/HST component. If the individual was a GST registrant earning business income, these GST/HST payments would generate input tax credits. However, employment is not considered to be a commercial activity and, as a consequence, employees who have no separate commercial activity cannot be registrants. This means that they will not be able to use the usual input tax credit procedure to obtain a refund of GST/HST amounts paid with respect to their employment expenses. A similar analysis applies to partners who have partnership related expenses that are not included in partnership net income or loss.

21-159.   The Employee and Partner GST/HST Rebate allows employees and partners to recover the GST/HST paid on their employment or partnership related expenditures, including vehicles and musical instruments, in a way that is similar to the input tax credits that they could have claimed if they were GST registrants. Form GST370 is used to claim the GST/HST rebate and is filed with the employee or partner's income tax return.

21-160.   To qualify for this rebate, the individual must be either an employee of a GST registrant, or a member of a partnership that is a GST registrant. Employees of financial institutions are not eligible for the rebate. However, employees of charities, not-for-profit organizations, universities, school boards, and municipalities are eligible as long as the organizations that they work for are registered. In addition, employees of provincial governments, Crown corporations, and the federal government qualify for the rebate. To claim the rebate, the individual must have unreimbursed expenses on which GST/HST was paid that are deductible against employment or partnership income.

Calculating The GST/HST Rebate Amount

21-161.   The GST/HST rebate is based on the GST/HST amounts included in those costs that can be deducted in the determination of employment income. In terms of calculations, this is accomplished by multiplying the GST/HST and non-refundable PST included in the cost by a fraction in which the GST/HST rate is the numerator and 100 plus the GST/HST rate is the denominator.

> **EXAMPLE** Marcia Valentino is employed in British Columbia. She has deductible cell phone expenses of $2,000. She paid $100 in GST (5%) and $140 in non-refundable PST (7%). She deducted $2,240 in her calculation of employment income.

> **ANALYSIS** Ms. Valentino's rebate would be $107 [($2,240)(5/105)]. This is more than the $100 in GST she paid as the rebate base includes the non-refundable PST.

21-162.   Eligible expenses exclude expenses for which a non-taxable allowance was received, zero-rated and exempt supplies, supplies acquired outside of Canada, supplies acquired from non-registrants, and expenses incurred when the employer was a non-registrant.

Example

21-163.   The following simple example illustrates the calculation of the GST/HST rebate for an employee:

> **EXAMPLE** Tanya Kucharik is a very successful sales manager employed in Ontario. She used her car 93 percent and her cell phone 80 percent for employment related purposes during 2018. She claimed the following expenses on Form T777, Statement of Employment Expenses, for 2018 (all HST taxable amounts include applicable HST at 13 percent):

Cell phone charges (80%)	$ 1,200
Gas, maintenance and car repairs (93%)	17,500
Insurance on car (93%)	1,023
Capital cost allowance (CCA) on car (93%)	3,100

The car on which the CCA was deducted was purchased during 2018. She did not own a car prior to this purchase. Note that car insurance is a financial service on which no HST is charged as it is an exempt supply.

ANALYSIS On Form GST370, her GST/HST rebate would be as follows:

	Eligible Expenses	HST Rebate (13/113)
Eligible Expenses Other Than CCA ($1,200 + $17,500)	$18,700	$2,151
Eligible CCA On Which HST Was Paid	3,100	357
Totals	$21,800	$2,508

21-164.   The employment related expenses that are listed in this calculation will be deducted in Ms. Kucharik's income tax return for 2018.   Under normal circumstances, the HST rebate for 2018 expenses will be claimed in Ms. Kucharik's 2018 tax return. As a result, this amount will be received in 2019, either as part of the 2018 refund or as a decrease in the amount owed for 2018.

21-165.   As the rebate constitutes a reduction in the incurred costs that were deducted by the employee, an adjustment of the deduction is required for amounts that are received. This is accomplished by including the $2,151 HST rebate on expenses other than CCA in Net Income For Tax Purposes in the year in which it is received (2019 in Ms. Kucharik's case). In similar fashion, the amount of any rebates received that related to CCA ($357) will be deducted from the capital cost of the relevant asset in the year in which it is received (again 2019, in the case of Ms. Kucharik). The GST/HST rebate she received in 2018 that was related to her 2017 income tax return would be added to her 2018 Net Income For Tax Purposes.

21-166.   While the rebate is normally claimed in the return in which the expenses are deducted, it can be claimed in any income tax return submitted within four years of the year in which the expenses are claimed.

We suggest you work Self Study Problem Twenty-One-7 at this point.

Residential Property And New Housing Rebate

General Rules For Residential Property

21-167.   Residential real estate is an area of considerable importance to most Canadians. Given this, it is not surprising that residential real estate is provided special treatment under the GST/HST legislation.

21-168.   In somewhat simplified terms, GST/HST applies to residential property only on the first sale of a new home. If a new home is resold in substantially unaltered condition, no GST/HST will apply on this later transaction. If the homeowner undertakes renovations, such as a kitchen, GST/HST will be charged on the materials and other costs going into the renovation. By contrast, if a used home is acquired and substantially renovated before the home is lived in by the purchaser, the acquisition will be treated as a new home purchase and the transaction will be taxable for GST/HST purposes. The CRA defines a substantial renovation as one in which 90 percent or more of the interior of an existing house is removed or replaced.

New Housing Rebate

Calculating The Rebate

21-169.   While sales of new homes attract both GST and HST at the applicable rates, rebates of the amount paid are available. In provinces that do not participate in the HST program, the rebate is equal to 36 percent of the GST paid. However, the situation with participating HST provinces is much more complex, including provincial variations in the HST rebate percentage, as well as the price thresholds. Because of this additional complexity, we will deal only with non-participating provinces in this section. The CRA has a detailed guide covering the many complexities in this area, "GST/HST New Housing Rebate" (RC4028).

21-170.   With its traditional aversion to providing tax incentives related to luxury expenditures, the government has limited this rebate to a maximum value of $6,300, the amount of the GST rebate on a $350,000 home [(36%)(5%)($350,000) = $6,300]. In addition, the rebate is phased out for houses costing more than $350,000 and completely eliminated for homes costing more than $450,000. All of these amounts are before the inclusion of GST.

21-171.   The government's policy goals are accomplished by calculating the rebate as follows:

$$[A][(\$450,000 - B) \div \$100,000],\text{ where}$$

A = The lesser of 36 percent of the GST paid and $6,300; and
B = The greater of $350,000 and the cost of the home.

21-172.   A simple example will illustrate the application of this formula.

EXAMPLE Gilles and Marie Gagnon acquire a new home with a cost of $420,000, paying an additional amount of $21,000 [(5%)($420,000)] in GST.

ANALYSIS As 36 percent of the GST paid is $7,560, an amount in excess of the limit of $6,300, the rebate available to Gilles and Marie will be $1,890 {[$6,300][($450,000 - $420,000) ÷ $100,000]}.

Implementing The Rebate

21-173.   While the GST could be included in the price paid by the home purchaser, with that individual claiming the rebate, this is not the usual industry practice. The usual practice is for the builder to charge the purchaser an amount that is net of the rebate, with the purchaser assigning rights to the GST rebate to the builder. In the case of our example, the builder would charge Gilles and Marie $439,110 ($420,000 + $21,000 - $1,890). From the point of view of convenience for the purchaser, this appears to be an appropriate practice.

We suggest you work Self Study Problems Twenty-One-8 and 9 at this point.

Sale Of A Business

Sale Of Assets

21-174.   The sale of the assets of a business is a taxable supply for GST purposes. This applies regardless of the legal form in which the business is carried on. However, where "all or substantially all" of the assets that the purchaser needs to carry on a business are being acquired by the purchaser, the GST/HST legislation allows the vendor and purchaser to elect to treat the supply as if it were zero-rated.

21-175.   This applies to businesses that provide exempt supplies, as well as to businesses that provide fully taxable or zero-rated supplies. The use of the election is not permitted when the vendor is a registrant and the purchaser is a non-registrant. However, without regard to the type of business, the election can be used when both the vendor and the purchaser are not GST registrants.

21-176.   If the election is made, the vendor does not collect GST/HST on the sale of taxable supplies, and the purchaser cannot claim an input tax credit. As a result, a transfer of the assets of a business can be made without payment of GST/HST. If the election is not made, GST/HST will be collected on the sale. Offsetting input tax credits may be available to the purchaser through the normal input tax credit procedures.

21-177.   In determining whether "all or substantially all" of the assets necessary to carry on the business are transferred, the CRA relies on a 90 percent or more test. The CRA has several policy papers on this election in order to provide registrants with guidance in determining compliance with the 90 percent or more test.

Sale Of Shares

21-178.   As a general rule, the sale of shares in a corporation is not a taxable supply because, under the GST/HST legislation, the sale of a financial instrument such as a share is an exempt supply. As a result, share for share exchanges are not taxable for GST/HST purposes.

Other Situations

Section 85 Rollovers

21-179.   When property used in a commercial activity is rolled into a corporation under Section 85 of the *Income Tax Act*, the rollover is a taxable transaction for GST/HST purposes. For example, if a sole proprietorship or partnership transfers property when a business is incorporated, the rollover of property will be deemed to be a taxable supply for consideration equal to the fair market value of the property. This amount will then be subject to GST/HST.

21-180.   A joint election may be available to avoid any related GST/HST liability, providing the vendor sells or transfers all, or substantially all (i.e., 90 percent or more) of the assets that can reasonably be regarded as being necessary for the purchaser to carry on the business. A further requirement is that, if the vendor is a GST registrant, the purchaser must also be a GST registrant.

21-181.   If the transfer of property is a taxable supply, GST/HST will be payable on the total fair market value of the share and non-share consideration exchanged for the property, with the elected amount under Section 85 of the *Income Tax Act* being irrelevant. If the transferred property is subsequently used in commercial activities, an input tax credit may be claimed by the transferee for any GST/HST paid on the transfer of the property.

Amalgamations, Mergers, Winding-Up Of A Business

21-182.   Where two corporations are merged or amalgamated into a single corporation, or the activities of one corporation are wound up through a merger with another corporation, the new corporation is generally treated for GST/HST purposes as a person separate from each of the predecessor corporations.

21-183.   If the transfer of assets involves an amalgamation under ITA 87 or a winding-up under ITA 88(1), the transfer of assets is deemed not to be a taxable supply for GST/HST purposes and no election is required. The asset or property transferred on the merger or amalgamation is not a taxable supply under the legislation. As a result, there are no GST/HST consequences.

Transfers Within Corporate Groups

21-184.   Transfers of goods and services between members of corporate groups will normally attract GST/HST. However, an election can be made to have such transfers deemed to be made for nil consideration (only for GST/HST purposes), resulting in no required payment of GST/HST.

21-185.   The conditions for this election are quite strict and require either the ownership of at least 90 percent of the voting shares of one corporation by the other, or that the companies be sister corporations owned by a parent corporation. In addition, the electing corporations must be Canadian residents and the supplies involved must be used exclusively (more than 90 percent) in a commercial activity.

Holding Companies

21-186.   Although many holding companies only hold shares or debt and do not carry on a "commercial activity" in the usual sense, GST/HST legislation allows holding companies to register for the GST/HST and claim input tax credits if they hold shares or debt in another company that owns property that is used at least 90 percent for commercial activities. These provisions allow holding companies to obtain refunds of GST/HST paid on the purchase of property or services solely related to the holding of the shares or debt.

Ceasing To Carry On Business

21-187.   When a person ceases to carry on a commercial activity, or becomes a small supplier and, as a result, ceases to be a registrant, the person is deemed to have sold all assets at fair market value upon deregistration. If the assets were used for commercial purposes, GST/HST will be payable on the deemed dispositions.

Specific Applications

21-188.   There are many GST/HST procedures that are specific to certain types of transactions or organizations (e.g., import transactions or charitable organizations). Detailed coverage of such procedures clearly goes beyond the scope of a text which focuses on income taxation. However, we do believe that it is useful to provide you with some general information on some of these specific areas:

- **Imports**   In general, imports are subject to GST/HST.

- **Exports**   In general, exports of goods and services from Canada are zero-rated. This means that while no GST/HST is charged on exports, input tax credits can be claimed by the exporter.

- **Charities**   In general, the revenues of registered charities are exempt from GST/HST. However, revenues from commercial activities (e.g., museum gift shop revenues) are fully taxable subject to the small supplier threshold of $50,000 (a special rule for charities expands the small supplier threshold from $30,000 to $50,000). A special provision provides for a 50 percent rebate of the federal GST paid on purchases related to exempt activities. In the HST provinces, there is a 50 percent rebate of the federal portion of the HST on such purchases, as well as an additional rebate of the provincial portion of the HST. The provincial rebate varies from province to province.

- **Not-For-Profit Organizations**   In general, the revenues of not-for-profit organizations are fully taxable (in contrast to the situation with registered charities). However, exemptions are provided for such services as subsidized home care and meals on wheels. As was the case with registered charities, qualifying not-for-profit organizations receive a 50 percent rebate of the federal GST paid on purchases related to exempt activities. In the HST provinces, there is a 50 percent rebate of the federal portion of the HST on such purchases, as well as an additional rebate of the provincial portion of the HST. The provincial rebate varies from province to province.

  To be classified as a qualifying not-for-profit organization, the organization must receive significant government funding. Such funding is regarded as significant when at least 40 percent of total revenues come from this source.

- **Government Bodies**   All federal government departments receive a full rebate of the GST/HST paid on purchases by means of a tax remission order. Each provincial and territorial government is registered as a separate entity for the GST/HST, and uses "certificates" to receive point of purchase relief from the GST/HST.

- **Crown Corporations**   Crown corporations are not GST/HST exempt and are registered as separate persons for purposes of the GST/HST.

- **Municipalities, Universities, Schools And Hospitals (MUSH)**   These organizations are classified as "Public Institutions" in the GST/HST legislation and, except where there are specific exemptions, their revenues are fully taxable. Examples of exemptions include property taxes for municipalities, course fees for universities, and medical services for hospitals. Rebates for the federal GST paid on purchases related to exempt activities are available, with the rates varying from 67 percent for universities to 83 percent for hospitals to 100 percent for municipalities. In the HST provinces, the same rebates are available for the federal portion of the HST, as well as an additional rebate of the provincial portion of the HST. The provincial rebate varies from province to province.

- **Financial Institutions**   The GST/HST legislation defines financial institutions to include "listed" financial institutions, such as banks and insurance companies, as well as deemed financial institutions (e.g., businesses with financial revenues exceeding specified threshold levels). Revenues from providing financial services are designated as exempt. This means that, for an institution where the bulk of its revenues is from the provision of financial services, only limited input tax credits will be available.

21-189.   These brief comments serve only to give a very general view of the approach taken to these specific types of transactions and organizations. If you are dealing with any of these applications you will, of course, have to consult a more specialized source of information.

Partnerships And GST/HST

General Rules

21-190.   The ITA treats a partnership as a person only for the purpose of computing income or loss to its partners. The *Excise Tax Act* considers partnerships to be persons that are generally required to register for the GST/HST with respect to commercial activities. In addition, anything a partner does with respect to partnership activities is considered done by the partnership and not by the partners themselves.

21-191.   The result is that it is the partnership, and not the partners, who is required to register for the GST/HST with respect to partnership business. Given this, partnerships are required to collect and remit GST/HST on taxable supplies and are eligible for input tax credits. Partners are jointly and severally liable however with respect to GST/HST that relates to the partnership business.

Partner Expenses

21-192.   Non-reimbursed expenditures for property or services incurred personally by individual partners, which relate to the partnership business and that are deductible for income tax purposes by the partners, are generally eligible for the Employee And Partner GST/HST Rebate. Such property and services include office expenses, travel expenses, meals and entertainment, parking, lodging and CCA on certain capital assets such as motor vehicles. This rebate was discussed beginning in Paragraph 21-158.

21-193.   A partner can only claim a rebate to the extent that the partnership could have otherwise claimed an ITC if it had incurred the expense directly. This means that, if a partnership provides only exempt goods or services, the partners would not be eligible to claim a GST/HST partner rebate for expenses that they deduct from their share of partnership income.

Disposition Of A Partnership Interest

21-194.   A partnership interest may be disposed of or acquired in many situations. These include the admission of a new partner or retirement of an existing partner. A partnership interest is considered a "financial instrument" and is exempt from the GST/HST. In addition, any legal and accounting fees related to the acquisition or disposition of a partnership interest are not eligible for an input tax credit since they relate to a financial instrument and not to the partnership's business. Finally, drawings and capital contributions that specifically relate to a partnership interest are considered "financial services" and are also exempt from the GST/HST.

Transfers Between Partners And Partnerships

21-195.   In general, there is no GST/HST counterpart to the rollover rule that allows property to be transferred by a partner to a partnership on a tax deferred basis. An exception to this is the case where a business is being transferred and 90 percent or more of the property that is necessary to carry on that business is also transferred. In such cases, the transfer is not subject to GST/HST as long as both transferor and transferee are registrants.

21-196.   Transfers of property between partnerships and partners may be subject to GST/HST, generally depending on the status of the transferor and transferee as registrants and whether they are engaged in commercial activities. GST/HST is not applicable to transfers of cash, accounts receivable, or debt however, since these are either not considered property for GST/HST purposes or are considered exempt financial services.

Reorganization Of The Partnership

21-197.   The admission of new partners or retirement of existing partners that terminate the old partnership and result in the creation of a new partnership will not cause the new partnership to register for GST/HST as a new person. As a result, there are no GST/HST implications on the transfer of the old partnership property to the new partnership.

21-198.   There are no GST/HST implications to the new partnership where a partnership has ceased to exist, more than half of its members form a new partnership, and transfer 90 percent or more of the property they receive on the cessation of the old partnership to the new partnership. The new partnership is considered to be a continuation of the old partnership for GST/HST purposes.

Trusts And GST/HST

21-199.   A trust is included in the definition of person under the *Excise Tax Act* and, as a consequence, a trust that is engaged in commercial activities is required to register and collect GST/HST on taxable supplies. However, an interest in a trust is considered to be a financial instrument, so the sale of an interest in a trust is an exempt financial service and is not subject to GST/HST.

21-200.   A distribution of trust property by a trustee to a beneficiary of a trust is treated as a supply by the trust. The consideration is the same as proceeds of disposition for purposes of the *Income Tax Act*. Distributions of non-commercial property by a trust in the process of the settlement of an estate are generally not considered to be in the course of commercial activities of the trust and are GST/HST exempt. Similarly, a distribution of financial securities is GST/HST exempt as a financial service. The GST/HST only applies to properties acquired by the trust that are used in a commercial activity.

21-201.   Where property is settled through the use of an inter vivos trust, including an alter ego or joint spousal or common-law partner trust, the consideration for the property transferred is deemed to equal the amount determined under the *Income Tax Act*. The supply is considered to be made at fair market value and GST/HST is payable on all taxable supplies. However, when an estate is settled, an election can be filed to distribute any property of a deceased registrant without the payment of GST/HST. In this situation, the beneficiary of the deceased's estate must be a registrant, and the beneficiary is deemed to have acquired the property for use exclusively in a commercial activity.

Additional Supplementary Self Study Problems Are Available Online.

Key Terms Used In This Chapter

21-202.   The following is a list of the key terms used in this Chapter. These terms, and their meanings, are compiled in the Glossary located at the back of the Study Guide.

Capital Personal Property	New Housing GST/HST Rebate
Commercial Activity	Partner And Employee GST/HST Rebate
Commodity Tax	Quick Method
Employee And Partner GST/HST Rebate	Registrant
Exempt Goods And Services	Streamlined ITC Accounting
Fully Taxable Goods And Services	Small Suppliers Exemption
Goods And Services Tax (GST/HST)	Supply
Harmonized Sales Tax (HST)	Transaction Tax
Input Tax Credit (ITC)	Value Added Tax (VAT)
MUSH	Zero-Rated Goods And Services

Problems For Self Study (Online)

To provide practice in problem solving, there are Self Study and Supplementary Self Study problems available on MyLab Accounting.

Within the text we have provided an indication of when it would be appropriate to work each Self Study problem. The detailed solutions for Self Study problems can be found in the print and online Study Guide.

We provide the Supplementary Self Study problems for those who would like additional practice in problem solving. The detailed solutions for the Supplementary Self Study problems are available online, not in the Study Guide.

The .PDF file "Self Study Problems for Volume 2" on MyLab contains the following for Chapter 21:

- 9 Self Study problems,
- 6 Supplementary Self Study problems, and
- detailed solutions for the Supplementary Self Study problems.

Assignment Problems

(The solutions for these problems are only available in
the solutions manual that has been provided to your instructor.)

Assignment Problem Twenty-One - 1

(Turnover Tax vs. GST)

You have been appointed tax policy advisor to a country that has never used taxes on goods or services. Because of the increasing need for revenues, the Finance Minister, Maximus Surplus, is committed to introducing a sales tax. He is considering two alternatives:

- A 5 percent value added tax using the same invoice-credit approach that has been incorporated into Canada's GST system.

- A turnover tax that is applied as goods move from the raw materials supplier, to the manufacturer, to the wholesaler, to the distributor, to the retailer, and finally to the consumer. Minister Surplus would like you to calculate the turnover tax rate that would produce the same amount of revenue as the alternative 5 percent GST.

In illustrating this to Minister Surplus, he would like you to assume a sale price of $250, plus tax, by the raw materials supplier to the manufacturer. At this and subsequent turnover points, he would like you to assume a markup by each seller equal to 40 percent of their before tax cost.

Required: Provide the requested information with an explanation of your calculations.

Assignment Problem Twenty-One - 2

(Registration Requirements)

Joan Kraft has always had a great love of flowers. After many years of working tirelessly for other unappreciative florists, she has worked up the courage to start her own business.

It will be called Joan's Own Flowers and will have a December 31 year end. Her store opens for business on July 1, 2017 and, during the first 18 months of operations has the following quarterly revenues:

July To September, 2017	$6,000
October To December, 2017	5,000
January To March, 2018	8,000
April To June, 2018	10,000
July To September, 2018	16,000
October To December, 2018	20,000
Total For 18 Months	$65,000

Required:

A.   Advise Joan as to when she must start collecting GST. Also advise her by what date GST registration must be completed.

B.   How would your answer differ if the revenues for the April to June, 2018 quarter had been $32,000 instead of $10,000?

Assignment Problem Twenty-One - 3
(Registration Requirements And GST Collectible)

After years of study, Martin believes that he has developed a process for making perfect maca-roons. He also believes that there is significant demand for these tasty treats. Based on this, on March 1, 2018, he opens a retail operation in an Edmonton mall.

His new business will have a December 31 year end. All of his sales will be in Alberta, a prov-ince that has no provincial sales tax. Martin wants to delay collecting GST for as long as legally possible.

Martin's Macaroons had monthly sales for 2018 as follows:

Month	Sales
March	$ 2,420
April	$ 4,650
May	13,780
June	13,240
July	$13,780
August	15,760
September	16,480
October	$16,670
November	18,490
December	21,750

Required:

A.   Indicate the date on which Martin's Macaroons will be required to start collecting GST and the date by which Martin will be required to register.

B.   Assume that Martin's Macaroons has elected to file GST on a quarterly basis . Calculate the GST collectible for each quarter of 2018 and specify the due date of each GST return and payment.

C.   Assume that Martin's Macaroons files GST on an annual basis. Calculate the GST collect-ible for 2018 and specify the due date of the GST return and payment.

D.   Assume that in January, 2018, Martin comes to you for advice on when he should register for the GST. What factors should he consider?

Assignment Problem Twenty-One - 4
(Regular GST Return)

Saul's Sports Sales And Service is an unincorporated business, owned and operated by Saul Bernstein. It is resident in Alberta and all of its capital assets are located in that province. However, the business features several unique products that are shipped to various other provinces. In addition to selling various sports oriented products, it also operates a small (but growing) medical clinic specializing in sports injuries. These services are only provided in Alberta.

Saul's Sports Sales And Service is an annual filer for GST purposes. Alberta does not participate in the HST program and does not have a provincial sales tax.

The following is a summary of the financial statement information for the current year. All amounts are presented without the inclusion of applicable GST.

Revenues (Note 1)		$836,339
Less Expenses:		
Cost Of Goods Sold (Note 2)	($427,386)	
Amortization Expense	(36,348)	
Salaries And Wages (Note 3	(123,746)	
Interest Expense	(6,783)	
Other Expenses (Note 4)	(62,477)	(656,740)
Net Income Before Income Taxes		$179,599

Note 1 The various components of the total revenues of the business were as follows:

Sales In The Alberta Store	$563,420
Goods Shipped To Ontario	163,450
Goods Shipped To Manitoba	62,341
Goods Shipped To Saskatchewan	34,782
Medical Clinic Revenues	12,346
Total Revenues	$836,339

Note 2 Purchases of goods during the year were as follows:

Purchases From Alberta Suppliers	$382,946
Purchases From Ontario Suppliers	32,468
Purchases From British Columbia Suppliers	46,982
Total Purchases	$462,396

Note 3 Of the total Salaries And Wages, 5 percent related to the medical clinic.

Note 4 Other Expenses, before the inclusion of applicable GST, included the following:

Business Meals And Entertainment	$12,466
Gym Membership Fee For Saul	456
Property Insurance For Building	4,683
Drugs For Medical Clinic (Zero-Rated Taxable Supplies)	4,000

All of the remaining Other Expenses related to the costs of operating the retail business (ex., office supplies, telephone, packaging etc.).

Capital expenditures for the current year were as follows:

- $872,000 for a building. Of the total space 35 percent is used for the medical clinic. The remainder is used for the retail operations of the business.

- $48,300 for a new automobile that is used 100 percent in the retail business.
- $32,345 for office equipment. This equipment is used 15 percent in the provision of medical services.

Required: Calculate the net GST payable or refund that Saul's Sports Sales And Service will remit or receive for the current year.

Assignment Problem Twenty-One - 5
(Regular HST Return)

Conan's Comics is an unincorporated business owned by Conan Barbarian. All of its operations are located in Newfoundland. The HST rate in that province is 15 percent.

The business is an HST registrant that sells both fully taxable and zero-rated goods. In addition, Conan's Comics provides exempt services. The business is an annual filer for HST purposes.

The Income Statement for the current year is as follows. All amounts are before the addition of applicable HST.

Revenues:		
Fully Taxable Goods	$643,431	
Zero-Rated Goods	311,412	
Exempt Services	416,253	$1,371,096
Less Expenses:		
Cost Of Fully Taxable Goods Sold	($489,567)	
Cost Of Zero-Rated Goods Sold	(203,642)	
Amortization	(106,911)	
Salaries And Wages	(62,435)	
Interest Expense	(16,243)	
Other Operating Expenses	(28,968)	(907,766)
Income Before Taxes		$ 463,330
Less: Federal And Provincial Income Taxes		(157,243)
Net Income		$ 306,087

Other Information:

1. Inventories of fully taxable goods decreased by $24,650 during this period, while inventories of zero-rated goods increased by $19,243. The zero-rated sales were generated by purchasing and selling zero-rated supplies.

2. Capital expenditures for this period amounted to $1,950,000, with HST being paid on all amounts. Of this total, $1,260,000 was for a building that will be used 35 percent for the provision of fully taxable supplies and 25 percent for the provision of zero-rated supplies. The remaining $690,000 was for equipment that will be used 38 percent in the provision of fully taxable supplies and 27 percent for the provision of zero-rated supplies. HST was paid on the acquisition of all assets on which amortization is being taken during this period.

3. Of the Other Operating Expenses, 62 percent were related to the provision of fully taxable and 24 percent to the provision of zero-rated supplies.

4. Of the Salaries And Wages, 65 percent were paid to employees involved in providing exempt supplies.

Required: Calculate the net HST payable or refund that Conan's Comics will remit or receive for the current year.

Assignment Problem Twenty-One - 6
(Quick Method)

John, Alice, Alex, and Jerry Rangi are quadruplets. Their father financed an unincorporated business for each of them 3 years ago. They were each allowed to select their own line of business. As an incentive, their father has indicated that the child who owns the business that generates the most income in the first 5 years will receive a gift of $1,000,000 in cash.

All of the businesses are located in Ontario, with all of the revenues being generated in that province. As all of the business were expected to have taxable supplies well in excess of $30,000, each business was registered for the Ontario HST at its inception.

The siblings provide you with the following annual information for their businesses. All amounts are reported inclusive of HST. None of the sales or purchases were zero-rated or exempt, and none of the businesses made any capital expenditures during the year.

	Type Of Business	Sales	Purchases
John	Computer Sales, Repairs And Tutoring	$ 103,960	$ 26,160
Alice	Bicycle Sales And Service	194,360	159,330
Alex	Menswear Sales And Custom Tailoring	126,560	47,460
Jerry	Tarot Card Reading And Cell Phone Sales	84,750	41,810

The HST rate in Ontario is 13 percent. The Quick Method remittance rates are 4.4 percent for resellers and 8.8 percent for service providers. When calculating the applicable remittance rate, assume the sales and purchases of the previous year were equal to those of the current year.

Required: Recommend whether any of the businesses should use the Quick Method to calculate net HST remittances. Show all of your calculations.

Assignment Problem Twenty-One - 7
(Regular And Quick Method GST Returns)

Johnny Dangerous has successfully engaged in criminal activity since he was 12 years old. Financially, he has been very successful and, to date, he has no criminal record. All of his activity is carried out in Ontario. The HST rate for Ontario is 13 percent. The Ontario quick method rates are 4.4 percent for businesses that purchase goods for resale and 8.8 percent for service providers.

Early in his career, his father taught him that the notorious Chicago gangster Al Capone was sent to jail, not for his many murders and other illegal acts, but for tax evasion. Taking this lesson to heart, Johnny has been very diligent about filing both income tax returns and GST returns on time. For the 2018 taxation year, his activities fall into three categories:

Contract Assassinations   Johnny accepts contracts for assassinations at a base rate of $15,000. He offers volume discounts and charges higher fees for particularly difficult cases. As he enjoys the work, Johnny handles all of this activity personally.

During 2018, his revenues from this work totaled $323,000. While he does not specifically advise his clients that they are paying HST, he files his GST return on the basis that the amounts collected are HST included.

Export Of Illegal Drugs   A growing part of Johnny's activities involve exporting heroin and other illegal drugs to the U.S. market. His 2018 revenues from this activity totaled $113,000.

Loan Sharking   As a service to his clients, he offers extremely high interest rate loans to individuals who cannot find other sources of financing. Revenue from this source totaled $87,000 for 2018.

Johnny has an assistant, Cruella Ratched, who works on a full time basis for his business. Since he lost his driver's licence two years ago, her duties include driving him to his jobs using her car. Her salary for 2018 is $85,000 which includes a $12,000 car allowance.

Johnny maintains an office which he rents for $4,000 per month, plus HST. During the year, miscellaneous office costs total $6,900 plus applicable HST. This includes $400 for business insurance. The furniture, fixtures and art in the office are leased at a cost of $2,000 per month, plus HST. Telephone and internet cost $125 per month, plus HST.

Johnny has calculated that these costs should be allocated to his three business activities as follows:

Contract Assassinations	65%
Export Of Illegal Drugs	25%
Loan Sharking	10%

Expenditures specific to his various activities are as follows:

Contract Assassinations   Johnny uses a Glock 9mm for this activity. He disposes of each gun after a single use, making this a significant cost of doing business. On January 1, 2018, he had 5 of these guns on hand. Their total capital cost was $3,101, plus HST and they had been allocated to Class 8. They were the only assets in this class and on January 1, 2018, the UCC for this Class was $2,792. During 2018, Johnny acquires an additional 19 guns at $549 each, plus HST. After using each weapon once, he disposes of 20 of his guns. There were no proceeds associated with the disposals.

His only other costs associated with this activity were for travel. Airline, hotel, and taxis totaled $12,000 plus HST. Meals while travelling totaled $7,492 plus HST.

Export Of Illegal Drugs   Costs associated with this activity are as follows:

Purchases Of Processing Equipment (Including HST)	$11,300
Security Service For Lab (Including HST)	5,650
Shipping Costs (No HST - Using Illegal Immigrants)	3,000
Bribes To Customs Officials (No HST)	4,500
Cost Of Materials Exported (No HST)	21,700

Loan Sharking   Johnny used bank loans to finance these loans. Interest on these loans for 2018 was $12,600. When he experienced difficulties with collections he used a former World Wrestling Foundation champion to enforce the payment of the loans. Costs for this service for 2018 were $4,800 (no HST - small supplier).

Required:

A. Determine Johnny's HST payable (refund) for the year ending December 31, 2018, using the regular method of determination.

B. Determine whether Johnny can use the quick method for determining his HST payment or refund for 2018.

C. Without regard to your conclusion in Part B, determine Johnny's HST payable (refund) for the year ending December 31, 2018, using the quick method.

Assignment Problem Twenty-One - 8
(Regular And Quick Method HST Returns)

For the year ending December 31, 2018, the Income Statement of Sloan Inc. is as follows (all amounts are without the inclusion of applicable HST):

Revenues:		
Sales of Fully Taxable Goods	$291,600	
Provision of Exempt Services	105,300	$396,900
Less Expenses:		
Cost Of Goods Sold	($166,050)	
Amortization Expense	(75,600)	
Salaries And Wages	(16,200)	
Rent	(56,700)	
Interest Expense	(12,150)	
Other Operating Expenses	(36,450)	(363,150)
Income Before Taxes		$ 33,750
Less: Federal And Provincial Income Taxes		(10,800)
Net Income		$ 22,950

Other Information:

1. Sloan Inc. is a retail business located in Ontario where all of the Company's revenues and expenses are incurred. The HST rate in Ontario is 13 percent. The quick method rates applicable to the province are 4.4 percent for businesses that purchase goods for resale, and 8.8 percent for service providers.

2. For the previous year ending December 31, 2017, Sloan's cost of goods purchased for resale totaled $148,500 and the revenue from sales of taxable supplies totaled $407,700. Both amounts are before HST.

3. Inventories of taxable goods decreased by $10,800 during the year.

4. All of the Other Operating Expenses involved the acquisition of fully taxable supplies and were acquired to assist in the provision of fully taxable supplies.

5. Of the Salaries And Wages, 52 percent were paid to employees involved in providing exempt services.

6. A capital expenditure was made during the year at an HST inclusive cost of $83,620. The expenditure was for furniture and fixtures that will be used 60 percent for the provision of fully taxable goods. HST was paid on the acquisition of all assets on which amortization is being taken during this period.

Required: For the year ending December 31, 2018:

A. Determine if Sloan is eligible to use the Quick Method and the Quick Method remittance rate that would be applicable.

B. Calculate the net HST payable or refund that Sloan Inc. will remit or receive using regular HST calculations.

C. Assume that Sloan is eligible to use the Quick Method. Calculate the net HST payable or refund that Sloan Inc. will remit or receive using the Quick Method.

Assignment Problem Twenty-One - 9
(Employee HST Rebate Including CCA)

Sarah Martin is a resident of Ontario, a participating province that assesses HST at a 13 percent rate. Her employer is a large public company with all of its operations in that province.

Sarah's work requires extensive travel on behalf of her employer. For this travel, she uses her own car. The car was purchased in 2017 at a price before HST of $27,500. HST raised the total cost to $31,075 [(113%)($27,500)]. In 2017 she claimed maximum CCA of $4,661 [(1/2)(30%)($31,075)]. The portion of her HST rebate related to her car CCA equaled $536 [(13/113)($4,661)]. Sarah indicates that she plans to claim maximum CCA in 2018.

The family uses her husband's car for all personal purposes so that Sarah's car is used 100 percent for employment related activities. Sarah does not receive any reimbursement or allowance from her employer for her travel or car expenses.

In her 2018 tax return, Sarah deducts the following amounts in the calculation of her net employment income:

Accommodation (Includes HST Of $1,560)	$13,560
Business Meals And Entertainment - Deductible Amount (Includes HST of $1,170)	10,170
Automobile Costs:	
Gas And Maintenance (Includes HST Of $1,430)	12,430
Interest On Automobile Loan	1,805
Insurance	1,460
Total Deductions Excluding CCA	$39,425

Required: Calculate the maximum CCA that Sarah can claim on his car for 2018. In addition, calculate the 2018 HST rebate that Sarah will claim as a result of her deductible expenses.

Assignment Problem Twenty-One - 10
(Regular And Streamlined HST Returns)

Adeedas Sports is a retail business located in Nova Scotia. All of its revenues occur and expenses are incurred in that province. It has no associated business and files its GST return on an annual basis. Nova Scotia has a 15 percent HST.

Adeedas's Income Statement for the current year is as follows. All amounts are shown without the relevant HST.

Revenues:		
Fully Taxable Goods	$397,523	
Exempt Services	109,564	$507,087
Less Expenses:		
Cost Of Goods Sold (All Taxable)	($201,372)	
Amortization Expense	(34,784)	
Salaries And Wages	(25,679)	
Rent	(27,841)	
Interest Expense	(75,964)	
Other Operating Expenses	(31,478)	(397,118)
Income Before Taxes		$109,969
Less: Federal And Provincial Income Taxes		(21,489)
Net Income		$ 88,480

Other Information:

1. Inventories of taxable goods decreased by $19,561 during the year.

2. A capital expenditure was made during the year at an HST inclusive cost of $105,294. The expenditure was for equipment that will be used 60 percent for the provision of fully taxable goods. HST was paid on the acquisition of all assets on which amortization is being taken during this period.

3. All of the Other Operating Expenses involved the acquisition of fully taxable supplies and were acquired to assist in the provision of fully taxable supplies.

4. The rent was not subject to HST as it was paid to a non-registrant. The proportion of the leased property that is used for the provision of exempt services is 20 percent.

5. Of the Salaries And Wages, 40 percent were paid to employees involved in providing exempt services.

Required:

A. Calculate the net HST payable or refund that Adeedas Sports will remit or receive for the current year using regular GST calculations.

B. Calculate the net HST payable or refund that Adeedas Sports will remit or receive for the current year using the Streamlined Input Tax Credit Method.

Assignment Problem Twenty-One - 11
(New Housing GST Rebate)

Rebecca Forma lives in Alberta and is planning to buy a home outside of Edmonton. Alberta does not participate in the HST program and does not have a provincial sales tax. The properties that are under consideration can be described as follows:

Property A is a 10 year old property that was built several years ago at a cost of $285,000. It will not require any renovations and is being offered to Rebecca for $423,000.

Property B is an old house that is being offered in "as is" condition for $225,000. In order to be livable, it will require major renovations involving over 90 percent of the interior floor space. The estimated cost of these renovations is $180,000. The vendor has agreed to make these renovations and will charge Rebecca $405,000 for the improved property.

Property C is a new house that is under construction. The basic price at this point is $325,000. To meet Rebecca's requirements, it will need significant upgrades. The builder will complete $60,000 of these improvements prior to the sale. Additional improvements will be carried out by Rebecca using materials that will cost $25,000.

Required: Before making any offer to purchase, Rebecca has asked you to determine what the GST and total out-of-pocket costs of each purchase would be.

INDEX

A

Abbreviations 39

Accounting
• *See* Generally Accepted Accounting
  Principles

Accounting Methods - GST . . . 991

Accounts Receivable
• business income 256
• election on sale of business . . 285
• reserves 257, 276
• transfer under section 85 . . . 766

Acquisition Of Control
• deemed disposition election . . 675
• deemed year end 672
• defined 672
• investment tax credits . . . 685
• loss carry overs 671
• restrictions on charitable donations . 673
• restrictions on losses . . . 673
• unrecognized losses at year end . 674

Active Business Income - Defined . 599

Additional Refundable Tax (ART) . . 633

Adjusted Cost Base
• change in use 369
• death of a taxpayer 437
• defined 352
• government grants and assistance . 353
• GST/HST/PST considerations . . 354
• income trusts 330
• interest - idle land 353
• investment tax credits . . . 682
• leaving Canada 375
• mutual funds 332
• negative amounts 354
• non-arm's length transactions . . 429
• property taxes - idle land . . 353
• stock option shares 353
• superficial losses 353

Adjusted Cost Base - Partnership Interest
• basic concept 869
• capital contributions 871
• capital gains and losses . . . 870
• charitable donations . . . 871
• death of a taxpayer 872
• dividends 870
• drawings 871

Adjusted Cost Base - Partnership Interest (Continued)
• limited partners 872
• negative amounts 871
• net business income . . . 869
• political contributions . . . 871
• timing of adjustments 869

Adoption Expenses Tax Credit . . 157

Advance Income Tax Rulings
• described 17

Adventure In The Nature Of Trade
• defined 251

Affiliated Persons
• defined 768
• losses on non-depreciable property . 768

Age Tax Credit 155

Aggregate Investment Income
• defined 630

Alimony
• *See* Spousal Support

Alimony Payments
• *See* Support Payments

Allocations To Partners
• capital gains and losses . . . 864
• charitable donations . . . 862
• dividend income 865
• foreign source income . . . 865
• foreign tax credits 865
• methods of allocation . . . 866
• political contributions . . . 863
• tax credits 866

Allowable Business Investment Loss
• defined 521
• lifetime capital gains deduction, effect 522
• special treatment 521

Allowances
• automobiles 109
• employee's perspective . . . 110
• employer's perspective . . . 110
• employment income . . . 107
• general rules 107
• retiring 403
• taxable vs. non-taxable . . . 108
• vs. reimbursement 107

Alter Ego Trust
• defined 899
• rollover to trust 902
• tax planning 917
• transfers to capital beneficiaries . 904

Alternative Minimum Tax
• adjusted taxable income computation 548
• carry forward provisions . . . 549
• defined 547
• tax credits allowed 549
• tax free dividends 736
• trusts 912

Amalgamations
• asset bump-up 822, 825
• comparison with ITA 88(1) wind-up 827
• GST considerations 1006
• loss carry overs 820
• non-tax considerations . . . 822
• position of the shareholders . . 821
• procedures 819
• tax planning 822, 827
• vertical amalgamations . . . 822

Amended Income Tax Returns . . I 66

Amortization
• compared to CCA 201

Ancillary Tuition Fees Tax Credit . 168

Annual Business Limit
• small business deduction . . . 601

Annual Gains Limit
• lifetime capital gains deduction . . 526

Annuities
• income inclusion 418
• RRSP transfers 476

Appeals
• Federal Court of Canada . . . 70
• general rules 67
• notice of objection 67
• Supreme Court of Canada . . 70
• Tax Court of Canada 69
• time limits 67

Appraisal Costs - Deductibility . . 264

Apprenticeship Job Creation Tax Credit 683

Artists - Special Inventory Rules . . 274

This index includes the entries for both Volume I and II. Volume II begins on page 511.

Assessment
- appeals 67
- tax returns 65

Associated Corporations
- control defined 679
- deeming rules 679
- definitions 678
- examples 679
- group defined 678
- related persons 678
- small business deduction . . 601, 677
- specified shares 678

Associated Persons
- GST 1001

At-Risk Rules
- at-risk amount calculations . . 874
- partnerships 874

Attendant Care Costs
- disability supports deduction . . 413

Automobiles
- CCA classes and rates . . . 207
- change in use 226, 375
- deductibility of milage costs . . 263
- deduction for employees . . . 127
- employee benefits 99
- employer supplied - tax planning . 106
- input tax credits 990
- leasing costs example . . . 271
- limits on CCA 269
- limits on deductions . . . 269
- limits on interest costs . . . 269
- limits on leasing costs . . . 270
- operating cost benefit . . . 103
- parking benefit 103
- payments to employer for use . . 103
- separate classes 205
- standby charge 100
- summary of employment benefits . 104

Available For Use Rules - CCA . . 204

Avoidance Of Tax
- described 71
- tax planning objective . . . 37

Awards
- employment income 94

B

Bad Debts
- deductibility 257
- example 257
- sale of a business 285
- sale of capital property . . . 359

Basic Federal Tax - Defined . . . 533

Beneficiary - Defined For Trusts . . 893

Benefits For Employees
- See Employment Income

Billed Basis Of Revenue Recognition . 283

Board And Lodging
- employment income 93

Bond Discount - Deductibility . . . 275

Bonus Arrangements
- tax planning 84

Bonusing Down
- CCPC active business income . . 723

Books And Records
- GST/HST requirements . . . 1001
- requirements to retain . . . 64

Boot - Defined 764

Buildings
- CCA classes and rates . . . 206
- terminal losses 360

Business
- See Also Deductions From Business Income
- defined 251
- See Business Income
- See Losses
- sale of an incorporated business . 833

Business Combinations
- share for share exchange . . 807

Business Expenses
- See Deductions From Business Income

Business Income
- adventure in the nature of trade . 251
- amounts received or receivable . 256
- Canada/U.S. tax treaty . . . 936
- crowdfunding 259
- definition 251
- example 278
- foreign source 334, 953
- gambling profits 260
- illegal activities 260
- inclusions 256
- integration 625, 627
- inventory valuation 273
- non-residents, earned by . . 20, 935
- reconciliation schedule . . . 277
- reserves 276
- vs. capital gains 252
- vs. employment income . . 86
- vs. GAAP 254
- vs. property income . . . 250, 305

Business Investment Loss - Defined . 521

Business Losses
- See Carry Overs

C

Canada Caregiver Tax Credit
- background 152
- calculation 153
- described 153
- for child under 18 152

Canada Education Savings Grants . 422

Canada Employment Tax Credit . . 156

Canada Learning Bonds 423

Canada Pension Plan
- employees 86
- payments on self-employed earnings 405
- payments received 402
- refund of excess contributions . . 171
- self-employed individuals . . . 86
- tax credits 171

Canada Revenue Agency
- administration 49
- collection and enforcement . . 72
- publications 17
- web site 16

Canada/U.S. Tax Treaty
- business income 936
- dispositions of taxable Canadian property 939
- dividends received 942
- employment income . . . 937
- foreign source capital gains . . 954
- foreign source employment income . 952
- general information 16
- interest income 941, 954
- pension income 944
- rents 942
- residence of individuals . . . 27
- residence vs. citizenship . . . 28
- royalties 942

Canadian Controlled Private Corporations
- additional refundable tax on investment income . . . 633
- allowable business investment loss . 521
- bonusing down 723
- decision to incorporate . . . 721
- defined 599
- dividend refund 645
- electing not to be a CCPC . . . 723
- excessive eligible dividend designation (EEDD) . . 657
- general rate reduction . . . 612
- instalment payments 61
- investment income . . . 633, 636
- limits on small business deduction . 604
- refundable Part I tax 636
- refundable taxes 645
- See Small Business Deduction

Canadian Partnership Defined . . 876

Capital Assets
- adjustments to cost 352
- capital dividend account . . . 688
- change in use 369
- deemed dispositions . . . 352
- defined 253, 350
- disposition defined 351
- proceeds of disposition . . . 352
- transfer under section 85 . . . 767
- transfers to a spouse . . . 432

Capital Cost
- assets transferred under section 85 . 774
- determination 202
- government assistance . . . 202
- GST/HST considerations . . . 202
- interest capitalization . . . 202
- investment tax credits . . . 682

This index includes the entries for both Volume I and II. Volume II begins on page 511.

Capital Cost (Continued)
- non-arm's length acquisition . . 202
- vs. current expenditure . . . 203

Capital Cost Allowance
- accounting procedures compared . 199
- additions to class 200
- assets transferred under section 85 . 774
- automobiles 207
- available for use rules . . . 204
- buildings 206
- buildings - terminal loss . . . 360
- change in use 369
- classes 204
- commonly used classes . . . 206
- compared to amortization . . 201
- computer hardware . . . 208
- computer software . . . 207
- disposals 216
- dispositions 201
- franchises 207
- general rules 199
- goodwill 208
- GST/HST considerations . . 202
- intangibles - limited life . . . 207
- intangibles - unlimited life . . 208
- interest capitalized . . . 202
- involuntary disposition election . 378
- leasehold interest (improvements) . 207
- manufacturing and processing assets 208
- methods 205
- non-residential buildings . . 206, 226
- partnerships 863
- patents 207, 208
- rates 206
- recapture of CCA . . . 218
- rental property 316
- replacement property . . . 378
- schedule for determining . . 223
- separate businesses . . . 205
- separate class election . . 205, 225
- separate classes . . . 205
- short fiscal periods . . . 211
- system software . . . 208
- tax planning 215
- terminal loss 219
- terminology 199
- trusts 910
- undepreciated capital cost . . 199
- unlimited life intangibles . . 208

Capital Dividend Account . . . 688

Capital Dividends
- election to designate . . . 693
- taxation of 333

Capital Gains
- 1972 tax reform 349
- adjusted cost base defined . . 352
- allocation to partners . . . 870
- attribution 439
- bad debts 359
- calculation 354
- capital dividend account . . 688
- change in use 369
- charitable donations . . . 541

Capital Gains (Continued)
- convertible property . . . 832
- criteria for identifying . . . 253
- *See* Death of A Taxpayer
- deemed dispositions . . . 369
- defined 253, 350
- depreciable capital property . . 218
- disposition defined . . . 351
- economic policy . . . 349
- election on shares . . . 351
- farm property 364
- foreign exchange . . . 366
- foreign source 954
- gifts 351
- identical properties . . . 355
- inclusion rate changes . . 350
- involuntary dispositions . . 378
- *See* Leaving Canada
- lifetime deduction . . . 524
- listed personal property . . 365
- non-arm's length transfers . . 775
- options 368
- partial dispositions of property . 356
- partnerships . . . 863, 864
- personal use property . . . 365
- principal residence . . . 362
- proceeds of disposition defined . 352
- real property - special rule . . 360
- reserves 357
- RRSP investments . . . 464
- small business deferral . . 376
- stripping 790
- tax planning 384
- taxation policy . . . 349
- voluntary dispositions . . 378
- vs. business income . . . 252
- warranties 356

Capital Gains Reserves
- example 358, 359
- general rules 357

Capital Gains Stripping
- applicability 791
- described 790
- example 792, 793

Capital Losses
- acquisition of control rules . . 673
- business investment loss . . 521
- calculation 354
- death of a taxpayer . . . 520
- foreign exchange . . . 366
- general rules 518
- listed personal property . . 365
- *See* Losses
- ordering rules . . . 530, 593
- personal use property . . . 365
- tax planning 384
- transfers to affiliated persons . 768

Capitalization Of Interest
- depreciable assets . . . 202

Carry Overs
- amalgamations 820
- general rules . . . 35, 513
- ordering of deductions . . 593

Cars
- *See* Automobiles

Cash Damming
- interest deductibility . . . 308

Ceasing To Carry On Business
- GST 1007

Cell Phones
- employment income . . . 93

Change In Use
- automobiles . . . 226, 375
- business to personal . . . 370
- capital gains 369
- example 371
- personal to business . . 370
- principal residence . . 373, 374

Charitable Contributions
- *See* Donations

Charitable Donations
- *See* Donations

Charities - GST 1007

Child Care
- employment income . . . 93

Child Care Expenses
- annual expense amount . . 409
- camp attendance . . . 410
- deduction 408
- earned income . . . 409
- eligible child 409
- example 411
- limits on amount . . . 409
- periodic expense amount . . 409
- salary vs. dividend decisions, effect 745
- supporting person . . . 409

Child Support
- defined 416

Class 14.1
- additions to the class . . . 212
- CEC balances . . . 212
- conversion of CEC balances . 229
- dispositions 220
- economic impact of change . 234
- goodwill . . . 212, 214
- intangibles other than goodwill . 212
- rates 213
- terminal losses . . . 223
- transitional rules . . . 227

Clawbacks
- EI benefits 178
- OAS payments . . . 177

Club Dues
- deductibility of costs . . . 262
- employment income . . . 95
- input tax credits . . . 990

Collection - CRA's Powers . . . 72

Commercial Activity - Defined For GST 986

Common-Law Partner
- tax credit 149

This index includes the entries for both Volume I and II. Volume II begins on page 511.

Computation Of Income
- allowances 107
- annuity payments 418
- automobile benefits for employees . 99
- Canada Pension Plan receipts . . 402
- capital gains 350
- death benefits 403
- *See* Deductions From Income
- *See* Employment Income . . . 83
- example for individual . . . 35
- net income of corporations . . 585
- ordering of deductions . . . 530
- ordering rules 32
- payments from deferred income plans 404
- pension receipts 402
- *See* Tax Credits, personal
- prizes 404
- research grants 404
- retiring allowances 493
- social assistance payments . . 405
- stock options 116
- taxable income of corporations . . 586
- taxable income of individuals . 144, 511
- workers' compensation payments . 405

Computers
- hardware - CCA 208
- software - CCA 207
- software (systems) - CCA . . 208

Connected Corporations - Defined . 641

Consent Form - Described . . . 67

Control - Associated Corporations . 679

Controlled Foreign Affiliate - Defined . 961

Convention Expenses - Deductibility . 276

Convertible Securities
- rollover provision 832

Co-Ownership
- compared to partnership . . . 857
- defined 857

Corporations
- acquisition of control 671
- actual dividend tax credits . . 629
- actual tax rates 628
- amalgamations 819
- associated 601, 677
- basic federal tax rate 595
- *See* Canadian Controlled Private Corporations
- decision to incorporate . . . 715
- electronic filing 59
- exchange of shares in reorganization 810
- federal tax abatement . . . 595
- filing deadlines 59
- foreign tax credits 634
- functional currency reporting . . 59
- income splitting 737
- instalment payments 60
- intercompany dividends . . . 587
- interest income 312
- interest on instalments . . . 62
- liability for tax 28
- *See* Losses
- *See* Manufacturing And Processing

Corporations (Continued)
- mutual fund 331
- net income 585
- *See* Non-Residents
- penalties 62
- permanent establishment . . . 593
- personal services business . . 606
- refundable Part I tax 636
- residence 28
- returns 59
- sale of an incorporated business . 833
- share for share exchange . . . 807
- *See* Tax
- taxable income 586
- transfers from shareholders . . . 761
- winding-up 823

Cost Base
- *See* Adjusted Cost Base

Court Decisions 18

CRA News Releases - Described . 17

Credits
- *See* Tax Credits

Crowdfunding
- business income 259

Crown Corporations - GST . . . 1007

Cultural Property - Donation . . 544

Cumulative Eligible Capital
- basic procedures 228
- conversion of balances . . . 229
- December 31, 2016 balances . . 213
- dispositions 220
- economic impact of transition . . 234
- transitional rules 227

Cumulative Gains Limit
- lifetime capital gains deduction . 528

Cumulative Net Investment Loss (CNIL)
- described 527
- salary vs. dividend decisions . . 744

D

Damage Receipts - Income Inclusion . 260

Death Benefits - Inclusion In Income . 403

Death Of A Taxpayer
- capital losses 552
- charitable donations 551
- deductions and credits . . . 555
- deemed dispositions . . . 437, 552
- donations 551
- farm and fishing property . . . 438
- filing deadlines 51
- filing returns 552
- final return 552
- final returns 59
- home buyers' plan 484
- lifelong learning plan 485
- medical expenses 551
- net capital losses 520
- partnership - negative ACB . . 872
- payment of taxes 556

Death Of A Taxpayer (Continued)
- representation 552
- rights or things return 553
- rollover to spouse or spousal trust . 437
- RRIFs 490, 552
- RRSP transfers to child or grandchild 484
- RRSP transfers to spouse . . 484
- RRSPs 483
- special rules at death 551
- TFSAs 421

Debt Forgiveness - Inclusion In Income 260

Debts, Bad
- *See* Bad Debts

Decision To Incorporate
- *See* Incorporating A Business

Deductions From Business Income
- appraisal costs 264
- automobile CCA 269
- automobile financing costs . . 269
- automobile leasing costs . . . 270
- automobile milage payments . . 263
- bad debts 257
- bond discount and premium . . 275
- capital expenditures 261
- CCA on automobiles 269
- club dues 262
- convention expenses 276
- cost of sales 273
- deferred income plan payments . 262
- deferred profit sharing plan contributions 276
- disability related costs 276
- exempt income 262
- financing costs 275
- fines 273
- foreign media advertising . . . 267
- home office costs 265
- illegal payments 273
- incorporation expenses . . . 275
- incurred to produce income . . . 261
- interest costs
  - ° automobiles 269
  - ° deductibility 275
  - ° land 263
  - ° thin capitalization 264
- landscaping costs 276
- lease costs 272
- legal fees 276
- life insurance premiums . . . 261
- limits on deductibility 261
- living expenses 262
- meals and entertainment . . . 268
- non-arm's length transactions . . 255
- penalties 273
- personal services business expenses 263
- political contributions 262
- prepaid expenses 265
- property taxes on land 263
- recreational facilities - cost of . . 262
- registered pension plan contributions 276
- repayment of loans to shareholders . 275
- reserves 256, 276
- RPP contributions 485

Deductions From Business Income
(Continued)
- sale of a business 285
- soft costs 263
- undelivered goods 258
- unpaid amounts 259
- unreasonable amounts . . . 255
- work space in home costs . . 265

Deductions From Income
- allowable business investment loss . 521
- capital element of an annuity . . 418
- child care expenses 408
- CPP contributions 405
- disability supports deduction . . 412
- donations by corporations . . 587
- employment insurance repayments . 414
- intercompany dividends . . 587
- lifetime capital gains deduction . 524
- moving expenses 405
- net capital losses 518
- non-capital losses 517
- ordering rules for corporations . 593
- ordering rules for individuals . . 530
- restricted farm losses . . . 523

Deemed Dispositions
- election on acquisition of control . 675

Deemed Dividends
- ITA 84(1) - increase in PUC . 693, 785
- ITA 84(2) - on winding up . . 695
- ITA 84(3) - redemption of shares . 697
- ITA 84(4) - corporate liquidation . 698

Deemed Resident - Described . . . 25

Deemed Year End
- acquisition of control 672

Deferral Of Taxes Through Incorporation
- CCPC
  - active business income . . 721
  - dividend income 725
  - investment income . . . 724
- imperfections in integration system . 729
- provincial rate considerations . . 729
- provincial rates
  - corporations 731
  - individuals 731
- public corporations 720

Deferral Of Taxes, tax planning . . . 38

Deferred Income Plans - Income . . 404

Deferred Profit Sharing Plans
- deductibility of contributions . . 276
- general rules 491
- pension adjustments . . . 469
- transfers to other plans . . 493
- withdrawals 404

Defined Benefit Plans
- described 462
- pension adjustments . . . 470

Defined Contribution Plans - Described . 462

Departure Tax - Security For . . . 948

Depreciable Property
- *See Also* Property
- additions 202
- capital gains on dispositions . . 218
- CCA 199
- change in use 369
- disposals 216
- government assistance . . . 202
- losses on non-arm's length transfers 770
- non arm's length transactions . 202
- non-arm's length transfers . . 433
- *See* Proceeds Of Disposition
- recapture of CCA 218
- terminal loss 219
- transfer on death 437
- transfer under section 85 . . 770
- transfers to a spouse . . . 432

Depreciation
- compared to CCA 201

Disability Insurance - Employee Benefits
- employment income . . . 111

Disability Related Costs - Deductibility 276

Disability Supports Deduction
- attendant care expenses . . 413
- described 412
- limits on amounts 412
- medical expenses 413

Disabled Persons - Tax Credit . . 166

Disallowed Capital Loss
- allocation 769
- transfers to affiliated persons . 768

Disappearing Source Rules . . . 309

Discount On Long-Term Debt . . . 310

Discounts On Merchandise
- employment income 94

Discretionary Trusts . . 908, 915

Disposition Of Capital Property
- accounting vs. tax 201
- capital gains 218
- deemed
  - change in use 369
  - death of a taxpayer . . . 437
  - leaving Canada 375
  - meaning 352
- deemed - leaving Canada . . 946
- defined 351
- depreciable property . . . 216
- involuntary dispositions . . 378
- partial 356
- Pre-2017 CEC Assets
  - allocation of capital cost . . 230
  - determination of capital cost . 230
- *See Also* Proceeds Of Disposition
- proceeds of disposition - defined . 352
- recapture of CCA 218
- replacement property . . . 378
- small business deferral . . 376
- terminal loss 219
- transfers to a spouse . . . 432

Distributions Of Corporate Surplus
- capital dividends 693
- cash dividends 690
- deemed dividends
  - under ITA 84(1) 693
  - under ITA 84(2) 695
  - under ITA 84(3) 697
  - under ITA 84(4) and (4.1) . . 698
- dividends in kind 692
- general rules 690
- stock dividends 691

Dividend Income
- allocation to partners - income effect 865
- partnership income, effect on . . 862

Dividend Stripping
- applicability 787
- background 786
- defined 786
- example 787

Dividend Tax Credit
- allocation to partners . . . 865
- alternative calculations . . . 629

Dividends
- assets other than cash . . . 692
- capital 333, 693
- capital dividend account . . 688
- capital gains stripping . . . 790
- cash 690
- classified 690
- deduction by corporations . . 587
- deemed
  - under ITA 84(1) 693
  - under ITA 84(2) 695
  - under ITA 84(3) 697
  - under ITA 84(4) and (4.1) . . 698
- determining partnership income . 862
- distributions of corporate surplus . 690
- eligible 321
- eligible and non-eligible . . 652
- eligible vs. non-eligible . . . 322
- example 322, 325
- from untaxed income . . . 588
- gross up and credit procedures 319, 626
- investment returns 327
- non-cash, paid in kind . . . 692
- non-residents, received by . . 942
- owner-manager 742
- partnership interest . . . 870
- refundable taxes on . . . 645
- shares sold for loss . . . 589
- stock 333, 691
- stop loss rule 589
- tax credit 318, 336
- term preferred shares . . . 589
- transfer to a spouse or common-law
  partner 539

Division B Income
- *See* Net Income For Tax Purposes

Donations
- acquisition of control restrictions . 673
- allocation to partners . . . 862
- calculating the credit . . . 161
- capital asset example . . . 542

Donations (Continued)

Donations (Continued)
- capital property 541
- carry forward provision . . . 162
- classified 540
- corporate 587
- cultural property . . . 544
- deemed fair market value . . 541
- ecologically sensitive land . . 543
- eligible amounts . . . 541
- eligible gifts 160
- limits on amounts claimed . 161, 544
- partnerships 862
- publicly traded shares . . 543
- shares acquired with stock options . 543
- tax credit 160

Drawings
- determining partnership income . . 862

Dual Residence
- corporations 29
- individuals 27

E

Earned Income
- child care expenses . . . 409
- RRSP purposes . . . 467

Ecologically Sensitive Land - Donation 543

Economic Objectives - Taxation . . 5

Education Related Benefits
- employment income . . . 94

Education Tax Credit
- carry forward 169

EFILE - Described 50

Election
- accounts receivable - sale of . 285, 766
- capital gains on shares . . . 351
- deemed disposition at emigration . 947
- deemed disposition on acquisition of control 675
- involuntary/voluntary dispositions . 378
- not to be a CCPC 723
- out of ITA 85.1 809
- pension income of non-residents . 944
- reallocation of replacement proceeds 383
- rental income of non-residents . . 942
- Section 85 763
- separate CCA class . . . 225
- share for share exchange . . 807
- spousal rollover - election out of . 433
- transfer of property to corporation . 763
- transfer of property to spouse . 433

Electronic Filing 50

Eligible Dependant
- defined 150
- tax credit 150

Eligible Dividends
- CCPS 654
- defined 321, 626
- designation 652
- example 322

Eligible Dividends (Continued)
- GRIP balance 654
- gross up procedures . . . 321
- vs. non-eligible dividends . . 321

Employee And Partner GST Rebate
- described 1003
- example 1003

Employment Income
- allowances 107
- automobile benefits . . . 99
- automobile expenses . . . 127
- benefits
  - awards 94
  - board and lodging . . . 93
  - cell phones 93
  - child care 93
  - club dues 95
  - debt forgiveness . . . 122
  - defined 90
  - disability insurance . . . 111
  - discounts on merchandise . 94, 122
  - education related . . . 94
  - employer provided meals . . 94
  - gifts 94
  - housing loss reimbursement . 122
  - insurance 111
  - internet services . . . 93
  - ITA 6(1) exclusions . . . 91
  - ITA 6(1) inclusions . . . 91
  - loans 112
  - loyalty points 94
  - medical expenses . . . 95
  - moving expenses . . . 95
  - parking 95, 103
  - pooled registered pension plans . 95
  - post-employment payments . 122
  - pre-employment payments . 122
  - premiums - provincial health care . 95
  - private health care . . . 95
  - professional dues . . . 95
  - recreational facilities . . . 95
  - social events 95
  - spousal travel expenses . . 95
  - stock options 116
  - taxable vs. non-taxable . . 90
  - tax-free savings accounts . . 96
  - tickets to events . . . 96
  - tool reimbursement . . . 96
  - transit passes 96
  - uniforms 96
  - valuation 90
- bonus arrangements . . . 84
- Canada Pension Plan contributions . 86
- cash basis 84
- deduction for RPP contributions . 486
- *See* Deductions From Income
- deductions from 123
- defined 83
- dues 126
- employment insurance . . . 86
- foreign source 952
- gratuities 83
- GST on taxable benefits . . 98
- home office costs . . . 127

Employment Income (Continued)
- imputed interest . . . 112
- inclusions
  - basic concepts . . . 90
  - fringe benefits . . . 91
  - legislative guidance . . 91
  - non-legislative guidance . . 93
  - non-salary benefits . . 91
  - salaries and wages . . 90
- non-residents 20
- non-residents, earned by . . 937
- rent paid 126
- retiring allowances . . . 493
- *See* Stock Options
- salaries and wages . . . 83
- salaries to an assistant . . 126
- salesperson's expenses . . 124
- tax planning 97
- travelling expenses . . . 125
- U.S./Canada tax treaty . . 937
- work space in home costs . . 127

Employment Insurance
- benefits in income . . . 414
- benefits repaid (clawback) . . 178
- employees 86
- refund of excess contributions . 171
- self-employed individuals . . 86
- tax credit 171

Enforcement - CRA's Powers . . 72

Entering Canada - Tax Consequences 946

Estate Freeze
- example 813
- gifts 920
- holding company . . . 921
- instalment sales . . . 921
- objectives 920
- reorganization of capital - ITA 86 . 810
- rollovers - Section 85 . . . 922
- share exchange - Section 86 . 921
- trusts 921

Estate Planning
- non-tax considerations . . 918
- tax considerations . . . 919

Estates
- tax returns 894

Evasion Of Tax - Described . . . 70

Examination Fees Tax Credit . . 168

Excessive Eligible
Dividend Designation (EEDD)
- defined 656
- for a CCPC 657
- for a non-CCPC . . . 657

Excluded Amounts Described . . 536

Excluded Shares Described . . . 536

Exempt Income - Deductions Prohibited 262

Exempt Supplies 983

Exempt Surplus
- defined 959

Exports - GST 1007

This index includes the entries for both Volume I and II. Volume II begins on page 511.

F

Fairness Package 74
Family Trust
• defined 899
• tax planning 915
FAPI (Foreign Accrual Property Income)
• defined 962
• dividends from 963
• taxation of 962
Farm Income (Loss)
• cash basis of income . . 282
• farm loss carry overs . . 523
• farm losses 281
Farm Property
• lifetime capital gains deduction . 524
• principal residence rules . . 364
• rollover to a child . . . 436
• transfer to a child at death . . 438
Federal Courts 70
Filing Deadlines
• corporations 59
• deceased individuals . . 51
• individuals 51
• proprietors and partners . 51
• trusts 63
Filing Requirements
• corporations 59
• deceased taxpayers . . 59
• individuals 50
• trusts 63
Financial Institutions - GST . . 1008
Financing Costs - Deductibility . 275
Fines - Deductibility 273
First Time Home Buyer's Tax Credit 159
First Year Rules
• CCA 209
• exceptions 210
Fishermen - Cash Basis . . . 282
Fishing Property
• lifetime capital gains deduction . 524
• rollover to a child . . . 436
• transfer to a child at death . . 438
Flat Tax Systems 8
Foreign Affiliate
• controlled 961
• defined 957
• dividends from exempt surplus . 959
• dividends from taxable surplus . 960
• tax concepts 958
Foreign Exchange
• capital transactions involving financing 367
• funds on deposit . . . 368
• gains and losses . . . 366
• income transactions . . 366
• securities transactions . . 367

Foreign Investment Reporting
• requirements, described . . 951
• specified foreign property, defined . 951
Foreign Media Advertising - Deductibility 267
Foreign Source Dividends
• controlled foreign entities . 961
• foreign affiliates . . . 957
• problems 955
• received by individuals . . 956
Foreign Source Income
• allocations to partners . . 865
• business income . . . 335, 953
• capital gains 954
• employment income . . 952
• general rules 334
• interest income 954
• investment income
  ◦ controlled foreign affiliates . 961
  ◦ FAPI 962
  ◦ foreign affiliate . . . 957
  ◦ reporting requirements for assets 951
• non-business income . . 335
• tax credit 337
Foreign Tax Credits
• adjusted Division B income . 614
• allocations to partners . . 865
• carry over 615
• computation 545
• corporations
  ◦ additional refundable tax . . 634
  ◦ foreign business income . 613
  ◦ foreign non-business income . 613
• foreign business income . . 953
• individuals
  ◦ foreign business income . 546
  ◦ foreign non-business income . 545
• tax otherwise payable . . 614
Franchises - CCA 207
Full Rate Taxable Income
• defined 611
Fully Taxable Supplies . . . 983
Functional Currency Reporting . 59

G

Gambling Profits
• exclusion from income . . 32
• inclusion in business income . . 260
Garnishment - CRA's Powers . . 72
General Anti-Avoidance Rule
• described 71
• GST application . . . 1002
General Partnership Defined . . 855
General Rate Income Pool (GRIP)
• amalgamations 820
• defined 654
• winding up - 90% owned subsidiary 824

General Rate Reduction
• application to private companies . 612
• application to public companies . 611
• full rate taxable income . . . 611
• manufacturing/processing deduction 608
Generally Accepted Accounting Principles
• amortization vs. CCA . . 199
• depreciation vs. CCA . . 199
• relationship to Division B income . 585
• vs. net income for tax purposes . 254
Gifts
• employment income . . 94
• estate planning . . . 920
• indirect under section 85 . 782
• non-arm's length transfers . 429
• proceeds of disposition . . 351
Goods and Services Tax
• accounting methods . . 991
• adjusted cost base . . 354
• amalgamations . . . 1006
• appeals 1002
• associated persons . . 1001
• background 975
• books and records . . 1001
• calendar quarter test . . 988
• CCA calculations . . . 202
• cessation of business . . 1007
• charities 1007
• commercial activity . . 986
• consideration - measurement of . 985
• credit 174
• crown corporations . . 1007
• current application . . 976
• employee and partner GST rebate . 1003
• employee benefits . . . 98
• example 978
• exempt supplies . . . 983
• exports 1007
• filing requirements . . . 1000
• financial institutions . . 1008
• financial statement presentation . 992
• fiscal period 1000
• frequency of filing . . . 1000
• fully taxable supplies . . 983
• general anti-avoidance rule . 1002
• government organizations . 1007
• holding companies . . 1007
• hospitals 1007
• imports 1007
• input tax credits . . . 989
• intercorporate transfers . 1006
• interest on amounts due . 1001
• introduction to 975
• last four calendar quarters test . 987
• liability for GST . . . 981
• mergers 1006
• municipalities 1007
• MUSH 1007
• new housing rebate . . 1004
• not-for-profit organizations . 1007
• notice of objection . . . 1002

This index includes the entries for both Volume I and II. Volume II begins on page 511.

Goods and Services Tax (Continued)

Goods and Services Tax (Continued)
- partnerships 1008
- payments 1000
- penalties 1001
- person defined 986
- place of supply rules . . . 984
- provincial harmonization . . 5
- quick method of accounting . . 995
- refunds 1001
- registration requirements . . 986
- remittance 985
- residence 987
- residential property . . . 1004
- sale of an incorporated business . 1005
- sale of shares 1006
- schools 1007
- section 85 rollovers . . . 1006
- small business relief . . . 995
- small suppliers exemption . . 987
- streamlined ITC accounting . . 998
- supply categories 982
- Tax court of Canada . . . 1002
- taxable entities 3
- taxable supplies 982
- taxation year 1000
- timing of liability . . . 999
- trade-ins 985
- trusts 1009
- universities 1007
- voluntary registration . . . 988
- wind up of business . . . 1006
- zero-rated supplies . . . 983

Goodwill
- basic concept 214
- CCA 208
- Class 14.1 214
- dispositions 220
- sale of incorporated business . . 836

Government Assistance
- capital assets 353
- effect on capital cost . . . 202
- inclusion in business income . . 260

Government Organizations - GST . 1007

Graduated Rate Estate
- alternative minimum tax . . . 912
- defined 897
- special rules 897
- tainted 911
- tax free dividends . . . 912
- tax payable 911
- taxation year 900

Gratuities - Inclusion In Income . . 83

Gross Up
- dividend 319

Group - Defined For Association . . 678

Harmonized Sales Tax
- adjusted cost base 354
- CCA calculations . . . 202
- current application . . . 976
- described 975
- example 978
- See Also Goods and Services Tax
- history 5
- introduction of 975
- place of supply rules . . . 984

Holding Companies
- estate freeze 921
- GST 1007

Home Accessibility Tax Credit
- described 158
- eligible dwelling 158
- eligible individuals . . . 158
- qualifying expenditures . . . 159
- qualifying individuals . . . 158

Home Buyers' Plan
- departures from Canada . . . 483
- departures from life . . . 484
- example of repayment . . . 481
- income inclusions . . . 404
- making withdrawals . . . 479
- repayment 480
- restricted RRSP contributions . . 480

Home Office Costs
- business income deduction . . 265
- employment income deduction . . 127

Hospitals - GST 1007

Housing Loss
- employment income . . . 122

I

Identical Properties
- general rules 355

Illegal Business Activity - Profits . . 260

Illegal Payments - Deductibility . . 273

Immigration - Tax Consequences . . 946

Imports - GST 1007

Inadequate Considerations
- non-arm's length transfers . . 429

Income
- accountant's concept . . . 30
- active business, integration . . 625
- annuity payments . . . 418
- See Business Income
- Canada Pension Plan payments . . 402
- capital receipts vs. income . . 252
- cash basis - farmers and fishermen . 282
- classification controversy . . 250
- classification of 248
- See Computation Of Income
- death benefits 403
- See Deductions From Income
- economist's concept . . . 30

Income (Continued)
- See Employment Income
- FAPI 962
- foreign source 334
- Income Tax Act view . . . 31
- See Manufacturing And Processing
- See Non-Residents
- payments from deferred income plans 404
- pension benefits 402
- pension splitting . . . 415
- prizes 404
- professional 283
- See Property Income
- registered disability savings plan . 427
- registered education savings plan . 422
- retiring allowances . . . 403, 493
- scholarships and bursaries . . 404
- shareholder benefits . . . 738
- support payments . . . 416
- See Taxable Income

Income Attribution
- anti-avoidance provisions . . 444
- avoiding attribution . . . 441
- basic rules 439
- business income . . . 440
- examples 442
- income subject to tax on split income 440
- income types 439
- inter vivos trusts . . . 912
- ITA 73(1) rollover . . . 441
- loans at commercial rates . . 441
- minor children 439
- other related parties . . . 443
- reversionary trusts . . . 913
- spousal RRSPs 478
- spouse or common-law partner . 439
- tax planning 444

Income Splitting
- described 38
- example 38
- family trusts . . . 915, 917
- incorporating a business . . 716
- objective 737
- problems 39
- salary vs. dividend decisions . . 744
- spousal RRSPs 477
- tax on split income (minors) . . 533
- tax planning 444

Income Tax Act
- administration 49
- described 12
- interpretive sources . . . 16
- Part I described 13
- Parts described 13
- structure 12

Income Tax Application Rules, 1971
- described 16

Income Tax Folios - Described . . . 17

Income Tax Guides - Described . . . 17

Income Tax Pamphlets - Described . . 17

Income Tax Regulations - Described . 15

H

Half-Year Rules - CCA 209

This index includes the entries for both Volume I and II. Volume II begins on page 511.

Income Tax Returns
- *See* Returns

Income Tax Rulings - Described . . 17

Income Tax Technical News - Described   18

Income Trusts
- adjusted cost base 330
- organization 327
- SIFT trusts, for real estate . . 328
- tax features 328
- tax procedures 330

Incorporating A Business
- advantages and disadvantages . . 716
- CCPC 721
- conclusions on advantages . . . 726
- decision to 715
- example 718
- imperfections in integration system . 716
- income splitting 716, 737
- management compensation . . 741
- tax deferral 715, 717
- tax reduction 715, 717

Incorporation Costs
- deductibility 213

Individual Pension Plans - Described . 496

Individuals
- computation of tax payable . 145, 511
- computation of taxable income   144, 511
- provincial taxes 146
- *See* Residence
- returns 50
- tax credit 152

Inducement Receipts
- inclusion in business income . . 260

Information Circulars - Described . . 17

Information Returns - Described . . 64

Inheritances
- exclusion from income . . . 32

Input Tax Credits
- capital assets 990
- current expenditures . . . 989
- described 989
- example 992, 993
- general rules 989
- quick method of accounting . . 995
- restrictions on certain costs . . 990
- streamlined ITC accounting . . 998
- summary of rules 991
- vendors of exempt supplies . . 991

Instalment Payments
- corporations
  - calculation - general . . . 60
  - calculation - small CCPCs . . 61
- CRA's instalment reminder . . 55
- individuals
  - calculation of amounts . . . 54
  - due dates 54
  - examples 55
  - requirement for . . . 53
- trusts
  - due dates 63

Insurance
- disability 111
- employee benefits 111
- life insurance for employees . . 111

Intangible Assets
- CCA calculations 208

Integration
- basic concept 318, 625
- business income 627
- dividend tax credit rates . . . 721
- effect of provincial tax rates . . 729
- eligible vs. non-eligible dividends . 321
- imperfections 729
- implementing 319
- investment income
  - connected corporation . . 642
  - Part IV tax 639
- portfolio dividends - Part IV tax . 641
- required corporate tax rates . . 628
- required dividend tax credits . . 628

Inter Vivos Trust
- defined 897
- tax credits 911
- tax payable 911

Interest
- capitalization 202
- deduction of 275
- discount and premium . . . 310
- financing on vacant land . . 263
- imputed - shareholder loans . . 740
- imputed on employee loans . . 112
- land - idle 353
- on GST balances 1001
- prepaid 265
- prescribed rate 57
- thin capitalization . . . 264
- unpaid tax instalments
  - corporations 62
  - individuals 56
  - trusts 64

Interest Deductibility
- cash damming 308
- direct vs. indirect use . . . 307
- disappearing source rule . . 309
- discount and premium . . . 310
- examples 308
- exceptions to direct use approach . 309
- filling the hole 309
- Folio S3-F6-C1 306
- general rules 306
- interest defined 306
- interest free loans . . . 309
- investments in common shares . . 309
- legislation 307
- Ludco case 307
- partnership capital contributions . 861
- replacing properties . . . 309
- restructurer borrowings . . 308
- RRSP borrowings 466
- Singleton case 307
- tracing current use . . . 308

Interest Income
- accrued interest at transfer . . . 314
- annual accrual method . . . 313
- corporations 312
- discount and premium . . . 314
- foreign source 954
- general provision 312
- individuals 313
- interest defined 306
- non-residents, earned by . . . 941
- partnerships 312

Interest On Student Loans Tax Credit . 168

International Tax Treaties
- described 16
- objectives 934

International Taxation
- residence 22
- subjects covered 933
- tax treaties 934

Interpretation Bulletins - Described . . 17

Inventories
- artists 274
- losses on non-arm's length transfers   768
- overhead absorption . . . 273
- sale of a business . . . 285
- tax vs. GAAP 274
- transfer under section 85 . . 767
- valuation for tax purposes . . 273

Investment Counselling Fees
- deductibility 306

Investment Income
- additional refundable tax (ART) . . 633
- aggregate defined . . . 630
- CCPC 633
- refundable Part I tax . . . 636
- refundable taxes . . . 630, 645
- specified investment business . . 600

Investment Tax Credit
- acquisition of control . . . 685
- apprenticeship job creation . . 683
- carry overs 685
- earned by individuals . . . 174
- eligible expenditures . . . 683
- procedures 682
- qualified property . . . 683
- rates 683
- refundability 684
- scientific research expenditures . . 683
- scientific research rates . . . 683

Investments
- foreign reporting 951

J

Joint Spousal Or Common-Law Partner Trust
- defined 899
- rollover to trust 903
- tax planning 918
- transfers to capital beneficiaries . 904

Joint Ventures
- compared to partnerships . . . 857
- defined 857
- tax procedures 858

K

Kiddie Tax 533

L

Labour Sponsored Funds Tax Credit
- described 173

Land
- interest on vacant parcels . . . 263
- interest/taxes as cost adjustments . 353

Landscaping Costs - Deductibility . 276

Leasehold Interest - CCA . . . 207

Leases
- cancellation costs 276
- deductible costs 272

Leaving Canada
- *See Also* Non-Residents
- deemed disposition . . . 375, 946
- elective dispositions . . . 947
- home buyers' plan 483
- lifelong learning plan . . . 483
- problems with current system . . 947
- RRSPs 483
- security for departure tax . . . 948
- short term residents . . . 949
- tax consequences . . . 375, 946
- unwinding the deemed disposition . 949

Legal Fees - Deductibility . . . 276

Liability For Tax
- background 18
- corporations 28
- general 19
- individuals 22
- non-residents 20
- trusts 30

Life Insurance Premiums
- deductibility 261
- employee benefit 111

Lifelong Learning Plan
- departures from Canada . . . 483
- departures from life . . . 485
- general rules 481
- income inclusions 404
- repayments 482
- withdrawals 481

Lifetime Capital Gains Deduction
- advantages of incorporation . . 716
- allowable business investment loss . 522
- amount available 526
- annual gains limit 526
- cumulative gains limit . . . 528
- cumulative net investment loss . . 527
- determining the amount . . . 525
- election described 524

Lifetime Capital Gains Deduction (Continued)
- elimination of the general provision . 524
- example 528
- history 349
- limits, current and future . . . 524
- non-qualifying real property . . 524
- qualified small business corporation . 524
- sale of an incorporated business . 837

Limited Liability
- advantages of incorporation . . 716

Limited Liability Partnership Defined . 856

Limited Partnerships
- at-risk amount calculations . . 874
- at-risk rules 874
- defined 856, 873
- losses 874
- negative adjusted cost base . . 872

Liquidating Dividends 698

Listed Personal Property
- capital gains and losses . . . 365
- carry over provisions . . . 516
- defined 365
- losses 516

Loans
- employee benefit example . . 115
- employees 112
- forgiveness of employee loans . . 122
- repayment of shareholder . . 275
- shareholders 738
- tax planning 114

Long-Term Debt
- discount and premium . . 310, 314

Loss Carry Overs
- *See* Carry Overs

Losses
- acquisition of control . . 671, 673
- business investment losses . . 521
- carry over rules 35, 513
- cumulative net investment loss . . 527
- death of a taxpayer . . . 520
- listed personal property . . . 516
- net capital losses 518
- non-capital - defined . . . 517
- non-capital for a corporation . . 590
- ordering of deductions . . 530, 593
- personal use property . . . 516
- rental property 317
- restricted farm 523
- superficial 353
- tax credits 515
- terminal 219

Lottery Winnings
- exclusion from income . . 32, 260

Low Rate Income Pool (LRIP)
- amalgamations 820
- defined 655
- winding up - 90% owned subsidiary . 825

Loyalty Points
- employment income 94

Ludco Case 307

Lump-Sum Payments
- alternative tax 513
- qualifying amounts 513
- tax treatment 512

M

Maintenance Payments
- *See* Support Payments

Management Companies 607

Management Compensation
- owner-managed corporations . . 741
- tax effective alternatives . . . 741

Manufacturing And Processing Assets
- CCA 208

Manufacturing And Processing Deduction
- calculating the deduction . . . 608
- constraints on the amount . . 609
- eligibility 610
- eligible income 610
- excluded activities 610
- foreign tax credits 609
- formula for calculating . . . 610
- general rate reduction . . . 611
- investment income limit . . . 609
- provincial rates 596
- qualified activities 610
- rate 608
- small business deduction limit . . 609
- taxable income limit . . . 609

Married Persons
- *See* Spouse

Meals
- employment income 94

Meals And Entertainment
- GST restrictions 990
- limitation on deductibility . . . 268

Medical Expense Tax Credit . . . 163

Medical Expenses
- 12 month period rule . . . 165
- calculating the credit . . . 164
- disability supports deduction . . 413
- employment income 95
- example 165
- refundable supplement . . . 175
- spouse and dependant expenses . 164

Mental Impairment
- tax credit 166

Mergers
- GST considerations 1006

Minimum Tax
- tax free dividends 736

Money Purchase Limit 467

Money Purchase Plans
- described 462
- pension adjustments . . . 469

Moving Expenses
- deduction 405
- employer reimbursements . . 407

Moving Expenses (Continued)
- employment income 95
- housing cost subsidies 407
- loss on old residence 407
- simplified vehicle/meal calculations . 407
- tax planning 408

Municipalities - GST 1007

Mutual Funds
- adjusted cost base 332
- distributions by corporations . . 332
- distributions by trusts . . . 331
- objective 331
- organization 331

My Account (CRA) - Description . . 64

N

Negative Adjusted Cost Base
- capital assets 354

Net Capital Losses
- carry over provisions 518
- conversion to non-capital carry over 518
- general rules 518

Net Income
- *See* Income

Net Income For Tax Purposes
- components 31, 247
- corporations 585
- example of computation . . 35
- rules for computing . . . 32
- structure 31
- trusts 905

NETFILE - Described 50

New Housing GST Rebate . . . 1004

Non-Arm's Length Transactions
- asset acquisition 202
- capital assets 429
- deductions from business income . 255
- defined 429
- depreciable asset transfers . . 433
- dividend stripping 786
- example 430
- general rules 429
- leasing arrangements . . . 431
- problems 428

Non-Capital Losses
- acquisition of control . . . 673
- carry over provisions . . . 518
- defined 517

Non-Competition Agreements
- *See* Restrictive Covenants

Non-Depreciable Capital Property
- losses on non-arm's length transfers 768

Non-Eligible Dividends
- defined 627
- example 325
- procedures 324

Non-Resident Entity
- controlled foreign affiliates . . 961
- FAPI 962
- foreign affiliate 957

Non-Residential Buildings
- CCA rates 206, 226

Non-Residents
- *See Also* Leaving Canada
- business income 20, 935
- dividends received . . . 942
- employment income . . . 20, 937
- filing requirements . . . 935
- interest income . . . 941
- liability for tax 20
- Part I tax 934
- pension income 944
- property income . . . 21, 940
- rental income 942
- royalties 942
- shareholder loans . . . 945
- tax payable 935
- taxable Canadian property, dispositions 938
- taxable income 935
- thin capitalization . . . 264

Northern Residents Deduction . . 145

Not-For-Profit Organizations - GST . 1007

Notice Of Objection
- general rules 67
- GST 1002
- large corporation rules . . 68
- statistics 68

O

Old Age Security Benefits
- clawback 177

Operating Cost Benefit
- alternative calculation . . . 103
- automobiles 103
- described 100
- example 104
- tax planning 106

Options
- capital gains 368
- stock 116

Ordering
- deductions for losses . . . 593
- deductions from income . . 144, 530
- example 531
- net income for tax purposes . . 32

Owner-Manager Remuneration
- dividends - tax free limit . . 734
- registered retirement savings plan . 745
- salary vs. dividend . . . 742
- shareholder loans . . . 738

P

Paid Up Capital
- defined 686
- ITA 85 reduction . . . 776
- shares issued in section 85 rollover . 776

Parking
- employment income . . . 95, 103

Part I Tax
- non-residents 934

Part IV Tax
- applicable dividends . . . 641
- connected corporation
  - definition 641
  - dividends 642
- described 639
- example 640
- portfolio dividends . . . 641
- rates 641
- subject corporations . . . 640

Part XIII Tax
- applicability 940
- dividends received . . . 942
- interest income . . . 941
- nature of 940
- pension benefits . . . 944
- rates 940
- rents 942
- royalties 942
- shareholder loans . . . 945

Participating Debt Interest
- described 941

Partnerships
- *See Also* Adjusted Cost Base - Partnership Interest
- accrual basis 860
- acquiring an interest . . . 867
- admission of a partner . . 867
- allocation of income . . . 866
- at-risk amount calculations . . 874
- at-risk rules 874
- business transactions with partners . 863
- Canadian partnership defined . 876
- capital contributions . . . 871
- capital cost allowance . . 863
- capital gains 863, 864
- charitable donations . . 862, 871
- classification 855
- co-ownership compared . . 857
- defined 854
- dividend allocation . . . 870
- dividend income . . . 862
- drawings 862, 871
- general partnership defined . . 855
- GST considerations . . . 1008
- income determination . . 858, 861
- interest income . . . 312
- interest on capital contributions . . 861
- joint ventures compared . . 857
- limited liability partnership defined . 856
- limited partnership defined . . 856

This index includes the entries for both Volume I and II. Volume II begins on page 511.

Partnerships (Continued)
- negative adjusted cost base . . . 871
- ownership of property 860
- partnership interest defined . . . 867
- personal expenditures of partners . 863
- political contributions . . . 863, 871
- provincial legislation 855
- recapture 863
- reserves 864
- retention of income characteristics . 860
- *See Also* Rollovers
- rollover
  - between partnerships 878
  - to corporation 879
  - to partnership 877
  - to proprietorship 879
- salaries and wages to partners . . 861
- sale of a partnership interest . . 872
- separate person assumption . . 858
- syndicates compared 857
- tax credits 858, 866
- tax status 853
- taxation year 859
- terminal losses 863
- transfers of property to partners . 877
- transfers of property to partnership . 876
- types 855
- withdrawal of a partner . . . 873

Past Service Pension Adjustments
- described 471
- example 471

Patents - CCA 207, 208

Payments
- final balance due
  - corporations 62
  - individuals - deceased . . . 59
  - individuals - living . . . 59
- instalment payments
  - corporations 60
- withholding from individuals . . 52

Penalties
- corporations 62
- deductibility 273
- examples of 73
- GST 1001
- individuals 58
- late instalments 58, 62
- tax return preparers 73
- taxpayer relief provisions . . . 74
- trusts 64

Pension Adjustment Reversals . . 472

Pension Adjustments
- defined benefit plans 470
- DPSPs 469
- example 469
- general rules 468
- money purchase plans . . . 469

Pension Income
- benefits received 402
- non-residents, received by . . . 944

Pension Income (Continued)
- splitting between spouses
  - general rules 415
  - RRIF withdrawals 489
  - RRSP withdrawals 476
  - tax planning 415

Pension Income Tax Credit . . . 156

Pension Plans
- defined benefit plans - defined . . 462
- lump sum transfers 492
- money purchase plans - defined . . 462

Permanent Establishment
- allocation of taxable income . . 594
- defined 593
- example 594

Person - Defined 19

Person - GST Definition . . . 986

Personal Services Corporations
- deductibility of expenses . . . 263
- small business deduction, ineligible . 606

Personal Tax Credits
- *See* Tax Credits

Personal Tax Rates
- *See* Tax Rates

Personal Trusts - Defined . . . 897

Personal Use Property
- change in use 369
- deemed $1,000 cost and proceeds . 365
- defined 364
- listed personal property . . . 365
- losses 516

Phased Retirement - Described . . 486

Physical Impairment
- tax credit 166

Place of Supply Rules
- GST and HST 984
- real property 985
- services 985
- tangible goods 984

Political Contributions
- deduction from business income . 262

Political Contributions Tax Credit
- allocation to partners . . . 863
- federal accountability act . . . 172
- partnerships 863
- tax rules 172

Pooled Registered Pension Plans
- described 487
- employment income 95

Portfolio Dividends - Defined . . 641

Preferred Beneficiary Election . . 905

Preferred Shares
- establishing market value . . . 812

Premium On Long-Term Debt . . 310

Prepaid Expenses - Deductibility . . 265

Prescribed Rate
- amounts owing to taxpayers . . . 57
- amounts owing to the CRA . . . 57
- defined 57
- general application 57

Principal Residence
- capital gains 362
- change from personal to rental . 373
- change from rental to personal . 374
- defined 362
- farms 364
- non-residential use 364
- options 368
- trusts 910

Private Corporations
- *See Also* Canadian Controlled Private Corporations

Private Health Care
- employment income 95

Prizes
- inclusion in income 404

Proceeds Of Disposition
- deemed 352
  - change in use 369
  - death of taxpayer 437
  - leaving Canada 375
- deemed - charitable donations . . 541
- defined 352
- gifts 351
- involuntary dispositions . . . 378
- leaving Canada 946
- non-arm's length transactions . . 429
- options 368

Professional Corporations . . . 607

Professional Dues
- employment income 95

Profit Sharing Plans
- general rules 492
- tax on excess amounts . . . 492

Progressive Taxes
- described 6
- evaluation 7

Prohibited Investments
- RRSPs and RRIFs 464

Property
- defined 248
- *See* Depreciable Property
- *See* Disposition Of Capital Property
- *See* Identical Properties
- *See* Property Income
- *See* Listed Personal Property
- *See* Personal Use Property
- role in income classification . . 248

Property Income
- *See Also* Income
- defined 252
- dividends 318
- foreign source 334
- interest 312
- non-residents - earned by . . 21, 940

Property Income (Continued)
- payments based on production/use . 315
- rents 315
- royalties 315
- shareholder benefits . . . 738
- shareholder loans . . . 738
- small business deduction . . 600
- specified investment business . . 600
- vs. business income . 250, 252, 305

Proportional Taxes - Described . . . 6

Proprietorship
- decision to incorporate . . . 715

Provincial Health Care
- employment income 95

Provincial Payroll Taxes
- rates 745

Provincial Tax
- corporations 4
  - allocation of income to provinces 594
  - permanent establishment . . 593
  - rates 596
- effect on incorporation decision . 729
- GST/HST 5
- individuals 4, 146
- residence of individuals . . . 147
- tax credits 148

Public Corporations
- decision to incorporate . . . 720
- low rate income pool (LRIP) . 655

Publicly Traded Shares - Donations . 543

Q

Qualified Property
- investment tax credits 683

Qualified Small Business Corporation
- defined 524
- dividend stripping 787
- sale of shares 837

Qualifying Student Defined . . . 404

Qualitative Characteristics Of Tax Systems 9

Quick Method - GST
- example 997
- general rules 995
- rates 996
- supply categories . . . 996

R

Real Estate Companies
- deductible interest 263

Reasonableness
- expense deductibility 268

Reassessments 65

Recapture Of CCA
- charitable donations . . . 541
- determination of partnership income 863
- disposal of capital asset . . . 218
- replacement property rules . . 378

Recapture Of CCA (Continued)
- trusts 910

Recreational Facilities
- deductibility of costs 262
- employment income 95

Redemption Of Shares 697

Reduction Of Taxes Through Incorporation
- CCPC
  - active business income . . 721
  - dividend income . . . 725
  - investment income . . . 724
- imperfections in integration system . 729
- provincial rates
  - corporations 731
  - individuals 731
- provincial tax rates on individuals . 730
- provincial taxes 730
- public corporations 720

Refundable Dividend Tax On Hand
- defined 646
- dividend refund 648
- example 649
- general rules 645
- investment income . . . 645
- Part I taxes paid 646

Refundable Investment Tax Credits . 684

Refundable Tax Credits
- general concept 174
- GST/HST credit 174
- medical expense supplement . . 175
- teacher school supply . . . 176
- working income tax benefit . . 176

Refundable Taxes
- basic concepts 630
- calculation of foreign tax credits . 634
- example
  - refundable Part I tax . . . 636
  - refundable Part IV tax . . 643, 644
- Part I tax on investment income . . 633
- Part IV
  - connected corporations . . 642
  - portfolio dividends . . . 641
  - tax on dividends received . . 639
- Part XI.3 retirement compensation . 494
- procedures 632

Refunds On Overpayments . . . 65

Registered Disability Savings Plans
- general procedures 427

Registered Education Savings Plan
- accumulated income payments . . 425
- Canada education savings grants . 422
- Canada learning bonds . . . 423
- contributions 422
- earnings 422
- education assistance payments . . 424
- evaluation 426
- general procedures 422
- payments to beneficiaries . . . 424
- refund of contributions . . . 424
- repayment of CESG contributions . 425
- repayment of CLB 425

Registered Education Savings Plan (Continued)
- types of plans 424

Registered Pension Plan Contributions
- deductibility 276

Registered Pension Plans
- contributions
  - employee 486
  - employer 485
  - restrictions on . . . 485
- establishment 485
- phased retirement 486
- pooled 487
- registration of the plan . . . 485
- retirement options . . . 486
- transfers to other plans . . . 493

Registered Retirement Income Funds
- administration fees 476
- death of the registrant . . . 490, 552
- establishment 489
- evaluation 491
- minimum withdrawals . . . 490
- pension income splitting . . . 489
- prohibited investments . . . 464
- transfers from RRSP . . . 477
- withdrawals 404

Registered Retirement Savings Plans
- administration fees 476
- capital gains 464
- conversion to income . . . 476
- death of the registrant . . . 483, 552
- deduction limit 466
- deduction limit statement . . . 467
- departure from Canada . . . 483
- dividends 464
- earned income 467
- establishment 463
- examples of deduction limits . . 473
- excess contributions . . . 474
- foreign content limit . . . 463
- home buyers' plan 479
- interest on loans 466
- investment options . . . 463
- involuntary termination . . . 477
- lifelong learning plan . . . 481
- past service pension adjustments . 471
- pension adjustment reversals . . 472
- pension adjustments . . . 468
- prescribed amount . . . 471
- prohibited investments . . . 464
- RRSP dollar limit 467
- salary vs. dividend decisions . . 745
- spousal plans 477
- terminations 476
- transfer to a RRIF 477
- transfers to other plans . . . 493
- undeducted contributions . . . 474
- unused RRSP deduction room . . 467
- vs. RESPs 426
- vs. TFSAs 426
- withdrawals 404
  - income inclusion . . . 463
  - retirement options . . . 476

Regressive Taxes
- described 6
- evaluation 7

Regulations
- *See* Income Tax Act

REITs 328

Related Persons
- associated corporations . . . 678
- defined 678
- *See* Non-Arm's Length

Rental Income
- earned by non-residents . . . 942
- Part XIII tax 942

Rental Property
- capital cost allowance . . . 316
- example 317
- general provisions 315
- loss restrictions 317
- separate CCA classes . . 205, 316

Reorganization Of Capital - ITA 86
- conditions for the rollover . . . 811
- example 813
- gift to a related person . . . 816
- key employee succession . . 819
- preferred shares - market value . 812
- procedures 812
- PUC reduction 813
- tax planning 819

Replacement Property Rules
- capital gains deferral . . . 378
- ITA 13(4) - application . . . 380
- ITA 44(1) - application . . . 379
- reallocation of proceeds . . . 383
- recapture of CCA deferral . . 378

Represent A Client - Described . . 67

Research Grants - Inclusion In Income 404

Reserves
- bad debts 257, 276
- general system 256
- goods and services not delivered . 258
- partnerships 864
- unpaid amounts 259

Residence
- corporations 28
- deemed residents 25
- defined 19
- dual 27
- GST registrants 987
- importance of 22
- individuals 22
- liability for tax 19
- part year 24
- residential ties 22
- sojourner 25
- temporary absence 23
- tests for terminating 23
- tie-breaker rules 27
- trusts 30
- vs. citizenship 28

Resident
- foreign source income
  - business income 953
  - capital gains 954
  - employment income . . . 952
  - interest 954

Residential Property - GST . . . 1004

Restricted Farm Losses
- calculation 282
- carry overs 523

Restrictive Covenants
- exceptions to general rule . . . 833
- inclusion in income 260
- sale of an incorporated business . 833
- sale of shares 837
- sale of total business assets . . 836

Retained Earnings
- tax basis 687

Retirement Compensation Arrangements
- defined 494
- Part XI.3 refundable tax . . . 494
- the problem 494

Retirement Savings
- basic system 459
- early contributions 461
- tax benefits 460
- tax free compounding . . . 461
- transfers between plans . . . 492

Retiring Allowances
- income 403
- transfer to RRSP 493

Returns
- adjustments to 66
- assessment 65
- corporations 59
- deceased taxpayers 59
- individuals 50
- information 64
- reassessments 65

Reversionary Trusts
- income attribution 913

Rights Or Things Return 553

Rollovers
- *See Also* Section 85 Rollovers
- alter ego trust 902
- amalgamations 819
- convertible properties . . . 832
- estate freeze 921, 922
- farm or fishing property at death . 438
- farm or fishing property to a child . 436
- GST 1006
- joint spousal trust 903
- pension plan transfers . . . 492
- RRIFs at death 490
- RRSPs at death 483
- *See* Section 85 Rollovers
- share for share exchange . . 807
- small business investments . . 376
- spousal or common-law partner trust 901
- to a spouse at death . . . 437

Rollovers (Continued)
- transfer from a partnership
  - to a corporation . . . 879
  - to a new partnership . . . 878
  - to a proprietorship . . . 879
- transfer from partner to partnership . 877
- transfers to a spouse . . . 432
- trust to beneficiaries . . . 903
- winding up of subsidiary . . 824

Royalties
- non-residents, earned by . . 942
- tax treatment 315

S

Safety Deposit Boxes
- non-deductibility of cost . . . 306

Salary And Wages
- *See Also* Owner-Manager Remuneration
- management compensation . . 741
- owner-manager, salary vs. dividend 742

Salary Deferral Arrangements . . . 495

Salary Vs. Dividend Decisions
- basic trade-off 742
- child care costs 745
- corporate taxes payable . . . 745
- CPP and employment tax credits . 746
- CPP, EI, and payroll taxes . . 746
- cumulative net investment loss . 744
- income splitting 744
- optimum mix of salary and dividends 748
- owner-manager considerations . 742
- payroll taxes 745
- provincial tax rates 743
- RRSP considerations . . . 745
- tax free dividends 734

Sale Of A Business
- accounts receivable 285
- general rules 285
- inventories 285

Sale Of An Incorporated Business
- alternative approaches . . . 833
- evaluation of alternatives . . . 837
- example 839
- goodwill 836
- GST implications 1005
- lifetime capital gains deduction . . 837
- restrictive covenants . . 833, 836
- sale of assets as a going concern . 835
- sale of individual assets . . . 834
- sale of shares 836

Sale Of Individual Corporate Assets
- applicability 834
- restrictive covenants. . . . 834

Sale Of Shares
- restrictive covenants . . . 837

Salesperson's Expenses
- employment income deduction . 124

Scholarships
- general rules 404

This index includes the entries for both Volume I and II. Volume II begins on page 511.

Scientific Research Expenditures
- investment tax credit 683
- refundable investment tax credits . 685

Section 85 Rollovers
- accounts receivable, transfer of . . 766
- adjusted cost base of:
  - acquired assets 774
  - consideration 773
- benefit to transferor 785
- boot defined 764
- capital gains on transfers . . . 775
- capital property, non-depreciable . 767
- comprehensive example . . . 779
- consideration to transferor . . . 763
- corporation's position 774
- depreciable property
  - order of disposition 771
  - transfer of 770
- elected values 763
- election procedures 763
- eligible assets 762
- establishing transfer price . . 763, 765
- estate freeze 922
- example, indirect gift rules . . 782
- excess consideration . . 784, 785
- general rules 762
- GST 1006
- indirect gift rules 782
- introduction 761
- inventories, transfer of . . . 767
- non-share consideration . . . 764
- normal application 765
- paid up capital of issued shares . 776
- paid up capital reduction . . . 776
- shareholders' position . . . 773
- tax planning - disallowed losses . 770
- terminal losses disallowed . . 772
- transferor and transferee . . . 762

Section 86 Rollovers
- *See* Reorganization Of Capital - ITA 86

Securities
- *See* Shares

Seizure Of Property - CRA's Powers . 72

Self-Employment
- fringe benefits 87
- income computation 86
- tax evasion 87
- tests for identifying 88

Separate Class Election
- eligible assets 225
- objective 225

Separate Classes - CCA
- exceptions to general rule . . . 205
- rental properties 316

Settlor - Defined For Trusts . . . 893

Share For Share Exchange
- application in practice 810
- described 807
- electing out 807
- estate freeze 921
- example 808, 921
- general rules 807

Share For Share Exchange (Continued)
- opting out 809
- restrictions on rollover 808

Shareholder Benefits . . . 336, 737

Shareholder Loans
- exceptions to the general rule . . 738
- general rules 738
- imputed interest benefit . . . 740

Shareholders
- benefits from corporation . . . 738
- benefits under ITA 85 . . . 785
- loans to non-residents . . . 945
- *See Also* Owner-Manager Remuneration

Shareholders' Equity - Tax Vs. GAAP . 686

Shares
- issuing expenses 275
- paid up capital 776
- share for share exchange . . 807

Short Fiscal Period
- CCA 211

SIFT trusts, for real estate . . . 328

Singleton Case 307

Small Business - GST Relief . . 995

Small Business Corporations
- capital gains deferral on share sales . 376
- defined 521
- lifetime capital gains deduction . . 524
- sale of an incorporated business . 837

Small Business Deduction
- active business income defined . . 599
- annual business limit . . . 601
- associated corporations . . 601, 677
- calculation of tax payable . . 602
- constraints on the amount . . 602
- electing out 723
- example 598
- federal rates 583
- general provisions 598
- general rate reduction . . . 612
- incidental property income . . 601
- large CCPCs phase out . . . 604
- management companies . . . 607
- personal services corporations . 606
- professional corporations . . 607
- property income
  - problem with definition . . 600
  - received from associate . . 601
- provincial rates 596
- specified investment business . 600
- taxable income constraint . . 602

Small Suppliers Exemption - GST
- calendar quarter test . . . 988
- four calendar quarters test . . 987
- ineligible registrants . . . 989

Social Assistance Payments
- deduction from income . . . 144
- inclusion in income . . . 405

Social Events
- employment income 95

Soft Costs
- described 263

Sojourners - Deemed Residence . . 25

Source Deductions
- non-employment sources . . . 53
- salaries and wages 52

Source Individual
- defined 535

Specified Class - Shares . . . 678

Specified Individual
- defined 535

Specified Investment Business
- defined 600

Split Income
- defined 535

Spousal Or Common-Law Partner Trust
- defined 899
- rollover to trust 901
- tax planning 917
- transfers to capital beneficiaries . 904

Spousal RRSP
- attribution rules 478
- described 477

Spousal Support
- conditions for deduction/inclusion . 417
- defined 416

Spousal Travel Expenses
- employment income 95

Spouse
- death benefit exclusion . . . 403
- tax credit 149
- transfer of capital property . . 432
- transfer of dividends . . . 539
- transfers at death 437
- transfers of credits . . . 172

Standby Charges On Automobiles
- calculation 100
- described 100
- example 104
- reduction 102
- tax planning 106

Statutory Amalgamations
- *See* Amalgamations

Stock Dividends
- tax procedures 691
- tax treatment of receipt . . . 333

Stock Options
- adjusted cost base of shares . . 353
- capital gains 368
- CCPCs 120
- donation of acquired shares . . 543
- economics of 116
- employee benefits 116
- example 119
- overview of tax rules . . . 117
- private vs. public companies . . 118
- public companies 119

This index includes the entries for both Volume I and II. Volume II begins on page 511.

Stop Loss Rule
- described 589

Streamlined ITC Accounting - GST   998

Students
- transfer of tuition credit . . . 169

Subject Corporations
- part IV tax 640

Subsidiaries
- winding-up 823

Subsidies
- *See* Grants And Subsidies

Superficial Losses - Disallowed . . 353

Supply
- exempt 983
- fully taxable 983
- GST concept 981
- taxable 982
- zero-rated 983

Support Payments
- tax treatment 416

Supreme Court Of Canada 70

Surtax 146

Syndicates
- compared to partnerships . . . 857
- defined 858

T

Target Benefit Plans, described . . 488

Tax
- alternative bases 1
- collection and enforcement . . . 72
- *See* Computation Of Tax
- *See* Tax Credits
- economic objectives 5
- expenditures 8
- flat tax systems 8
- goals of corporate system . . . 597
- incidence 8
- income levels 6
- *See* Integration
- *See* Liability For Tax
- *See* Tax Planning
- progressive systems 6
- qualitative characteristics of systems 9
- *See* Refundable Tax
- regressive systems 6
- tax policy concepts 5
- taxable entities - GST 3
- taxable entities - income tax . . . 2

Tax Avoidance
- described 71
- general anti-avoidance rule . . . 71

Tax Court Of Canada
- GST disputes 1002
- procedures 69

Tax Credits
- adoption expenses 157
- age 155

Tax Credits (Continued)
- ancillary tuition fees credit . . . 168
- calculation - basic approach . . . 148
- Canada caregiver 152
- Canada caregiver for child . . . 152
- Canada employment 156
- Canada Pension Plan 171
- carry forward of tuition credit . . 169
- charitable donations . . . 160, 540
- common-law partner 149
- disability 166
- dividend 319, 320
- eligible dependant 150
- employment insurance 171
- examination fees 168
- example 179
- first time home buyers 159
- foreign taxes paid 545, 590
- GST refundable 174
- home accessibility tax credit . . 158
- interest on student loans . . . 168
- investment 174, 682
- loss carry overs, effect of . . . 515
- married persons 149
- medical expenses
  - example 165
  - qualifying medical expenses . . 163
- pension income 156
- personal 149
- political contributions 172
- provincial 148
- refundable medical
  expense supplement 175
- scientific research and development   683
- single individuals 152
- spouse - transfer of credits to . . 172
- transfer of credits
  - disability 166
- transfer of tuition 169
- trusts 911
- tuition fees 168
- volunteer firefighters 160
- volunteer search and rescue workers 160
- working income tax benefit . . . 176

Tax Evasion - Described 70

Tax Free Savings Accounts
- death of a taxpayer . . . 421, 552
- evaluation 426
- general procedures 421

Tax Legislation
- court decisions 18
- draft legislation 15
- income tax application rules . . . 16
- income tax regulations 15
- international tax treaties 16
- interpretation of the income tax act . . 16
- other income tax references . . . 15
- structure of the federal income tax act   12

Tax On Split Income
- 2018 changes 533
- applicability 535
- background 533
- calculation 537

Tax On Split Income (Continued)
- capital gains on qualified property . 537
- evaluation 539
- example 538
- excluded shares 536
- impact on ITA 86 810
- income attribution rules 440
- marriage breakdown agreements . 537
- reasonableness test 537
- retirement income splitting . . . 537
- split income defined 535
- types of income 535

Tax Payable
- basic corporate rate 595
- basic federal tax 533
- basic system for individuals . . . 145
- corporation
  - federal tax abatement . . . 595
  - foreign tax credit 590
  - full rate taxable income . . . 595
  - general rate reduction . . . 595
  - M&P deduction 608
  - provincial tax rates 596
  - small business deduction . . 602
- dividend tax credit 321, 324
- federal rates for individuals . . . 145
- income not earned in a province . . 148
- investment income of a CCPC . . 633
- overview for individuals 532
- provincial tax for individuals . . . 146
- provincial taxes
  - capital 597
  - payroll taxes 597
- surtax 146
- tax on split income 533
- types of income 147

Tax Planning
- advantages of incorporation . . . 715
- alter ego trusts 917
- amalgamations 822
- attribution of income 444
- basic principles 37
- bonus arrangements 84
- capital gains or losses 384
- CCA 215
- CCPC
  - active business income . . . 723
  - dividend income 725
  - investment income 724
- CEC transition 234
- CNIL 527
- deferral 38
- deferred profit sharing plans . . . 491
- disallowed capital losses . . . 770
- dividend rates of return 327
- employee benefits 97
- employee vs. self-employed . . . 86
- employer provided automobiles . . 106
- estates 918
- excess RRSP contributions . . . 475
- family trusts 915
- gifts 920
- imperfections in integration system . 729
- income attribution 441

This index includes the entries for both Volume I and II. Volume II begins on page 511.

Tax Planning (Continued)
- income splitting 38
- income splitting with incorporation . 737
- investment returns 327
- joint spousal trusts 918
- loans to employees 114
- loss carry overs 515
- moving expenses 408
- pension income splitting . . . 415
- profit sharing plans 492
- registered retirement income funds . 491
- reorganizations of capital . . . 819
- RESPs vs. RRSPs 426
- RESPs vs. TFSAs 426
- retirement savings benefits . . . 460
- salary vs. dividend decisions . . 742
- spousal RRSPs 477
- spousal/common-law partner trusts . 917
- terminal losses 772
- TFSAs vs. RRSPs 426
- winding up of subsidiary . . . 827

Tax Policy Concepts 5

Tax Rates
- federal for individuals 145
- provincial for individuals . . . 146

Taxable Benefits
- *See* Employment Income

Taxable Canadian Property
- Canada/U.S. tax treaty 939
- compliance certificates 939
- defined 20
- dispositions by non-residents . 20, 938

Taxable Income
- calculation for individuals . . 37, 511
- corporations 586
- deduction for payments . . . 144
- deductions for individuals . 144, 512
- defined 19
- individuals 144
- northern residents deduction . . 145
- ordering of deductions and losses . 530
- ordering of deductions/losses . . 144
- stock option deduction . . . 116
- trusts 907

Taxable Surplus
- defined 959

Taxation Year
- defined 19
- general rules 279
- GST 1000
- non-calendar year ends . . . 280
- partnerships 859
- short fiscal period 211
- unincorporated businesses . . 280

Taxes Payable
- *See* Tax Payable

Tax-Free Savings Accounts
- employment income 96

Taxpayer Relief Provisions . . . 74

Taxpayers
- liability for tax 19

Teacher School Supply Credit
- described 176

Term Preferred Shares
- dividends 589

Terminal Losses
- buildings 360
- Class 14.1 223
- determination of partnership income . 863
- general provisions 219
- non-arm's length transactions . . 772
- separate class election . . . 225
- trusts 910

Testamentary Trust
- defined 897
- tainted 911
- tax credits 911
- tax payable 911
- use of multiple 911

Thin Capitalization Limitation . . . 264

Tickets To Events
- employment income 96

Tie-Breaker Rules
- corporations 29
- individuals 27

Tips - Inclusion In Income . . . 83

Tool Reimbursement
- employment income 96

TOSI
- *See* Tax On Split Income

Trade-Ins
- GST considerations 985

Transaction Taxes
- general concepts 977
- multi-stage 978
- single stage 978

Transfers
- *See* Rollovers
- *See* Spouse

Transit Passes
- employment income 96

Travel Expenses
- deduction from employment income . 125
- meals and entertainment - 50% limit . 268

Trustee - Defined 893

Trusts
- allocations to beneficiaries . . . 907
- alter ego
  - defined 899
  - rollover to trust 902
  - tax planning 917
- amounts deemed not paid . . . 906
- amounts paid or payable . . . 907
- beneficiary defined 893
- capital cost allowance . . . 910
- capital gains on trust assets . . 904
- capital gains, flow through provisions . 908
- certainties required 895
- classification of 63, 896
- contributions, taxation of . . . 900

Trusts (Continued)
- deemed disposition of trust assets . 904
- definition 893
- discretionary 908, 915
- dividends, flow through provisions . 908
- establishing 895
- estate freeze 921
- estates, compared to 894
- executor's fees 905
- family
  - defined 899
  - tax planning 915
- graduated rate estate
  - defined 897
  - special rules 897
  - taxation year 900
- GST 1009
- income 327
- income attribution 912
- income, taxation of 900
- inter vivos
  - defined 897
  - tax payable 911
- joint spousal or common-law partner
  - defined 899
  - rollover to trust 903
  - tax planning 918
- legal perspective 893
- lifetime capital gains deduction . . 908
- minor beneficiaries 906
- mutual fund 331
- net income for tax purposes . . 905
- non-discretionary 908
- non-tax uses 896
- personal tax credits 911
- personal trusts 897
- preferred beneficiary election . . 905
- principal residence exemption . . 910
- purchase of an interest . . . 914
- recapture of CCA 910
- residence 30
- returns 63
- reversionary 913
- revoking 893
- rollovers to beneficiaries . . . 903
- sale of an interest 914
- settlor defined 893
- spousal or common-law partner
  - defined 899
  - rollover to trust 901
  - tax planning 917
- tax definition 894
- tax free dividends 912
- taxable income 907
- taxation of 900
- taxation year 900
- terminal losses 910
- testamentary
  - defined 897
  - tax payable 911
  - use of multiple 911
- transfer to spouse at death . . . 437
- transfers to beneficiaries . . . 900
- trustee defined 893
- trustee's fees 905

Trusts (Continued)
- twenty-one (21) year
  deemed disposition rule . . . 904
- varying trust arrangement . . . 893

Tuition
- employer provided 94

U

Undepreciated Capital Cost - Defined . 199

Uniforms
- employment income 96

Unincorporated Business
- taxation year 280

Universities - GST 1007

Unreasonable Amounts
- deductions from business income . 255

V

Value Added Tax (VAT)
- accounts-based approach . . . 979
- invoice-credit approach 979

Vertical Amalgamations 822

Voluntary Registration
- GST/HST 988

Volunteer Firefighters Tax Credit . 160

Volunteer Search And Rescue Workers
Tax Credit 160

W

Wages
- *See* Salary and Wages

Warranties - Capital Gains . . . 356

Web Site (CRA) 16

Winding Up - 90% Owned Subsidiary
- acquisition of assets 824
- asset bump-up 825
- comparison with amalgamation . . 827
- deferral of loss carry forwards . . 825
- disposition of shares 827
- GRIP and LRIP balances . . . 824
- nature of the transaction . . . 823
- tax planning considerations . . 827

Winding Up - Canadian Corporation
- example 829
- GST considerations 1006
- ITA 84(2) deemed dividend . . 695
- nature of transaction 829

Withholdings
- non-employment sources . . . 53
- salaries and wages 52

Work Space In Home Costs
- business income deduction . . 265
- employment income deduction . 127

Workers' Compensation Payments
- deduction from taxable income . . 144
- inclusion in income 405

Working Income Tax Benefit
- calculation 176
- described 176

Z

Zero-Rated Supplies 983

This index includes the entries for both Volume I and II. Volume II begins on page 511.

NOTES

Notes

Notes

Notes